Preface to the ninth edition

The ninth edition has again seen some changes in relation to the contributions to the book. Elizabeth has stepped back, basically only dealing with three chapters in this edition (exemption clauses, exemption clauses and legislation, and unfair terms). The rest of the work has been undertaken by Ruth, with the exception of two chapters (misrepresentation, and duress and undue influence) the work on which was kindly undertaken by Dr Jens Krebs.

The aims of the book remain the same today as they were when the project was started: to provide a clear, non-technical account of the law of contract, which is accessible to university students new to the study of law, whilst maintaining academic rigour. Unlike the eighth edition, there has been no major restructuring this time. What has occurred is a full updating, taking account of major developments. Chief of these on the legislative front is the Consumer Rights Act 2015, which now encompasses, and makes some changes to, the unfair terms regime, which was previously provided by the Unfair Terms in Consumer Contracts Regulations 1999, as well as removing, and taking on board, the consumer elements of the Unfair Contract Terms Act 1977. There have, of course, also been many new cases to take account of, such as *Armchair Answercall Ltd* v *People in Mind Ltd, Blue* v *Ashley, Cavendish Square Holding BV* v *Talal El Makdessi, ParkingEye Ltd* v *Beavis, Globalia Business Travel S.A.U. (formerly TravelPlan S.A.U.) of Spain* v *Fulton Shipping Inc of Panama, Marks and Spencer plc* v *BNP Paribas Securities Services Trust Company (Jersey) Ltd, MWB Business Exchange Centres Ltd* v *Rock Advertising Ltd, Patel* v *Mirza, Phones 4U Ltd (In Administration)* v *EE Ltd.*

We are very grateful to Natasha Ellis-Knight and her colleagues at Oxford University Press for their patience, efficiency, and encouragement.

Elizabeth Macdonald
Ruth Atkins
March 2018

I would like to take this opportunity to thank Ruth, for her commitment and a great deal of hard work, in so ably taking on the vast bulk of the writing which was required for this edition. Ruth has remained a bastion of good humour, and good sense, throughout a demanding process.

Elizabeth Macdonald
March 2018

Addendum

At the proof stage, we have been able to take some account, in Chapters 4, 5, & 7, of the decision of the Supreme Court in *Rock Advertising Ltd* v *MWB Business Exchange Centres Limited* [2018] UKSC 24, which was only handed down in May 2018, after our original text was completed and sent to OUP.

EM and RDA
June 2018

Koffman & Macdonald's

Law of Co

Ninth Ec

Elizabet
Professor of Lav
Ruth Atl
Lecturer in Law

With contr

Jens Kr
Senior Lecture

OXFORD
UNIVERSITY PRESS

Great Clarendon Street, Oxford, OX2 6DP,
United Kingdom

Oxford University Press is a department of the University of Oxford. It furthers the University's objective of excellence in research, scholarship, and education by publishing worldwide. Oxford is a registered trade mark of Oxford University Press in the UK and in certain other countries

Sixth edition 2008
Seventh edition 2010
Eighth edition 2014

Impression: 1

Published in the United States of America by Oxford University Press
198 Madison Avenue, New York, NY 10016, United States of America

British Library Cataloguing in Publication Data
Data available

Library of Congress Control Number: 2018951469

ISBN 978–0–19–875284–4

Printed in Great Britain by
Bell & Bain Ltd., Glasgow

Preface to the first edition

The impetus for writing this book came from our experience, over many years, of teaching the Law of Contract to first-year law students. We found that although the established textbooks on the subject are admirable in many respects, they are longer and more detailed than required by the average student. Our aim was to produce a book which has sufficient detail to meet the needs of students taking law degrees, but which does not contain more information than students ever require. Obviously we have been selective in deciding which topics merit more detailed exposition, but we hope that our selection reflects the emphasis of most Contract courses.

Although the book is written primarily with law students in mind, we hope that our approach to the subject will also appeal to those studying Contract as part of a business studies course. We think that a book on Contract should be readily intelligible to students new to law, as the subject is usually taught in the first year of a law degree. For this reason, the emphasis of the book is on explanation of the law in clear and non-technical terms. In particular, we have tried to give a full explanation of the important case law in order to assist students towards an understanding of how the common law works. We have preferred to provide a firm grounding in the case law, rather than to espouse or develop any individual 'theory' of contract law.

In writing the book we have been helped by more people than it is possible to name individually. But we are particularly grateful to those tutoring in Contract at Aberystwyth for reading and commenting helpfully on drafts of certain chapters. We also wish to thank Lillian Stevenson and the staff of the Hugh Owen library for their good-natured and patient assistance. We are indebted to our publishers for their initial interest in the idea of the book and for the encouragement which they gave us to write it. Special thanks are owed to Indira Carr for her advice on computers, and to Valerie Koffman for her help with proofreading. Our greatest debt of gratitude is owed to our families and friends who encouraged and supported us throughout the writing of the book. More particularly, Laurence Koffman wishes to thank his wife Valerie and daughter Angela, for their patience and constant support. Elizabeth Macdonald would like to express her thanks to her parents, Pat and Stan Macdonald, for all their support and help.

We have attempted to state the law as at 15 September 1991.

Laurence Koffman
Elizabeth Macdonald
Aberystwyth
February 1992

Outline contents

Detailed contents

Table of Legislation

Paragraph references printed in **bold** type indicate where the legislation is set out in part or in full.

References to W1 and W2 relate to web chapter 1 (Capacity) and web chapter 2 (An outline of the law of restitution) which can be found on the Online Resource Centre.

United Kingdom Statutory Instruments

United Kingdom Rules

European Legislation

Directives

Regulations

International Treaties and Conventions

Other National Legislation

Germany

United States

Table of Cases

Paragraph references in **bold** type indicate where there is a quotation from the case. References to W1 and W2 relate to web chapter 1 (Capacity) and web chapter 2 (An outline of the law of restitution) which can be found on the Online Resource Centre.

Chapter 1

Introduction to the study of contract law

What is a contract?

1.1 A contract is a legally enforceable agreement giving rise to obligations for the parties involved. The law of contract determines which agreements are enforceable and regulates those agreements, providing remedies if contractual obligations (undertakings or promises) are broken. Under a contract, the parties voluntarily assume their obligations or undertakings: for example, S promises to supply a new car to B by the end of the month, whilst B promises to pay, on delivery, the price of the vehicle. Their agreement to perform these undertakings is a contract. There is no legal duty to enter into such an agreement, but if the parties choose to do so, it will give rise to legal obligations. Therefore, the law of contract is distinct from branches of law where duties are imposed: for example, there is a general duty (in the law of tort) to take care that we do not injure other people by our careless actions. The doctor whose treatment of a patient falls below the professional standard expected of an ordinary practitioner of medicine may be liable for negligence. This liability is not based on a contract (indeed, there is no contractual relationship between a general practitioner and a National Health Service patient); it is a general duty of care imposed by law.

1.2 The word 'contract' suggests to most people a formal or technical document drawn up and understood only by lawyers. Contracts can take this form, and certain types of contract (for instance, for the sale of land or any interest in land) must be in writing; but generally a contract can be made orally, without any legal jargon or formality. We all make numerous contracts as part of everyday life and we rarely give thought to legal technicalities. Making a contract is simply a way of facilitating, amongst other things, the exchange of goods and services. It is merely a method of commercial or consumer transaction. Of course, the transaction can vary enormously in complexity and in value—from the purchase of a chocolate bar to the multi-million-pound takeover of a large company—but it is based on a contract nevertheless.

1.3 To illustrate the importance of contracts in our society, let us consider a day in the life of a fairly ordinary person (X), from the point of view of his contractual relationships. In the morning, the milkman delivers two pints to X's house and X buys a newspaper on the way to work. Both transactions are contracts for the sale of goods. X goes to work on the train, riding under a contract of carriage, and performs various tasks at work under a contract of employment. Later, X returns to a house which is probably subject to a very important contract, namely a lease or a mortgage. X is having the house redecorated, under a contract for the provision of services and materials. X takes a ride in the car that X is buying under a hire purchase agreement, and which is protected by a contract of insurance. On returning home, X watches a DVD which is hired from a local shop. Finally, X walks the dog—no contract there!

The law of contract/s

1.4 There are particular types of contract, such as contracts of employment and contracts for the sale of land, which are subject to their own specialized rules of law and detailed legislation. The law of contract, however, has long survived as such, and is the study of the legal principles which underlie all contracts. It is not (generally) concerned with particular types of contracts and their specialized rules, but provides the important foundation for these specific areas.

1.5 The law of contract is a common law subject: it is primarily derived from the decisions of the courts (precedent), and these judicial rulings constitute the relevant law. Many principles of contract law owe their existence to decisions dating back hundreds of years, whilst some are of comparatively recent origin.

1.6 There are, of course, some important statutes in the general law of contract, for example the Law Reform (Frustrated Contracts) Act 1943, the Misrepresentation Act 1967, the Contracts (Rights of Third Parties) Act 1999, and the Unfair Contract Terms Act 1977. However, there is an increasing volume of consumer contract legislation. In the consumer context, there is the Consumer Rights Act 2015; this covers a much broader range of clauses than the Unfair Contract Terms Act 1977 (UCTA), albeit limited to the consumer context, and UCTA does not now apply in the consumer context. The Law Commissions took the view that consumers need clearer, simpler, and more effective rights in relation to misleading and aggressive trade practices than are provided by the general contract law on duress and misrepresentation,[1] and the Consumer Protection (Amendment) Regulations 2014 bring that about, by making changes to the Consumer Protection from Unfair Trading Regulations 2008. Such an increasing volume of broad consumer legislation may start to create a much more significant division of contract law than anything which has previously occurred—into commercial and consumer contract law.

1.7 Although contract is common law subject, a study of appeal court decisions can create the misleading impression that contracts lead inevitably to disputes and conflict. A contract

1 The Law Commissions, *Consumer Redress for Misleading and Aggressive Practices* (Law Com No 332, Scot Law Com No 226) para. S.18.

law book or course deals with what is comparatively rare (namely legal action in the courts). Traditional approaches tell us little about business practice and how it differs from the formal law. It is particularly important in the area of contractual remedies that we do not overemphasize the importance of lawyers and the courts. As we have noted, a contract is simply a means of facilitating exchange (of goods, services, etc.) and if there is a dispute over its interpretation, or even if one party clearly breaks the agreement, this does not inevitably lead to litigation and the courts. The costs of a legal action can be prohibitive and only the very wealthy can contemplate protracted litigation without considerable unease.

1.8 Even where the parties can afford to go to court there may be good reasons to try to avoid doing so. In commercial practice, some breaches of contract are seen less as a legal problem and more as a commercial one. Companies will want to avoid any damage to their reputation that might be caused by litigation. A legal action, with its formal style, its conflict approach, and its demands on time and money, can be damaging to continuing relationships in the business world. Even if successful, a party will normally fail to recover all the expenses that were incurred. For these and other reasons, business people often try to resolve disputes without recourse to the courts. The same also applies to the consumer, who, generally, can ill afford to take a claim to law. It is better to try negotiation and persuasion in the event of a contractual dispute.

'Freedom of contract'/Inequality of bargaining power

1.9 Many important contractual principles, as expounded by the leading decisions of the courts, were established in the eighteenth and nineteenth centuries. The 'classical' view of contract was that the parties entered into an agreement or bargain freely, and therefore there should be as little state regulation or intervention as possible. It was not the task of the law to ensure that a fair bargain had been struck. This attitude was consistent with the laissez-faire philosophy which was so influential in the thinking of the time; it was consistent with the idea that contracts should be made by the parties (with freedom of choice) and not be imposed on them by the state. It was thought to be consonant with a free market economy and the spirit of competition.

1.10 Even in its historical context, this approach raises obvious questions. It assumes a particular model of contractual activity: namely that between business people of fairly equal resources. It assumes the existence of genuine competition. Of course there never was true equality—a prerequisite for functional freedom of contract. How could such a doctrine apply as between employer and employee, for example? In a more modern context, such a laissez-faire world-view seems absurd. It fails to take account of groups who are particularly susceptible to exploitation, such as consumers, tenants, and employees.

1.11 However, the important concept of inequality of bargaining power came to be recognized. A major influence in the decline of the freedom-of-contract philosophy was the emergence of the consumer as a contractual force. The traditional model of contracts as a means of exchange between business people had to accommodate the idea of exchange between a business person and a consumer. Inevitably, inequality of bargaining strength (in relation to wealth, resources, and experience) had to be acknowledged. The twentieth century saw a move towards greater state regulation of many types of contract. A good example is the Unfair Contract Terms Act 1977, which went further in regulating and restricting the use of exclusion clauses than any previous control provided by the courts. There is also public law regulation of consumer affairs and the increasing influence of European directives.

1.12 There is acceptance of the idea that certain contracting parties need the protection of the law against economic exploitation and oppression. Major legislation has gradually helped to prevent the exploitation of tenants and employees and to reduce the incidence of gender discrimination. However, the extent of protection which is needed and the extent of the departure from freedom of contract which should occur are still hotly disputed. The law of contract is often engaged in trying to balance traditional market liberalism with the need to protect those who may be exploited. As we shall see, one of the most recent contexts in which the battle between the opposing forces of market liberalism and consumer welfarism has been fiercely fought is in relation to the scope of the legislation derived from the Unfair Terms in Consumer Contracts Directive, which is now in the Consumer Rights Act 2015.

Europe

1.13 The European Union has had significant impact upon English contract law. It has brought about significant legislation, such as that implementing the Unfair Terms in Consumer Contracts Directive. It has also simply made English lawyers more aware of the law of other European states, which has particularly occurred through projects like the drafting of the *Principles of EU Contract Law*,[2] produced by a group of academic lawyers from different member states. Such awareness brings consideration of alternative legal strategies which might be adopted by English law. There has also, of course, been much discussion about harmonizing the law of contract in the member states of the European Union. The existence of separate, national laws of contract can be seen to impede the development of an internal market. However, we are now faced with Brexit, and the question of what that may bring in relation to maintaining, or stepping back from, some of the changes that have come through EU law. Whatever happens, the common law currently seems to be alive and well, and continuing to evolve.

Further reading

P. Atiyah, *The Rise and Fall of Freedom of Contract*, Clarendon, 1979

H. Collins, *The European Civil Code: The Way Forward*, Cambridge University Press, 2008

K. Kryczka, 'Electronic Contracts and the Harmonisation of Contract Laws in Europe—An Action Required, A Mission Impossible?' (2005) 13(2) ERPL 149

2 O. Lando and H. Beale (eds), *Principles of EU Contract Law*, Oxford University Press, 2000, parts I and II, and O. Lando, *Principles of EU Contract Law*, Oxford University Press, 2003, part III.

E. McKendrick, 'English Contract Law: A Rich Past, An Uncertain Future' (1997) 50 CLP 25

L. Miller, 'The Common Frame of Reference and the Feasibility of a Common Contract Law in Europe' (2007) (June) JBL 378

D. Staudenmayer, 'The Commission Communication on European Contract Law and the Future Prospects' (2002) 51 ICLQ 673

W. Van Geren, 'Codifying European Private Law? Yes, If' (2002) 27 ELR 156

Chapter 2

Formation of the contract

Agreement

2.1 Whichever definition of the law of contract we use, the word 'agreement' will be central to it. Broadly, a contract is a legally enforceable agreement giving rise to obligations for the parties to it. However, not all agreements are legally binding contracts. For example, social and domestic agreements are generally presumed to lack any intention to create legal relations, and no contract will be found in those situations unless there is very clear evidence of an intention to create legal relations between the parties (see *Balfour* v *Balfour* (1919)): the courts do not want to be overrun by social or domestic agreements being inappropriately disputed before them. More significantly, it is generally not simply agreements which the law will enforce, but 'bargains'. Something of value must normally be supplied by each party, to the other, to make the agreement into a contract. This is the requirement of 'consideration', which is fundamental to 'simple' contracts (those not made by deed—see **Chapter 4**). In *Re Hudson* (1885):

> Hudson had promised to pay £4,000 a year for five years to a religious charity to help it pay off chapel debts. He died before the two final instalments could be paid and his executors claimed that his estate was not liable for the remaining £8,000 as there was no binding contract in law. The judge ruled that no consideration had been given by the charity in exchange for Hudson's promise. The promise was gratuitous, and there was no contract in any legal sense of the word. Thus Hudson's estate was not liable for the remaining instalments.

However, if a promise such as Hudson's was made in writing by deed, it would be enforceable. That formality would give it legal force, even without the presence of consideration. But most contracts are not made in this way and, generally, they depend upon agreement and consideration. A contract generally, therefore, is an agreement with undertakings (promises or obligations) on each side, where there is an intention for the agreement to have legal consequences.

In fact, the appropriateness of applying the contract label to the situation where there is simply a deed, but no consideration and no agreement, is questioned:

> The affinity of the deed is with gift not with bargain, and it is fair to say that the so-called 'contract by deed' has little in common with agreement save its name and its history, and that it does not seem to require detailed consideration in a modern book upon the law of contract.[1]

It is the 'simple' contract, not that by deed, which is our principal concern.

2.2 The agreement is often said to require a meeting of minds between the contracting parties, which is sometimes described as a *consensus ad idem*. However, such statements are apt to mislead, as our law takes a predominantly objective approach to agreement. The law is not generally concerned with what is in the minds of the parties, but with what can be inferred from what was said and done. Statements of this are legion. In *Storer* v *Manchester City Council* [1974] 3 All ER 824, for example, Lord Denning stated (at 828):

> In contracts you do not look into the actual intent in a man's mind. You look at what he said and did. A contract is formed when there is, to all outward appearances, a contract.

More recently, in *RTS Flexible Systems* v *Molkerei Alois Müller GmbH & Co KG* (2010), Lord Clarke stated (at [45]):

> Whether there is a binding contract between the parties, and if so, upon what terms depends upon what they have agreed. It depends not upon their subjective state of mind, but upon a consideration of what was communicated between them by words or conduct, and whether that leads objectively to a conclusion that they intended to create legal relations and had agreed upon all the terms which they regarded or the law requires as essential for the formation of legally binding relations.

2.3 The legal test to establish formation of contract has been most recently explored in two interesting and rather entertaining High Court decisions—*Blue* v *Ashley* [2017] EWHC 1928 (Comm) and *MacInnes* v *Gross* [2017] EWHC 46 (QB).

In *Blue* v *Ashley* (2017):

> The question facing the court was whether a statement made by Mr Ashley to Mr Blue, during an informal meeting in the Horse & Groom public house, that he would pay him a £15 million consultancy fee if he could raise the company's share price to £8 amounted to an enforceable oral contract. Mr Ashley owned the majority shares in Sports Direct and Mr Blue had been employed to provide consultancy services. During the conversation in the meeting in the pub, when both parties consumed a notable amount of alcohol, Mr Ashley allegedly

1 M. Furmston, *Cheshire, Fifoot & Furmston's Law of Contract*, 16th edn, Oxford University Press, 2012, p. 37.

> agreed to pay Mr Blue £15 million if he was able to raise the company share price from its current standing of £4 to £8. The following year, in February 2014, the price hit £8 but Mr Ashley refused to pay £15 million, responding with a far lower payment of £1 million, a payment which he argued was for unconnected reasons.

The court decided that no reasonable person present would have thought that the offer to pay Mr Blue £15 million was serious and had intended to create a legally binding contract. Reference was made to eight main reasons for the finding, including the discussion setting, the nature and tone of the conversation, the apparent lack of commercial sense, the vagueness of the offer, and the perceptions of the parties. As Leggatt J concluded (at 142):

> no one who was actually present in the Horse & Groom that evening—including Mr Blue—did in fact think at the time [that the offer to pay was serious and intended to create a binding contract]. They all thought it was a joke. The fact that Mr Blue has since convinced himself that the offer was a serious one, and that a legally binding agreement was made, shows only that the human capacity for wishful thinking knows few bounds.

In *MacInnes* v *Gross* [2017] EWHC 46 (QB) the court considered whether a contract was formed during a conversation over dinner at a restaurant.

MacInnes was an investment banker who claimed that Gross had reached an oral agreement to pay him a fee for his services in a business sale. When Gross did not pay, MacInnes tried to recover the sum, which he calculated at €13.5 million, arguing the contract had been formed in conversation over dinner. MacInnes had sent an email to Gross after dinner, writing (at para. 40): 'I am delighted we are agreed on headline terms'. This was the only contemporaneous record of the discussions which MacInnes relied upon to claim a legally binding contract had been made; therefore it was for the court to determine whether an agreement had been reached and, if so, on what terms.

Although each party was perceived by the court to be credible, it was evident that both had left the restaurant with two very different views of what had happened. Coulson J found that the informality of the setting was held not to preclude a binding agreement being formed, although it did require the court to closely scrutinize whether there was an intention to create legal relations. As no agreement had been reached on the critical issue of MacInnes's remuneration and the email had contained no reference to key fundamental terms, this represented insufficient certainty of the services to be provided (see further **Chapter 3**) and accordingly MacInnes's claim failed.

In both decisions, *Blue* v *Ashley* (2017) and *MacInnes* v *Gross* (2017), the judiciary relied upon the Supreme Court statement of Lord Clarke in *RTS Flexible Systems* (2010), as noted in para. **2.2**, emphasizing the objective nature of the test of the parties' intention as understood by a reasonable person.[2]

2 Note however a possible limitation on the objective nature of the test where one party's subjective intention is actually known to the other: *Novus Aviation Ltd* v *Alubaf Arab International Bank BSC(c)* [2016] EWHC 1575 (Comm).

2.4 The reason for this predominantly objective approach to establishing the formation of a contract is the difficulty of ascertaining a person's subjective intention. Unlike the criminal law, which deals with the liability of the defendant only, and assesses intent from a subjective perspective, the law of contract has to be fair to *both* parties to an apparent agreement. In the interests of fairness, certainty, and commercial convenience, one party has to be able to rely on the words and conduct of the other, even if it turns out that they were not an accurate reflection of the other party's private or subjective intentions. For example, if a person appears to indicate a willingness to enter into a contract on a particular set of terms, the law will look at how a reasonable person would have understood it. The law will not concern itself with the subjective intention of the apparent maker of the offer, as to do so would be unfair to the other party.[3]

2.5 In the majority of cases there will, of course, be both actual and objective agreement. But the law will not allow the general, objective approach to be abused. If one party *knows* either that the other has no intention of contracting with him or is mistaken as to the proposed terms, despite an objective appearance of agreement, the law will not simply apply the objective test (see *Hartog* v *Colin & Shields* (1939)).

2.6 Whether it is the 'meeting of minds' or agreement which is referred to, the tendency is to think simply in terms of two parties bargaining, and then reaching agreement. However, first, we should not lose sight of the fact that there may, of course, be far more than two parties to a particular contract, and they will each need to intend to contract and supply consideration. Secondly, we must take on board the idea of the 'unilateral contract'. The normal contract with two parties is called a bilateral contract, and the same rules will apply if there are more parties (multilateral). Unilateral contracts do differ from the others in important respects, however, as we shall see at various points. Here we should merely note what is meant by a unilateral contract. The name, '*uni*lateral', comes from the fact that only one party becomes bound to do anything. The immediate reaction to this might be to ask, 'what about consideration, then?', but each party will supply consideration. This is not the puzzle it sounds. A unilateral contract will be of the form 'A promises to do X, if B does Y'. The most common example of such contracts is that for a reward, where, for example, A has promised to pay £10 to anyone who returns his lost dog, Spot. B sees the reward poster, B returns Spot, and A is contractually bound to pay the £10 to B. It is a unilateral contract, with only one party ever coming under an obligation, because B was never contractually bound to find and return Spot. However, when B returned Spot, B's actions supplied consideration for A's promise, and fulfilled the condition under which A became obliged to pay. As has been

3 It should be noted that there are differing views on precisely what is meant by an 'objective' approach to agreement: from which perspective should the reasonable person view any statements/actions—from that of the 'fly on the wall' or that of one of the relevant parties? For further discussion, see, e.g., Howarth, 100 LQR 265; De Moor, 106 LQR 632; and Friedmann, 119 LQR 68, but note what has become the predominant approach in the context of interpretation: 'Interpretation is the ascertainment of the meaning which the document would convey to a reasonable person having all the background knowledge which would reasonably have been available to the parties in the situation in which they were at the time of the contract': *Investors Compensation Scheme Ltd* v *West Bromwich Building Society* [1998] 1 All ER 98, Lord Hoffmann at 114.

indicated, unilateral contracts will need to be referred to at points, but it must not be forgotten that they are not the commonly occurring, usual type of contract; that is the bilateral contract.

Offer and acceptance

2.7 In deciding whether the parties have reached contractual agreement, the law generally looks for an offer by one party and an acceptance of the terms of that offer by the other. In the bargaining process, one party will finally propose terms (price, date of delivery, etc.) and express a willingness to be bound by them if the other party signifies acceptance of them, and a contractual agreement is found when the other party accepts. The 'offer and acceptance' analysis generally determines whether or not there is sufficient agreement to form a contract, but it should be noted, at the start, that it is not absolutely required to be used. In *Gibson* v *Manchester City Council* (1979), Lord Diplock stated:

> My Lords, there may be certain types of contract, though I think they are exceptional, which do not fit easily into the normal analysis of a contract as being constituted by offer and acceptance, but a contract alleged to have been made by an exchange of correspondence between the parties in which the successive communications other than the first are in reply to one another is not one of these.

There are some situations which simply do not fit the offer and acceptance analysis (see, for example, *Clarke* v *Earl of Dunraven* (1897) for an unusual contract scenario which did not fit the traditional analysis), and some situations, such as the 'battle of the forms', which is considered later in the chapter, which can place its use under great strain.

Offer

2.8 An offer is a promise by one party (the offeror) to enter into a contract, on a particular set of terms, with the intention of being bound as soon as the other party (the offeree) signifies his or her acceptance. An offer may be made either to an individual person or to a particular group of people, or it may be made to the general public (as in the case of a reward offered for the provision of information). An offer may be written, spoken, or implied by conduct, and it may be made with varying degrees of complexity. Although this is simple enough to state, and to understand, it may be difficult to apply it to a particular set of facts. During the bargaining process, there may be a series of communications between the parties as they move towards a final agreement and it may be difficult to determine whether a particular statement was an offer or something else, and the cases are not always easy to reconcile on their facts.

Offer or invitation to treat?

2.9 The question of whether there was an offer is usually put in terms of whether there was an offer or an invitation to treat. There is no particular significance to the phrase 'invitation to treat', other than that it is the one which we generally use to distinguish, from an offer, a statement which is merely indicating a willingness to commence, or continue, negotiations. The offer is the legally significant statement, and offer is the legally significant terminology, so we do not need to define an invitation to treat. All we need to do is distinguish it from an offer: the offer will contain the intention to be bound, if the other party accepts. An invitation to treat will not contain that intention. This is a distinction which is easy to state, but again, it may be difficult to decide on which side of the line a particular communication falls.

2.10 An illustration of the difficulty in distinguishing between an offer and an invitation to treat is provided by *Gibson* v *Manchester City Council* (1979). The facts were:

> The Conservative-controlled Manchester City Council advertised details of a scheme for tenants to buy their council houses from the corporation and C expressed interest and asked to be told the price of buying his house. The city treasurer wrote in reply: 'The corporation may be prepared to sell the house to you at . . . £2,180', but the letter was not to be 'regarded as a firm offer of a mortgage'. C had to fill in a form to make a formal application, which he did, leaving blank the purchase price and listing certain defects in the property. He was told by the council that the price had been fixed in accordance with the condition of the property, and wrote that he wished to go ahead on the basis of his application. The council took the house off the list of tenant-occupied houses which had to be maintained by them, and put it on their house purchase list. As a result of a local election, Labour gained control of the council and reversed the policy of selling council houses. They would sell only those houses where a legally binding contract had already been concluded.

The trial judge and the Court of Appeal decided that there was a contract and ordered specific performance (i.e. an order compelling Manchester Council to sell the property to C). In the Court of Appeal, Lord Denning stated that the parties appeared to have reached agreement on all the material terms, and this was evidenced by their correspondence and conduct. He thought that it did not matter that 'all the formalities had not been gone through'.[4] He was critical of the traditional offer and acceptance approach, and that received the response from Lord Diplock, indicated earlier, that although there are exceptional situations where it is not appropriate, it generally is, particularly in a case concerned with a chain of communications, each in response to the other.

2.11 The House of Lords allowed the council's appeal and made it clear that the council's statement of the price of the house was not an offer to Mr Gibson. It was merely one stage in the negotiating process. The language of the treasurer's letter indicated this with the phrase 'may be prepared to sell'. In reply to the argument that the parties' agreement could be shown by their conduct, it can be said that their conduct was equivocal. The house was taken off the list of properties maintained by the council, but this could merely indicate that the house was expected to be sold in the near future, and not that agreement had been reached. In addition to the force of the use of the phrase 'may be prepared to sell' as indicating that the treasurer's letter was not an

4 See [1978] 2 All ER 583 at 586.

offer, there was also uncertainty over whether C would be granted a mortgage: would C have wanted to go ahead if he had been unable to obtain one? Would he have expected to be obliged to do so? The successive communications between the parties show that they were feeling their way towards agreement, but that the negotiations had not yet ripened into a contract. (Contrast *Storer* v *Manchester City Council* (1974).)

2.12 As *Gibson* v *Manchester City Council* (1979) illustrates, the statement of a price by one party does not necessarily indicate that there is an offer to sell at that price, without further negotiations. Obviously, there is unlikely to be an offer without some statement of the price, or as to the means of determining it (for example, the market price on a specified date), but its presence is not determinative that there is an offer. It is important to look at all the surrounding circumstances. In *Harvey* v *Facey* (1893), C sent a telegram to D: 'Will you sell us Bumper Hall Pen? Telegraph lowest cash price.' D's telegram replied: 'Lowest price for Bumper Hall Pen, £900.' C's final telegram purported to accept this 'offer' and 'agreed' to buy the property for £900. The Privy Council held that there was no contract, as D was not making an offer merely by responding to C's request for information. There was no clear intention by D to be bound simply by C's expression of assent. (For a similar result, see *Clifton* v *Palumbo* (1944).)

2.13 The distinction between an offer and an invitation to treat is often difficult to draw. One has to consider the communications between the parties and try to ascertain the intention with which a statement was made. Does the statement show a willingness to be bound if the other party expresses agreement? It may be necessary to look at a series of statements, or letters, which pass between the parties during the negotiating process, to assess the overall impression conveyed by these communications. In *Bigg* v *Boyd Gibbins Ltd* [1971] 2 All ER 183, during the course of negotiations for the sale of his property to D, C stated that 'for a quick sale [he] would accept £26,000'. D replied by letter that he accepted this offer. C wrote back, expressing his pleasure at D's decision and stating that he was putting the matter in the hands of his solicitor to proceed with the sale. The Court of Appeal held that the impression given by these communications was that the parties 'intended to and did achieve the formation of a . . . contract' (per Russell LJ at 185).

2.14 The use of the word 'offer' by one party is not decisive. It might not be being used in its technical sense. In *Spencer* v *Harding* (1870) LR 5 CP 561, D sent out a circular: 'We are instructed to offer [certain business stock] to the wholesale trade for sale by tender.' C's tender for the stock was the highest that D received, but D refused it. C's contention was that the circular amounted to an offer and contained a promise to sell to the highest bidder. Generally, advertisements are not regarded as offers, but C tried to draw an analogy with advertisements of rewards for information (dealt with later), where there is a promise to pay the first person who supplies the information. But the court rejected this line of reasoning; there was no promise to sell to the highest bidder. In finding for the defendant, Willes J stated (at 563):

> [T]he question is, whether there is here any offer to enter into a contract at all, or whether the circular amounts to anything more than a mere proclamation that the defendants are ready to chaffer for the sale of goods, and to receive offers for the purchase of them . . . Here there

> is a total absence of any words to intimate that the highest bidder is to be the purchaser. It is a mere attempt to ascertain whether an offer can be obtained within such a margin as the sellers are willing to adopt.

2.15 However, the circumstances in each case will be important, and the words used may make it clear that there is an intention to be bound, and an offer, rather than an invitation to treat, and there may even be a subsidiary offer, alongside a more important invitation to treat. In *Harvela Investments Ltd* v *Royal Trust Co. of Canada* (1984):

> D(1) owned a parcel of shares which would give effective control of a company to either C or D(2), who were rivals bidding for the shares. D(1) invited both parties to submit, by sealed bid, a 'single offer' for the whole parcel by a particular time and date. In making the invitation, they stated: 'we bind ourselves to accept [the highest] offer.' C made a single bid, but D(2)'s bid was really two bids, being (a) for a fixed monetary amount (which was less than that bid by C); and (b) a referential bid which offered $101,000 in excess of any other offer that D(1) received. D(1) accepted D(2)'s referential bid and entered into a contract with them for the sale of the shares. C claimed that D(2)'s successful bid was not valid as it was not within the terms of the original invitation to bid (because it was not a 'single offer'). C succeeded in this action. (Despite reversal in the Court of Appeal, the House of Lords restored the original decision in C's favour.)

In this case we can see a different intention on the part of the sellers, when inviting bids, from that in *Spencer* v *Harding* (1870). In *Harvela*, the sellers bound themselves to accept the highest offer. This statement was an offer rather than a mere invitation to treat, which C accepted by the submission of its bid.

2.16 On the particular facts of a case, the court may be willing to find other subsidiary offers, alongside invitations to treat. In *Blackpool and Fylde Aero Club Ltd* v *Blackpool Borough Council* [1990] 3 All ER 25 the facts were as follows:

> The defendant council owned an airport, from which it permitted an air operator to run pleasure trips. This concession had been granted to the claimant club (C) on previous occasions. On the expiry of the last concession, the council invited C and six other parties to tender for the rights to operate pleasure flights from the airport. A very clear procedure for submitting bids was laid down by the council, and it was stated that tenders received after noon on 17 March 1983 would not be considered. Only C and two others responded to this invitation. C's tender was put in the Town Hall letter box one hour before the deadline, but due to an oversight the letter box was not cleared by council staff at noon that day as it was supposed to be. (The council accepted that this was due to administrative error.) C's tender was recorded as late, and was not considered. C contended that the council was contractually bound to consider any tender that was validly made, and received, by the deadline. It sought damages from the council.

It was clear from the wording of the council's invitation to tender that it was not promising to accept the highest tender it received. But was it bound at least to consider all tenders submitted within the specified period? The Court of Appeal held that the council was liable in damages to the club for breach of contract. It held that, in certain circumstances, an invitation to tender could give rise to a contractual undertaking by the invitor to consider tenders which conformed with the stipulated conditions of tender. Bingham LJ stated (at 30):

> [W]here, as here, tenders are solicited from selected parties all of them known to the invitor, and where a local authority's invitation prescribes a clear, orderly and familiar procedure . . . the invitee is in my judgment protected at least to this extent: if he submits a conforming tender before the deadline he is entitled, not as a matter of mere expectation but of contractual right, to be sure that his tender will after the deadline be opened and considered in conjunction with all other conforming tenders or at least that his tender will be considered if others are.

The council was not obliged to accept any tender. Alternatively, it could have awarded the concession to any tenderer, so long as the decision was taken in good faith. But the council was contractually bound to consider C's tender before making its decision.[5]

Offer or invitation to treat: some common situations

2.17 Undoubtedly, it can be difficult to know how the offer and acceptance analysis should apply in every case, but there have come to be generally accepted analyses of certain commonly occurring situations, which will normally be adopted in those situations, but which could, of course, be departed from in the face of a contrary intention being clearly shown.

Advertisements

2.18 Advertisement of goods for sale are not generally regarded as offers. In *Partridge* v *Crittenden* (1968) the appellant was charged, under legislation for the protection of wild birds, with unlawfully offering for sale a wild bird. He had placed an advertisement in a magazine: 'Bramblefinch cocks and hens, 25s each.' The Divisional Court held that the appellant was not liable for the statutory offence as he had not offered the birds for sale; the advertisement was an invitation to treat.

2.19 Similarly, the particular type of 'advertisement' which is in the form of a catalogue or circular with a price list will not generally be regarded as making an offer to sell those goods.

5 Such cases raise difficult issues in relation to the point at which, short of the 'main contract' coming into being, legal obligations should be triggered. They raise questions as to whether the courts are not really finding subsidiary contracts but surreptitiously requiring compliance with some limited duty to behave in good faith during negotiations, which, occasionally, a party steps outside of. We say 'surreptitiously' as certainly no such duty is openly recognized in English law.

If a person sees a price list and places an order, the seller is not normally bound to supply the goods. In *Grainger & Son* v *Gough* [1896] AC 325, Lord Herschell said (at 334):

> The transmission of such a price-list does not amount to an offer to supply an unlimited quantity of the wine described at the price named, so that as soon as an order is given there is a binding contract to supply that quantity. If it were so, the merchant might find himself involved in any number of contractual obligations to supply wine of a particular description which he would be quite unable to carry out, his stock of wine of that description being necessarily limited.

A seller of goods wants to be able to provide information about his or her goods (i.e. advertise them) without risking being bound to sell more of the specified items than he or she has (and it is in the interests of fostering a competitive market that he or she should be able to do so). This is seen as indicating that adverts are not generally intended as offers, but merely invitations to treat. Of course, the problem might equally have been met by generally implying that an advertised offer was subject to stock availability, but it is the accepted line that adverts are generally not offers, but merely invitations to treat.

2.20 An advertisement of reward is, however, generally an offer. They are of course unusual offers, in that they are offers of unilateral, rather than normal bilateral, contracts. Similarly, *Carlill* v *Carbolic Smoke Ball Co* (1893)—which is a very famous case, and one where an advert was found to be an offer—was about an offer of a unilateral contract, and its membership of that unusual category must not be forgotten.

The defendant company placed an advertisement in the newspaper offering a reward of £100 to anyone who bought one of its smoke balls and used it in the prescribed manner, and yet caught influenza. The advert stated that, to show its 'sincerity in the matter', the company had deposited £1,000 with its bank. Relying upon the advertisement, C bought a smoke ball and used it as directed—and, needless to say, still caught influenza. C sued successfully for the £100 reward and the defendant company appealed against the decision.

A variety of arguments were put forward by the defendants to defeat C's claim. It was argued that the advert was too vague and that the defendants did not intend to be bound by it. These arguments were rejected by the Court of Appeal which held that both the meaning and the effect of the advertisement were clear, particularly with the statement as to the deposit of £1,000. (It was also argued that there was no contract, as C had not notified the defendants of her acceptance. However, although acceptance does generally have to be communicated, this is not the case where the offer is unilateral. The contract is made by carrying out the relevant act or condition.[6])

6 See also *Bowerman* v *Association of British Travel Agents Ltd* (1996) and *Vehicle Control Services Ltd* v *Revenue and Customs Commissioners* (2013).

Items displayed in shops

2.21 It might be supposed that goods displayed in shop windows or on shop counters, with the prices clearly marked, are being offered for sale. In certain types of shops or markets a limited degree of bargaining (or 'haggling') may be possible, but in the vast majority of shops, stores, and supermarkets this is neither possible nor expected; goods are to be sold at the prices shown and no negotiation takes place between retailer and customer. Yet it is firmly established that the display of goods in a shop is generally not an offer to sell those goods, but merely an invitation to treat. In *Pharmaceutical Society of Great Britain* v *Boots Cash Chemists (Southern) Ltd* [1953] 1 QB 401:

> It had to be decided at what point a contract is concluded in a 'self-service' shop where the goods are priced and displayed on shelves, selected by customers, and then taken to the cash desk for payment. The case arose under s 18(1) of the Pharmacy and Poisons Act 1933 which stated that 'it shall not be lawful—(a) for a person to sell any [listed] poison, unless . . . the sale is effected by, or under the supervision of a registered pharmacist'. The case was brought to establish whether the defendants were breaking the law by positioning their registered pharmacist adjacent to the cash desk. If the display of goods on the shelves were regarded as an offer to sell, and could be accepted by the customer when they were picked up and put into the basket provided, then the defendants were breaking the law, as the sale would not be supervised by the pharmacist as required by the statute. But if the display of items was merely an invitation to treat and it was the customer who made the offer at the cash desk, then Boots were complying with the law.

It was decided that the contract was concluded at the cash desk. The customer made the offer, and this could be accepted or rejected by the defendants. Therefore, sales were supervised by the registered pharmacist. The court took the line (per Somervell LJ) that if the display of items on the shelf amounted to an offer, a customer who picked up items and put them into the basket provided would thereby accept the offer and be contractually bound to pay for the goods even if the customer later changed his or her mind and did not want the goods. Somervell LJ stated (at 406):

> I can see no reason for implying from this self-service arrangement any implication other than that . . . it is a convenient method of enabling customers to see what there is and choose, and possibly put back and substitute, articles which they wish to have, and then go up to the cashier and offer to buy what they have so far chosen.

2.22 It could be argued with equal force that if the display of goods were regarded as an offer, the acceptance by the customer would take place only when the goods are presented at the cash desk for payment, and not when they are placed into the basket. However, it is the accepted line that the display of goods in a self-service shop, supermarket, or shop window does not amount to an offer to sell those goods. In *Fisher* v *Bell* (1961), it was, for example, also held that the display of a 'flick-knife' in a shop window was not an offer to sell it. (It does not affect the contractual outcome, but it is worth noting that if a shop lures in customers with displays of goods at a low price, and then refuses to sell them to the customer at that price, it may well be an offence under the Consumer Protection from Unfair Trading Regulations 2008 (SI 2008/1277), which implemented Directive 2005/29/EC of the European Parliament and of the council concerning unfair business-to-consumer practices.)

Auctions

2.23 Where an auctioneer asks for bids, he or she is not making an offer to sell the goods to the highest bidder. It was established in *Payne* v *Cave* (1789) that the auctioneer is merely inviting offers from bidders, which he can either accept or reject. This rule is now encapsulated in s 57(2) of the Sale of Goods Act 1979, which states:

> A sale by auction is complete when the auctioneer announces its completion by the fall of the hammer, or in other customary manner; and until the announcement is made any bidder may retract his bid.

2.24 The advertisement of an auction sale is not an offer to sell particular goods (*Harris* v *Nickerson* (1873)). But is there a binding promise to sell the goods to the highest bidder where an auction sale, which is advertised as 'without reserve', actually takes place? The point was not resolved entirely by the case of *Warlow* v *Harrison* (1859), despite *obiter dicta* supporting the view that such an advertisement may include a separate and binding promise by the auctioneer to sell to the highest bona fide bidder. The decision of the Court of Appeal in *Barry* v *Davies (t/a Heathcote Ball & Co.)* (2001), however, confirmed that this is the correct approach. In that case, two machines were advertised for sale by auction without reserve. B, the claimant, was the sole bidder and his bid of £200 for each of them fell a long way short of the commercial value of the machines. D, the auctioneer, refused to sell the machines to B and withdrew them from sale. The trial judge and the Court of Appeal held that, in doing this, D was in breach of contract. In an auction sale without reserve, it was not open to the auctioneer to reject the highest bid—in this case the only bid—simply because it was not high enough. This may appear a harsh decision in these circumstances, where the bid was far below the estimated value of the goods. However, if the seller wishes to avoid such a risk, a reserve price can be stipulated.[7]

Advertisements on websites

2.25 It is increasingly common for customers to buy goods by selecting items advertised on websites and making payment for them by credit card. Such websites combine the attributes of both advertisements and shops, and it seems likely that the normal inference will be that they are making invitations to treat, and not offers, unless there is something on the website that clearly shows that the site intends to be bound.[8] It is more likely, however, that the website will expressly provide that it is not making an offer, that the customer makes an offer when his or her 'order' is submitted, and

7 For further discussion, see F. Meisel, 'What Price Auctions Without Reserve?' (2001) 64 Mod LR 468.

8 Electronic Commerce (EC Directive) Regulations 2002 require, unless parties who are not consumers have agreed otherwise, the service provider to explain to customers in plain terms, where a contract is made by electronic means, the *technical steps* to follow to complete a binding agreement (reg. 9(1)).

that there will be no acceptance until the customer is notified that the goods have been dispatched. Amongst other things, this will serve to protect the website against pricing mistakes it makes—customers will not be able to claim that they have a contract to buy the television mistakenly advertised at £3.99 (instead of £399), just because they have placed an 'order'. Article 11 of the UN Convention on the Use of Electronic Communications in International Contracts, which is not binding on the courts of England and Wales but merely of interest in relation to such contracts, provides:

> A proposal to conclude a contract made through one or more electronic communications which is not addressed to one or more specific parties, but is generally accessible to parties making use of information systems, including proposals that make use of interactive applications for the placement of orders through such information systems, is to be considered as an invitation to make offers, unless it clearly indicates the intention of the party making a proposal to be bound in the case of acceptance.

Termination of offers

2.26 There are a number of ways in which an offer may be terminated before an acceptance has taken place. We should briefly consider them, before looking at acceptance.

Revocation (or withdrawal)

2.27 Obviously an offer cannot be withdrawn once it has been accepted, but it may be revoked at any time before acceptance has occurred (see *Payne* v *Cave* (1789)). In fact, the offeror may generally withdraw the offer even if it was expressly stated that it would remain open for a fixed period (*Routledge* v *Grant* (1828) 130 ER 920), unless there was consideration for such a promise (i.e. a separate contract that the main offer would remain open for a specified period). In *Routledge* v *Grant* (1828) the defendant offered to take a lease of the claimant's premises, giving the claimant six weeks to make up his mind. Three weeks later, the defendant withdrew the offer and, afterwards, the claimant purported to accept within the six-week period. The court held that there was no contract, as the defendant was free to withdraw the offer at any time before acceptance by the offeree. Despite the defendant's promise, the offer did not have to remain open for six weeks. Best CJ said (at 923):

> [I]f six weeks are given on one side to accept an offer, the other side has six weeks to put an end to it. One party cannot be bound without the other.

2.28 As has been indicated, the situation will, of course, be different if the offeree provides consideration for the offeror's promise to keep the offer open (for example, pays £x for it). In this case there will be a separate or 'collateral' contract between the parties; the offeror's promise will no longer be one-sided.

2.29 Although an offer may be withdrawn at any time before the offeree has accepted it, the withdrawal has to be communicated to the offeree. It is not sufficient for the offeror merely to change his or her mind without informing the offeree. In particular, it should be noted that the 'postal rule'—which, as we shall see, makes a posted acceptance effective on posting, rather than requiring its communication—does not apply to a posted revocation (*Byrne & Co* v *Leon Van Tienhoven & Co.* (1880)).

2.30 Although the withdrawal of an offer must be communicated to the offeree, it appears that the offeree does not have to be notified of the withdrawal by the offeror. In *Dickinson* v *Dodds* (1876) 2 Ch D 463, D made an offer to C for C to buy certain land from D for £800, and D promised that the offer would remain open for two days (until 9 a.m. on 12 June). But D sold the land to someone else on 11 June, and C learned of this later the same day, by chance, via a third party. C then proceeded to notify D of his acceptance of the offer before 9 a.m. on 12 June. The Court of Appeal held that C's action for specific performance failed, as there was no contract between C and D. We have seen already that a promise to keep an offer open for a specific period is not, by itself, binding on the offeror. But was the withdrawal of the offer effectively communicated to the offeree? James LJ (at 472) had no doubt that it was:

> [I]n this case, beyond all question, the [claimant] knew that Dodds was no longer minded to sell the property to him as plainly and clearly as if Dodds had told him in so many words, 'I withdraw the offer'.

Of course, an offer may be withdrawn by someone whom the offeror has authorized to communicate that to the offeree, but that was not what occurred in *Dickinson* v *Dodds,* and unless the offeree believes the offer has been withdrawn, third party notification of withdrawal should be restricted to the situation where the third party would be seen as a reliable source of that information, whom the reasonable person would believe.

Rejection

2.31 An offer is terminated if the offeree rejects the offer. It is not possible for the offeree to subsequently change his or her mind and accept. It will be seen that a counter offer amounts to a rejection of the original offer (*Hyde* v *Wrench* (1840)), but the offeree does not make a counter offer where he or she merely seeks further information from the offeror (See *Stevenson, Jacques, & Co.* v *McLean* (1880)). See further paras 2.39 and 2.40.

Lapse of time

2.32 An offer may come to an end due to lapse of time. If A, on Monday, offers to sell his car to B and says 'I must have your answer by Friday at the latest', B cannot accept the offer on Saturday. In many cases, the offeror does not stipulate that the offer must be accepted within a specified period. However, it would be impracticable if offers could last indefinitely, and where no time limit is specified, they will lapse after a reasonable time. What amounts to a reasonable time will depend on the circumstances of the case and must take account of the subject matter of the offer. In *Ramsgate Victoria Hotel Co.* v *Montefiore* (1866), an offer to buy shares that was made in June could not be accepted in November.

Where the offer is conditional

2.33 An offer may be expressed as subject to the occurrence of some condition. For example, A may offer to sell goods to B subject to his being able to obtain supplies himself. If A subsequently cannot obtain supplies, the offer will come to an end. The offer was conditional on a particular state of affairs, which did not occur. The courts can also imply a condition into an offer where it has not been expressly stated by the offeror. If A offers to buy goods, or to take them on hire purchase, it will be implied that the offer is subject to the condition that the goods will remain in (substantially) the same state that they were in at the time of the offer. (See *Financings Ltd* v *Stimson* [1962] 3 All ER 386, especially Donovan LJ at 390.)

Death

2.34 What is the position where the offeror dies after making an offer but before the offeree has accepted? If it is an offer of a 'personal' contract (involving a personal service such as employment or agency), the offer should come to an end with the death of the offeror. Otherwise, it is possible for an offer to continue even after the death of the offeror, where the offeree accepts without knowing of the offeror's death (see *Bradbury* v *Morgan* (1862)). In this event the obligations under the contract will fall on the offeror's personal representatives.

2.35 Where the offeree dies after an offer has been made, it seems both likely and sensible that the offer comes to an end. It must be acknowledged, however, that the cases are not conclusive. In *Reynolds* v *Atherton* (1921), Warrington LJ stated that an offer 'made to a living person who ceases to be a living person before the offer is accepted . . . is no longer an offer at all', but the case was actually decided on different grounds.

Acceptance

2.36 As has been indicated, the usual way to decide if the necessary agreement is present for there to be a contract is to look for offer and acceptance. We have discussed various aspects of offers, and we will now look at what will amount to acceptance.

2.37 What constitutes acceptance of an offer? It is the final expression of assent, by words or conduct, to the offer or proposal. It is important that the acceptance is both final and unequivocal. It must be an acceptance of the offeror's proposal without varying the terms or adding new terms. (For obvious reasons, this is sometimes referred to as the 'mirror image rule'.) A purported acceptance which attempts to introduce new terms, or vary those contained in the offer, will be a counter offer and not an acceptance of the original offer.

2.38 In *Jones* v *Daniel* (1894) D wrote and offered to buy C's property for £1,450, and received a reply from C's solicitor which purported to accept the offer and enclosed a contract for D's signature. However, the document contained important new terms, which were not part of D's original offer, and D refused to sign it. It was held that there was no contract between the parties. The letter from C's solicitor (with its draft contract) was not an acceptance but a counter offer, which D was free to accept or reject. Similarly, if a person offers to pay a fixed price for services and materials, this will not be accepted by a promise to provide those services and materials at a variable price.[9]

2.39 As has been indicated, a counter offer amounts to a rejection of the original offer, which cannot thereafter be accepted. In *Hyde* v *Wrench* (1840), D made a written offer to sell his farm to C for £1,000, to which C replied that he would give £950 for it. D refused to sell at the lower price and, a few days later, C wrote to D agreeing to pay £1,000 for the property. D had not withdrawn his original offer, but he now refused to sell to C. The court held that there was no contract. C's counter offer (of £950) was a rejection of D's original offer and brought it to an end. It could not be revived afterwards by C simply purporting to accept it.

2.40 However, there are situations where the offeree does not put forward a new proposal, but merely seeks clarification of the offer, or further information about it, from the offeror. In such a case the offer is not to be regarded as rejected and it is still open to the offeree to accept it. This is illustrated by the case of *Stevenson, Jacques & Co.* v *McLean* (1880) 5 QBD 346:

> D wrote to C offering to sell a quantity of iron at '40s per ton net cash', and stating that the offer would remain open until the following Monday. It was clear from communications between the parties that C, in turn, was looking for buyers and that the market was unsettled. Early on Monday morning, C sent D a telegram: 'Please wire whether you would accept forty for delivery over two months, or if not, longest limit you would give.' D did not answer C's question and sold the iron to a third party. On Monday afternoon, C (having had no reply) sent another telegram accepting D's offer to sell at 40s cash. C's final telegram was sent before D's withdrawal of the offer reached C. C sued for breach of contract, and D claimed that C's telegram of Monday morning amounted to a counter offer and therefore a rejection of D's offer.

Was C's first telegram a fresh proposal, or did it merely seek to clarify an aspect of D's offer? The distinction can be a very fine one, but the court ruled in C's favour. Lush J held that C did not make a counter offer: 'Here there is no counter proposal . . . there is nothing specific by way of offer or rejection, but a mere enquiry, which should have been answered and not treated as a rejection of the offer' (at 350).

Communication of acceptance

2.41 Unsurprisingly, the general rule is that an acceptance must be communicated to be effective and create a contract.[10] As in many other ways, unilateral contracts are exceptional and do not require communication, and there is an odd, but longstanding, exception for posted acceptances in relation to our normal bilateral contracts. We shall look at these exceptional

9 See *North West Leicestershire District Council* v *East Midlands Housing Association* (1981).

10 *Entores Ltd* v *Miles Far Eastern Corp* (1955); *Brinkibon Ltd* v *Stahag Stahl und Stahlwarenhandelgesellschaft mbH* (1983).

situations later, but here we should firmly emphasize that the general rule is that acceptance must be communicated.[11] Obviously acceptance can be communicated not only by spoken or written words but also by conduct, and *Brogden* v *Metropolitan Rly Co.* (1877) 2 App Cas 666 provides an example of that:

> B had supplied the Metropolitan Railway Co. with coal for some years without a formal agreement. The parties decided to formalize their transactions and the Metropolitan Railway Co. sent B a draft agreement. B completed certain details in the draft which had been left blank, including the name of an arbitrator, and B then signed it and wrote 'approved', and returned it to the Metropolitan Railway Co., whose manager put it in his desk. Nothing further was done formally with the document, but for some time the parties acted in accordance with its arrangements by supplying and paying for the coal. Finally a disagreement arose and B denied that there was a binding contract between the parties.

The addition of the arbitrator's name by B was a new term, and therefore a counter offer. Did the Metropolitan Railway Co. accept this offer? Obviously, the manager merely putting the document in his desk could not amount to acceptance. Not only was it an equivocal action, but it also did nothing to communicate to the other party. However, the Metropolitan Railway Co. placed an order for, and accepted coal, on the basis of the agreement. As Lord Cairns stated (at 680):

> [A]pprobation was clearly given when the company commenced a course of dealing which is referable . . . only to the contract, and when that course of dealing was accepted and acted upon by [B] in the supply of coals.

2.42 Although it will be extremely rare, as the meaning of silence is generally not unequivocal, it would seem that there can be cases where silence can communicate acceptance.[12] However, it is clear that one party cannot force another to have to take positive action, to deny they are accepting, if they are to avoid becoming bound. X cannot create a contract out of Y's silence by writing to Y stating: 'I will sell you my car for £1,000. If I do not hear from you within seven days, I shall assume that you accept.' The law will not allow X to take advantage of the common human tendency to inaction in this way. Y will not become contractually bound to buy X's car simply on the basis that Y has not communicated a denial of acceptance to X.

2.43 Something of this type of situation arose in *Felthouse* v *Bindley* (1862). In that case:

> C entered into negotiations with his nephew, J, for the purchase of J's horse. He wrote to J shortly after, offering to buy the horse and stating: 'If I hear no more about him, I consider the horse is mine at £30 15s.' J did not reply to his uncle's letter, but he did instruct the auctioneer

11 *Entores Ltd* v *Miles Far Eastern Corp* (1955); *Brinkibon Ltd* v *Stahag Stahl und Stahlwarenhandelgesellschaft mbH* (1983).

12 *The Hannah Blumenthal* (1983); *Vitol SA* v *Norelf Ltd* [1996] AC 800 per Lord Steyn at 810.

(D) not to sell the horse along with his, J's, farming stock. D forgot this instruction and six weeks after C's letter, the horse was sold by D to another person. C sued D for conversion (in tort) basing his action on the contention that there was a concluded contract between C and J for the sale of the horse, and that, therefore, the horse belonged to C at the time of the auction. But was there a binding agreement between C and his nephew?

The court decided that the action for conversion failed. Although the nephew may have decided to sell the horse to his uncle, there was no communication of this decision to the uncle. Accordingly, there was no binding agreement between C and J, and the horse never became the uncle's property. This illustrates that X cannot turn Y's silence into acceptance, merely by stating that is to be the case.

2.44 However, the situation may well be different if Y is claiming that X should be bound. Whilst X cannot trap Y in a contract against Y's wishes in this way, it would seem that Y should be able to say that he or she has a contract with X. X may be seen to have 'waived' communication, and so be unable to deny there is a contract without it.

Acceptance by post

2.45 The general rule, then, is that for an acceptance to be effective, it must be communicated to the offeror.[13] As has been indicated, however, there is a rule of great age, and very limited justification, that this does not apply to posted acceptances, but rather we have an exception which is known as 'the postal rule'.

2.46 The postal rule is an exception to the 'general rule . . . that a contract is formed when acceptance of an offer is communicated by the offeree to the offeror' (*Brinkibon Ltd* v *Stahag Stahl und Stahlwarenhandelsgesellschaft mbH* [1983] 2 AC 34 at 41). It stems from *Adams* v *Lindsell* (1818), and under it a contract is formed when a letter of acceptance is posted. It applies when it is reasonable to use the post (*Henthorn* v *Fraser* (1892)), and is subject to the offeror not ousting its application (*Holwell Securities Ltd* v *Hughes* (1974)). It means that an offer can no longer be revoked once the acceptance has been posted (*Re Imperial Land Co of Marseilles (Harris' case)* (1872)), and it is generally irrelevant that the acceptance never arrives, or arrives late (*Household Fire and Accident Insurance Co* v *Grant* (1879)), although the postal rule will not apply if loss or delay is due to the fault of the offeree, who has, for example, not put the correct stamps on it, or has misaddressed it (*L J Korbetis* v *Transgrain Shipping BV* [2005] EWHC (QB) 1345 at [15]). It is also said that it will give way to 'manifcst inconvenience and absurdity' (*IIolwell Securities* v *Hughes* (1974)). We should enlarge on some of these points before considering the basis of the rule and its extension to other forms of communication.

13 *Entores Ltd* v *Miles Far Eastern Corp* (1955); *Brinkibon Ltd* v *Stahag Stahl und Stahlwarenhandelgesellscaft mbH* (1983).

2.47 The postal rule stems from the case of *Adams* v *Lindsell* (1818):

> D wrote to C offering to sell wool and requested a reply 'in the course of post'. D misdirected the letter and this caused it to be delayed for a couple of days. On receiving the letter, C replied immediately, by posting a letter of acceptance. After C's acceptance was posted, but before it arrived, D sold the wool to a third party, in the belief that C was not interested.

The court decided that a contract was concluded between D and C when the letter of acceptance was posted by C. Obviously this produced a just result in the instant case. However, as a general rule for postal communication, it has its difficulties, and lacks justification, to which we shall return.

2.48 As has been indicated, the postal rule means that it is generally irrelevant that the postal acceptance never arrives, or arrives late (*Household Fire and Accident Insurance Co* v *Grant* (1879)), but the rule will not apply if that loss or delay is due to the fault of the offeree, who has, for example, not put the correct stamps on it, or misaddressed it. Under the postal rule, the offeror takes the general risk of the post office losing or delaying the acceptance. The offeror should not bear the risk of loss or delay where it has been increased through the offeree's fault.[14]

2.49 The offeror can oust the application of the postal rule. He or she can specify that acceptance will have to be received to be effective. In *Holwell Securities Ltd* v *Hughes* (1974):

> D offered to sell a house to C in the form of an option 'exercisable by notice in writing to the intending vendor [D] at any time within six months'. Within the six-month period, C's solicitors wrote to D, notifying him of C's acceptance of the offer. The letter was correctly stamped, addressed, and posted, but it never arrived. (A copy was received by D's solicitor, but C admitted that this was not sufficient notice.) No other written acceptance was given or sent to D before the time limit expired. C claimed specific performance, arguing that a contract was concluded on posting the letter of acceptance to D.

14 *L. J. Korbetis* v *Transgrain Shipping BV* (2005) per Toulson J at [15]:

The topic of misdirected letters of acceptance has been considered by text book writers. Chitty, at paragraph 2–056, has the following passage:

'Misdirected letter of acceptance. A letter of acceptance may be lost or delayed because it bears a wrong or an incomplete address, or because it is not properly stamped. Normally such defects would be due to the carelessness of the offeree, and although there is no English authority precisely on point, it is submitted that the postal rule should not apply to such cases. Although an offeror may have to take the risk of accidents in the post, it would be unreasonable to impose on him the further risk of the acceptor's carelessness. These arguments do not apply where the misdirection is due to the fault of the offeror, e.g. where his own address is incompletely or illegibly given in the offer itself. In such a case, the offeror shall not be allowed to rely on the fact that the acceptance was misdirected, except perhaps where his error in stating his own address was obvious to the offeree, for in such a case the offeror's fault would not be the effective cause of the misdirection of the acceptance. It is submitted that a misdirected acceptance should take effect, if at all, at the time which is least favourable to the party responsible for the misdirection.'

The Court of Appeal decided that the offer, by stipulating actual 'notice to [D]', could not be accepted merely by C posting a letter of acceptance. The offer was so framed as to require that the acceptance be received by the offeror, and therefore the postal rule did not apply.

2.50 So, we now have some idea of the effect of the postal rule and the limits of its application. However, obviously, there are now a great number of means of communication besides the post, and as each new method comes along, the question of whether the postal rule should apply tends to be asked. As the postal rule is an exception to the general rule, it would have been more appropriate to simply assume the application of the general rule unless a strong case for departing from it could be made out. Nevertheless, the question has been put in terms of 'should the postal rule apply?' (giving that postal rule more status than it deserves), and we should address it. On a terminological point, we should note that the postal rule is sometimes more broadly referred to as a 'dispatch rule', and the general rule as a 'receipt rule'.

2.51 In the early days of its existence, the postal rule was extended to acceptances sent by telegram. However, when it came to be considered whether it should be extended to communication by telex,[15] the courts, in *Entores Ltd* v *Miles Far East Corporation* (1955) and *Brinkibon Ltd* v *Stahag Stahl und Stahlwarenhandelsgesellschaft mbH* (1983), concluded that it should not be: the general rule applied, and acceptance was not effective until received.

2.52 Both of the telex cases were concerned with whether the postal rule or the general rule applied to decide when the contracts were made, in order to determine the underlying question of where they were made, as that question needed to be answered to decide if the English courts had jurisdiction.[16] Both cases took the line that the general rule applied to telex, not the postal rule, so the telex had to be received for the acceptance to be effective, and this meant that the contract was made at the location of the offeror's telex machine—in England in *Entores* and Austria in *Brinkibon*.

2.53 In both cases there is considerable reference to 'instantaneous' communication, and they have come to be seen as providing a rule that the postal rule does not apply to an 'instantaneous' means of communication. So in *David Baxter Edward Thomas and Peter Sandford Gander* v *BPE Solicitors (a firm)* (2010) the view was taken that the postal rule was not applicable to email as it was 'instantaneous' (at [86]). One problem with this is that there is no consensus as to whether

15 Telexes can be likened to faxes, but here the message is actually typed into the machine.

16 It was recognized that in relation to contracts made between parties in different countries, by a means of distance communication, which country the contract happened to be made in was a poor basis for determining which court should hear a dispute; however, they did what they could by simply focusing on the question of when the contract was made, and letting 'where' logically follow. In *Brinkibon*, Lord Wilberforce said ([1983] 2 AC 34 at 40): 'In the case of successive telephone conversations it may indeed be most artificial to ask where the contract was made: if one asked the parties, they might say they did not know—or care . . . Unfortunately it remains in Order 11 as a test for the purpose of jurisdiction, and courts have to do their best with it.' More recently, in *Apple Corps Ltd* v *Apple Computer Inc* [2004] EWHC 768, [2004] 2 CLC 720, Mann J suggested that, for the purposes of jurisdiction, a contract made by one party speaking to another on the telephone, should be viewed as being made in both locations (see [36]–[37]).

email is 'instantaneous',[17] but this is hardly surprising. The courts in the telex cases were not applying a factual test of whether a telex was 'instantaneous'; they were asking whether it should be treated like situations, such as that of two people talking to one another on the telephone, which clearly are instantaneous. So, for example, in *Brinkibon*, Lord Wilberforce asked (at 41–2):

> [W]ith a general rule covering instantaneous communication inter praesentes, or at a distance, with an exception applying to non-instantaneous communication at a distance, how should communications by telex be categorised?

He answered the question by recognizing that in '*Entores Ltd. v. Miles Far East Corp* the Court of Appeal classified them with instantaneous communications' (at 41). This was not a matter of establishing that factually telex satisfied a test of instantaneousness, but of deciding to treat telex as in the same category as communications which did.

2.54 So, if there was no factual test being used of whether or not telexes were instantaneous, and when we have nevertheless tried to apply an 'instantaneousness' test to email, it is not surprising that we cannot agree on a conclusion. How should we decide whether the postal rule applies to email, or any other new form of communication? We should go back to fundamentals and ask what the postal rule does, and should do, in order to decide if it is needed to perform that role in relation to email.

2.55 First, there have been lots of ideas put forward to try to justify the postal rule which simply do not stand up to scrutiny. These include the meeting of minds,[18] the idea of the post office as an agent,[19] the notion that the offeror chose the method of communication and anyway could have stated that the postal rule was not to apply,[20] that it is necessary to avoid an endless chain

17 Contrast *Chwee Kin Keong and Others* v *Digilandmall.com Pte Ltd* (2004) with the case noted in the text, in relation to judicial views; and contrast, e.g., S. Hill, 'Flogging a Dead Horse—The Postal Acceptance Rule and E-Mail' (2001) 17 JCL 151, 158–9 and A. Murray, 'Entering into Contracts Electronically: The Real w.w.w.' in L. Edwards and C. Waelde, *Law & the Internet: A Framework for Electronic Commerce*, Hart Publishing, 2000, p. 25, in relation to academic views.

18 The traditional idea of meeting of minds, or *consensus ad idem*, may be seen as providing a basis for *Adams* v *Lindsell* (1818). If the contract was made when the acceptance was dispatched then in that case, it was at a time when both intended the contract, and there would have then been a meeting of minds, in the sense of both of them intending a contract at that point. There is, however, the problem that that had not been manifested to the offeror, and in any event, in later cases it was recognized that acceptance is effective on posting even where the offeror has changed his or her mind prior to that time (*Henthorn* v *Fraser* (1892)), 'so that there is not even such residual *consensus*' (S. Gardner, 'Trashing with Trollope: A Deconstruction of the Postal Rules in Contract' (1992) 12 Ox Jo LS 170, 171).

19 In *Household Fire and Carriage Accident Insurance Co Ltd* v *Grant* [1874–80] All ER Rep 919 (at 922), the postal rule was seen as being based on the idea of the post office as agent for the parties, so that handing over the acceptance to this 'agent' was communication to the offeror. The very unsatisfactory nature of this reasoning was pointed out in *Henthorn* v *Fraser* [1892] 2 Ch 27 per Kay LJ at 35–6: the post office is only a carrier, it does not deal with the content of the communication. Any justification of the postal rule on the basis that the post office is an agent has been long 'discredited' (see M. Furmston and G. J. Tolhurst, *Contract Formation—Law and Practice*, Oxford University Press, 2010, 4.102).

20 It is said, in justification of the postal rule, that the offeror chose, or contemplated, the use of the post as a method of communication (*Henthorn* v *Fraser* (1892) 2 Ch 27 at 33). The postal rule might then be seen as based on waiver, but again this does not provide sufficient explanation, as the same line should then have been taken in relation to communication by telex (R. A. Samek, 'A Reassessment of the Present Rule Relating to Postal Acceptance' of correspondence,[21] and that it is the better rule evidentially.[22] They have been so completely dismissed that they are not dealt with in the text, but they are nevertheless raised from time to time, and the footnotes may be consulted for explanations. That they do not, however, stand up to scrutiny is evident in the *obiter* comment in the recent Australian case of *Wardis* v *Agriculture and Rural Finance Pty Ltd* (2012). Campbell JA (at [133]) took the line that:

> It is hard to find a convincing explanation for the posting of an acceptance sometimes being a sufficient acceptance of an offer, beyond the urgent practical necessity of having some rule to decide by what act and at what time people who are negotiating for a contract, but are not in each other's presence become bound.

This is in keeping with the view that the postal rule merely deals with a 'co-ordination problem', so that, like the rule as to which side of the road we drive on, it is there because *a* rule is needed, rather than *the* rule.[23] It is hardly surprising that Campbell JA went on to express the opinion that the 'future existence of the postal acceptance rule . . . might be in doubt' (at [134]). However, there are two explanations of the postal rule which deserve further scrutiny before we should be content to arrive at any such conclusion.

2.56 As we have seen, offers are generally revocable at common law, even if it has been stated that they will remain open for a set time. The need for consideration is seen to stand in the way of irrevocability (*Routledge* v *Grant* (1828)), and revocability is significant in relation to the postal rule. The particular difficulty which is occasioned by revocation, and is dealt with by the postal rule, is that of a revocation which arrives with the offeree after an acceptance has been dispatched, but before the acceptance is received by the offeror. This was identified as a

(1961) 35 ALJ 38, 40). The point is also made that the offeror can specify that the postal rule is not to apply (*Holwell Securities Ltd* v *Hughes* (1974); *Household Fire and Carriage Accident Insurance Co Ltd* v *Grant* (1879)). This latter point, however, does not actually provide any argument for the postal rule as such, but is rather a means of presenting it as not needing to cause unfairness (Gardner, 'Trashing with Trollope', p. 174). Even in relation to that limited object, a moment's reflection will indicate its inadequacy. Leaving aside the basic difficulty that the postal rule is counterintuitive, and that the offeror may assume that there will not be a contract until the acceptance has been received (P. Fasciano, 'Internet Electronic Mail: A Last Bastion for the Mailbox Rule' (1997) 25 Hofstra LR 971), the party who is the offeror may not have any power in relation to the terms of the offer. In fact, the terms may well be the offeree's standard terms, as would normally be the case when, e.g., a consumer seeks to make a contract through the post in response to an advertisement. The advertisement will generally be an invitation to treat (e.g. *Partridge* v *Crittenden* (1968); *Grainger & Son* v *Gough* (1896)), the consumer will be the offeror, and the business, which has dictated the standard terms, will be the offeree.

21 In *Adams* v *Lindsell* (1818) the justification was put forward that the postal rule was needed to avoid an endless chain of correspondence: '[If] the defendants were not bound by their offer when accepted by the [claimants] till the answer was received, then the [claimants] ought not to be bound till after they had received the notification that the defendants had received their answer and assented to it. And so it might go on *ad infinitum*.' This can be simply dealt with. It is just a matter of a line needing to be drawn. It 'would be perfectly possible to hold that the acceptance took effect when it came to the notice of the offeror, whether the offeree knew of this or not': E. Peel, *Treitel's Law of Contract*, Sweet & Maxwell, 2011, 2.031.

22 For swift and clear dismissal of the idea that the postal rule is the better rule from the evidentiary perspective see, e.g., I. R. Macneil, 'Time of Acceptance: Too Many Problems for a Single Rule' (1964) 112(7) Pa LR 947, 965 and P. H. Winfield 'Some Aspects of Offer and Acceptance' (1939) 120 LQR 499, 509–10.

23 S. A. Smith, *Contract Theory*, Oxford University Press, 2004, p. 192.

matter of concern by Mellish LJ in *In Re Imperial Land Co. of Marseilles (Harris's case)* (1872) LR 7 Ch 587. He said (at 594) that he had been

> forcibly struck with the extraordinary and very mischievous consequences which would follow if it were held that an offer might be revoked at any time until the letter accepting it had been actually received.

He gave several examples of this mischief, including (at 594):

> Suppose that a dealer in Liverpool writes to a dealer in New York and offers to buy so many quarters of corn or so many bales of cotton at a certain price, and the dealer in New York, finding that he can make a favourable bargain, writes an answer accepting the offer. Then, according to the argument that has been presented to us to-day, during the whole time that the letter accepting the offer is on the Atlantic, the dealer who is to receive it in Liverpool, if he finds that the market has fallen, may send a message by telegraph and revoke his offer. Nor is there any difference between an offer to receive shares and an offer to buy or sell goods. And yet, if the argument is sound, then for nearly ten days the buyer might wait and speculate whether the shares were rising or falling, and if found they were falling he might revoke his offer.

Mellish LJ identified this 'revocation issue' as a matter of serious concern, and we should note that it is recognized as the key basis of the 'mailbox rule' in the US, which is very like our postal rule,[24] and such revocation is prevented by other means in other systems.[25]

2.57 The other effect of the postal rule which we should look at is its impact in relation to lost or delayed acceptances which are not the fault of the offeree. Under the postal rule, the risk of such loss or delay is placed on the offeror; there will be a contract even if the acceptance is lost, or delayed beyond the point when the offer would have expired. In *British & American Telegraph Co. Ltd* v *Colson* (1871) LR 6 Exch 108, 112, Kelly CB saw an acceptance effective on posting as working 'great and obvious injustice in a variety of mercantile transactions of constant occurrence', and it was to this risk that he was referring. He gave examples, including (at 112):

> A merchant in London writes to another merchant at Bristol offering to sell him a quantity of merchandise at the price of 1000l., and the Bristol merchant by return of post accepts the offer and agrees to become the purchaser; but the letter miscarries and is never received. Would the Bristol merchant be entitled a week afterwards to bring an action for the non-delivery of the goods, when the London merchant, from having received no answer to his letter, has sold them to another person?

24 See the comments on s 63 of the US Restatement (2d) Contracts.

25 Under German law an offer is generally irrevocable unless otherwise stated (ss 146–149 BGB), and it is commented that under German law the postal rule is not adopted 'largely because the irrevocability of offers (made possible . . . by the absence of the doctrine of consideration) means that the offeree is sufficiently protected during a reasonable period after an offer has reached him': B. S. Markesinis, H. Unberath and A. Johnston, *The German Law of Contract: A Comparative Treatise*, 2nd edn, Hart Publishing, 2006, p. 74.

Kelly CB (at 112) thought it 'absolutely impossible that such can be the law of this country'. Bramwell B similarly provided examples of this effect of the postal rule, and he viewed it as 'wholly unjust and unreasonable' to make liable 'the person who had never received the letter' of acceptance (at 118).[26]

2.58 In the light of such forceful criticism, it might well be queried as to why we still have a postal rule producing this effect today. The answer would seem to be bad timing. The postal rule was revived, in relation to a lost acceptance, in *Household Fire and Carriage Accident Insurance Co* v *Grant* (1879), but that should be seen in context. Gardner has pointed out that, at the time, there was considerable concern that those who had sought shares in a company which then rapidly proved to be worthless (as was happening on an appreciable number of occasions at the time) were evading liability by denying receipt of the letters accepting their offers to become shareholders. If the letters were effective on posting, this avenue of escape was denied to them (S. Gardner, 'Trashing with Trollope: A Deconstruction of the Postal Rules in Contract' (1992) 12 Ox Jo LS 170 at 185).

2.59 In Scotland, although the basic postal rule was adopted, it may not be carried to its logical conclusion in relation to a lost acceptance. In *Mason* v *Benhar Coal Co* (1882) 9 R 883, Lord Shand stated, *obiter* (at 890), that if delivery of the acceptance was not established he would 'not hold that the contract was completed by mere posting', and the recommendations of the Scottish Law Commission would not maintain the postal rule merely a means of dealing with the revocation issue (Scots Law Com 2012, para. 3.21). Similarly, although again there was no need to pursue the point, the Irish Supreme Court, in *Kelly* v *Cruise Catering Ltd* [1994] 2 ILRM 394, thought it 'no doubt correct' that 'it might be unjust to hold a party to a contract when he had never received the acceptance'.

2.60 However, the postal rule, with its allocation of the risk of loss or delay of the acceptance to the offeror, has been justified on the basis that it is economically efficient. Posner takes the view that the postal rule is economically efficient as it

> enables the offeree to begin performance (or preparatory measures) but does not delay the offeror's performance, which in any event cannot begin until the offeror received the acceptance, for until then he wouldn't know whether there was a contract. (R. A. Posner, *Economic Analysis of Law*, 7th edn, Aspen Publishers, 2007, p. 103)

One response to this might be that it depends upon the individual transaction as to the commencement of which of the parties' performances is important, and it is undoubtedly the case that it may well be the start of the offeror's which is significant. However, this would be to miss the point that Posner is making a statement at a more general level and, under the postal

26 Although Kelly CB and Bramwell B were anxious to reject the postal rule because of its impact in relation to lost acceptances, they nevertheless did not dismiss the need for protection of the offeree from revocation. They envisaged the possibility that, although an acceptance would only be effective once received, its effect would then be backdated to the point of dispatch (at 116, 121).

rule, both parties can perform as quickly as possible. As far as it goes, the argument is clear: the postal rule is economically efficient because it allows performance to commence as soon as possible.

2.61 However, the postal rule may be seen as economically inefficient because it results in the risk of loss or delay not being placed on the party best able to minimize such risk:

> If anything, one would have thought it was more efficient to make each type of letter effective only on delivery. After all, it is the sender, rather than the addressee, who is in control of a letter's transmission. This would mean reversing the rule regarding acceptances. If the rule were against the offeree (that is, required delivery to the offeror), he could respond by using the recorded delivery service, sending multiple communications, etc. As things stand however it is the offeror the law encourages to guard against accidents in the post, yet . . . he is much less well placed to do so. (Gardner, 'Trashing with Trollope', 177)

It is the offeree who can send an acceptance in a way which involves least risk of it being delayed or going astray and, as it is the offeree who knows that the acceptance has been dispatched, it is he or she who is best situated to check on its arrival; there are now multiple cheap, fast means of doing so. The offeror cannot realistically keep asking the offeree whether an acceptance has been sent. Loss or delay will cause problems; putting the non-fault risk of either occurring on the offeree would minimize them.

2.62 When the issue of economic efficiency and the postal rule is considered, the entire impact of the rule cannot be seen as economically efficient; a weighing or balancing exercise is in question and the balance point of economic efficiency can be strongly contended to be different in relation to more modern, and much faster, means of communication. There are now multiple fast, cheap means by which the offeree can accept and can check receipt of acceptance. They not only markedly reduce the potential for an intervening revocation, they also very significantly diminish the time before performance by both parties can safely commence. Allocating the non-fault risk of loss or delay of the acceptance to the inappropriate party—the offeror—should no longer be viewed as a price which has to be paid for the benefit of performance commencing swiftly. To the contrary, unless a very strong approach is taken to the reasonableness of using the post, which would simply render the postal rule meaningless, even maintaining the postal rule just in relation to the post may be seen to be inefficient. Its allocation of the non-fault based risk of loss or delay to the offeror would provide a reason for the offeree to post an acceptance rather than use a much faster means of communication,[27] and a posted acceptance could substantially delay the offeror's ability to commence performance.

2.63 In summary, the problem of a revocation intervening whilst a communication was in transit provided a justification for the postal rule, but only to the extent that it was needed

27 A. Rawls, 'Contract Formation in an Internet Age' (2009) 10 Columbia Science and Technology LR 200, 228.

to deal with that problem. There is certainly no justification now to allow it also to put the risk of a lost or delayed acceptance on the offeror. It is arguably time to abandon the postal rule in relation to the post, and we certainly should not extend it to email. The best solution would, however, be one which dealt with the revocation issue, but did not have the other 'side effect' of the postal rule in relation to lost or delayed acceptances. That could be achieved by legislation, reflecting the line taken under the United Nations Convention on International Sale of Goods (CISG, Art 16(2)), and the Draft Common Frame of Reference (DCFR, Art II-4:202). Under both, although the acceptance will not be effective until received by the offeror, an offer cannot be revoked once the offeree has dispatched an acceptance. Similarly, the Scottish Law Commission has proposed that Scots law should not continue to use the postal rule, but that a revocation should not be effective if it reaches the offeree after dispatch of an acceptance (Scots Law Com 2012, para. 3.21).[28]

2.64 Of course, even if it is merely that the postal rule is not extended, and the postal rule continues to be applied to the post, the question arises as to what will satisfy the normal rule that an acceptance must be communicated to be effective. It is an objective question, so there can be no issue of requiring a message actually to be read, and the question is usually put in terms of when the acceptance is 'received' by the offeror. In relation to the telex, it was indicated that it would normally be when it arrived on the offeror's machine. However, the question of 'office hours' was raised (Lord Wilberforce, *Brinkibon* at 42), and the line generally taken was that a telex arriving outside of office hours would be received, and effective, when office hours recommenced. More broadly, 'accessibility' seems to be becoming recognized as determinative of the time of receipt of an electronic message generally.[29] Article I.-1:109 of the Draft Common Frame of Reference adopts 'accessibility' in relation to the time of receipt of an electronic message, and the Scottish Law Commission stated that

> in a context where the concept of office hours is relevant, a communication that reaches the addressee's system outside of those hours will become accessible for the purposes of the DCFR . . . when the next period of business hours opens. (Scot Law Com 2012, para. 2.17)

There should be scope for saying that an acceptance has become effective if its 'inaccessibility' is due to the offeror's fault (e.g. through inappropriate email security settings).

Prescribed method of acceptance

2.65 As we saw in *Holwell Securities Ltd* v *Hughes* (1974), the offeror can stipulate that the acceptance must be made in a particular way. He or she may require it to be sent to a certain place, or to take a particular form, such as by letter or fax. In order to complete a binding

28 For a suggestion as to how it might be achieved at common law, and for further analysis and explanation of the telex cases and how they fit with the analysis described, see E. Macdonald, 'Dispatching the Dispatch Rule? The Postal Rule, E-Mail, Revocation and Implied Terms' [2013] (2) Web Journal of Current Legal Issues.

29 Article 11, E-Commerce Directive, Art 10(2), UN Convention on the Use of Electronic Communications in International Contracts.

agreement the offeree must normally comply with the prescribed method of acceptance. If the offeror stipulates a particular form of acceptance, and states that only the stipulated form will suffice, the offeree must comply with the offeror's requirement in order for there to be an effective acceptance. However, the offeror may have requested a particular method of acceptance for a specific purpose, for example to obtain a speedy reply. If the offeree uses some other method which equally achieves the offeror's purpose, this should be a valid acceptance (see *Tinn* v *Hoffman* (1873)). In *Manchester Diocesan Council of Education* v *Commercial and General Investments Ltd* [1970] 1 WLR 241, Buckley J stated (at 246):

> Where . . . the offeror has prescribed a particular method of acceptance, but not in terms insisting that only acceptance in that mode shall be binding, I am of the opinion that acceptance communicated to the offeror by any other mode which is no less advantageous to him will conclude the contract . . . If an offeror intends that he shall be bound only if his offer is accepted in some particular manner, it must be for him to make this clear.

In *Reveille Independent LLC* v *Anotech International UK Ltd* [2016] EWCA Civ 443, the Court of Appeal considered when a contract containing a stipulation requiring signature will become effective despite not having been signed. Cranston J, with whom Underhill and Elias LJJ agreed, set out the following propositions (at [40]–[41]):

> (i) acceptance can be by conduct provided that, viewed objectively, it is intended to constitute acceptance; (ii) acceptance can be of an offer on the terms set out in a draft agreement but never signed; (iii) if a party has a right to sign a contract before being bound, it is open to it by clear and unequivocal words or conduct to waive the requirement and to conclude the contract without insisting on signature; (iv) if signature is the prescribed mode of acceptance, the offeror will be bound if it waives that requirement and acquiesces in a different mode of acceptance; (v) a draft agreement can have contractual force, although the parties do not comply with a requirement that to be binding it must be signed, if essentially all the terms have been agreed and their subsequent conduct indicates this, albeit a court will not reach this conclusion lightly.

Although signature was the prescribed mode of acceptance and was intended for the benefit of the offeree, as the offeree accepted in an alternative way (in the instant case, by their conduct), the court held that should be treated as effective unless it could be shown that the failure to sign had prejudiced the offeror.

Acceptance in unilateral contracts

2.66 In a unilateral contract, the offeror promises to do something, or make a payment (for example, a reward), if certain acts are carried out (see e.g. *Carlill* v *Carbolic Smoke Ball Co.* (1893)). The offeree does not have to communicate acceptance to the offeror, and the offeree never becomes obliged to do anything. It is simply that, if the offeree carries out the relevant acts, the offeror is obliged to make the promised payment, or carry out the promised act. Therefore, the acceptance is an acceptance by conduct (see *Vehicle Control Services Ltd* v

Revenue and Customs Commissioners [2013] EWCA Civ 186). It is an essential element and a well-established principle that in the case of a unilateral or 'if' contract, such as an 'option', the terms of exercise are fully complied with (see *Siemens Hearing Instruments Ltd* v *Friends Life Ltd* [2014] EWCA Civ 382; [2015] 1 All ER (Comm) 1068). (Remember, we call such situations *uni*lateral contracts because only one party comes under an obligation.)

2.67 As we have seen, an offer of a bilateral contract can be revoked at any time up until acceptance, unless there is a separate contractual obligation to keep it open for a specified time. Revocation of unilateral offers raises a particular difficulty. Can O, the offeror of a unilateral offer, withdraw the offer once A has started to carry out the stipulated act? To take the classic example known to generations of law students: O offers a reward of £100 to anyone who walks from, say, Aberystwyth to Swansea. Can O revoke his or her offer once A has started, but not yet completed, the walk to Swansea? Certainly O is not bound to pay the £100 unless, and until, A completes the walk, but should O be able to withdraw at any time until A has completed the walk, even when A has nearly reached Swansea? This question arose in a more realistic form in *Errington* v *Errington and Woods* [1952] 1 KB 290. The facts were:

> A father wanted to provide his son and daughter-in-law with a home and he bought a house for £750, borrowing £500 on a mortgage from the building society. The ownership of the house remained in the father's name, and he also paid the rates. He promised his son and daughter-in-law that if they continued to occupy the house and paid all the mortgage instalments, he would transfer the property to them. Until the father's death nine years later, the couple occupied the house and paid the mortgage. On the death of the father, all of his property (including the house occupied by the couple) was left to his widow. The son left the daughter-in-law and moved out of the house. The widow brought an action for possession against the daughter-in-law.

The Court of Appeal decided that the widow was not entitled to possession. Denning LJ stated (at 295):

> The father's promise was a unilateral contract—a promise of the house in return for their act of paying the instalments. It could not be revoked by him once the couple entered on performance of the act, but it would cease to bind him if they left it incomplete and unperformed, which they have not done.

The general reaction to this is that it was an appropriate result, but orthodox explanations for it are difficult to find. It is generally suggested that there is a collateral contract, formed when A starts to perform, that O will not withdraw as long as A continues to perform.[30] See *Daulia Ltd* v *Four Millbank Nominees Ltd* [1978] 2 All ER 557 (at 561, 566, and 570).

2.68 However, the offeror was allowed to withdraw without penalty in *Luxor (Eastbourne) Ltd* v *Cooper* (1941). In that case, C was promised commission if he introduced a buyer for two

30 It might more easily be seen as a matter of good faith, but English law is unwilling to accept a duty of good faith, particularly in the pre-contractual context—see generally Furmston and Tolhurst, *Contract Formation*.

cinemas and the introduction resulted in the sale of the properties. Although C introduced a willing purchaser, the vendors changed their minds and decided against selling the properties. C claimed damages, arguing that the offer implied that the vendors would not refuse to sell to a buyer that he had introduced. The Court of Appeal refused to imply such a term and rejected C's claim. The case can be distinguished from *Errington* in relation to its commercial context: the estate agent was inherently taking a risk for a large reward if a sale was made, so it would have been inappropriate to imply an obligation on the offeror.

Is knowledge of the offer required?

2.69 This issue has tended to arise in the context of unilateral offers of reward, where someone performs an act or service (for example, by returning an item of lost property to the owner), and later learns that a reward was in fact offered for the performance of this act. In one sense, such a person has fulfilled the terms of the offer, and it could be argued that he or she is entitled to claim the reward. But can someone create a contract 'accidentally'? The impetus to the objective approach, for the sake of certainty, is very strong. In *Gibbons* v *Proctor* (1891) 64 LT 594, the court appeared to decide that ignorance of an offer did not preclude a person from claiming a reward where he gave information and then later learned of the existence of the offer. However, another report of the case suggests that C did know of the reward by the time the information was passed, via C's agents, to the appropriate person (see (1891) 55 JP 616).

2.70 The situation was given extensive consideration in the Australian case of *R* v *Clarke* (1927) 40 CLR 227. It concerned an offer of a reward for information leading to the arrest of certain murderers, and a pardon to any accomplice giving the information. C gave the required information but admitted that he had forgotten about the reward at the time that he supplied it (i.e. when he was in custody, himself charged with the murders). C's claim for the £1,000 reward was rejected by the High Court of Australia, and the case was treated as if he had never known of the reward. Higgins J stated (at 241):

> Clarke had seen the offer indeed; but it was not present to his mind—he had forgotten it, and gave no consideration to it, in his intense excitement as to his own danger. There cannot be assent without knowledge of the offer; and ignorance of the offer is the same thing whether it is due to never hearing of it or forgetting it after hearing . . . But for this candid confession of Clarke's it might fairly be presumed that Clarke, having once seen the offer, acted on the faith of it, in reliance on it; but he has himself rebutted that presumption.

2.71 In the context of these reward cases, it might be argued that the reward should be paid. It encourages the performance of socially useful acts, and the offeror expected to pay. It would also maintain the generally objective approach, and the certainty which goes with it. The question of whether there is a contract is not particularly worrying in the unilateral context, because the person who does not know of the offer can never become bound to do anything. It is only a question of the offeror's liability, and the offeror knew perfectly well what he or she was doing. The objective approach could be maintained without discomfort. However, the issue would be far more vexed in relation to a bilateral contract. It is not simply whether X should get the reward which Y promised, but whether X should come under contractual obligations accidentally. This question has been unlikely to be asked in the bilateral context, until now. However, it might now arise in the context of 'browse-wrap contracting', where the owner of a website specifies that the visitor to it, Y, will make a contract imposing certain obligations just by performing certain acts on the website, which Y might perform anyway. The simple answer is that such actions are unlikely to unambiguously convey objective acceptance, or they may well be regulated by other means.[31]

2.72 Even if knowledge of an offer is required for there to be a valid acceptance, the motive for performing an act which fulfils the terms of an offer is irrelevant. So where a person knows of an offer of a reward for information, but gives the requested information for another reason (such as remorse), he is still entitled to claim the reward. (See *Williams* v *Cowardine* (1833) and, for a discussion, see P. Mitchell and J. Phillips 'The Contractual Nexus: Is Reliance Essential?' (2002) 22 OJLS 115.)

2.73 A related issue is that of 'cross offers'. For example, A writes to B offering to sell him his computer for £100 and B, without knowing of the offer, writes to A and offers to buy that computer for £100. It could be argued that there is a meeting of the minds, but clearly any 'agreement' between the parties is merely by chance. It is thought that there is no contract in this situation unless one of the parties replies to the other and accepts the other's offer. It would lead to uncertainty if cross offers, with nothing further, amounted to a binding agreement. The problem is hardly one of great practical significance, as indicated by the paucity of case law on the subject. (The case which discusses the problem, *obiter*, is *Tinn* v *Hoffman* (1873). The majority of the judges thought there was no contract.)

'Battle of the forms'

2.74 Assessing whether there is sufficient agreement for a contract by means of offer and acceptance has raised particular problems in relation to the 'battle of the forms', and we should now consider that phenomenon. We are, of course, again talking about bilateral contracts.

2.75 We have already noted that when he was considering whether offer and acceptance analysis should be used in *Gibson* v *Manchester City Council* [1979] 1 WLR 294, Lord Diplock stated (at 297):

> My Lords there may be certain types of contract, though I think they are exceptional, which do not fit easily into the normal analysis of a contract as being constituted by offer and acceptance, but a contract alleged to have been made by an exchange of correspondence between the parties in which the successive communications other than the first are in reply to one another is not one of these.

31 For further discussion of an old conundrum in a new context, see E. Macdonald, 'When Is a Contract Formed by the Browse-Wrap Process' (2011) 19 International Journal of Law and Information Technology 285–305.

Prima facie, according to this, the 'battle of the forms' situations should be prime candidates for offer and acceptance analysis. They are concerned with an exchange of correspondence in which each communication is in reply to the previous one. The problem is, however, that large parts of each communication are ignored, and certainly not responded to.

2.76 The so-called 'battle of the forms' arises when X and Y set out to make a contract. They negotiate with one another via a series of letters. Each of them focuses on such matters as price, quantity, and time of delivery, and they gradually reach agreement on these obviously significant elements. The problem is that on the back of each letter from X and Y are their standard terms, and their standard terms are different in significant ways, but their correspondence does not address those differences. This means that even when the terms on the front of their letters are agreed, they have not agreed the terms on the back. In effect, whatever the front of the letters look like, they keep throwing counter offers at one another, and not reaching agreement. They may be doing this on purpose, to try to make their standard terms the standard terms of the contract. Hence the name 'battle of the forms'. But they might also be doing it simply because they are not thinking about the law, but rather about making a deal on what seems to them to be the important matters.[32] For whatever reason it comes about, the lack of negotiation on the standard terms during the contracting process causes difficulties when issues arise which are dealt with differently under the two sets of standard terms. It may be that the courts will find that there was actually no contract at all, although they tend to strive to avoid that conclusion when the parties have started performing on the assumption that there is a contract.

2.77 Applying the traditional rules of offer and acceptance, the party who last gets in his or her standard terms, which the other party then acts upon, wins. This is often put in terms of the party who fired the last shot winning. This is illustrated in *British Road Services Ltd* v *Arthur V Crutchley & Co. Ltd* (1968). The claimants delivered goods to the defendants' warehouse and presented a delivery note which stated: 'All goods are carried on [the claimants'] conditions of carriage . . .' However, when the claimants' driver presented the delivery note to the defendants, it was 'rubber-stamped' by the defendants with the words: 'Received under [the defendants'] conditions.' In this way the delivery note was transformed into a note of receipt and handed back to the claimants' driver. In the course of an action for negligence against the defendants, it was disputed whose conditions prevailed. Although the defendants were liable to the claimants in negligence for not adequately protecting the goods against theft, the Court of Appeal held that the defendants' liability was limited in accordance with their conditions which were incorporated into the contract between the parties. The defendants', rather than the claimants', conditions prevailed as they got in the final word or 'shot', without any further riposte from the claimants.

2.78 Another example is provided by *Butler Machine Tool Co. Ltd* v *Ex-Cell-O Corpn. (England) Ltd* (1979), which is a case in which, in a sense, the 'last shot' did not win. The facts were:

32 See H. Beale and A. Dugdale, 'Contracts between Businessmen' (1975) 2 Br Jo Law & Soc 45.

> In response to D's enquiry, C made a quotation on 23 May, offering to sell a machine tool to D for £75,535. The offer was stated to be subject to certain conditions which were to 'prevail over any terms in the buyer's order'. These conditions included a price variation clause: that is, that any increase in the cost of the goods, by the date of delivery (which was to be in ten months' time), would be added to the purchase price. On 27 May, D replied, ordering the machine, but on their own terms and conditions which did not include a price variation clause. At the foot of D's order form there was an acknowledgement section to be torn off, stating: 'We accept your order on the terms and conditions stated thereon.' On 5 June, C completed and signed the acknowledgement, returning it to D together with a letter stating that D's order was being entered in accordance with C's quotation of 23 May. When the machine was delivered, C claimed the price had increased by £2,892, and D refused to pay the increase in price. C's action was based on the contention that they were entitled to increase the price under the price variation clause contained in their offer. C argued that the contract was on the buyer's terms and these did not include such a clause.

The Court of Appeal decided that the contract did not include the price variation clause and C could not claim the extra £2,892. It was held that D's order of 27 May was a counter offer which brought to an end the offer made by C on 23 May, and that C accepted D's counter offer by completing and returning the acknowledgement of the order on 5 June. The contract was therefore on D's terms, and the price variation clause did not apply.

2.79 It might be asked how this occurred when C's original quotation had stated that its conditions were to 'prevail over any terms in the buyer's order'. However, what must be remembered is that under the offer and acceptance rules, such a clause could not prevail in the face of D's counter offer, on different terms. It is the rule about counter offers which generally means that the 'last shot' wins. Of course, the 'last shot', in the sense of the last written communication, did not win in this case. It might be described as a 'blank': C lost by signing the tear-off slip and failing to successfully reintroduce their standard terms.

2.80 Although the majority of the Court of Appeal arrived at their conclusion using traditional offer and acceptance analysis, Lord Denning MR adopted a different approach from the majority, whilst arriving at the same conclusion. He argued that the documents must be considered as a whole:

> If [the terms and conditions of both parties] can be reconciled so as to give a harmonious result, all well and good. If differences are irreconcilable, so that they are mutually contradictory, then the conflicting terms may have to be scrapped and replaced by a reasonable implication.

Such an approach does offer flexibility, but it is uncertain.

2.81 In *Tekdata Interconnections Ltd* v *Amphenol Ltd* (2009), the court emphasized the use of the traditional offer and acceptance analysis, and it was indeed a case in which the 'last shot' won, but it did leave scope for 'rare cases' where that analysis would be departed from. *Tekdata* was not such a rare case, but in *GHSP Inc* v *AB Electronic Ltd* (2010) it had been so clear during their protracted negotiations that the parties were never going to reach agreement on the issue of the extent of liability that the judge found that the contract was on neither parties' terms, but that terms implied by the Sale of Goods Act 1979 should simply be used.

Summary

- Agreement is central to the making of a contract.
- The law takes a predominantly objective approach to agreement.
- The traditional method of establishing agreement is through the process of offer and acceptance.
- This process may be an accurate description of how many, but not all, contracts are made.
- An offer is an expression by the offeror of a willingness to enter into a contract, on a particular set of terms, with the intention of being bound if the other party (the offeree) signifies acceptance.
- An offer must be distinguished from an invitation to the other party to make an offer (i.e. an invitation to treat).
- An acceptance is the final expression of assent to the offer by the offeree.
- A purported acceptance which attempts to introduce new terms, or to vary those contained in the offer, is a counter offer (and a rejection of the original offer).
- A counter offer must be distinguished from a request by the offeree for further information about the offer, which is not a rejection of the offer.
- Acceptance may take a variety of forms depending on the terms of the offer.
- As a general principle, acceptance must be communicated to the offeror.
- Outside of unilateral contracts, the major exception to this is the 'postal rule'.
- As a whole, the postal rule is very hard to justify. There is a debate about whether it should be extended to more modern forms of communication, but there certainly seems to be no justification for doing so to its full effect.
- There is a problem in relation to revocation of unilateral offers, once the offeree has started to carry out the stated acts.
- There are particular difficulties in applying offer and acceptance analysis to certain business transactions, sometimes described as the 'battle of the forms'.

Further reading

R. D. Atkins, 'Co-op Group v. ICL: Loyalty Scheme Pays "Dividend" for Supplier' (2004) 12 (2) IJLIT 157

R. Austen-Baker, 'Offeree Silence and Contractual Agreement' (2006) 35 (4) CLWR 247

D. Friedmann, 'The Objective Principle and Mistake and Involuntariness in Contract and Restitution' (2003) 119 LQR 68

W. Howarth, 'The Meaning of Objectivity in Contract' (1984) 100 LQR 267

E. Macdonald, 'When Is a Contract Formed by the Browse-Wrap Process' (2011) 19 IJLIT 285–305

E. Macdonald, 'Dispatching the Dispatch Rule? The Postal Rule, E-mail, Revocation and Implied Terms' [2013] (2) Web JCLI

E. McKendrick, 'Invitations to Tender and the Creation of Contracts' [1991] LMCLQ 31

F. Meisel, 'What Price Auctions Without Reserve?' (2001) 64 MLR 468

P. Mitchell and J. Phillips, 'The Contractual Nexus: Is Reliance Essential?' (2002) 22 OJLS 115

J. Steyn, 'Contract Law: Fulfilling the Reasonable Expectations of Honest Men' (1997) 113 LQR 433

Chapter 3

Certainty and formalities

Introduction

3.1 In **Chapter 2** we saw that contracts are normally based on agreement. Although courts will try to give effect to apparent agreements, it may be difficult to do so in cases where the parties have expressed themselves in vague or incomplete terms. Much will depend on how far a court is willing to go in filling in any gaps left by the parties. Whilst not wishing to 'incur the reproach of being the destroyer of bargains' (per Lord Tomlin in *Hillas & Co. Ltd* v *Arcos Ltd* (1932) 147 LT 503 at 512), a court may find it impossible to give effect to an uncertain 'agreement'. For example, in the Court of Appeal decision in *Schweppe* v *Harper* (2008) at [72]–[76] and [80]–[81], the majority held that there was no binding contract between the parties because of uncertainty over important terms of the alleged agreement, with Sir Robin Auld stating (at [81]) that 'the notion of "reasonable finance" is too uncertain to be given any practical meaning'. Such disputes must be viewed within the confines of legal principle; if no contractual bargain exists, it is not for a court to invent one.

3.2 However, in the business world it is not uncommon for negotiating parties to leave matters vague for as long as possible. For example, this may arise where there may be some understandings between the parties, but where these have not been expressed with any certainty or finality. (For a broader discussion, see S. Mouzas and M. Furmston, 'From Contract to Umbrella Agreement' (2008) 67 CLJ 37.) This may be desirable in certain circumstances because the 'agreement' in question might be conditional on one of the parties securing another contract with a third party. (For example, where company A uses a 'letter of intent' to indicate to company B that a subcontract is likely to be entered into with them if A's tender for a major contract with company C is successful. But the more widespread use of letters of intent, especially in the construction industry, may be a cause for concern. For a discussion of this practice and some of the resulting case law, see C. Hoar, 'We Do Intend to Contract with You, and May Actually Just Have' (2008) *Construction Newsletter* May/June 4–5.) The parties may even proceed as if a concluded contract has been made, despite the fact that in a technical (legal) sense there is no final agreement. (For examples of this problem, see *British Steel Corpn* v *Cleveland Bridge and Engineering Co. Ltd* (1984) and *G Percy Trentham Ltd* v *Archital Luxfer Ltd* (1993); and for a more recent approach see *RTS Flexible Systems Ltd* v *Molkerei Alois Müller GmbH & Co KG* (2010).) We have considered further examples of this in relation to the 'battle of the forms' (see **Chapter 2**) and it will be recalled that commercial practice may depart from the finer points of legal theory. It is difficult to lay down general rules about the extent of a court's power to fill in the gaps left by the parties and, for this reason, some of the cases that follow may appear to be inconsistent with one another. Much depends on the factual situation in each case rather than on any consistent or underlying precepts.

The need for certainty

3.3 Where contractual intention is expressed in such imprecise terms that no clear meaning can be given to it, there will be no binding agreement. For example, in *Gould* v *Gould* (1969), a husband promised his wife £15 per week 'so long as he could manage it', that is, as long as his business was doing well. On appeal, it was held that this agreement was too vague and uncertain to be enforceable. (Also, in *Loftus* v *Roberts* (1902), an agreement to employ an actress at a 'West End salary' was held to be too vague. For a more recent example, see *Cook* v *Norlands Ltd* (2001).) In other cases, the parties may clearly have intended to enter into a contract, but may have used some vague or ambiguous expression. In *G Scammell and Nephew Ltd* v *Ouston* (1941), the facts were:

> Ouston (C) wrote to the defendant company (D) ordering a new Commer motor van, stating that the 'order is given on the understanding that the balance of purchase price can be had on hire purchase terms over a period of two years'. The order was accepted, but the defendants dropped out before any specific hire purchase agreement was entered into. C sued D for non-delivery and D claimed that there was no final agreement between the parties. The trial court and the Court of Appeal decided that there was a binding contract between the parties, and D appealed to the House of Lords.

It was held that there was no contract, as the phrase 'on hire purchase terms' was too vague to constitute a binding agreement. This was because different types of hire purchase agreements existed (imposing different obligations on the parties) and therefore there was an ambiguity in the apparent agreement. If C could have shown, by reference to previous dealings with D or by reference to trade practice, that one particular meaning could be given to the phrase 'hire purchase terms', he may well have succeeded. But this was not possible in this instance and the contractual intention of the parties may not have been identical.

3.4 In *Peter Lind & Co. Ltd* v *Mersey Docks and Harbour Board* (1972), C submitted two tenders to build a container freight terminal. The first offer was to build the terminal for a fixed price, whilst the second was to do the work for a price which was subject to variations in the cost of labour and materials. D purported to accept C's tender without making it clear which one. It was decided that there was no contract on the terms of either of C's tenders as there was an obvious ambiguity that could not be resolved by the court.

3.5 In contrast, there are instances where a court is able to make sense of vague statements and to give effect to the contractual intention of the parties. For example, in *Hillas & Co. Ltd* v *Arcos Ltd* (1932), C had previously agreed to buy a quantity of timber, 'of fair specification', from D. The contract gave C an option to buy a further 100,000 standards of timber the following year, but it failed to specify the size or type of timber. D argued that the vagueness of this 'agreement' prevented it from being binding on the parties. But this argument was rejected by the House of Lords. In contrast to the case of *G Scammell and Nephew Ltd* v *Ouston* (1941), the uncertainty in the agreement could be resolved by the court. It was possible to make reference to the previous dealings between the parties and the custom of the timber trade. In this way, the court could fill in the gaps left by the parties without making an entire contract for the parties. Clearly, the distinction between this type of case and that of *Scammell* is a fine one.[1] In the case of *Baird Textile Holdings Ltd* v *Marks and Spencer plc* (2002), the Court of Appeal rejected a claim by Baird that M&S was in breach of a contractual obligation to order garments from Baird in quantities and at prices which were reasonable in all the circumstances. The court decided that this alleged obligation lacked certainty, as there were no objective criteria by which a reasonable quantity or price could be ascertained. It was held that the lack of certainty confirmed a lack of intention to create legal relations.

3.6 The issue of lack of certainty was also raised in *Walford* v *Miles* [1992] 1 All ER 453. This case involved negotiations for the sale of a photographic business. The parties entered into a so-called 'lock-out' agreement whereby the seller, in exchange for good consideration, agreed not to negotiate with any other party in respect of the sale of the business. Although such agreements can be enforceable, the House of Lords held that this one was not, because it was of unspecified duration. It was stated that no term could be implied by the court to give effect to the agreement. However, if the seller had agreed not to negotiate with any other party for a specified period of time, the agreement could have been enforced (see Lord Ackner's judgment at 461–2).

3.7 It is important to distinguish between a clause in a contract which has still to be agreed (such as 'hire purchase terms' in *G Scammell and Nephew Ltd* v *Ouston* (1941)) and a clause which is simply meaningless. The former may lead to a court deciding that no contract exists, whereas the latter can often be disregarded. Much will depend on the importance attached to the clause by the parties. For example, if it is of central importance in defining the contractual obligations of the parties, the vagueness of the clause may negate agreement (see *Bushwall Properties Ltd* v *Vortex Properties Ltd* (1976)). In *CPC Consolidated Pool Carriers GmbH* v *CTM Cia TransMediterranea SA* (1994), the negotiations between the parties, for the shipment of a jet foil, were said to be 'subject to details/logical amendments'. Potter J held that there was no concluded contract, as it was intended by the parties that a formal contract was still to be drawn up later. The expression 'subject to details' left matters too vague, as these terms and

1 *Quaere*: In *Hillas & Co. Ltd* v *Arcos Ltd* (1932), did the option to buy timber constitute an agreement, or was it merely an agreement to make an agreement? The ambit of the decision was also considered more recently by the Court of Appeal in *iSoft Group plc* v *MISYS Holdings Ltd* (2003) (see, especially, [43]–[44]).

details needed to be finalized. But if the clause is 'severable' from the main part of the agreement (i.e. of little significance, or even superfluous), then it can be ignored without affecting the validity of the contract. If this were not so, those in breach of contract might look for any vague phrase in the agreement as a means of escaping liability.

3.8 In *Nicolene Ltd* v *Simmonds* [1953] 1 QB 543, for example, C ordered 3,000 tons of steel bars from D. D's letter of acceptance of the order included the phrase that it was assumed that 'the usual conditions of acceptance apply'. D, who failed to supply the steel and was sued for breach of contract, claimed that due to the uncertainty caused by the words 'usual conditions of acceptance', there was no binding agreement. This argument was rejected by the Court of Appeal. In the words of Lord Denning (at 552):

> [T]here was nothing yet to be agreed. There was nothing left to further negotiation. All that happened was that the parties agreed that the "usual conditions of acceptance apply". That clause was so vague and uncertain as to be incapable of any precise meaning. It is clearly severable from the rest of the contract. It can be rejected without impairing the sense or reasonableness of the contract as a whole, and it should be so rejected. The contract should be held good and the clause ignored.

Is there a complete contract?

3.9 Provided that the main terms of a contract have been agreed by the parties, the fact that further terms have still to be negotiated will not necessarily prevent there being a concluded contract (see *Pagnan SpA* v *Feed Products Ltd* (1987), applied recently in *Bear Sterns Bank Plc* v *Forum Global Equity Ltd* (2007); and *De Jongh Weill* v *Mean Fiddler Holdings Ltd* (2003) at [22]). In other instances the parties may negotiate a contract and reach agreement in principle but leave certain details to be decided later. (See for example *RTS Flexible Systems Ltd* v *Molkerei Alois Müller GmbH & Co KG* (2010) discussed at para. **3.16**.) As a matter of strict theory it might appear that this does not constitute a binding agreement, especially if important terms are left undecided. This may well be the result in practice too, as illustrated by *Willis Management (Isle of Man) Ltd* v *Cable & Wireless plc* (2005). In this case, the Court of Appeal held that an agreement by the parties, to agree an essential term in the future, was incomplete and unenforceable. The court was not prepared to make an agreement for the parties where further discussion and agreement was still required from them. More recently, in *Barbudev* v *Eurocom Cable Management Bulgaria Eood* (2012), the Court of Appeal held that a side letter signed by both parties was not a legally enforceable agreement but simply an 'agreement to agree', given that essential terms were not dealt with. Here, it was concluded that the side letter was not sufficiently certain to be an enforceable contract. But much will depend on the circumstances of the case (as discussed in *J Murphy and Sons Ltd* v *ABB Daimler-Benz Transportation (Signal) Ltd* (1999) and further emphasized in *RTS Flexible Systems Ltd* v *Molkerei Alois Müller GmbH & Co KG* (2010)). It is not the role of a court to make an agreement for the parties where none exists, but it may be able to give effect to contractual intention (e.g. by implying terms) where there is an agreement which has not been fully expressed. (For a discussion of this distinction, see *Scancarriers A/S* v *Aotearoa International Ltd* (1985).)

3.10 In some commercial contexts it may be necessary to allow the price to be fixed, or adjusted, after the agreement has been concluded. For example, in a contract between an oil company and a petrol station owner for the supply of petrol over a number of years, it would not be too uncertain an agreement to allow the price to be adjusted periodically by the supplier. In *Shell (UK) Ltd* v *Lostock Garage Ltd* [1977] 1 All ER 481, the buyer agreed to pay for his supply of petrol 'at a price which shall be the wholesale schedule price ruling at [the] date and place of delivery'. Of course, such an agreement may be declared unenforceable by the court where it gives rise to an unreasonable restraint of trade, or even (perhaps) where it simply operates in an unfair and unconscionable way (*Shell* case at 489–93). But it is not void for lack of completeness.

3.11 As examples of contracting parties leaving important points unsettled, it is instructive to contrast the cases of *May and Butcher Ltd* v *R* [1934] 2 KB 17 and *Foley* v *Classique Coaches Ltd* [1934] 2 KB 1. In the former, the facts were:

> C agreed to buy surplus tentage from the Controller of the Disposals Board. The agreement provided: 'The price . . . to be paid, and the date or dates on which payment is to be made by the purchasers to the Commission for such old tentage shall be agreed upon from time to time between the Commission and the purchasers.' The trial judge decided that this 'agreement' did not amount to a contract, and this was affirmed by the Court of Appeal.

The House of Lords held that such a vague and incomplete agreement was not enforceable and that there was no binding contract between the parties. Lord Buckmaster stated (at 20):

> It is, of course, perfectly possible for two people to contract that they will sign a document which contains all the relevant terms, but it is not open to them to agree that they will in future agree upon a matter which is vital to the arrangement between them and has not yet been determined.

3.12 The failure of the parties to an agreement to fix a price for the goods need not prevent a binding contract from being concluded. The Sale of Goods Act 1979, s 8(1) provides that if the price of goods is not fixed by the contract of sale, it may alternatively 'be left to be fixed in a manner agreed by the contract, or may be determined by the course of dealing between the parties'. If the parties have not fixed a price for the goods then, under s 8(2), the buyer must pay a reasonable price. These provisions were not applicable in *May and Butcher Ltd* v *R* (1934) because the parties had made it clear that the price was to be settled by future negotiation between them. This tends to indicate an incomplete agreement. (Also note *King's Motors (Oxford) Ltd* v *Lax* (1970), where a lease contained an option for the tenant to accept a further lease 'at such rental as may be agreed upon between the parties'. It was held that, in the absence of an arbitration clause or some supplementary agreement fixing the rent to be paid, the option was void for uncertainty.)

3.13 Although the decision in *May and Butcher Ltd* v *R* (1934) is defensible and probably correct, the law must be careful not to thwart the reasonable expectations of business people. (For further discussion on the reasonable expectations of contracting parties, see J. Steyn, 'Contract Law: Fulfilling the Reasonable Expectations of Honest Men' (1997) 113 LQR 433.) Wherever possible, an attempt should be made to give effect to the clear contractual intention of the parties. (See P. Nicholls, 'My Word is My Bond' (2008) 158 NLJ 122, for a discussion of how the law 'seeks to uphold commercial transactions and is wary of technical attempts by parties to avoid their contracts'.) For example, in *Foley* v *Classique Coaches Ltd* (1934), the following facts occurred:

> C agreed to sell a piece of land, adjoining C's garage, to the defendants. The sale of the land ('Contract One') was conditional on the defendants, who ran a motor coach business, entering into a second agreement with C for the supply of all their petrol requirements ('Contract Two'). Although the two agreements were contained in separate documents, the sale of the land was clearly conditional on the defendant's agreement to buy petrol from C 'at a price to be agreed by the parties in writing and from time to time'. (*Note:* There was also an arbitration clause included in the second contract to deal with any dispute between the parties arising out of the agreement.) After the conveyance of the land, the defendants bought their petrol from C for three years, but then they repudiated the second agreement. C sued for damages and sought a declaration that the agreement concerning the supply of petrol was binding on the defendants.

The Court of Appeal held that there was a binding contract despite the fact that the price was 'to be agreed by the parties . . . from time to time'. It may seem that this decision is inconsistent with that of *May and Butcher*; but on closer examination the decisions are clearly distinguishable. In *Foley*, the agreement had been acted upon by the parties for three years. (See also *F & G Sykes (Wessex) Ltd* v *Fine Fare Ltd* (1967).) This was not the case in *May and Butcher*. Furthermore, the arbitration clause in *Foley* enabled the parties to resolve any problems caused by an incomplete agreement. One of the grounds put forward by the defendants in *Foley* for repudiating the second agreement with the claimant was that it constituted an unreasonable restraint of trade. This argument was rejected by the court and it was stated that it would have been unfair to allow the defendants to escape from their contractual obligations, having obtained a good deal on the purchase of the land in the first place. Therefore the respective behaviour of the parties in *Foley* also appears to be of some significance.[2]

3.14 An interesting point arose in *Sudbrook Trading Estate Ltd* v *Eggleton* [1983] 1 AC 444. If the parties to an agreement provide some procedure for resolving the uncertainty of that

2 See the speech of Scrutton LJ at 7.

agreement, and that procedure is subsequently unsuccessful, can the court still give effect to the clear contractual intention of the parties? The facts were as follows:

> The claimants were tenants of four adjoining properties let to them by the defendants. Each lease gave the claimants an option to purchase the freehold reversion of the leased properties at a price to be agreed by two valuers. Each party was to nominate a valuer, and if agreement was not reached by them, an umpire was to be appointed by both valuers. When the claimants tried to exercise the options contained in the four leases, the defendants argued that the option clauses were void for uncertainty and refused to name a valuer. (They argued that the options were nothing more than agreements to agree in the future.) Although the options to purchase were declared valid by the trial court judge, the defendants' appeal was allowed by the Court of Appeal on the basis that there was no complete agreement which the court could enforce. The claimants appealed to the House of Lords.

The claimants' appeal was allowed and the options were ordered to be specifically performed. The purpose of the option clauses had been to provide for the sale of the properties at a fair and reasonable price and a procedure had been provided to ensure this. The machinery for ascertaining the value of the property was merely subsidiary and non-essential to this main purpose. It would have been unfair if the defendants, by their own breach of contract, had been able to defeat this clear contractual purpose by their refusal to appoint a valuer. Because the procedure laid down by the parties was not essential, there was no reason why the court could not substitute its own machinery to prevent the contract from being unenforceable. Accordingly, it ordered an enquiry into the fair value of the properties. (But see Lord Russell's dissenting judgment in this case.[3])

Agreement reached 'subject to contract'

3.15 A different problem arises where parties negotiate the terms of a contract, expressing their agreement 'subject to contract', and one of the parties incurs costs in preparing for the intended contract, which then fails to materialize. This occurred in *Regalian Properties plc* v *London Dockland Corpn* [1995] 1 All ER 1005, where C's offer to build a residential development was accepted by D subject to contract. There were long delays for various reasons and, two years later, after a sharp decrease in land prices, D abandoned the project. There was clearly no complete contract between the parties, but could C claim £3 million for costs already incurred in relation to the proposed contract? This claim was rejected by Rattee J who stressed that the dealings between C and D had been 'subject to contract' only, and that D had not led C to believe that such costs would be paid for. The judge stated (at 1024) that in this situation the parties should understand 'that pending the conclusion of a binding contract any costs incurred by [C] in preparation for the intended contract will be

3 His Lordship ([1982] 3 All ER 1 at 12) made the following observations: 'Why should it be thought that the potential vendor and purchaser intended the price to be "fair"? The former would intend the price to be high, even though unfairly so. And the latter vice versa. Vendors and purchasers are normally greedy.' *Quaere*: Is this an apposite criticism of the view of the majority in *Sudbrook Trading Estate Ltd* v *Eggleton* (1982)?

incurred at his own risk in the sense that [C] will have no recompense for these costs if no contract results'.[4]

3.16 The difficulties which can arise when an agreement is expressed to be 'subject to contract' were most recently illustrated by the Supreme Court case of *RTS Flexible Systems Ltd* v *Molkerei Alois Müller GmbH & Co KG* (2010). Here a dispute arose between the parties, who had entered into negotiations for the supply and installation of automated packaging machinery. Although the parties had intended to enter into a detailed written contract, work began before the terms were finalized. Whilst continuing to negotiate the full contract terms, Müller and RTS entered into a contract formed by a Letter of Intent. This provided details of the full agreed contract price which extended beyond the price of the work to take place during the currency of the Letter of Intent contract. It also included a term which stated that the full contractual terms were to be based on Müller's final draft version of contract terms known as the MF/1 terms. After four weeks, the Letter of Intent expired but as work on the project continued beyond that time, it was questioned whether the parties had entered into a contract and if so, on what terms.

3.17 The Supreme Court hearing recognized that the problems fell under two heads, both of which arose out of the parties agreeing to start work before execution of a formal written contract, 'in accordance with the parties' common understanding' (at [46]). The first problem concerned the effect of the parties' understanding that the contract would not become effective until they had executed and exchanged an agreement in written form. However, this had never occurred. Second, it needed to be questioned whether the parties had agreed upon all the terms which they objectively regarded, or the law required, as essential for the formation of legally binding relations. In the instant case, this related to the terms on which the work was being carried out, agreement on the price or remuneration, and the rights and obligations of the supplier.

3.18 The judge at first instance held that after the Letter of Intent had expired, the parties had entered into a contract whereby RTS would carry out the agreed work for the agreed price but that this contract did not include the final draft version of the MF/1 terms. The Court of Appeal overturned that decision and found that there was no contract between the parties. The Supreme Court recognized that a third possible conclusion could be reached (at [57]), namely that agreement had been reached between the parties and this had been reached on wider terms.

3.19 The Supreme Court found, (at [85]–[86]), evidence of unequivocal conduct on the part of both RTS and Müller indicating that there was agreement that the project would be carried out by RTS for the agreed price, on the terms which the parties had agreed by 5 July and as varied on 25 August. When the agreement was varied in August, this was treated as a variation of the agreement which had been reached in July. At this juncture, no suggestion was made that there was no contract between the parties and therefore no terms to vary. Rather, it was not until November, by which time the parties were in dispute, that points were taken as to whether there was a contract.

4 If D had encouraged C to incur costs beyond those which fell within the category of normal business risks in this situation, the result may have been different, especially if D had encouraged C to think such costs would be remunerated. See *William Lacey (Hounslow) Ltd* v *Davis* (1957), which was distinguished by Rattee J in the *Regalian* case. For a more recent discussion of the 'subject to contract' issue, see the House of Lords' decision in *Cobbe* v *Yeoman's Row Management Ltd* (2008).

3.20 Given that all essential terms had been agreed, and with reference to the standard of the reasonable honest businessman (see [86]), the Supreme Court overturned the Court of Appeal decision, concluding that a binding agreement had been reached. As the essential aspects of the project, including what sums would be paid, were clear, this created sufficient certainty of terms for there to be a binding contract (also see *Pamela Allen* v *Fisher Jones Greenwood (A Firm)* (2013)). The *RTS* case offers a useful summary of the existing position on contractual certainty and completeness and serves as a cautionary tale of the possible perils of beginning a project before agreeing the precise basis upon which it is to be carried out. In the words of Lord Clarke (at [1]): 'The moral of the story is to agree first and to start work later.'

3.21 In *Bieber v Teathers (in Liquidation)* (2014) an agreement was reached between the parties, via email and through their solicitors, to settle their dispute. Here, although the negotiations had begun 'subject to contract', when objectively tested and determined by the court, this condition was found to have been waived. This remained unaffected by the fact that the parties had not reached agreement on the precise terms of the settlement. A willingness 'to negotiate concerning the terms of a settlement agreement [did] not necessarily lead to the conclusion that the parties had not earlier entered into a binding agreement to settle the dispute' (at [57]). (As an alternative, see *Taylor v Burton* (2015), which concerned a dispute over a right of way and where submission of a draft order with a deed attached by one party did not demonstrate both parties' agreement to expunge the 'subject to contract' qualification.)

Uncertainty and incompleteness

3.22 The apparent willingness of both parties to make a contract does not necessarily amount to a legally binding agreement. Essential terms, such as price and date of completion, should not normally be left incomplete and the intentions of the parties should not be couched in vague or ambiguous terms. (See *Wallis* v *Learonal (UK) plc* [2003] EWCA Civ 98 at [14]–[15].)

3.23 However, this basic principle is limited by the desire of the courts to give effect, particularly in business contexts, to the contractual intentions of the parties (for example, see *Perry* v *Suffields Ltd* (1916)). The law has to remain in touch with commercial reality and it is correct that problems of uncertainty and incompleteness are not decided purely on the basis of technical legal requirements. (See *Liverpool City Council* v *Walton Group plc* (2001), which illustrates the flexible attitude of the courts when faced with lack of certainty in commercial agreements. In this case, the draft lease did not include a commencement date, but the judge held that it was not void for uncertainty as the document was intended by both parties to have commercial effect.)

3.24 As we have seen, the courts are frequently able to fill in gaps left by the parties, and this judicial invention is assisted by the provisions of the Sale of Goods Act 1979 (s 8, for example) and the Supply of Goods and Services Act 1982 (see s 15(1)). Furthermore, a court is more likely to give effect to an incomplete or uncertain agreement which has been acted on by one or both of the parties than to one where the obligations on each party are in the future. This is both fair and commercially realistic.

Formalities

3.25 It is commonly assumed that a contract is something which must be made in writing and signed. This assumption however has been borne from matters of common sense and practicality rather than from legal principles. In *Blue* v *Ashley* [2017] EWHC 1928 (Comm) it was said (at [49]):

> Generally speaking, it is possible under English Law to make a contract without any formality, simply by word of mouth. Of course, the absence of a written record may make the existence and terms of a contract harder to prove. Furthermore, because the value of a written record is understood by anyone with business experience, its absence may—depending on the circumstances—tend to suggest that no contract was in fact concluded. But those are matters of proof: they are not legal requirements.

Usually, therefore, contracts require no formalities—most can be made orally—although a deed may substitute for consideration (see para. **4.2**). As a recent example, see *MacInnes* v *Gross* [2017] EWHC 46, where the court was required to consider whether there was any intention to form an agreement based on an alleged oral contract, finding that the terms of the alleged contract were both too complex and too uncertain to be enforceable.

3.26 Formality requirements are restricted to a few specific types of contract, and these requirements vary. For example, a contract for the sale or other disposition of an interest in land is unenforceable unless in writing (Law of Property (Miscellaneous Provisions) Act 1989, s 2). Certain contracts of guarantee are unenforceable unless evidenced in writing (Statute of Frauds 1677, s 4).

3.27 Formalities may be required for a number of reasons (see L. Fuller, 'Consideration and Form' (1941) 41 Col LR 799; and Law Com Rep No 164 (1987)). They may be there to promote certainty by requiring clear evidence of the terms. They may be used to encourage the parties to give full consideration to the legal obligations being undertaken. Increasingly, they may also be required for paternalistic reasons, that is, to provide protection for people in a weaker bargaining position, such as consumers. The practical benefits of committing a contractual relationship to writing are notable and a written record of rights and responsibilities will undoubtedly promote clarity and certainty in the parties' arrangement.

Electronic contracting

3.28 Requirements of 'writing' or 'signature' may cause difficulties in the e-commerce context. It may be argued that they can be fulfilled by communications by email (see *J Pereira Fernandes SA* v *Mehta* (2006) and *Orton* v *Collins* (2007) at [21]) or over the internet, but mere uncertainty as to the position can be detrimental to the efficient growth of e-commerce and action has been taken at both the EC and UK levels. Article 9 of the EC Directive on Electronic Commerce (2000/31/EC) requires member states to 'ensure that their legal system allows contracts to be concluded by electronic means' and, in particular, to 'ensure that the legal requirements applicable to the contractual process do not create obstacles for the use of electronic contracts or result in such contracts being deprived of legal effectiveness and validity on account of their having been made by electronic means'. Member states are allowed to exempt from this:

(a) contracts that create or transfer rights in real estate, except for rental rights;
(b) contracts requiring by law the involvement of the courts, public authorities or professions exercising public authority;
(c) contracts of suretyship granted and collateral securities furnished by persons acting for purposes outside their trade, business, or profession;
(d) contracts governed by family law or the law of succession.

This takes the approach of requiring the removal of any formality barriers to electronic contracting in all but a small number of exceptional cases. As has been indicated, there are relatively few situations in which formalities are required for contract formation in English law.

3.29 There has been legislation in the UK in the form of the Electronic Communications Act 2000. The Act is more wide-ranging than the EC Directive, in that its coverage extends beyond the contracting process to requirements for 'signature', 'writing', 'documents', or 'notices', for example, which are legally significant in other ways. It does not in itself make any changes to the legislation under which such requirements are set out, but s 8 allows the 'appropriate minister' to amend any such legislation by statutory instrument, 'for the purpose of authorising or facilitating the use of electronic communications or electronic storage . . . for any purpose mentioned in subsection (2)'. The purposes mentioned in subs (2) are wide-ranging, but here it is relevant to note that they include:

(a) the doing of anything which under any such provision is required to be or may be done or evidenced in writing, or otherwise using a document notice or instrument;

...

(b) the doing of anything which under any such provision is required to be or may be authorized by a person's signature or seal, or is required to be delivered as a deed or witnessed.

Where necessary, this legislation may allow law in the UK to be brought into line with the requirements of the EC Directive. However, the Law Commission has advised the government that, generally, requirements of writing and signature may be fulfilled by some electronic form of communication without any change in the law, so 'that it is only in very rare cases that the statute book will conflict with Article 9 [of the Electronic Commerce Directive]'. (See 'Electronic Commerce: Formal Requirements in Commercial Transactions', Advice from the Law Commission, December 2001, para. 3.49 and paras 10.1–10.3.) The Law Commission also stated that despite a 'lack of consensus on these issues, statutory requirements for "writing" and a "signature" are generally capable of being satisfied by emails and by web-site trading' (at para. 10.1). (For further discussion of the Law Commission's views, see H. Beale and L. Griffiths, 'Electronic Commerce: Formal Requirements in Commercial Transactions' (2002) LMCLQ 467.)

3.30 The introduction of the Electronic Identification and Trust Services for Electronic Transactions Regulations (2016/696), which implement the provisions of Regulation (EU) 910/2014 known as 'the eIDAS Regulation', has been a notable development, particularly in respect of electronic signatures. The eIDAS Regulation repeals and revokes the Electronic Signatures Regulations (2002/318) and makes amendments to section 7 of the Electronic Communications Act 2000, both of which implemented the Directive on a Community framework for electronic signatures (1999/93/EC). The main objective of the eIDAS Regulation is to facilitate 'secure and seamless electronic cross-border transactions between businesses, citizens and administrations and introduce a regime for the mutual recognition of electronic signatures, electronic seals, electronic time-stamping and acceptance of electronic documents and website authentication' [at Recital 2]. It is perhaps too early to assess the true impact of the eIDAS Regulation within the UK but if contracting parties acquire an increased sense of security through the implementation and protection of its provisions, there will undoubtedly be an increase in the effective and appropriate use of e-signatures for legal transactions in the future.

Summary

- The courts will try to give effect to apparent agreements by filling in the gaps left by the parties.
- However, there are limits to how far the courts will go in making agreements for the parties.
- There is often a need for flexibility in business contracts, which may not always conform to technical requirements of the law in relation to offer and acceptance.
- The courts will try to make sense of imprecise terms, except where the ambiguity is central to the contractual obligations, or where the imprecision suggests a lack of contractual intention.
- In some commercial contexts it is permissible to allow a price to be fixed, or adjusted, after the agreement is made.
- Courts are more likely to give effect to an incomplete or uncertain agreement which has been acted on by one or both of the parties.
- It is commonly, but wrongly, thought that a contract has to be in writing. Most contracts do not require any formalities.

Further reading

H. Beale and L. Griffiths, 'Electronic Commerce: Formal Requirements in Commercial Transactions' (2002) 4 (Nov) LMCLQ 467

I. Brown, 'The Contract to Negotiate: A Thing Writ in Water?' [1992] (Jul) JBL 353

L. Fuller, 'Consideration and Form' (1941) 41 Columbia Law Review 799

Law Commission, 'Electronic Commerce: Formal Requirements in Commercial Transactions', 2001

D. McLauchlan, 'Rethinking Agreements to Agree' (1998) 18 NZULR 77

S. Mouzas and M. Furmston, 'From Contract to Umbrella Agreement' (2008) 67 CLJ 37

P. Nicholls, 'My Word Is My Bond' (2008) 158 NLJ 122

J. Steyn, 'Contract Law: Fulfilling the Reasonable Expectations of Honest Men' (1997) 113 LQR 433

Chapter 4

Consideration

Introduction

4.1 The law of contract has to have some means of distinguishing between those agreements which are enforceable and those which are not. It would be clearly impracticable and inconvenient if all agreements were legally binding. Some agreements may lack certainty or completeness (see **Chapter 3**) and will be ineffective for this reason. In some cases there will be no intention to create legal relations, and in certain situations, such as social and domestic agreements, the law presumes that there is no such intention (see **Chapter 6**). Another method of limiting the enforceability of agreements is to require that the contract be expressed in a particular form, such as in writing. This is a rather time-consuming and inflexible method which tends to be employed either for evidential reasons or in circumstances where the law wishes to protect certain groups from possible exploitation.

4.2 A gratuitous promise made in writing by deed is legally binding because of the form in which it is expressed. It does not matter whether anything is given in return for such a promise. However, most contracts are not of this type. 'Simple' contracts do not normally require any particular form in order to be effective. As we have seen, an enforceable agreement can be made orally or in writing. The test of enforceability which is used under our law of contract is the requirement of consideration. This is the symbol of bargain and reciprocal obligations. The law does not enforce gratuitous promises; the promise of a gift, for example, to a charity will not be binding unless it is by deed (see *Re Hudson* (1885)). Similarly, a promise is not enforceable simply because it is morally right that a promisor should keep his or her word (see *Eastwood* v *Kenyon* (1840)). The law requires that the promisor asks for and receives something in return for his or her promise. The courts are not generally concerned with whether the promisor made a good bargain. All that is required is that there is some element of exchange.

4.3 The historical origins of the doctrine of consideration are the subject of much academic debate, which need not concern us here. It is sufficient to note that the doctrine survived the challenge of an eminent judge, Lord Mansfield, in the mid-eighteenth century, when he attempted to argue that it was not a necessary contractual requirement, but merely one method of proving the intention of the parties to be bound.[1] In Lord Mansfield's view, some other evidence of the parties' contractual intention, such as writing, would equally suffice. This was rejected in *Rann* v *Hughes* (1778) and despite criticisms of the doctrine, some of which we will consider in due course, consideration is a basic requirement of all simple contracts and is therefore central to our understanding of the subject.

4.4 But a word of warning is necessary at the outset. Although we refer to *the* doctrine of consideration, it must be stressed that this doctrine in fact consists of a number of different rules, developed over a long period, some of which are more defensible than others. To debate whether the doctrine is a good or bad thing is to miss the point of its importance. The various rules which we call 'consideration' simply represent the method that our law has developed for distinguishing between enforceable and unenforceable promises. In doing so, it has emphasized the idea of bargain and exchange in contractual dealings. This was clearly in keeping with the spirit of classical contract law and the laissez-faire philosophy which influenced it.

4.5 If the doctrine were to be abolished, some alternative test of enforceability would still be required. This is not to suggest that all the present rules are satisfactory. It is only the resourcefulness of the judiciary and the malleability of the common law which have enabled the doctrine to survive in its present form without being subjected to the attentions of the legislature (e.g. see the development of the doctrine of promissory estoppel, in **Chapter 5**). Some of the rules of consideration appear to be capable of producing unfair results, whilst others are perhaps out of touch with commercial practice. Some of these anomalies have been smoothed out by the judges, but certain fundamental issues still need to be resolved. For example, what is the nature of the interrelationship between the traditional exchange model of contracts and the more modern emphasis on estoppel and reliance? These are matters to which we shall return.

Can consideration be defined?

4.6 As the doctrine is in fact a loose assortment of different rules, it tends to defy any standard or broadly accepted definition. Yet attempts at such a definition abound. The traditional definitions tended to concentrate on the ideas of benefit and detriment. For example, in *Currie* v *Misa* (1875) LR 10 Ex 153, Lush J stated (at 162):

> A valuable consideration, in the eyes of the law, may consist either in some right, interest, profit, or benefit accruing to the one party, or some forbearance, detriment, loss, or responsibility given, suffered or undertaken by the other.

1 In *Antons Trawling Co. Ltd* v *Smith* (2003), Baragwanath J argued, at [93], that 'the importance of consideration is as a valuable signal that the parties intend to be bound by their agreement, rather than an end in itself'.

This type of definition stressed the exchange nature of contracts in terms of some kind of economic advantage. (See also *Thomas* v *Thomas* (1842) 2 QB 851 at 859.) In other words, the promisor must receive something which the law recognizes as a 'benefit', namely something of value. If a seller promises to deliver goods to a customer, the latter provides consideration by paying for them, or by his or her promise to pay for them. The customer suffers a detriment by so doing, in exchange for the benefit conferred upon him or her by the seller.[2]

4.7 The problem with the traditional definition is that in many instances the consideration in question does not, in fact, confer any economic benefit on the promisor. The idea of something of value, given in exchange for a promise, is interpreted very widely. In the absence of fraud or any other vitiating factor, the courts are not generally concerned with the nature of the bargain struck by the parties. It may well be that, in economic terms, the consideration is inadequate; the courts will not interfere. The doctrine represents the symbol, rather than the reality, of bargain. It is a technical requirement of the law of contract, and the parties can easily ensure that it is met by the provision of some nominal consideration.

4.8 For these reasons, more modern definitions of consideration tend not to be expressed in terms of benefit and detriment. Reference is made more loosely to one party paying the 'price' of the other's promise. For example, Sir Frederick Pollock stated: 'An act or forbearance of one party, or the promise thereof, is the price for which the promise is bought and the promise thus given for value is enforceable.'[3] (This statement was approved in *Dunlop Pneumatic Tyre Co. Ltd* v *Selfridge & Co. Ltd* [1915] AC 847 at 855.) If a party promises something and asks for nothing in return, there is no consideration and, therefore, the promise is not legally enforceable. But where the promisor asks for something in exchange for his or her promise, the promisee provides consideration by giving the promisor what he or she has requested. The promisor might have requested a specific act, such as the provision of information in exchange for a reward. This is referred to as 'executed' consideration. Alternatively, the promisor might request a promise (for example, of payment for goods to be delivered in the future). This is known as 'executory' consideration.

4.9 The various definitions of consideration have their respective supporters, but it is not particularly important which one we adopt. This is because the courts take an essentially pragmatic view of the requirement. (See Steyn (1997) 113 LQR 433 at 437.) The decisions under the different rules which are discussed in this chapter are not always consistent with one another. In some circumstances, where justice demands, the courts may be seen to 'invent', or 'find', consideration so as to make the promise in question binding. As we saw in the earlier chapters of this book, the common law is flexible and the law of contract cannot be reduced to a set of axioms. With this warning in mind, the main rules which comprise the doctrine of consideration will now be considered.

2 In many commercial transactions there is such a benefit and detriment, although some might argue that there is no detriment where the contract is wholly executory (i.e. by the exchange of promises). For an interesting discussion, see P. Atiyah, *The Rise and Fall of Freedom of Contract*, Oxford University Press, 1979, pp. 448–54.

3 See his work on *Contract*, 13th edn, p. 133.

Consideration must not be past

4.10 Where the promisor (P) requests a specific act in return for his or her promise, then performance of the act by the promisee will be good consideration. If all the other ingredients of a binding contract are present, P's promise will be enforceable. It will be remembered that in *Carlill* v *Carbolic Smoke Ball Co.* (1893), the defendant company offered a reward of £100 to anyone who bought one of their smoke balls, used it in the prescribed manner, and yet caught influenza. The claimant, who bought a smoke ball and used it, provided consideration for the company's promise. (Obviously she could not have claimed the reward unless she in fact caught flu, but this can hardly be described as part of the consideration.) The act done in return for the promise is referred to as 'executed' consideration.

4.11 An exchange of promises by the parties, known as 'executory' consideration, will also amount to an enforceable agreement. For example, X promises to deliver a new car to Y in three weeks' time, and Y promises to pay for the vehicle on delivery. Despite the fact that no performance of the undertakings has yet taken place—the performances are still in the future—there is good consideration. Both parties are getting what they requested in return for their promises. For commercial reasons it is important that the law recognizes the validity of such agreements, as this facilitates forward planning by the parties.

4.12 Executed and executory consideration are commonly referred to as 'good consideration'. However, a promise which is made after an act has been performed is generally not enforceable. This is rather confusingly referred to as 'past' consideration, and it is not recognized as good consideration. The reason for this is that the act or performance in question was not part of any bargain or exchange; it was gratuitous. Therefore, any subsequent promise is not part of any contractual bargain and remains unenforceable (although there are some important exceptions which will be considered later). A vivid illustration of the basic rule is provided by *Eastwood* v *Kenyon* (1840):

> The claimant had become the guardian of Sarah, a young heiress, on the death of Sarah's father. He spent money on improving her estate and on her education, and he had to borrow £140 in order to do so. When she came of age, she promised to pay the claimant the amount of the loan. After her marriage to the defendant, he (her husband) repeated this promise of reimbursement to the claimant.

The claimant could not enforce the defendant's promise, due to lack of consideration. The guardian's acts were gratuitous; they were not given in return for the defendant's (or Sarah's) promise. The case clearly shows that a moral obligation to fulfil a promise is not sufficient to lead the court to enforce that promise. Even when confronted by an unjust result, as in this case, the court will require something given in exchange for a promise for it to be enforceable.

4.13 A similar decision was reached in *Re McArdle* (1951), which also shows that the use of the term 'consideration' by the parties themselves is not necessarily of any significance. The facts were:

> The five children of a family were to inherit a house (by their father's will) after the death of their mother. One of the sons, and his wife, lived in the house with his mother until she died. During this period the daughter-in-law made some improvements and alterations to the property, which she paid for herself. She had not been asked to do this. However, about a year later, all five children signed a document addressed to her, in which they promised to repay her £488 from the estate when it was eventually distributed. The document specifically stated that this payment was 'in consideration of [her] carrying out certain alterations and improvements to the property'. When the mother died, the daughter-in-law tried to enforce the promise made in this document.

The Court of Appeal held that her claim failed. The promise was not given in exchange for her act. She had already carried out the improvements without any such promise of reimbursement being made. This was a clear instance of past consideration and the promise was, accordingly, unenforceable, despite the apparently unequivocal way in which the document expressed the contractual intention of the five children.

4.14 Another example is provided by *Roscorla* v *Thomas* (1842). In that case, C bought a horse from D for £30. After the sale, D promised that the horse was 'sound and free from vice', a fact which turned out to be untrue. It was held that this promise was not enforceable, as it was given after the contract between the parties had been concluded. Nothing was given by C in exchange for D's promise.

Instances where consideration is not past

4.15 There are certain well-established circumstances where what appears to be past consideration will be regarded as good consideration by the courts. They will look at the whole transaction between the parties and not rely simply on whether the promise was made after a particular act or service was performed by the promisee. These circumstances were helpfully summarized by Lord Scarman in the Privy Council decision in *Pao On* v *Lau Yiu Long* [1979] 3 All ER 65 at 74, where he stated:

> An act done before the giving of a promise to make a payment or to confer some other benefit can sometimes be consideration for the promise. The act must have been done at the promisor's request, the parties must have understood that the act was to be remunerated either by a payment or the conferment of some other benefit, and payment, or the conferment of a benefit, must have been legally enforceable had it been promised in advance.

4.16 An early illustration is provided by *Lampleigh* v *Brathwait* (1615). The facts were:

> Brathwait had killed a man and he requested that Lampleigh should try to get him a pardon from the King. Lampleigh did as requested, which involved making journeys at his own expense, and obtained a pardon for Brathwait. Afterwards, Brathwait promised to pay him £100 for his endeavours. He then failed to pay Lampleigh and was sued by him. Brathwait's defence was that the act had been performed before the promise of a reward was made.

The court found in favour of Lampleigh and rejected the argument that the consideration was past. It stressed that the claimant's service was performed at the request of the defendant and his later promise to pay for it was binding. This is because the later promise was clearly related to the earlier request for help: essentially, it was all part of the same transaction. The idea is that, as Lord Scarman said, 'the parties must have understood that the act was to be remunerated either by a payment or the conferment of some other benefit'.

4.17 The requirements put forward by Lord Scarman are further illustrated by *Re Casey's Patents (Stewart* v *Casey)* (1892). The facts were:

> Stewart and Charlton, the joint owners of certain patent rights, wrote to Casey stating that, in consideration for his services as practical manager in working their patents, they promised to give him a one-third share of the patents. They later transferred the letters patent to Casey. After the death of Stewart, it was argued by Charlton and by Stewart's executor that Casey was not entitled to possession of the letters patent. Casey contested this and argued that, as owner of a one-third share in the patents, he was entitled to possession.

The question for the Court of Appeal to decide was whether Casey provided consideration for the promise made to him by Stewart and Charlton in the letter. The claimants contended that it was a case of past consideration, but this argument was rejected by the court, which found in favour of the defendant. The court was willing to imply an understanding between the parties, at the time the services by Casey were performed, that they would be remunerated. The later promise was, therefore, part of the same transaction: it merely fixed the amount of remuneration for which the service was originally rendered. Accordingly, consideration is not past in these circumstances, despite appearances to the contrary.[4]

4.18 The general rule about past consideration is also subject to certain statutory exceptions: for example, in relation to negotiable instruments. Under the Bills of Exchange Act 1882, s 27(1) provides that 'valuable consideration for a bill may be constituted by: (a) Any consideration sufficient to support a simple contract; (b) An antecedent debt or liability. Such a debt or liability is deemed valuable consideration whether the bill is payable on demand or at a future time.'[5]

4 For a more recent example, where Lord Scarman's three requirements were held to be satisfied, with the result that there was good consideration despite the defendant's argument that his promise was in exchange for past consideration, see *Foster* v *Matania* (2009).

5 Of interest on this subject, see *Thoni GmbH & Co. KG* v *RTP Equipment Ltd* (1979).

Consideration must move from the promisee

4.19 As a general principle, A can enforce a promise made to him or her only if A, him or herself, provided consideration for that promise (see *Price* v *Easton* (1833)). But what if A is promised some benefit by B, but the consideration for the promise has been supplied by C? In such a situation, A has given nothing in exchange for B's promise; A has not paid the price of it, or suffered any detriment. The traditional view of the law has been that A will not normally be able to enforce B's promise, as consideration has not been provided by A. For example, in *Tweddle* v *Atkinson* (1861) 1 B & S 393, the facts were:

> John Tweddle and William Guy agreed (at first orally, and later in writing) each to pay a sum of money to a couple on their marriage. The couple in question were their son and daughter, respectively. The claimant, John Tweddle's son, tried to enforce his father-in-law's promise, when William Guy failed to make the agreed payment. (In fact, the action was brought against the executor of the deceased William Guy.)

The son's action failed as he did not provide any consideration for his father-in-law's promise. Crompton J stated (at 398) that:

> [T]he consideration must move from the party entitled to sue upon the contract. It would be a monstrous proposition to say that a person was a party to a contract for the purpose of suing upon it for his own advantage, and not a party to it for the purpose of being sued.

An alternative way of expressing the justification for not allowing the son's action to succeed in *Tweddle* v *Atkinson* is that there was no privity of contract between him and his father-in-law. (The contract was between John Tweddle and William Guy.) This principle of contract law is dealt with in **Chapter 17**, together with the important Contracts (Rights of Third Parties) Act 1999, which has introduced significant changes to this area of law. The extent to which the rule that 'consideration must move from the promisee' has been affected by the new legislation, implicitly if not formally, will be considered in **Chapter 17**, as this principle is closely related to the doctrine of privity. It was the view of the Law Commission that it is not possible 'even at a formal level, [to] reform the privity doctrine while leaving untouched the rule that consideration must move from the promisee.' (See Law Commission Report, No 242, Privity of Contract: Contracts for the Benefit of Third Parties, 1996, para. 6.5.)

Must the consideration be adequate?

4.20 The doctrine of consideration represents the idea of bargain and mutual obligations. The law will enforce only those promises for which something is given in return; it will not enforce gratuitous promises. One of the difficulties with the traditional definition of consideration in terms of 'benefit' and 'detriment' is that the promisor might request some act or forbearance from the promisee which is of little or no economic value. But as long as this is what he requests, and is given, the court will not interfere with the 'bargain' struck by the parties (see

Bainbridge v *Firmstone* (1838)). Thus consideration represents the idea of bargain rather than the reality of it.

4.21 This apparent failure to question the adequacy (value) of consideration is perhaps more defensible than it might seem at first sight. If the parties have bargained for a particular consideration, then it can usually be assumed that they achieved what they wanted from the exchange. Where a party appears to have made a particularly bad bargain there may be some other factor present which may vitiate the agreement, such as fraud or duress, but in the absence of any vitiating factor, the courts will not generally intervene in order to ensure a fair bargain has been struck. An important point here is that the law of contract is not, in general, the most suitable means of monitoring or controlling prices and ensuring fairness. Regulation through other measures can achieve this end more effectively. Moreover, although there is perhaps no general doctrine in our law which protects parties simply on the basis that they have entered into a bad bargain, the law of contract is capable of considerable flexibility in the pursuit of a fair result. In other words, the courts may rely on the various techniques at their disposal in order to promote the idea that a contract should not involve an unfair exchange or a very one-sided bargain.[6]

Adequacy of consideration: the general rule

4.22 Although it is commonly stated that consideration must be of some economic value, as we have seen, it is generally not a matter for the courts to judge the adequacy of consideration. So the provision of nominal consideration will suffice to meet the technical requirement of the law. For example, in *Mountford* v *Scott* [1975] Ch 258 the payment of £1 by C was sufficient to secure an option to purchase D's house. The Court of Appeal held that this option agreement was enforceable against D and that it was irrelevant that the consideration provided by C could be described as a token payment. In reaching this conclusion, reference was made to the 'mass of English authority to the effect that anything of value, however small the value, is sufficient consideration to support a contract at law' (per Cairns LJ at 265). There may, occasionally, be problems in differentiating between a contract supported by consideration and a conditional gift. These issues are well illustrated by the case of *Thomas* v *Thomas* (1842). The facts were:

> C's husband had made it clear that if his wife survived him, she should have the use of his house. After her husband's death, C agreed with the defendant, her husband's executor, that she should have the use of the house as long as she did not remarry. Her husband's executor made the agreement largely in deference to the deceased's clearly expressed wishes. But C was also asked to pay £1 per year to the executors under the agreement. Had C provided consideration for the promise, or was the payment of £1 per year no more than a condition attached to a gift?

It was held that C provided consideration for the executor's promise. It would not have been a legally enforceable agreement if the executor had merely wished to honour the deceased's

6 See further **Chapter 16**.

wishes and requested nothing further. It would have been a gratuitous promise. But in this case, something of value, no matter how inadequate, was asked for by the promisor. It was more than a conditional gift, it was a binding agreement; the court did not have to enquire into the adequacy of the consideration provided by the promisee under the contract.

4.23 Generally, consideration must be of some economic value, no matter how slight. Less tangible benefits may fail to supply consideration. In *White* v *Bluett* (1853), the defendant borrowed money from his father and gave him a promissory note. This was followed by bitter complaints from the defendant that he had been treated less favourably by his father than the other children in the family. In order to gain some peace, and out of affection for his son, the father promised to discharge the defendant from his obligation to repay the loan. On the father's death, his executor brought a successful action to recover the loan. It was held that no consideration had been provided by the defendant for his father's promise, as refraining from making complaints was thought not to be of any economic value.

4.24 However, we should consider the case of *Ward* v *Byham* (1956). The facts were:

> The claimant (C) lived with the defendant (D) for five years as an unmarried couple. C gave birth to their daughter during this period, but the couple eventually separated. Initially, D was responsible for looking after the child, as C had been forced to leave their home. But when C found a housekeeping job, where she could have her daughter with her, D agreed to let her have the child and an allowance of £1 per week, provided that C could prove that their daughter was 'well looked after and happy'. The daughter, who was allowed to decide with which parent she wanted to live, went to her mother's. D made the £1 weekly payments, but stopped these when C married her employer. C brought an action for the £1 per week promised by D.

The Court of Appeal decided in favour of C and held that she did provide consideration for D's promise. In fact, C was under a legal obligation (as the mother of an illegitimate child) to look after her daughter (National Assistance Act 1948, s 42). The view was generally held that performance of a statutory duty could not provide consideration. However, it was argued that she went beyond her statutory duty by undertaking that the child was well looked after and happy. As we shall see, going beyond a statutory duty was well recognized as sufficient to provide consideration, and this would seem to be the line taken by the majority. However, treating doing so in this way, as consideration, makes a difficult contrast with *White* v *Bluett*, and it should not be thought that the general idea of something of economic, rather than purely emotional, value being needed to supply consideration will be easily departed from. (The courts can be fairly inventive in finding consideration for a promise where it is felt that justice requires such an approach.) Further, Denning LJ's approach was somewhat different to the rest of the court. He took the line that C could provide consideration for D's promise simply by fulfilling her statutory duty. This is an idea which may be seen to be a much more acceptable explanation of the case in the light of the developments made in relation to the doctrine of consideration by the case of *Williams* v *Roffey Bros & Nicholls (Contractors) Ltd* (1990) (see later).

4.25 However, there may be questions about something which is tangible being of any economic value, and being consideration.[7] In *Chappell & Co. Ltd* v *Nestlé Co. Ltd* [1960] AC 87, the facts were:

> The Nestlé Company (D) offered a record entitled 'Rockin' Shoes' to the public for 1s 6d (7.5p) plus three Nestlé chocolate bar wrappers. The requirement of sending in the wrappers in addition to the money was in order to promote the company's chocolate; the wrappers were thrown away on receipt. The action arose because the claimant, who owned the copyright in 'Rockin' Shoes', argued that he received insufficient royalties on the sale of the record. D paid a percentage based on the price of the record, which was 1s 6d. The claimant argued that the wrappers were also part of the consideration.

The House of Lords decided the case in favour of the claimant. The wrappers were part of the consideration. They were requested by the Nestlé Company and were given by members of the public, together with money, in exchange for the record. It was held to be irrelevant that the wrappers were of no intrinsic value to the company (at 114 per Lord Somervell). Parties to a contract could ask for whatever consideration they wanted, and it was not for the court to assess its adequacy. It might also be observed that the wrappers represented something of value to the Nestlé Company, namely the successful promotion of the company's products. This was acknowledged by Lord Reid (at 108) who stated that 'the requirement that wrappers should be sent was of great importance to the Nestlé Co . . . it seems to me quite unrealistic to divorce the buying of the chocolate from the supplying of the records'.

Forbearance to sue and compromise as consideration

4.26 Where X is threatened by Y with legal action to enforce a claim, they might reach a compromise whereby Y's promise to refrain from suing is 'bought' by X's counter promise to pay an agreed amount. This exchange of promises is binding, because something of value is given by both parties. (For example, see *Horton* v *Horton (No 2)* (1961): in this case there was only a possibility that an action might have been brought by the wife against her husband in relation to their separation agreement. But giving up this possible claim was still regarded by the court as consideration. For a more recent example of a case raising some similar issues, see *Papanicola* v *Fagon* (2008). Here a wife's forbearance from petitioning for divorce was held to be consideration for her husband's transfer to her of the beneficial ownership of the matrimonial home.) One party gives up a claim whilst the other agrees to pay compensation. It is in the interest of the legal system to encourage parties, wherever possible, to reach a compromise over disputes. Similarly, if X is faced with a claim by Y (for example, for an outstanding debt), and requests further time to pay, Y's forbearance from pursuing the claim can amount to consideration for any new promise made by X. So where a debtor promises to give additional security for a debt, in exchange for more time to pay, this will again be regarded as a binding agreement.

7 See *Revenue and Customs Commissioners* v *Debenhams Retail plc* (2005).

4.27 If X is threatened with a legal action which Y knows to be without foundation, Y's forbearance from proceeding will not amount to consideration for any new promise given by X. To hold otherwise would encourage vexatious and frivolous claims and be contrary to public policy (see *Wade* v *Simeon* (1846)). But as long as Y honestly believes that the action is reasonable, and might succeed, then forbearance from proceeding with a doubtful or even a bad claim is capable of amounting to consideration. (For a discussion of this issue, see *Freedman* v *Union Group plc* (1997).) Y must not conceal any information from X which might affect X's ability to resist the claim (see *Miles* v *New Zealand Alford Estate Co* (1886)).

4.28 Is it necessary for Y specifically to promise X some degree of forbearance from bringing an action, or need there only be some forbearance in fact which can be inferred from the dealings between the parties? This question was considered in *Alliance Bank Ltd* v *Broom* (1864) 2 Drew & Sm 289, where the facts were:

> The defendants, a firm of Liverpool merchants, owed £22,000 to the claimant bank and were asked by the bank to provide additional security for the debt. The defendants promised to assign to them the documents of title to certain goods by way of additional security. It is important to note that, in return, the bank made no express counter promise not to sue the defendants. The defendants failed to provide the promised security and the bank tried to enforce the promise. Had the bank given anything in return for the defendants' promise?

It was held that the bank had given consideration by their actual forbearance and were entitled to claim specific performance. The reason given was that in the circumstances the defendants received the benefit of 'a certain amount of forbearance which [they] would not have derived if [they] had not made the agreement' (at 292). Apparently, it did not matter that no specific promise to forbear was given by the bank, nor was it necessary that the actual forbearance should last for a substantial period of time. The decision is, perhaps, unfortunate. The court seems to have enforced a very one-sided exchange in circumstances where the extent of any forbearance was, to say the least, unclear. (For a contrasting decision, see *Miles* v *New Zealand Alford Estate Co* (1886).) In the opinion of two commentators, the unsatisfactory decisions on forbearance should be seen not as laying down any useful contractual principles, but more as a reflection of 'the policy objective of the courts' desire to encourage out of court settlements' (see P. Mitchell and J. Phillips, 'The Contractual Nexus: Is Reliance Essential?' (2002) OJLS 115 at 127).

Performance of a legal duty as consideration

4.29 We noted earlier that the law does not look at the adequacy of consideration. That is, however, contrasted with looking at its 'sufficiency'. Obviously the two words can mean much the same in everyday terms, but here the question of 'sufficiency' of consideration is about whether what is in question is something which is, in law, capable of constituting consideration. It is in the context of existing legal duties that the question has come to the fore in recent times.

4.30 The rules relating to sufficiency of consideration are not always entirely consistent, tending sometimes to reflect the exigencies of public policy rather than logic. This is particularly the case in relation to the performance of an existing legal duty in exchange for another person's promise. This can arise in three distinct factual situations, which will be considered in turn: (a) the performance of a duty owed already to a third party; (b) the performance of a public duty; and (c) the performance of a duty owed already to the promisor.

Performance of a duty owed to a third party

4.31 The law in this situation is well established. The type of situation is where X makes a promise to Y in exchange for Y doing (or promising to do) something which Y is already obliged to do under an existing contract with Z. At first sight it seems, as a matter of logic, that Y provides no consideration for X's promise. However, X does obtain a direct contractual right against Y. If Y does not perform, he or she is not only liable to Z, but also to X. Consideration has long been found in this situation, where the existing contractual duty is to a third party (*Shadwell* v *Shadwell* (1860) 9 CB NS 159, *Chichester* v *Cobb* (1866) and *Scotson* v *Pegg* (1861)). In *Pao On* v *Lau Yiu Long* [1979] 3 All ER 65, Lord Scarman stated (at 76):

> Their lordships do not doubt that a promise to perform, or the performance of, a pre-existing contractual obligation to a third party can be valid consideration.

4.32 *New Zealand Shipping Co. Ltd* v *AM Satterthwaite & Co. Ltd, The Eurymedon* [1974] 1 All ER 1015, provides an example. In that case, the claimant cargo owners (C) promised the defendant stevedore company (D) that they would not be liable for any damage to the goods arising out of their (D's) negligence. The cargo was damaged as a result of D's negligence during unloading. Could D rely on C's promise? D had already been bound to unload the goods under an existing contract with a third party, the carrier. Could the unloading of the goods be regarded as consideration provided by D in exchange for C's promise not to sue in the event of damage to the goods? The Privy Council held (at 1020–1) that the work done in unloading the cargo was good consideration for C's promise, as the claimants obtained the benefit of a direct obligation, which they could enforce.

Performance of a public duty

4.33 We have already seen an illustration of this type of case. In *Ward* v *Byham* (1956) (see para. **4.24**) the claimant was under a statutory duty to look after her illegitimate daughter, but it was held that she provided consideration, for the defendant's promise to pay her £1 per week, by doing that. It was argued by Morris LJ that the consideration consisted in going beyond her statutory duty by ensuring that the child was both well looked after and happy, as requested by the promisor. But, as we have seen, it is unlikely that keeping the child 'happy' can itself amount to something of value for the purposes of the law (see *White* v *Bluett* (1853), discussed at para. **4.23**). Lord Denning's assessment of the facts in *Ward* v *Byham* was, perhaps, more realistic. He acknowledged that, in looking after her daughter, the claimant was only fulfilling her legal obligation. However, he thought that such a performance of an existing duty (or the promise of such performance) was good consideration. He concentrated on the benefit that this performance conferred upon the promisor.[8]

4.34 The traditional view is not in accord with Lord Denning's opinion, as expressed in *Ward* v *Byham* (1956). In *Collins* v *Godefroy* (1831), C was subpoenaed to give evidence on D's behalf at a trial in which D was involved. C claimed that D promised him one guinea (£1.05) per day for attending court. But C was unsuccessful in his attempt to enforce D's promise, as he failed to provide consideration for this promise. C was already under a legal duty to attend court because of the subpoena, and the case is thought to have established a general principle that a person does not provide consideration for another person's promise by simply performing an existing legal duty.

4.35 Such a principle is, however, open to question. There can be no doubt that it is in the public interest to prevent certain professional groups from bargaining for services that they are under a public duty to render. It would be unthinkable for a police constable or a firefighter to be able to enforce a promise of a reward made to them by a member of the public in urgent need of their help, simply for carrying out their public duties. But the reason for not upholding such an agreement is not necessarily based on lack of consideration, but rather on the grounds of public policy and the prevention of extortion.[9]

4.36 However, it has long been accepted that there is consideration where the public duty is exceeded. (This was the explanation given by the majority of the court for the decision in *Ward* v *Byham* (1956), on the dubious ground that the mother also promised to ensure the child was 'happy'.) An example is provided by *Glasbrook Bros Ltd* v *Glamorgan County Council* (1925), where mine-owners, during a miners' strike, were fearful of violence occurring. Their assessment of the amount of police protection that they needed differed from that of the police whose job it was to provide it. Eventually, the police did agree to mount a stationary guard, which they did not think necessary, but they did so on the basis that it would be paid for by the company. The company agreed to pay £2,200 for this more extensive police operation, but later refused to make the payment, claiming that there was no consideration given for their promise. The House of Lords held that the police were entitled to recover the payment as they had done more than perform their existing legal duty.

4.37 The decision in *Glasbrook Bros Ltd* v *Glamorgan County Council* (1925) is not open to criticism as long as the police's original assessment of the company's security requirements was a reasonable one. If it was, the police clearly gave something of value, over and above their public duty, in exchange for the company's promise. Of course, if there is the slightest suggestion of extortion in this type of case, the agreement should not be enforceable on the grounds of public policy. It is submitted that a case like *Glasbrook Bros Ltd* cannot be resolved purely on the basis of any technical requirement of consideration in the law of contract. In reality, such cases would seem to

8 See the discussion of this issue in the Law Revision Committee's 6th Interim Report, Cmnd 5449, 1937, para. **36**.

9 It will be remembered that in *Gibbons* v *Proctor* (1891) a policeman was able to claim a reward for providing information leading to the arrest of an offender. (See also *England* v *Davidson* (1840).)

involve issues of public policy.[10] The decision in *Williams* v *Roffey Bros & Nicholls (Contractors) Ltd* (1990) (para. **4.42**), which found consideration for a new promise where one party performed what they were already obliged to do under an existing contract with the other party, may move the basis of the discussion, in such cases, from consideration to duress and public policy. It may eventually be found that Denning LJ took the appropriate line in *Ward* v *Byham*.

Performance of a duty owed to promisor

4.38 This type of case involves the following conundrum: X makes a promise to Y in exchange for Y doing (or promising to do) something which Y is already obliged to do under an existing contract with X. If Y does (or promises) nothing more than he is already bound to do, it is difficult to see how he can be said to have provided consideration for X's promise. However, as we have seen, the requirement of consideration can be satisfied very easily if the parties remember to include something extra, of nominal value, to be provided by Y. Increasingly the question has come to be recognized as more complex than the issue of the provision of some nominal, additional consideration. Obviously, it would be clearly undesirable if a person who had already contracted to perform a particular service could extort more money from the promisor for performing the same service. (Making the original contract may have narrowed X's options, leaving X more vulnerable to a threat of non-performance by Y.) On the other hand, if the situation has become such, in relation to the original contract, that Y cannot perform without charging more, for example, it may be beneficial to X to pay more, maintain his working relationship with Y, and get performance. In such circumstances, it may be argued that the new situation is beneficial to both parties and the new agreement should be enforced, even though the parties have forgotten to include some additional, token new consideration on Y's part. Increasingly the situation is recognized as more complex than should be dealt with simply on the basis of whether or not some technical consideration is present. (The question of when a contract will be voidable for duress is looked at in the chapter dealing with duress, **Chapter 14**.)

4.39 We should, however, start by looking at the traditional view that the performance of an existing duty already owed to the promisor (as described earlier) could not amount to consideration, and the case of *Stilk* v *Myrick* (1809). The facts arose out of a return voyage from London to the Baltic, during which two sailors had deserted and the captain was unable to find replacements for them. He promised to divide the wages of the two deserters amongst the remaining crew members in exchange for their sailing the ship short-handed on the home voyage. The action brought by one of the crew to enforce this promise failed. The crew members provided no consideration for the captain's promise, as they were only fulfilling their existing contractual obligations by sailing the ship home, and the case was long regarded as based on this consideration point. There would, however, also seem to have been concerns that a ship's crew should not be able to extort additional payments to get a ship home.

4.40 Of course, there was consideration in such a situation if a crew could be seen as providing something extra. In *Hartley* v *Ponsonby* (1857), a crew of 36 was reduced by desertions to

10 See also S. Weatherill, 'Buying Special Police Services' [1988] Public Law 106.

one of 19, of which only a handful were experienced sailors. This situation was distinguishable from that of *Stilk* v *Myrick* (1809) and the claimant was able to enforce the captain's promise of an additional £40. The situation was exceptional: continuing with the voyage was so dangerous that the remaining crew members were not simply fulfilling their existing obligations. Consideration was provided for the captain's promise.

4.41 The basic rule laid down in *Stilk* v *Myrick* (1809) has increasingly been questioned. Consideration can be provided by something additional which is of little value: a bar of chocolate; a cheap biro. When there is no more done, for extra payment, the real questions are about such issues as duress, and the encouragement, or discouragement, of the parties amending the agreement when circumstances change. The situation may be one in which Y can no longer afford to carry out the contractual performance. X may be willing to pay more to assist Y, maintain their working relationship, and get performance on time. There is much more to be looked at here, in these additional payment situations, than whether some technical extra consideration has been provided. Again, this will be considered further in the chapter dealing with duress (see **Chapter 14**). Here we should look at the development of the law away from simply labelling the issue as one of consideration.

4.42 The rule in *Stilk* v *Myrick* was 'refined' and 'limited', and the emphasis thrown upon duress, in *Williams* v *Roffey Bros & Nicholls (Contractors) Ltd* [1990] 1 All ER 512. The facts were:

> The defendant building contractors were under contract to refurbish a block of 27 flats. They sub-contracted the carpentry work to the claimant (C) for £20,000. After completing some of the work, and receiving interim payments under the sub-contract, C found that he was in financial difficulties because the remuneration under his contract with the defendants was too low and he had failed to supervise his workmen properly. The defendants were liable under a 'penalty' clause in the main contract if the work was not completed on time, and they were aware that C was in difficulty because the carpentry work had been underpriced. They called a meeting with C at which they promised an extra £10,300 to ensure that C continued with the work and finished it on time. The extra payment thus agreed was to be at the rate of £575 per flat on completion. C continued working, but the defendants did not keep up the additional payments which they had agreed. C then stopped work on the remaining flats and sued the defendants for the additional sum promised. The defendants argued that no consideration had been provided by C for the promise of extra payment.

The Court of Appeal held that C was entitled to the additional payments for the flats completed. There was no evidence of economic duress; the original contract underpriced the work and the defendants understood this and themselves commenced the process of renegotiation. The defendants also gained a benefit under this later agreement. It was important to them to be sure that the work was completed promptly; they were faced with a penalty clause under the main contract. The court took the line that C provided consideration for the defendants' promise of additional payment. D gained a 'practical' benefit, the agreement was not affected by duress, and it was binding.

4.43 It might be objected that the claimant in *Williams* v *Roffey Bros & Nicholls (Contractors) Ltd* agreed to do nothing more than he was already bound to do by the original sub-contract with the defendants. In finding in his favour, it appears that the court did (despite its protestations to the contrary) seek to depart from, rather than apply, the decision in *Stilk* v *Myrick* (1809). Glidewell LJ rationalized the decision in the following way (at 522):

> If it be objected that the propositions above contravene the principle in *Stilk* v *Myrick*, I answer that in my view they do not: they refine and limit the application of that principle, but they leave the principle unscathed, e.g. where [the promisor] secures no benefit from his promise. It is not in my view surprising that a principle enunciated in relation to the rigours of seafaring life during the Napoleonic wars should be subjected during the succeeding 180 years to a process of refinement and limitation in its application in the present day.

4.44 Although controversial,[11] the decision in *Williams* v *Roffey Bros & Nicholls (Contractors) Ltd* (1990) has opened the way to a broader consideration of the issues involved when someone promises to pay more to obtain a performance they were already entitled to. It has thrown the emphasis upon the question of whether the promise to pay more was obtained in unacceptable circumstances: by duress. Nevertheless, as we shall see in the next section, it sits uneasily beside the decision of the House of Lords in *Foakes* v *Beer*, in relation to the question of the consideration for a promise to accept a lesser sum in full discharge of the debt, when all the debtor does is pay part of what was already owed. In *MWB Business Exchange Centres Ltd* v *Rock Advertising Ltd* (2016), the Court of Appeal were bringing that situation more into line with *Williams* v *Roffey*, but the Supreme Court (2018) decided that the consideration issue did not need to be discussed, and left the clash between *Williams* v *Roffey* and *Foakes* v *Beer*, all the more exposed (see para. **4.54**ff). Until there is a decision of the Supreme Court, controversy will remain in this area.

Part payment of a debt

4.45 The question arises as to the enforceability of a particular promise in the situation in which Y owes a debt to X, and X promises to accept from Y payment of part of the debt, in exchange for releasing Y from the rest of it. The issue is whether that promise is enforceable. First we will consider the traditional approach.

4.46 The classic statement is to be found in *Pinnel's Case* (1602), where it was held that payment of part of an existing debt could not amount to consideration for the creditor's promise to accept this lesser sum as full settlement and to forgo the balance. But if, in addition or instead, something other than money was given by the debtor, in exchange for the creditor's promise, this would provide good consideration. (Lord Coke famously referred to the provision of 'a horse, a hawk, or a robe').[12] Similarly, payment of a lesser sum by the debtor at an earlier time than originally agreed, at the creditor's request, can also amount to consideration. In these situations, some benefit to the creditor can be discerned. But where there was simply part payment, and nothing more, there was no consideration given by the debtor.

11 *Williams* v *Roffey* was criticized in *South Caribbean Trading* v *Trafigura Beheer BV* (2004) per Colman J at [108].

12 He actually used the phrase 'the gift of a horse, a hawk, or a robe, etc, in satisfaction is good'. However, if anything was handed over as a true 'gift', it would not be consideration: it would not be provided in return for the dispensation from the rest of the payment.

4.47 With some misgivings, this rule was approved by the House of Lords in *Foakes* v *Beer* (1884) 9 App Cas 605. The facts were as follows:

> Julia Beer had obtained a judgment in the High Court against John Foakes for £2,090 19s. More than a year later, Dr Foakes requested time to pay. It was agreed by the parties, in writing, that if Dr Foakes paid £500 immediately and then paid biannual instalments of £150 until the debt was fully paid, Mrs Beer would 'not take any proceedings whatever on the said judgment'. Dr Foakes paid the debt, in the agreed way, and then Mrs Beer claimed interest. (Dr Foakes was liable to pay interest on a judgment debt, but their agreement had made no reference to this.) Dr Foakes argued that Mrs Beer had promised not to take any action on the debt if he paid in the prescribed manner. But even assuming that the agreement covered the question of interest, did Dr Foakes provide any consideration in return for Mrs Beer's promise?

The House of Lords found in favour of Mrs Beer and upheld her claim for the interest. Opinion was divided on whether the agreement was, in fact, intended to cover the question of interest. But, whatever the true construction of the agreement might have been, it was held that payment of part of the debt could not be good consideration for Mrs Beer's promise to forgo the balance (that is, the interest). The 'rule in *Pinnel's case*' was seen as too long established to reject. Lord Blackburn did, though, have serious misgivings at the extent to which it was out of keeping with business practice. He said (at 622):

> What principally weighs with me in thinking that Lord Coke made a mistake [in *Pinnel's Case*] . . . is my conviction that all men of business, whether merchants or tradesmen, do every day recognise and act on the ground that prompt payment of a part of their demand may be more beneficial to them than it would be to insist on their rights and enforce payment of the whole. Even where the debtor is perfectly solvent, and sure to pay at last, this often is so. Where the credit of the debtor is doubtful it must be more so.

This will be returned to later in the chapter.

4.48 One of the benefits of the *Foakes* v *Beer* approach has been seen to be that it meant that a debtor could not force an impecunious creditor to accept a lesser sum, in final settlement, by threatening that otherwise they would get nothing. *D&C Builders* v *Rees* (1966) provides an example.

> The claimants were a small firm of builders who had done some work for the defendant, as a result of which the defendant still owed them £482. The claimants were in financial difficulty and the defendant, having delayed payment of the debt, instructed his wife to offer the builders £300 and no more. The financial problems of the claimants (which were allegedly known to the debtors) led them to accept the offer of £300 in full settlement. They later sued for the balance.

The Court of Appeal held that the builders were entitled to claim the rest of the debt from the defendant, who had given no consideration in exchange for the claimants' promise to accept part payment of the debt. The rule in *Foakes* v *Beer* was thus used to defeat the unconscionable behaviour of the debtor in this case.

4.49 However, such situations could now be directly tackled by reference to economic duress (see **Chapter 14**). The problem with the rule in *Foakes* v *Beer* is that it is undiscriminating: not differentiating between those agreements made in unacceptable circumstance and those which should be enforced.

Limitations on the rule in *Foakes* v *Beer*

4.50 Some limitations on the rule did come to be established. We have already seen that, in *Pinnel's Case* (1602) itself, it was recognized that whilst part payment of a debt is not good consideration to forego part of the debt, supplying something different (a horse, hawk, robe, or chocolate bar, for example) could be.[13]

4.51 A further limitation on the rule in *Foakes* v *Beer* (1884) can also be simply illustrated. X owes Y £1,000. Y promises to accept £700 from Z in full settlement of X's debt. Y is not able to go back on his promise and sue X for the balance (see *Hirachand Punamchand* v *Temple* (1911)). It might be argued that in such a situation X provides no consideration for Y's promise to forgo the remainder of the debt. However, it would be manifestly unjust, to Z in particular, if Y were able to go back on his promise. (It would be a breach of Y's contract with Z.) Another restriction on the rule is where X owes money to a number of creditors and is unable to meet the debts in full. He may come to a composition agreement with them, under which they all promise to accept a lesser amount than they are in fact owed. If the creditors accept such a payment by X, based on a division of his assets, in full satisfaction of their claims against him, they cannot go back on this and sue for the balance.

4.52 A final point should also be made here. It is common practice for services to be rendered, by plumbers, builders, etc., under a contract which fails to fix the price of the work to be done. The amount owed will not necessarily be the amount claimed by the workman. It may well be that the customer disputes the account when it is finally presented. If the tradesperson agrees to accept, in full settlement, a lesser sum than he or she originally claimed, he or she is bound by such an agreement. It is only where the creditor's claim is 'liquidated' (and undisputed) that his promise to accept part payment of the debt in full settlement will not be binding.

Williams v Roffey Bros

4.53 We have seen Lord Blackburn's concern that the approach in *Pinnel's Case* was out of keeping with commercial practice, and the commonly perceived practical benefit of getting part of a debt paid rather than being left to sue for the whole. Obviously, the question arises

13 The line was even taken in *Sibree* v *Tripp* (1846) that this extended to the situation where a debtor gave his creditor promissory notes for a lesser amount than the actual debt. Thus, if X owed Y £1,000, and Y promised to accept £900 in full settlement, Y could go back on this and later claim the full amount. But if Y promised to accept from X promissory notes for £500 in full settlement, Y was bound by that promise and could not claim the residue. The line was taken that the promissory note was something different: a negotiable security. The court refused to extend this approach to a cheque, however, in *D & C Builders Ltd* v *Rees* (1966).

as to the application of the approach taken in *Williams* v *Roffey Bros* in this context. Accepting less, and releasing someone from the rest of a debt, poses the same problem as a larger payment for the original amount of work. The logic of applying the *Williams* v *Roffey* approach, in the context of a promise to accept part payment of a debt for release from the whole debt, was acknowledged by the Court of Appeal in *Re Selectmove* (1995). However, the line was taken that as *Foakes* v *Beer* was a House of Lords' authority, it had to be followed, in the context of part payment of a debt, until the House of Lords (now the Supreme Court) said otherwise.[14] The Court of Appeal took the opportunity to return to the issue in *MWB Business Exchange Centres Ltd* v *Rock Advertising Ltd* (2016), but the Supreme Court (2018) decided the case on different grounds, leaving the consideration question still to be looked at by that Court.

4.54 We should now consider *MWB Business Exchange Centres Ltd* v *Rock Advertising Ltd* in the Court of Appeal (2016) and the Supreme Court (2018). The facts of the case were as follows:

> Rock Advertising (RA) entered into a licence agreement to occupy office premises in central London which were managed by MWB Business Exchange Centres (MWB). When RA fell into arrears on their licence payments, MWB exercised its right under the licence to exclude them from the premises, gave notice of termination, and brought a claim for arrears and damages. RA counterclaimed for loss and damage for wrongful exclusion from the premises, submitting that an oral agreement had been made with MWB's credit controller for a revised payment schedule to clear the arrears. MWB denied this agreement, claiming that it would in any event be unenforceable as it lacked consideration and that any oral variation to the licence was explicitly prohibited by the written agreement, which contained an express provision requiring any variations to be in writing and signed by both parties.

At first instance, the judge found that an oral agreement had been entered into, which was supported by consideration in the practical benefit that Rock Advertising would honour some and hopefully all of its obligations, but that this agreement was unenforceable due to the anti-oral variation clause in the licence. Rock appealed against the judge's finding on the effect of the 'no oral variation clause', and MWB against the finding that there was consideration.

4.55 The Court of Appeal decided in favour of Rock Advertising. They regarded the 'no oral variation' clause as giving way in the face of a new (oral) agreement, on the basis that the autonomy of the parties prevailed in relation to the making of such a new agreement. On the question of consideration, the Court of Appeal accepted the application of the practical benefit approach as taken in *Williams* v *Roffey*. They found a means to distinguish *Foakes* v *Beer* by taking the line that the practical benefit was greater than simply receiving part payment, or deferred payment, as MWB also had a benefit in the building not standing empty. This suggested that

14 Although, logically, *Pinnel's Case* and *Stilk* v *Myrick* raise the same underlying issue, the two questions, and lines of authority, have been kept distinct.

Foakes v *Beer* was in the process of being distinguished out of existence, with the result, ultimately, that whilst consideration was required for the creation of a contract, it would not be required for its variation. However, the Supreme Court completely retreated from any such line, deciding instead that the 'no oral variation clause' prevented there being an effective oral variation, even if there was consideration. They emphasized the certainty which 'no oral variation clauses' provide, and said that, as there was no need to discuss the consideration issue, they would not do so. They saw it as too important to be addressed in what would merely be an *obiter dictum*. They took the line that 'any decision on' the consideration issue was 'likely to involve a re-examination of the decision in *Foakes* v *Beer*' (at [18]). That decision was stated to be 'probably ripe for re-examination', but that if it was to be 'overruled or its effect substantially modified' this was not the appropriate situation in which to do it (at [18]). The Supreme Court may have seen the power given to the 'no oral variation' clause as providing the benefit of certainty, but they allowed great uncertainty to continue in relation to consideration and the variation of contracts, even casting doubts on *Williams* v *Roffey* in pointing out that, in that case, 'the Court of Appeal held that an expectation of commercial advantage was good consideration', but that 'the problem about this [is] that practical expectation of benefit was the very thing which the House of Lords held not to be consideration in *Foakes* v *Beer*' (at [18]). Proponents of change in this area, who applaud the line taken in *Williams* v *Roffey*, must emphasize the Supreme Court's acknowledgement that, in relation to *Williams* v *Roffey* and *Foakes* v *Beer*, there 'are arguable points of distinction', even though 'somewhat forced' (at [18]), as well as highlighting the Court's view that the 'reality is that any decision' on the consideration issue 'is likely to involve a re-examination of the decision in *Foakes* v *Beer*', and that it is 'probably ripe for re-examination' (at [18]).

The equitable approach

4.56 Through equity, attempts have been made to circumvent the common law rules on consideration and part payment of a debt.[15] A recent illustration is provided by *Collier* v *P and MJ Wright (Holdings) Ltd* (2008) (discussed at para. **5.17**). Here, the court found the alleged agreement was not contractually binding (at [23–[28]), as there was a lack of consideration from C in relation to W's promise to accept part payment of the debt. However, there was a triable issue that C could nevertheless use promissory estoppel to prevent W from enforcing the rest of the debt (at [40] and [50]). Using promissory estoppel as a means of circumventing the common law rules on consideration and part payment of a debt is discussed in **Chapter 5.**

Summary

- Contracts do not, generally, have to be made in a particular form in order to be effective.
- The main test of enforceability in our law of contract is the requirement of consideration.
- Traditionally, this symbolizes the bargain or exchange nature of contracts.

15 See A. Burrows, 'We Do This at Common Law But That in Equity' (2002) 22 OJLS 1–16.

- Consideration can be described as the 'price' paid by one party for the other party's promise.
- Consideration must not be 'past': but there are important exceptions to this rule.
- Courts will not normally judge the 'adequacy' of consideration.
- The various rules relating to the 'sufficiency' of consideration are not always consistent or coherent.
- The controversial decision in *Williams* v *Roffey Bros* (1990) has changed the situation where there is performance of an existing duty and payment of an additional sum.
- It has been a long-standing authority that part payment of an existing debt cannot amount to consideration for a creditor's promise to forgo the balance (see *Foakes* v *Beer* (1884)).
- However, the rule in *Foakes* v *Beer* can be criticized as out of step with commercial practice. It is argued that the line taken in *Williams* v *Roffey Bros* should be extended to this context but, although the Court of Appeal in *MWB* v *Rock Advertising* (2016) took that approach, when the case went to the Supreme Court (2018), they decided it without dealing with consideration, and the issue of consideration and contractual variation remains controversial.

Further reading

J. Adams and R. Brownsword, 'Contract, Consideration and the Critical Path' (1990) 53 MLR 536

P. Atiyah, 'Consideration: A Restatement' in *P. Atiyah*, *Essays on Contract*, Oxford University Press, 1986, pp. 179–244

B. Coote, 'Considerations and Variations: A Different Solution' (2004) 120 LQR 19

R. Hooley, 'Consideration and the Existing Duty' [1991] JBL 19

P. Mitchell and J. Phillips, 'The Contractual Nexus: Is Reliance Essential?' (2002) 22 OJLS 115

J. Morgan, 'Contracting for Self-Denial: On Enforcing "No Oral Modification" Clauses' (2017) 76 (3) CLJ 589

J. O'Sullivan, 'In Defence of *Foakes* v *Beer*' (1996) 55 CLJ 219

E. Peel, 'Part Payment of a Debt Is No Consideration' (1994) 110 LQR 353

A. Phang, 'Consideration at the Crossroads' (1991) 107 LQR 21

M. Roberts, 'MWB Business Exchange Centres Ltd: The Practical Benefit Doctrine Marches On' (2017) 80 (2) MLR 339

J. Steyn, 'Contract Law: Fulfilling the Reasonable Expectations of Honest Men' (1997) 113 LQR 433

A. Trukhtanov, '*Foakes v Beer*: Reform of the Common Law at the Expense of Equity' (2008) 124 LQR 364

S. Weatherill, 'Buying Special Police Services' [1988] Public Law 106

Chapter 5

Promissory estoppel

Introduction

5.1 In *Foakes* v *Beer* (1884), the House of Lords established that a debtor's payment of part of an existing debt (or promise to do so) cannot amount to consideration for a creditor's promise to accept a lesser sum in full settlement.

5.2 However, in the light of *Williams* v *Roffey Bros & Nicholls (Contractors) Ltd* (1990) (see **Chapter 4**), the whole question of consideration and the performance of existing obligations needs to be re-examined. This became even clearer with the decisions of the Court of Appeal, and then the Supreme Court, in the case of *MWB Business Exchange Centres Ltd* v *Rock Advertising Ltd* (2016) and (2018) (see para. **4.54**). There seems to be little justification for the law to hold that A's performance of a service already owed to B is capable of amounting to consideration if it confers some practical benefit on B, whilst simultaneously maintaining that payment of part of an existing debt can never provide good consideration for a creditor's promise regardless of the practical advantages to the creditor. But, whilst the Court of Appeal in *MWB* v *Rock*, plainly sought to extend *Williams* v *Roffey* to the context of part payment of a debt, the Supreme Court found it unnecessary to address the consideration issue. It recognized that the distinctions between *Williams* v *Roffey* and *Foakes* v *Beer*, were 'somewhat forced' but basically left consideration to be looked at subsequently, with Lord Sumption stating (at [18]):

> The reality is that any decision on this point is likely to involve a re-examination of the decision in *Foakes* v *Beer*. It is probably ripe for re-examination. But if it is to be overruled or its effect substantially modified, it should be before an enlarged panel of the court and in a case where the decision would be more than obiter dictum.

The weight of the authority of Foakes v Beer, as a longstanding decision of the House of Lords, which was itself following a very long-established rule, the significant place of consideration in English Law generally, as well as the issues of principle which are raised, seem to be troubling to the Supreme Court, when the prospect of turning away from it arises.

5.3 However, there can be little doubt that the decision in *Foakes* v *Beer* is capable of producing unfair results and of defeating reasonable commercial expectations. As has been indicated, in *Foakes* v *Beer* itself, Lord Blackburn expressed misgivings about the rule ((1884) 9 App Cas at 622). He observed that businessmen frequently do decide to accept part payment in full satisfaction of an outstanding debt. There was further criticism in the report of the Law Revision Committee (Cmnd 5449, 1937) on the doctrine of consideration. A major objection to the rule is that where a creditor (Y) promises to accept a lesser sum in full settlement and the debtor (X) relies on this promise, altering his or her position in some detrimental way, it is unjust to permit Y to go back on Y's promise. X may, for instance, incur other financial liabilities (for example, to Z) in the belief that the debt owed to Y has been fully settled.

Development of the doctrine

5.4 The opportunity to put forward a different solution to the problem of part payment of a debt arose in *Central London Property Trust Ltd* v *High Trees House Ltd* [1947] KB 130. In this famous case, widely referred to as *High Trees*, the facts were as follows:

> The claimants let a block of flats to the defendants in September 1937, for a term of 99 years at a rent of £2,500 per year. A few years later, due to wartime conditions and fear of bombing raids, many of the flats were not let. The claimants agreed in 1940 to reduce the defendants' rent to £1,250. When the war ended in 1945, the flats were no longer empty, and the claimants wanted to claim the full rent (i.e. £2,500) from the defendants. In order to test whether they could claim the full rate, retrospectively, for the period when many of the flats were empty, the claimants claimed the full rent for the last two quarters of 1945.

After less than a year as a High Court judge, Denning J delivered a famous judgment, described by Arden LJ in *Collier* v *P & MJ Wright (Holdings) Ltd* [2008] 1 WLR 643 at [42] as a 'brilliant *obiter dictum*'. He held in favour of the claimants' argument on the basis that the agreement to accept the lower rent was intended only to cover the period when many of the flats were empty. As this was no longer the case by the second half of 1945, the claimants were entitled to go back to charging the defendants the full rent that had been agreed originally between the parties in 1937. What is significant about the judgment, however, is his opinion that any attempt by the claimants to recover the full rent for the period 1940–5 would not be successful. In other words, apparently contrary to the established rule in *Foakes* v *Beer* (1884), the claimants would not be permitted to go back on the promise made to the defendants (in 1940) to accept a lesser rent whilst wartime conditions prevailed and many flats remained empty.

5.5 On the basis of the principles discussed in **Chapter 4**, it would seem that Denning J's opinion was without legal foundation. The defendants did not provide any consideration for the claimants' promise in 1940. Thus, the 1940 agreement did not satisfy all the requirements that we look for in a legally binding contract. But Denning J was undeterred in his search for a means of preventing the promisor from going back on his promise, and insisting on his full legal rights. He chose the idea of estoppel as the basis for his assault on the rule in *Foakes* v *Beer* (1884). Put simply, this doctrine encapsulates the idea that if X makes an unequivocal statement of fact to Y which he intends X to rely upon, and which Y does in fact rely upon to his or her detriment, X is prevented from later acting inconsistently with that representation (i.e. by denying the truth of his or her statement). The difficulty with estoppel, as a means of evading the common law rule, was that it was held in *Jorden* v *Money* (1854) that the doctrine applied only to a representation of existing fact,[1] whereas in *High Trees* (1947) the representation made by the claimants in relation to reducing the rent was one of intention, rather than of existing fact (i.e. a promise).

5.6 However, starting as he meant to go on as a judge, Denning J did not allow this established meaning of the doctrine of estoppel to present an insurmountable barrier to achieving justice in the instant case. He distinguished *Jorden* v *Money* (1854), on rather tenuous grounds, and proceeded to promulgate an analogous doctrine of promissory estoppel. He argued that the law had moved on since *Jorden* v *Money* to provide a broader principle than that traditionally represented by the doctrine of estoppel by representation. This principle extended to cases in which a promise was made by X to Y, with the intention that it would be acted upon by Y, and was in fact acted upon by Y. Denning J thought that it was now established that X's promise must be honoured insofar as X would be prevented from acting inconsistently with it, despite a lack of consideration by Y. (It should be noted that X could not be sued for breach of such a promise.) Of course, this wider principle of promissory estoppel covered the *High Trees* situation. But was there any authority for Denning J's view? He argued in *High Trees* ([1947] KB 130 at 134) that the principle that he was putting forward was the 'natural result of a fusion of law and equity'. He continued:

> In my opinion, the time has now come for the validity of such a promise to be recognised. The logical consequence, no doubt, is that a promise to accept a smaller sum in discharge of a larger sum, if acted upon, is binding notwithstanding the absence of consideration: and if the fusion of law and equity leads to this result, so much the better.

5.7 It might be objected that Denning J's interpretation of the law appeared to ignore the binding precedent of the House of Lords in *Foakes* v *Beer* (1884). He argued that the equitable principle had not been considered in *Foakes* v *Beer*, and instead he chose to rely on another House of Lords decision: *Hughes* v *Metropolitan Rly Co.* (1877) 2 App Cas 439. The facts were:

> A landlord gave his tenant six months' notice to repair the premises. The tenant faced forfeiture of the lease if he did not comply with the notice. The tenant agreed to do the repairs but also suggested that the landlord might wish to purchase the lease. The tenant indicated that he would not start the repairs whilst negotiations for the sale of the lease were in progress. One month after giving him the notice to repair, the landlord began negotiations with the tenant for the purchase of the lease, but these proved fruitless and were discontinued the following month. The tenant had, meanwhile, failed to repair the premises. When six months had passed from the date of giving the tenant notice to repair, the landlord tried to treat the lease as forfeited.

1 See also *Argy Trading Development Co. Ltd* v *Lapid Developments Ltd* (1977).

The House of Lords rejected the landlord's claim. The tenant was entitled to relief in equity against forfeiture. By starting negotiations for the purchase of the lease the landlord had led the tenant to believe that he would not enforce his strict legal rights while the negotiations continued. It would have been unfair to allow the landlord to go back on this implied promise. Once the negotiations did break down, he should have given the tenant reasonable time to do the repairs. Accordingly, the six-month notice period was to run from the point at which the negotiations were broken off. It was stated by Lord Cairns (at 448):

> It is the first principle upon which all courts of equity proceed, that if parties who have entered into definite and distinct terms involving certain legal results—certain penalties or legal forfeiture—afterwards by their own act or with their own consent enter upon a course of negotiation which has the effect of leading one of the parties to suppose that the strict rights arising under the contract will not be enforced, or will be kept in suspense, or held in abeyance, the person who otherwise might have enforced those rights will not be allowed to enforce them where it would be inequitable having regard to the dealings which have thus taken place between the parties.

This statement offered possibilities of a broader doctrine, which can be summarized in the following way. Where X, who has contractual rights against Y, by his conduct induces Y to believe that these rights will be suspended or will not be strictly enforced for a certain period, he will be prevented from enforcing those rights until that period has elapsed.[2] This was Denning J's solution to the problem posed by *Foakes* v *Beer* (1884). The ingenuity of his approach cannot be questioned, but it sits uneasily beside *Foakes* v *Beer*, and it has created uncertainty.

5.8 It should not be forgotten that *Foakes* v *Beer* (1884) was decided seven years after *Hughes* v *Metropolitan Rly Co.* (1877) and the *Hughes* case was not seen as relevant in *Foakes*. It could hardly have been forgotten! It is more plausible that the House of Lords did not think that the two situations were truly analogous. All that was being sought in *Hughes* was relief from forfeiture.

5.9 It should also be recognized that Denning J's judgment in *High Trees* (1947) extended the scope of estoppel (see para. **5.6**). His suggested doctrine of promissory estoppel was not restricted to representations of fact. Further, the doctrine of estoppel by representation requires detrimental reliance. In *High Trees* it seemed that there was no such reliance, and no such requirement.[3] In assessing Denning J's novel formulation of an equitable doctrine of promissory estoppel, it is fair to conclude that it was born with a far from unimpeachable pedigree. However, despite that, it has been the subject of extensive discussion, both in later cases and in academic literature. Of course, it would cease to be needed in the part payment of a debt situation if *Williams* v *Roffey* was suitably extended, but as was said in *Rock Advertising Limited* v *MWB Business Exchange Centres Limited* (2018) (see para. **4.54**), that will need a decision of the Supreme Court.

2 See *Birmingham and District Land Co.* v *London and North Western Rly Co.* (1888).

3 See *Collier* v *P & MJ Wright Ltd* (2008) per Arden LJ at [39].

Scope of the doctrine

5.10 It is necessary to examine the scope, and limitations, of the doctrine. This is no easy matter as, despite much discussion of the doctrine, there have been relatively few cases decided exclusively on this ground.

The doctrine does not create a cause of action

5.11 By itself, promissory estoppel does not create a cause of action; if it did, it would be very difficult to reconcile with the doctrine of consideration. In *Combe* v *Combe* (1951), a husband agreed to pay his wife £100 a year (free of tax) at the time of their divorce. He failed to make any payment and she sued him, after six years, for arrears of £600. She gave no consideration for her husband's promise. She chose not to apply to the Divorce Court for maintenance; she did not refrain from doing so at her husband's request. (In fact, she had a greater annual income than her husband.) However, the trial judge, by applying the doctrine of promissory estoppel, held that the husband's promise was enforceable. The husband had made a clear promise, which he intended to be binding and to be acted upon, and which was acted upon by his wife.

5.12 This proposed extension of the doctrine was potentially far-reaching. Promissory estoppel was not being relied upon here as a defence; it was being used to create a cause of action. If the trial judge (Byrne J) in *Combe* v *Combe* had been correct, this would have been a fundamental challenge to the traditional requirement of consideration in contracts. The Court of Appeal allowed the husband's appeal, and Denning LJ (as he had now become) was quick to dispel fears that promissory estoppel posed such a threat to the doctrine of consideration. He explained that the *High Trees* principle did not create new causes of action where none previously existed. It operated only to prevent a person from insisting on his or her strict legal rights, when it would be unjust for him or her to do so in view of the dealings which had taken place between the parties. To this extent only was promissory estoppel intended to modify the legal requirement of consideration. Denning LJ continued ([1951] 2 KB 215 at 220):

> Seeing that the principle never stands alone as giving a cause of action in itself, it can never do away with the necessity of consideration when that is an essential part of the cause of action. The doctrine is too firmly fixed to be overthrown by a side-wind . . . it still remains a cardinal necessity of the formation of a contract, though not of its modification or discharge.

This limitation on the principle of promissory estoppel is not accurately encapsulated by the phrase that it is 'a shield and not a sword', for such a phrase tends to suggest, misleadingly, that the principle cannot be relied upon by a claimant. In fact, the limitation means only that promissory estoppel cannot stand alone as giving a cause of action.

5.13 The operation of estoppel was considered by the Court of Appeal in *Baird Textile Holdings Ltd* v *Marks and Spencer plc* (2001). Baird had been a leading supplier of garments to M&S for 30 years when M&S suddenly notified Baird of its decision not to place any more orders. This led to an action by Baird claiming that M&S was precluded, both by contract and estoppel, from ending this long-term commercial relationship without reasonable notice. The lack of certainty in the alleged agreement between the parties meant that the claim in contract failed. Baird tried to establish an 'equity generated by estoppel' to protect its reliance interest, arguing that the doctrine of estoppel is a flexible one. Although the court (especially Judge LJ) expressed some interest in the potential development of estoppel and its flexibility, it rejected Baird's claim. It held that the alleged obligation lacked certainty and that the law, as it stands, 'does not enable the creation or recognition by estoppel of an enforceable right of the type and in the circumstances relied on in this case' (at [38]).[4]

Does it merely suspend rights?

5.14 It will be remembered that in *Hughes* v *Metropolitan Rly Co.* (1877) the landlord's right to treat the lease as forfeited was not lost altogether. The case simply decided that, due to his implied promise to the tenant, he could rely on those rights only after six months' notice from the point of the breakdown of their negotiations. However, extinguishment of rights would seem to be what Denning J proposed in *High Trees* (1947), and in *D & C Builders Ltd* v *Rees* (1966) he was even more forthright in stating that the equitable principle was capable not simply of suspending a promisor's strict legal rights, but could operate 'so as to preclude the enforcement of them'. Such a view poses a direct challenge to the House of Lords' decision in *Foakes* v *Beer* (1884).

5.15 The effect of the principle on the promisor's rights was considered by the House of Lords in *Tool Metal Manufacturing Co. Ltd* v *Tungsten Electric Co. Ltd* (1955). The facts were:

> Tool Metal (TM) owned the patents of certain hard metal alloys and, under a contract in 1938, granted Tungsten Electric (TE) a licence to manufacture and sell these metals. The agreement provided that the standard royalty to be paid by TE was 10 per cent, but that a higher rate of 30 per cent (described as 'compensation') was payable if TE used more than a specified amount of the alloys in any month. After the outbreak of war, TE stopped paying compensation to TM at the higher royalty rate, and TM agreed (in the national interest) not to enforce their right to 30 per cent, and to allow payment at the basic rate of 10 per cent. In 1944, TM proposed a new agreement which included compensation payments once again, but this was rejected by TE. In 1945, TM sought compensation (i.e. the waived 20 per cent) in respect of the material used by TE since June 1945. The Court of Appeal held that, under the principle of *Hughes* v *Metropolitan Rly Co.* (1877), TM's agreement to suspend compensation payments was binding in equity until proper notice was given of their intention to resume insistence upon their strict legal rights. (The draft agreement of 1944 did not amount to reasonable notice.) In 1950, TM claimed compensation from TE dating from January 1947. Had TM given reasonable notice to TE of their intention to insist once more on their strict legal rights?

4 For further comment on *Baird Textile* v *Marks & Spencer*, see C. Mitchell, 'Leading a Life of Its Own? The Rules of Reasonable Expectation in Contract Law' (2003) 23 OJLS 639 at 649–50.

The House of Lords held in favour of TM's claim to compensation. They had effectively revoked their promise, made during the war, to suspend their strict legal rights. The first action, brought in 1945, constituted reasonable notice of their intention. The case suggests that the promisor's strict legal rights are merely suspended, and can be resumed by giving adequate notice to the other party.

5.16 In *Ajayi* v *RT Briscoe (Nigeria) Ltd* [1964] 1 WLR 1326 at 1330, the Privy Council stated a number of limitations on promissory estoppel. Amongst these was the qualification that the promisor is able to go back on his or her promise, on giving reasonable notice, providing the promisee with a reasonable opportunity of resuming his or her position; the line has been taken that it is only if it is not possible for the promisee to resume his or her position that the promise would be irrevocable.[5] However, in *Collier* v *P & MJ Wright (Holdings) Ltd* (2008) at [37], Arden LJ argued that although the effect of the doctrine 'is usually suspensory only', the creditor's right to recover the debt may be extinguished in circumstances where to go back on the promise is merely 'sufficiently inequitable'.[6]

5.17 The facts of *Collier* v *P & MJ Wright (Holdings) Ltd* (2008) were as follows:

> W was owed a judgment debt of £46,800 for which C and his two former property development partners were jointly liable. The three partners were to pay this debt jointly, by monthly instalments of £600. Although C kept up his share of the payment, his partners became bankrupt, and W claimed the whole of the debt from C. In contesting this demand, C tried to rely on an alleged agreement with W to the effect that, as long as C continued to pay his share of the debt, W would not pursue him for the balance owed by his former partners. C argued that, by entering into this alleged agreement with W, he provided consideration for W's promise to treat him as owing only one-third of the judgment debt. He argued also that W was prevented by a promissory estoppel from claiming more than a one-third share of the debt from him.

As a preliminary matter the Court of Appeal had to consider whether C had raised a triable issue, and it found that he had. The alleged agreement, under which W agreed with C to accept part payment from him of just a one-third share, was not contractually binding (at [23]–[28]): there was a lack of consideration from C in relation to W's promise to accept part payment of the debt. However, they thought that there was a triable issue that C could nevertheless use promissory estoppel to prevent W from enforcing the rest of the debt (at [40] and [50]).

In line with Arden LJ's comments in *Collier*, therefore it would seem that the doctrine is merely suspensory, and can be reactivated by reasonable notice, but becomes irrevocable when it would

5 See *Brikom Investments Ltd* v *Carr* (1979).

6 For a critical view of this see A. Trukhtanov, '*Foakes* v *Beer*: Reform of Common Law at the Expense of Equity' (2008) 124 LQR 364 at 368.

be 'sufficiently inequitable' (at [37]). More recently, in *MWB Business Exchange Centres Ltd* v *Rock Advertising Ltd* [2016] EWCA Civ 553 (discussed at para. **4.54**), Kitchen LJ stated at [61]:

> It may be the case that it would be inequitable to allow the promisor to go back upon his promise without giving reasonable notice, as in the *Tool Metal Manufacturing Co. Ltd* case [1955] 1 WLR 761; or it may be that it would be inequitable to allow the promisor to go back on his promise at all with the result that the right is extinguished. All will depend upon the circumstances.

Other limitations on the doctrine of promissory estoppel

5.18 For the principle to operate, there must be a promise (by words or conduct), and its effect must not be vague or equivocal.[7] In *IMT Shipping and Chartering GmbH* v *Chansung Shipping Co. Ltd* (2009) at [30] it was also stated that 'the promise must be intended to affect the parties' legal relations and must be understood to be a promise that will be acted upon by the promisee'. In *Northstar Land Ltd* v *Maitland Brooks* (2006), it was stressed that the promise (by words or conduct) has to be a 'clear, unequivocal, unambiguous promise or assurance which was intended to affect the legal relations between them or was reasonably understood by the other to have that effect' (Ward LJ at [21]).[8]

5.19 The principle is equitable in nature and therefore it should not be used to help a promisee, or debtor, who has behaved in an unconscionable or inequitable way. In *D & C Builders Ltd* v *Rees* (1966), for example, the defendant took advantage of the financial hardship of his creditor, who had little choice but to accept the defendant's offer of a lesser sum in full settlement of the debt. The decision of the Court of Appeal was consistent with the common law rule in *Foakes* v *Beer* (1884); the creditor was entitled to go back on his promise and sue successfully for the balance of the debt. However, the case was decided after the principle of promissory estoppel had been established, and Lord Denning's reason for finding in favour of the creditor was that the defendant had behaved inequitably and, therefore, should not be allowed to rely on the equitable defence.

Reliance

5.20 Promissory estoppel draws upon an analogy with the doctrine of estoppel by representation. As we have seen, the latter form of estoppel requires, inter alia, reliance by the representee to his or her detriment, but what of promissory estoppel? In *High Trees* (1947) itself there appears to have been no detriment suffered by the defendants; they simply paid less rent than was agreed under the original lease.[9] They relied on the claimants' promise and Lord Denning argued that detriment is not required for the *High Trees* principle to operate (see *WJ Alan & Co.* v *El Nasr Export and Import Co* [1972] 2 QB 189 at 212).

7 See *Woodhouse AC Israel Cocoa SA* v *Nigerian Produce Marketing Co. Ltd* (1972).

8 See also *Kim* v *Chasewood Park Residents Ltd* (2013).

9 For further discussion see M. Thompson, 'Estoppel and Change of Position' [2000] Conv and Prop Law 548.

5.21 This aspect of the doctrine is still a matter for debate. In *Collier* v *P & MJ Wright Ltd (Holdings) Ltd* (2008), Longmore LJ, although agreeing with the other judges that the applicant had a triable issue in relation to promissory estoppel, pointed out (at [45]–[46]) that there had been no 'detriment' to the applicant as a result of the alleged promise, and that there was no evidence that he had 'relied on it [in] any meaningful way'. In contrast, as we have seen, Arden LJ took a less restrictive view (at [42]), arguing that for the creditor to go back on the alleged promise would, in itself, be inequitable, appearing to suggest that no detriment need be proved. This would certainly seem to be the line which has to be taken if the defence is to be generally available in relation to the promise to accept part payment of a debt in discharge of the whole. In *MWB Business Exchange Centres Ltd* v *Rock Advertising Ltd* (2016), Arden LJ has since qualified her comments, making it clear that they need to be interpreted in the context of the *Collier* case where the question was just that of a 'genuine triable issue' and that the court was not in a position to decide on it, and did not need to, but there was

> evidence from the debtor that, if the creditor had not, as the debtor alleged, agreed to accept part payment from him of one third of the debt, he would have pursued the other partners to ensure that they paid their share of the debt and that he had potentially been prejudiced because he was no longer able to do so.

In other words, she had not reasoned that simply paying part of the debt was necessarily enough to make it inequitable for the creditor to go back on his promise.

5.22 Even so, perhaps the debate over whether the equitable principle requires detrimental reliance is not particularly apposite. The following reconciliation of views can be put forward. It is unlikely that 'detriment' is a strict requirement, and it may be inequitable to allow the promisor to go back on his promise even in the absence of detrimental reliance. It may simply be that it is just more likely to be inequitable to allow a promisor to resile from his or her promise where the other party has acted on the promise, not only in reliance, but also to his or her disadvantage or 'detriment'.[10] In *Emery* v *UCB Corporate Services Ltd* (2001), Peter Gibson LJ stated (at [28]):

> [T]he fact that the promisee has not altered his position to his detriment is plainly most material in determining whether it would be inequitable for the [promisor] to be permitted to act inconsistently with his promise.

Conclusion

5.23 There is much that remains unclear about the doctrine of promissory estoppel, and about its development. The apparent approach of Arden LJ in *Collier* would have opened it up as a readier means of dealing with the problems posed by *Foakes* v *Beer*, but in *MWB Business Exchange Centres Ltd* v *Rock Advertising Ltd* (2016) she explained it should not be viewed as

10 For a useful discussion, see *Société Italo-Belge Pour le Commerce et l'Industrie SA (Antwerp)* v *Palm and Vegetable Oils (Malaysia) Sdn Bhd* [1982] 1 All ER 19 at 26–7 per Robert Goff J.

so extensive. Of course, promissory estoppel would not be so needed if *Williams* v *Roffey* was extended to the part payment of a debt situation, but the Supreme Court in *Rock* v *MWB* (2018) has curtailed any such ready extension, at least for now.

5.24 Elsewhere, however, promissory estoppel has been used even more innovatively, to create rights. The decision of the High Court of Australia in *Walton Stores (Interstate) Ltd* v *Maher* (1988) represents an interesting and potentially far-reaching challenge to the traditional view of the relationship between estoppel and consideration. In that case, M (a builder) negotiated with W (a large retail company) for a construction and lease contract under which M would demolish an existing building on his own land and build a new one to W's specifications, which would then be leased by W. The parties were very close to concluding the deal, but as no formal exchange of contracts had taken place, there was no binding agreement. Believing that W's completion of the relevant documents was no more than a formality, M started work on the project so as to enable him to meet the deadline for completion. He demolished the old building and laid the foundations for the new one. W was, in fact, having second thoughts about the deal, but did not communicate these to M despite being aware that M had already started work on his land. W told him of its decision to pull out only after he had carried out a substantial amount of work. Although no formal contract had been completed between the parties, M brought an action claiming specific performance or, as an alternative, damages against W. M argued that W had made an implied promise that it would enter into a binding agreement with him and that W was now estopped from resiling from this. The problem with this contention was that, as there was no existing contract between the parties, M was seeking to use the idea of estoppel to establish a cause of action.

5.25 The High Court of Australia found in favour of M, holding that in certain cases the ambit of promissory estoppel could be extended so as to permit the creation of a cause of action. It was argued (by the majority of the court) that as the decision was based on an estoppel and not on a contract, the absence of consideration was not a problem. The court held that the purpose of the equitable doctrine was to avoid the detriment which M suffered as a result of W's unconscionable behaviour in going back on its promise. (In other words, the object was not to compensate M for expectation loss for a breach of contract by W.) By this reasoning, the court found that promissory estoppel was not limited to cases where there is an existing legal relationship between the parties. It was argued that the doctrine has a wider function of providing equitable relief against unconscionable conduct, even in the context of non-contractual promises. One question is whether the English courts will be tempted, at some point, to adopt the Australian approach.[11]

Summary

- Part payment of an existing debt cannot amount to consideration for a creditor's promise to accept a lesser sum in full settlement (the rule in *Foakes* v *Beer* (1884)).

11 *Baird Textile Holdings Ltd* v *Marks and Spencer plc* [2001] EWCA Civ 274, [2002] 1 All ER (Comm) 737 at [38]–[40], [52]–[54] and [96]–[98].

- The developments in *Williams* v *Roffey Bros* (1990) could, potentially, overtake the rule in *Foakes* v *Beer.*
- The rule in *Foakes* v *Beer* is capable of producing unfair results where a debtor has relied on a promise by the creditor to accept part payment in full satisfaction, and where the debtor has altered his or her position in reliance on such a promise.
- The *High Trees House* case (1947) saw the innovative, but controversial, decision of Denning J (as he then was) to the effect that a promise to accept a lesser sum might be binding under the equitable principle of promissory estoppel.
- Promissory estoppel is not restricted to representations of fact, but applies also to promises and representations of intention.
- Promissory estoppel has created some uncertainty in the law, and the ambit of the doctrine is still unclear (as illustrated recently in *Collier* v *P and MJ Wright (Holdings) Ltd* (2008)).
- However, certain principles appear to be established in relation to the operation of the doctrine:
  - it does not create a cause of action
  - the effect of promissory estoppel is, generally, suspensory, but see comments in *Collier* v *P and MJ Wright (Holdings) Ltd* (2008)
  - there must be a promise (by words or conduct), which is clear and unambiguous
  - the promise must have been relied upon by the promisee
  - where a promisee has behaved inequitably, he or she cannot rely on the doctrine.

Further reading

R. Austen-Baker, 'A Strange Sort of Survival for Pinnel's Case: *Collier v P & MJ Wright (Holdings) Ltd*' (2008) 71 MLRP 611

E. Cooke, 'Estoppel and the Protection of Expectations' (1997) 17 LS 258

A. Duthie, 'Equitable Estoppel, Unconscionability and the Enforcement of Promises' (1988) 104 LQR 362

R. Halson, 'The Offensive Limits of Promissory Estoppel' [1999] LMCLQ 256

R. Lee and L. Ho, 'Disputes over Family Homes Owned through Companies: Constructive Trust or Promissory Estoppel?' (2009) 125 LQR 25

C. Mitchell, 'Leading a Life of Its Own? The Rules of Reasonable Expectation in Contract Law' (2003) 23 OJLS 639

J. O'Sullivan, 'In Defence of *Foakes v Beer*' (1996) 55 CLJ 219

A. Phipps, 'Resurrecting the Doctrine of Common Law Forbearance' (2007) 123 LQR 286

A. Robertson, 'Reliance and Expectation in Estoppel Remedies' (1998) 18 LS 360

M. Thompson, 'Estoppel and Change of Position' [2000] Conv and Prop Law 548

A. Trukhtanov, '*Foakes v Beer*: Reform of the Common Law at the Expense of Equity' (2008) 124 LQR 364

Chapter 6

Intention to create legal relations

Introduction

6.1 Not all agreements are legally enforceable. We have seen that the main test of enforceability which is applied in our law of contract is the requirement of consideration. Even if the parties intend to enter into a contract, the law requires an element of exchange between the parties; this represents, in theory at least, the idea of reciprocal obligations. It might be thought that if this requirement is satisfied, and if the contract does not need to be expressed in a particular form, then an agreement will be enforceable. There is, however, a further requirement: an intention to create legal relations.

6.2 In fact, in commercial transactions it will generally be presumed (usually correctly) that the parties did intend to create legal relations, unless there is an express statement to the contrary. In the case of social and domestic agreements it will usually be presumed that they did not intend such consequences. In the vast majority of such agreements this will undoubtedly be a valid assumption. But although the word 'intention' is used, it is arguable that the test is really one of judicial policy. It is a method of restricting the enforceability of social and domestic arrangements. It could be argued that if both parties to an agreement provide consideration, there should be no need for any further requirement of an intention to create legal relations. But our law has not followed this line of reasoning. It has attempted to limit the enforceability of certain types of agreement. This may be a sound policy for pragmatic reasons, but it is difficult to see why it should be described today in terms of contractual intention.

Social and domestic agreements

6.3 Every day, people make family, or social, agreements. For instance, two friends might agree to operate a rota for taking their young children to school, so that only one car is required for each journey. Agreement and reciprocal obligations are both present here, but it is unlikely that the two friends intend any legal consequences to arise from their agreement.[1] A parent may agree to give 'pocket money' to his or her child in return for the performance of simple household chores; a person may agree to make a meal for a friend, who in turn promises to bring a bottle of wine.

6.4 In all of the above examples of social and domestic agreements, it is fair to say that the parties do not intend legal consequences to flow from their arrangements, but also if such agreements are broken, it is not an appropriate use of the legal process to allow one party to pursue another.[2] To prevent frivolous claims, and a waste of court time, it is better that disputes over such arrangements are left to the parties to settle for themselves, informally.

6.5 However, in other instances of family and domestic agreements, the presumed lack of intention to contract is more questionable. A significant example of the court strongly embracing the exclusion of a finding of a contractual relationship, in the context of an agreement between husband and wife, is *Balfour* v *Balfour* [1919] 2 KB 571. In that case, the facts were:

> D, who worked as a civil servant stationed abroad, left his wife (C) in England; C had been advised by her doctor that her health was not sufficiently good to accompany her husband. Before departing, D promised to pay C an allowance of £30 a month whilst they were apart. C sued D for breach of his promise. The trial judge found that there was consideration given for D's promise and he ruled in C's favour.

The Court of Appeal reversed the trial judge's decision, and held that D's promise was not enforceable. Even if C had given consideration for the promise (which is arguable), there was no intention to create legal relations. It was seen as a purely domestic agreement. Lord Atkin stated (at 578):

> [T]here are agreements between parties which do not result in contracts within the meaning of that term in our law . . . and one of the most usual forms of agreement which does not constitute a contract appears to me to be the arrangements which are made between husband and wife . . . and they do not result in contracts even though there may be what as between other parties would constitute consideration for the agreement.

6.6 Although the justification for the decision in *Balfour* v *Balfour* (1919) was expressed in terms of the parties' lack of contractual intention, it is clear from other parts of Lord Atkin's

1 Of interest on a related issue, see *Buckpitt* v *Oates* (1968) and *Coward* v *Motor Insurers' Bureau* (1963). Cases on this issue have tended to arise as a result of accidents caused by the driver's negligence. But now see Road Traffic Act 1988, s 149.

2 But, surprisingly, a prosecution for theft may succeed in the circumstances where a man gives his 'de facto' wife a sum of money for her to pay certain debts and to meet household expenses and, instead of doing so, she spends the money on herself. In *Cullen* (1972) (unreported), the Court of Appeal seems to have assumed that the defendant was under an obligation to deal with the money in the manner prescribed and in no other way. Her conviction for theft overlooked the fact that it arose out of a domestic arrangement which was not intended to create legal relations. Her behaviour could not have amounted to a breach of contract—so why should it have been regarded as theft?

judgment that he was concerned with the perceived inappropriateness of the husband–wife agreement being governed by contract law ('each house is a domain into which the King's writ does not seek to run'), and by the prospect of the 'small courts of this country' being inundated with domestic disputes (over 'housekeeping' arrangements and the like). Although he perhaps overstated the likelihood of such a flood of litigation, there is a sound policy reason for encouraging trivial domestic disputes to be settled by the parties, without recourse to law. But did the agreement in *Balfour* v *Balfour* fall into this category? It was clearly a borderline case, and the court's bald assertion that the parties lacked contractual intention is not particularly helpful.

6.7 However, *Balfour* v *Balfour* (1919) was distinguished in *Merritt* v *Merritt* (1970), where the parties were separated at the time of the agreement:

> A husband (H) left his wife (W), moving out of the house that was in their joint names, and went to live with another woman. H and W later met to discuss their financial arrangements for the future. They agreed that H would pay £40 per month to W, and W was to make the outstanding mortgage payments on the house out of this sum. W insisted upon a written acknowledgement by H of their agreement; this stated: 'In consideration of the fact that you will pay all charges in connection with the house . . . until such time as the mortgage repayment has been completed . . . I will agree to transfer the property into your sole ownership.' W paid off the mortgage, but H refused to transfer the house to her.

The Court of Appeal held that W was the sole owner of the matrimonial home based on the enforceable agreement made between H and W. The court stated that the *Balfour* principle does not apply in the case of couples who are not on friendly terms but are about to separate or, indeed, have separated.[3]

6.8 More broadly, it should be recognized that social circumstances have changed markedly since *Balfour* v *Balfour* was decided in relation to a 'Victorian marriage'.

> Where the emphasis was on status, it is now on autonomy. For role identification we now have role distance. The 'self' and individual choice have replaced role and obligation as central organizing concepts.[4]

There may, today, be many financial arrangements between husbands and wives which should readily be seen to involve an intention to create legal relations. In *Radmacher v Granatino* (2010), Lady Hale commented (at [142]):

> There is nothing to stop a husband and wife from making legally binding arrangements, whether by contract or settlement, to regulate their property and affairs while they are still

3 A further limitation of the *Balfour* principle relates to the situation where parties carry out promises, under what would otherwise be an unenforceable domestic agreement, by making improvements or additions to the matrimonial home. See *Pettitt* v *Pettitt* [1970] AC 777 and especially Lord Diplock's comments at 822.

4 M. Freeman, 'Contracting in the Haven: *Balfour* v *Balfour* Revisited' in R. Halson (ed.), *Exploring the Boundaries of Contract*, Dartmouth, 1996, p. 75.

> together . . . These days, the commonest example of this is an agreement to share the ownership or tenancy of the matrimonial home, bank accounts, savings or other assets. Agreements for housekeeping or personal allowances, on the other hand, might run into difficulties.[5]

6.9 Of course, the presumption against an intention to create legal relations is general to the domestic sphere, and not confined to the relationship of husband and wives. In *Jones* v *Padavatton* [1969] 1 WLR 328, the facts were:

> A mother (M) promised her daughter (D) that she would give her an allowance of $200 a month if she gave up her job in Washington DC and went to England to study for the Bar. (M lived in Trinidad, where she hoped D would practise when qualified.) Despite not wishing to leave Washington DC, D accepted M's proposal and went to England and commenced her studies to become a barrister. Two years later, M and D varied the agreement. M bought a house in London for D to live in, and by renting out some of the rooms, D was able to maintain herself instead of receiving the $200 a month. Three years later, M and D quarrelled, and M claimed possession of the house. D still had not passed her Bar exams.

The Court of Appeal found in M's favour. It was held (by the majority) that the arrangement between the parties was not intended to have legal consequences and therefore M was entitled to possession. This followed the broader reasoning in *Balfour* v *Balfour* (1919). The opening comments of Danckwerts LJ (at 329) reveal the majority's concern that disagreements of this type should not be aired in a court of law. He stated:

> This action . . . is really deplorable. The points of difference between the two parties appear to be comparatively small, and it is distressing that they could not settle their differences amicably and avoid the bitterness and expense which is involved in this dispute carried as far as this court.

The case is instructive. It not only shows the general presumption that family agreements are not enforceable, but also illustrates, again, that there are policy reasons at work. In fact, although Salmon LJ arrived at the same decision as the other two judges, he reached it by way of a different route. He thought that there was an intention to create legal relations at the time of the original agreement, but that this agreement was to last only for a reasonable time and it had therefore ended by the time that five years had elapsed. M could never have intended to pay indefinitely whilst her daughter made repeated and unsuccessful efforts to pass the exams.

6.10 Salmon LJ's judgment seems to represent a much sounder basis for deciding the case than those of his two colleagues. If the test is really one of an intention to create legal relations, then surely the agreement (at least initially) satisfied this requirement. D reluctantly gave up a

5 *Radmacher* v *Granatino* [2010] UKSC 42, [2011] 1 AC 534.

good job and commenced studies in England at M's request. If M had ceased to pay D her allowance within a few months of D arriving in England, was it really intended by the parties that D would have no legal redress?

6.11 Of course, the presumption against an intention to create legal relations extends beyond the family sphere into the social one, and it can be difficult to draw a line between those where a contract will be found and those where it will not. In *Simpkins* v *Pays* (1955), a lodger (C), her landlady, and her landlady's granddaughter entered a competition run by a newspaper. Their weekly entries were a joint effort with an agreement that, if successful, the prize would be shared. The entries were sent in the landlady's name and she refused to share the prize when they won. It was held that there was a binding agreement, and that C was entitled to claim one-third of the prize.

6.12 No contract was found in the more recent case of *Wilson* v *Burnett* (2007). The case involved a claim that three friends had made a binding agreement that they would share any winnings equally between them if they were successful in an evening spent playing bingo. One of them won not only a small local prize of £153, but also a very large national prize of £101,211 during the course of the evening. The claim of her two friends that this prize should be divided equally was unsuccessful at first instance, partly on the basis of conflicting evidence about whether there was in fact a binding agreement. The Court of Appeal (May LJ giving judgment) dismissed the appeal of the two friends, stating that the issue was essentially a narrow one of whether there was a binding agreement between the three friends, made prior to playing bingo, of sufficient certainty. It was held that, on the available evidence, the conversations between the parties fell short of concluding a binding and enforceable agreement.

6.13 *Blue* v *Ashley* (2017) and *MacInnes* v *Gross* (2017) (discussed at para. **2.3**) both illustrate the situation where business parties have conducted oral discussions in social settings and the creation of a contract has been disputed. In each case the claimant failed to establish a legally binding agreement had been reached. However, as reasoned by Coulson J in *MacInnes* v *Gross* (at 81):

> The mere fact that the discussion took place over dinner in a smart restaurant does not, of itself, preclude the coming into existence of a binding contract. A contract can be made anywhere, in any circumstances. But I consider that the fact that this alleged agreement was made in a highly informal and relaxed setting means that the court should closely scrutinise the contention that, despite the setting, there was an intention to create legal relations.

Any agreement—and particularly one involving large sums of money, such as the alleged £15 million in *Blue* v *Ashley* (2017) and €13.5 million in *MacInnes* v *Gross* (2017)—will more readily demonstrate the requisite intention if expressed with clarity and precision of the key terms. In *MacInnes* v *Gross* (2017) a finding that the terms of the alleged contract were too complex and too uncertain was a factor in itself which led to a failure in the decision that a binding agreement had been reached.

6.14 In *Wilson* v *Burnett*, there was an issue of uncertainty, and it is likely that many agreements between friends, or members of a family, are not enforceable because they are too uncertain. In *Gould* v *Gould* (1969) a husband promised his wife, when leaving her, £15 per week as long as his business was all right. (The actual words used were disputed.) The majority of the court thought that the vagueness of the arrangement showed a lack of contractual intention, but uncertainty may in itself prevent a contract being found. In *Jones* v *Padavatton*, the second agreement, concerning occupation of the house and the use of funds derived from letting out rooms, might have been regarded as unenforceable because of its evident vagueness. There were several details left unsettled, and perhaps this would have been a better basis for allowing M's claim for possession.

6.15 Lack of certainty in the agreement may be a basis, in itself, for saying that there is no contract (see **Chapter 3**), or it may provide evidence to underpin the presumption against intention to create legal relations. In contrast, significant reliance may point towards a finding that there was an intention to create legal relations. In *Tanner* v *Tanner* (1975), D gave birth to twins of which C was the father. D and C were unmarried, but D took C's name. C bought a house for them both to live in, with the children, and D gave up her rent-controlled flat. Later, C moved out and wanted to evict D (and he succeeded at first instance). On appeal, the court held that C was contractually bound by his promise to D, who was awarded compensation (having already been evicted).

6.16 The important fact about cases of this type is that one of the parties to the agreement has acted in reliance upon the other's promise and, in doing so, has given up something of value. Although such actions do not appear to have impacted on the views of the majority in *Jones* v *Padavatton* (1969), it can be argued that they provide objective evidence of an intention to create legal relations. However, it can also be suggested that, in cases of this type, the general policy of denying legal consequences to domestic agreements would produce such an unjust result that the courts depart from their general policy. In *Parker* v *Clark* (1960), the Clarks invited a younger couple, the Parkers, to share their house. (Mrs C was the aunt of Mrs P.) In order to go ahead with the arrangement the Parkers sold their own house. It was held that the agreement was legally binding.

Commercial agreements

6.17 In commercial transactions, it is generally presumed that there is an intention to create legal relations. The courts are anxious to uphold the validity of commercial dealings. But in certain situations, the general presumption may be rebutted. For example, manufacturers of products may make boastful but vague claims about the effectiveness of their products. These statements (known as 'mere puffs'), contained in advertisements and other promotional literature, will generally not be regarded as having any legal effect.[6] (Although note the effect of

6 See *Lexmead (Basingstoke) Ltd* v *Lewis* (1982).

the Consumer Rights Act 2015 ss 11–12 relating to goods contracts, ss 36–37 covering digital content contracts, and s 50 for the supply of services, as discussed in **Chapter 13**.)

6.18 However, in exceptional cases, what might otherwise be a 'mere puff' will be expressed in such a way that the courts will infer a definite intention to create legal relations. In *Carlill* v *Carbolic Smoke Ball Co.* (1893), the company's advertisement of a reward was held to be an offer to members of the public who bought the smoke ball and used it in the prescribed manner, and still caught influenza. The company's attempt to argue that there was no contractual intention was rejected; the claimant was entitled to recover the reward. The fact that the company stated that it had deposited £1,000 with its bank as evidence of its 'sincerity in the matter' indicated that the advertisement was more than just a mere puff.

6.19 Problems may arise in determining whether an agreement is of a commercial rather than social nature. In *Sadler* v *Reynolds* (2005), a dispute arose between the claimant (S) and the defendant businessman (R) over an oral agreement that S should be the 'ghost writer' of R's autobiography. S claimed that he had proposed the title of the book to R and outlined its first chapter before R changed his mind and entered into an agreement with another author to write the book. The case involved, inter alia, a dispute over whether there was a contract, and Slade J held that an oral contract had been concluded on terms that the profits would be divided equally between S and R. Of interest here is the judge's comment that there was initially some uncertainty over whether the parties' agreement was a commercial transaction or merely a social exchange. The judge stated that, in these circumstances, the onus was on S to establish an intention to create legal relations, but that this burden would be less onerous than if the agreement had arisen out of a purely social relationship. On the facts, the judge held that S had established an intention to create legal relations.[7] Commercial arrangements reached in a social setting may also generate problems for the parties; see for example *MacInnes* v *Gross* (2017), where the claimant failed to establish an intention to create legal relations. This decision also highlights an important principle relating to burden of proof, noting that 'where there is no express agreement, the onus is on the party claiming that a binding agreement had been made to prove that there was an intention to create legal relations' (at 77); see further *Assuranceforeningen Gard* v *IOPC Fund* [2014] EWHC 3369 (Comm).

6.20 In some commercial situations the parties might, as part of their agreement, expressly deny that they intend to create legal relations.[8] For example, in *Jones* v *Vernons Pools* [1938] 2 All ER 626, C claimed to have filled in his pools coupon and sent it off, but the Vernon Pools company alleged that they had not received it. (C's entry, if received, would have been successful.) It was a condition of entry, known to C, that the sending in of the coupon should not be attended

7 For further discussion, see A. Taylor, 'Law of Ghosts' (2005) 16 Entertainment LR 132.

8 In agreements for the sale of houses, for instance, it is a common practice to state that they are 'subject to contract'. The agreement will not have legal force until a formal contract has been entered into. Also, in *Regalian Properties plc* v *London Dockland Development Corpn* (1995), an agreement for a building development was 'subject to contract'. The project was later abandoned and P's claim for wasted expenditure was unsuccessful, as such costs were incurred at their own risk (see **Chapter 3**).

by or give rise to any legal relationship, or be legally enforceable, or be the subject of litigation. It was stated in the conditions of entry, therefore, that the arrangements of the pools were binding in honour only. Atkinson J held that the agreed conditions prevented C from succeeding against the defendants in any action to enforce payment of prize money. As there was no intention to create legal relations, there was no need for the court to decide whether C did, in fact, post the coupon. Atkinson J stated (at 629):

> It seems to me that the purpose of these rules [for entry] is this. The defendants wish it to be made quite clear that they are conducting these pools on certain clear lines, and they intend to say by these conditions: 'Everybody who comes into these pools must understand that there are no legal obligations either way in connection with these pools . . . money must be sent in [with entries] on the clearest understanding that this is a gentlemen's agreement, an agreement which carries with it no legal obligations on either side, and confers no legal rights'.

6.21 In *Rose and Frank Co* v *JR Crompton & Bros Ltd* [1925] AC 445, an arrangement was made between an American company and an English company whereby the American company was established as sole agent for the sale, in the USA, of tissues (for carbonizing paper) supplied by the English company. Their original agreement was extended and a document was drawn up to regulate their dealings. This stated:

> This arrangement is not entered into, nor is the memorandum written, as a formal or legal agreement, and shall not be subject to legal jurisdiction in the Law Courts either of the U.S. or England, but it is only a definite expression and record of the purpose and intention of the . . . parties concerned, to which each honourably pledge themselves.

A dispute eventually arose between the parties and the English company determined the agreement without notice. Before this, the American firm had placed an order, which had been accepted by the English firm. The American company brought an action for breach of contract. The House of Lords held that the agreement did not constitute a legally binding contract.[9] Accordingly, there was no obligation on the American company to order goods, or on the English firm to accept an order. But any actual transaction between the parties gave rise to the usual legal rights, 'for the fact that it was not of obligation to do the transaction did not divest the transaction when done of its ordinary legal significance' (per Lord Phillimore at 455).

6.22 If a plainly commercial transaction is not intended by the parties to give rise to legal relations, the courts will require clear evidence to that effect. This is illustrated by *Edwards* v *Skyways Ltd* (1964), where the facts were:

---

9 Contrast *Home Insurance Co.* v *Administration Asigurarilor* (1983).

C was employed as a pilot by the defendant company ('the company'), and he was a member of the company's contributory pension fund. The company informed C that he was to be made redundant. It also promised C an 'ex gratia' payment 'equivalent to' (the actual words were disputed) the defendant's contribution to the pension fund. Later, the defendant company failed to make the 'ex gratia' payment to C. The company defended C's action for breach of contract by arguing that the agreement about the 'ex gratia' payment was not intended to create legal relations, and that it was too vague to be enforceable.

It was held that where (as in this case) the subject of the agreement between the parties related to business matters, the onus of negativing contractual intention was on the defendant company. It was a heavy onus and one which the company had failed to discharge. The court found in favour of C. The fact that the payment was described as 'ex gratia' did not show that the company's promise lacked contractual intention.

6.23 The issue of contractual intention has been considered by the courts in relation to the use, in business, of 'letters of comfort'.[10] This is a practice which occurs where a party is considering lending money to X, and receives some encouragement, in the form of a 'comfort letter' from Y, to go ahead and do so. This can be illustrated by the facts of *Kleinwort Benson Ltd* v *Malaysia Mining Corpn Sdn Bhd* [1989] 1 All ER 785:

The claimant merchant bank (KB) agreed with the defendants (D) to a make a loan of up to £10 million available to D's wholly owned subsidiary (M), which traded in tin on the London Metal Exchange. As part of this credit arrangement, D provided KB with two 'letters of comfort' which both stated, in para. 3, that 'it is our policy to ensure that the business of [M] is at all times in a position to meet its liabilities to you under the [loan facility] arrangements'. A year later, the tin market collapsed, at a time when M owed KB the whole amount of the facility. M went into liquidation, and KB sought from D payment of the amount owing. At first instance, the court held that KB could recover the money from D, who appealed on the ground that the letters of comfort did not have contractual effect.

It was held, allowing D's appeal, that the letters of comfort in question did not constitute a contractual promise. Ralph Gibson LJ stated (at 792):

> In my judgment the defendants made a statement as to what their policy was, and did not in para 3 of the comfort letter expressly promise that such policy would be continued in future. It is impossible to make up for the lack of express promise by implying such a promise, and indeed, no such promise was pleaded. My conclusion rests on what is the proper effect and meaning which . . . is to be given to para 3 of the comfort letters.

10 See also I. Brown, 'The Letter of Comfort: Placebo or Promise?' [1990] JBL 281.

It might be argued that as the letters occurred in a commercial context, the usual presumption of contractual intention should have applied, and that there should have been more than just a moral responsibility on D's part to meet M's debt. Of course the parties can, if they wish, expressly disclaim any contractual intention, but is it clear that this was done in the *Kleinwort Benson* case? In each case, the specific wording will be important.

6.24 *Mahmood* v *The Big Bus Co.* (2017) offers a recent illustration of the application of the rebuttable presumption of contractual intention in a commercial context. Here, the dispute centred on a 'Heads of Terms' document which was drafted but not formally agreed between the business parties, who were seeking to replicate a London open-top tourist bus scheme to operate in Dubai. When called to determine whether there was a legally enforceable agreement under UAE law, the court found that although the parties had not entered into the disputed joint venture agreement on particular terms, the rest of the contractual agreement should have been contemplated. This included consideration of three recitals and agreement clauses which were couched in obligatory language, including an agreement to agree. The summary judgment had therefore been incorrect in stating that there were too many uncertainties in the agreement and the claimant did have a real prospect of establishing his case at trial. (See also *MacInnes* v *Gross* (2017), where the claimant had emailed the defendant following their meeting over dinner to say he was delighted they had agreed on headline terms, but at trial the judge found that when the parties had left the restaurant that evening they clearly had very different views on what had taken place.)

6.25 There may be commercial transactions where the value of the goods involved is so small that the parties are most unlikely, in practice, to take the matter to court, but the question of whether there was a contract, and intention to create legal relations, may come before a court for other reasons. For example, where a 'free gift' is offered, as part of a sales promotion, to purchasers of certain goods, it may be asked if there is any intention to create legal relations in relation to it. This issue arose in *Esso Petroleum Co. Ltd* v *Customs and Excise Comrs* (1976), where the facts were:

> Esso distributed millions of 'World Cup' coins to petrol stations which supplied their (Esso's) petrol, as part of a sales promotion scheme. One coin (depicting a member of the English soccer team) was to be given away with every four gallons of petrol bought by motorists. The coins were of little value, but the scheme was potentially lucrative because motorists were encouraged to buy Esso petrol in order to collect the set of 30 coins. Large posters and extensive advertisements were used to publicize the scheme. The Customs and Excise Commissioners claimed that the coins were chargeable to purchase tax (under the relevant legislation) on the basis that they had been 'produced in quantity for general sale'.

On the point of tax law in question, the House of Lords held that the coins had not been 'produced . . . for . . . sale' (within the relevant legislation) and were not therefore chargeable to purchase tax. The majority held (with Lord Fraser dissenting) that this was because the coins were not supplied under a contract of 'sale'. The consideration for the transfer of the coins was not a money payment, but the undertaking by the customer to enter into a collateral contract to buy the requisite amount of petrol. However, the majority were then divided on whether there was any intention to create a legally binding contract (of any sort) to supply the coins to customers who bought the petrol. The majority, including Lord Fraser, appear to have favoured the view that there was contractual intention. But it is possible that the dissenting judges (Lords Dilhorne and Russell) were correct in their interpretation of the transaction between the parties. Their lordships doubted whether there was any intention to create legal relations because of the way in which the advertisements referred to 'free gifts', and also because of the lack of intrinsic value of the coins.

Summary

- It is usually stated that the parties to a contract must intend to create legal relations.
- In fact, the law proceeds on the basis of two rebuttable presumptions: that parties to commercial transactions *do* intend to create legal relations; and that parties to social or domestic agreements do *not* intend legal consequences.
- The courts do not want to get involved in domestic disputes and, generally, this is consistent with the parties' intentions.
- But there are certain situations where this policy is capable of producing an unfair outcome.
- In some cases it is the element of reliance which provides the objective evidence of an intention to create legal relations, and is capable of rebutting the general presumption.
- In commercial transactions there is a general presumption that the parties intend to create legal relations. This is rebuttable, but the courts will require clear evidence of this.

Further reading

I. Brown, 'The Letter of Comfort: Placebo or Promise?' [1990] JBL 281

M. Freeman, 'Contracting in the Haven: *Balfour v Balfour* Revisited' in R. Halson (ed.), *Exploring the Boundaries of Contract*, Dartmouth, 1996, pp. 68–82

S. Hedley, 'Keeping Contract in Its Place—*Balfour* v *Balfour* and the Enforceability of Informal Agreements' (1985) 5 OJLS 391

D. McClean, 'In the Service of the Saints: A Consideration of the Draft Ecclesiastical Offices (Terms of Service) Measure—The Legal Background' (2008) 10 ECCLJ 310

M. Nash, 'Family Trouble' (2007) 157 NLJ 620

Pey-Woan Lee, 'Letters of Comfort Revisited' [2002] LMCLQ 169

A. Taylor, 'Law of Ghosts' (2005) 16 Entertainment LR 132

Chapter 7

Express and implied terms

Introduction

7.1 Here we are concerned with the contents of the contract, its terms, and the obligations undertaken by the parties. They may be either express or implied, and both possibilities are considered.

Express terms

Introduction

7.2 As we have seen, most contracts can be made orally or in writing, or there may be a combination of oral and written terms. Of course, there is much to be said about when a written clause is treated as part of a larger written or, otherwise, oral contract. However, such questions commonly arise in relation to exemption clauses, and they are therefore dealt with, at length, in Chapter 9. What we are concerned with here is the spoken word, and the problem of whether what was said became part of a contract, or was a mere representation. But what we can briefly state here is a reminder that where a written contract has been made which contains a clause precluding oral variation of it (a 'no oral variation clause'), then a variation will need to be in writing. This conclusion was reached by the Supreme Court in *Rock Advertising Limited v MWB Business Exchange Centres Limited* (2018) (see para. **4.54**ff), which favoured the certainty which maintaining adherence to such a clause produced. But it is the basic question of an oral statement becoming a term, without the complication of any such clauses, to which we must now turn, and focus upon.

7.3 It is possible that a statement may be found to be a term not of the main contract, but of a collateral contract. Collateral contracts often serve to avoid some difficulty involved in finding that the statement is a term of the main contract (for example, the statement may be found to be a term of a collateral contract where the person injured is not a party to the main contract, thus evading the rule relating to privity of contract (see **Chapter 17**)). Collateral contracts are considered at para. **7.17**.

Representations and terms

7.4 A statement made before the contract may become a term of the contract or it may be a mere representation. It may relate to some present fact or to some future act, event, or circumstance. If the statement is a term, a remedy will lie for breach of contract if it is untrue or does not occur. If it is a mere representation, and it is untrue or does not occur, there will be no remedy for breach, although a remedy may be available for misrepresentation (see **Chapter 13**). The basic test for distinguishing terms and representations is that of the parties' intention. It is the type of test which leaves considerable scope for the court to be influenced by the result which will ensue from a decision. Such influence particularly needs to be borne in mind when considering some of the older decisions where terms were found. Before the mid-1960s, damages for misrepresentation were much more limited in their availability than they are now, with the result that the courts had a greater impetus to find that the statement in question was a term and not merely a representation.

7.5 A preliminary point should be made on the terminology adopted by the courts. The question whether or not X's statement was a term of X's contract with Y may be put in terms of whether X warranted what he or she was saying. 'Warrant' is being used simply to mean promise or guarantee, that is, it is being used to ask whether X intended to take upon him or herself the risk that the statement was untrue, or would not be fulfilled, by making it a term. Similarly, 'warranty' may be used simply to mean a term of the contract, but some care must be taken. The courts also use it more technically, to contrast with condition and innominate term, to mean a term with a particular legal consequence flowing from its breach (i.e. only a claim in damages with no right to terminate the contract for its breach, as there would be for breach of a condition, and might be for breach of an innominate term). To avoid confusion, 'term' will be used here to denote the simple fact that a statement was a term, but not to indicate that it was of any particular type. The use of 'warranty' in that sense will be avoided wherever possible.

The basic test

7.6 The basic test of whether a statement is a term is one of intention. This was recognized by the House of Lords in *Heilbut, Symons, & Co.* v *Buckleton* (1913). The facts were:

> Heilbut, Symons, & Co. were rubber merchants who were underwriting an issue of shares in a company called Filisola Rubber and Produce Estates Ltd. Heilbut, Symons, & Co. contacted Johnston, their manager in Liverpool, and told him to obtain applications for shares in the Filisola company. Johnston had seen a prospectus for that company but he did not have one in the Liverpool office. Buckleton telephoned Johnston and said: 'I understand you are bringing out a rubber company.' The reply was 'we are'. On being informed that Johnston did

> not have any prospectuses, Buckleton enquired 'if it was all right'. The response was, 'we are bringing it out'. Buckleton replied, 'that is good enough for me'. After Buckleton had bought shares in the company, it was discovered that there were considerably fewer rubber trees on the estate than the prospectus had stated. The shares fell in value. Buckleton tried to claim damages from Heilbut, Symons, & Co. on the basis (a) of a fraudulent misrepresentation, or (b) that Heilbut, Symons, & Co. had contracted with him that the company was a rubber company.

The claim of fraud was dismissed at first instance, but the assertion that there had been a breach of a contract term—that the company was a rubber company—was successful until the case reached the House of Lords. There it was held that the company could not properly be termed a 'rubber company' and there was no contractual promise by Heilbut, Symons, & Co. that the company was a rubber company. When Buckleton had spoken to Johnston on the telephone, what had clearly been important was that the company was being 'brought out' by Heilbut, Symons, & Co. They had not been considering whether it should, or should not, technically be referred to as a 'rubber company'.

7.7 It should be emphasized that the intention test is not subjective, but objective.[1] Denning LJ, in *Oscar Chess Ltd* v *Williams* [1957] 1 WLR 370, said at 375:

> It is sometimes supposed that the tribunal must look into the minds of the parties to see what they themselves intended. That is a mistake ... The question of whether a warranty was intended depends on the conduct of the parties, on their words and behaviour, rather than on their thoughts. If an intelligent bystander would reasonably infer that a warranty was intended, that will suffice.

The objective nature of the test is well illustrated by *Thake* v *Maurice* [1986] 1 All ER 497. In that case, the facts were:

> Mr and Mrs Thake did not wish to have any more children, and so Mr Thake decided to have an operation which would sterilize him. The defendant, the surgeon who undertook the operation, had explained beforehand that it was irreversible. He had not told them that there was a slight possibility that it might reverse itself naturally even after the usual checks on Mr Thake's sperm count had shown that the operation had been successful. The couple believed that Mr Thake must be sterile after the operation, and they did not realize that Mrs Thake was pregnant until it was too late for her to have an abortion. Mr Thake's operation had been carried out with due care, and his sperm count had been correctly checked, but a natural reversal of the operation had subsequently occurred.

1 On objectivity in contract, see generally W. Howarth. 'The Meaning of Objectivity in Contract' (1984) 100 LQR 265; A. De Moor, 'Intention in the Law of Contract: Elusive or Illusory?' (1990) 106 LQR 632.

Mr and Mrs Thake argued that it had been a term of their contract with the surgeon that the operation would render Mr Thake sterile, and that term had been breached. The Court of Appeal did not accept that argument. It was held that the surgeon had merely guaranteed to carry out the operation with care and skill. However, Mr and Mrs Thake were awarded damages on the basis that the surgeon had been negligent in failing to warn them of the possibility of natural reversal.

7.8 On the question of whether the surgeon had guaranteed that the operation would render Mr Thake sterile, the court recognized the objective nature of the search for intention as the determinant of the terms of the contract. Mr and Mrs Thake both left the surgeon's consulting room thinking that he had guaranteed that the operation would render Mr Thake sterile, but, equally, the surgeon had not intended to give any such guarantee. Both parties held opposing views of what the terms were. Objectively, no term guaranteeing the success of the operation was found. The court thought that a reasonable person in the position of Mr and Mrs Thake would have known that medical science was not certain and would not have thought that the surgeon was guaranteeing the success of the operation. Nourse LJ said (at 511):

> The function of the court in ascertaining, objectively, the meaning of words used by contracting parties is one of everyday occurrence. But it is often exceedingly difficult to discharge it where the subjective understandings of the parties are clear and opposed. Here the [claimants] understood that Mr Thake would be permanently sterile. The defendant himself recognised they would have been left with that impression. On the other hand, he did not intend, and on the state of his knowledge he could not have intended, to guarantee that that would be the case. Both the understanding and the intention appear to them, as individuals, to have been entirely reasonable, but an objective interpretation must choose between them. In the end the question seems to be reduced to one of determining the extent of the knowledge which is to be attributed to the reasonable person standing in the position of the plaintiffs.

This illustrates the objective approach and the need for it.

Indicators of intention

7.9 The test of the parties' intention can be difficult to apply, but certain factors are regarded by the courts as indicators of whether a statement was intended as a term. Some of the factors have been given more importance than others but, as Lord Moulton emphasized in *Heilbut, Symons & Co.* v *Buckleton* [1913] AC 30 at 50, none of them is decisive. They are all only aids to establish the parties' intention. With that in mind we may now consider some of the factors the courts have recognized as indicators of whether a statement was intended as a term.

Importance of the statement

7.10 It may be clear to both sides that a certain factor was very important to one of the parties in the decision to contract. A statement on that factor, by the other party, may then well be found to have been intended as a guarantee, as a term. In *Bannerman* v *White* (1861):

> Brewers were refusing to use hops contaminated with sulphur. Bannerman offered hops to White, and White asked if sulphur had been used to grow them. Bannerman said 'no' and White said that he would not even discuss the price if it had. A contract was made for the sale of the hops; later it was established that Bannerman had forgotten that sulphur had been used in growing a small proportion of them.

It was held that it was a term of the contract that sulphur had not been used in growing the hops. It had been clear to both parties that the question of the use of sulphur was very important to White and that he would not have contracted without the assurance that no sulphur had been used on Bannerman's hops.

Reliance

7.11 An indication that a statement by one party can be relied upon, and need not be verified, may show that it should be regarded as a term. For example, a prospective seller may indicate to a potential buyer that he or she can rely upon the seller's statement as to the condition of the goods and need not check the goods. This may then lead to the conclusion that the seller's statement is a term of the contract of sale. In *Schawel* v *Reade* [1913] 2 IR 64:

> The claimant wished to purchase a horse for stud purposes. He visited the defendant's stables and while he was inspecting a horse, Mallow Man, the defendant said, 'You need not look for anything; the horse is perfectly sound. If there was anything the matter with the horse I would tell you.' The claimant ceased his inspection and three weeks later he bought Mallow Man. The horse was unfit for stud purposes because of a hereditary eye disease.

The House of Lords held that the soundness of the horse was a term of the contract. It was clearly indicated that the buyer could rely upon the seller, that is, that the seller was taking the risk of the horse being unsound. Lord Moulton said (at 86):

> The essence of such warranty is that it becomes plain by the words, and the action, of the parties that it is intended that in the purchase the responsibility of the soundness shall rest upon the vendor; and how ... could a vendor more clearly indicate that he is prepared and intends to take upon himself the responsibility of the soundness than by saying: 'You need not look at that horse because it is perfectly sound', and sees that the purchaser thereupon desists from his immediate independent examination.

This can be contrasted with *Ecay* v *Godfrey* (1947), where a boat was being sold. Although the seller, Mr Godfrey, said that it was sound, he also suggested a survey to the buyer, Señor Ecay. It was held that it was not a term of the contract of sale that the boat was sound. Equally, a similar conclusion may be reached where, although the statement of soundness is not followed by any express warning to carry out a check, there is a trade practice that such statements are not terms.[2]

2 Trade practice seems to be the explanation of *Hopkins* v *Tanqueray* (1864).

Relative knowledge of the parties

7.12 It is relevant to consider the question of which of the two parties was in the best position to know or ascertain the truth of a statement made. It is connected with the above indicator. It could be put in terms of whether it was reasonable to rely upon the statement made, or whether one party can be taken to have assumed the risk of the statement being untrue. The court will be more inclined to find that the statement is a term if it was made by the person in the best position to have ascertained its truth. Two cases can be contrasted here: *Oscar Chess Ltd* v *Williams* (1957) and *Dick Bentley Productions Ltd* v *Harold Smith (Motors) Ltd* (1965).

7.13 In *Oscar Chess Ltd* v *Williams* (1957):

> The defendant sold a Morris car to the claimant, a car dealer who was familiar with the car as he had been given lifts in it. The log book had shown it to be a 1948 model and the defendant had innocently described it as such and produced the log book. Before the defendant acquired the car the log book had been tampered with and the car was, in fact, a 1939 model. There was no difference in appearance between a 1948 and a 1939 model. The claimant would have paid £115 less for a 1939 model than for a 1948 model. Eight months after the sale, the claimant discovered the alteration of the log book and sought £115 from the defendant for breach of a term that the car was a 1948 model.

The Court of Appeal held that there was no term that the car was a 1948 model. The defendant was in no better position than the claimant to assess the age of the car. The defendant had simply relied upon the date stated in the log book. There was no reason to suppose that he had intended to take upon himself the risk that the car was not a 1948 model by making the age of the car a term of the contract.

7.14 *Oscar Chess Ltd* v *Williams* (1957) contrasts with *Dick Bentley Productions Ltd* v *Harold Smith (Motors) Ltd* (1965), where the person making the statement was in the better position to establish its truth, and the statement was found to be a term. In *Dick Bentley*:

> Dick Bentley asked a car dealer, Smith, to find him a well-vetted Bentley car. Smith found a car and showed it to Dick Bentley, telling him that since a new engine had been fitted the car had done only 20,000 miles, the mileage shown on the odometer. Dick Bentley purchased the car, which proved to be unsatisfactory, and it was discovered that it had done far more than the mileage shown on the odometer since the new engine had been fitted.

The Court of Appeal held that the mileage had been a term of the contract. The case was distinguished from *Oscar Chess Ltd* v *Williams* (1957) on the basis of the position of the person making the statement. A car dealer was in a far better position than his customer to establish the accuracy of the mileage recorded on the odometer.

The parol evidence rule

7.15 Where there is a written document containing contract terms, the question arises whether evidence can be given to show that the parties agreed to additional terms which are not contained within the written document. It has been said that 'it is firmly established as a rule of law that parol evidence cannot be admitted to add to, vary or contradict a deed or other written document' (*Jacobs* v *Batavia and General Plantations Trust Ltd* [1924] 1 Ch 287 at 295 per Lawrence J). However, although this is commonly referred to as the parol evidence rule, its status as a rule is very doubtful. On closer examination it does nothing more than express a presumption. In *Gillespie Bros & Co.* v *Cheney, Eggar & Co.* [1896] 2 QB 59, Lord Russell CJ said (at 62):

> [A]lthough when the parties arrive at a definite written contract the implication or presumption is very strong that such contract is intended to contain all the terms of their bargain, it is a presumption only, and it is open to either of the parties to allege that there was, in addition to what appears in the written agreement, an antecedent express stipulation not intended by the parties to be excluded, but intended to continue in force with the express written agreement.

In other words, a written agreement, which looks like a complete contract, leads to the presumption that it is the complete contract, but that presumption can be rebutted. If it is shown that other terms were intended, in addition to those contained in the written document, then there is no rule preventing the admission of evidence of those other terms. If the written document was intended to embody the entire contract between the parties, there is clearly no room to admit evidence of any other statements of the parties as terms: they cannot be terms. On this basis the Law Commission concluded that the parol evidence rule is 'a proposition of law which is no more than a circular statement' (Law Com 154 (1986); G. Marston, 'The Parol Evidence Rule: The Law Commission Speaks' [1986] CLJ 192).

7.16 The Law Commission also concluded that even if the parol evidence rule was viewed as of some substance, it was unlikely to work injustice because of the numerous exceptions to it. For example, evidence can be used to show that it had been orally agreed that the contract embodied in the written document was not intended to be immediately effective but was to become so only when certain conditions had been fulfilled (*Pym* v *Campbell* (1856)), or evidence of custom can be used to add to written contracts on matters on which the writing is silent (*Hutton* v *Warren* (1836)—see para. **7.52**). The device of the collateral contract has also been used to avoid the parol evidence rule, so that if the parol evidence rule meant that the court felt unable to find that a statement was a term of the main contract, it could still find that it was a term of a collateral contract.[3]

3 For further 'exceptions' to the parol evidence 'rule', see G. Treitel, *The Law of Contract*, 13th edn by E. Peel, Sweet & Maxwell, 2011, 6–013–6–030.

Collateral contracts

7.17 The courts may occasionally find that, although a statement is not part of the main contract, it is part of a collateral contract.[4] The statement can then found an action for breach of contract just as it would have done had it been part of the main contract. The collateral contract is often of the form, 'if you will enter into the main contract then I guarantee that . . .'. In *Heilbut, Symons, & Co.* v *Buckleton* [1913] AC 30, Lord Moulton stated (at 47):

> It is evident, both on principle and on authority, that there may be a contract the consideration for which is the making of some other contract. 'If you will make such and such a contract I will give you one hundred pounds,' is in every sense of the word a complete legal contract. It is collateral to the main contract, but each has an independent existence, and they do not differ in respect of their possessing to the full the character and status of a contract.

7.18 The collateral contract has proved to be a useful device when there is a reason why the court cannot find that the statement in question is a term of the main contract. It has, for example, provided the courts with a means of avoiding the rule as to privity of contract (see **Chapter 17**), formality requirements, and the parol evidence rule (earlier in this chapter), where it 'eases the consciences of those who believe that the parol evidence rule is a strict and meaningful prohibition' (Wedderburn [1959] CLJ 58 at 69).

7.19 The usual requirements for a valid contract apply to a collateral contract just as to any other. The consideration for the promise in the collateral contract is usually the act of entering into the main contract, that is, 'if you will enter into the main contract then I guarantee that . . .' (e.g. *City and Westminster Properties Ltd* v *Mudd* (1959)).

7.20 There is a terminological difficulty in this area. Warranties are sometimes referred to as 'collateral terms' or 'collateral warranties', that is, terms subsidiary to the main terms, the conditions, but properly speaking still part of the main contract. Nevertheless, it is sometimes difficult to discern whether the judges think they are discussing a warranty in the main contract or in a collateral contract (for example, *Heilbut, Symons, & Co.* v *Buckleton* (1913)) and sometimes, although recognizing the two different possibilities, they treat them as interchangeable (e.g. *J Evans & Son (Portsmouth) Ltd* v *Andrea Merzario Ltd* (1976)).

Implied terms[5]

Introduction

7.21 Often the parties will not expressly deal with every query which could arise under the contract. They may have thought that some things were too obvious to express, they may not

4 Wedderburn [1959] CLJ 58.

5 A. Phang, 'Implied Terms Revisited' [1990] JBL 394; A. Phang, 'Implied Terms in English Law—Some Recent Developments' [1993] JBL 242; A. Phang, 'Implied Terms Again' [1994] JBL 255; and R. Hooley, 'Implied Terms after Belize Telecom' [2014] 73(2) CLJ 315.

have considered every possible eventuality, or they may have avoided covering a particular issue with an express term, because they did not think they could reach agreement about it, or that it was worth spending the time on. When a problem arises which has not been dealt with by the express terms of the contract, then it may be argued that a term can be implied. There are basically three types of implied term which we need to consider: terms implied in fact, terms implied in law, and terms implied by custom.

Terms implied in fact

7.22 In implying terms in fact, the courts will state that they are endeavouring merely to find the objective intention of the parties. In particular, the courts will often emphasize that they are not rewriting the parties' bargain.[6] Traditionally the courts have not simply applied a test of the parties' intentions, but rather have sought that intention through two narrow tests: first, the 'business efficacy' test; secondly, the 'officious bystander test'. Under the 'business efficacy' test it is said that the implication of the term must be 'necessary to give the transaction such business efficacy as the parties must have intended' (per Bowen LJ in *The Moorcock* (1889)), that is, the term must be required to make the contract workable. In addition, the 'officious bystander' test is often cited:

> Prima facie that which in any contract is left to be implied and need not be expressed is something so obvious that it goes without saying; so that, if while the parties were making their bargain an officious bystander were to suggest some express provision for it in the agreement, they would testily suppress him with a common 'Oh, of course'. (*Shirlaw* v *Southern Foundries Ltd* [1939] 2 KB 206 at 227 per Mackinnon LJ)

7.23 In *The Moorcock* (1889):

> The defendants owned a wharf on the Thames and made a contract with the claimant shipowner for him to unload his vessel at their wharf. Both parties knew that the vessel was such that, whilst at the wharf, it must ground at low tide. The vessel grounded and was damaged.

It was held to be an implied term of the contract that the defendants had taken due care to ascertain that the bed of the river adjoining the wharf was not such as to damage the vessel when it grounded. The defendants were in breach of the implied term.

7.24 In *Shirlaw* v *Southern Foundries (1926) Ltd* (1939):

> On 1 December 1933 Mr Shirlaw was appointed managing director of Southern Foundries for ten years. Subsequently, Federated Foundries became the beneficial owners of Southern Foundries and in 1936 they changed the articles of association of Southern Foundries to enable them to remove Mr Shirlaw as a director. They removed him from his directorship, and he could not continue as managing director once he ceased to be a director.

6 For example, *Trollope & Colls Ltd* v *North West Metropolitan Regional Hospital Board* [1973] 2 All ER 260 at 268.

The original articles of association of Southern Foundries did not allow Mr Shirlaw's removal in that way. The court found a breach of an implied term that such removal would not occur before the ten-year period expired.

7.25 However, a different approach to the law in this area was taken by Lord Hoffmann in delivering the decision of the Privy Council in *Attorney General of Belize* v *Belize Telecom Ltd* [2009] 2 All ER (Comm) 1.

> The case was concerned with whether provision should be implied into a company's articles of association to provide for the removal of directors appointed by the holders of a 'special share' when their ordinary shareholding fell below the percentage shareholding which was stated in the articles to give them the power to appoint or remove such directors. The Privy Council found that such a provision should be implied. With that shareholding below the required percentage, the express terms of the articles did not confer on anyone the power to remove those directors. Further, the articles of association expressly protected the interests of the holders of the special share in carefully graduated stages, corresponding with their economic interest in the company.

However, what is of significance here is not the specific facts of the case but Lord Hoffmann's general statements on implying terms in fact. He equated the implication of terms in fact with the construction of the contract (i.e. the interpretation of the contract) so that what is in question is ascertaining the objective intention, that is, what the reasonable person with the background knowledge of the parties would have thought that the contract meant. He said (at [17]–[18]):

> The question of implication arises when the instrument does not expressly provide for what is to happen when some event occurs. The most usual inference in such a case is that nothing is to happen ... the loss lies where it falls.
>
> In some cases, however, the reasonable addressee would understand the instrument to mean something else. He would consider that the only meaning consistent with the other provisions of the instrument, read against the relevant background, is that something is to happen. The event in question is to affect the rights of the parties. The instrument may not have expressly said so, but this is what it must mean. In such a case, it is said the court implies a term as to what will happen if the event in question occurs. But the implication of a term is not an addition to the instrument. It only spells out what the instrument means.

Lord Hoffmann took the line that the 'business efficacy' test and the 'officious bystander' tests are not 'different or additional tests'; they have just assisted the courts to determine what the contract means, as there 'is only one question: ... what the instrument, read as a whole against the relevant background, would reasonably be understood to mean' (at [21]). Further, he indicated that the 'business efficacy' and 'officious bystander' tests must be treated with caution, as merely guides, not displacing the test he identified.

7.26 Lord Hoffmann's specific arguments, in concluding that the traditional tests have merely assisted the courts, are open to considerable criticism.[7] However, his idea of recognizing the underlying link between interpretation and implication is a strong one and has been accepted, albeit within restricted boundaries (see e.g. *Mediterranean Salvage & Towage Ltd* v *Seamar Trading & Commerce Inc* (2009)).

7.27 Most recently in *Marks and Spencer plc* v *BNP Paribas Securities Services Trust Company (Jersey) Ltd* (2015) however, the Supreme Court reasserted the 'business efficacy' and the 'officious bystander' tests, thereby disposing of the idea that the implication of terms in fact is to be treated in the same way as construing the written terms (see in particular Lord Neuberger's comments at [26], although note Lord Carnwath's difference of opinion with reference to Lord Hoffmann and the Board's approach in *Attorney General of Belize* v *Belize Telecom Ltd* (2009) and its subsequent interpretation by judges and commentators [at 58–74]).

7.28 In *Marks and Spencer plc* v *BNP Paribas Securities Services Trust Company (Jersey) Ltd* (2015) the facts were:

> Marks and Spencer ('M&S') had rented premises and the lease required them to pay rent to the landlords on a quarterly basis, in advance. The lease contained a break clause, providing that the tenant could terminate the lease as long as there were no rent arrears on the break date. M&S exercised its right under the break clause to terminate the lease and paid the full quarter's rent due immediately before the break date. The issue in dispute was whether M&S was entitled to recover from the landlords the portion of prepaid rent for the period after the break date up until the next quarter date. There was no express term to that effect in the lease, which was a detailed and lengthy document, and the question was, therefore, whether such term should be implied.

The High Court held that a term to that effect should be implied, finding in favour of M&S, but the Court of Appeal held that it should not and overturned that decision. The Supreme Court agreed with the Court of Appeal, ruling unanimously in favour of the landlords.

7.29 The Supreme Court judgment in *Marks and Spencer plc* v *BNP Paribas Securities Services Trust Company (Jersey) Ltd* (2015) delivers a useful clarification of when a term may be implied into a contract. Lord Neuberger (at [14–20]) referred to the numerous judicial observations made in earlier case law, regarding the nature of the requirements which must be satisfied before a term can be implied into a contract (for example, Lord Simon's summary in *BP Refinery (Westernport) Pty Ltd* v *President, Councillors and Ratepayers of the Shire of Hastings* (1977) ALJR 20 at 26, extended by Sir Thomas Bingham in *Philips Electronique Grand Public SA v British Sky Broadcasting Ltd* (1995) and exemplified in *The APJ Priti* [1987] 2 Lloyd's Rep 37). Lord

7 See further, E. Macdonald, 'Casting Aside Officious Bystanders and Business Efficacy' (2009) 26 Journal of Contract Law 97.

Neuberger concluded [at 21] that whilst 'the judicial observations so far considered represent a clear, consistent and principled approach' and although 'it could be dangerous to reformulate the principles', there were six comments he would wish to add. He said (at 21):

> [First ...] the implication of a term was 'not critically dependent on proof of an actual intention of the parties' when negotiating the contract. If one approaches the question by reference to what the parties would have agreed, one is not strictly concerned with the hypothetical answer of the actual parties, but with that of notional reasonable people in the position of the parties at the time at which they were contracting. Secondly, a term should not be implied into a detailed commercial contract merely because it appears fair or merely because one considers that the parties would have agreed it if it had been suggested to them. Those are necessary but not sufficient grounds for including a term. However, and thirdly, it is questionable whether Lord Simon's first requirement, reasonableness and equitableness, will usually, if ever, add anything: if a term satisfies the other requirements, it is hard to think that it would not be reasonable and equitable. Fourthly ... I would accept that business necessity and obviousness ... can be alternatives in the sense that only one of them needs to be satisfied, although I suspect that in practice it would be a rare case where only one of those two requirements would be satisfied. Fifthly, if one approaches the issue by reference to the officious bystander, it is 'vital to formulate the question to be posed by [him] with the utmost care' (Lewison, *The Interpretation of Contracts* 5th ed (2011), para 6.09). Sixthly, necessity for business efficacy involves a value judgment. It is rightly common ground on this appeal that the test is not one of 'absolute necessity', not least because the necessity is judged by reference to business efficacy ... [A] term can only be implied if, without the term, the contract would lack commercial or practical coherence.

7.30 In reaching its decision, the Supreme Court emphasized that although a clause that the landlord should reimburse the tenant the apportioned sum would seem to be a reasonable and equitable one, in the instant case this was not found to be a term which should be implied into the agreement. The lease was a very carefully considered contract, which included express obligations similar to the proposed implied term—namely, financial liabilities in connection with the tenant's right to break—and the proposed implied term would sit uneasily with those provisions (see Lord Neuberger's discussion at 53).

7.31 The judgment in *Marks & Spencer plc* clarifies that merely being reasonable and equitable does not justify the implication of a term into the contract, even if it may seem unfair to refuse implying a term into the contract. Subsequent case law, in the Court of Appeal hearing of *Kason Kek-Gardner Ltd* v *Process Components Limited* [2017] EWCA Civ 2132, has reaffirmed (at 54–55):

> a term will not be implied into a detailed commercial contract unless it is necessary to give the contract business efficacy or it is so obvious that it goes without saying. It is not enough that it would have been sensible to agree the term, or that with hindsight, the terms actually agreed operate to the disadvantage of one of the parties ... The 'necessity' required by the test is for the business efficacy *of the contract*; not for a wider business purpose of a contracting party.

Thus, we are reminded that if, in taking into account all circumstances, the Court is of the view that it was not the parties' intention to imply such a term and implication of a term is not necessary to give business efficacy, it will not interfere with the wording of a professionally drafted contract.

7.32 An underlying rationale of implying terms in fact has always been the objectively determined intention of the parties, and cases concerned with that, even in the context of the traditional tests, therefore remain of relevance.

Knowledge

7.33 That one party could not reasonably have knowledge of the subject matter of a proposed implied term has obviously been of importance to such implication, and remains so. In *Spring* v *National Amalgamated Stevedores and Dockers Society* [1956] 1 WLR 585 such a factor was put in the context of the 'officious bystander' test:

> In 1939, at Bridlington, the Trades Union Congress drew up an agreement for the transfer of members between one union and another—the Bridlington Agreement. In breach of that agreement, the NASDS allowed Mr Spring to become a member. He had been a member of the Transport and General Workers Union. In deciding the ensuing dispute between the two unions, the TUC told the NASDS to exclude all the members, like Mr Spring, that it had enrolled in contravention of the Bridlington Agreement.

When the NASDS attempted to expel Mr Spring, he asked the court for a declaration that the union was acting ultra vires, illegally and unconstitutionally, and that his expulsion was void. The union tried to argue that an implied term in Mr Spring's contract of membership justified his expulsion to bring the union back within the terms of the Bridlington Agreement.

7.34 The court granted Mr Spring's request for a declaration. On the question of the implied term, and applying the 'officious bystander' test, Sir Leonard Sachs V-C said (at 599):

> If … the bystander had asked the [claimant] … 'won't you put into it some reference to the Bridlington Agreement?', I think (indeed I have no doubt) the [claimant] would have answered 'What's that?'.

Although the court's discussion is put in terms of Mr Spring's actual knowledge, it is undoubtedly the 'objective' intention of the parties which is the basis of the implication, and what should be relevant is what the reasonable person in his position would have known. It seems likely that it would have been clear that the reasonable person would similarly have had no knowledge of the Bridlington Agreement.

Would both parties have agreed to the term?

7.35 *National Bank of Greece SA* v *Pinios Shipping Co* [1989] 1 All ER 213[8] illustrates another factor relevant to the implication of terms based on intention. The court asks whether, at the

8 The case went to the House of Lords on another point—[1990] 1 All ER 78.

time of contracting, both parties would have agreed to the term which one of them is contending should be implied. Again, the objective nature of what is under consideration should be emphasized. So it is a matter of whether it would have been plain that one party would not have agreed to it.

A ship was built for Pinios in Japan. Pinios paid 30 per cent of the price on delivery but the rest of the purchase price was borrowed on the basis of a mortgage of the ship. Pinios failed to pay the first instalment of the money owed. The bank could have declared Pinios in default and the ship would have been sold, but the sale of the ship at that point would not have recovered all the money owed, and another course was taken. The bank made a three-party agreement with Pinios and Glafki for Glafki to manage the ship in the best interest of Pinios and the bank. It was a term of the mortgage that Pinios should insure the ship for 130 per cent of the amount secured, and Pinios had done so when the ship was initially delivered. The management contract specifically made it an obligation of Glafki to insure the vessel in accordance with the requirements of the mortgage. Glafki allowed the value of the insurance to fall. When the ship sank, the insurance did not cover the sums owed by Pinios. Pinios successfully sued Glafki for negligent management of the ship, but could not obtain payment. Pinios sued the bank for Glafki's neglect.

The question before the court was whether the bank was also responsible to Pinios for Glafki's failure to insure the vessel fully. Pinios argued that a term should be implied that the bank would oversee Glafki's insurance of the vessel and that they were liable for not doing so. Pinios contended that the term should be implied because otherwise their interests were not protected, as Glafki was only subject to control by the bank and not Pinios. The Court of Appeal rejected this argument as, although Pinios would have agreed to such a term, it was not thought that the bank would have done so. The 'officious bystander' test could not be satisfied; both parties would not have said 'Oh, of course'. The management agreement had put Glafki under the control of the bank, and not Pinios, but the agreement was very much in Pinios's interests. But for the bank deciding on the management agreement, rather than simply selling the vessel, Pinios would not have remained the ship's owner. As long as Pinios owned the ship, their financial situation would improve if the market improved. In addition, it was thought that the parties would have envisaged Pinios recovering from Glafki in the sort of situation which occurred. They would not have envisaged Glafki refusing to honour the judgment. Dealing with the 'officious bystander' test, Lloyd LJ said (at 218):

> the judge was … understating the position when he said that it was by no means obvious that the bank would have agreed to act as 'guarantor' for Glafki, more especially as Glafki was Pinios's own nominee to act as manager. To my mind it is obvious that it would not.[9]

9 See also *Bank of Nova Scotia v Hellenic Mutual War Risk Association (Bermuda) Ltd, The Good Luck* [1989] 3 All ER 628 at 667; *El Awadi v Bank of Credit and Commerce International SA* [1989] 1 All ER 242 at 252.

Care must be taken not to slip into a consideration of the parties' subjective intentions. Nevertheless, clearly, if it is plain that one party would not have agreed, then the implication would not be spelling out what the 'instrument read against the relevant background, would reasonably be understood to mean'.

Several possible formulations of implied term; detailed express terms

7.36 *Trollope & Colls Ltd* v *North West Metropolitan Regional Hospital Board* (1973) provides an example of two factors against the implication of a term based on the parties' intention. In that case:

> T&C had contracted to build a hospital for the Board. The hospital was to be constructed in phases. Phases I and II were concurrent, but Phase III was to commence only six months after the issue of the Certificate of Practical Completion of Phase I. The date for the completion of Phase I was specified, and there was provision for extension of that time if the delay was due to certain specified factors. There was no provision for an alteration of the date for completing Phase III because of delay in completing Phase I, although there was provision for extension of the Phase III completion date in certain other specified circumstances. The completion of Phase I was delayed to such an extent that there were only 16 months in which to construct Phase III by the specified date. There would have been 30 months available for construction of Phase III had Phase I been completed by the date specified.

The House of Lords had to decide whether to imply a term allowing the delay on completion of Phase I to extend the completion date for Phase III. Two factors indicated that no term should be implied. First, there were detailed express terms in the contract. Those terms even dealt with some reasons for extending the completion date of Phase III. Under those circumstances it was not clear that the omission of any reference to an extension because of the late completion of Phase I was not deliberate. Second, it was not clear what the content of any implied term should be. There were various reasons for the delay in the completion of Phase I. Some of that delay was allowed under the contract for one reason, and some for other reasons, and some of it was not allowed at all. It was not clear how much of the delay any implied term should encompass. There were four or five possibilities. Doubts over the substance of the term meant that the court was not prepared to find that the parties would have included any particular version of it.[10] (But see McCaughran (2011) CLJ 607.)

Terms implied in law

7.37 Statutes imply terms into certain types of contract. For example, the Sale of Goods Act 1979 implies terms into contracts for the sale of goods that the goods should be of satisfactory

10 See also *Shell UK Ltd* v *Lostock Garage Ltd* [1977] 1 All ER 481 at 488; *Liverpool City Council* v *Irwin* (1975).

quality and reasonably fit for the buyer's purpose (see s 14).[11] In any particular case, whether a statute implies a term will depend upon whether the statutory requirements for its implication are present. In relation to s 14 of the Sale of Goods Act, for example, the above terms are only implied if the goods are sold 'in the course of a business'. Similarly, whether the parties can exclude the implication will depend upon the statute. Terms implied by statute are the most obvious type of term implied in law, but they will not be considered further here—as has been indicated, the implication is dependent upon the particular statute. What requires further consideration here is the implication of terms in law at common law. Like statute, such implication is not based upon the particular contract, but on the type of contract, and there are many types of regularly occurring contracts where certain implied terms have become standard for the type of contract in question—contracts for the lease of a furnished house (e.g. *Smith* v *Marrable* (1843)), contracts of employment (e.g. *Lister* v *Romford Ice and Cold Storage Co* (1957); *Malik* v *BCCI* (1997)), and contracts between banker and customer (e.g. *London Joint Stock Bank Ltd* v *Macmillan* (1918)). The standard implied terms are implied in the particular case unless they would contradict the express terms.[12]

7.38 However, although there are established terms which are implied in law, consideration must now be given to how a type of contract will be addressed and a term implied in law generated.

Terms implied in law are not based on the intention of the parties

7.39 In *Liverpool City Council* v *Irwin* [1976] 2 All ER 39 Lord Cross distinguished between terms implied in fact on the basis of the, objectively determined, intention of the parties, and terms implied in law because of the type of contract. He said (at 47):

> When it implies a term the court is sometimes laying down a general rule that in all contracts of a certain type—sale of goods, master and servant, landlord and tenant, and so on—some provision is to be implied unless the parties have expressly excluded it ... Sometimes however there is no question of laying down any prima facie rule applicable to all cases of a defined type ... Here ... the court ... must be able to say that the insertion of the term is necessary to give ... 'business efficacy' to the contract and that if its absence had been pointed out at the time both parties—assuming them to be reasonable men—would have agreed to the insertion.

Although this is put in terms of the traditional test for implication in fact, the basic point is clear. 'Terms implied in fact are individualised gap fillers, depending on the terms and circumstances

11 Note that since the introduction of the Consumer Rights Act 2015, in a consumer contract for the supply of goods, digital content, or services, the legislation does not refer to implied terms, instead referring to 'a term treated as included in the contract'. For example, see s 9(1) which states: 'Every contract to supply goods is to be treated as including a term that the quality of goods is satisfactory.'

12 The Court of Appeal seems to be making an inroad on the parties' intention here in envisaging the application of the Unfair Contract Terms Act 1977 to an express term precluding the implied term—*Johnstone* v *Bloomsbury Health Authority* [1991] 2 All ER 293 (see para. **10.103**).

of a particular contract. Terms implied in law are in reality incidents attached to standardised contractual relationships' (*Society of Lloyd's* v *Clementson* [1995] CLC 117 at 131 per Steyn LJ). 'Such implied terms operate as default rules' (*Malik* v *BCCI* [1997] 3 All ER 1 at 15 per Lord Steyn).

7.40 *Liverpool City Council* v *Irwin* (1976) itself provides an example of the difference between implying a term in fact and implying a term in law:

> Liverpool City Council owned a tower block which was in a very bad state of repair. Many of the problems were due to vandalism. The lifts frequently did not work and stairwells were often unlit. Rubbish chutes were frequently blocked. When Liverpool City Council sued the tenants for non-payment of rent, the tenants claimed that Liverpool City Council was in breach of an implied term as to the maintenance of the premises.

The House of Lords implied a term that Liverpool City Council should take reasonable care to maintain the common parts of the block in a reasonable state of repair. Unfortunately for the tenants, the court also found that a lack of reasonable care by Liverpool City Council had not been established, and that the implied term had not been breached.

7.41 At a time when the traditional tests undoubtedly applied in relation to terms implied in fact, how did the House of Lords imply a term when the 'officious bystander' test was not satisfied, as it was clear that Liverpool City Council would not have agreed to the term? The majority of the Court of Appeal had refused to imply a term on the only argument before them, that a term should be implied in fact, on the basis of the parties' intention. The House of Lords was able to imply a term as it did not look to the parties' intention, but to the type of contract in question. In this case the contract was a landlord-and-tenant contract, but in a multi-occupancy building where the only access to the flats was via the common areas, the stairs, and the lifts. The only express terms set out the obligations of the tenants and they did not deal with the maintenance of the common parts of the building, such as the stairs and the lifts. There were no express obligations on Liverpool City Council. The situation demanded that someone had to be responsible for those common parts and, in the absence of any express allocation of responsibility amongst the tenants, the obligation was held to fall on Liverpool City Council, which had kept control of those areas.

When will a term be implied in law?

7.42 There are two basic requirements for the implication of a term in law. As has been indicated, terms implied in law are implied because the contract is of a particular type and so the first test is often stated as a requirement that the contract is of a 'defined type'. The second requirement has tended to be put in terms of 'necessity'. So, for example, it has been stated:

> the first requirement is that the contract in question should be a contract of a defined type ... The second requirement is that the implication of the term should be necessary. (*El Awadi* v *Bank of Credit and Commerce International SA* [1989] 1 All ER 242 at 253)

However, although the second test, or requirement, has been stated as one of necessity, it is clearly a test embracing much broader considerations. It may also be that the courts are starting to become more willing explicitly to recognize that. Both requirements for the implication of a term implied in law should now be given further consideration and, in particular, the nature of the second test will be returned to later.

A contract of a defined type

7.43 We saw earlier that Lord Cross provided examples of the type of contract into which a term may be implied in law—'sale of goods, master and servant, landlord and tenant'. As he indicated, they are all commonly occurring types of contract. We can identify two basic factors relevant to determining whether the contract in question is a contract into which a term may be implied in law: a contract of a defined type. They are, first, that the contract is of a recognizable commonly occurring type and, secondly, that the express terms of the particular contract do not differ too greatly from the 'ordinary' terms of those contracts normally regarded as falling within that type.

7.44 Sale of goods contracts, master and servant contracts, and landlord and tenant contracts are all contracts of a recognizable commonly occurring type and there will often be no difficulty in deciding if the contract is of such a type. Hutchinson J had no doubts that he was dealing with a contract of that type in *El Awadi* v *Bank of Credit and Commerce International SA* (1989), where the contract was for the sale of traveller's cheques by a bank to its customer. Hutchinson J thought that the sale of traveller's cheques was 'self evidently' a contract in which the implication of a term in law was a possibility. It was a contract of common occurrence.[13]

7.45 However, the type of contract in which a term may be implied may be more specifically delimited. There is an interaction between the identification of the type of contract in which the term in question is to be implied and whether the second test is satisfied; that is, narrowing the scope of the 'type' of contract being considered may make it possible for the courts to find a term which can be implied in keeping with the second requirement. This will be returned to later (see para. **7.51**ff).

7.46 The second point to be made here is that it is not simply a matter of commonly occurring contractual relationships (for example, landlord and tenant) or contracts commonly occurring to deal with a specific subject matter (for example, sale of goods, sale of traveller's cheques by bank to customer): the contents of the contract must also be such that, in its express terms, it is an 'ordinary' contract of that type. *National Bank of Greece SA* v *Pinios Shipping Co* [1989] 1 All ER 213 has already been discussed in the context of whether or not a term could be implied in fact (see para. **7.35**). Here we need to consider the alternative argument, that a term should be implied in law. Lloyd LJ dismissed the possibility (at 219):

> Can the present case be brought within a defined type? If we were concerned with the ordinary relationship of banker and customer the law would imply certain obligations ... But we

13 But see *Shell UK Ltd* v *Lostock Garage Ltd* [1977] 1 All ER 481 at 488 per Lord Denning MR.

> are not here concerned with the ordinary relationship of banker and customer. We are concerned with a carefully drawn one-off contract between three parties, made for a particular purpose in special circumstances, and apparently making full provision for that purpose. I cannot imagine a contract which it would be more difficult to fit into a 'defined type'.

Although contracts between banker and customer could be of a 'defined type' (see, e.g., *Tai Hing Cotton Mill Ltd* v *Liu Chong Hing Bank Ltd* (1985)), this contract was not. The court was not faced with the 'ordinary' relationship of banker and customer but with a 'one-off' contract. All contracts are 'one-off' in the sense that they will have terms unique to them. The question therefore relates to the degree of departure from the 'ordinary' contract of the type in question. For example, how far does the contract in question depart from the 'ordinary' banker and customer contract? It will be relevant to consider which terms are specific to the particular contract. Are they those terms which are specific to the 'ordinary' contract between banker and customer?

The second test

7.47 It has been emphasized that the term should be 'necessary' (*Liverpool City Council* v *Irwin* (1976); *Tai Hing Cotton Mill Ltd* v *Liu Chong Hing Bank Ltd* (1985)), and that is understandable: the courts would not want to be seen to be too readily making an implication which is not based on the parties' intentions. It is, however, clear that this reference to necessity is not to be equated with the traditional *Moorcock* test, for implication in fact, as to whether the term is 'necessary' to give the contract 'business efficacy' (*The Moorcock* (1889)). In *Scally* v *Southern Health and Social Services Board* [1991] 4 All ER 563, Lord Bridge said (at 571):

> A clear distinction is drawn ... between the search for an implied term necessary to give business efficacy to a particular contract, and the search, based on wider considerations for a term which the law will imply as a necessary incident of a definable category of contractual relationship.

The distinction is important: it is the 'wider considerations' which must be emphasized, rather than 'necessity'.

7.48 In *Crossley* v *Faithful & Gould* (2004), referring to Peden (2001), Dyson LJ gave clearer recognition to what is occurring when a term is implied in law. He stated (at [36]):

> It seems to me that rather than focus on the narrow concept of necessity, it is better to recognise that to some extent at least, the existence and scope of standardised implied terms raise questions of reasonableness, fairness and the balancing of competing policy considerations.

'There is much to be said for that approach' (*Société Générale* v *Geys* (2012) at [56]). A term implied in law is based on an 'ought': it is a matter of what should be present in the 'type' of contract, rather than what the parties can be found to have intended. If that 'ought' means that a term should be present, then the term is necessary to effectuate the 'ought'. It is a 'necessary incident' of the category of contract. Necessity is, indeed, not what should be focused on. What is important is the difficult question of determining the 'ought', which will vary from one 'type' of contract to another, and in relation to the problem for that 'type' of contract. It is not surprising that the generation of the 'ought' is expressed in vague terms such as 'fairness, reasonableness, and competing policy considerations', or 'justice and [s] ocial policy' (*The Star Texas* [1993] 2 Lloyd's Rep 445 at 526). Further, it can be emphasized that there is usually 'some justice on each side' of a case where a term implied in law is in question,[14] so that what is generally of concern is, indeed, the 'balancing of competing policy considerations' (Peden at 467). It is plain that implying a previously unrecognized term in law will rarely be simple.

7.49 In *Malik* v *BCCI* [1997] 3 All ER 1 it was also recognized that the considerations which will be relevant to an implication in law will change over time, with changing social attitudes. In that case, the House of Lords accepted that there should be implied into contracts of employment a term that both parties would not engage in conduct likely to undermine the trust and confidence required if the employment relationship was to continue. They saw such implication as part of the 'history of the development of employment law in this century' (at 15). They recognized the

> [c]hanges which have taken place in the employer/employee relationship, with far greater duties imposed on the employer than in the past whether by statute or by judicial decision, to care for the physical, financial and even psychological welfare of the employee. ([1997] 3 All ER 1 at 15, quoting *Spring* v *Guardian Assurance plc* [1994] 3 All ER 129 at 161 per Lord Slynn)

The term was regarded as making little difference to the obligations of employees, who had long been seen as under obligations to serve their employers loyally and not to act contrary to their business. Its importance was perceived to be in its impact upon the employer's obligations. The term was regarded as 'apt to cover the great diversity of situations in which a balance has to be struck between an employer's interest in managing his business as he sees fit and the employee's interest in not being unfairly and improperly exploited' ([1997] 3 All ER 1 at 15–16 per Lord Steyn).

7.50 At times, broad considerations of justice and social policy may lead to the conclusion that a term should be implied but the courts will, nevertheless, refuse to imply a term on the basis that the issue is not one which can appropriately be dealt with in that way. Public policy was looked at in *Reid* v *Rush & Tompkins Group plc* [1990] 1 WLR 212 and the implication of a term was viewed as desirable, but the issue was regarded as too complex for the courts to deal with by such means. It was said (at 220):

> As to treating such a term as implied by law, the arguments in favour of a social policy, which would require employers to provide some level of personal accident insurance for the benefit of men and women working overseas, and for their dependants, are obvious but there appears to be no way in which the court could 'embody this policy in the law without the assistance of the legislature'.

14 T. D. Rakoff, 'The Implied Terms of Contracts: Of "Default Rules" and "Situation-Sense"' in J. Beatson and D. Friedmann (eds), *Good Faith and Fault in Contract Law*, Oxford University Press, 1995, p. 198.

7.51 The final point to consider here is that, as has been indicated, it may be necessary to consider an interaction between the width of the 'type' of contract, identified in the first test, and the issue of whether the second test is satisfied. This is exemplified by *Scally* v *Southern Health and Social Services Board* [1991] 4 All ER 563. *Scally* was concerned with doctors' contracts of employment. They included a contributory pension scheme which required 40 years' contribution for maximum benefit. However, the terms were varied to give the employees an opportunity, for a limited period, to purchase extra years of contribution to make their pensions equivalent to one based on 40 years' service, if the employees would not achieve that period of actual service. The problem arose because the claimants were not informed of that opportunity and did not exercise their right. The question was whether there was an implied term in the contract requiring the employer to give notice of that opportunity. It was held that a term requiring notice could be implied in law. The contracts in which such an implication would be made were of a carefully stated 'defined type'. Lord Bridge said (at 571):

> I would define it as the relationship of employer and employee where the following circumstances obtain: (1) the terms of the contract of employment have not been negotiated with the individual employee but result from negotiation with a representative body or are otherwise incorporated by reference; (2) a particular term of the contract makes available to the employee a valuable right contingent upon action being taken by him to avail himself of its benefit; (3) the employee cannot, in all the circumstances, reasonably be expected to be aware of the term unless it is drawn to his attention.

Stating the type of contract into which the term would be implied in this narrow way limited the impact upon contracts of employment more generally of implying such a term in law. In stating this limited 'type' of contract, Lord Bridge recognized that at first instance 'Carswell J accepted the submission that any formulation of an implied term of this kind must be too wide in its ambit to be acceptable as of general application'. Policy issues as to the 'acceptability' of implying a term were dealt with by a narrow statement of the contracts into which it would be implied. In contrast, in *Crossley* v *Faithful & Gould* [2004] 4 All ER 447 at [43] the Court of Appeal denied the implication into contracts of employment generally of the much broader term that the employer will take reasonable care of the economic well-being of the employee. The term was viewed as one which would impose an 'unfair and unreasonable burden on employers'.

Terms implied by custom

7.52 There may be contractual terms which are implied on the basis that they are customary in a particular trade, profession, or locality.[15] In *Hutton* v *Warren* (1836) 1 M & W 466:

> The tenant of a farm was given notice to quit by the landlord. He had worked and planted the land and the landlord would obtain the benefit of that when the tenant left. It was held that the tenant was entitled to an allowance for the seeds and labour on leaving. There was no express term to that effect, but he was so entitled on the basis of a local custom.

15 See, e.g., *National Bank of Greece SA* v *Pinios Shipping Co.* (1990).

Baron Parke indicated the rationale of implying terms on the basis of custom. He said (at 475):

> It has long been settled that, in commercial transactions, extrinsic evidence of custom and usage is admissible to annex incidents to written contracts, in matters with respect to which they are silent. The same rule has also been applied to contracts in other transactions of life, in which known usages have been established and prevailed; and this has been done upon the principle of presumption that, in such transactions, the parties did not mean to express in writing the whole of the contract by which they intended to be bound, but to contract with reference to those known usages.

However, despite the reference to intention by Baron Parke, the situation is more akin to terms implied in law than to terms implied on the basis of the parties' intention (i.e. terms implied in fact). Terms implied by custom are implied on the basis that the contract is of a certain type and there is a custom which implies certain terms into contracts of that type. Also, as with terms implied in law, the intention of the parties is only of limited relevance. Here, the term will be excluded if the contract evidences a contrary intention:

> An alleged custom can be imported into a contract only if there is nothing in the express or necessarily implied terms of the contract to prevent such inclusion and further that a custom will only be imported into a contract where it can be so imported consistently with the tenor of the documents as a whole. (*London Export Corpn Ltd* v *Jubilee Coffee Roasting Co* [1958] 1 WLR 661 at 675 per Lord Jenkins)

In *Walford's* case (*Affréteurs Réunis SA* v *Walford* (1919)), for example, a custom that a broker's commission was payable only when hire was earned under a charter could not be implied into a contract with an express term stating that the owners were to pay commission on the signing of a charter.

7.53 It is not easy to establish the existence of a particular custom or usage. It has been said that it must be:

> certain, in the sense that the practice is clearly established; it must be notorious, in the sense that it is so well known in the market in which it is alleged to exist, that those who conduct business in the market contract with the usage as an implied term; and it must be reasonable. (*Cunliffe-Owen* v *Teather & Greenwood* [1967] 1 WLR 1421 at 1438 per Ungoed Thomas J)

More recently, the House of Lords has viewed the situation as requiring 'evidence of a universal and acknowledged practice of the market' (*Baker* v *Black Sea and Baltic General Insurance Ltd* [1998] 2 All ER 833 at 842). If a custom is unreasonable, 'the courts have said that they will not recognise it as binding on people who do not know of it and who have not consented to act upon it' (*Perry* v *Barnett* (1885) 15 QBD 388 at 393 per Brett MR).

Summary

The first part of the chapter is concerned with express spoken terms.

- What is said before the contract is made may become express terms of the contract.
- The basic test is the intention of the parties, that is, did the parties intend the statement to be a term?—*Heilbut, Symons & Co.* v *Buckleton* (1913).
- The test is objective, not subjective.
- The courts have identified indicators of the parties' intentions:
  - importance of the statement: was it clear to both parties that the statement was important in the contract being made (e.g. *Bannerman* v *White* (1861))?
  - reliance: did one party make it clear that the other was intended to rely upon his statement (e.g. *Schawel* v *Reade* (1913))?
  - relative knowledge of the parties: did one party have more knowledge/expertise in relation to the subject matter of the statement so that he would have been more likely to have taken upon him(her)self the risk of it being untrue (e.g. *Dick Bentley Productions* v *Harold Smith Motors* (1965))?
- It has been stated as a 'rule' that 'parol evidence' cannot be admitted to show that there are terms additional to those contained within a written agreement. However, this has been seen not as a rule but simply as a circular statement—a written agreement which looks like a complete contract leads to the presumption that it is, but the presumption can be rebutted and if it is shown that other terms were intended then evidence of them will be admitted. Even if the 'parol evidence rule' has some substance as a rule, there are so many exceptions that it is unlikely to work injustice.
- A statement may be found to be part of a collateral contract, rather than the main contract. This device is usually used to avoid some difficulty in finding it is part of the main contract, such as formalities or the privity rule.

The second part of the chapter is concerned with implied terms.

- There are three sorts of implied terms at common law:
  - terms implied in fact
  - terms implied in law
  - terms implied by custom.
- There are also terms implied by statute.
- Terms implied in fact are derived from the objective intention of the parties but traditionally there has not been a simple test of the intention of the parties applied to ascertain them.
- Traditionally, the 'business efficacy' test from *The Moorcock* (1889) and the 'officious bystander' test from *Shirlaw* v *Southern Foundries* (1939) have been applied.
- These restrictive tests have been applied, rather than simply the intention test, to confine terms implied in fact to the least disputable possible terms, so that the courts can make it clear that they are not rewriting/improving the parties' bargain.

- In *Attorney General of Belize* v *Belize Telecom* (2009), a Privy Council case, Lord Hoffmann linked interpretation and implication of terms in fact, and has indicated a change to a test simply based upon a search for the parties' (objective) intentions: 'what the instrument, read as a whole against the relevant background, would reasonably be understood to mean' (at [21]).
- However, in *Marks and Spencer plc* v *BNP Paribas Securities Services Trust Company (Jersey) Ltd* (2015), the Supreme Court reasserted the 'business efficacy' and the 'officious bystander' tests, and disposed of the idea that the implication of terms in fact is to be treated in the same way as construing the written terms.
- Terms implied in law are not based on the intention of the parties—*Liverpool City Council* v *Irwin* (1976).
- The intention of the parties is only relevant to the extent that a term will not be implied in law if there is an express contrary term.
- There is a two-stage test for terms implied in law:
  - First, the contract in which it is sought to imply a term must be a type of contract, not a one-off contract.
  - The second test has traditionally been put in terms of whether it is 'necessary' to imply the term, for example, *Tai Hing Cotton Mill* v *Liu Chon Hing Bank* (1985).
- However, the courts have taken into account factors which do not come within any normal use of the term 'necessary' and they may now be starting to recognize that the second test is a more broadly based policy question: see, for example, *Crossley* v *Faithful & Gould* (2004)—'questions of reasonableness, fairness and the balancing of competing policy considerations'.
- Terms may be implied on the basis that they are customary in a particular trade, profession, or locality.
- Terms will not be implied on the basis of custom if the contract evidences a contrary intention.
- It is difficult to establish the existence of a relevant custom.

Further reading

R. D. Atkins, 'Contract Classification and the Implications of Change: Software, Computers and the Law of Implied Terms' (2013) 30(2) JCL 156

R. Hooley, 'Implied Terms after Belize Telecom' (2014) 73(2) CLJ 315

A. Kramer, 'Implication in Fact as an Instance of Contractual Interpretation' (2004) 63 CLJ 384

Law Commission Report, No 154, 'The Law of Contract: The Parol Evidence Rule', 1986

E. Macdonald, 'Casting Aside Officious Bystanders and Business Efficacy' (2009) 26 JCL 97

J. McCaughran, 'Implied Terms: The Journey of the Man on the Clapham Omnibus' 70 (2011) CLJ 607

E. Peden, 'Policy Concerns behind Implication of Terms in Law' (2001) 117 LQR 459

K. Wedderburn, 'Collateral Contracts' (1959) 18 CLJ 58

Chapter 8

Classification of terms

Introduction

8.1 Some terms of the contract are more important than others. In particular, the breach of some terms will give the injured party the right to terminate the contract. That is a significant right for the injured party. For example, they may be able to terminate and obtain a substitute performance from elsewhere. A distinction is made between terms which are conditions, warranties, and innominate terms and, basically, the three types of term are differentiated by the legal consequences that flow from the breach of each of them. When a condition is breached the injured party has the right to sue for damages and also to terminate the contract.[1] A breach of warranty gives rise only to the right to sue for damages. When an innominate term is breached, the legal consequence of the breach depend upon its factual consequences, that is, there is a right to terminate the contract, in addition to suing for damages, only if the breach of an innominate term is such as to deprive the injured party of substantially all the benefit which he or she was intended to derive from the contract.

8.2 For a long time it was thought that terms were either conditions or warranties. That was probably due to the fact that the definitions of condition and warranty given above were only satisfactorily settled with the enactment of the Sale of Goods Act 1893, which Act referred only to conditions and warranties. It was the judgment of Diplock LJ in *Hong Kong Fir Shipping Co.* v *Kawasaki Kisen Kaisha* (1962) that made it clear that the division into conditions and warranties was not complete but had to be supplemented by the innominate term.

1 There is what may be regarded as an exception to this in s 15A of the Sale of Goods Act 1979. Under certain circumstances, breaches which would otherwise be labelled by the statute as breaches of condition are 'deemed' to be breaches of warranties. This occurs in business-to-business contracts where the breach is so slight that it would be unreasonable to reject the goods.

8.3 There is a need to be careful with terminology. The Sale of Goods Act 1893 settled the technical meaning to be given to conditions and warranties in one context (i.e. when the effect of a breach is under consideration), but the words are still used in other senses. For example, both condition and warranty may be used non-technically simply to mean a term of the contract, without it carrying any implication as to the legal consequences of a breach. Warranty is often used non-technically in that way, to mean a term, when the question being asked is whether a statement is a term or a mere representation. The words 'condition' and 'warranty' must be approached with some caution to ascertain the sense in which they are being used. That caution must be all the greater when dealing with some of the older cases decided before the enactment of the Sale of Goods Act 1893.

8.4 A further mention regarding terminology must be made, and that is the recent change introduced by virtue of the Consumer Rights Act 2015. In relation to consumers, terms (in the technical sense) are no longer classified as warranties or conditions but rather the new statute stipulates how a breach of the particular term in question will be treated. (For example, see the Consumer Rights Act 2015, s 42 in respect of the rights and remedies available for breach of terms pertaining to the supply of digital content.)

The test

8.5 Statute may sometimes classify a term, as in the Sale of Goods Act 1979. In other cases the question of how it is to be decided whether a term is a condition, a warranty, or an innominate term can be easily answered in theory, but its application may be more problematic as it is based upon the parties' intention (objectively ascertained, of course). The parties may have expressly classified the term;[2] otherwise the test to be applied derives from *Bentsen* v *Taylor, Sons, & Co. (No 2)* [1893] 2 QB 274. In that case, it was held that the term in the charter party describing the ship as 'now sailed or about to sail from a pitch pine port to the United Kingdom' was a condition. Such a statement provided the charterer's only basis for his calculations as to when he would be able to load the ship in the United Kingdom. It was the importance of the term to the whole charter that led to its construction as a condition. In coming to that conclusion, Bowen LJ delivered what is now the classic test for distinguishing the different types of term. He said (at 281):

> There is no way of deciding that question except by looking at the contract in the light of the surrounding circumstances, and making up one's mind whether the intention of the parties, as gathered from the instrument itself, will best be carried out by treating the promise as a warranty sounding only in damages, or as a condition precedent by the failure to perform which the other party is relieved of his liability.

This provides the test for determining whether the term is a condition or a warranty, despite the reference to a 'condition precedent'—there are difficulties with terminological usage in

2 Express classification itself may not be without difficulties. See para. **8.30**ff.

this area! To that formulation of the test should now be added the third possibility: that the intention of the parties will best be carried out by classifying the term as innominate. In *Bunge Corpn* v *Tradax Export SA* (1981) (see para. **8.18**ff) the House of Lords made it clear that this is the correct approach to the classification of terms—even innominate terms. The application of this test for deciding if a term is a condition, warranty, or innominate term is considered further later.

8.6 One aspect of the classification test should be emphasized here, if the importance of the innominate term is to be understood. That aspect is the point in time against which the intention of the parties is to be assessed in determining the classification of a term. In *Bentsen* v *Taylor, Sons, & Co. (No 2)* [1893] 2 QB 274, after the dictum given earlier, Bowen LJ continued (at 81):

> One of the first things you would look to is to what extent the accuracy of the statement—the truth of what is promised—would be likely to affect the substance and foundation of the adventure which the contract is intended to carry out . . . it may well be that such a test can only be applied after getting the jury to say what the effect of a breach of such a condition would be on the substance and foundation of the adventure; not the effect of the breach which has in fact taken place, but the effect likely to be produced on the foundation of the adventure by any such breach of that portion of the contract.

As will be seen, a term is more likely to be classified as a condition if it can be regarded as an important term of the contract; and the effect of any breach of it is relevant to an assessment of its importance. However, the point to be noted here, and which Bowen LJ emphasized, is that the importance of the term is to be assessed against the effect of possible breaches rather than the actual breach. The classification of terms is based upon the intention at the time of contracting and not the time of the breach.[3] Basically, the actual breach is considered only if the term is innominate. It is then that the actual breach becomes relevant to deciding if the injured party can terminate the contract.

8.7 However, there is a statutory exception to this. The Sale of Goods Act 1979 was amended by the Sale and Supply of Goods Act 1994. A new section, s 15A, was inserted into the Sale of Goods Act 1979 and, in business-to-business sales, that section deems a breach of the conditions implied by ss 13–15 of that Act to be merely a breach of warranty where the breach is so slight that it would be unreasonable to reject the goods. This creates the exception to the point made earlier. The implied terms are generally conditions but, because they can be deemed to be merely warranties in the light of the actual breach, the actual breach is relevant to the terms' 'deemed' classification at least. Section 15A of the Sale of Goods Act 1979 is considered further later.[4]

3 Of course, the actual breach will be known to the court and, particularly prior to the identification of the innominate term, the courts have sometimes been tempted to act on the basis of hindsight. See, e.g., *Poussard* v *Spiers* (1876).

4 Similar provision is made for other supply of goods contracts, where there are similar statutorily labelled conditions, in the Sale and Supply of Goods Act 1994.

Recognition of the innominate term

8.8 In *Hong Kong Fir Shipping Co. Ltd* v *Kawasaki Kisen Kaisha Ltd* [1962] 2 QB 26 it was shown that the traditional division of terms into conditions and warranties is not complete, and that there are also innominate terms. In that case:

> The shipowner hired a ship, *The Hong Kong Fir*, to the charterer for 24 months. On a voyage to deliver coal to Osaka, the ship spent five weeks being repaired. The engines were old and needed to be well maintained by efficient staff. The engine-room staff were insufficient in number and inefficient. When the ship arrived in Osaka the engine-room staff were replaced, and a further period of 15 weeks was required to make it ready for sea again. The charterer claimed to be able to terminate the contract for failure to deliver a seaworthy ship because of the state of the engines and the inadequacy of the staff.

The shipowner sued the charterer for wrongful termination of the contract, that is, the shipowner claimed that the breach of the term that the vessel was seaworthy did not entitle the charterer to terminate the contract. Although the owner had been in breach, in failing to provide a seaworthy ship, the Court of Appeal held that the breach had not entitled the charterer to terminate. The charterer was in breach in wrongfully terminating the contract. The owner was entitled to substantial damages as the market had dropped considerably since the charter had been made.

8.9 The importance of *Hong Kong Fir Shipping Co. Ltd* lies in the treatment by Diplock LJ of the charterer's claim that seaworthiness was a condition and that, as a consequence, any breach of it entitled the charterer to terminate the contract (see also Upjohn LJ). He made it clear that whether termination was possible, for the breach of the term as to seaworthiness, did not depend upon the classification of the term as a condition or warranty but upon the factual consequences of the breach. The factual consequences of the breach determined the legal consequences. If the factual consequences were sufficiently serious, termination was possible—but not otherwise. Diplock LJ said (at 70):

> There are however many contractual undertakings of a more complex character which cannot be categorised as being 'conditions' or 'warranties' . . . Of such undertakings all that can be predicated is that some breaches will and others will not give rise to an event which will deprive the party not in default of substantially the whole benefit which it was intended that he should obtain from the contract; and the legal consequences of a breach of such an undertaking . . . depend upon the nature of the event to which the breach gives rise and do not follow automatically from a prior classification of the undertaking as a 'condition' or a 'warranty'.

The term as to seaworthiness is such that it is particularly appropriate that the legal consequences of a breach should depend upon the particular breach. It is a term which can be breached in many ways. Some of the possible defects which it encompasses are very serious whilst others may be fairly trivial. A ship will not be seaworthy 'if a nail is missing from one of the timbers of a wooden vessel or if proper medical supplies or two anchors are not on board at the time of sailing' (at 62 per Upjohn LJ). It is particularly inappropriate to label such a term as a condition or warranty from the inception of the contract. In *Hong Kong Fir* it was decided that the need for 20 weeks of repairs, and the replacement of the engine-room staff, were not sufficiently serious to give the charterer the right to terminate when the charter, the hire of the ship, was for 24 months. The breach was not one which deprived the charterer of 'substantially the whole benefit which it was the intention of the parties . . . that he should obtain' (see dictum of Diplock LJ given earlier).

8.10 If the term is an innominate or intermediate term, what is the test which is applied to determine if the breach gives the injured party a right to terminate as well as to claim damages? What makes the breach of an innominate term equivalent, in the legal result it produces, to a breach of a condition? As has been indicated, the test has been put in terms of whether the breach substantially deprives the innocent party of the whole of the benefit which he, or she, was intended to derive from the contract (see also *Bunge Corpn* v *Tradax Export SA* (1981)). This was the formulation adopted by Diplock LJ in *Hong Kong Fir Shipping Co. Ltd* v *Kawasaki Kisen Kaisha Ltd* (1962). The test has also been put in terms of whether the breach went to the root of the contract (for example, *Cehave NV* v *Bremer Handelsgesellschaft mbH, The Hansa Nord* [1975] 3 All ER 739 at 747 per Lord Denning MR, at 757 per Roskill LJ).

Flexibility—the benefit of the innominate term classification[5]

8.11 A better understanding of the intention the parties would have had in making the contract as to the classification of a term can be ascertained if the major benefits and drawbacks of the classifications are recognized. The benefit of the innominate term classification is its flexibility, which contrasts with the fixed nature of the other classifications, where the consequences of the breach are simply determined by the classification. So, for example, if a term is a condition, then, outside the special statutory exceptions noted earlier (see further para. **8.16**ff), even a trivial breach of it will justify the innocent party in terminating. There is no necessary connection between the seriousness of the factual consequences of the breach and its legal consequences. For example, in *Arcos Ltd* v *EA Ronaasen & Son* (1933):

> There was a contract for the sale of barrel staves half an inch thick. There was held to be a breach of the condition that the goods should correspond with their description when the staves varied from that thickness by up to one-sixteenth of an inch. The variation caused no problems with their use, but this did not prevent the finding of a breach of condition.[6]

5 Brownsword (1992) JCL 83.

6 See also *Re Moore & Co. Ltd and Landauer & Co. Ltd* [1921] 2 KB 519 at [8.16].

The party in breach may lose the entire contract because of a breach of condition which has little practical effect. This is obviously not the case where the term is innominate and the factual consequences of the breach are directly related to the availability of the right to terminate. The innominate term classification allows the law to be flexible in its approach to the legal consequences of a breach.

8.12 One aspect of termination being related to the seriousness of the breach is that a minor breach cannot be used by the innocent party to escape from a contract which has ceased to be a 'good deal' from their point of view. In *Hong Kong Fir Shipping Co. Ltd* v *Kawasaki Kisen Kaisha Ltd* (1962) the owners of the vessel received substantial damages in the wake of the charterer's wrongful termination of the contract. This was because the charter market had dropped. Any substitute charter had to be at a much lower rate than that provided for by the relevant contract. The drop in the market probably explains why the charterer was eager to claim to be entitled to terminate the contract. By the time he did so he could get another ship more cheaply. Had the term been a condition, the charterer could have escaped from the contract and hired another ship more cheaply. This would have defeated part of the object of the contract, the allocation of the risk of market changes for the period of the charter. The flexibility of the innominate term classification prevents a minor breach from being used in this way.

8.13 *Cehave NV* v *Bremer Handelsgesellschaft mbH, The Hansa Nord* (1975) provides a good example of the benefits of the flexibility of the innominate term. The facts were as follows:

> A German company had contracted to sell citrus pulp pellets to a Dutch company for about £100,000. The pellets had to come from Florida and it was a term of the contract that they should be shipped 'in good condition'. On arrival it was discovered that some of the pellets had been damaged by overheating, and by that time the market price for sound goods had dropped to about £86,000. The purchasers refused to take delivery and claimed to be entitled to terminate the contract on the basis that the goods had not been shipped 'in good condition' and that it was a condition of the contract that they should be. Whilst the dispute was in progress the pellets were sold to a third party for about £30,000. That third party then sold them for that same reduced price, approximately £30,000, to the original purchasers. The original purchasers were able to use them as originally intended in the manufacture of cattle food, although in slightly reduced proportions.

The Court of Appeal had to decide whether the purchasers had been correct in their claim to be able to terminate for breach of the term that the goods would be shipped 'in good condition'. It was held that the purchasers were not correct. The breach entitled them to damages but not to terminate, and they were themselves liable for wrongful termination. The Court of Appeal refused to regard the term as a condition. It was a term, the legal consequences of the breach of which depended upon its factual consequences; that is, it was an innominate term. The particular breach was not sufficiently serious to give rise to the right to terminate. It did not go to the root of the contract. This was evident from the fact that the pellets had been used to make cattle food in almost exactly the same way as they would have been, had they not been damaged.

8.14 The advantages of the innominate term classification are obvious in *The Hansa Nord*. Had the term been a condition, the breach would have allowed the purchaser to terminate. This would have been his right despite the fact that the grounds for his decision to terminate were obviously purely pecuniary, rather than based on the actual breach. The damage to the goods barely affected the purchaser's use of them. The flexibility provided by the innominate term classification allowed the court to look at the seriousness of the breach to determine the availability of a right to terminate.[7]

8.15 The attempt to avoid trivial breaches giving rise to the right to terminate can also be seen in other situations. As has already been indicated, the legal effect of breaches of the conditions implied by Sale of Goods Act 1979, ss 13–15 has been modified by a new s 15A, inserted by the Sale and Supply of Goods Act 1994. In business-to-business contracts, where the breach is so slight that it would be unreasonable for the buyer to reject, the term is deemed not to be a condition but a warranty, and the buyer cannot reject the goods but has only a right to claim damages. Before the amendment made by the Sale and Supply of Goods Act 1994, the implied terms always remained conditions in the full sense and the buyer had a right to reject the goods for any breach, even the most trivial. *Re Moore & Co. Ltd and Landauer & Co. Ltd* (1921) provides an example. In that case:

> The contract concerned the sale of tinned fruit. The tins were stated to be packed in cases containing 30 tins each. The correct number of tins was delivered, but they were packed in cases containing 24 tins each.

The court held that the difference in the number of tins per case meant that there was a breach of the statutorily implied condition that the goods should correspond with their description.

8.16 It was in keeping with the post-*Hong Kong Fir* approach that the Law Commission should recommend that, in contracts between business people, a breach of the implied conditions in the Sale of Goods Act 1979 should cease to give rise to an automatic right to terminate, however trivial the breach (Law Com No 160, Cmnd 137, 1987). In relation to contracts between business people, the Law Commission recommended that a breach of such a term should be treated as a breach of warranty where the breach is so slight that it would be unreasonable for the buyer to terminate. It was this recommendation which led to the enactment of the Sale and Supply of Goods Act 1994 and the addition of s 15A to the Sale of Goods Act 1979, modifying the legal effect of breach of the conditions implied by ss 13–15 of that Act. This does not equate such terms with innominate terms, as the right to terminate is absent only if the breach is fairly minor. If a term is innominate, the right to terminate is present only if the breach is serious. The emphasis is different, but the changes in the law moved the sale of goods legislation more into line with the flexible *Hong Kong Fir* approach which links the availability of the right to terminate to the seriousness of the factual consequences of the breach.

7 But see A. Weir, 'The Buyer's Right to Reject Defective Goods' [1976] CLJ 33.

Conditions and the benefit of certainty

8.17 As we have seen, the benefit of the innominate term classification is its flexibility—matching the availability of the right to terminate with the seriousness of the breach. The desirability of such flexibility will indicate that the parties intended a term to be innominate. However, a condition is not merely inflexible; it also has the benefit of certainty, and the situation may be one in which the parties would have desired that certainty and the indications will then be of a condition classification.

8.18 However, initially after the development of the innominate term approach in *Hong Kong Fir Shipping Co. Ltd* v *Kawasaki Kisen Kaisha Ltd* (1962) the argument arose that, in the absence of a label being placed on a term expressly by the parties or by statute, the classification of the term depended entirely upon the factual effects of the breach. In other words, the argument was that, in the absence of an express classification, all terms were innominate and a breach gave rise to the right to terminate only if it deprived the innocent party of substantially all the benefit that it was intended he or she should derive from the contract. This argument was dismissed by the House of Lords in *Bunge Corpn* v *Tradax Export SA* (1981),[8] where it was affirmed that the question whether the breach is such as substantially to deprive the innocent party of all the benefit it was intended that he or she should derive from the contract is relevant only after it has been decided that the term is innominate. The first question which must be asked is what sort of a term it is, that is, a condition, a warranty, or an innominate term. If the term has not been labelled by statute or expressly by the parties, the test is that stated by Bowen LJ in *Bentsen* v *Taylor, Sons & Co. (No 2)* [1893] 2 QB 274 at 281 (see para. **8.5**), that is, which classification will fulfil the intention of the parties.

8.19 In *Bunge Corpn* v *Tradax Export SA* [1981] 1 WLR 711 the term in question was found to be a condition despite the lack of any statutory or express classification. In that case:

> The contract concerned the sale of soya bean meal. The meal was to be shipped by the end of June 1975. By cl 7 the buyers had to give the sellers at least 15 days' notice of the probable readiness of the vessel to load the meal. The 15 days were to allow the sellers time to nominate a loading port and make sure the meal could be shipped from there at the appropriate time. The buyers gave notice on 17 June. The last shipment day within the contract was 30 June, and the notice provided less than the required 15-day interval. The sellers claimed to terminate the contract. The buyers disputed that termination.

The House of Lords held that cl 7 was a condition of the contract and breach of it gave the sellers the automatic right to terminate, whatever the factual consequences of that breach. Lord Roskill said (at 727):

> While recognising the modern approach and not being over-ready to construe terms as conditions unless the contract clearly requires the court so to do, none the less the basic principles of construction for determining whether or not a particular term is a condition remain as

8 See also *Maredelanto Compania Naviera SA v Bergbau-Handel GmbH, The Mihalis Angelos* (1971).

> before, always bearing in mind on the one hand the need for certainty and on the other the desirability of not, when legitimate, allowing rescission where the breach complained of is highly technical and where damages would clearly be an adequate remedy.

In *Bunge Corpn* the court was dealing with a time clause in a mercantile contract, and this indicated the need for the certainty obtained by classifying the term as a condition; that is, if the term is a condition, the innocent party knows that he or she has the right to terminate upon any breach of that term and can do so immediately and can quickly try to find a substitute contract. The injured party does not have to weigh up the seriousness of the consequences of the breach to see if he or she can terminate. If the term was innominate, the injured party might decide that it was necessary to wait to see further what the actual consequences of the breach were before risking claiming to be able to terminate.

8.20 Beyond the simple fact that the clause was a time clause in a mercantile contract, there were other factors pointing to the clause being a condition in *Bunge Corpn*. First, the contract was one of a chain of sales of the soya bean meal. Timely performance is obviously all the more important where a whole chain of sales is involved. Secondly, the sellers had to act upon the buyers' notification; they had to nominate a suitable port and ensure that the soya bean meal could be shipped from there on time. The dependence of the sellers' performance upon the buyers' timely notification indicated that the sellers should be able to terminate for any breach of the time clause.

Classification of terms not expressly labelled by the parties

8.21 The general impetus is towards the labelling of terms as innominate rather than as conditions because of the flexibility provided by that classification, but in 'suitable cases' conditions will be found:

> It remains true, as Lord Roskill said in *Cehave NV* v *Bremer Handelsgesellschaft mbH, The Hansa Nord*, that the courts should not be too ready to interpret contractual clauses as conditions. And I have myself commended, and continue to commend, the greater flexibility in the law of contracts to which *Hong Kong Fir* points the way . . . But I do not doubt that in suitable cases, the courts should not be reluctant, if the intention of the parties as shown by the contract so indicates, to hold that an obligation has the force of a condition and that indeed they should usually do so in the case of time clauses in mercantile contracts. (Lord Wilberforce in *Bunge Corpn* v *Tradax Export SA* [1981] 1 WLR 711 at 715–16)

8.22 Before addressing ourselves to what constitutes a 'suitable case', it is worth noting that the question is basically whether the term is a condition or an innominate term. The warranty label is unlikely to be used in the absence of a clear express, or statutory, classification (e.g. Sale of Goods Act 1979, s 12(2)). The innominate term classification will be used instead. It does not matter if most breaches of the term in question would have minor factual consequences; they will give rise only to the right to damages and not to the right to terminate, but the innominate term classification also allows for termination in the odd case where the breach has very serious consequences (*Re Olympia and York Canary Wharf Ltd (No 2)* [1993] BCC 159 at 166–7).

8.23 In *Bunge Corpn* v *Tradax Export SA* [1981] 1 WLR 711 Lord Wilberforce distinguished the time clause in that case, and the seaworthiness clause in *Hong Kong Fir Shipping Co. Ltd* v *Kawasaki Kisen Kaisha Ltd* (1962). He pointed out (at 715) that a term as to seaworthiness can be breached in many different ways:

> the breaches which might occur of the [seaworthiness clause are] various. They might be extremely trivial, the omission of a nail; they might be extremely grave, a serious defect in the hull or in the machinery.

He considered that this made the term one in which it was appropriate for the legal consequences of the breach to depend upon the factual consequences. A time clause was 'totally different in character . . . As to such a clause there is only one kind of breach possible, namely to be late.'

8.24 However, although a clause such as that in *Hong Kong Fir* can be breached in many different ways, and will usually be appropriately classified as an innominate term, the jump cannot be made from that conclusion to stating that a term which can be breached in only one way will normally be classified as a condition or a warranty. Even though a term may be breached in only one way, for example by being late, it will normally be capable of being breached to different degrees and there may be variations in the seriousness of the consequences which flow from any breach. An exception to this would seem to be in relation to an agreement to sell goods where the purported seller does not have title to the goods. In *Barber* v *NWS Bank plc* [1996] 1 All ER 906 the court had to consider the classification of an express term of a conditional sale agreement that, at the time the contract was made, the supplier was the owner of the goods. That was not the case, as the goods were still subject to an earlier hire purchase agreement, and the court found that the term was a condition, enabling the purchaser to terminate the contract. The view was taken that the term was distinguishable from those which admit 'of different breaches, some of which are trivial' (at 911). All breaches of the term were viewed as sufficiently serious to justify termination and, thus, the term had to be classified as a condition.

8.25 It should be emphasized that the question of classification is a matter of the parties' intention. However, as we have seen, the starting point should favour the innominate term and the basic question should be whether there is a reason to classify the term as a condition rather than as an innominate term. The basic pointers to a term being a condition are that the term is important to the contract as a whole and that certainty is required. The need for certainty, as an indicator of the intention that the term should be a condition, was referred to in *Bunge Corpn* v *Tradax Export SA* (1981) (see para. **8.19**) and reference to the importance of the term is well established (e.g. *Bentsen* v *Taylor, Sons & Co. (No 2)* [1893] 2 QB 274 at 281 per Bowen LJ (see para. **8.5**)). The more important a term is perceived to be to the substance of the contract, the more likely it is to be found that it was intended to be a condition (see also *Glaholm* v *Hays* (1841) 2 Man & G 257 at 266). Consideration of the importance of the term, in deciding upon its classification, has been put in terms of its 'commercial significance' (see *State Trading Corpn of India* v *M Golodetz Ltd* (1989) at para. **8.28**)—but the same point is being made. Although the main indicators of whether a term is to be construed as a condition are the importance of the term and the need for certainty, each case must be assessed as a whole to determine the parties' intention.

8.26 In *Bunge Corpn* the House of Lords indicated that time clauses in mercantile contracts will normally be conditions because of the need for certainty. Consideration of time clauses will illustrate how the need for certainty and the importance of the term, or otherwise, aid its classification.

8.27 A time clause had to be considered in *Compagnie Commerciale Sucres et Denrées* v *C Czarnikow Ltd, The Naxos* (1990):

> There was a contract for the sale of sugar. Delivery was to be to a vessel which was to be ready to load during May or June. The buyer was to give the seller not less than 14 days' notice of expected readiness to load. By rule 14 of the standard term contract the buyer was entitled to call for delivery at any time within the contract period, provided he had given the requisite notice. The buyers gave the requisite notice for loading on 29 May. The sellers did not have the sugar ready to load on 29 May; on 3 June, having warned the sellers, the buyers terminated the contract and purchased a replacement cargo.

The House of Lords had to decide whether rule 14 was a condition giving the buyers the right to terminate when the sellers failed to deliver on the date specified for loading. The House of Lords held (Lord Brandon dissenting) that rule 14 was a condition and the buyers had been entitled to terminate. The clause was a time clause in a mercantile contract, but there were also more specific indications that the term was to be construed as a condition. The court found that compliance with the time clause was 'crucially important' to the buyers. Had there been no delay it would, in turn, have enabled the buyers punctually to perform their own obligations to their customers. The situation was, as in *Bunge Corpn* v *Tradax Export SA* (1981), that of a chain of sales.

8.28 Of course, time clauses in mercantile contracts will not always be construed as conditions. The situation as a whole must be considered. In *State Trading Corpn of India* v *M Golodetz Ltd* [1989] 2 Lloyd's Rep 277, Kerr LJ said (at 283):

> At the end of the day, if there is no other more specific guide to the correct solution to a particular dispute, the court may have no alternative but to follow the general statement of Bowen LJ in *Bentsen* v *Taylor* . . . by making what is in effect a value judgment about the commercial significance of the term in question.

In that case the term in question contained a time limit and the contract was mercantile, but its 'commercial significance', or importance to the contract as a whole, meant that it was not construed as a condition. In that case:

> The contract was for the sale of a cargo of sugar. The sugar was to be paid for by a letter of credit, which the buyers undertook to open within seven days. The sellers undertook to open two guarantees within seven days—one in respect of the sugar sale and the other in respect of another undertaking which they had made, to purchase from the buyers, within six months, goods to the value of 60 per cent of the sugar contract.

The Court of Appeal was asked to decide whether the provision of the second guarantee, the countertrade guarantee, within seven days was a condition of the contract. It was held that it was not. The 'commercial significance of the term' indicated that it should not be treated as a condition. It did not affect the buyer's performance of the sugar contract. It was a time clause, but it did not relate to the main and immediate transaction, only to one which was to occur within six months. It was also relatively unimportant in financial terms. The more important guarantee was that relating to performance of the sugar contract, and the timely giving of that guarantee was expressly prevented from being a condition. It was felt that the provision of the countertrade guarantee, within seven days, could not be a condition when the undertaking to provide a guarantee of the sugar contract was much more important to the contract, and was not a condition.

8.29 A time clause may be such that it does not require the certainty of the 'condition' label. A time clause was not construed as a condition in *Bremer Handelsgesellschaft mbH* v *Vanden Avenne-Izegem PVBA* (1978) because the clause did not set a definite time limit. The clause in question stated that the sellers were to advise the buyers 'without delay' if shipment had become impossible for any one of a number of stated reasons. The question was whether it was a condition that such notification be made 'without delay'. Without a quantification of delay in terms of a stated time period, the House of Lords did not think that the term was to be construed as a condition. It was an innominate term. Similarly, 'as soon as reasonably practicable' was too indefinite to be construed as a condition in *British and Commonwealth Holdings plc* v *Quadrex Holdings Inc.* (1989). In that case the contract was for the sale of shares in an unquoted private company trading in a very volatile sector. The possibility of changes in the value of the shares would have made the time of completion of the sale a condition had it been more specific. However, it must be remembered that the parties may have intended a term which looks indefinite to be a condition. For example, a term requiring notice 'as soon as possible' might be construed as a condition if it was seen as very important to the contract. Such a conclusion would be assisted if trade practice made it possible to read 'as soon as possible' as the more specific 'within 24 hours' (see *Société Italo-Belge pour le Commerce et l'Industrie SA* v *Palm and Vegetable Oils (Malaysia) Sdn Bhd* (1981)).

Express classification

8.30 The parties can expressly make a term a condition, in the technical sense of that word, so that any breach of it, no matter how trivial, gives rise to the right to terminate. However, the word 'condition' may be used in many different senses and a court may decide that it is not being used in its technical sense to indicate that a breach is to give the right to terminate. In particular, they will be slow to find that it has been used in that sense where they are faced with a term which could obviously be breached in trivial ways. If finding that a term is a condition in the technical sense will lead to an unreasonable result, the courts will regard it as unlikely that the parties intended that and will need the term to be very clearly drafted to be convinced that such a result was intended.

8.31 In *L Schuler AG* v *Wickman Machine Tool Sales Ltd* [1973] 2 All ER 39, the word 'condition' was used in relation to a term but it was not construed in its technical sense. In that case:

> Schuler, a German manufacturing company, made an agreement with Wickman for Wickman to have the sole right to sell Schuler's goods in the UK for about four and a half years. The agreement contained provisions relating to the promotion of Schuler's goods by Wickman. Clause 7 stated that it was a 'condition' that one of two named representatives of Wickman should visit six named UK automobile manufacturers each week. Clause 11 laid out the procedure for termination of the contract upon a 'material breach' of the contract occurring, that is, notice was to be given to remedy it within 60 days and if it was not remedied the contract could be terminated. In breach of clause 7, Wickman failed to carry out all of the specified visits to the six named automobile manufacturers.

Schuler argued that clause 7 was expressly made a condition of the contract and thus there was a right to terminate the contract for any breach of it, no matter how trivial. Schuler argued that even one failure to visit, out of the 1,400 visits required during the course of the contract, gave them the right to terminate. The House of Lords (Lord Wilberforce dissenting) refused to accept that argument. It pointed out that the word 'condition' had many meanings other than its technical one. In addition, their Lordships thought that a construction was to be avoided if it produced an unreasonable result, and there was an alternative construction available which did not. The court thought it would be unreasonable if any single breach of clause 7 gave the right to terminate, no matter how little at fault Wickman had been. The alternative found by the court to help it avoid that unreasonable result was to link clause 7 with clause 11. The use of the word 'condition' in clause 7 was construed as relating to whether the breach was 'material' within clause 11.

8.32 Lord Reid thought that the use of the word 'condition' was a 'strong indication' that the parties intended termination to be available on any breach of clause 7, but (at 45):

> The fact that a particular construction leads to a very unreasonable result must be a relevant consideration. The more unreasonable the result the more unlikely it is that the parties can have intended it, and if they do intend it the more necessary it is that they should make that intention abundantly clear.

Any intention to use 'condition' in its technical sense had not been made clear enough, under the circumstances, for Lord Reid and the other members of the majority in the House of Lords.

8.33 However, Lord Wilberforce thought that 'condition' should have been construed technically. He gave little weight to the argument that such a construction was to be avoided on the grounds that it produced an unreasonable result. He said (at 55):

> to call the clause arbitrary, capricious, or fantastic, or to introduce as a test of its validity the ubiquitous reasonable man . . . is to assume, contrary to the evidence, that both parties to this contract adopted a standard of easygoing tolerance rather than one of aggressive, insistent punctuality and efficiency. This is not an assumption which I am prepared to make, nor do I think myself entitled to impose the former standard on the parties if their words indicate, as they plainly do, the latter.

8.34 The initial reaction to the construction put upon the word 'condition' in *L Schuler AG* v *Wickman Machine Tool Sales Ltd* (1973) might be that if the parties want to make it clear that they intend a term to be a condition in the technical sense, they should specify that breach of it is to give rise to the right to terminate. However, that may not be sufficient when unreasonable results are in issue. The express statement of a right to terminate may be seen simply as an express right to terminate, rather than as making clear that the term is a technical condition. (Obviously, this does give the injured party the right to terminate, but damages will be different from what they would be if the term was technically a condition. They will not encompass the loss of the rest of the contract (see, for example, *Financings Ltd* v *Baldock* (1963)).)

8.35 However, it may be made clear that terms are technical conditions. In *Lombard North Central plc* v *Butterworth* (1987) there was a term stating that time was 'of the essence' in relation to the payment of each of the 19 instalments due under what was, in effect, a hire purchase contract. The Court of Appeal held that the phrase 'time of the essence' was so well established as meaning that a time term was a technical condition, that they had to interpret it as such.

Summary

- Not all contract terms are of equal importance.
- Terms may be conditions, warranties, or innominate.
- The breach of any term gives a right to damages.
- The classification of terms as conditions, warranties, or innominate terms is of significance when the injured party's right to terminate for breach is in question.
  - Any breach of condition gives the right to the injured party to terminate.
  - A breach of a warranty does not give the injured party the right to terminate.
  - A breach of an innominate term gives the injured party the right to terminate if the breach is such as to deprive the injured part of substantially all the benefit he or she was intended to derive from the contract (*Hong Kong Fir* (1962)).

- Determining whether a term is a condition, warranty, or innominate is a matter of the (objective) intention of the parties at the time the contract was made (*Bentsen* v *Taylor, Sons & Co. (No 2)* (1893); *Bunge* v *Tradax* (1981)).
- In deciding what classification of a term the parties would have intended when the contract was made, it is relevant to consider the benefits and drawbacks of the classification.
- There is an impetus to classify a term as innominate, because it has the benefit of flexibility, providing some correlation between the seriousness of the breach and the availability of the right to terminate.
- Some terms may be important to the contract and require the benefit of the certainty of the condition classification.
- The parties may themselves state that a term is a condition. However, the word 'condition' has many meanings. The courts will be slow to find that the parties intended the technical meaning here considered if that would lead to an unreasonable result (for example, *Schuler* v *Wickman* (1973)).

Further reading

R. Brownsword, 'Retrieving Reasons, Retrieving Rationality? A New Look at the Right to Withdraw for Breach of Contract' (1992) 5 JCL 83

J. W. Carter, 'Intermediate Terms Arrive in Australia and Singapore' (2008) 24 JCL 226

G. H. Treitel, '"Conditions" and "Conditions Precedent"' (1990) 106 LQR 185

G. H. Treitel, 'Types of Contractual Terms' in G. Treitel, *Some Landmarks of Twentieth Century Contract Law*, Clarendon Press, 2002, pp.103-8

S. Whittaker, 'Termination Clauses' in A. Burrows and E. Peel (eds), *Contract Terms*, Oxford University Press, 2007, pp. 277–83

Chapter 9

Exemption clauses

Introduction

9.1 Exemption clauses have proved to be one of the most interesting areas of contract law in recent years. It is an area which has provoked litigation and legislation, and often involves a balancing of the competing interests of protection of the consumer, and of weaker parties more generally, and freedom of contract. The main general legislation in relation to exemption clauses was the Unfair Contract Terms Act 1977 (UCTA), which is considered in detail in **Chapter 10**. For some years, this was accompanied in the consumer sphere by the Unfair Terms in Consumer Contracts Regulations 1999,[1] which overlapped with UCTA but extended to unfair terms more generally—but only in the consumer sphere—and which were an implementation of the EC Directive on Unfair Terms in Consumer Contracts (see **Chapter 11**). However, having two overlapping regimes created undesirable complexity, and the 1999 Regulations have now been replaced by the Consumer Rights Act 2015, which has also stripped from UCTA its provisions dealing with consumers and taken that role within its purview. This restricts UCTA's coverage to the business context (see **Chapters 10** and **11**). However, although there will obviously be reference to legislation, the focus of this chapter is the common law.

Definitions

9.2 At a basic level an exemption clause is one which excludes or limits, or appears to exclude or limit, liability for breach of contract, or other liability arising by way of tort, bailment, or statute. It should be noted that the exemption clause may seek to exclude a liability totally or merely to limit it. The terms 'exemption clause' and 'exclusion clause' are often loosely used to encompass both situations but, in an effort to avoid confusion, the practice adopted here is to

1 Previously the Unfair Terms in Consumer Contracts Regulations 1994.

use 'exemption clause' as a general term, encompassing both exclusion and limitation clauses. The term 'exclusion clauses' will be restricted to those clauses which remove, or purport to remove, liability. The label 'limitation clause' will be used solely for those clauses which do not remove, or purport to remove, liability entirely but, for example, restrict or purport to restrict damages payable on a breach of contract to a specified sum.[2]

9.3 Coote identified a problem with the above type of basic definition (Coote, *Exception Clauses*, Sweet & Maxwell, 1964, chs 1 and 10). An example will help to explain the difficulty. Consider the situation where X has agreed to sell goods to Y and to deliver them by a certain date. The contract contains a clause designed to prevent X having to pay damages for breach if late delivery is caused by industrial action. X may have put in a term stating that liability for late delivery is excluded where it is caused by industrial action. Alternatively, X may have specified that he is obliged to deliver by that stated date only if there is no industrial action. The same end result can be achieved by two different forms of clause. The first possible way of achieving the desired result is by using a straightforward exclusion clause. The second possibility is to use a clause which defines the initial obligation in such a way that there is no obligation to deliver by the stated time if industrial action occurs. The fact that the same result can be achieved by the two different approaches leads to the argument that an exclusion clause cannot be regarded as a distinct type of clause but merely as one of the clauses defining the obligations under the contract, whatever form it takes.[3] For the most part, the courts assume that an exclusion clause is a distinct type of clause, removing liability for breach of an existing obligation. They may even be content to regard a clause as an exclusion clause without any consideration of the fact that it is, in form, a definition of the obligation (e.g. *J Evans & Son (Portsmouth) Ltd* v *Andrea Merzario Ltd* (1976)). However, it must be borne in mind that an exclusion clause can simply be seen as part of the definition of the obligation. In particular, difficult borderline cases arise under the Unfair Contract Terms Act 1977. It is sometimes necessary to determine whether a clause should be regarded as an exclusion clause, and subject to the Act, or merely a definition of the parties' obligations, and not subject to the Act (see E. Macdonald, 'Exception Clauses: Exclusionary or Definitional? It Depends!' (2012) 29 JCL 47; J. Adams and R. Brownsword, 'The Unfair Contract Terms Act: A Decade of Discretion' (1988) 104 LQR 94).

9.4 It should be noted that this problem, in relation to the identification of exclusionary and definitional clauses, cannot arise in relation to a limitation clause. Such a clause concedes the existence of the initial obligation and merely purports to place a limitation upon what happens when that obligation is not fulfilled. It is distinct from the definition of the initial obligation. Further, in the consumer context, the problem is largely obviated by legislation that applies to terms quite generally, rather than merely exemption clauses.

2 See D. Yates, *Exclusion Clauses in Contracts*, 2nd edn, Sweet & Maxwell, 1982, pp. 33–41; and H. Beale, W. Bishop, and M. Furmston, *Contract Cases and Materials*, 5th edn, Oxford University Press, 2008, p. 975 for a more extensive breakdown of types of exemption clause.

3 For contrasting judicial approaches on this, see *Photo Production Ltd* v *Securicor Transport Ltd* [1980] AC 827 at 842–3 per Lord Wilberforce and at 851 per Lord Diplock.

Standard form contracts

9.5 Where one party has a set of standard form terms, the other party may find themselves in a 'take it or leave it' position in relation to the terms because of an inferior bargaining position; hence the alternative label of 'contracts of adhesion'. Further, long standard form contracts may well mean that that other party has no knowledge of many of the terms of the contract. In such circumstances it would hardly be surprising if the fairness of the terms was questioned, and this potential for unfairness particularly came to the fore in relation to exemption clauses.

9.6 This sort of problem led to the enactment of the Unfair Contract Terms Act 1977. The Act prevents the use of some exemption clauses entirely and renders others ineffective unless they satisfy the requirement of reasonableness. Before the Act the common law tried to respond to the problem of objectionable exemption clauses. It was possible for the courts to take a restrictive approach to the construction of an exemption clause and limit its effectiveness by finding that it did not cover the particular breach which had occurred. Similarly, the courts found some flexibility in the rules relating to incorporation of contract terms. They could find that the exemption clause was not part of the contract at all. Some of the older case law relating to exemption clauses must now be viewed with caution. The existence of the legislation means that the devices developed by the common law to deal with exemption clauses may now be used more sparingly by the courts. The legislation has the advantage that it often allows the court openly to weigh the factors indicating whether the clause is 'reasonable', or fair. Such calculations of reasonableness, or fairness, must have influenced the courts' approach to their use of the common law devices, but the question can now often be considered openly, with arguments from both sides specifically directed to it. However, it should be borne in mind that not all types of contract are subject to such legislative controls and the courts may be more willing to use the common law devices when faced with a contract which is not so covered. Of course, UCTA is now accompanied by the consumer unfair terms regime which, in its latest incarnation in the CRA, has displaced UCTA's coverage of exemption clauses in the consumer context, as well as addressing the unfairness of terms in consumer contracts more generally. Nevertheless, not all situations of unreasonable, or unfair, terms will be dealt with by legislation. Small businesses, in particular, may find themselves with little, or no, more bargaining power than a consumer when faced with the standard terms of a very large business. They have the protection of UCTA, but not of the CRA 2015.

9.7 Of course, it should not be assumed that standard form contracts are always devices for the abuse of a superior bargaining position. There are advantages to be gained from the use of standard form contracts. A standard form contract may be used to speed up the contracting process and reduce the costs involved in arriving at a concluded contract. This is desirable and, indeed, unobjectionable if the standard form contract embodies a fair bargain between the parties. The standard form may be one used throughout a particular trade, arrived at by negotiation, on equal terms, between representatives of those using it on both sides (for example, both buyers and sellers of a particular commodity, or hirers and those to whom they hire a type of equipment). Under such circumstances, the exemption clause, for example, may merely represent an allocation of risk to the person best able to insure against it. A limitation of risk may be accompanied by a low charge to the other party.

Three basic questions

9.8 When considering exemption clauses, there are three basic questions to be considered:

1. Incorporation—is the clause part of the contract?
2. Construction—is the clause appropriately worded to cover what has occurred?
3. Legislation—basically, is the clause affected by the Unfair Contract Terms Act 1977 or the legislative regime dealing with unfair terms in consumer contracts, which is now contained in UK law in the Consumer Rights Act 2015?

Questions (1) and (2) are discussed at para. **9.9**ff and para. **9.60**ff respectively. Question (3) is dealt with in **Chapters 10** and **11**.

Incorporation

Introduction

9.9 The first question to be considered is whether the exemption clause (or indeed any clause) has become a term of the contract. This is the issue of incorporation. It should be noted that the same basic rules apply to incorporation of all terms, whether or not they are exemption clauses. The discussion of incorporation largely takes place here, in the context of exemption clauses, because it is in relation to such clauses that the issue is often raised. Under consideration here are clauses in written documents; it is unlikely that an exemption clause will have simply been stated orally by one party to another, but on the question generally of whether an oral statement is a term of the contract, see para. **7.6**ff.

9.10 At first sight the question of incorporation of a clause might be thought of as an uncomplicated matter, simply requiring the determination of what the parties agreed to. Certainly, incorporation poses no problems where both parties have actual knowledge of all the terms contained in the offer which was accepted. Problems arise because there is often no actual knowledge of all the terms, and incorporation cannot be said to be based upon any simple notion of what the parties agreed to. Even when one party has been alerted that a document contains important clauses, designed to be part of the contract, he or she will not always read it. He or she may even sign it without reading it. Such signature will normally ensure that the clauses become terms of the contract even though that party has no actual knowledge of their content (see para. **9.12**ff). Incorporation of clauses from unsigned documents can also occur, even though there is no actual knowledge of their content (see para. **9.22**ff). In short, incorporation is not a matter of subjective agreement to the terms, but it is often not a search even for objective agreement to the terms in any real sense. It has become a question of whether or not the parties are to be taken to have 'agreed to' a particular set of terms according to a very artificial set of rules worked out by the court for determining the question of incorporation.

9.11 To allow incorporation without actual knowledge, and even without signature, obviously opens the way for one party to take advantage of another. This is particularly so where one party has a set of standard terms which he wishes to incorporate into each contract he makes.

This is often the case with contracts between business people and consumers, and the lack of any real opportunity to become acquainted with terms may be relevant to their reasonableness, or fairness, under the appropriate legislative regime. It could be said that if one party is not sufficiently careful of his or her own interests to inform him or herself of all the terms on which the contract is being made, then he or she cannot blame anyone else for any unacceptable terms. However, with long standard form documents it is understandable that all clauses may not be read before the document is signed and, where there has been incorporation without signature, there may not even have been knowledge of the existence of the clauses. Particularly in the business/consumer situation, there may also be a feeling that there is no point in reading the standard clauses as they will not be open to negotiation. Against this background, when the issue of incorporation has arisen, the courts have attempted to maintain some balance between the parties (see para. **9.34**ff). In other words, the cases show some reaction against the perceived unfairness produced by the basic rules on incorporation. It is also interesting to note that Atiyah has identified those basic rules as stemming from the courts' reaction to juries favouring consumers in litigation against railway companies, and the then perceived need to protect those companies.[4] However, it should again be emphasized that legislation will now often provide a direct means of attacking 'objectionable' exemption clauses and, in the consumer context, other 'unfair' clauses which have become terms of the contract.

Signature

9.12 Incorporation of a clause by signature is basically a very mechanical process. It leaves little room for any questioning of the incorporation of the clause into the contract and has the benefit of certainty. The relevant clause will be incorporated into the contract if it is contained in a contractual document which has been signed by the person seeking to deny that the clause is part of the contract. This is obviously subject to a claim of fraud, or misrepresentation, or *non est factum* but, in the absence of such a claim, signature will act to incorporate the clause whether the person signing had any knowledge of the clause or not. *L'Estrange* v *F Graucob Ltd* (1934) illustrates this point:

> Miss L'Estrange was the owner of a cafe in Llandudno. She purchased a cigarette vending machine from Graucob Ltd. The machine proved to be defective. She claimed that Graucob Ltd were in breach of an implied term that the machine was reasonably fit for its purpose. Graucob Ltd denied that any such term could be implied. They relied upon a clause in the order form, which the claimant had signed, which said 'any express or implied condition, statement, or warranty, statutory or otherwise not stated herein is hereby excluded'. This clause was in 'regrettably small print' and Miss L'Estrange had not read it and did not know of its contents.

The court decided that Miss L'Estrange's signature on the order form containing the clause meant that her total lack of awareness of the exemption clause was irrelevant. The clause

4 P. S. Atiyah, *Rise and Fall of Freedom of Contract*, Oxford University Press, 1979, p. 731.

prevented the term from being implied, and Graucob were not in breach of contract despite the defects in the vending machine.

9.13 In the case of *Grogan* v *Robin Meredith Plant Hire Ltd* (1996) it was emphasized that in order for signature to incorporate terms, the document signed must be a contractual one. Signature of a time sheet, which had an obvious and purely administrative purpose in the working of an existing contract, did not incorporate clauses printed on it as it did not 'purport to have contractual effect'. More generally, the question seems to be how the reasonable person would have viewed the document, taking account of 'the nature and purpose of the document' and the 'circumstances of its use between the parties', that is, in that context would the reasonable person have viewed it as a document intended to contain contract terms?[5] This does not make any significant inroads on the approach taken in *L'Estrange* v *F Graucob Ltd* (1934) and should be distinguished from incorporation of unsigned documents through 'reasonably sufficient notice' (see para. **9.22**ff). In the context of a signed document there is no requirement of notice. It is merely that, in the absence of knowledge, a signing party should not be contractually bound by clauses printed on what would not generally be seen as a non-contractual document.

9.14 However, misrepresentation as to the effect of the exemption clause came to the aid of the person seeking to deny the effectiveness of that clause in *Curtis* v *Chemical Cleaning and Dyeing Co. Ltd* (1951):

> Mrs Curtis took a white satin wedding dress to the defendants' shop to be cleaned. The assistant asked her to sign a document headed 'Receipt'. Mrs Curtis asked about the 'Receipt' and was told that it stated that the cleaners would not accept liability for damage to beads and sequins. The 'Receipt' actually contained a clause stating: 'This article ... is accepted on condition that the company is not liable for any damage however arising.' Owing to the cleaners' negligence the fabric of Mrs Curtis's dress was stained, but the cleaners argued that they were not liable for this damage because of the exemption clause in the 'Receipt'.

The wording of the exemption clause was very wide and could have covered damage to the fabric of the dress, but, despite Mrs Curtis's signature, the Court of Appeal held that the cleaners could not rely upon the clause to remove their liability. The contents of the exemption clause had been innocently misrepresented as confined to limiting liability for negligent damage to the beads and sequins. It could not assist them when damage had occurred to the fabric of the dress.[6]

9.15 The restrictions on the basic approach taken in *L'Estrange* v *F Graucob Ltd* (1934) are very limited, and it is a very artificial approach to determining the content of the parties' agreement. On occasion, this artificiality has been noted. In *McCutcheon* v *David MacBrayne Ltd* [1964]

5 See also *Noreside Construction* v *Irish Asphalt Ltd* (2011).

6 The basis of the conclusion in *Curtis*, and what the case should be regarded as authority for, was questioned by Rix LJ in *Axa Sun Life Services Ltd* v *Campbell Martin* (2011) at [99]–[105].

1 WLR 125 Lord Devlin considered what difference it should make whether the document in question had been signed or not. He said (at 133):

> If it were possible for your Lordships to escape from the world of make-believe which the law has created into the real world in which transactions of this sort are actually done, the answer would be short and simple. It should make no difference whatever. This sort of document is not meant to be read, still less to be understood. Its signature is in truth about as significant as a handshake that marks the formal conclusion of a bargain.[7]

It is not without irony that Lord Denning MR characterized *L'Estrange* as part of 'a bleak winter for our law of contract',[8] when, as Mr A. T. Denning, he had acted as counsel for the sellers.

9.16 Elsewhere there has been a move away from the basic approach in *L'Estrange* v *F Graucob Ltd* (1934). In the Canadian case of *Tilden Rent-A-Car Co.* v *Clendenning* (1978), unusual and onerous printed clauses were not incorporated and the line was taken that signature can only be relied upon as showing assent to a document when it is reasonable for the person relying on the signed document to believe that the signatory assented to its contents.

9.17 Here there have been suggestions that the reasoning on the 'red hand' rule in *Interfoto Picture Library Ltd* v *Stiletto Visual Programmes Ltd* (1988) in the context of incorporation by notice (see para. **9.34**ff) could provide a basis for a requirement that the signatory's attention be drawn to unusual or unreasonable clauses if they are to be incorporated by signature.[9] The 'red hand' rule mitigates the impact of the general rule—that clauses can be incorporated from unsigned documents or signs by using 'reasonably sufficient notice'—by requiring a greater degree of notice to pass that test where clauses are unusual or unreasonable. Limited support for the extension of that approach into the context of incorporation by signature might be found in an *obiter* comment made by Evans LJ in *Ocean Chemical Transport Inc.* v *Exnor Craggs Ltd* (2000) at [48]. In response to counsel's suggestion that 'the *Interfoto* test … has to be applied, even in a case where the other party has signed an acknowledgment of the terms and conditions and their incorporation', Evans LJ said it seemed to him that counsel 'could be right in what might be regarded as an extreme case, where signature was obtained under pressure of time or other circumstances'.

9.18 However, the comments of the courts more generally are against the extension of the 'red hand' rule into the context of incorporation by signature,[10] and, despite the artificialities involved in the *L'Estrange* approach, it is suggested that the line taken by the Canadian court is

7 See also *Jones* v *Northampton Borough Council* (1990) Times, 21 May, per Ralph Gibson LJ; *Levison* v *Patent Steam Cleaning Co. Ltd* [1978] QB 69 at 78 per Lord Denning MR; *Bridge* v *Campbell Discount Co. Ltd* [1962] 1 All ER 385 at 399 per Lord Denning.

8 George Mitchell (Chesterhall) Ltd v Finney Lock Seeds Ltd [1983] 1 QB 284, 297.

9 L. Rutherford and S. Wilson, 'Signature of a Document' (1998) 148 NLJ 380; A. Downes, *Textbook on Contract Law*, 5th edn, Blackstone, 1997, pp. 160–1.

10 *Yoldings Ltd* v *Swann Evans* (2000); *Jonathan Wren & Co Ltd* v *Microdec plc* (1999); *Bankway Properties Ltd* v *Penfold-Dunsford* (2001) at [41]; *HIH Casualty & General Insurance Ltd* v *New Hampshire Insurance Co.* (2001) at [209]–[213].

unlikely to be adopted here at common law. It was developed by the Canadian court at about the same time as the Unfair Contract Terms Act 1977 was introduced in the UK to deal with objectionable exemption clauses. In *Toll (FGCT) Pty Ltd.* v *Alphapharm Pty Ltd* (2004) at [48], in reasserting the *L'Estrange* approach, the High Court of Australia commented that 'as a result of' that type of legislative control 'there is no reason to depart from principle and every reason to adhere to it'.[11] It should be recognized that the *L'Estrange* approach provides a great deal of certainty in relation to the issue of incorporation, and that is very significant. In *Peninsula Business Services Ltd* v *Sweeney* (2004) at [23] the Employment Appeal Tribunal said:

> It would make for wholly unacceptable commercial uncertainty if it were open to B who has signed a written agreement to say that he was not bound by one of the terms expressly contained in it because A had not first drawn his attention expressly to it.

Also, the comment has been made that the *L'Estrange* approach is one which 'underpins the whole of commercial life; any erosion of it would have serious repercussions far beyond the business community' (*Peekay Intermark Ltd* v *Australia and New Zealand Banking Group* (2006) per Moore-Bick LJ at [43]. See also *Coys of Kensington Automobiles Ltd v Pugliese* (2011) at [40]).

9.19 One question which now arises is what will amount to a signature, to invoke the rule in *L'Estrange* v *Graucob*, when a contract is made electronically. In particular, it is controversial as to whether the action of clicking an 'I agree' button could amount to such signature. The Law Commission took a very broad approach to what should constitute a signature to satisfy statutory formality requirements:

> Digital signatures, scanned manuscript signatures, typing one's name (or initials) and clicking on a website button are, in our view, all methods of signature which are generally capable of satisfying a statutory signature requirement (*Electronic Commerce: Formal Requirements in Commercial Transactions* Advice from the Law Commission (Dec. 2001), **para. 3.29**).

Further, they concluded that, in that formalities context, clicking on a website button should be regarded as the functional equivalent to a signature on the basis that it demonstrates a validating intention and is not purely oral. They also made an analogy with the historically accepted manuscript 'X' signature, made by those who cannot sign their names in the usual manuscript form.

9.20 However, it is suggested that the everyday manuscript signature has an alerting function for the consumer, in particular, which simply clicking on a website button does not have.[12] It is a commonplace, albeit one seldom acted upon, that 'you should read a contract before signing it'. It seems unlikely that the consumer, in particular, will have that reaction before clicking the relevant button.

11 E. Peden and J. Carter, 'Incorporation of Terms by Signature: *L'Estrange* Rules' (2005) 21 JCL 1.

12 The point might be made that a typed name or a rubber stamp may constitute signature in the off-line world (e.g. *Goodman* v *Eban* (1954)) but whilst businesses may be familiar with these forms of signature, it is suggested that the consumer is not.

9.21 The rule in *L'Estrange v Graucob* is very artificial, and capable of creating considerable unfairness. That may now often be dealt with by legislation, but should we really extend that rule to this new, and very commonplace, context? Contracting by clicking such a button could be regarded as equivalent to merely stating one's agreement, and the rules about notice would then be required to be satisfied to incorporate the relevant standard terms.[13]

Notice

9.22 Unsigned documents or signs provide the main problems in relation to incorporation.[14] As there is no signature, it must be asked what other means can be used to establish that the clauses on the document or sign are part of the contract. There is no difficulty where there is actual knowledge of the clause. It will then clearly be part of the contract. It is the situation when this knowledge is absent which needs to be considered.

Timing

9.23 The first point to be made is that clauses cannot be incorporated from unsigned documents or signs if those documents or signs are not introduced into the transaction until after the contract has been concluded. Once offer and acceptance have occurred, one party cannot say to the other: 'Oh, by the way, these clauses are part of our agreement.' The contract is on the terms of the offer, which was accepted. A case which illustrates the need to ensure that the unsigned document or sign is introduced into the transaction before offer and acceptance are complete, and the contract is made, is *Olley* v *Marlborough Court Ltd* (1949). In that case:

> Mrs Olley and her husband made a contract to stay in the hotel. The contract was made at the reception desk on their arrival. They were then shown to their room. There was a sign in the room which purported to exclude the hotel's liability for the theft of guests' property unless deposited with the manageress for safekeeping. Mrs Olley returned to her room one day to discover that her furs had been stolen as a result of the hotel's negligence. The hotel sought to rely upon its exemption clause to exclude its liability for her loss.

The Court of Appeal held that the clauses on the sign in the bedroom could not form part of the contract between the hotel and Mrs Olley. The contract had been made at the reception desk before there had been any opportunity to see the sign.

The test

9.24 The basic rule for incorporation of a clause contained in an unsigned document or sign is that such a clause is part of the contract if there has been reasonably sufficient notice of it. This

13 See further E. Macdonald, 'Incorporation of Standard Terms in Website Contracting—Clicking "I Agree"' (2011) 27 JCL 198.

14 See generally Clarke [1976] CLJ 51.

test is derived from *Parker* v *South Eastern Rly Co.* (1877), where the court was concerned with the terms on which goods were deposited in a railway station cloakroom. In that case:

> On depositing a bag in the cloakroom, Mr Parker was handed a ticket which he did not read and which contained a clause purporting to limit the railway company's responsibility to packages not exceeding £10 in value. Mr Parker's bag was of greater value than £10 and, on its loss from the cloakroom, the question was whether the clause on the ticket limited the liability of the railway company.

The result of the case was that a retrial was ordered. The judge at first instance had misdirected the jury on the test for incorporation. The court decided that the basic test to determine whether incorporation had occurred in this type of situation is that of reasonably sufficient notice, that is, whether reasonably sufficient notice of the clause had been given.

9.25 The need to order a retrial in *Parker* v *South Eastern Rly Co.* (1877) emphasizes the factual nature of the test (*Hood* v *Anchor Line (Henderson Bros) Ltd* [1918] AC 837 at 844). So, for example, there is unlikely to be reasonably sufficient notice of a clause printed on the back of a ticket if the front of the ticket does not say 'for conditions see back' (*Henderson* v *Stevenson* (1875)), but it will depend upon all the facts of the particular case. Equally, a ticket which would in normal circumstances provide reasonably sufficient notice might not do so if it had been folded over (*Richardson, Spence, & Co.* v *Rowntree* (1894)) or the relevant clause had been obscured by a date stamp (*Sugar* v *London, Midland, and Scottish Rly Co.* (1941)).

Type of document

9.26 The type of document in which a clause is found is relevant to its incorporation. It may simply be said that a non-contractual document will not incorporate terms.[15] However, in the context of a general requirement of reasonably sufficient notice, the type of document is also relevant to that requirement. In *Parker* v *South Eastern Rly Co.* [1877] 2 CPD 416, Mellish LJ gave an example (at 422):

> If a person driving through a turnpike-gate received a ticket upon paying the toll, he might reasonably assume that the object of the ticket was that by producing it he might be free from paying toll at some other turnpike-gate, and might put it in his pocket unread.

Although this is quite an old example, the general point is clear. It was referred to by Slesser LJ in *Chapelton* v *Barry UDC* [1940] 1 KB 532 (at 538), and that case provides us with a further example:

---

15 See *Grogan* v *Robin Meredith Plant Hire* (1996)—**para. 9.13**—in the context of signed documents.

> Mr Chapelton was at the beach at Cold Knap in Barry. There was a sign indicating the hire charge for deckchairs and requesting those using the chairs to obtain a ticket from the attendant and retain it for inspection. Mr Chapelton took a chair and obtained a ticket. He put the ticket in his pocket without reading what was printed on it. When he sat down in the chair the canvas gave way and he fell and injured himself. Barry UDC, from whom he had hired the chair, claimed to be able to rely upon a clause on the ticket to exclude liability for his injuries.

The court decided that the clause on the ticket was not part of the contract. The ticket was not the sort of document on which a contract term would be expected. It appeared merely to be proof that Mr Chapelton had paid his 2d hire charge.

9.27 When the type of document is discussed in relation to the issue of incorporation, the point is sometimes put in terms of whether the document is a 'mere receipt'. Mellish LJ clearly envisaged the ticket from the turnpike gate as a mere receipt and that is also how the court in *Chapelton* v *Barry UDC* (1940) perceived the deck-chair ticket, that is, those tickets were seen as evidence of payment and nothing more. However, there is no reason why a document headed 'receipt' should not be used to incorporate clauses into a contract successfully if the circumstances indicate its true role to the reasonable person (*Watkins* v *Rymill* (1883)). It should be borne in mind that a clause cannot be incorporated into a contract by a document which is introduced after the contract is concluded; if a document is intended to be a receipt, in the sense of evidence of payment, it may have been introduced too late, after offer and acceptance have occurred. The timing of the introduction of the ticket was another reason for the decision in *Chapelton*.

9.28 A further point, related to that of the type of document, is that the transaction may be one in which it is commonly known that there will be standard terms. The question of incorporation from a particular document will then be viewed against this background and it will be easier to establish that reasonably sufficient notice has been provided. In *Alexander* v *Railway Executive* [1951] 2 KB 882 it was regarded as relevant to the question of reasonably sufficient notice that 'most people nowadays know that railway companies have conditions subject to which they take articles into their cloakrooms' (at 886).[16]

Reference

9.29 It is not necessary for the document or sign itself to contain the terms. There may be incorporation by reference. In *Thompson* v *London, Midland Scottish Rly Co.* (1930) the railway ticket said on its front, in 'quite big print and quite legible print', 'for conditions see back'. On the back the passenger was referred to the railway timetable to ascertain the conditions. Despite the fact that the clause was only to be found upon p. 552 of the timetable, which itself cost 6d when Mrs Thompson's ticket cost only 2s 7d, the clauses were held to be incorporated and removed the railway's liability for the negligent injury to Mrs Thompson.

16 See also incorporation by a course of dealing and *British Crane Hire Corpn Ltd* v *Ipswich Plant Hire Ltd* (1975) (**para. 9.56**).

9.30 The reaction to *Thompson* v *London, Midland Scottish Rly Co.* (1930) may be that it is a fairly extreme case. A decision by a passenger to ascertain the content of the terms would have entailed a search of the timetable and some expense. Undoubtedly it was easier for the court to accept that the terms were incorporated in this case because it did not regard the exemption clause as unreasonable. Mrs Thompson had purchased an excursion ticket, at half the ordinary fare for the journey. Restricted liability was not regarded as unreasonable when a reduced fare was being paid.

9.31 As will be seen, at common law the courts have now proved themselves willing to link the question of incorporation by notice and the unreasonableness, or unusualness, of the content of a clause. That occurs through the 'red hand' rule (see para. **9.34**ff), which applies to incorporation by notice generally, and in the context of incorporation by reference (*O'Brien* v *MGN Ltd* (2002)). It should, however, also be noted that artificiality of incorporation will also be relevant to the reasonableness test under UCTA 1977, and the fairness test in the consumer unfair terms regime, which is now contained in the Consumer Rights Act 2015. In particular, the latter contains a relevant term in its 'grey list' of terms which may be regarded as unfair (see para. **11.55**). Schedule 2 of the CRA, containing the 'grey list', includes para. 10, which covers:

> A term which has the object or effect of irrevocably binding the consumer to terms with which the consumer has had no real opportunity of becoming acquainted before the conclusion of the contract.

In contracts between consumers and sellers or suppliers, this requires consideration of the accessibility of any clauses that it is sought to incorporate by reference. If they are inaccessible, then the term referring to them may be found to be unfair. Under those circumstances, it would not bind the consumer and there would then be no effective term to incorporate the clauses it referred to.

Objective nature of the test

9.32 A variation on the facts of *Thompson* v *London, Midland Scottish Rly Co.* (1930) provides a useful way to emphasize the objective nature of the notice test. In that case the passenger was illiterate but the ticket was purchased by her agent (her daughter), who could read. The legal position of an agent is such that what the agent had notice of, Mrs Thompson would also have notice of, and her illiteracy could not be relevant to the question of incorporation. However, even without the agent, Mrs Thompson's illiteracy should not be relevant to the question of reasonably sufficient notice, and this is the tenor of the judgments in the case. The test is objective. The question is one of sufficiency of notice for the reasonable person, not the particular individual. In *Parker* v *South Eastern Rly Co.* (1877) 2 CPD 416, Mellish LJ said (at 423):

> The railway company ... must be entitled to make some assumptions respecting the person who deposits luggage with them; I think they are entitled to assume that he can read, and that he understands the English language.

The situation would be modified if the person who wished to include his or her exemption clauses knew, or should have known, that the person with whom he or she was contracting was illiterate. That factor would then enter into the assessment of whether there had been reasonably sufficient notice (*Geier* v *Kujawa, Weston, and Warne Bros (Transport) Ltd* (1970)).

9.33 More generally, the situation may be that the person wishing to incorporate his or her standard terms knows, or should know, that he or she will be contracting with individuals from a particular group who share some characteristic affecting their ability to acquire knowledge from a particular form of notice. In *Richardson, Spence, & Co.* v *Rowntree* [1894] AC 217 one of the elements mentioned by the court in relation to sufficiency of notice of the exemption clause was that the tickets were for steerage class passengers, 'many of whom have little education and some of them none' (at 221). That specific factor is obviously a product of its time, but it is possible to conceive of situations where the problem of communication with a particular group might be raised today. For example, a travel company setting out to provide holidays suitable for the blind would have to give serious consideration to the method used to incorporate an exemption clause into the contract with a blind person for such a holiday.

The 'red hand' rule

9.34 *Thompson* v *London, Midland and Scottish Rly Co.* [1930] 1 KB 41 at 53 and 56 contains some comments on whether it is possible to incorporate an unreasonable clause by notice.[17] Such comments can be found in various cases,[18] but there is no such accepted restriction upon this method of incorporation. However, it is understandable that there should be a reaction against the idea that unreasonable clauses can be incorporated into a contract by notice, and used against someone who has not read them and who has not even been alerted to be on guard by the necessity of signing the document containing them. The courts have developed a technique for restricting incorporation of unusual or unreasonable clauses by notice. In *J Spurling Ltd* v *Bradshaw* [1956] 1 WLR 461 Denning LJ, as he then was, said (at 466):

> the more unreasonable a clause is, the greater the notice which must be given of it. Some clauses which I have seen would need to be printed in *red ink on the face of the document with a red hand* pointing to [them] before the notice could be held to be sufficient. (emphasis added)

Spurling itself provides no further guidance on what will, for obvious reasons, be termed the 'red hand' rule. The reference to the rule in *Spurling* was a lone *obiter dictum*.

9.35 The rule was given further consideration in *Thornton* v *Shoe Lane Parking Ltd* [1971] 2 QB 163. *Thornton* involved an attempt by the owners of a car park to escape liability for the negligently caused personal injury of Mr Thornton, who was injured when he returned to the

---

17 See E. Macdonald, 'The Duty to Give Notice of Unusual Contract Terms' [1988] JBL 375; H. McClean, 'Incorporation of Onerous or Unusual Terms' [1988] CLJ 172; E. Macdonald, *Exemption Clauses and Unfair Terms*, 2nd edn, Tottel, 2006, pp. 19–23.

18 E.g. *Parker* v *South Eastern Rly Co.* (1877) 2 CPD 416 at 428; *Van Toll* v *South Eastern Rly Co.* (1862) 12 CBNS 75 at 85 and 88.

car park to collect his car. The car-park owners were seeking to rely upon an exemption clause printed on the sign inside the car park and referred to on a ticket received at the entrance to the car park. It was argued that the ticket arrived too late to incorporate any clause into the contract, but the court also considered what the situation would be if that was not the case. The clause purported to exclude liability not only for damage to property but also for personal injury. Lord Denning MR considered it (at 170) to be an example of the type of clause which he had in mind in *J Spurling Ltd* v *Bradshaw* (1956) when propounding the 'red hand' rule (i.e. an unreasonable clause) and one which would require additional notice to incorporate it. Megaw LJ also thought (at 172) that the clause would require extra notice in order to be incorporated, but he considered that unusual clauses were the ones which should be treated in this way. (See Clarke [1976] CLJ 51 at 69–71.)

9.36 After *Thornton* v *Shoe Lane Parking Ltd* (1971) it seemed that the 'red hand' rule should be stated as being that the more unreasonable or unusual a clause is, the greater the degree of notice required to incorporate it, and this basic approach is confirmed by the judgments of the Court of Appeal in *Interfoto Picture Library Ltd* v *Stiletto Visual Programmes Ltd* (1988). In *Interfoto*:

> An advertising agency, Stiletto, telephoned Interfoto, who ran a library of photographic transparencies, to obtain material for a presentation to a client. Stiletto had not dealt with Interfoto before. Interfoto dispatched to Stiletto a bag containing 47 transparencies and a delivery note containing nine 'Conditions'. 'Condition 2' stated that a holding fee of £5 per transparency per day would be charged for any transparency kept beyond a 14-day period. Stiletto failed to return the transparencies within 14 days and, on the basis of 'Condition 2', Interfoto claimed more than £3,500 from Stiletto. The question was whether or not that clause was a term of the contract.

At first instance it was held that 'Condition 2' was part of the contract, but this was reversed by the Court of Appeal. The clause in question was not an exclusion clause, but the court said that the same rules for incorporation applied, and in particular what has here been termed the 'red hand' rule. The judgments in the Court of Appeal can be synthesized into the formulation of the 'red hand' rule indicated earlier, that is, the more unusual or unreasonable a clause, the greater the notice required for there to be reasonably sufficient notice. The court considered 'Condition 2' to be both unusual and onerous. There was evidence of the holding fees of ten other agencies. Most of them charged less than £3.50 per transparency per week: only one charged more (£4 per week). The court held that there was not sufficient notice to incorporate 'Condition 2', and Interfoto were entitled to a quantum meruit of £3.50 per transparency per week, instead of the £5 per transparency per day claimed.

9.37 It should be acknowledged that the judges referred to 'onerous' rather than 'unreasonable' clauses, but onerousness is merely the particular form of unreasonableness encountered in the case, which was that of a term imposing an unreasonable burden. That is likely to be the important form of unreasonableness for the 'red hand rule' in the future commercial cases, as

UCTA will deal with many exemption clauses, but it is not relevant to a clause imposing liability, as was the situation in *Interfoto*. In relation to consumer contracts, the controls of the CRA are not limited to exemption clauses. The 'red hand' rule now seems most likely to play a significant role in relation to clauses which are not exemption clauses, in contracts between small businesses and large ones. Nevertheless, the more general restriction of unreasonable clauses, rather than merely onerous ones, should not be thoughtlessly discarded just because it will not often be needed.

9.38 However, we also should note that the type of liability which it was sought to exclude in *Thornton* would not now simply be subject to the reasonableness test/fairness test in UCTA/CRA. Such an attempt to exclude or restrict liability for negligently caused personal injury would be automatically ineffective under s 2(1) UCTA/s 65 CRA. In *Goodlife Foods Ltd* v *Hall Fire Protection Ltd* (2017) the judge took the line that the aspect of a clause which was automatically ineffective under s 2(1) of UCTA should not be considered in deciding if the clause fell within the 'red hand' rule. Obviously, this is some reduction in the scope of the rule. Its overall impact depends upon the line which the judge also took, that the part of the clause falling within s 2(1) was simply excised and did not impact upon the whole clause, the rest of which was therefore subject to the reasonableness test under s 2(2) in relation to the exemption of liability for other negligently caused loss or damage. This does not sit very comfortably alongside *Stewart Gill Ltd* v *Horatio Myer & Co. Ltd* [1992] 2 All ER 257, where the court took the line that in applying the requirement of reasonableness under UCTA the clause needed to be considered as a whole, on the basis that the 'time frame' in relation to which reasonableness had to be considered was that of the making of the contract. When the contract is made, it is obviously not known which element of a clause will be used, and what for (see further **para. 10.58**).

9.39 We should now consider the 'red hand' rule more broadly. Its importance here does not simply lie in its impact within the law of contract as a specific rule. The development of the 'red hand' rule is worth considering also because it will make us think about the way in which the common law evolves, and this is of great importance in relation to an area of law, like contract, which is largely based upon judicial decisions rather than statute. The 'red hand' rule says that notice varies with the contents of a clause. Its effect is that where clauses (a), (b), and (c) are printed on a ticket, in exactly the same size type, and (b) is a very unreasonable clause whilst the other two are not, there may be sufficient notice to incorporate clauses (a) and (c) but not clause (b). Is this logical? How can the degree of notice required to incorporate a clause depend upon its contents? Can the contents of a clause affect its legibility? Consideration of these questions makes obvious the problem of establishing the basis of the rule. It certainly cannot be regarded as merely a logical derivation from *Parker* v *South Eastern Rly Co.* (1877).[19] The contents of a clause cannot affect its legibility. However, the common law develops in response to the problems which the courts encounter. The general principle of incorporation by notice can be perceived as producing unfairness in some situations. One party may use it to introduce very unreasonable, or unusual, terms into his or her contract with the other party and that other party will have no

19 R. Brownsword, 'Incorporating Exemption Clauses' (1972) 35 MLR 183.

actual knowledge of the terms and will not even have been alerted to be on guard by the necessity of signing the document. The decision in *Interfoto* represents the view that it is appropriate for the courts to interfere with the parties' apparent bargain in such circumstances. The court has acted to limit what it has seen as an abuse of the general notice principle, and to protect the injured party against that common human failing of not reading everything. The decision will be approved by those who favour an interventionist role for the courts.

9.40 *Interfoto Picture Library Ltd* v *Stiletto Visual Programmes Ltd* (1988) will be criticized by those who strongly favour the idea of freedom of contract. The court has interfered with the parties' apparent bargain. It could, however, be argued that the form of the 'red hand' rule does not place an absolute bar upon the incorporation of unusual or unreasonable clauses, and is not a real interference with freedom of contract, being merely an interference with the manner of the terms' incorporation and not with their content. It can be seen as aimed at ensuring that there is real freedom of contract through trying to address the problem of the artificiality of incorporation of contract terms, and the lack of real choice and consent that engenders. *Interfoto* is the type of case in which the court has to base its decision upon its view of a very fundamental idea, such as that of freedom of contract, and precedent can be of only limited help. In the end the result will depend upon whether or not the court leans towards intervention in such situations.

The general test—a further clarification of Parker

9.41 As we have seen, the basic test for incorporation of an unsigned document is that of reasonably sufficient notice. However, it is not uncommon to encounter a dictum of Mellish LJ in *Parker* v *South Eastern Rly Co.* (1877) 2 CPD 416 which appears to provide a fuller test, and which is worth considering now that the basic test has been explored. Mellish LJ thought the appropriate test was (at 423):

> that if the person receiving the ticket did not see or know that there was any writing on the ticket, he is not bound by the conditions; that if he knew there was writing, and knew or believed that the writing contained conditions, then he is bound by the conditions; that if he knew there was writing on the ticket, but did not know or believe that the writing contained conditions, nevertheless he would be bound, if the delivering of the ticket to him in such a manner that he could see there was writing upon it, was ... reasonable notice that the writing contained conditions.

A number of points must be noted here in order to avoid confusion. First, Mellish LJ said that there will not be incorporation if the person to whom the ticket was given did not know that there was writing on it. This cannot be regarded as a general rule. As has been seen, the test of reasonably sufficient notice depends upon the facts in each case, and is not dependent upon providing sufficient notice for the particular individual (see the discussion of *Thompson* v *London, Midland and Scottish Rly Co.* (1930) at para. **9.29**). That the person to whom the ticket was delivered did not know that there was any writing on it cannot determine the issue. At most it is evidence that the reasonable person would not have realized that there was writing on the ticket, and that there was not reasonably sufficient notice.

9.42 The second point to be made is in relation to Mellish LJ's second statement—that if the person to whom the ticket is handed knows that it contains conditions, then he will be bound by them even though he does not know of the content of the conditions. An analogy can be made with incorporation by reference (see para. **9.32**). The individual is in a position to ascertain the contents of the terms. One qualification needs to be made: this situation should also be subject to the 'red hand' rule. If the person to whom the ticket is given does not know of the content of the terms, but merely of their existence, he should be given extra notice of any unusual or unreasonable terms.

9.43 Finally, Mellish LJ's third point must be considered. It is close to a formulation of the general test. Again, the point which needs to be made is that the test is one which depends upon the facts in each case (*Hood* v *Anchor Line (Henderson Bros) Ltd* [1918] AC 837 at 844). It cannot be regarded as a general rule that, in order for there to be reasonably sufficient notice, the ticket must be delivered, so that the person to whom it is delivered can see that there is writing on it. The dictum of Mellish LJ should be treated with some care.

Consistent course of dealing

The test

9.44 There may sometimes be incorporation based upon the previous dealings between the parties.[20] *J Spurling Ltd* v *Bradshaw* [1956] 1 WLR 461 provides an illustration of this:

> Bradshaw stored casks of orange juice in Spurling's warehouse. When Bradshaw went to collect his casks it was discovered that the juice was either gone or ruined, and he refused to pay the storage charge. When Spurling sued for the storage charge, Bradshaw counterclaimed for breach of contract by negligent storage. To defeat the counterclaim, Spurling sought to rely upon an exemption clause contained in a document which was sent to Bradshaw only some days after the contract of storage had been concluded.

The document containing the exemption clause had obviously arrived too late to incorporate terms into that particular contract. However, Bradshaw conceded that he had received such documents on previous occasions when he had dealt with Spurling and this led the Court of Appeal to conclude that 'by the course of business and conduct of the parties [the clause was] part of the contract' (at 471).

9.45 In *J Spurling Ltd* v *Bradshaw* (1956) the clause had been incorporated despite the late arrival of the document containing it. It is in this sort of situation, where the document has arrived too late in the instant case, that the argument for incorporation by a course of dealing

20 See generally E. Macdonald, 'Incorporation of Contract Terms by a "Consistent Course of Dealing"' (1988) 8 LS 48; Macdonald, *Exemption Clauses and Unfair Terms*, 2nd edn, pp. 25–31.

usually arises. *Henry Kendall & Sons* v *William Lillico & Sons Ltd* (1969) provides another example:

> The seller sold Brazilian groundnut extract to the buyer to be used to compound cattle and poultry food. The contract between the parties had been made over the telephone but was followed the next day by the dispatch of a document, a sold note, which contained an exemption clause. The conclusion of an oral contract followed by the dispatch of the sold note was the practice which the parties had followed for three years. During that time there had been three or four transactions a month following that pattern. In the instant case the groundnut extract contained a substance poisonous to poultry.

The question arose as to the seller's liability for the poisonous state of the Brazilian groundnut extract. One argument was that the seller was protected by the exemption clause. This raised the issue of incorporation. The House of Lords was willing to accept that, although the document arrived too late to incorporate the clause into the particular transaction, the clause was part of the contract on the basis of the previous dealings between the parties. In the event this did not assist the sellers, as the court also concluded that the clause was not appropriately worded to cover the breach which had occurred.

9.46 *Henry Kendall & Sons* v *William Lillico & Sons Ltd* (1969) helps us towards a general test for incorporation by past dealings. In the Court of Appeal ([1966] 1 WLR 287, sub nom *Hardwick Game Farm* v *Suffolk Agricultural and Poultry Producers' Association Ltd*), Diplock LJ stated the test (at 339) as 'what each party by his words and conduct reasonably led the other party to believe were the acts he was undertaking a legal duty to perform'. In the House of Lords, Lord Wilberforce agreed with Diplock LJ ([1969] 2 AC 31 at 130) and Lord Pearce formulated a general test in similar terms. He said (at 113): 'The court's task is to decide what each party to an alleged contract would reasonably conclude from the utterances, writings or conduct of the other.' More recently, a similar formulation has been applied. It has been asked 'what each party by his words and conduct would have led the other party as a reasonable man to believe he was accepting'.[21]

9.47 To settle on an exact formula for the test for incorporation by a course of dealing we need to consider the mechanism by which such incorporation occurs. In each case the court is concerned with what was included, unspoken, in the offer and acceptance on the basis of the previous dealings between the parties and what they have said and done in the instant case in relation to the offer and acceptance. In both *J Spurling Ltd* v *Bradshaw* (1956) and *Henry Kendall & Sons* v *William Lillico & Sons Ltd* (1969) a document containing the clauses in question had been sent, but it had been sent after offer and acceptance had occurred. The lateness of this document did not prevent the clauses from being incorporated, because it is not the document dispatched in relation to the particular transaction which is the basis of incorporation of the

21 *SIAT di del Ferro* v *Tradax Overseas SA* [1978] 2 Lloyd's Rep 470 at 490; *Johnson Matthey Bankers Ltd* v *State Trading Corpn of India* [1984] 1 Lloyd's Rep 427 at 433; *Circle Freight International Ltd* v *Medeast Gulf Exports Ltd* [1988] 2 Lloyd's Rep 427 at 433.

clauses in the instant case. In *Kendall* v *Lillico*, for example, the incorporation of the exemption clause should be seen as based upon the 'sold note' delivered in relation to each of the previous transactions over the preceding three years. Because of the past transactions, each party, as a reasonable person, should have assumed that the offer and acceptance, in the instant case, included the seller's standard terms. In *Petrotrade Inc.* v *Texaco Ltd* (2000), on the basis of five previous transactions on the same terms, and for the same commodity, in the space of 13 months, Clarke LJ concluded (at 1349): 'Given the course of dealing … both parties will have made the oral agreement on the basis that the contract would be subject to the same terms as before'. Obviously the situation would be different if one party had indicated by his words or actions that the particular transaction was not to be on the same basis as previous transactions. Bearing all this in mind, it is possible to formulate the test for incorporation from a course of dealings. The test should be whether, at the time of contracting, each party, as a reasonable person, should infer from the past dealings and the actions and words of the other in the instant case that the standard clauses are part of the instant contract.

Acts/words in the instant case

9.48 In the context of incorporation by a course of dealing, further consideration needs to be given to the relevance of the acts or words of the parties in the instant case. On a factual level their relevance is obvious. For many years the parties may have contracted frequently and always used one party's standard terms. In the instant case it may be clear that past practice is to be departed from and that the standard terms are not to form part of the contract. Equally, it should be possible to find incorporation by a course of dealing when there are some differences between the instant case and past transactions, provided that the situation as a whole is such that the parties, as reasonable people, would still assume the standard terms to be part of the contract. For example, incorporation of one party's standard terms should be possible where those terms have been incorporated in each previous transaction by a document providing reasonably sufficient notice and, in the instant case, the contract is concluded over the telephone without any express reference to those standard terms (see *British Crane Hire Corpn.* v *Ipswich Plant Hire Ltd* (1975) at para. **9.56**). However, *McCutcheon* v *David MacBrayne Ltd* (1964) indicated that the acts or words in the instant case must be given some special legal significance beyond that which they would naturally have on a factual level, and this should be considered.

9.49 In *McCutcheon* v *David MacBrayne Ltd* (1964):

> McSporran arranged for a car belonging to his brother-in-law, McCutcheon, to be shipped from the Hebrides to the mainland by MacBrayne. McCutcheon had shipped various items three or four times in the past and so had McSporran. On each previous occasion McCutcheon had signed a risk note, but McSporran had done so only twice. The ship sank and McCutcheon sought to recover the cost of his car from MacBrayne. MacBrayne sought to rely upon an exemption clause, and one of the ways in which he argued that it had been incorporated was by a course of dealing. The clause was contained in the risk note which, on this occasion, McSporran had not been asked to sign.

In this case the House of Lords found that the past dealings were not appropriate to incorporate the clause. On the facts there is no difficulty with this. The previous transactions were limited in number and not consistent in the introduction of the risk note.

9.50 The reasoning in *McCutcheon* v *David MacBrayne Ltd* [1964] 1 WLR 125 must be considered. The judgment of Lord Reid poses no problems. He took the line which is the basis of the general test indicated earlier. He thought (at 128) that the court's task is 'to decide what each [party] was reasonably entitled to conclude from the attitude of the other'. It is the judgments of the other members of the House of Lords which present some difficulties. They favour the idea that for incorporation by a course of dealing there must be complete consistency, not only in the past transactions, but also between the previous transactions and the instant case. If this were so, incorporation by a course of dealing could occur only in the *Henry Kendall & Sons* v *Williams Lillico & Sons Ltd* (1969) type of case, the 'complete consistency' case, where the document containing the relevant clauses arrived too late in the instant case and has always arrived too late in the past, that is, the document has always arrived after offer and acceptance.

9.51 Incorporation by a course of dealing should not be regarded as restricted to the situation where the instant case follows entirely the pattern of past dealings (and the Court of Appeal seems to have assumed that it was not so restricted in *PLM Trading Ltd* v *Georgiou* (1986)). Two points must be made. First, the need for complete consistency between past transactions and the instant case would create an unacceptable uncertainty. This is illustrated if we look again at the facts of *Henry Kendall & Sons* v *Williams Lillico & Sons Ltd* (1969). The contract in the instant case was concluded over the telephone. In the previous dealings the telephone conversation had been followed by the dispatch of the 'sold note' containing the exemption clause. If a course of dealing could not incorporate a clause unless there was complete consistency between past transactions and the instant case, it would not be clear whether the instant contract included the clause until the 'sold note' had been dispatched or, possibly, received. There would be a time, after the making of the contract, during which it would not be clear what the terms of the contract were. Clearly that would be an unacceptable situation (A. Hogget, 'Changing a Bargain by Confirming it' (1970) 33 MLR 518 at 520–1).

9.52 The second point to be made is that circumstances have changed since *McCutcheon* v *David MacBrayne Ltd* [1964] 1 WLR 125 was decided, and the reason why the majority of the House of Lords favoured a restrictive approach to incorporation by a course of dealing no longer applies. The line taken by the majority in *McCutcheon* is explained by their view that such incorporation is another way in which the business person has an unfair advantage over the consumer (per Lord Pearce at 139, Lord Hodson at 130, Lord Guest at 131, Lord Devlin at 136). They saw it as simply giving the business person yet another opportunity to rely upon standard terms with exemption clauses. It should be remembered that *McCutcheon* was decided prior to the Unfair Contract Terms Act 1977, and the subsequent unfair terms legislation.

9.53 It seems unlikely that the approach of the majority in *McCutcheon* v *David MacBrayne Ltd* (1964) will be revived today. Comments upon *McCutcheon*, such as that in *Circle Freight*

International Ltd v *Medeast Gulf Exports Ltd* [1988] 2 Lloyd's Rep 427 (see para. **9.58**), therefore need to be treated with care. In that case Taylor LJ said (at 431) of *McCutcheon*:

> [Lord Pearce] was pointing out that whereas some of the previous dealings in that case had involved a contractual document, on the occasion of the sinking the contract was purely oral. It was the departure from the ordinary course of business which excluded the condition.

Such a comment should merely be seen as an acceptance of the natural factual relevance of differences between the past transactions and the instant case.

Failure to incorporate in past transactions

9.54 Incorporation by a course of dealing in the *Henry Kendall & Sons* v *William Lillico & Sons Ltd* (1969) type of case is worth further consideration. Each time the parties contracted, the document containing the standard terms was introduced by one party only after offer and acceptance had occurred. It is the cumulative effect of these documents which means that a point is reached when the other party, as a reasonable person, must be taken to know that the offer is made on the basis of those standard terms and, in the absence of some indication to the contrary, his or her acceptance will encompass them. This is simply to re-emphasize the mechanism by which incorporation by a course of dealing occurs. The point to be made here is that there is no possibility of incorporation by a course of dealing when the failure to incorporate standard terms by the document produced in each particular past contract, and the instant case, is due not to the timing of delivery of that document but rather to its not providing 'reasonably sufficient' notice, that is, where, in relation to each transaction, the terms have been present before offer and acceptance but they are insufficiently prominent to be incorporated by notice. Under these circumstances the party seeking to rely upon his or her standard terms never puts the other party in the situation where, as a reasonable person, he or she should assume that the offer encompasses those terms. The reasonable person would make no such assumption in relation to terms of the existence of which he or she has not been given sufficient notice. By definition, there is no reason why he or she should know of the terms. Where incorporation occurs because of the cumulative effect of a series of late deliveries of standard terms, the situation must be such that those terms would have been incorporated in each individual transaction, had they arrived on time.

Consumer/business distinction

9.55 When considering whether incorporation by a course of dealing has occurred, the courts have shown themselves less willing to find such incorporation where one party is a consumer than where both are business people. In *Hollier* v *Rambler Motors (AMC) Ltd* (1972):

> Rambler Motors had repaired Mr Hollier's car on three or four occasions over a five-year period. On at least two occasions Mr Hollier had signed a form containing Rambler's standard terms, including an exemption clause. In the instant case the parties contracted over the telephone, without any mention of the standard terms. Whilst the car was in the garage it was damaged by fire due to Rambler's negligence.

The court decided that the exemption clause did not cover the breach which had occurred, but it also considered the issue of incorporation. On that question the court concluded that three or four transactions over a five-year period were not sufficient to incorporate the standard terms into the oral contract. This was obviously not a strong case for such incorporation, but it should be noted that in considering this case the Court of Appeal in *British Crane Hire Corpn Ltd* v *Ipswich Plant Hire Ltd* (1975) (see **para. 9.56**) emphasized that Mr Hollier was a consumer. It should be easier to incorporate terms by a course of dealing into a contract between two business people than into a contract between a business person and a consumer.

9.56 *Hollier* v *Rambler Motors (AMC) Ltd* (1972) should be contrasted with *British Crane Hire Corpn Ltd* v *Ipswich Plant Hire Ltd* (1975). In that case:

> Ipswich Plant Hire (IP) were draining marsh land and carrying out other engineering works on it. IP were also in the business of hiring out equipment, but on this occasion they themselves needed to hire a crane. As their need was urgent they telephoned British Crane Hire (BC) and arranged to hire a crane from them. Subsequently BC sent IP a printed form setting out conditions of hire. IP did not sign or return the form to BC. On two previous occasions BC had hired equipment to IP and those contracts had been made on the basis of BC's printed form. The crane sank into the marsh.

The question arose as to who was to pay for the removal of the crane from the mud. BC relied on their standard terms to argue that IP should pay. The question was whether those terms were part of the contract. Both parties were business people involved in the same trade. BC's standard terms were similar to those used throughout the trade and resembled those used by IP themselves when they were hiring out their machinery. Two prior transactions, by themselves, might not have been sufficient to incorporate the terms but the question of incorporation had to be viewed against the background of trade practice, and that decided the issue in BC's favour. BC's terms were incorporated because the contract was between two business people in the same trade.

9.57 The court seemed inclined to view trade background as a distinct basis of incorporation from course of dealing. However, even if it could work independently, trade background can add to the effect of past dealings between the parties when incorporation by a course of dealing is considered. In *SIAT di del Ferro* v *Tradax Overseas SA* [1978] 2 Lloyd's Rep 470 Donaldson J considered *British Crane Hire Corpn Ltd* v *Ipswich Plant Hire Ltd* (1975) and the course of dealing cases. He said (at 490):

> I do not think that they are different. They are two different examples of a much wider concept, namely, that a contract is not made in a vacuum, but against a background of present and past facts ... and that its terms ... are to be gathered ... from conduct viewed against that background.

Common trade background affects what each party, as a reasonable person, is entitled to infer that the other is agreeing to (*Fal Bunkering of Sharjah* v *Grecale Inc of Panama* (1990)). Trade background can feed into the test for incorporation by a course of dealing. The two may combine and they should be viewed as so doing in *British Crane Hire*. When two business people contract, it may well be easier to say that reasonable people in their situation would infer the use of one party's standard terms after a very brief course of dealing. The knowledge of business practice which can be imputed to business people, particularly within the same trade, is obviously greater than that which can be imputed to a consumer.

Course of dealing and reasonably sufficient notice

9.58 In *Circle Freight International Ltd* v *Medeast Gulf Exports Ltd* [1988] 2 Lloyd's Rep 427 some consideration was given to the relationship between incorporation by a course of dealing and the rule from *Parker* v *South Eastern Rly Co.* (1877). The facts of *Circle Freight* provide us with another useful illustration of incorporation by a course of dealing. In *Circle Freight*:

> Medeast exported goods to the Middle East. Circle Freight were freight forwarding agents. They had acted as such for Medeast on a number of occasions when Medeast were exporting dresses. Circle Freight were suing Medeast for money owed. Medeast were counterclaiming in relation to a consignment of dresses stolen whilst Circle Freight's driver left them unattended in Fleet Street. In relation to the counterclaim, Circle Freight sought to rely upon an exemption clause in the standard terms of the Institute of Freight Forwarders. Each contract between the parties was made orally, over the telephone, and was followed by an 'invoice'. The standard terms were referred to on the 'invoice' which had been sent to Medeast on at least 11 occasions over the six months preceding the lost consignment. Medeast were a commercial company and knew that freight forwarders usually dealt on standard terms.

The court concluded that the standard terms were incorporated. Taylor LJ said (at 433):

> I consider that [Medeast's] conduct in continuing the course of business after at least eleven notices of the terms and omitting to request a sight of them would have led and did lead [Circle Freight] reasonably to believe [Medeast] accepted their terms.

As can be seen, this is an application of the test indicated above for incorporation by a course of dealing, that is, whether, at the time of contracting, each party, as a reasonable person, should infer from the past dealings and the actions and words of the other in the instant case that the standard clauses are part of the instant contract. However, the question of reasonably sufficient notice was also raised and was regarded as interchangeable with the more specific test for incorporation by a course of dealing. There seems to be every justification for this. Both tests are based upon an objective view of the contracting process. Both are concerned with what a reasonable person should be taken to have agreed to. However, although it is desirable to recognize the link, as such recognition may help with any further development of the law, there is something to be said for maintaining a separate test for the course of dealing cases. The separate test draws attention to the factors specific to incorporation in that manner.

9.59 Why is incorporation by a course of dealing required? Empirical work undertaken in relation to contract law has revealed that business people do not always have the rules of contract law at the forefront of their minds when contracting.[22] The primary interest is in 'clinching the deal'. When this attitude is combined with the use of standard terms, it can create problems. Perhaps the best-known example of this is the 'battle of the forms'. The contention that terms have been incorporated by a course of dealing can also be seen as a product of this attitude. It is usually raised when one party has attempted to introduce standard terms into the contract after it has been made, that is, when not much thought has been given to the correct procedure, within the law of contract, to ensure that his or her standard terms are part of the contract.

Construction

Introduction

9.60 When considering the construction of the contract, we are looking at its interpretation. In relation to exemption clauses the question being asked is whether the clause used is appropriately worded to cover what has occurred. However, before considering in detail the interpretation of exemption clauses, we should first briefly look at construction more generally, and also the trends in relation to the approach taken to the construction of exemption clauses.

Construction in general

9.61 The objective when construing or interpreting a contract is that of determining the parties' intention. It is a matter of objective ascertainment, of course, so what is looked at is the meaning which the contract would convey to the reasonable person, having all the background knowledge of the parties, at the time of contracting. Traditionally, there was an overwhelming emphasis upon the written words used and a restrictive approach to what further evidence could be considered. However, in *Investors Compensation Scheme Ltd* v *West Bromwich Building Society* [1998] 1 All ER 98 at 114, the House of Lords took the view that a 'fundamental change ... has overtaken this branch of the law' and that the result has largely been:

> to assimilate the way in which such documents are interpreted by judges to the common sense principles by which any serious utterance would be interpreted in ordinary life. Almost all the old intellectual baggage of 'legal' interpretation has been discarded.

9.62 In *Investors Compensation Scheme Ltd* v *West Bromwich Building Society* [1998] 1 All ER 98 Lord Hoffmann provided a summary of principles, which is now frequently referred to by the courts. He said (at 114):

> 1. Interpretation is the ascertainment of the meaning which the document would convey to a reasonable person having all the background knowledge which would reasonably

22 S. Macauley, 'Non-Contractual Relations in Business' [1963] Am Soc Rev 45; H. Beale and A. Dugdale, 'Contracts Between Businessmen: Planning and the Use of Contractual Remedies' (1975) 2 Brit J Law and Soc 18.

have been available to the parties in the situation in which they were at the time of the contract.

2. The background was famously referred to by Lord Wilberforce as the 'matrix of fact', but this phrase is if anything an understated description of what the background may include. Subject to the requirement that it should have been reasonably available to the parties and to the exception mentioned next, it includes absolutely anything which would have affected the way in which the language of the document would have been understood by a reasonable man.

3. The law excludes from the admissible background the previous negotiations of the parties and their declarations of subjective intent. They are admissible only in an action for rectification. The law makes this distinction for reasons of practical policy and, in this respect only, legal interpretation differs from the way we would interpret utterances in ordinary life.

...

4. The meaning which a document (or any other utterance) would convey to a reasonable man is not the same thing as the meaning of its words. The meaning of words is a matter of dictionaries and grammars; the meaning of the document is what the parties using those words against the relevant background would reasonably have been understood to mean. The background may not merely enable the reasonable man to choose between the possible meanings of words which are ambiguous but even (as occasionally happens in ordinary life) to conclude that the parties must, for whatever reason, have used the wrong words or syntax (see *Mannai Investments Co. Ltd* v *Eagle Star Life Ass Co. Ltd* [1997] 3 All ER 352).

...

5. The 'rule' that words should be given their 'natural and ordinary meaning' reflects the commonsense proposition that we do not easily accept that people have made linguistic mistakes, particularly in formal documents. On the other hand, if one would nevertheless conclude from the background that something must have gone wrong with the language, the law does not require judges to attribute to the parties an intention which they plainly could not have had.

So, as has been indicated, the interpretation of contracts is objective, and on the basis of Lord Hoffmann's first point, just quoted, it is 'the ascertainment of the meaning which the document would convey to a reasonable person having all the background knowledge which would reasonably have been available to the parties in the situation in which they were at the time of the contract'. We will consider what this background can encompass, but we should also note that, more recently, the Supreme Court has sought to stress that it is the words of the contract that come first, and that the 'reliance on commercial common sense and surrounding circumstances ... should not be invoked to undervalue the language of the provision which is to be construed' (*Arnold v Britton* (2015), Lord Neuberger at [17]. See also *Rainy Sky SA v Kookmin Bank* (2011)).

9.63 We should nevertheless consider the background knowledge, or 'matrix of fact'. It is 'subject to the requirement that it should have been reasonably available to both parties' at the time of contracting. Subject to certain exceptions (see later), that includes 'absolutely anything which would have affected the way in which the language of the document would have been understood by a reasonable man' (point (2) above), although Lord Hoffmann has subsequently had to emphasize that he 'meant anything which a reasonable man would have regarded as relevant' (*Bank of Credit and Commerce International* v *Ali* [2001] UKHL 8 at [39]). It includes 'evidence of the "genesis" and objectively of the "aim" of the transaction' (*Prenn* v *Simmonds* [1971] 1 WLR 1381 per Lord Wilberforce).

9.64 It has also been said that in general, business contracts should be construed in a way which makes 'good commercial sense'. 'If a detailed semantic and syntactical analysis of words in a commercial contract is going to lead to a conclusion that flouts business common sense, it must be made to yield to business common sense' (*Antaios Cia Naviera SA* v *Salen Rederierna AB* [1985] AC 191 at 121 per Lord Diplock). Further, there has also been pressure against a construction which achieves an unreasonable result, and the 'more unreasonable the result the more unlikely it is that the parties can have intended it, and if they do intend it the more necessary it is that they [should] make that intention abundantly clear' (*L Schuler AG* v *Wickman Machine Tool Sales Ltd* [1974] AC 235 at 251 per Lord Reid). However, as has been indicated, there has been re-emphasis on the words that the parties agreed upon, and the courts must avoid substituting 'for the bargain actually made one which the court believes could better have been made' (*Charter Reinsurance Co. Ltd* v *Fagan* [1996] 2 WLR 726 at 759 per Lord Mustill); in *Rainy Sky SA* v *Kookmin Bank* (2011), it was emphasized that if there is no ambiguity in the language used in the contract, that unambiguous meaning will have to be applied, even if the result is improbable (at [23]–[24]).

9.65 It was indicated earlier that the general approach to the background which should be considered in determining the parties' intentions is a (nearly) all-embracing one, covering (nearly) everything which is relevant and was reasonably available to both parties at the time of contracting. However, in his third point, Lord Hoffmann did indicate the inadmissibility of evidence of the subjective declarations of the parties and their previous negotiations, and it is also well established that evidence of the parties' conduct subsequent to the making of the contract is also inadmissible (*Schuler* v *Wickman Machine Tool* (1974)). There has been considerable criticism of the maintenance of the latter two exclusions.[23] However, with Lord Hoffmann delivering the principal judgment, in *Chartbrook* v *Persimmon Homes* (2009) the House of Lords re-asserted the exclusion of evidence of the parties' negotiations. In *Prenn* v *Simmonds* [1971] 1 WLR 1381 at 1384 Lord Wilberforce had identified the basis of the exclusion as being that the evidence is 'simply unhelpful,' as 'by the nature of things, where negotiations are difficult, the parties' positions, with each passing letter are changing and until final agreement, though converging, still divergent'. This led to the contention that there are occasions when such evidence would be helpful and the courts simply need to treat such evidence with care, rather than not look at it at all. However, against that are raised fears of greater costs

23 G. McMeel, 'Prior Negotiations and Subsequent Conduct—The Next Step Forward for Contractual Interpretation' (2003) 119 LQR 272; D. Nicholls, 'My Kingdom for a Horse: The Meaning of Words' (2005) 121 LQR 577.

of cases through more evidence needing to be considered, and also increased uncertainty in the interpretation of contracts. The House of Lords concluded that there was nothing to suggest that the drawbacks to making evidence of negotiations admissible in interpreting the contracts were outweighed by the cases in which such evidence would improve the results. The well-established rule excluding evidence of negotiations would not be displaced. Lord Hoffmann said (at 41):

> The conclusion I would reach is that there is no clearly established case for departing from the exclusionary rule. The rule may well mean, as Lord Nicholls has argued, that parties are sometimes held bound by a contract in terms which, upon a full investigation of the course of negotiations, a reasonable observer would not have taken them to have intended. But a system which sometimes allows this to happen may be justified in the more general interest of economy and predictability in obtaining advice and adjudicating disputes.

Trends in the approach to exemption clauses

9.66 The process of construing the contract, with its search for the 'intention of the parties', is one which allowed the courts sufficient flexibility for the desirability of the end result to play a part in the conclusion reached. Prior to the enactment of the controls imposed upon exemption clauses by UCTA 1977, the courts used the rules of construction inventively in order to mitigate the effects of such clauses. This was described by Lord Denning MR in the Court of Appeal in *George Mitchell (Chesterhall) Ltd* v *Finney Lock Seeds Ltd* [1983] QB 284 at 297:

> Faced with this abuse of power—by the strong against the weak—by the use of small print conditions—the judges did what they could to put a curb upon it. They still had before them the idol, 'freedom of contract'. They still knelt down and worshipped it, but they concealed under their cloaks a secret weapon. They used it to stab the idol in the back. This weapon was called 'the construction of the contract'. They used it with great skill and ingenuity. They used it so as to depart from the natural meaning of the words of the exemption clause and to put upon them a strained and unnatural construction.

9.67 The courts' ability to stretch the rules of construction so as to arrive at the result they thought appropriate was used to its fullest extent before UCTA 1977. Since then the use of 'strained construction' has been deprecated. In *Photo Production Ltd* v *Securicor Transport Ltd* [1980] AC 827, Lord Diplock said (at 851):[24]

> the reports are full of cases in which what would appear to be very strained constructions have been placed upon exclusion clauses, mainly in what today would be called consumer contracts and contracts of adhesion ... any need for this kind of judicial distortion of the English language has been banished by Parliament's having made these kinds of contracts subject to the Unfair Contract Terms Act 1977.

24 See also, e.g., *George Mitchell (Chesterhall) Ltd* v *Finney Lock Seeds Ltd* [1983] 2 AC 803 at 810.

Since then the courts have become 'more accepting' of exemption clauses, recognizing that 'exclusion and limitation clauses are an integral part of pricing and risk allocation', at least in relation to 'commercial contracts made between parties of equal bargaining power'.[25]

9.68 In addition to the particular trend in relation to the treatment of exemption clauses, the more general evolution of construction in general since *Investors Compensation Scheme Ltd* v *West Bromwich Building Society* (1998) must also be emphasized. Plainly, that more general development has an impact in relation to exemption clauses.[26] It will be further considered in this chapter in referring to specific issues.

Basic approach to exemption clauses

9.69 Traditionally, the contra proferentem rule applied generally and in relation to exemption clauses, where it meant that any ambiguity in the clause was resolved against the person seeking to rely upon it. The words used had to clearly cover what had occurred if the clause was to be effective. *Wallis, Son, and Wells* v *Pratt & Haynes* (1911) provides an example:

> P & H sold seed to W as 'common English sanfoin' seed. In fact the seed supplied was giant sanfoin, a different and inferior variety. There was a clause in the sale contract stating that the 'sellers give no warranty expressed or implied as to the growth, description or any other matters'.

The House of Lords decided that the exemption clause did not cover what had occurred. It was a condition of the contract that the seed supplied was common English sanfoin. A breach of that term could not be covered by a clause which merely referred to warranties.[27] (A reference to 'warranties' could be understood in a broad sense, as simply another word for 'terms', but it also has a narrower, more technical sense, as a particular type of term, distinct from conditions (and now innominate terms). It could be seen as ambiguous.)

9.70 The impact of the general evolution of construction since *Investors Compensation Scheme Ltd* v *West Bromwich Building Society* (1998), alongside the change in attitude to exemption clauses post-UCTA, is still being worked out.[28] However, even before *Investors*, the point was made that 'it would be wrong to use [the contra proferentem rule] to create an ambiguity where

25 *Interactive E-Solutions JLT v O3B Africa Ltd* [2018] EWCA Civ 62 at [14].

26 See, e.g., Lord Hoffmann's judgment in *Bank of Credit and Commerce International* v *Ali* (2001).

27 But see now *KG Bominflot Bunkergesellschaft für Mineralöle mbH & Co v Petroplus Marketing AG (The Mercini Lady)* [2010] EWHC Civ 1145, [2011] 2 All ER (Comm) 522 and *Air Transworld Ltd v Bombardier Inc* [2012] EWHC 243 (Comm), [2012] 2 All ER (Comm) 60.

28 Contrast *KG Bominflot Bunkergesellschaft für Mineralöle mbH & Co v Petroplus Marketing AG (The Mercini Lady)* [2010] EWHC Civ 1145, [2011] 2 All ER (Comm) 522 and *Air Transworld Ltd v Bombardier Inc* [2012] EWHC 243 (Comm), [2012] 2 All ER (Comm) 60.

none realistically exists, and then to resolve the question by reference to it' (*Singer Co. (UK)* v *Tees and Hartlepool Port Authority* [1988] 2 Lloyd's Rep 164 at 169). The contra proferentem rule still exists,[29] but it is emphasized that in 'relation to commercial contracts, negotiated between parties of equal bargaining power, that rule now has a very limited role':[30]

> The words used, commercial common sense, and the documentary and factual context, are, and should be, normally enough to determine the meaning of a contractual provision.[31]

9.71 The final point to be made here is that the EC Directive on Unfair Terms in Consumer Contracts itself contains what can be regarded as a version of the contra proferentem rule. It is now contained in s 69 of the Consumer Rights Act 2015, and is, of course, limited to the consumer context.

Liability for negligence

9.72 The courts long dealt with the issue of whether an exemption clause covers liability based on negligence by developing a three-stage test: the *Canada Steamship* rules.[32] However, before considering that test, it should be emphasized that many such clauses will now fall within the controls of UCTA 1977 or the CRA 2015, depending upon whether it is a consumer contract which is in question. Where the clause purports to exclude or restrict liability for negligently caused personal injury or death, it is automatically ineffective under UCTA 1977, s 2(1) or CRA 2015, s 65. In relation to attempts to exclude or restrict liability for other negligently caused loss or damage, the clause is subject to UCTA 1977's requirement of reasonableness under s 2(2), or the CRA 2015's fairness test under s 61.[33] (Section 61 of the CRA 2015 is the section subjecting terms in consumer contracts to the fairness test generally. When there is such a provision, no special arrangement is needed to mirror the effect of s 2(2) of UCTA.)

9.73 Consideration should now be given to the test which has been used by the courts when faced with the question of whether an exemption clause covers negligence. The three-stage test, derived from *Canada Steamship*, is:

1. If the exemption clause expressly refers to liability for negligence, then effect must be given to it, to cover negligence liability.

---

29 *Transocean Drilling UK Ltd* v *Providence Resources plc* [2016] 2 All ER (Comm) 606, at [20]; *Nohabar-Cookson* v *The Hut Group Ltd* [2016] EWCA 128 at [37]–[38].

30 *Persimmon Homes Ltd* v *Ove Arup & Partners Ltd* [2017] EWCA Civ 373 at [52]; *Interactive E-Solutions JLT* v *O3B Africa Ltd* [2018] EWCA Civ 62 at [14].

31 *K/S Victoria Street* v *House of Fraser (Stores Management) Ltd* [2011] EWCA Civ 904 at [68]; Quoted in *Persimmon Homes Ltd* v *Ove Arup & Partners Ltd* [2017] EWCA Civ 373 at [52].

32 This section refers to Macdonald, *Exemption Clauses and Unfair Terms*, 2nd edn, pp. 50–62; J. Carter, 'Commercial Construction and the *Canada Steamship* Rules' [1995] 9 JCL 69.

33 These provisions not only cover contractual clauses dealing with liability for negligence, but also non-contractual notices. In relation to negligence liability it may simply be liability in tort which is in question, rather than any contractual liability.

2. If there is no express reference to negligence, it must be asked whether the words used are wide enough, in their ordinary meaning, to cover liability for negligence; any doubt must be resolved against the party in breach.
3. Even if the words used are wide enough to cover liability for negligence, it must be asked whether the party in breach could be liable on some ground other than that of negligence. If he or she could be, and if that other ground is not so fanciful or remote that the party in breach cannot be supposed to have desired protection against it, then it is likely that the words will be taken to refer to the non-negligent liability only.

As has been indicated, this is based upon the three-stage test formulated by Lord Morton in giving the judgment of the Privy Council in *Canada Steamship Lines Ltd* v *R* [1952] AC 192 at 208.[34] There are three initial points which must be made before the stages of the test are considered further.

9.74 First, the approach is based upon the idea that 'it is inherently improbable that one party to the contract should intend to absolve the other party from the consequences of the latter's own negligence' (*Gillespie Bros & Co. Ltd* v *Roy Bowles Transport Ltd* [1973] 1 All ER 193 at 203).

9.75 Second, it has been suggested that there is no such 'high degree of improbability' that a limitation of liability (rather than an exclusion of liability) would be agreed to, and that a less strict approach should be taken to the construction of limitation than exclusion clauses. The idea of making a general distinction of this type between limitation clauses and exclusion clauses is considered more generally, and criticized, later (para. **9.88**).

9.76 Third, the impact on the *Canada Steamship* test of the changes in relation to the construction of exemption clauses, and also of the general evolution in the approach to construction after *Investors Compensation Scheme Ltd* v *West Bromwich Building Society* (1998) (see para. **9.87**), will need to be considered. It will be addressed after the stages of the test have been considered further.

9.77 It is obvious that there should be no difficulty in finding that a clause covers negligence if it expressly refers to negligence. Any other conclusion would run contrary to the idea of freedom of contract and the basic principle that in construing a clause it is the intention of the parties which is being sought. It has not, however, always been clear what should amount to an express reference to negligence. Although it has been suggested that nothing short of the use of the term 'negligence' itself will suffice (*Lamport and Holt Lines Ltd* v *Coubro and Scrutton (M&I) Ltd, The Raphael* [1982] 2 Lloyd's Rep 42 at 48), if the clause uses some synonym for it (*Smith* v *South Wales Switchgear Co. Ltd* [1978] 1 WLR 165 at 168 and 172), such as the phrase 'neglect or default' (*Monarch Airlines Ltd* v *London Luton Airport Ltd* [1997] CLC 698 at 706), that should also be sufficient. In *Smith* v *South Wales Switchgear* (1978) the House of Lords made it clear

34 See also *George Mitchell (Chesterhall) Ltd* v *Finney Lock Seeds Ltd* [1983] QB 284 at 312; *Alderslade* v *Hendon Laundry Ltd* [1945] KB 189 at 192.

that the addition of words such as 'howsoever caused' to a reference to loss or damage could not amount to express references to negligence.

9.78 Clauses explicitly referring to negligence are not unknown (for example, *Spriggs* v *Sotheby Parke Bernet & Co.* (1986)), but do not occur very often. Such a clause could dissuade the party against whom it might be used from contracting. In *EE Caledonia Ltd* v *Orbit Valve plc* [1994] 2 Lloyd's Rep 239, Steyn LJ said (at 246):

> Why was an express reference to negligence not inserted? ... I have no doubt that the draftsman on the Underground to whom such a question was addressed would say 'one does not want to frighten off one or other of the parties'. Omissions of express reference to negligence in contracts drafted by lawyers tend to deliberate.

9.79 The second part of the rule would seem to require consideration of what the clause 'plainly means to any ordinary literate and sensible person' (*Lamport and Holt Lines Ltd* v *Coubro and Scrutton (M&I) Ltd, The Raphael* [1982] 2 Lloyd's Rep 42 at 52), although, in appropriate circumstances, specialized commercial knowledge may be relevant. A clause may refer to loss or damage 'howsoever caused', directing attention to the cause of the loss (*Joseph Travers & Sons Ltd* v *Cooper* [1915] 1 KB 73 at 93 and 101), and that is sufficient for the second part of the rule. Less explicit general clauses may also be sufficient. The words 'any act or omission' have been seen as 'certainly wide enough to comprehend negligence' (*The Raphael* at 45 per Donaldson LJ). The second and third stages of the test can combine to put the person seeking to rely on the clause 'on the horns of a dilemma', that is, in some cases, arguing that the clause is wide enough to satisfy the second part of the test will result in it covering 'other' liability within the third (*Shell Chemicals UK Ltd* v *P & O Roadtankers Ltd* [1995] 1 Lloyd's Rep 297 at 301 per Balcombe LJ).

9.80 The third stage of the test indicated above could be regarded as part of the second stage. In considering whether there could be liability without negligence, the question being asked is merely whether a general clause is ambiguous because of one particular factor: the number of ways in which liability may occur. In some cases liability may occur in more than one way. It may arise on the basis of negligence or it may occur strictly, without fault. Where there can be liability without negligence the courts tended to find that a generally worded exemption clause was intended to cover only the strict liability and not that based on negligence. In *Alderslade* v *Hendon Laundry Ltd* [1945] KB 189 (see para. **9.83**), Lord Greene MR gave this example (at 192):[35]

> [A common carrier's] liability in respect of articles entrusted to him is not necessarily based on negligence. Accordingly if a common carrier wishes to limit his liability for lost articles and does not make it quite clear that he is desiring to limit it in respect of his liability for negligence, then the clause will be construed as extending only to his liability on grounds other than negligence.

35 See also *Rutter* v *Palmer* [1922] 2 KB 87 at 94.

9.81 A further illustration is provided by *White* v *John Warwick & Co. Ltd* (1953):[36]

> Mr White was in business as a newsagent and tobacconist. He contracted with the defendants for the hire of a tradesman's tricycle. The defendants supplied him with a tricycle with a defective saddle which caused him to fall off and injure himself. The contract of hire contained a clause which stated 'nothing in this agreement shall render the owners liable for any personal injury to the riders of the machines hired'.

Mr White sued the defendants for damages for his injuries. He had two grounds for his claim:

1. breach of contract for failure to supply a tricycle which was reasonably fit for its purpose (strict liability);
2. liability for negligently failing to see that the cycle was kept in good repair.

The defendants sought to rely upon the exemption clause in the contract of hire. The Court of Appeal concluded that the exemption clause should be construed as merely applying to the strict liability and not to the liability for negligence. (In such a case the exclusion of liability for negligently caused personal injury would now be prevented by UCTA 1977, s 2.) See also *EE Caledonia Ltd* v *Orbit Valve plc* (1994).

9.82 One point which should be emphasized is that not every alternative basis of liability would be relevant to the third part of the test. To be relevant to the question of construction, an alternative basis of liability must not be too 'fanciful or remote' so that it 'would not have been within the contemplation of the parties when the terms of the [contract] were agreed' (*Canada Steamship Lines Ltd* v *R* [1952] AC 192 at 210). The question of whether or not any alternative basis of liability is too 'fanciful or remote' will depend upon the facts of the particular case, but it should be borne in mind that:

> When two commercial concerns contract with one another, they do not ... concern themselves with ... legal subtleties ... We should look at the facts and realities of the situation as they did or must be deemed to have presented themselves to the contracting parties at the time the contract was made, and ask what potential liabilities the one to the other did the parties apply their minds, or must be deemed to have done so. (*Lamport and Holt Lines Ltd* v *Coubro and Scrutton (M&I) Ltd, The Raphael* [1982] 2 Lloyd's Rep 42 at 50 per May LJ (see also Stephenson LJ at 51))

9.83 Up to this point we have discussed the situation where there is a generally worded exemption clause and negligence is not the only basis of liability. The converse of that situation is where there is a generally worded clause but there is no liability, and no breach of contract, in the absence of negligence. Where the sole basis of liability is negligence, the courts have more readily found that a generally worded exemption clause covers negligence. In

36 L. Gower, 'Exemption Clauses—Contractual and Tortious Liability' (1954) 17 MLR 155.

Alderslade v *Hendon Laundry Ltd* (1945) it was successfully argued that the exemption clause covered negligence. In that case:

> Mr Alderslade left ten Irish linen handkerchiefs with the laundry to be washed. The laundry lost the handkerchiefs. The contract contained a clause which stated: 'The maximum amount allowed for lost or damaged articles is twenty times the charge made for laundering.'

When sued by Mr Alderslade, the laundry sought to rely upon the clause to limit its liability. The loss of the handkerchiefs constituted a breach of contract only if the laundry had been negligent; there was no strict liability for the loss. It was decided that the clause covered the breach: the negligent loss of the handkerchiefs.

9.84 In *Alderslade* v *Hendon Laundry Ltd* [1945] 1 KB 189 Lord Greene MR considered the third stage of the test, and used language which indicated that the presence, or absence, of an alternative basis of liability to negligence is determinative of the question of construction of a widely worded, general, exemption clause. In that case there was no liability in the absence of negligence and he was influenced by the fact that, if the court had concluded otherwise, the exemption clause would have served no purpose at all. He said (at 192) that the clause must be construed as relating to negligence, in the absence of other possible liability for it to cover (see also Lord Morton in *Canada Steamship Lines* v *R* [1952] AC 192 at 208). However, this was to take too rigid a line. In *Alderslade* Mackinnon LJ took the approach that 'if the only liability of the party pleading the exemption is a liability for negligence, the clause will more readily operate to exempt him' (at 195, quoting Scrutton LJ in *Rutter* v *Palmer* [1922] 2 KB 87 at 92). Similarly, in relation to the converse case, it has been emphasized that the presence of an alternative, non-negligent ground of liability is merely an indicator of the parties' intentions:

> If there is a head of liability upon which the clause could bite in addition to negligence then, because it is more unlikely than not that a party will be ready to excuse his other contracting party from the consequence of the other's negligence, the clause will generally be construed as not covering negligence ... the court asks itself what in all the relevant circumstances the parties intended the alleged exemption clause to mean. (*Lamport and Holt Lines Ltd* v *Coubro and Scrutton (M&I) Ltd, The Raphael* [1982] 2 Lloyd's Rep 42 at 50 per May LJ)

In short, it must be borne in mind that even in looking at the three-stage test, we are not considering a rule of law, but merely an aid to construction (*Smith* v *South Wales Switchgear Co. Ltd* [1978] 1 WLR 165 at 178 per Lord Keith).

9.85 *Hollier* v *Rambler Motors (AMC) Ltd* (1972) illustrates the point that the three-part test merely assists construction. Mr Hollier's car was on the Rambler Motors' premises for repair when it was damaged by a fire caused by their negligence. Rambler Motors had a standard form document containing the clause: 'The company is not responsible for damage caused by fire to customers' cars on the premises.' The Court of Appeal decided that Rambler Motors had not incorporated that clause into the particular contract with Mr Hollier (see para. **9.55**). However, the court also considered whether the clause would have covered what had occurred had it been incorporated. It was argued that, as there was no breach unless the fire had been caused by Rambler Motors' negligence, the clause had to cover a negligent breach or it would serve no purpose. The court did not take that line. It considered how an ordinary person in the position of Mr Hollier would have viewed the clause and concluded that he would have seen it as merely indicating that there was no strict liability for fire damage. The case before the court was contrasted with *Alderslade* v *Hendon Laundry Ltd* [1945] 1 KB 189, which the court thought had dealt with a situation where 'any ordinary man or woman would have known that all that was being excluded was the negligence of the laundry' (at 80). The clause before the court in *Hollier* was construed not as covering negligence but rather as a warning to customers that Rambler Motors were not liable if a car was damaged by a fire occurring without negligence.[37] (For a discussion of the case, see E. Barendt, 'Exemption Clauses: Interpretation and Incorporation' (1972) 85 MLR 644.)

9.86 As we have seen, in applying the three-stage test, the courts looked at the clause in context; they considered such matters as the understanding of the ordinary person and whether a possible liability is too 'fanciful or remote' for the parties to have considered it when contracting. Clearly this left sufficient flexibility for the courts' view of the justice of the case to influence their legal reasoning. It must be remembered that *Hollier* v *Rambler Motors (AMC) Ltd* (1972) did not concern a dispute between two business people but rather one between a consumer and a businessman. However, the tools which the courts have available to assist them to achieve a desired result vary from time to time. When they acquire a new tool their use of an old one may change. It must be emphasized that *Hollier* is a pre-UCTA 1977 case, and post-UCTA the courts acknowledged that they should no longer resort to 'strained construction' to restrict the operation of exemption clauses.[38]

9.87 In addition, some final consideration should be given to the *Canada Steamship* rules, not only in relation to the fact that there is now frequently statutory policing of exemption clauses, but also in relation to the evolution in the approach to construction generally since *Investors Compensation Scheme Ltd* v *West Bromwich Building Society* (1998). In *BCCI* v *Ali* [2001] UKHL 8 at [66], [2002] 1 AC 251 at [66], Lord Hoffmann indicated that a change has occurred in relation to the use of the *Canada Steamship* rules. Of course, the *Canada Steamship* approach has been seen as based on an assumption about the improbability of one party intending to excuse the other's negligence (for example, *Gillespie Bros & Co. Ltd* v *Roy Bowles Transport Ltd* [1973] 1 All ER 193 at 203), and in *HIH Casualty and General Insurance Ltd* v *Chase Manhattan Bank* [2003] 1 All ER (Comm) 349, Lord Hoffmann was of the view that in that case there was 'no inherent improbability' that the intention was to exclude liability for negligence. Rather, he saw negligence as 'a risk which the parties could reasonably have been expected to allocate' and the

37 Where there is no other head of liability, the clause may be seen as not covering negligence but merely avoiding doubt about the existence of other liability—*Dorset County Council* v *Southern Felt Roofing* (1990).

38 E.g. *Photo Production Ltd* v *Securicor Transport Ltd* [1980] AC 827 at 851 per Lord Diplock; *George Mitchell (Chesterhall) Ltd* v *Finney Lock Seeds Ltd* [1983] 2 AC 803 at 810.

Canada Steamship approach was not applied to confine the coverage of the clause in question to strict liability (at [67]). Similarly, in *Lictor Anstalt* v *MIR Steel UK Ltd* (2012) the court concluded that it was clear that 'the whole point' of the clause was to shift the 'entire risk and burden of any claim' even in relation to torts of intentional wrongdoing (at [42]). Moreover, in *Persimmon Homes Ltd* v *Ove Arup & Partners* (2017) Jackson LJ emphasized that in major construction contracts exemption clauses are 'merely part of the contractual apparatus for distributing risk' and 'there is no need to approach such clauses with horror or with a mindset determined to cut them down' (at [57]). He saw the *Canada Steamship* rules as being of little assistance in the instant case (at [59]).[39] It would seem that, at least in a commercial contract between parties of equal bargaining power, the parties' intentions as to the coverage of negligence by an exemption clause will often be clear,[40] and there will simply be no need to refer to *Canada Steamship.*

Limitation of liability

9.88 The House of Lords has distinguished the construction of clauses which totally exclude liability from the construction of those which merely limit it. In *Ailsa Craig Fishing Co. Ltd* v *Malvern Fishing Co. Ltd* [1983] 1 WLR 964, their Lordships stated that limitation clauses are to be construed differently from total exclusion clauses. In that case:

> Securicor had undertaken to provide a security service for the boats belonging to a fishing association whilst those vessels were in Aberdeen harbour. Ailsa Craig were members of that association. One night their vessel, the *Strathallan*, fouled another boat and sank. Ailsa Craig claimed £55,000 damages from Securicor. Securicor conceded that they had been negligent and breached their contract, but sought to rely upon a clause in the contract to restrict their liability to £1,000.

The House of Lords decided that the clause was effective to limit Securicor's liability to £1,000.

9.89 The general comments on the construction of limitation clauses in *Ailsa Craig* should be noted. Such clauses were still to be construed contra proferentem (at 966 and 971), but Lord Wilberforce stated (at 966) that limitation clauses are not to be treated with 'the same hostility as clauses of exclusion'. Lord Fraser thought (at 971) that the rules for the construction of exclusion clauses should not be applied in 'their full rigour' to limitation clauses. The same line was taken by the House of Lords in *George Mitchell (Chesterhall) Ltd* v *Finney Lock Seeds Ltd* [1983] 2 AC 803. There Lord Bridge, with whom the rest of the court agreed, stated (at 814) that the principles used for the construction of total exclusion clauses 'cannot be applied in their full rigour to limitation clauses'.

39 Although he did then show that the same conclusion, that the clause covered negligence, would be arrived at under the *Canada Steamship* rules.

40 *HIH Casualty and General Insurance Ltd* v *Chase Manhattan Bank* (2003); *National Westminster Bank* v *Utrecht Finance Co* (2001) at [47]; *Re-Source America International Ltd* (2004) at [55].

9.90 The natural reaction to this stated distinction between limitation and exclusion clauses is that it is wholly unrealistic, as 'a limitation clause may be so severe in its operation as to be virtually indistinguishable from that of an exclusion clause'. Such indeed was the reaction of the High Court of Australia when refusing to take the same approach to the construction of a limitation clause as the House of Lords (*Darlington Futures Ltd* v *Delco Australia Pty* (1986) 68 ALR 385 at 391). The Australian High Court thought that the same basic approach should be taken to the interpretation of limitation and exclusion clauses.

9.91 It seems unlikely that the distinction drawn by the House of Lords in *Ailsa Craig* could now survive any significant challenge to it as a general approach. In *HIH Casualty and General Insurance Ltd* v *Chase Manhattan Bank* [2003] 1 All ER (Comm) 349 Lord Hoffmann doubted that Lord Fraser had been intending to create a 'mechanistic' rule in *Ailsa Craig* (at [63]). More broadly, we have seen the waning of the contra proferentem rule, and the hostile treatment of exemption clauses, in general.

9.92 Further, we should consider the justification which the House of Lords put forward for the different treatment of limitation and exclusion clauses. In *Ailsa Craig Fishing Co. Ltd* v *Malvern Fishing Co. Ltd*, Lord Wilberforce said ([1983] 1 WLR 964 at 966):

> Clauses of limitation are not to be regarded with the same hostility as clauses of exclusion; this is because they must be related to other contractual terms, in particular to the risks to which the defending party may be exposed, the remuneration which he receives, and possibly also the opportunity of the other party to insure.

(See also Lord Fraser at 970.) This is to take the line that a limitation clause, unlike an exclusion clause, will represent a carefully agreed allocation of risks, and price, between the parties and, on that basis, is not to be construed 'hostilely'; but such a correlation of risk and price may be present when there is an exclusion clause (*Photo Production Ltd* v *Securicor Transport Ltd* (1980)) and may not be present when there is a limitation clause (*George Mitchell (Chesterhall) Ltd* v *Finney Lock Seeds Ltd* (1983)), and we have seen the recognition of the significance of such correlation on a more general basis. In *Persimmon Homes* v *Ove Arup* (2017) where, although the particular issue was concerned with an exclusion clause, the contract contained both limitations and exclusions, Jackson LJ said (at [57]):

> In major construction contracts the parties commonly agree how they will allocate the risks between themselves and who will insure against what. Exemption clauses are part of the contractual apparatus for distributing risk. There is no need to approach such clauses with horror or with a mindset determined to cut them down. Contractors and consultants who accept large risks will charge for doing so and will no doubt take out appropriate insurance. Contractors and consultants who accept lesser degrees of risk will presumably reflect that in the fees which they agree.

These comments may have been made in relation to 'major construction contracts', the type of contract with which the case was specifically concerned, but it was also said of the contra proferentem rule that 'it now has a very limited role' in relation to 'commercial contracts negotiated between parties of equal bargaining power' (at [52]). It would seem that the comment about the agreed allocation of risk through exemption clauses should also extend to this more general category of contracts, particularly as it can be emphasized that the true relevance of the correlation of the risk allocation and the pricing is in relation to the 'reasonableness' of the exemption clause, whether it is one excluding or limiting liability, and legislation will often now allow the courts to directly examine the 'reasonableness', or fairness, of the clause and avoid 'strained construction'.

9.93 There is one situation in which there is a basic difference in principle between a clause which merely limits and one which excludes liability (see (1983) 99 LQR 163). An exclusion clause could be so extensive that the court would be faced with the question of whether the person relying upon it was under any obligation at all, that is, if X and Y have made an agreement, X could have inserted an exclusion clause which is so extensive that X appears to have no legal liability, whatever he or she does or does not do, and so has no initial legal obligation under the agreement. In this situation the court would have to determine whether X and Y had intended to make a legally enforceable contract at all. If it concluded that they had, it would have to find a way of construing the exclusion clause to leave some binding obligation upon X.[41] This singular situation can never arise in relation to a limitation clause. In seeking to limit liability, the parties acknowledge the existence of the obligation on which that liability is founded. When dealing with a limitation clause, the question of whether the parties in fact intended a legally enforceable contract cannot arise in the way that it can in relation to a total exclusion clause. (See *George Mitchell (Chesterhall) Ltd* v *Finney Lock Seeds Ltd* [1983] QB 284 at 304 per Oliver LJ.) However, interesting as this distinction may be (see B. Coote, *Exception Clause*, Sweet & Maxwell, 1964, ch 1; Macdonald (2012) 29 JCL 47), it would not justify the wide, and unqualified, general distinction made by the House of Lords between exclusion and limitation clauses.

Fundamental breach

9.94 There have been attempts to introduce a rule of law preventing 'fundamental breaches', or breaches of 'fundamental terms', being covered by exemption clauses, no matter how aptly worded the clause (e.g. *Karsales (Harrow) Ltd* v *Wallis* (1956)). However, in *Suisse Atlantique Société d'Armement Maritime SA* v *NV Rotterdamsche Kolen Centrale* [1967] 1 AC 361 the House of Lords disagreed with any such attempts, and in *Photo Production Ltd* v *Securicor Transport Ltd* (1980) it 'gave the final quietus to the doctrine that a "fundamental breach" of contract deprived the party in breach of the benefit of a clause in the contract excluding or limiting his liability' (*George Mitchell (Chesterhall) Ltd* v *Finney Lock Seeds Ltd* [1983] 2 All ER 737 at 741 per Lord Bridge). The purpose of the Court of Appeal, in attempting to create fundamental breach as a rule of law, was to deal with objectionable exemption clauses in a way which the draftsman could not overcome. However, the usefulness of fundamental breach as a rule of law had been considered in *Suisse Atlantique*. There it had been pointed out that it was an undiscriminating

41 See the arguments raised in *Mitsubishi Corp.* v *Eastwind Transport Ltd* (2005).

approach to the problem of objectionable exemption clauses, as it could strike down clauses arrived at as a fairly negotiated allocation of risk between businesses. It was indicated that to deal with objectionable exemption clauses, a more discriminating tool than fundamental breach would have to be provided by legislation. (See Lord Reid at 406.) By the time *Photo Production* was decided, Parliament had provided the courts with a means of attacking exemption clauses in a more discriminating way: UCTA 1977.

9.95 Once fundamental breach had been disposed of as a rule of law, the point could be made that it

> is always necessary when considering an exemption clause to decide whether as a matter of construction, it extends to exclude or restrict the liability in question, but, if it does, it is no longer permissible at common law to reject or circumvent the clause by treating it as inapplicable to a 'fundamental breach'. (*Edmund Murray Ltd* v *BSP International Foundations Ltd* (1993) 33 Con LR 1 at 16 per Neill LJ)

In this context, it was never entirely clear what was meant by a 'fundamental breach' or a 'fundamental term', and it now seems unnecessary to be overly concerned with those questions or to use the terminology. What should be given some brief consideration here are some of the approaches and rules which were, in effect, the foundations upon which the attempt was made to construct 'fundamental breach' as a rule of law. Some care has to be taken, though, not to resurrect that idea, and it must be remembered that there have been significant changes in the approach to the construction even of exemption clauses since the advent of UCTA 1977 and the *Investors case*.

'Peas and beans'; main purpose of the contract; four corners rule

9.96 Here, brief consideration can be given to some of the approaches and rules which were, in effect, the foundations upon which the attempt was made to construct 'fundamental breach' as a rule of law. Some care has to be taken, though, not to resurrect that idea.

9.97 The argument may arise that an exemption clause does not cover what has occurred, because it was only intended to relate to the situation in which the contract was being performed (albeit in some way defectively) and what has occurred is not a performance of the contract, even a defective one. In other words, it is argued that the clause was not intended to apply in such circumstances because they are beyond the boundaries of the contract by which the clause was intended to be limited. In *Chanter* v *Hopkins* (1838) 4 M & W 399, Lord Abinger said (at 404):

> If a man offers to buy peas of another, and he sends him beans, he does not perform his contract. But that is not a warranty; there is no warranty that he should sell him peas; the contract is to sell peas, and if he sends him anything else in their stead, it is a non-performance of it.

If there is a contract between two parties, X and Y, and X has contracted to deliver peas to Y, but he delivers beans instead, it will be contended that he cannot rely upon any clause of the contract excluding his liability for defective performance because what occurred was not a performance at all, even a defective one. (Of course, care must be taken in ascertaining exactly what the contractual obligations were. The contract may have been one for the supply of peas or beans or, even, any green vegetable—see Lord Devlin, 'The Treatment of Breach of Contract' [1966] CLJ 192 at 212.) But this type of argument has been seen as going beyond delivery of goods which are clearly of an entirely different kind to that contracted for, to the situation where the goods delivered are, at one level, the type of goods contracted for, but are argued to be so defective that their delivery cannot be regarded as within the performance of the contract (e.g. *Karsales (Harrow) Ltd* v *Wallis* (1956)). However, such an approach must now be regarded as of very restricted application. In *George Mitchell Ltd* v *Finney Lock Seeds Ltd* [1983] 2 All ER 737, where there was a contract for the sale of Dutch winter white cabbage seed and an inferior autumn variety was supplied which led to a valueless crop, the House of Lords refused to apply this type of approach. The view was taken that acceptance of that argument in the Court of Appeal and at first instance 'came dangerously near to reintroducing by the back door the doctrine of fundamental breach' (at 741). The relevant clause was seen as applying to 'seeds' and 'seeds' had been supplied.

9.98 However, there are other situations in which arguments arise that an exemption clause was not intended to apply to what has occurred because it has gone beyond the boundaries of the contract. That line may be taken in relation to the situation in which a ship unjustifiably deviates from its route, or a bailee stores goods other than in the place contracted for or hands them over to a subcontractor without authority. In each case it is, of course, necessary to determine what the boundaries of the contract are; a clause may give a ship 'liberty to deviate', for example, and effect will be given to such a clause. However, faced with wide clauses serving to stretch the contractual boundaries, the courts may find that such clauses are intended to be restricted by the 'main purpose', or the 'four corners', of the contract. In *Glynn* v *Margetson & Co.* (1893), when a clause in a contract for the shipment of a perishable cargo stated that the ship

> should have liberty to proceed to and stay at any port or ports in any station in the Mediterranean, Levant, Black Sea, or Adriatic, or on the coasts of Africa, Spain, Portugal, France, Great Britain or Ireland, for the purpose of delivering coals, cargo, or passengers, or for any other purpose whatsoever,

that clause did not prevent the shipowners from being liable for the damage to the cargo, when it had gone 350 miles off of the direct route. The clause provided liberty to deviate, but the approach taken was that it had to be read in the light of the main purpose of the contract, ascertained from reading it as a whole, and that the main purpose of getting a perishable cargo from A to B would be defeated if the liberty to deviate was not read as confined to ports along the route from A to B. Similarly, in *Sze Hai Tong Bank* v *Rambler Cycle Co. Ltd* (1959), where there was a clause stating that 'the responsibility of the carrier ... shall be deemed ... to cease absolutely after the goods are discharged from the ship' but the contract also provided that delivery should only be made on production of the bill of lading, the court viewed delivery of the goods without production of the bill of lading as defeating the main object of the contract and as outside the protection of the other clause. The situation was equated with what would have occurred if the carriers had burnt the goods or thrown them into the sea. However, this type of reasoning must be used with care to avoid resurrecting fundamental breach. The reasoning in *Motis Exports Ltd* v *Dampskibsselskabet* (2000), in extending the *Rambler Cycle* case, just discussed, to hold liable carriers who had handed over goods in response to a forged bill of lading, has been seen as 'coming perilously close to, if not actually to be, the doctrine of fundamental breach' (B. Davenport, 'Misdelivery: A Fundamental Breach?' [2000] LMCLQ 455 at 456). More recently, the court refused to extend this type of approach to goods stored on deck when the obligation was to store them below deck, at much less risk (*Daewoo Heavy Industries Ltd* v *Klipriver Shipping Ltd* (2003)), and plainly the impetus to avoid the artificiality of such a doctrine as fundamental breach has only been added to with the general approach to construction taken in *Investors*.[42]

Summary

- To be incorporated, terms must be introduced before a contract is made.
- Subject to very limited restrictions, signature of a contractual document will incorporate terms.
- Terms on an unsigned document or sign are incorporated if reasonably sufficient notice has been supplied of them.
- Terms may be incorporated because of a course of past dealings between the parties.
- The basic approach to construction generally has evolved since the *Investors* case, which brought a new emphasis to the background to the contract, but it has become clear that that should not generally be allowed to overwhelm the words.
- Rules such as the contra proferentem (i.e. if there is any ambiguity in a clause it will be construed against the proferens) and the *Canada Steamship* approach to the coverage of liability by an exemption clause will now be used sparingly in the context of commercial parties of equal bargaining power.
- The idea that a limitation clause will be construed less strictly than an exclusion clause must now be very doubtful, in the light of the movement away from any special treatment of exemption clauses generally.

Further reading

M. Clarke, 'Notice of Contractual Terms' (1976) 35 CLJ 51

H. Collins, 'Objectivity and Committed Contextualism in Interpretation' in S. Worthington, (ed.), *Commercial Law and Commercial Practice*, Hart Publishing, 2003, pp. 189–209

A. Kramer, 'Common Sense Principles of Contract Interpretation and How We've Been Using Them All Along' (2003) 23 Ox Jo LS 173

42 See the judgment of Lord Hoffmann in *Bank of Credit and Commerce International* v *Ali* [2001] 1 All ER 961, particularly at [66].

E. Macdonald, 'Incorporation of Standard Terms in Website Contracting—Clicking "I Agree"' (2011) 27 JCL 198

E. McKendrick, 'The Interpretation of Contracts: Lord Hoffmann's Re-Statement' in S. Worthington (ed.), *Commercial Law and Commercial Practice*, Hart Publishing, 2003, pp. 139–62

G. McMeel, 'Prior Negotiations and Subsequent Conduct—The Next Step Forward for Contractual Interpretation' (2003) 119 LQR 272

D. Nicholls, 'My Kingdom for a Horse: The Meaning of Words' (2005) 121 LQR 577

J. R. Spencer, 'Signature, Consent and the Rule in *L'Estrange v Graucob*' (1973) 32 CLJ 104

Lord Sumption, 'A Question of Taste: The Supreme Court and the Interpretation of Contracts' (2017) 17(2) Oxford University Commonwealth Law Journal 301.

Chapter 10

Exemption clauses and legislation

Introduction

10.1 In the previous chapter, it was seen that the problem of unfair exemption clauses had impacted upon, and distorted, the construction of exemption clauses, but the courts took the line that the need for 'strained' construction had been removed with the advent of the Unfair Contract Terms Act 1977 (UCTA). It is UCTA which is largely considered in this chapter.

10.2 Despite its title, UCTA has only ever been concerned with exemption clauses, and since 1994, because of the Directive on unfair terms in consumer contracts, there has been legislation in the UK dealing with unfair terms more generally. The coverage of the Directive is not restricted to exemption clauses, but it is only concerned with consumer contracts, whereas UCTA dealt with exemption clauses in relation to both consumer and business-to-business contracts.

10.3 The Directive was originally implemented in the UK by the Unfair Terms in Consumer Contracts Regulations 1994, which were then replaced by the 1999 Regulations of the same name. There was an overlap between the Regulations and UCTA, and the situation was not straightforward. The Regulations and UCTA had different approaches to identifying which contracts should be treated as those where a consumer was involved, and whereas UCTA applied a test of 'reasonableness' to some exemption clauses, and made some automatically unfair, the Regulations used a test of 'fairness'. Such a complicated situation was particularly undesirable in relation to consumer protection.

10.4 The complex overlapping regimes provided the background to the eventual enactment of the Consumer Rights Act 2015,[1] Part 2 of which now contains the UK's implementation of the

1 *Unfair Terms in Contracts*, Law Com No 292, Scot Law Com No 199; Law Com, Scot Law Com, Issues Paper *Unfair Terms in Consumer Contracts: a new approach?* (2012)); Law Com, Scot Law Com, *Unfair Terms in Consumer Contracts: Advice to the Department for Business, Innovation and Skills* (2013).

Directive, and which has also taken the consumer protection elements out of UCTA. In places, UCTA went further in relation to the protection of consumers than did the Directive and, to a large extent, that has been maintained in the CRA.

10.5 This chapter is concerned with exemption clauses. It will principally deal with UCTA, but point out where the CRA impacts, rather than UCTA. The broader provisions of the CRA, such as the fairness test, and the 'core exemption', which exempts some terms from the fairness test, are however left for detailed consideration in **Chapter 12**, which deals with the fairness regime in the CRA more generally.

10.6 However, before we begin to look at the legislative policing of exemption clauses, we should acknowledge the impact of UCTA. That Act clearly interferes with freedom of contract. It affects the agreement which the parties made for themselves but, as Lord Reid pointed out in *Suisse Atlantique* [1967] 1 AC 361, the situation in which an 'objectionable' exemption clause is found may be one in which one party's freedom of contract is very limited. He said:

> Probably the most objectionable are found in the complex standard conditions which are now so common. In the ordinary way the customer has no time to read them, and if he did read them he probably would not understand them. And if he did understand and object to any of them, he would generally be told he could take it or leave it. And if he then went to another supplier the result would be the same.

To a large extent UCTA can be seen to be policing exemption clauses where freedom of contract is not operating as it should.

10.7 Obviously, the CRA 2015 also interferes with freedom of contract, but only in the consumer context, and in *Kasler* the CJEU emphasized (at [39]) that it has

> consistently held that the system of protection introduced by Directive 93/13 is based on the idea that the consumer is in a position of weakness vis-à-vis the seller or supplier, as regards both his bargaining power and his level of knowledge, a situation that leads to his agreeing to terms drawn up in advance by the seller or supplier without being able to influence the content of those terms.

In other words, the Directive is based on the idea of policing terms where freedom of contract is not operating properly between the parties. The Directive is confined to terms which are not individually negotiated, as had been its implementation in the UK prior to the CRA 2015 (Unfair Terms in Consumer Contracts Regulations 1994 and then the Unfair Terms in Consumer Contracts Regulations 1999). Most of those will be in standard form contracts, the basic problems which they may occasion being set out by Lord Reid above, and which are echoed in the CJEU's views of the 'idea' behind the Directive. The Law Commissions took the step of recommending extending the coverage of the fairness regime in what has become the CRA 2015 to individually negotiated terms, because UCTA 1977's protection from unreasonable exemption clauses did so, in the consumer context, and also because 'Consumers seldom have sufficient understanding of the possible impact of non-core terms to make any negotiation meaningful'.[2] (As we shall see in **Chapter 11**, 'core terms' are generally exempt from the fairness test.)

10.8 There is one final issue to be looked at before consideration of UCTA and the CRA's coverage of exemption clauses can begin, and that is the need to identify which Act should be looked at to see if it impacts in relation to a particular contract. This is determined by whether the contract is a consumer contract within the definition set out in the CRA. The definition of 'deals as consumer' which used to be in s12 of UCTA has been repealed.

Consumer contracts

10.9 Looking at s 61 CRA, we can see that a 'consumer contract' is one between a 'consumer' and a 'trader'. Section 2(3) CRA states:

> 'Consumer' means an individual acting for purposes that are wholly or mainly outside the individual's trade, business, craft or profession.

And s 2(2) CRA states:

> 'Trader' means a person acting for purposes relating to that person's trade, business, craft or profession, whether acting personally or through another person acting in the trader's name or on the trader's behalf.[3]

The burden of proving that an individual is not a consumer lies on the trader (s 2(4)).[4]

10.10 We can first consider the meaning of 'consumer', and note that the definition refers to 'an individual'. Like the reference to 'a natural person' in the Directive, and previous definition in the Regulations, this is intended to preclude purely 'legal persons', such as companies, from being counted as consumers. This differs from the approach which was taken under UCTA, where a company could 'deal as consumer'.[5]

10.11 The CRA basically adopts the approach of the Directive. It does, however, contain a specific addition to the definition to deal with mixed transactions which are partly business and partly private. In *Gruber* v *Bay Wa AG* (2005) the CJEU had indicated a very restrictive line on such transactions, making it 'irrelevant that the private element is predominant' and confining the consumer classification to the situation where 'the trade or professional purpose is so

2 Law Com No 292, Scot Law Com No 199 (2005), *Unfair Terms in Contracts* 3.51.

3 Under s 76(2), these definitions also apply under Part 2 of the CRA, which provides the broad coverage of unfair terms generally (see Chapter 11).

4 These definitions, and the statement of the burden of proof, are extended to Part 2 of the CRA, which contains the general consumer fairness regime (see Chapter 11), by s 76.

5 For example, *R & B Customs Brokers Co. Ltd* v *United Dominion Trust Ltd* (1988).

limited as to be negligible in the overall context of the supply',[6] and this was followed in *Overy* v *Paypal (Europe) Ltd* (2012). The approach taken under the CRA is less restrictive, with its reference to 'purposes that are wholly *or mainly* outside' the individual's 'trade, business, craft or profession' (emphasis added). The Law Commissions were concerned with situations where, for example, 'a sole trader buys a car primarily for private use but with the intention of occasionally using it for business'.[7] Further, para 36 of the explanatory notes to the CRA states that

> a person who buys a kettle for their home, and works from home one day a week and uses it when working from home would still be a consumer. Conversely a sole trader that operates from a private dwelling who buys a printer of which 95% of its use is for the purposes of the business, is not likely to be held to be a consumer.

10.12 Broader assistance as to who will be a 'consumer' under the Act can be gleaned from the case law, including that of the CJEU dealing with other EC measures using basically the same 'consumer' classification. First, it can be emphasized that the type of approach taken under UCTA 1977, allowing someone to 'deal as consumer' if the transaction was not integral to their business or regularly occurring,[8] is not followed. In the *Di Pinto* case [1991] ECR I-1189, in the context of the meaning of 'consumer' in the doorstep-selling Directive (Council Directive 85/577/EEC), the ECJ stated that a distinction could not be drawn between the 'normal' acts of a business and those which are 'exceptional in nature'. Further, in considering the 1999 Regulations, the Scottish court in *Prostar Management* v *Twaddle* 2003 SLT (Sh Ct) 11 pointed out 'the absurdity of a major trader claiming the protection afforded to a consumer whenever he stepped out of his habitual line of business' ([12]). Rather, the line indicated by the CJEU as to the definition of consumer is whether the contract is to satisfy 'requirements other than family or personal requirements of a trader' (*Di Pinto* at [16]) or is 'for the purpose of satisfying an individual's own needs in terms of private consumption' (*Benincasa* v *Dentalkit Srl* [1997] ECR I-3767 at [16]). That approach was considered when the meaning of 'consumer' under the Unfair Terms Directive and the Brussels Convention fell to be addressed by Longmore J in *Standard Bank London Ltd* v *Apostolakis* (2002). That case was concerned with foreign exchange investment contracts made with the bank by a wealthy couple who were a civil engineer and a lawyer. Longmore J took the basic line that entering into foreign exchange contracts was 'not part of a person's trade as a civil engineer or a lawyer' and that 'the only question' was whether they 'were engaging in the trade of foreign exchange contracts as such'. He did not believe that they were. He took the view that 'they were disposing of income which they had available. They were using money in a way which they hoped would be profitable but merely to use money in a way one hopes would be profitable is not enough ... to be engaging in trade'. In relation to the line taken in *Benincasa*, he thought that the description there of contracts 'concluded for the purpose of satisfying an individual's own needs in terms of private consumption' was met in the instant case—'the contracts made ... were for the purpose of satisfying the needs of Mr and

6 *Gruber* v *Bay Wa AG* (C-464/01) [2005] ECR I-439, at [54].

7 *Unfair Terms in Contracts* (2005) Law Com No 292, Scot Law Com No 199, para. 3.36.

8 *R & B Customs Brokers Co. Ltd* v *United Dominion Trust Ltd* (1988).

Mrs Apostoliakis, defined as an appropriate use of their income, and that the need was a need in terms of private consumption'. He made the point that 'consumption cannot be taken as literally consumed so as to be destroyed but rather consumed in the sense that a consumer consumes, viz he uses or enjoys the relevant product'. Undoubtedly a contract for the investment of disposable income must be capable of being a contract made by a consumer. However, it can be suggested that, in the future, greater account should be taken of the level of investment. The case was concerned with 28 contracts with a total exposure of $7 million. There must come a point at which a secondary means of making money becomes a secondary trade or business. When the issue came before a Greek court, the view was taken that the couple could not be classified as consumers (the type of investment and its scope were seen as putting it outside of the consumer classification [2003] I L Pr 29), and in *Maple Leaf Macro Volatility* v *Rouvray* (2009), Andrew Smith J 'question[ed] the conclusion' of Longmore J (at [209]).

10.13 Lastly, it should be noted in relation to the definition of 'consumer' that the CJEU has indicated the adoption of something like the specific exclusion, which was present in UCTA, of someone from 'dealing as consumer' if they held themselves out as contracting in the course of a business. In *Gruber* v *Bay Wa AG* (2005) it was indicated that account should be taken of the person claiming to be a consumer behaving 'in such a way as to give the other party to the contract the legitimate impression that he was acting for the purpose of his business'. In *Overy* v *Paypal (Europe) Ltd* (2012) this was followed in relation to the opening of a type of account on PayPal which was confined to businesses. The claimant was a professional photographer who was primarily (at least initially) using the account in an attempt to realize the value in his home in an unusual way, by a form of lottery or draw.

10.14 Finally, as has already been indicated, the CRA relates to contracts between consumers and 'traders'. We have seen that a trader is 'a person acting for purposes relating to that person's trade, business, craft or profession'. 'Business includes the activities of any Government department or local or Public authority' (s 2(7)). Contracts between consumers and traders do not include contracts of employment or apprenticeship (s 61(5)).

Basic structure of the legislation

Introduction

10.15 Not all exemption clauses are covered by either UCTA or the CRA, and not all exemption clauses to which one of those Acts applies are subject to the test of 'reasonableness' (under UCTA) or fairness (under the CRA). Some clauses are automatically ineffective under the relevant statute, without their 'reasonableness' (under UCTA) or 'fairness' (under the CRA) needing to be considered. If the contract comes within the basic scope of one of the Acts, a section must be identified which deals with it, and then it must be asked what that section does to the clause. If the section states that the clause is effective only if it satisfies the requirement of reasonableness (UCTA), or if is fair (CRA), then tests of reasonableness or fairness become relevant. Whether dealing with UCTA or the CRA, it is a matter of identifying the relevant 'Active' section and what it says should happen to the exemption clause in question.

10.16 It is important to take note of a significant difference in the enforcement regime of the CRA from that under UCTA. While UCTA provides a means of an exemption clause being rendered ineffective in an action by one party to the contract against another, the CRA does not only operate at that level. It provides for enforcement at a more general level, to have a standard term struck down in an action by the Competition and Markets Authority, so that it does not then impact upon particular consumers by misleading them.

Exemption clauses within the legislation

10.17 Before the 'active' sections are considered, some thought should be given to the basic scope of the legislation. As we have seen, the CRA is concerned with 'consumer contracts', which are those between 'consumers' and 'traders'. Apart from this basic requirement, further coverage of its scope, such as the 'core exemption' from the fairness test, and its disapplication in relation to terms reflecting mandatory provisions of statutes and regulations, are left for **Chapter 11**, where the fairness regime, in general, in the CRA, is discussed in detail.

10.18 Here it is the scope of UCTA to which more consideration must be given. Basically, UCTA 1977 only applies to business liability. Sections 2–7, subject to the exception in s 6(4) (which is very limited in its effect), apply only to business liability, that is, liability for breach of obligations or duties arising (a) from things done or to be done by a person in the course of a business, or (b) from the occupation of premises used for the business purposes of the occupier (s 1(3)). Business is not defined, but it includes 'a profession and the activities of any government department or local or public authority' (s 14).

10.19 UCTA 1977, Sch 1 lists certain types of contract which are excluded wholly or in part from its operation. They include contracts of insurance, or any contract insofar as it relates to the creation or transfer of an interest in land (see *Electricity Supply Nominees Ltd* v *IAF Group plc* (1993)) or intellectual property (patents, trade marks, etc.); the formation or dissolution of a company or its constitution, and the creation or transfer of securities (para. 1); charter parties and carriage of goods by ship or hovercraft, etc. (paras 2 and 3); and contracts of employment (para. 4) (see s 1).

10.20 Sections 26, 27, and 29 set boundaries for UCTA in relation to contracts with an international element.

The active sections

10.21 In considering the active sections, frequent reference will be made to the requirement of 'reasonableness' which is set out in s 11 of UCTA, and the fairness test in s 62 CRA. These concepts, as such, are considered later.

Negligence

10.22 Section 2 is an important and widely applicable section of UCTA. It deals with liability arising from negligence, which, for the purposes of UCTA 1977, is defined in s 1. Section 1 states that negligence means the breach:

> (a) of any obligation, arising from the express or implied terms of a contract, to take reasonable care or exercise reasonable skill in the performance of the contract;
>
> (b) of any common law duty to take reasonable care or exercise reasonable skill (but not any stricter duty);
>
> (c) of the common duty of care imposed by the Occupiers' Liability Act 1957.

The duty may arise in contract or tort or under the Occupiers' Liability Act 1957, and UCTA 1977, s 2 not only relates to contract terms purporting to exclude or restrict liability for negligence, but also covers non-contractual notices attempting to affect such liability in tort.

10.23 UCTA 1977, s 2(1) prevents entirely the exclusion or restriction of liability for negligently caused death or personal injury. There is no need to consider whether the clause is reasonable.

10.24 UCTA 1977, s 2(2) deals with negligently caused loss or damage not covered by s 2(1). Under it, the term or notice will only be effective to exclude or restrict liability for such negligently caused loss or damage if the term or notice satisfies the requirement of reasonableness.

10.25 UCTA 1977, s 2(3) enigmatically states:

> Where a contract term or notice purports to exclude or restrict liability for negligence a person's agreement to or awareness of it is not of itself to be taken as indicating his voluntary acceptance of any risk.

This seems to be intended to limit claims to rely upon the tort defence of *volenti non fit injuria*.

10.26 Section 65 CRA basically reproduces the effect of s 2(1) UCTA in relation to consumer contracts and also consumer notices, rendering them simply ineffective against the consumer. There is no need for a specific provision dealing with terms or notices attempting to exclude or restrict liability for 'other' negligently caused loss or damage. Such terms or notices are subject to the fairness test under the CRA's general fairness regime, that is, they are ineffective against the consumer unless fair under s 62.

10.27 The existence of legislation dealing with terms or notices attempting to exclude or restrict liability means that there is less need for a very restrictive approach to be taken to the construction of exemption clauses which are claimed to deal with liability for negligence. It is worth considering whether the Court of Appeal would have viewed the construction of the exemption clause in *Hollier* v *Rambler Motors (AMC) Ltd* (1972) in the same way had such legislation been available to it (see para. **9.86**).

Contracts where one party deals on the other's 'written standard terms of business'

10.28 Section 3 provides UCTA 1977's broadest coverage as it is not limited to dealing with any particular kind of obligation or liability, whereas, for example, s 2 is limited to liability based on negligence and ss 6 and 7 to obligations stemming from certain implied terms in goods contract. Section 3 also used to cover contracts where one party dealt as a consumer. Obviously, that was removed by the CRA, and there was no need to replace it with a specific provision in the CRA. Rather, the fairness test in s 62 CRA is generally relevant to exemption clauses in consumer contracts, although there are more specific sections to apply in some situations, such as in relation to specified obligations in contracts for the supply of goods, reflecting the protection previously afforded to those who dealt as consumers by s 6 of UCTA (see para **10.45**).

'Written standard terms'

10.29 The phrase 'written standard terms' is important in determining the scope of UCTA 1977's broadest provision. It raises a number of questions. In most cases, it will be clear that the terms are written (but see para. **10.34**ff), and what will fall to be determined is (a) whether the relevant party has standard terms, and (b) whether the parties dealt on them in the instant case. It is for the party claiming that the contract is made on the other party's standard terms, and so falls within s 3 of UCTA, to prove that is the case (*African Export-Import Bank v Shebah Exploration and Production Co Ltd* (2017) at [18]).

The existence of the relevant party's standard terms

10.30 In the context of s 17 of UCTA 1977, which is the equivalent of s 3 in the Scottish part of the Act, the phrase used is 'standard form contract', rather than 'written standard terms of business'. In the context of s 17, in *McCrone* v *Boots Farm Sales Ltd* 1981 SLT 103, Lord Dunpark referred (at 105) to a standard form contract as one where there are 'a number of fixed terms or conditions invariably incorporated in contracts of the kind in question'. However, whilst a set of terms 'invariably' incorporated into contracts of the appropriate type would clearly be standard terms, a set of terms may be 'standard terms' even though not used 'invariably'. 'If this were not so the statute would be emasculated'—UCTA 1977, s 3 could be avoided simply by not using the relevant terms on one or two isolated, and unimportant, occasions.[9] It is nevertheless quite a demanding standard which is required. It was indicated in *British Fermentation Products Ltd* v *Compair Reavell Ltd* (1999) that it would suffice if the terms were 'usually used' by the relevant party, and, following that line, the Court of Appeal in *African Export-Import Bank v Shebah Exploration and Production Co Ltd* (2017) adopted the approach that it had to be shown that the relevant party 'habitually uses those terms of terms of business' (at [19]). This should depend upon the pattern of dealing on the terms in question, when the contract is of the type to which they are appropriate. However, if the relevant party has only just started to use a set of terms, intention as to their use might suffice.

10.31 One question which might take matters beyond the simple question of the pattern of use of the terms is whether a standard form which is common throughout a particular trade, and has been devised by a third party, such as a trade association, should fall within UCTA

9 *Chester Grosvenor Hotel Co Ltd* v *Alfred McAlpine Management Ltd* (1991) 56 BLR 115. But see *Hadley Design Associates* v *Westminster London Borough Council* (2003).

1977, s 3. Can it be regarded as the written standard terms of business of the relevant party? Certainly, the Contractors Plant Association model conditions were assumed to be the written standard terms of the relevant party in *Cox Plant Hire (London) Ltd* v *Dialbola* (1983) and *USA* v *ARC Construction Ltd* (1991). It was considered in *British Fermentation Products Ltd* v *Compair Reavell Ltd* (1999) whether a contract made on the basis of the Institute of Mechanical Engineers Model Form General Conditions of Contract Form C could constitute the defendant's written standard terms of business. There was no proof of the manner in which the terms were used by the defendant and the judge took the line that if s 3 could apply to 'model forms drafted by an outside body', there would need to be proof of their adoption by the relevant party as his or her standard terms, 'either by practice or by express statement'. Further, in *African Export-Import Bank* v *Shebah Exploration and Production Co Ltd* (2017), although there were considerable negotiations and changes to the set of terms of the Loan Market Association which the relevant party was using, the indications are that it is a matter of looking at the facts of the relevant party's usage of a third party's standard form to see whether a contract falls within s 3. That approach, alongside recognition of the potential for adoption by 'express statement', would seem to be the appropriate line to take.[10] The coverage of s 3 is too significant to the role of UCTA for such contracts to be left outside its remit, particularly when it is remembered that UCTA may be the only straightforward means of providing protection for small businesses (without again resorting to 'strained construction'), which often have no more bargaining power than consumers when dealing with large businesses.

10.32 Of course, some model standard terms will be arrived at by consultation with representatives of both sides of those involved in the transaction to which the terms relate and may not carry the same risk of one-sided terms as some other standard form contracts, but such factors can be considered in the application of the 'requirement of reasonableness'.

The instant case

10.33 If the relevant party has 'written standard terms of business', the question is whether they were used in the instant case. In *McCrone* v *Boots Farm Sales Ltd* (1981) Lord Dunpark indicated that for the instant contract to have been made on the relevant party's standard terms, they should have been used 'without material variation'. However, it should not be too easy to argue that the relevant party's standard terms have been sufficiently departed from to take the contract outside of the scope of UCTA 1977, s 3. It must be a question of degree whether the variation in terms is such that the parties are not contracting on the 'standard terms'. Of course, some terms are inherently dependent upon the particular contract (*St Alban's City and District Council* v *International Computers Ltd* [1995] FSR 686 at 706 per Scott Baker J), and the mere insertion of matter such as quantities to fill in 'blanks' is obviously not indicative of departure from standard terms (*Yuanda (UK) Co Ltd* v *V W Gear Construction Ltd* (2010) at [21]). Nevertheless, although we should leave aside the inherently individualized terms, the

10 There having been considerable negotiation and redrafting, there was little difficulty in concluding that the contract was not on the relevant party's standard terms. The relevant party's (undecided) contention that the Loan Market Association's terms (of which there were multiple sets) always required addition or amendment is a different and subsidiary question to the treatment of third party model terms in general.

general approach which was indicated in the Court of Appeal in *African Export-Import Bank* v *Shebah Exploration and Production Co Ltd* (2017) is that it is 'relevant to inquire whether there have been more than insubstantial variations',[11] and that 'if there have been substantial variations, it is unlikely to be the case that the party relying on the Act will have discharged the burden on him to show that the contract has been made "on the other's written standard terms of business"' (at [25]). There could be a major gap between 'insubstantial variations' and 'substantial variations', but the Court's approval of the approach taken in *Yuanda (UK) Co Ltd* v *V W Gear Construction Ltd* (2010) and *Hadley Design Associates* v *Westminster London Borough Council* [2003] EWHC 1617 (TCC) indicates that it will not require a great deal of alteration to take a case outside of s 3.

Written terms

10.34 A question arises in relation to the situation which occurs when terms are incorporated by a 'consistent course of dealing'. Offer and acceptance often occur orally in such cases. Is a set of 'standard terms' then incorporated as written terms? To answer the question in the context of UCTA 1977, s 3, we need to consider the basic mechanism for incorporation by a course of dealing. The mechanism is that, although there is no specific reference to standard terms in making a particular contract, the past dealings between the parties are such that, in the absence of any contrary indication, those terms are taken to have been included in the offer and acceptance (see para. **9.47**ff). They should be regarded as incorporated as 'written' terms if they have been embodied in a written document in the past. An analogy can be made with incorporation by reference. The terms are incorporated as terms recorded in the written standard document in which they previously appeared.

10.35 The final question to be considered here relates to contracts made using computers via email or simply on the internet. There is no definition of writing in UCTA 1977 but, in general, writing 'includes typing, printing, lithography, photography and other modes of representing words in a visible form' (Interpretation Act 1978, Sch 1). Although when contracts are made using computers the words generally appear on the computer screen,[12] they are actually represented, and recorded, by electrically charged particles. Nevertheless, the Law Commission takes the view that such transitory visibility is sufficient to satisfy the Interpretation Act definition of writing for the purposes of formalities. It would seem that the same approach should be taken to the reference to 'written' terms in s 3 ('Electronic Commerce: Formal Requirements in Commercial Transactions' Advice from the Law Commission, Dec. 2001, **para. 3.8**).

11 Approving the decisions in *Yuanda (UK) Co Ltd v V W Gear Construction Ltd* (2010) and *Hadley Design Associates* v *Westminster London Borough Council* [2003] EWHC 1617 (TCC).

12 The exception is where computer-to-computer 'automated' contracting occurs using a structured Electronic Data Interchange (EDI) system. It is not intended that the messages be read by a human being, but merely by computer. There is not even transitory visibility of the message to satisfy the Interpretation Act definition—see Law Com Advice, **paras 3.19–3.20**.

Section 3(2)(a)

10.36 In relation to contracts where one party deals on the other's 'written standard terms of business', UCTA 1977, s 3(2)(a) prevents that 'other' party from restricting or excluding his or her liability for breach of contract by the use of a contract term, except insofar as that term satisfies the requirement of reasonableness. This is a very wide provision. It relates to the situation where there is a breach and the party in breach is claiming that the relevant term excludes or restricts his or her liability for breach. It should be emphasized that the term will be effective only 'in so far as [it] satisfies the requirement of reasonableness'.

Section 3(2)(b)—exclusion clauses 'in disguise'

10.37 Under UCTA 1977, s 3(2)(b), a person contracting on his or her 'written standard terms of business' cannot by reference to any contract term:

> claim to be entitled—
>
> (i) to render a contractual performance substantially different from that which was reasonably expected of him, or
>
> (ii) in respect of the whole or any part of his contractual obligation, to render no performance at all,
>
> except in so far as ... the contract term satisfies the requirement of reasonableness.

This is less straightforward than s 3(2)(a). It applies to situations where there is apparently no breach. Section 3(2)(b) is an attempt to deal with what can be termed exclusion clauses 'in disguise'.

10.38 The point was made earlier (see para. **9.3**) that there is a problem in identifying exclusion clauses. An exclusion clause may be rewritten so that it is, in form, part of the definition of the obligation. This has led to the argument that an exclusion clause is not a distinct type of clause at all (B. Coote, *Exception Clauses*, Sweet & Maxwell, 1964). However, the Unfair Contract Terms Act 1977 assumes that an exclusion clause is a distinct type of clause. On that basis, the Act recognizes that an exclusion clause can take the form of part of the definition of the obligation and still be an exclusion clause. Its form is then perceived as a possible means of evading provisions dealing with exclusion clauses. Section 3(2)(b) is one of the parts of the Act designed to bring exclusion clauses 'in disguise' within its operation. The Law Commission, in considering the proposed Act to deal with exclusion clauses, recognized that what mattered about such clauses was not their form but their substance. It was said (Law Com Rep No 69 (1975), para. 146):

> We do not propose to define exemption clauses in general terms; we regard this expression not as a legal term of art but as a convenient label for a number of provisions which may be mischievous in broadly the same way. Their mischief is that they deprive or may deprive the person against whom they are invoked ... *of rights which the promisee reasonably believed the promisor had conferred on him.* (emphasis added)

Section 3(2)(b)(i) deals with the 'mischief' of clauses which deprive the promisee of rights which he or she reasonably believed the promisor had conferred on him or her.

10.39 The reaction to this might be to ask how the promisee's reasonable expectations can differ from the actual obligations embodied in the contract. The answer to this is the artificial way in which terms can be incorporated, and the difficulty of understanding a long standard form document, can present a danger that 'the relatively unsophisticated or unwary party will not realize what or how little he has been promised, although the legal scope and effect of the contract may be perfectly clear to a lawyer' (Law Com Rep No 69 (1975), para. 145). In other words, the contracting process is so artificial that the expectations of the promisee, as a reasonable person, may differ from the obligations which lawyers would find in the contract. At times there does still seem to be a reluctance to recognize this and to consider whether such artificialities were present (for example, *Peninsula Business Services* v *Sweeney* (2004)). Nevertheless, it seems plain how s 3(2)(b)(i) should operate.

10.40 UCTA 1977, s 3(2)(b)(i) encompasses, for example, what have been seen as 'trap' provisions—'cases in which the application of small print provisions would enable a party to perform a contract in a substantially different manner from that which could reasonably have been expected from a perusal of its primary terms' (*Liberty Life Insurance Co.* v *Sheikh* (1985) per Kerr LJ). Another situation which may fall within s 3(2)(b)(i) is where one term apparently states what the proferens' (the person putting forward the clause) performance is to be, but another confers on the proferens a discretion as to that performance. It may be recognized as reasonable for the other party to expect that discretion to be exercised within narrow bounds, and for s 3(2)(b)(i) to apply if it is not. In relation to a contract for the supply of a service by British Telecom, which contained a clause stating that BT could terminate the contract on one month's notice, Sir Thomas Bingham MR said:

> If a customer reasonably expects a service to continue until BT has substantial reason to terminate it, it seems to me at least arguable that a clause purporting to authorise BT to terminate without reason purports to permit partial or different performance from that which the customer expected. (*Timeload Ltd* v *British Telecommunications plc* (1995))

(But see *Hadley Design Associates* v *Westminster London Borough Council* (2003).)

10.41 The claimed extent of a discretion was an element in an example given by the Law Commission of the type of case which they thought might fall within what became UCTA 1977, s 3(2)(b). The clause was also relatively obscurely positioned. The case was that of *Anglo-Continental Holidays Ltd* v *Typaldos (London) Ltd* (1967) and the facts were:

The claimant travel agent booked cabins for clients on the defendant's ship *Atlantica* for a Mediterranean cruise commencing on 12 August. On 2 August the defendant notified the claimant that the clients could not be accommodated on the *Atlantica* but had been booked on the *Angelika*. The *Atlantica* was a large ship with two swimming pools. The *Angelika* was

> a 'small old crate'. The itinerary of the *Angelika* differed from that of the *Atlantica*. The latter would have spent two days in Haifa, allowing time for trips further into Israel. The former was to spend only eight hours in Haifa. The two days in Haifa would have been the climax of the trip for the claimant's clients as they were a Jewish group. Printed on the back of the defendant's handbook for travel agents was a clause which said 'Steamers, Sailing Dates, Rates and Itineraries are subject to change without prior notice'.

On being informed of the change of ship and itinerary, the claimant cancelled the arrangements and claimed damages for breach. The defendant sought to rely upon the clause on the back of the handbook. The Court of Appeal held that the clause could not assist the defendant, who was liable for breach. The clause could not be used to alter the substance of the transaction. It had to be limited so that effect could be given to the main object of the contract.

10.42 In *Typaldos* the court recognized that the clause, as it appeared, was not in keeping with the 'substance' and the 'main object' of the contract. Effect was given to the 'substance' of the contract by construction of the contract.[13] Similar facts to *Typaldos* could now fall under UCTA 1977, s 3(2)(b)(i) as the defendant was claiming to render a performance substantially different from that which was reasonably expected. The case emphasizes the artificial nature of standard terms. The court was willing to recognize that the terms specific to the particular contract might well reflect its substance better than the standard terms used by one party in many contracts. A similar approach would now provide work for s 3(2)(b)(i).[14]

10.43 However, the point should be made that if UCTA 1977, s 3(2)(b)(i) is to cover terms conferring a discretion on the proferens, the discretion must relate to the performance of the proferens and not that of the other party. In *Paragon Finance plc* v *Staunton* (2001) it was held not to apply to a term conferring a discretion on a lender as to the interest rate to be paid by the borrower. (Clearly, setting the interest rate could literally be regarded as part of the proferens' performance. The court's approach embodies the underlying assumption that even the broadest parts of UCTA 1977 should be restricted to terms which can, in some sense, be seen as exemption clauses.) (For further discussion, and much more detailed analysis, of the difficulties of distinguishing clauses excluding liability from those defining the obligation, and giving meaning to s 3(2)(b)(i) and (ii), see E. Macdonald, 'Exception Clauses: Exclusionary or Definitional? It Depends!' (2012) 29 JCL 47.)

10.44 Some final points need to be made in relation to UCTA 1977, s 3(2)(b)(i). The first is to emphasize that it contains a recognition both of the difficulty of distinguishing between the actual contract terms and the party's reasonable expectations and of the uncertainty that such an exercise could create. It subjects to the requirement of reasonableness only those clauses on which one party seeks to rely to render a performance '*substantially* different from that which was reasonably expected' (emphasis added). The assessment is a broad one. The second point to

13 See also *Sze Hai Tong Bank Ltd* v *Rambler Cycle Co. Ltd* (1959) and *Glynn* v *Margetson & Co.* (1893).

14 See the example provided in *Axa Sun Life Services plc* v *Campbell Martin* (2011) at [50].

be noted is that before s 3(2)(b) is applied there is, apparently, no breach. There is no apparent breach because one party is claiming that a specific term prevents whatever he or she has done, or has not done, from being a breach. Section 3(2)(b) subjects that term to the requirement of reasonableness. If the term does not satisfy the requirement of reasonableness, then it is ineffective and there is a breach.

10.45 However, the ultimate point to be made is to re-emphasize the fact that consumer contracts no longer fall within UCTA, and there is no need for concern that there is no equivalent provision to s 3(2)(b) in the CRA. The CRA does not need to make special provision for exemption clauses 'in disguise' because its application is not limited to exemption clauses, but deals with unfair terms much more generally.

Goods (ss 6 and 7)

10.46 UCTA 1977, s 6 deals with exemption clauses relating to certain implied terms in contracts for the sale or hire purchase of goods. Section 7 makes analogous provision for contracts where possession or ownership of goods passes and the contract is not one of sale or hire purchase. The sections often accorded more extensive protection for the acquirer of goods who 'dealt as consumer'. The CRA excises the reference to 'deals as consumer' from the sections and removes terms in 'consumer contracts' from their coverage, itself providing similarly extensive protection for consumers acquiring goods under 'consumer contracts'.

10.47 Section 6(1)(a) provides that liability for breach of the terms implied by s 12 of the Sale of Goods Act 1979 cannot be excluded or restricted. The terms implied by s 12 relate to title to the goods. It should be noted that such an exemption clause is automatically ineffective. There is no need to consider whether it satisfies the requirement of reasonableness. Section 6(1)(b) makes the same provision for the terms implied into contracts of hire purchase. Consumers are now similarly protected by CRA, s 31.

10.48 Under what is now UCTA 1977, s 6(1A), but was previously s 6(3), attempts to exclude or restrict liability for breach of the terms implied by Sale of Goods Act 1979, ss 13–15 are effective, but only so far as they satisfy the requirement of reasonableness. The terms implied by ss 13–15 relate to the conformity of the goods with description and sample, and their fitness for purpose and satisfactory quality. Again, s 31 CRA makes such terms simply ineffective against consumers, without any question of fairness arising (and extends to a greater number of obligations of the supplier).

10.49 UCTA 1977, s 7 makes similar provision to s 6 for contracts under which possession or ownership of goods passes, but which are not contracts of sale or hire purchase. The sort of contracts covered are contracts of hire or contracts for work and materials. Similar amendments to s 7 as have been made to s 6 are contained in the CRA. (In relation to the supply of digital content, and the supply of services, to consumers, exemption clauses relating to specified obligations of the trader are made ineffective against the consumer under ss 47 and 57 CRA, respectively.)

Indemnities by consumers (s 4) and 'Guarantee' of consumer goods' (s 5)

10.50 UCTA 1977, s 4 is repealed by the CRA, and did not require specific replacement in that Act. Such terms will fall within the general fairness test in s 62 CRA. Again, UCTA 1977, s 5 has been repealed.

Two contracts (s 10)

10.51 Section 10 of the Unfair Contract Terms Act 1977 deals with the situation where there are two contracts and a clause in the second affects rights arising under the first. Section 10 states:

> A person is not bound by any contract term prejudicing or taking away rights of his which arise under, or in connection with the performance of, another contract, so far as those rights extend to the enforcement of another's liability which this Part of this Act prevents that other from excluding or restricting.

The drafting of this section is somewhat obscure. It does not reflect the style generally adopted in the Act as it does not refer to the exclusion or restriction of liabilities, or even rights, but rather to 'prejudicing or taking away rights'.

10.52 The provisions of the CRA oust the application of s 10 to 'secondary contracts' where the 'main contract' is a consumer contract: they remove the application of the other provisions of UCTA to such 'main contracts'. Similar provision for secondary contracts is, however, made in the CRA, s 72, dealing with the situation where the 'main contract' is a consumer contract whether or not the secondary contract is a consumer contract. The CRA also provides answers, in that context, for some of the problems which have arisen in relation to s 10.

10.53 One major problem with the borderlines of s 10 was resolved by *Tudor Grange Holdings Ltd* v *Citibank NA* [1991] 4 All ER 1, in which it was held that the section did not apply to an agreement settling a contractual dispute. It is made explicit in s 72(5), CRA that the section 'does not apply if the secondary contract is a settlement of a claim arising under the main contract'. More generally, in *Tudor Grange*, Browne-Wilkinson V-C did not think that UCTA 1977, s 10 dealt with the situation where both contracts were between the same parties. He gave an example of the type of contract which he thought s 10 was designed to cover. He said (at 13):

> Under contract 1, the supplier (S) contracts to supply a customer (C) with a product. Contract 1 contains no exemption clause. However, C enters into a servicing contract, contract 2, with another party (X). Under contract 2, C is precluded from exercising certain of his rights against S under contract 1. In such a case s 10 operates to preclude X from enforcing contract 2 against C so as to prevent C enforcing his rights against S under contract 1.

This would seem to be an inappropriate approach. There is nothing in the wording of s 10 to suggest it, and it would provide an opportunity for evasion of UCTA 1977 if s 10 was confined to the situation where both contracts are not between the same parties. It is expressly stated in s 72(3)(a) of the CRA that it is irrelevant under that section 'whether the parties to the secondary contract are the same as the parties to the main contract'.

Definitions

'Deals as consumer' (s 12)

10.54 As has been made clear, this categorization is repealed by the CRA. What is now significant is whether the contract is a 'consumer contract' under s 61 CRA (see **para. 10.9**).

The requirement of reasonableness (s 11)

10.55 Under UCTA, the active sections often render a clause ineffective except insofar as it satisfies the requirement of reasonableness. Meaning is given to that requirement in UCTA 1977, s 11, with guidelines in Sch 2. It should again be emphasized that the CRA has taken consumer contracts outside of UCTA, and its fairness test is dealt with in Ch 11. UCTA's reasonableness test nevertheless continues to be of significance in relation to exemption clauses in the business-to-business context, and in fact, it is in relation to contracts between businesses that that test has mainly fallen to be applied by the courts. Of course, although some cases involving a consumer are referred to below, their context should not be forgotten, but it is also worth bearing in mind that the relative bargaining power of a small business in relation to a large one may not be very different from that of a consumer to a business.

10.56 Section 11(5) places the burden of proof upon the person claiming that the contract term satisfies the requirement of reasonableness. The basic test is one involving the weighing of multiple factors to decide if it was 'fair and reasonable' to have included the clause in the contract (s 11(1)). The 'Court must entertain a whole range of considerations, put them in the scales on one side or another and decide at the end of the day on which side the balance comes down' (*Mitchell* v *Finney Lock Seeds* [1983] 2 AC 803 at 816).

10.57 It should briefly be noted that there was a predecessor to the UCTA 1977 test of reasonableness in the Supply of Goods (Implied Terms) Act 1973. This was preserved, for contracts made between 18 May 1973 and 1 February 1978, by s 55 of the Sale of Goods Act 1979 (originally Sale of Goods Act 1893). Some of the cases referred to later in this chapter were decided under this predecessor to the 1977 Act, and some differences between the two tests of reasonableness must be noted to assess the significance of those cases today. These will be returned to at relevant points.

Timeframe—irrelevance of the particular breach

10.58 UCTA 1977, s 11(1) states:

> In relation to a contract term, the requirement of reasonableness ... is that the term shall have been a fair and reasonable one to be included having regard to the circumstances which were, or ought reasonably to have been, known to or in the contemplation of the parties when the contract was made.

The reasonableness of the clause is to be assessed on the basis of the circumstances known to or contemplated by, or which should have been known to or contemplated by, the parties at the time of contracting. The particular breach is not directly relevant. It can be relevant only to the extent that it was one of the possibilities the parties contemplated, or should have contemplated, at the time of contracting. Assessing the reasonableness of the clause in relation to the circumstances at the time of contracting should assist contract planning. A clause should not be rendered unreasonable because it appears unreasonable in the light of unforeseeable events which occurred once the contract had been made, and the 'court should not be too ready to focus on remote possibilities or to accept arguments that a clause fails the test by reference to relatively uncommon or unlikely situations' (*F G Wilson Engineering Ltd* v *John Holt & Co (Engineering) Ltd* (2012) at [96]).

10.59 It was UCTA 1977, s 11(1) and the question of timing which the Court of Appeal focused on in *Stewart Gill Ltd* v *Horatio Myer & Co. Ltd* [1992] 2 All ER 257, in deciding that the reasonableness of a clause must be assessed as a whole and not merely the part of the clause being relied upon in the instant case.[15] In that case:

> The defendants had contracted with C for the supply and installation of an overhead conveyor system for a price of £266,400. The defendants were to pay in stages, and it was the last 10 per cent which gave rise to the dispute. C were asking for summary judgment for the remaining 10 per cent of the price. The defendants contended that summary judgment should not be given as C had committed certain breaches which gave rise to claims which could be set off against the unpaid 10 per cent of the price. C relied upon clause 12.4 of their standard form contract to meet the defendants' contention. Clause 12.4 stated:
>
>> the Customer shall not be entitled to withhold payment of any amount due to the Company under the contract by reason of any payment set off counterclaim allegation of incorrect or defective goods or for any other reason whatsoever which the Customer may allege excuses him from performing his obligations hereunder.

At first instance C's application for summary judgment was refused. The clause was not in the form of a simple exclusion or restriction of liability, but the Court of Appeal concluded that the clause was brought within UCTA 1977, s 3 by s 13(1)(b), and so its effectiveness depended upon whether it satisfied the requirement of reasonableness. Although of the view that the exclusion

15 E. Peel, 'Making More Use of the Unfair Contract Terms Act' (1993) 56 MLR 98; I. Brown and A. Chandler, 'Unreasonableness and the Unfair Contract Terms Act' (1993) 109 LQR 41.

of the right of set-off—the part of the clause relied upon in the instant case—might be reasonable, the court did not view the clause as a whole as reasonable. It was not viewed as reasonable that the defendants should not be entitled to withhold payment to C by reason of any 'credit' owing by C to the defendants or by reason of any payment made by the defendants to C (for example, an over-payment under some other contract).

10.60 The Court of Appeal concluded that it must assess the clause as a whole because of UCTA 1977, s 11(1). The 'time frame' of assessment required by s 11(1) meant that the actual events in relation to which the clause would be used could not be taken into account and, on that basis, it was not relevant that a clause might be reasonable in relation to what actually occurred. It could nevertheless be unreasonable because that was outweighed by the unreasonableness of its other coverage. After considering s 11(1), Stuart-Smith LJ said (at 262):

> Although the question of reasonableness is primarily one for the court when the contract term is challenged, it seems to me that the parties must also be in a position to judge this at the time the contract is made. If this is so, I find it difficult to see how such an appreciation can be made if the customer has to guess whether some, and if so which, part of the term will alone be relied upon.

10.61 The simplest point to be made from *Stewart Gill Ltd* v *Horatio Myer & Co. Ltd* (1992) is that draftsmen might be advised to include several narrow exemption clauses rather than one wide clause, such as that given here, so that at least some of their exemptions may survive. However, to a very limited extent the court will treat what appears as a single clause as composed of several distinct units in applying the requirement of reasonableness. So, the two sentences written as a single clause in *Watford Electronics Ltd* v *Sanderson CFL Ltd* (2001) were nevertheless treated as two clauses. What was set out as clause 7(3) of the contract stated:

> Neither the Company nor the Customer shall be liable to the other for any claims for indirect or consequential losses whether arising from negligence or otherwise. In no event shall the Company's liability under the Contract exceed the price paid by the Customer to the Company for the Equipment connected with any claim.

The two sentences were considered as separate exclusion and limitation clauses, respectively, by the court.

10.62 One qualification which should be noted in relation to the above is that it generally means that, even if what is written as one clause can be seen as distinct clauses, each of those distinct clauses should be looked at as a whole in applying the requirement of reasonableness, except in relation to a part of it which would be automatically ineffective under UCTA. At least, that was the line taken in *Goodlife Foods Ltd* v *Hall Fire Protection Ltd* (2017). In applying the requirement of reasonableness to the clause, the judge disregarded the reference to 'persons' in a clause dealing with liability for negligence. He did so on the basis that such an attempted exemption was automatically ineffective under s 2(1) of UCTA, and did not then need to be considered when the reasonableness of the clause was assessed. He distinguished *Stewart Gill*.[16]

10.63 Finally, it should be noted here that the time at which reasonableness is assessed is one of the differences between the reasonableness test under the Unfair Contract Terms Act 1977 and its predecessor in what became Sale of Goods Act 1979, s 55. Under the previous legislation the question was whether it was fair and reasonable to allow reliance upon the term, and the question of reasonableness thus fell to be judged in the light of the breach and its consequences. Although cases decided under s 55 will offer some guidance on the operation of the reasonableness test in UCTA 1977, s 11, this difference in timing will affect the current relevance of some factors in those earlier cases. The test of fairness in the CRA uses the same 'time frame' as the 1977 Act. The assessment of fairness is made on the basis of the circumstances at the time of contracting (see para. **11.32**).

Guidelines

10.64 UCTA 1977, Sch 2 contains guidelines for the application of the requirement of reasonableness. The factors in Sch 2 are:

> **(a)** the strength of the bargaining position of the parties relative to each other, taking into account (among other things) alternative means by which the customer's requirements could have been met;
>
> **(b)** whether the customer received an inducement to agree to the term, or in accepting it had an opportunity of entering into a similar contract with other persons, but without having to accept a similar term;
>
> **(c)** whether the customer knew or ought reasonably to have known of the existence and extent of the term (having regard, among other things, to any custom of the trade and any previous course of dealing between the parties);
>
> **(d)** where the term excludes or restricts any relevant liability if some condition is not complied with, whether it was reasonable at the time of the contract to expect that compliance with that condition would be practicable;
>
> **(e)** whether the goods were manufactured, processed or adapted to the special order of the customer.

By s 11(2) these guidelines are applicable when the contract is one covered by s 6 or s 7 of UCTA 1977, but even in that context, they are not exhaustive. Outside of ss 6 and 7, the guidelines will not apply by 'legislative prescription', but the factors set out in the guidelines are still likely to be factually relevant to the reasonableness of an exemption clause.[17] In *Phillips Products Ltd*

---

16 He relied instead on *Trolex Products Ltd* v *Merrol Fire Protection Engineers* (1991), which, like *Stewart Gill*, was a decision of the Court of Appeal, and decided shortly before it. *Trolex* was, however, unreported, only transcripts being available on Lexis and Westlaw, and there has been little awareness of it. *Goodlife* is to be appealed.

17 See, e.g., *Singer Co. (UK) Ltd* v *Tees and Hartlepool Port Authority* [1988] 2 Lloyd's Rep 164 at 169; *Stewart Gill Ltd* v *Horatio Myer & Co. Ltd* [1992] 2 All ER 257 at 262; *Schenkers Ltd* v *Overland Shoes Ltd* [1998] 1 Lloyd's Rep 498 at 505.

v *Hyland* [1987] 2 All ER 620 the Court of Appeal thought that the judge at first instance had been wrong to assume that the case did not fall within s 7 but found that in any event, that did not affect the way in which the decision on reasonableness, which had been applied under s 2, had been taken. Those factors from Sch 2 which were relevant to the case had been taken into account not because they were within the statutory guidelines, but simply because they were factually relevant (at 628).

Limitation of liability to a specified sum

10.65 UCTA 1977, s 11(4) makes two factors particularly relevant to the question of the reasonableness of a clause which purports to limit liability to a specified sum. When someone tries to use such a clause, regard is to be had to:

> (a) the resource which he could expect to be available to him for the purpose of meeting the liability should it arise; and
>
> (b) how far it was open to him to cover himself by insurance.

The cases show that the availability and cost of insurance are important factors generally, not only in relation to clauses limiting liability (see para. **10.70**ff).

10.66 In the context of UCTA 1977, s 11(4), it should not be thought that when the factors in that subsection point towards the clause being unreasonable, this necessarily decides the issue. All the relevant factors present must be taken into account and this may lead to a different conclusion (for example, *Singer Co. (UK) Ltd* v *Tees and Hartlepool Port Authority* (1988)).

10.67 More generally it has been indicated that when liability is limited to a specific sum, that sum has to be justified in order to satisfy the requirement of reasonableness. In *Salvage Association* v *CAP Financial Services Ltd* (1995) it was seen as relevant to ask whether the sum related to the turnover or insurance of the party seeking to rely on it, the contract price, or the uninsurable risk to which the other party is exposed. In *St Albans City and District Council* v *International Computers Ltd* (1995), Scott Baker J said:

> There are some types of agreement where ordinary risks fall within a particular sum, and there may be good reasons for limiting liability to that sum and leaving the purchaser to carry any additional risk.

In relation to standard terms it may be easier to establish that a monetary limit is reasonable if it is regularly reviewed (*Singer Co. (UK) Ltd* v *Tees and Hartlepool Port Authority* (1988)).

10.68 *Overseas Medical Supplies Ltd* v *Orient Transport Services Ltd* [1999] 1 All ER (Comm) 981 raises the issue of the use of a single limitation clause in relation to different types of liability. C, the suppliers of medical equipment, employed the defendants as freight forwarders to transport equipment to and from a trade exhibition. The defendants were specialists in dealing with that type of contract. The defendants' terms included a clause requiring C to insure, either through the defendants themselves or independently, against loss or damage to the equipment, and another clause limited the defendant's liability to £600. C opted to insure through the defendants—there had been no realistic possibility that they would do otherwise, it being far easier for the defendants to do so, due to their general work in the area. The equipment was lost on the return journey from the exhibition, at a cost to C of some £8,500. The defendants had failed to effect the insurance requested by C. The limitation was held to be unreasonable and ineffective under UCTA 1977 because it covered liability not only for loss or damage to the equipment being transported but also for the defendant's failure to insure—leaving C without any worthwhile recompense for their loss, had it been effective. More broadly, the point was made as to the unreasonableness of limitation clauses covering very different types of loss. The point was made (at [21]) that whereas a 'broad brush approach to limitation of liability will be reasonable' in relation to 'certain package services', the position of the defendants in the instant case:

> was that of [a] trading organisation which, under a single contract had agreed to combine at least two activities or functions in respect of which the nature of the work undertaken, the incidence of risk as between the parties, and the effect of a breach of duty by the appellants were all of a different character, yet were to be treated without distinction as subject to a single limitation of liability of only £600.

Such an approach was unreasonable. The appropriateness of the limitation must be considered in relation to each of the different types of breach which it is stated to cover.[18]

Inequality of bargaining power

10.69 Inequality of bargaining power is referred to in para. (a) of the guidelines in UCTA 1977, Sch 2. It is one of the most basic factors to be considered in relation to the question of the reasonableness of an exemption clause. When the parties are regarded as of equal bargaining power and knowledge the courts may not be reluctant to find a clause reasonable (see **para. 10.96**, *Watford Electronics v Sanderson* (2001)).

10.70 In looking at relative bargaining power, it will be relevant to ask whether the customer could have gone elsewhere to contract for the required goods or services. However, in 'relation to the question of equality of the bargaining position, the court will have regard not only to the question of whether the customer was obliged to use the services of the supplier, but also the question of how far it would have been practicable and convenient to go elsewhere'

18 Although we are here concerned with monetary limits there are also other types of limitation clause, such as those setting time limits for a claim. What may be unreasonable coverage of a clause setting one type of limit may not be unreasonable coverage for a clause setting a different type of limit. *Overseas Medical* was distinguished in *Granville Oil and Chemicals Ltd* v *Davies Turner and Co. Ltd* (2003). In the latter case the issue was again a clause covering loss and damage as well as failure to insure. However, what was in question was not a monetary limitation but a clause limiting the time within which a claim could be made. The same time limit was not seen as inappropriate in relation to those different types of breach.

(*Overseas Medical Supplies Ltd* v *Orient Transport Services Ltd* [1999] 1 All ER (Comm) 981 at [3]). Standard terms, used throughout a particular trade, may indicate that one side of a common transaction is always in a better bargaining position than the other, but this is not necessarily so. Whether standard terms throughout a trade indicate inequality of bargaining power will depend upon how the standard terms were arrived at. For example, in *RW Green Ltd* v *Cade Bros Farms* (1978) (see para. **10.75**) the standard form contract, containing the exemption clause, was used throughout the trade by sellers of seed potatoes, but the standard form had been arrived at after discussions between the National Association of Seed Potato Merchants and the National Farmers' Union. It had not simply been imposed by the seedsmen upon their purchasers. The use of a standard form did not indicate inequality of bargaining power.[19]

Insurance

10.71 As we have seen, the possibility of obtaining insurance to cover a potential liability is made specifically relevant to the reasonableness of a limitation clause by s 11(4). It is also a factor which the courts have indicated as being of general significance. The reasonableness of the risk allocation in the exemption clause is assessed against the possibilities open to either party to insure against it (*Flamar Interocean Ltd* v *Denmac Ltd* (1990)).

10.72 In *Photo Production Ltd* v *Securicor Transport Ltd* (1980) UCTA 1977 was not applicable because of the date when the events occurred, but the House of Lords commented upon the reasonableness of the exemption clause in general terms. In that case:

> Securicor had contracted to provide a security patrol of Photo Production's factory. One of Securicor's employees, Musgrove, whilst carrying out a patrol of the factory, decided one night to start a fire, and the factory burnt down. The question was whether Securicor was liable for the destruction of the factory. Securicor wished to rely upon an exemption clause.

The main issue was that of the construction of the clause. However, having held that the clause was appropriately worded to cover the events which had occurred, the House of Lords also considered, *obiter*, whether the clause was reasonable; the court thought that it was. The contract was one between two businesses of equal bargaining power. The risk of fire damage had been allocated to the party who could most appropriately insure against it. Photo Production had to insure their factory against fire damage generally. Securicor might not have been able to obtain the appropriate insurance and, even if it had, paying for insurance cover would have increased Securicor's costs and prevented the provision of the security service at the cheap rate given to Photo Production. (See also *Goodlife Foods Ltd* v *Hall Fire Protection Ltd* (2017).)

10.73 It should be emphasized that what must be asked is not merely whether a party could have insured but also at what cost.[20] *George Mitchell Ltd* v *Finney Lock Seeds Ltd* (1983) contrasts

19 See also *Singer Co. (UK) Ltd* v *Tees and Hartlepool Port Authority* (1988); *George Mitchell Ltd* v *Finney Lock Seeds Ltd* (1983); *Schenkers Ltd* v *Overland Shoes Ltd* (1998).

20 See also *Singer Co. (UK) Ltd* v *Tees and Hartlepool Port Authority* [1988] 2 Lloyd's Rep 164 at 169.

with *Photo Production Ltd* v *Securicor Transport Ltd* (1980). In *Mitchell* v *Finney Lock Seeds*, a case decided under s 55 of the Sale of Goods Act 1979, the person seeking to rely upon the clause could have insured without materially increasing his prices, and this was one factor which led the court to conclude that the exemption clause was unreasonable. *Mitchell* v *Finney Lock Seeds* concerned the sale of cabbage seed. The seed should have been of a variety of winter cabbage but what was negligently supplied was autumn cabbage seed of an inferior quality. The plants produced were very poor, without hearts. The entire crop was useless and had to be ploughed in. The farmers sought to claim for their lost year's production (about £61,000). Finney Lock claimed to rely upon a clause which limited their liability to the cost of the seed (about £200). In deciding that it was not fair and reasonable to allow reliance on the clause, the court indicated that it was relevant that the sellers could have insured against the risk of crop failure caused by supplying the wrong seed and that such insurance would not have led to a significant increase in the price of their seed.

10.74 It is clear that exemption clauses may be employed to circumvent the need to pay for insurance against the risk of having to pay damages. As in *Photo Production Ltd* v *Securicor Transport Ltd* (1980), this may be regarded as a reasonable course to have taken. Y may be in a better position to insure than X and, if X does not have to bear the cost of insurance, X may offer Y a better contract price. However, an exemption clause may still be regarded as unreasonable even where its ineffectiveness will mean that the person who sought to rely upon the clause will have to insure in the future and increase his or her contract price accordingly. Such increased costs may sometimes be seen as preferable to the consequences which would follow if the exemption clause were to be effective This point is illustrated by *Smith* v *Eric S Bush* (1989), which, it should be emphasized, was a case concerning a consumer. In that case:

> Mrs Smith wished to purchase a house. In order to do so she applied to a building society for a mortgage. The building society instructed a firm of valuers, Eric S Bush, to report on and value the property. Mrs Smith paid the building society a fee and signed an application form which stated that the society would provide her with a copy of the mortgage valuation. The form contained a disclaimer to the effect that neither the society nor its valuer warranted that the valuation would be accurate and that the valuation would be supplied without any acceptance of responsibility. When Mrs Smith received the valuation, it too contained the disclaimer. The valuation stated that no essential repairs were required and valued the house at £16,500. Relying upon the report and without obtaining an independent survey, Mrs Smith purchased the house for £18,000, £3,500 coming from the mortgage. The valuers had been negligent in their inspection of the house and had failed to notice the lack of support for a chimney which fell through the roof 18 months later, causing considerable damage.

Mrs Smith claimed damages from the valuers in tort because of their negligent valuation. The House of Lords found that a duty of care was owed to Mrs Smith by the valuers and considered the disclaimer. Its reasonableness fell to be considered under UCTA 1977, s 2(2). That section deals with non-contractual notices purporting to exclude liability in tort as well as contractual exemption clauses, and it is the House of Lords decision on the reasonableness of the clause which is of interest here. The court noted that, although it was open to someone purchasing a house to commission a full survey, the purchaser in this case had relied upon the mortgage valuation rather than arranging for her own survey to be carried out, and such reliance was common practice in house purchases. Purchasers often could not afford to pay for the valuation and a separate survey. Those factors indicated that the disclaimer was not reasonable. The court also considered the practical consequences if the disclaimer was effective. It would mean one individual would bear the loss involved, and that would be likely to cause hardship. Individuals could find themselves with an uninhabitable dwelling and a mortgage still to be paid on it. If the disclaimer was ineffective, leaving the valuer with the consequences of his negligence, it would merely result in his increasing his insurance cover. The cost of increased insurance would be borne by a small price increase to all his clients, and the whole of the risk of his negligence would not fall on one unfortunate house purchaser. In this case the likely increase of valuers' fees to meet their new insurance premiums was a preferable, and more reasonable, outcome to that which would follow if the disclaimer was effective.[21]

Availability of alternatives

10.75 Paragraph (b) of UCTA 1977, Sch 2 deals with the availability of an alternative form of contract, without the exemption clause in question, and this is also a factor which has been prominent in the case law. *Woodman* v *Photo Trade Processing Ltd* (1981)[22] is a consumer case illustrating this factor but, as will be seen, the availability of alternatives, as a factor in relation to reasonableness, is certainly not restricted to the consumer context. In that case:

> Mr Woodman had taken photographs at his friends' wedding. He had intended to give them the photographs as a wedding present. There was no other photographer present. He took his film into a shop which acted as an agent for Phototrade Processing Ltd (PTP). On the counter in the shop was a sign containing an exemption clause limiting PTP's liability to replacement of lost films with new ones. PTP negligently lost Mr Woodman's film.

Mr Woodman claimed damages in excess of the cost of a replacement film because of the distress caused by the loss. The question was whether the exemption clause was effective to prevent this from being successful. As negligence was involved, UCTA 1977, s 2(2) rendered the clause ineffective except insofar as it satisfied the requirement of reasonableness. It was argued that the clause was reasonable because it enabled PTP to operate a cheap mass production service. The judge considered such a service to be good enough for the majority of photographers whose pictures were not valuable. He also thought that the majority might complain if they had to pay a higher rate in order to protect the interest of the minority whose pictures were of greater value. However, there was no choice for the minority who required greater care to be

21 See also *St Albans City and District Council* v *International Computers Ltd* (1995); this point was affirmed in the Court of Appeal [1996] 4 All ER 481.

22 Unreported, but see (1981) 131 NLJ 935.

taken with their photographs. In addition, the code of practice of the photographic industry, as agreed with the Office of Fair Trading, recognized the possibility of a two-tier system of liability for photographic processors. This code envisaged the customer being offered the choice of a cheaper service and very limited liability for the processor, or a more expensive service with the processor accepting greater liability. PTP did not offer their customers a more expensive/greater liability alternative service and this was taken as decisively indicating that the exemption was unreasonable. (See also *Singer Co. (UK) Ltd* v *Tees and Hartlepool Port Authority* [1988] 2 Lloyd's Rep 164 at 170.)

10.76 In *RW Green Ltd* v *Cade Bros Farms* (1978), the availability of more expensive seed potatoes, which would be more likely to be healthy, indicated that the exemption clause was reasonable in relation to the purchase of cheaper seed potatoes. In that case:

> Seedsmen RW Green sold 20 tons of King Edward seed potatoes to a farmer on the standard terms of the National Association of Seed Potato Merchants. The potatoes were infected with a virus which was undetectable until the crop started to grow. The standard terms contained an exemption clause which stated that any claim had to be notified to the sellers within three days of delivery and which also limited liability to the cost of the seed.

When RW Green claimed the price of the seed, the farmers counterclaimed for their lost profit on the crop (about £6,000). The counterclaim depended upon whether the exemption clause passed the reasonableness test in the predecessor to UCTA 1977. It was decided that it was not fair and reasonable to allow reliance upon the three-day time limit as the virus could not be detected until the crop started to grow. In contrast, the limitation of liability to the cost of the seed (£634) passed the reasonableness test. The parties were of equal bargaining power. The standard terms were the result of discussions between the seedsmen's association and the National Farmers' Union. This counterbalanced the fact that the same terms were used throughout the trade and the farmers could not have made such a purchase without the exemption clause being a part of the contract. The reasonableness of the limitation was also indicated by the fact that those standard terms had been used for about 20 years and the parties had dealt together for five or six years, so that they both should have known of the exemption clause. More specifically, the fact that the farmers had the alternative of purchasing certified seed at a higher price indicated that limiting liability to a specified sum was reasonable. Certified seed would have come from a crop which had been inspected for signs of virus the previous year and purchasing such seed would have provided 'a very real safeguard' against the risk of obtaining infected seed. The farmer had chosen to buy cheaper seed with a higher risk of the virus being present in it.

10.77 It is clear that the availability of an alternative is important to the reasonableness of the exemption clause. However, it must be borne in mind that not all alternatives will render the exemption clause reasonable. The reality of the alternative must be borne in mind. In *Smith* v *Eric S Bush* (1989) (see para. **10.92**), it will be recalled, the House of Lords had to consider the reasonableness, under UCTA 1977, of the disclaimer of liability by a valuer in relation to a mortgage valuation of a dwelling house. The consumer purchaser could have obtained her own survey but the court considered the reality of this possible alternative. It was recognized that most consumer purchasers of dwelling houses relied on the valuation carried out for the building society. It was regarded as impracticable and too expensive for such purchasers to obtain a separate survey. The consumer purchaser had to pay for the valuation for the mortgage, and often could not afford to pay again. The possibility of a separate survey was not an alternative which rendered reasonable the disclaimer of liability on the mortgage valuation. In addition, the reality of the alternative will be considered from another perspective. If a condition 'works in such a way as to leave little time to put such option into effect this may effectively eliminate the option as a factor indicating reasonableness' (*Overseas Medical Supplies Ltd* v *Orient Transport Services Ltd* [1999] 1 All ER (Comm) 981 at 987). Further, it has been indicated that a party seeking to rely on an exemption clause cannot simply use a clause stating that he or she has an alternative available if there is no intention to make such alternative contracts (*Overseas Medical*). However, in *Goodlife Foods Ltd* v *Hall Fire Protection Ltd* (2017) the relevant provision concluded by stating:

> As an alternative to our basic tender, we can provide insurance to cover the above risks. Please ask for the extra cost of the provision of this cover if required.

Hall Fire had never been asked about such provision, and did not have any plan for providing it. The exemption was nevertheless reasonable. The parties were of 'roughly equal bargaining power' (at [79]). Sensibly, Goodlife needed to insure against fire damage for reasons beyond the failure of Hall Fire's fire suppression system. If they did not have such insurance, the clause drew attention to the need for it, and indicated Hall Fire's willingness to arrange it (at [80]). The judge had 'no real doubt' that if a customer took them up on the question of the 'alternative' of the addition of insurance cover, Hall Fire would simply have passed that customer to an insurance broker who would have discussed appropriate cover for fire as a whole (at [81]). (See also the discussion of *Photo Production v Securicor* at **10.71**.)

Knowledge/consent

10.78 UCTA 1977, Sch 2(c) refers to the factor of knowledge, that is, whether there was, or should have been, knowledge of the exemption clause on the part of the person against whom the clause is being used. Such knowledge, actual or constructive, could indicate that the clause is reasonable. More broadly, there is the factor of whether the injured party should be taken to have consented to the clause.

10.79 In *Stevenson* v *Nationwide Building Society* [1984] EGD 934 the situation was very similar to that in *Smith* v *Eric S Bush* (1989) except that the person purchasing the property was himself an estate agent. He had 'trade' knowledge of the house purchasing process and the disclaimer of liability for a negligent valuation was considered reasonable. It was said (at 935):

> When I bear in mind that the person affected by the disclaimer is someone well familiar with the possibility of obtaining a survey, and also familiar with the difference between a building society valuation and a survey and their different costs, it seems to me perfectly reasonable to allow the building society, in effect to say to him that if he chooses the cheaper alternative he must accept that the society will not be responsible for the content to him.

10.80 However, it should be emphasized that the whole picture must be considered. Even actual knowledge of the clause may not indicate that the clause is reasonable if there is inequality of bargaining power. In such circumstances the clause may have been knowingly accepted on the basis that there was no realistic alternative (*Phillips Products Ltd* v *Hyland* [1987] 2 All ER 620 at 629).

10.81 It has been said that 'it is necessary, in order to assess reasonableness, to consider to what extent the party has actually consented to the clause' (*AEG (UK) Ltd* v *Logic Resources Ltd* [1996] CLC 265 at 279), but as has been indicated, it should not be thought that it is only actual subjective knowledge which is relevant; what the relevant party should have known, as a reasonable person, should also be looked at, although there may be greater weight to be given to actual knowledge (*Britvic Soft Drinks* v *Messer UK Ltd* (2002) at [21]). In fact, the question of knowledge will often be a matter of whether the relevant party should have known of the proferens' terms, rather than actual knowledge. However, although when the reasonableness of a contract term is under consideration, the question of 'knowledge' is looked at 'in circumstances where ex hypothesi the term has been validly incorporated in the contract' (*AEG* at 274), it should be recognized that incorporation does not necessarily mean that there is even objective knowledge (*Britvic* at [21]). Factors similar to those looked at in relation to incorporation of contract terms will often be examined to determine what the reasonable person should have known, but here the artificiality with which the facts are often clothed by the rules on incorporation should be avoided. As was seen earlier, incorporation by notice or signature has little to do with any real agreement to, or even objective knowledge of, the terms and may be a very artificial process.

10.82 Knowledge and understanding of the clause were found where a party used a similar clause when contracting on its own standard terms (*Watford Electronics Ltd* v *Sanderson CFL Ltd* (2001)). Trade practice and a long course of dealing between the parties indicated knowledge of the clause and pointed to its reasonableness in *RW Green Ltd* v *Cade Bros Farms* (1978). Similarly, in *Singer Co. (UK) Ltd* v *Tees and Hartlepool Port Authority* (1988) an indicator of the reasonableness of the clause was the wide distribution, and ready availability, of the port authority's standard terms (see also *Schenkers Ltd* v *Overland Shoes Ltd* [1998] 1 Lloyd's Rep 498 at 507). Also relevant to the question of actual or constructive knowledge of a clause is its legibility and intelligibility. In *Stag Line Ltd* v *Tyne Ship Repair Group Ltd, The Zinnia* [1984] 2 Lloyd's Rep 211, Staughten J commented (*obiter* at 222) that he was inclined to find the exemption clauses unreasonable because the print was so small that it was barely legible, and also because 'the draftsmanship was so convoluted and prolix that one almost need[ed] an LL.B. to understand them'. Similarly, it indicated the unreasonableness of the clause in *Overseas Medical Supplies Ltd* v *Orient Transport Services Ltd* [1999] 1 All ER (Comm) 981 that there was 'insufficient clarity in the conditions to bring home to the plaintiffs the effect of' the clause' (at [20]).

The width of the clause

10.83 The width of the clause may be relevant to its reasonableness under UCTA 1977. For example, it may be easier to find that an exemption clause is reasonable if it has been construed as applying only to non-negligent breaches (see *Stag Line Ltd* v *Tyne Ship Repair Group Ltd, The Zinnia* [1984] 2 Lloyd's Rep 211 at 223), and in general a narrow construction of a clause may make it more likely to be found reasonable than a wider one (*Regus (UK) Ltd* v *Epcot Solutions Ltd* (2008)). It should be emphasized that s 11(1) requires the reasonableness of the clause to be assessed on what was known or contemplated, or what should have been known or contemplated, by the parties at the time of contracting. The fact that the working of the exemption clause might be perfectly reasonable in relation to the specific breach which has occurred does not mean that the clause will pass the reasonableness test. The clause may be unreasonable because of the breaches which it potentially covers,[23] but, as has been indicated, the 'court should not be too ready to focus on remote possibilities or to accept arguments that a clause fails the test by reference to relatively uncommon or unlikely situations'.[24] (See also, however, the disregarding of an element of the clause which was rendered ineffective by s 2(1) in *Goodlife Foods Ltd* v *Hall Fire Protection Ltd* (2017). See para. **10.61**.)

Settlement of past claims

10.84 In *George Mitchell Ltd* v *Finney Lock Seeds Ltd* (1983), the 'decisive factor' in the House of Lords' conclusion that the exemption clause was unreasonable was the seed sellers' past practice. In the past they had settled claims which they regarded as justifiable for sums in excess of the limit set by the exemption clause. The sellers had even attempted to negotiate a settlement in the instant case. This 'decisive factor' needs to be given further consideration. First, it is necessary to consider whether any account of it should be taken in applying the test in UCTA 1977, s 11. Second, once it is decided that it is a potentially relevant factor, it should be asked what conclusions should be drawn from it in relation to that test of reasonableness.

10.85 It should be remembered that the reasonableness of the exemption clause in *George Mitchell Ltd* v *Finney Lock Seeds Ltd* (1983) fell to be determined under what became s 55 of the Sale of Goods Act 1979 rather than under UCTA 1977, s 11. It must be emphasized again that the test under s 55 was whether it was fair and reasonable to allow reliance on the clause. As that test relates to reliance, the events after formation of the contract were relevant to the question

23 *Stewart Gill Ltd* v *Horatio Myer & Co. Ltd* (1992) (see para. **10.58**ff). See also the discussion of *Overseas Medical Supplies Ltd* v *Orient Transport Services Ltd* (1999) in relation to the unreasonableness of a clause limiting different types of liability to a single sum at para. **10.67**.

24 *F G Wilson Engineering Ltd* v *John Holt & Co (Engineering) Ltd* (2012) at [96].

of reasonableness. Under s 55 the fact of an attempted settlement in the particular case could come within the range of factors to be considered. Equally, because of the difference in the test in UCTA 1977, s 11, any attempted settlement of the particular case cannot be relevant to 'reasonableness' under that Act. Section 11 looks at the time at which the contract was made. However, there was a past practice of settling claims in *Mitchell* v *Finney Lock Seeds,* and it seems that this past practice should have been one of the factors contemplated by the parties at the time of contracting. If the past practice has been such that the parties should have contemplated it at the time of contracting, it would be possible to take account of such past settlements under the s 11 test of reasonableness. Such a factor has been considered in coming to a decision on the application of s 11. In *Rees Hough Ltd* v *Redland Reinforced Plastics Ltd* (1985) the parties' past practice of settling claims rather than relying upon the exemption clause was regarded as the most important factor against the clause, and it was decided that the clause did not satisfy the requirement of reasonableness in s 11.[25]

10.86 Under UCTA 1977, s 11 it is possible to consider a past practice of settling claims rather than relying upon the exemption clause, but what is its relevance? In *George Mitchell Ltd* v *Finney Lock Seeds Ltd* [1983] 2 AC 803 at 817 such practice was taken to indicate that the sellers themselves did not regard it as reasonable to rely upon the clause. It can be contended that such a conclusion will often not be appropriate. Business people often may not take a legalistic view, and seek to enforce strict contractual rights, because they do not wish to endanger their business relationship with the other party. Negotiation and settlement are more conducive to the continuance of relationships than is a legal battle. The business community in which the parties operate may even regard the use of legal action as an inappropriate way to settle disputes.[26] In *Schenkers Ltd* v *Overland Shoes Ltd* [1998] 1 Lloyd's Rep 498 the Court of Appeal distinguished *Mitchell* v *Finney Lock* on its facts and refused to accept the argument that non-reliance on the clause in past transactions showed that it was unreasonable. Pill LJ said (at 508):

> In the present circumstances, I see little merit in the defendant's argument that the clause had not in practice been relied upon. The give and take practised by the parties in the course of substantial dealings ... was admirable and conducive to a good business relationship but did not prevent the [claimants], when a dispute arose, relying upon the terms agreed.

The mere fact of a past practice of settling claims will often not be indicative that a clause is unreasonable. What matters is whether the clause was put into the contract as a fair allocation of risk.

Conditions placed on claims

10.87 UCTA 1977, Sch 2(d) relates to exclusion or restriction of liability unless a condition is complied with. This relates to the situation where one party seeks to use an exemption clause to

25 But see *Stewart Gill Ltd* v *Horatio Myer & Co. Ltd* (1992)—see para. **10.58**ff.

26 See S. Macauley, 'Non-Contractual Relations in Business' (1963) 28 Am Soc Rev 55; H. Beale and T. Dugdale, 'Contracts between Businessmen: Planning and Use of Contractual Remedies' (1975) 2 Br J Law and Soc 45. For discussion of this factor in relation to the requirement of reasonableness, see Adams and Brownsword (1988) 104 LQR 94.

place a condition upon his or her liability. For example, he or she may state that the other party must notify him or her of any claim within a specified time (for example, *RW Green* v *Cade Bros Farms* (1978)). The test of reasonableness in UCTA 1977, s 11 requires some consideration in relation to such restrictions.

10.88 The facts which can be taken into account under UCTA 1977, s 11 in looking at conditions on claims should be considered. In *RW Green* v *Cade Bros Farms* (1978) the exemption clause was in two parts. The first stated that any claim had to be notified to the sellers within three days of delivery of the seed potatoes. The second part limited any claim to the contract price of the seed potatoes. It will be recalled that although the second part of the exemption clause was found to be reasonable, the time limit was not. It was not reasonable because the problem with the potatoes was a viral infection, which could be detected only after the crop started to grow. Obviously, that would be outside the three-day limit. That case was decided under the previous test of reasonableness. It should be emphasized that, under s 11, the reasonableness of such a time limit cannot be assessed in relation to the particular breach which occurred. The possibility of the potatoes being defective because of such a virus can be considered only to the extent that it was, or should have been, contemplated by the parties at the time of contracting.

10.89 If the condition is one which will, within the contemplation of the parties, lead to erratic results, that may indicate that the exemption is unreasonable. For example, if a clause in a ship repair contract requires the return of the ship to the repairer's yard for any defect to be remedied, this may be unreasonable because it is capricious. 'The apportionment of risk is made to depend upon where a casualty happens to occur, and whether the owner happens to find it convenient and economic to return his vessel to the yard' (*Stag Line Ltd* v *Tyne Ship Repair Group Ltd, The Zinnia* [1984] 2 Lloyd's Rep 211 at 223).

Negligence

10.90 One factor relevant to holding the exemption clause unreasonable in *George Mitchell Ltd* v *Finney Lock Seeds Ltd* (1983) was the fact that the breach involved negligence.

Customer's detailed specifications

10.91 UCTA 1977, Sch 2(e) specifically makes relevant to the requirement of reasonableness 'whether the goods were manufactured, processed or adapted to the special order of the customer'. In *Edmund Murray Ltd* v *BSP International Foundations Ltd* (1993) the sellers manufactured a drilling rig for the buyers. The contract contained detailed specifications as to the technical standards which the rig was required to meet, and it was made clear exactly how the buyers wished to use the rig. Against that background, the court considered it unreasonable for the sellers to restrict their liability to replacement of defective parts.

10.92 However, what matters is whether there is a reason for any restriction on the customer's remedies and whether the customer has been left with sufficient remedies. In *British*

Fermentation Products v *Compare Reavell* [1999] 2 All ER 389 the point was made that in *Murray* v *BSP* 'the purchaser was left without any remedy when the machinery failed to do what was required of it' (at 404). In contrast, in *British Fermentation* the contract provided the purchaser with several opportunities to reject the goods if they did not comply with the specifications and, effectively, the purchaser would have been able to replace the goods at the supplier's expense. Against that background it was seen as reasonable that, if the purchaser did not take the opportunity to reject, the supplier's clause should protect it from £1 million damages for reduced production over the lifetime of the machine. The machinery failed to comply with its specification and so was less productive than it should have been, but the exemption clause left the purchaser with an adequate means of dealing with that. The judge made the point that, without the exemption clause, the suppliers 'would no doubt have wished to reconsider the price quoted, having regard to the totally different level of risk undertaken' (at 404).

Risk

10.93 In *Smith* v *Eric S Bush* (1989) Lord Griffiths gave an indication of some factors which might be of general relevance in applying the requirement of reasonableness, and included the degree of difficulty or risk involved in the performance.

> When a difficult or dangerous undertaking is involved there may be a high risk of failure which would certainly point towards the reasonableness of excluding liability as a condition of doing the work.

This type of factor was taken into account in *Watford Electronics Ltd* v *Sanderson CFL Ltd* (2001), where it was one of the elements pointing towards the reasonableness of the clause. It was recognized that in the supply of software which had been customized to meet the particular needs of a complex business, there was a significant risk that the software might not perform to the customer's satisfaction and involve considerable loss of expected savings or profits, and other losses. Clauses limiting liability for direct loss to the contract price, and excluding liability for consequential loss, were regarded as reasonable.

Appeals and precedent

10.94 The courts have given some consideration to the approach to be taken to an appeal from a decision on the requirement of reasonableness in UCTA 1977, s 11. In *George Mitchell Ltd* v *Finney Lock Seeds Ltd* [1983] 2 AC 803 Lord Bridge, with whom the other members of the court agreed, said (at 816) in relation to the test of reasonableness under s 11 (and Sale of Goods Act 1979, s 55):

> There will sometimes be room for a legitimate difference of opinion as to what the answer should be, where it will be impossible to say that one view is demonstrably wrong and the other demonstrably right. It must follow … that, when asked to review such a decision on appeal, the appellate court should treat the original decision with the utmost respect and refrain from interference with it unless satisfied that it proceeded upon some erroneous principle or was plainly and obviously wrong.

This indicates that decisions on the requirement of reasonableness will often provide very limited guidance for the future. Another judge might have weighed the factors in the same case differently, come to the opposite conclusion, and still not be overturned on appeal.[27] *Phillips Products Ltd* v *Hyland* (1987) provides an example of the way this approach to appeals works. In that case, the court was concerned with a standard form, widely used by those in the business of hiring out plant. Despite the fact that the Court of Appeal took a different view from the trial judge on several of the factors relevant to the issue of reasonableness, it declined to overrule his decision. It accepted the approach to appeals indicated in *George Mitchell Ltd* v *Finney Lock Seeds Ltd* (1983). In keeping with this, the Court of Appeal emphasized that it was considering the reasonableness of the clause in the particular contract between the particular parties. The contract was made on the basis of a widely used standard form, but the court indicated that its decision did not mean that the exemption clause was to be taken to be unreasonable in every transaction in which the standard form was used. The decision on reasonableness related to the instant case. Even in relation to a standard form contract, this must follow from the adoption of the above approach to appeals.

10.95 This approach to appeals inevitably creates uncertainty as to what is required for an exemption clause to pass the reasonableness test in UCTA 1977, s 11. This presents some hindrance to contract planning. It is difficult for a person in business to decide whether to pay for insurance and increase his or her costs, and contract price, if there is uncertainty concerning the efficacy of the exemption clause which he or she had designed to obviate the need for insurance.

10.96 However, in some cases of standard forms, the factors indicating that the clause is unreasonable may be present so often when the form is used that a case may be widely relevant to the issue of reasonableness. The House of Lords decision in *Smith* v *Eric S Bush* [1989] 2 All ER 514 is such a case. The House of Lords thought its decision on the reasonableness of the disclaimer in the mortgage valuation to be of general application to the purchase, via a mortgage, of a dwelling house of 'modest value'. It was known in relation to such transactions that purchasers did not usually obtain their own survey but relied on the mortgage valuation. Lord Griffiths said (at 532):

> It must, however, be remembered that this is the sale of a dwelling house of modest value in which it is widely recognised by surveyors that purchasers are in fact relying on their care and skill. *It will obviously be of general application in broadly similar circumstances.* But I expressly reserve my position in respect of quite different types of property for mortgage purposes, such as industrial property, large blocks of flats or very expensive houses. In such cases it may be that the general expectation of the behaviour of the purchaser is quite different. (emphasis added)

27 See also *Cleaver* v *Schyde Investments Ltd* (2011).

Trends

10.97 Although precedent is of limited value in this area, there is a final point to be made here as to indications, in the commercial context, of a trend favouring a non-interventionist basic approach by the courts. In this context, further consideration should be given to *Watford Electronics Ltd* v *Sanderson CFL Ltd* (2001):

> Watford had found the need for a computer system to deal with their mail order business and to perform accounting functions. They contracted with Sanderson for standard software which was to be modified to meet their needs. Basically, the contract was made on Sanderson's standard terms, but Watford had successfully negotiated for a price reduction and some modification of the terms. The significant term was the exemption clause, which stated:
>
>> Neither the Company nor the Customer shall be liable to the other for any claims for indirect or consequential losses whether arising from negligence or otherwise. In no event shall the Company's liability under the Contract exceed the price paid by the Customer to the Company for the Equipment connected with any claim.

The dispute arose because the system did not perform as Watford had wanted. There was a contractual claim which totalled about £5.5 million and an alternative claim under the Misrepresentation Act 1967 (or for negligent misstatement) for about £200,500. Watford had paid £104,596. A number of matters were ordered to be tried as preliminary issues, including whether the exemption clause satisfied the requirement of reasonableness.

10.98 As has been indicated, the court, in fact, viewed the clause as separate exclusion and limitation clauses (see para. **10.60**) and concluded that both were reasonable. In making that assessment, it recognized that there may be significant risks in supplying a customized computer system. It also recognized that the parties were of roughly equal bargaining power and that they knew of the risks and the need to insure, as well as that the price related to the allocation of the risks in the exemption clause. However, what should be emphasized here is that the court may be seen as signalling a restrained approach to the use of the requirement of reasonableness in commercial contexts between parties of equal bargaining power. Chadwick LJ said (at [55]):

> Where experienced businessmen representing substantial companies of equal bargaining power negotiate an agreement, they may be taken to have had regard to the matters known to them. They should, in my view be taken to be the best judge of the commercial fairness of the agreement which they have made; including the fairness of each of the terms in that agreement. They should be taken to be the best judge on the question whether the terms of the agreement are reasonable. The court should not assume that either is likely to commit his company to an agreement which he thinks is unfair, or which he thinks includes unreasonable terms. Unless satisfied that one party has, in effect, taken unfair advantage of the other—or that a term is so unreasonable that it cannot properly have been understood or considered—the court should not interfere.' (See also Peter Gibson LJ at [63].)

There have been other indications of this type of approach.[28] However, care must be taken with such general statements. Every case must depend upon its particular facts.

Exemption clauses (s 13)

10.99 The active sections frequently refer to clauses which 'exclude or restrict' liability. A fairly narrow interpretation could have been given to that phrase and such an interpretation would have limited the clauses falling within the operation of the Act. UCTA 1977, s 13 makes it clear that the Act is not so restricted. Section 13(1) states:

> To the extent that this Part of this Act prevents the exclusion or restriction of any liability it also prevents—
>
> **(a)** making the liability or its enforcement subject to restrictive or onerous conditions;
> **(b)** excluding or restricting any right or remedy in respect of the liability, or subjecting a person to any prejudice in consequence of his pursuing any such right or remedy;
> **(c)** excluding or restricting rules of evidence or procedure;
>
> and (to that extent) sections 2, 6 and 7 also prevent excluding or restricting liability by reference to terms and notices which exclude or restrict the relevant obligation or duty.

Paragraphs (a) to (c) ensure that clauses which have the effect of excluding or restricting liability, but in a slightly round-about way, are dealt with as if they limited or excluded liability more simply (see, e.g., *Stewart Gill Ltd* v *Horatio Myer & Co. Ltd* (1992)). For example, (a) covers a clause stating that any claim must be made within a certain time period, and (b) covers a clause which allows recovery of damages but which purports to remove any right to terminate the contract for breach. A clause stating that signature was proof that the goods delivered met the requirements of the contract falls within (c). It is the last part of s 13(1) which presents difficulties, and requires further consideration.

10.100 It has already been seen that UCTA 1977, s 3(2)(b) deals with exclusion clauses in the form of part of the definition of the obligation. The last part of s 13(1) is similarly a provision to prevent evasion of the Act by exclusion clauses in 'disguise'. Section 13(1) ensures that some clauses which, in form, define the obligation will be identified as exclusion clauses, in substance, for the purposes of ss 2, 6 and 7. The difficulty is that it does not indicate how to determine which clauses are to be treated in this way.

10.101 We have already seen that a clause in the form of an exclusion of liability could have been drafted instead as a clause in the form of part of the definition of the obligations

28 E.g. *SAM Business Systems Ltd* v *Hedley & Co.* (2002) at [67]; *Granville Oil and Chemicals* v *Davies Turner & Co. Ltd* (2003) at [31]; *Frans Maas (UK)* v *Samsung Electronics* (2005) at [158]; *Air Transworld Ltd* v *Bombarier Inc* (2012) at [133]. See also previously *Photo Productions Ltd* v *Securicor Transport Ltd* [1980] AC 827 at 843 per Lord Wilberforce.

(see para. **9.3**). Both forms of clause mark out the boundaries within which a legal remedy is available. A clause in the form of an exclusion of liability does that by removing the legal remedies for breach of what would be, but for the clause, an obligation. A clause in the form of part of the definition of the obligations simply states the obligations. The problem presented by the last part of s 13(1) is to determine which clauses, in the form of part of the definition of the obligation, it requires to be treated in the same way as clauses in the form of exclusions of liability. The lack of any clarification of this in the Act means that there is a conceptual hole at the centre of UCTA 1977.

10.102 The House of Lords considered the coverage of the final part of UCTA 1977, s 13(1) in *Smith* v *Eric S Bush (a firm)* [1989] 2 All ER 514. The case was considered earlier in the context of the court's conclusion that the surveyor's disclaimer of his tortious liability for negligence did not satisfy the requirement of reasonableness applied by s 2(2) of the Act. The point to be considered here is the surveyor's prior argument that the disclaimer was not subject to s 2(2) because it did not exclude or restrict the surveyor's liability, but rather prevented the duty of care from arising. The House of Lords did not agree with that contention. It was concluded that the disclaimer fell within the relevant part of s 13(1), and so was brought within s 2(2). Lord Griffiths arrived at that conclusion by applying the 'but for' test. He said (at 530): 'the existence of the common law duty of care ... is to be judged by considering whether it would exist "but for" the notice.' In other words, the approach taken was simply to ask whether there would be an obligation in the absence of the clause. If there was, then the clause was to be regarded as excluding it, and so within the relevant part of UCTA 1977, s 13(1). (This reflects the approach indicated by the Court of Appeal in *Phillips Products Ltd* v *Hyland* [1987] 2 All ER 620 in the contractual context.)[29]

10.103 The 'but for' test would also seem to be indicated by *Johnstone* v *Bloomsbury Health Authority* (1991). The case concerned the contract of employment of a junior hospital doctor. The contract provided that he should work for 40 hours a week and be on call for up to a further 48 hours a week. It was the express term concerning the hours on call which was at the centre of the dispute. The doctor claimed that his health had been damaged by the long hours which he had worked, and argued that the health authority was in breach of an implied term that it had a duty to take care not to foreseeably damage his health. The Court of Appeal was asked to strike out his action, but his claim survived. A term will not be implied in the face of an express contradictory term, but the majority of the court thought that the express term did not contradict the implied term contended for, and merely set the limits within which the health authority should exercise its discretion in relation to the 'on call hours'. However, the point of interest here is that all three members of the court agreed that, if the express term prevented the implication, then that express term would be regarded as a clause falling within the final part of UCTA 1977, s 13(1) and would thus be rendered ineffective by s 2(1).

29 In considering whether there had been a breach of an obligation to take reasonable care, Slade LJ said (at 625):

> the court has to leave out of account at this stage the contract term which is relied on by the defence as defeating the plaintiff's claim for breach of such obligation or duty.

10.104 The idea of using UCTA 1977 in the way in which the court envisaged in *Johnstone v Bloomsbury Health Authority* (1991) illustrates how wide the compass of the Act would be under the application of the 'but for' test. It would seem to render subject to the Act any express term contradicting a term which would, in the absence of the clause, be implied into a contract falling within the Act (provided that the liability existing in the absence of the clause is appropriate to bring the clause within one of the relevant 'active sections'). 'But for' the clause the implication would be made. In addition, the 'but for' test would seem to make it impossible for the parties to define an obligation to take due care by stating it widely and then qualifying it, without its being subject to s 2 of the Act.

10.105 The 'but for' test is very mechanical, which means that it is easy to apply. However, that ease of application is paid for by a lack of discrimination. The 'but for' test is too wide, bringing clauses inappropriately within the Act.

10.106 It can be contended that an exclusion clause can be identified 'in substance' by looking at the reality of the contracting process. A relevant clause should be found to be exclusionary, rather than definitional, when it is in small print, being used against an unsophisticated party, and only a term because it is a contractual document which that party signed, and could not reasonably be expected to know the content of. In contrast, when what is in question is a transaction involving legally sophisticated parties, who can be expected to have taken on board the impact of the relevant clause in a standard form contract, so that it reflects the reality of the transaction, it should be regarded as definitional.[30] (For further discussion, and analysis of the identification of exclusion clauses in substance, see E. Macdonald, 'Exception Clauses: Exclusionary or Definitional? It Depends!' (2012) 29 JCL 47.)

Summary

- Basically, the Unfair Contract Terms Act 1977 (UCTA) applies to exemption clauses (i.e. clauses excluding or restricting liability (s 13 ensures a narrow approach is not taken to identifying such clauses)), but coverage of such clauses in 'consumer contracts' has now been removed from UCTA and is dealt with in the Consumer Rights Act 2015. It subjects some of the clauses to which it applies to automatic ineffectiveness and renders others ineffective unless they satisfy the requirement of reasonableness.
- The Act basically applies to business liability. There are some contracts excluded from its scope (Sch 1) and there are also limits on its application in relation to contracts with an international element (ss 26, 27, 29).
- The provisions of the CRA excise the references to 'deals as consumer' from the Act, and take 'consumer contracts' and 'consumer notices' outside of the scope of UCTA, bringing

30 See, e.g., *Raiffeisen Zentralbank Österreich AG v Royal Bank of Scotland* (2010); *Avrora Fine Arts Investment Ltd v Christie, Manson & Woods* (2012).

them within one distinct consumer regime relating to unfair terms, removing the complexity of two overlapping regimes.

- If the Act is going to impact upon a particular exemption clause, an 'active section' which covers the situation must be found. The relevant active section will then state what is to happen to the clause in question, that is, whether it is automatically ineffective or subject to the requirement of reasonableness. The principal active sections are ss 2, 3, 6, and 7.
- Section 2 is the active section which deals with attempts to exclude or restrict liability for negligence. Under s 2(1) liability for negligently caused death or personal injury cannot be excluded or restricted (automatic ineffectiveness). Under s 2(2) liability for other negligently caused loss or damage can be excluded or restricted if the requirement of reasonableness is satisfied. (This section covers non-contractual disclaimers as well as contractual exemption clauses.) The provisions of the CRA now deal with such clauses in consumer contracts.
- Section 3 covers contracts under which the party against whom the exemption clause is used deals on the 'other party's written standard terms of business'. Section 3(2)(a) subjects to the requirement of reasonableness clauses excluding or restricting liability in such contracts. Section 3(2)(b) subjects 'disguised' exemption clauses to the requirement of reasonableness. (Section 3 also used to cover contracts where the relevant party 'dealt as consumer', but consumer contracts now fall within the CRA.)
- Sections 6 and 7 cover clauses excluding or restricting liability in relation to certain implied terms in goods contracts. The removal of those sections' coverage of consumer contracts is provided for by the CRA, which provides equivalent coverage.
- Section 11 assists with the meaning of 'the requirement of reasonableness' but it is a weighing exercise, requiring the consideration of all the relevant factors. The time frame for identifying relevant factors is that of the making of the contract, that is, it is relevant factors which were known to, or ought reasonably have been known to, the parties when they made the contract. Some factors are identified in Sch 2 and s 11(4). Others have been identified by the courts. Relevant factors include, for example, relative bargaining power of the parties, insurance, availability of alternatives, knowledge (objective and subjective) of the clause, width of the clause, settlement of past claims, conditions placed on claims, negligence, and risk.

Further reading

J. Adams and R. Brownsword, 'The Unfair Contract Terms Act 1977: A Decade of Discretion' (1988) 104 LQR 94

H. Beale, 'Unfair Terms in Contracts: Proposals for Reform in the UK' (2004) 27 Journal of Consumer Policy 289

B. Coote, *Exception Clauses*, Sweet & Maxwell, 1964

Law Commission and Scottish Law Commission, *Unfair Terms in Contracts*, Law Com 292, Scot Law Com No 199

E. Macdonald, 'Exception Clauses: Exclusionary or Definitional? It Depends!' (2012) 29 JCL 47

Chapter 11

Unfair terms in consumer contracts

Introduction

11.1 The EC Directive on Unfair Terms in Consumer Contracts (93/13/EEC) is a highly significant EC measure in the sphere of consumer contracts. Under it, member states have had to subject non-individually negotiated terms in contracts between consumers and sellers or suppliers to a fairness test, with unfair terms not binding consumers. As can immediately be seen, this is a significant inroad on the basic idea of freedom of contract in the consumer context. Pat Edwards, Legal Director of the Office of Fair Trading, said:[1]

> that cherished principle [of freedom of contract], instilled in the course of academic studies and practice had, of course, been much under attack well before 1995 in its application to some aspects of consumer contracts. But nothing had hitherto actually turned on its head, as the Directive does, the general duty of the lawyer to draft wholly and exclusively in the interests of the client, in whatever language is adapted to preserve and enhance the client's legal position … Now in order properly to serve their clients, legal advisers must have a wider perspective than taking into account only those client's interests.

Indeed, the idea behind the Directive is that of providing some rebalancing between the position of the parties, where the inequalities of bargaining power and knowledge prevent freedom of contract from operating properly. We have seen that in *Kasler*, the Court of Justice of the European Union (CJEU) emphasized (at [39]) that it has

> consistently held that the system of protection introduced by Directive 93/13 is based on the idea that the consumer is in a position of weakness vis-à-vis the seller or supplier, as regards

1 'The Challenge of the Regulations', OFT Bulletin No 4 on Unfair Contract Terms, p. 19.

> both his bargaining power and his level of knowledge, a situation that leads to his agreeing to terms drawn up in advance by the seller or supplier without being able to influence the content of those terms.

There are, however, exclusions from the Directive's fairness test, particularly what is commonly referred to as the 'core exemption', which, very broadly, covers terms defining the main subject matter of the contract, and the question of the appropriateness of the price. This core exemption is key to the extent of the impact on freedom of contract, and its scope has proved controversial in the UK.

11.2 The Directive is a minimum Directive, so that, whilst member states cannot fall below the level of consumer protection which it provides, they can go further. In the UK, initially by the Unfair Terms in Consumer Contracts Regulations 1994 (SI 1994/3159) and then by the replacement Unfair Terms in Consumer Contracts Regulations 1999 (SI 1999/2083), it was largely implemented simply by 'copy out', with the Regulations basically just reproducing the Directive; the 1999 Regulations did so more closely than the 1994 version. There was an obvious drawback to this in the significant overlap with the Unfair Contract Terms Act 1977 (UCTA). A great deal of complexity was occasioned by having two such regimes which used different tests and definitions, with, for example, UCTA giving a very different meaning to 'deals as consumer' than did the Regulations to who was a 'consumer' and what was a 'consumer contract'.

11.3 In 2005 the Law Commission and the Scottish Law Commission produced a report, and a draft Bill, to provide one unified piece of unfair terms legislation;[2] however, that was overtaken by proposals for new EU measures, which would have brought together, and changed, EU law in a number of important consumer areas, including unfair terms. The proposed Consumer Rights Directive was intended as a maximum Directive, requiring the same level of protection by all member states. The idea was to make it easier for businesses to trade in different member states, without having to deal with different requirements, and for consumers to have confidence to buy in different member states, knowing they would get the same level of protection. The promotion of cross-border e-commerce within the EU was a key driver. However, whilst it is easy, and not generally controversial, to produce uniform consumer protection in relation to such matters as how many days a consumer has to cancel a contract made by distance communication, such as telephone, post, or online, there were major concerns about this approach in relation to the unfair terms regime. The proposals would have reduced the protection provided in some member states, which had gone further than the Unfair Terms Directive required, as they were allowed to do under a minimum Directive. In any event, it seems unlikely that the situation could, or should, have been produced in which a term which was fair before the courts of one member state would be found to be fair in the courts of all the other member states. As we shall see, fairness under the Directive has been recognized as having a contextual, societal element, and the potential for different conclusions on the fairness of a particular term in different member states. In its final form, the Consumer Rights Directive did not include a new version of the Unfair Terms Directive.

2 Law Commissions, *Unfair Terms in Contracts* (2005), Law Com No 292, Scot Law Com No 199.

11.4 The limited coverage of the final version of the Consumer Rights Directive left the way open for the UK to return to the reform of its unfair terms legislation, in order to rid itself of the complexities of two overlapping regimes; after further work by the Law Commissions,[3] the Consumer Rights Act 2015 (CRA) was finally enacted to replace the Regulations and the consumer aspects of UCTA, which were repealed. Of course, UCTA did not simply deal with consumer contracts; it also applied to exemption clauses in many business-to-business contracts, and that has been left largely unchanged. It is the consumer protection elements which are stripped out of UCTA by CRA, to provide a single consumer protection regime in relation to unfair terms, and indeed unfair notices,[4] although the focus here will be on terms. As UCTA's protection, in the consumer context, was not limited to non-individually negotiated terms, neither is that of the CRA. In addition, largely reflecting what had happened under UCTA, there are also some terms (and notices) which are simply not binding on the consumer, without the fairness test needing to be applied (ss 31, 47, 57, 65).[5] In addition, just as UCTA dealt with avoidance by means of a secondary contract (s 10, UCTA 1977), so the CRA does to a term in a secondary contract what it would have done to it had it been in the primary contract (s 72 CRA).

Enforcement

11.5 Much of the significance of the unfair terms regime stems from enforcement mechanisms which operate at a general level. However, before emphasizing that, we should first note its action in the individual case. The protection of the CRA can be used, like UCTA was, by an individual consumer in dispute with a particular trader, and an unfair term does not bind the consumer (s 62(1)), although this does not prevent the consumer from relying on the term if he or she chooses to do so (s 62(3)). Also, the consumer is obviously not bound by those terms which the CRA simply states are not to bind him or her, without any need for the application of the fairness test (ss 31, 47, 57, 65). The contract continues to have effect, so far as is 'practicable', in every other respect (s 67).

11.6 A court may assist a consumer in an individual dispute as it may find a term unfair even if the consumer does not raise that point. That line was taken by the CJEU in Cases C-240/98 to C-244/98, *Oceano Grupo Editorial SA* v *Quintero* (2000), and in Case C-243/08 *Pannon GSM Zrt* v *Gyorfi* (2009) it was viewed as 'a duty' for the court to consider the unfairness of a term even where it has not been raised by the consumer, albeit that the court would need to have 'available to it the legal and factual elements necessary for the task' (at [32]). This is a practical limitation: 'a court cannot hold a term unfair if it does not so appear from the case presented to it.'[6]

3 The Law Commission and the Scottish Law Commission, *Unfair Terms in Consumer Contracts: A New Approach?* (2012), The Law Commission and the Scottish Law Commission, *Unfair Terms in Consumer Contracts: Advice to the Department for Business, Innovation and Skills* (2013).

4 Reflecting the fact that UCTA's coverage is not limited to terms, but also covers non-contractual notices in relation attempts to exclude or restrict liability for negligence in s 2.

5 There are also some others which are deemed unfair to fulfill the requirements of other EU Directives on distance marketing (see s 63(6)).

6 S. Whittaker, 'Judicial Interventionism and Consumer Contracts' (2001) 117 LQR 215.

The CRA now specifically provides for the duty, and also recognizes its effective limits, stating that it does not apply 'unless the court considers that it has before it sufficient legal and factual material to enable it to consider the fairness of the term' (s 71).

11.7 However, the most important enforcement mechanism is the general one. The 1994 Regulations gave the Director General of Fair Trading power to apply for injunctions to prevent the continued use, or recommendation for the use, of unfair terms. Under the 1999 Regulations, that power lay with the Office of Fair Trading (OFT) and was also extended to other 'qualifying bodies', as set out in Sch 1. The Director General of Fair Trading and the OFT achieved the removal or modification of many terms in standard form consumer contracts—mostly by negotiation rather than having to resort to litigation—and that can be seen in the Bulletins published by the OFT to show how complaints about terms were dealt with. Such a general enforcement mechanism is important in the consumer context because consumers do not generally litigate and often do not know their rights. The OFT even encountered terms which would have been automatically ineffective under the 1977 Act (for example, Bulletin 3 at 1.2). Any terms which cannot have the effect they may appear to the consumer to have may be used to intimidate the consumer (Bulletin 3 at 4.4), but they cannot have that impact, or even simply mislead the consumer as to his or her rights,[7] if the general level of enforcement ensures their removal from the trader's terms, so that they are not, thereafter, encountered by the consumer. Under the Consumer Rights Act 2015, the primary role in relation to the general level of enforcement falls to the Competition and Markets Authority (CMA) and there are other 'regulators' (Sch 3, para. 8). Their powers extend not to just unfair terms, but also to terms which are simply not binding on the consumer without any need to apply the fairness test (Sch 3, para. 2).

11.8 The CRA also deals with a long disputed aspect of the enforcement of the Directive/Regulations. The Directive appears to state a requirement that terms should be in 'plain intelligible language' (art. 5). However, neither it nor the Regulations provided any mechanism for enforcement of that, and its existence as a requirement, as such, was therefore open to dispute. Under the CRA, there is a requirement that a written term (or notice) is 'transparent'. A term (or notice) is transparent if it is 'expressed in plain intelligible language and it is legible' (s 68), and there is specific provision for the CMA and other regulators to obtain injunctions to prevent the use, or continued use, of terms (or notices) which fail to meet this requirement (Sch 3). (See further para. **11.61**.)

EC background

11.9 Of course, we do not know what is to happen with Brexit so, until matters are clarified on that front, the current position must be stated. As matters stand with the UK as a member state, when interpreting any legislation purporting to implement a Directive, every endeavour must be made to construe it so that it implements that Directive, and some of the terms

7 In *Skerratt* v *Linfax Ltd* (2003) the misleading effect of a clause which was automatically ineffective under s 2(1) of UCTA 1977 was raised as a factor when C was asking to bring an action out of time.

used in the legislation may need a European interpretation through the CJEU. In *Freiburger Kommunalbauten GmbH Baugesellschaft & Co. KG* v *Hofstetter* Case C-237/02 (2004) the CJEU indicated that it would not provide a view as to the fairness of a particular term, but that it was its role to 'interpret general criteria used by the community legislature in order to define the concept of unfair terms' (at [22]).[8] This division of responsibility was confirmed by the CJEU in *VB Penzugyi Lizing Zrt* v *Ferenc Schneider* (2010):

> the jurisdiction of the Court of Justice extends to the interpretation of the concept of 'unfair term' used in art.3(1) of the Directive and in the annex thereto, and to the criteria which the national court may or must apply when examining a contractual term in the light of the provisions of the Directive, bearing in mind that it was for that court to determine, in the light of those criteria, whether a particular contractual term was actually unfair in the circumstances of the case.

The interpretation of the concept and the criteria which may be used to determine fairness under the Directive are matters for the CJEU, but the fairness of a term is left to be decided by the courts with an understanding of its legal and social context (*Aziz v Caixa d'Estalvis de Catalunya* (2013)). This means that a term may be fair in one member state and unfair in another. It is not sought to achieve the certainty which a business wanting to trade in several member states, in particular, might regard as desirable on this point. However, apart from any technical arguments as to the extent of the powers of the CJEU, there is the basic point that to seek to achieve greater uniformity would have been to fail to recognize the great differences in the broader laws and societies of the member states. Gunther Teubner wrote, in relation to 'good faith', that:[9]

> an interpretation of good faith which is oriented to the peculiarities, opportunities, risks and dangers of a specific production regime would indeed result in widely divergent rules in different countries, even in contradictory decisions in apparently equal cases. These cleavages cannot and should not be papered over by European zeal for harmonization ... European efforts at harmonization have not yet seriously taken into account the 'varieties of capitalism', the difference in production regimes.

Basic scope of the unfair terms regime

11.10 As has been indicated, the Directive applies a fairness test to terms in non-individually negotiated consumer contracts, specifying that unfair terms do not bind the consumer. Subject to some terms simply not binding the consumer, without the need to apply the fairness test, the CRA basically does the same, but it also encompasses individually negotiated terms. The test

8 See also Case C-243/08 *Pannon GSM Zrt* v *Gyorfi* (2009) at [42].

9 G. Teubner, 'Legal Irritants: Good Faith in British Law or How Unifying Law Ends Up in New Divergences' (1998) 61 MLR 11 at 31.

of unfairness requires that, contrary to the requirement of good faith, there should be a significant imbalance in the rights and obligations of the parties to the detriment of the consumer (s 62(4)).[10] In addition, as in the Directive, the CRA has a 'grey list' of terms which may be unfair (Sch 2). The Directive and the CRA also contain the core exemption from the fairness test, so that the question of adequacy/appropriateness of the price, as against the subject matter of the contract, and the terms defining the main subject matter of the contract, are not subject to the fairness test (s 64(1)). The Directive made such exemption subject to the terms being in 'plain intelligible language'. In the CRA this has become restriction to terms which are 'transparent and prominent' (s 64(2)), with 'transparency' being a matter of 'plain intelligible language' and, in relation to written terms, 'legibility' (s 64(3)). Further, terms are 'prominent' if they are 'brought to the consumer's attention in such a way that the average consumer would be aware of the terms' (s 64(4)). It was said of the Regulations that they did not apply to terms implied at common law, and the same line would seem to apply under the CRA.[11] The Directive and the CRA specifically put outside their scope terms reflecting certain legislation or international conventions. Section 73(1) states:

> This Part does not apply to a term of a contract, or to a notice, to the extent that it reflects –
>
> **(a)** mandatory statutory or regulatory provisions, or
>
> **(b)** the provisions or principles of an international convention to which United Kingdom or the EU is a party.

The reference to 'mandatory statutory or regulatory provisions' includes 'rules which, according to law, apply between the parties on the basis that no other arrangements have been established' (s 73(2)). If the reflection of the statutory or regulatory provisions or of the convention is not a sufficiently accurate one, there should be scope for the application of the Directive/Regulations, as has been indicated by the CJEU (Case C-473/00 *Cofidis SA* v *Jean-Louis Fredout* (2002) at [22]).

11.11 It can be re-emphasized that the unfair terms regime in the CRA is not restricted to non-individually negotiated terms. The Directive is a minimum Directive, so implementing legislation can go further, and it is not just an implementation of the Directive, but also the creation of a unified consumer unfair terms regime from both the Directive and UCTA. Extension beyond non-individually negotiated terms was recommended by the Law Commissions in their 2005 report. UCTA's controls of exemption clauses in contracts where one party 'deals as consumer' were not confined to non-individually negotiated, or standard, terms, so maintaining UCTA's level of protection for consumers would have necessitated maintaining separate protection against exemption clauses, unless the requirement of 'non-individually negotiated terms'

10 Art. 3.

11 *Baybut* v *Eccle Riggs County Park Ltd* (2006). It is in any event difficult to imagine that such terms would be unfair. However, any general exclusion of implied terms from the Regulations should not encompass terms incorporated by a course of dealing. In a sense these are implied terms, as they are not expressly brought within the particular contract, but the mechanism is very different from that importing other terms by implication. Inevitably what is in question when terms are incorporated by a course of dealing is simply one party's set of standard terms and there will be as much scope for them to be unfair as in any other set of standard terms.

was dropped across the broad coverage of the unfair terms regime.[12] Such simplification is one reason for not confining the CRA's unfair terms regime to non-individually negotiated terms. It was also thought that, in any event, outside of the core terms, 'consumers seldom have sufficient understanding of the possible impact of [the terms] to make any negotiation meaningful'.[13] Further there was uncertainty over when a term was 'non-individually negotiated',[14] and also evidence of exploitation by some businesses of the fact that the Regulations did not cover non-individually negotiated terms.[15]

11.12 Although UCTA only deals with exemption clauses, it sometimes does more to those clauses than simply subject them to its 'reasonableness test'. Obviously, in order to maintain, or improve, the level of consumer protection, the CRA had to impact similarly on certain terms. Thus, UCTA's provision of automatic ineffectiveness for terms excluding or restricting liability for negligently caused death or personal injury, without any scope for arguments as to reasonableness or fairness, is maintained in the CRA in s 65. Of course, UCTA's coverage of exemptions for negligence is not restricted to terms but also covers notices, and the CRA is also, more broadly, able to cover a notice (s 61(4)):

> to the extent that it
> **(a)** relates to rights or obligations between a trader and a consumer, or
> **(b)** purports to exclude or restrict s trader's liability to a consumer.

The automatic ineffectiveness which was provided under ss 6 and 7 of UCTA of terms excluding or restricting liability against someone 'dealing as consumer', in relation to certain implied terms in goods contracts, has been repealed and is now provided more broadly in the first part of the CRA in relation to specified obligations relating to goods (s 31), services (s 57), and digital content (s 47).

Consumer contracts

11.13 The Directive and the CRA are concerned with providing protection for consumers who are contracting with businesses. In the CRA this is put in terms of 'consumer contracts' (s 61), which are contracts between 'traders' and 'consumers', both of which are defined in s 2,[16] with the CRA also extending its protection to 'consumer notices' (s 61(4)). We looked at when a contract is a 'consumer contract' in **Chapter 10**, as it is necessary to do so when deciding whether an exemption clause requires consideration of UCTA or the CRA. The reader should therefore turn to paras 10.9–10.14 for discussion of when a contract is a 'consumer contract'

12 *Unfair Terms in Contracts* (2005) Law Com No 292, Scot Law Com No 199, para. 3.51.

13 *Unfair Terms in Contracts* (2005) Law Com No 292, Scot Law Com No 199, para. 3.51.

14 *Unfair Terms in Contracts* (2005) Law Com No 292, Scot Law Com No 199, para. 3.52.

15 *Unfair Terms in Contracts* (2005) Law Com No 292, Scot Law Com No 199, para 3.52.

16 These definitions in s 2 are extended to Part 2 of the CRA by s 76(2).

within the CRA. It is, however, worth emphasizing that where a trader claims that an individual is not a consumer, the burden lies on that trader to prove it (s 76(3)).

The 'core' exemption

11.14 Article 4(2) of the Directive states:

> Assessment of the unfair nature of terms shall relate neither to the definition of the main subject matter of the contract nor to the adequacy of the price and remuneration, on the one hand as against the services or goods supplied in exchange, on the other, in so far as those terms are in plain intelligible language.

This is commonly referred to as the 'core exemption' from the fairness test. What is covered by it has proved to be a problematic and controversial question. Its scope is of great importance to the effectiveness of the fairness regime and the extent of the interference with freedom of contract. The tension between consumer protection and freedom of contract is central to the difficulty it has occasioned. Something of this can be seen in what is commonly regarded as its origin, in an article about the original draft of the Directive, which did not contain any such exemption.[17] That article by Brandner and Ulmer stated:[18]

> In a free market economy parties to a contract are free to shape the principal obligations as they see fit. The relationship between the price and the goods or services provided is determined not according to some legal formula but by the mechanisms of the market. Any control by the courts or administrative authorities of the reasonableness or equivalence of this relationship is anathema to the fundamental tenets of a free market economy.

Brandner and Ulmer went on to qualify this, giving some acknowledgement to the circumstances which may limit the effective operation of freedom of contract. They recognized the need for a requirement of 'transparency', because of[19]

> terms which may conceal the principal obligations or the price and thus would make it difficult for the consumer to obtain an overview of the market and to make what would (relatively speaking) be the best choice in a given situation.

The tension which can be seen to exist between freedom of contract and the control of unfair terms is plain, just as it is that the core exemption is a significant point of focus for it.

17 Hugh Beale ed., *Chitty on Contracts* (30th edn, Sweet & Maxwell, 2008) para. 15–050. *Office of Fair Trading v Abbey National plc and others* [2009] UKSC 6, [2010] 1 AC 696, [6], [109].

18 H. E. Brandner and P. Ulmer, 'The Community Directive on Unfair Terms in Consumer Contracts: Some Critical Remarks on the Proposals Submitted by the EC Commission' (1991) 28 CMLR 647, 656.

19 H. E. Brandner and P. Ulmer, 'The Community Directive on Unfair Terms in Consumer Contracts: Some Critical Remarks on the Proposals Submitted by the EC Commission' (1991) 28 CMLR 647, 656.

11.15 In relation to the core exemption as a point of focus for the tension between consumer protection and freedom of contract, and more generally, it should be emphasized that both the CJEU in *Matei* and now, specifically, the CRA in s 64(6) made it clear that the core exemption is subject to the grey list of terms in Sch 2 which may be unfair. If a term falls within the grey list the fairness test applies to it, even if it would otherwise fall within the core exemption. Further—and again, this point is important in relation to the tension between consumer protection and freedom of contract, and more generally—the CJEU has made it clear that the core exemption must be construed narrowly, as an exception to the protection provided by the Directive. In *Kasler*, the CJEU started (at [42]):

> Article 4(2) of Directive 93/13 thus laying down an exception to the mechanism for reviewing the substance of unfair terms, such as that provided for in the system of consumer protection put in place by that directive, that provision must be strictly interpreted.

11.16 In the CRA, the core exemption is contained in s 64, with s 64(1) stating:

> A term of a consumer contract may not be assessed for fairness under section 62 to the extent that—
>
> **(a)** it specifies the main subject matter of the contract, or
>
> **(b)** the assessment is of the appropriateness of the price payable under the contract by comparison with the goods, digital content or services supplied under it.

The restriction of the exemption to terms which are in 'plain intelligible language' is replaced by one limiting the exemption to terms which are 'transparent and prominent' (s 64(2)). It is explained, in s 64(3), that a term is 'transparent' if it is in 'plain intelligible language and (in the case of a written term) is legible'. In addition, s 64(4) states that a term is 'prominent' if 'it is brought to consumers' attention in such a way that the average consumer would be aware of the term' and in s 64(5) it is explained that the 'average consumer means a consumer who is reasonably well informed, observant and circumspect'. In other words, this does not involve the true 'average consumer' revealed by the empirical work of behavioural psychologists, but rather is a standard set by the legislation. The reference to the 'average consumer', who is endowed with such virtues beyond those of the empirically identified 'average' person, comes from the CJEU.[20] That court has set a demanding standard for the requirement of 'plain intelligible language',[21] so that it is not satisfied by terms being merely 'formally and grammatically intelligible'[22] but rather takes the view that it is 'of fundamental importance for the purpose of complying with the requirement of transparency' that the consumer could 'foresee, on the basis of clear, intelligible criteria, the economic consequences for him which derive from' the term.[23] Against this

20 *Matei v SC Volksbank Romania SA* Case C-143/13 (26th Feb, 2015) [2015] 1 WLR 2385 at [75]; *Arpad Kasler v OTP Jelzabalogbank Zrt* (2014), at [74].

21 See **n 20**.

22 *Kasler* at [71].

23 *Kasler* at [73].

background, the references to 'legibility' and 'prominence' in the CRA may add little to the simple reference in the Directive to 'plain intelligible language', and despite the identification of the 'average consumer' as an artificial construct, there is a fairly demanding limitation of the scope of the core exemption here.

11.17 Turning to the substantive elements of the core exemption, we should remember that in *Kasler* the CJEU emphasized that it must be 'strictly interpreted', as an exception to the review of the fairness of terms generally provided by the Directive (at [42]). More specifically, in relation to the part of the core exemption which is referred to in s 62(1)(a) as covering a term to the extent that 'it specifies the main subject matter of the contract', the CJEU in *Kasler* also stated, in relation to the Directive (at [49]–[50]):

> However, taking account also of the fact that Article 4(2) of Directive 93/13 represents a derogation and the ensuing necessity of its being interpreted strictly, contractual terms falling within the notion of the 'main subject-matter of the contract', within the meaning of that provision, must be understood as being those that lay down the essential obligations of the contract and, as such, characterise it.

The CJEU added:

> By contrast, terms ancillary to those that define the very essence of the contractual relationship cannot fall within the notion of the 'main subject-matter of the contract' within the meaning of Article 4(2) of Directive 93/13.

Here we find the idea of the restriction of terms falling within the first part of the core exemption—with its reference to terms which 'define the main subject matter of the contract', in the words of the Directive, or which 'specify the main subject matter of the contract', in the words of the CRA—to those which 'lay down the essential obligations of the contract' and 'as such, characterise it'. A contrast is made between such terms and those which are 'ancillary terms'.

11.18 In the English courts, there has been some running together of the first part of the core exemption, referring to terms defining the main subject matter of the contract, and the second part, relating to the price. It was also less clear, in the earlier implementation of the Directive in English law, that the second part of the core exemption merely related to the specific question of the 'adequacy' or 'appropriateness' of the price as against the goods, services, or digital content supplied, and that can also be seen in the discussion in the cases. This should be borne in mind in considering the judgments of the English courts. Nevertheless, we can see, in the basic approach of the House of Lords in *Director General of Fair Trading* v *First National Bank*, a line which is not too different to that of the CJEU in relation to the first element of the core exemption.

11.19 *Director General of Fair Trading* v *First National Bank* (2001) was concerned with one of the terms in First National's standard form contract for lending money to borrowers through regulated agreements under the Consumer Credit Act 1974. The particular term allowed for the continuance of the contractual rate of interest after judgment for default. The significance of the term was that, without it, First National would have ceased to have a right to interest on the amount outstanding once judgment had occurred. In the absence of such a term, the contractual right to interest would have 'merged' with the judgment and, as judgment had to be sought in the county court, no interest could be awarded because what was in question was a regulated agreement. The court had power to order payment by instalments of the sum for which judgment was given, but that did not include future interest to cover the further time taken to repay the principal. The court also had powers under s 136 of the Consumer Credit Act 1974, when making a 'time order' to allow repayment over a period of time, to amend any term of the agreement. However, what caused a problem was that the county court would give judgment for First National on the consumer's default, and make an order allowing for repayment by instalments. The consumer would duly make those instalment payments and then be shocked to discover that a considerable sum was still owed because, under the relevant contractual term, the contractual rate of interest had continued to be payable after the judgment. That interest could not be covered by the payments ordered by the court and the court had not, when making the order, considered whether to provide any relief from it. The consumer had not understood the interaction of the term and the legislation. There were two basic arguments to be considered by the court: first, that the situation fell within the core exemption and was not covered by the fairness test; second, that it was, in any event, fair. The High Court ([2000] 1 All ER 240), the Court of Appeal ([2000] 2 All ER 759), and the House of Lords ([2002] 1 All ER 97) all found that the core exemption did not apply, but only the Court of Appeal regarded the term as unfair. The approach taken to the core exemption is the matter of interest here. It was the 1994 Regulations on Unfair Terms in Consumer Contracts with which the courts were concerned, but the broad approach is still of significance.

11.20 It should be emphasized that the House of Lords took the line that a restrictive approach was needed in relation to the core exemption if the purpose of the Regulations was not to be frustrated.[24] In deciding that the term in question was not within the core exemption, Lord Bingham accepted the distinction between terms 'which express the substance of the bargain and "incidental" (if important) terms which surround them' (at [12]). Similarly, Lord Steyn thought that the term in question was not within the core exemption and was a 'subsidiary' term (at [34]). This is not unlike the subsequent comments of the CJEU in *Kasler*. It is also worth noting that Lord Steyn specifically made the point that a restrictive approach should be taken to the 'core', to avoid the 'main purpose of the scheme [being] frustrated by endless formalistic arguments as to whether a provision is a definitional or exclusionary provision' (at [34]).[25] However, at its narrowest, the *First National Bank* case could be seen as merely deciding that a term dealing with the situation after default was not within the core.[26]

11.21 The 1999 Regulations on Unfair Terms in Consumer Contracts fell to be considered by the Supreme Court in *Office of Fair Trading* v *Abbey National* (2009). It involved an action by the OFT against seven banks and one building society ('the Banks'). The terms in question were those which impose charges (the 'relevant charges') in relation to overdrafts which have not been agreed in advance, or in relation to unsuccessful 'requests' for such overdrafts (not the

24 Lord Bingham at [15], Lord Steyn at [34].

25 On the problems of distinguishing definitional and exclusionary terms see para. 9.3.

26 Lord Bingham at [12], Lord Steyn at [34], Lord Hope at [43].

terms imposing interest payments on the overdrafts).[27] Such overdrafts may be successfully or unsuccessfully 'requested' in a number of ways, such as a cheque being presented, direct debits becoming payable, a withdrawal from an ATM, or even the debiting from an account of an amount to cover interest or fees payable to the bank. The courts were asked to consider whether the 'relevant charges' were covered by the core exemption or could be subject to the fairness test. At first instance, and in the Court of Appeal,[28] a narrow approach was taken to the core exemption, and it was found that it did not cover the terms.

11.22 The Court of Appeal emphasized the distinction made by the House of Lords in *First National Bank* between terms falling within the 'core' and incidental or subsidiary terms. It developed this approach to confine 'core terms' to those embodying the 'essential bargain' (at [86]), whether they fell within the first or second element of the core exemption, and with the identification of the essential bargain not being simply a matter of interpretation of the contract, but one of how it would be viewed by the consumer. That line was taken to ensure 'protection in respect of the kind of issues that a consumer will not have in focus when entering the bargain' (at [86]). Whether freedom of contract was properly operating would be considered before the core exemption ousted the operation of the fairness test.

11.23 However, the line taken by the Supreme Court was very different. It gave much greater scope for the core exemption, and the judges thought the core exemption clearly applied. The Supreme Court confined the *First National Bank* case to its narrowest line; the term there was not exempt as it was a default term. The Court took the approach that, subject to the protection of the consumer by the requirement of 'plain intelligible language', the scope of the core exemption was simply a matter of construction of the contract. Lord Mance stated:[29]

> [T]he identification of the price or remuneration for the purposes of … Regulation 6(2) is a matter of objective interpretation for the court. The court should no doubt read and interpret the contract in the usual manner … [There] is no basis for requiring it to do so … by confining the focus to matters on which it might conjecture that [the consumer] would be likely to focus. The consumer's protection under the … Regulations is the requirement of transparency … That being present, the consumer is assumed to be capable of reading the relevant terms and identifying whatever is objectively the price and remuneration under the contract into which he or she enters.

27 These relevant charges formed part of the charging structure adopted by the banks in relation to current accounts, and that was described by Andrew Smith J at first instance ([2008] EWHC 875 (Comm)) at [53] as follows:

> The charging structure adopted by the Banks in relation to current accounts is commonly known as 'free-if-in-credit banking' … under this structure customers do not pay bank charges for the day-to-day operation of the account while it is in credit (although there are often charges for additional services such as, for some banks, stopping cheques written by the customer or supplying additional bank statements). The Banks do, however, have the benefit of customers' credit balances … and also interest will be incurred and fees may be incurred if the customer's account goes into debit or in other circumstances. These fees include the Relevant Charges.

28 [2009] EWCA Civ 116, [2009] 1 All ER (Comm) 1097.

29 [2009] UKSC 6, [2010] 1 AC 696 at [113].

In the view of the Supreme Court, the coverage of the core exemption was basically a matter of construction—whether the terms deal with 'the main subject matter of contract' or the price, with protection of the consumer's decision making provided by the requirement that the relevant terms be 'plain intelligible language'.

11.24 Of course, the Supreme Court acknowledged that the core exemption should be construed 'restrictively' and limited to terms falling 'squarely within it' (at [43]). Lord Walker stated that he was agreeing with the line taken by Lord Bingham in *First National Bank* on this ([43]). However, the more specific comments do not fit easily with any such idea. Lord Walker had stated (at [40]):

> [A] supply of services may be simple (an entertainer booked to perform for an hour at a children's party) or composite (a week's stay at a five-star hotel offering a wide variety of services). Again, there is no principled basis on which the court could decide that some services are more essential to the contract than others and again the main subject matter must be described in general terms—hotel services.

Such comments obviously relate to the first part of the core exemption, and would have made it very broad indeed. There has been no further indication of an approach as restrictive of the core exemption as that of the Court of Appeal in *Abbey National*, and relating it as much to the operation of freedom of contract, but we should remember that the CJEU has now emphasized that the core exemption must be strictly construed, and that its first element should be limited to those terms which 'lay down the essential obligations of the contract and, as such, characterise it'. It certainly seems that the 'wide variety of services' provided in a week's stay at a five-star hotel should not all, or even nearly all, fall within the first element of the core exemption. They will not 'characterize' the contract.

11.25 The approach of the Supreme Court was much criticized. The heavy emphasis on construction invites issues in relation to distinguishing clauses in substance rather than just form, as in relation to whether a clause in the form of part of the definition of the obligation is an exclusion clause, or whether a payment is part of the price or is, in substance, a payment after default. Lord Steyn had recognized the potential for the first type of problem in *First National Bank* (see para. **11.22**), and *Bairstow Eves London Central Ltd* v *Smith* (2004), which the Supreme Court approved of in *Abbey National*, illustrates the latter.[30]

30 The case was concerned with an estate agent's fees, which had, mistakenly, not been paid by the vendor's solicitors at the time of the sale. The contract provided for a 'standard commission rate' of 3 per cent and an 'early payment discounted rate' of 1.5 per cent. The standard rate became payable if the estate agents were not paid at the 'discounted rate' within ten days of the sale. The question arose as to the application of the 1999 Regulations to the term requiring 3 per cent commission. The estate agents argued it was covered by the core exemption and not subject to the fairness test. Gross J concluded that it was not covered by the core exemption. He thought it 'plain that both parties contemplated an agreed operative price of 1.5 per cent with a default provision of 3 per cent' (the market for estate agents was such that the estate agents recognized that they were unlikely to obtain business at 3 per cent and the negotiations had focused on 1.5 per cent).

11.26 More broadly, the Supreme Court's approach was seen as taking insufficient account of the aim of the Directive as a consumer protection measure, and as having a detrimental impact upon the consumer.[31] An OFT Market Study which was 'not primarily about which terms contravene specific legislation, but about which terms harm consumers' (and was not guidance on the interpretation of the legislation)[32] took the line in relation to the 'price' exemption that:[33]

> the exclusion from assessment ... in our view, should only apply to terms concerning the main value-for-money proposition as it is fact understood by both parties including the consumer. Consequently we believe that many terms imposing charges should be assessable, including any such charges shown to be outside of ordinary consumers' considerations whether because they are payable on a remote contingency or for other reasons.

11.27 There was considerable concern that the line taken by the Supreme Court would mean that the Regulations would not provide protection for consumers from many unfair terms. In relation to the first part of the core exemption, the question is whether the courts will step back, to a meaningful extent, from the approach indicated in *Abbey National* in the light of what was said by the CJEU in *Kasler*, or simply modify their language somewhat to better echo that of the CJEU, with its references to terms which 'characterize' the contract. It should, however, be remembered that the core exemption is now recognized as limited by the 'grey list' of terms which may be unfair.

11.28 In relation to the second part of the core exemption, there was recognition in the Supreme Court, in *Abbey*, of its limited nature, that is, that it is only the question of the adequacy, or appropriateness, of the price, in relation to the goods or services provided, which is ousted from consideration under the fairness test. Lord Phillips stated, for example (at [80]), that:

> It may be open to question whether it is fair to subsidise some customers by levies on others who experience contingencies that they did not foresee when entering into their contracts.

In that case, there was a 'significant amount of cross subsidy' from the 12 million customers who regularly incurred unauthorized overdraft charges to the 42 million who did not,[34] but the court only had to decide whether the charges fell within the core exemption, as part of the price or remuneration, so that the adequacy question could not be asked under the fairness test. However, that it is only the adequacy/appropriateness of the price, as against the goods or services provided, which is ousted by the second part of the core exemption is also emphasized by

31 M. Chen-Wishart, 'Transparency and Fairness in Bank Charges' (2010) 126 LQR 157; P. Davies, 'Bank Charges and the Supreme Court' (2010) 69 CLJ 2; P. Morgan, 'Bank Charges and the Unfair Terms in Consumer Contracts Regulations 1999: The End of the Road for Consumers?' [2010] LMCLQ 21; S. Whittaker, 'Unfair Terms, Unfair Prices and Bank Charges' (2011) 74 MLR 106. But see A. Arora, 'Unfair Contract Terms and Unauthorised Bank Charges: A Banking Lawyer's Perspective' [2012] JBL 44.

32 OFT, *Consumer Contracts Market Study* (February 2011) p. 6.

33 OFT, *Consumer Contracts Market Study* (February 2011) para. 6.13.

34 *Abbey National*, at [1].

the pragmatic reason which the CJEU saw in *Kasler* for that element of the exemption that 'no legal scale or criterion exists that can provide a framework for, and guide, such a review'.[35] A contrast can be made with Brandner and Ulmer's rationale of the fundamentals of a 'free market economy', and it can again be emphasized that the 'grey list' prevails over the core exemption.

Unfair terms

11.29 Whereas the Unfair Contract Terms Act 1977 uses a test of 'reasonableness', the unfair terms regime has one of 'fairness' and, under art. 3 of the Directive, a term is unfair 'if, contrary to the requirement of good faith, it causes a significant imbalance in the parties' rights and obligations arising under the contract, to the detriment of the consumer'. This has basically been mirrored in the various incarnations of the implementing legislation in the UK, with s 62(4), CRA now stating:

> A term is unfair if, contrary to the requirement of good faith, it causes a significant imbalance in the parties' rights and obligations under the contract to the detriment of the consumer.

There are basically two elements here:

1. significant imbalance in the parties' rights and obligations to the detriment of the consumer;
2. the requirement of good faith.

(The test in relation to notices is basically the same, only worded appropriately for notices—s 62(6) CRA.) The reference to 'to the detriment of the consumer' merely 'serves to make clear that the Directive is aimed at significant imbalance against the consumer'.[36]

11.30 However, before those elements are considered further, two preliminary points should be made. First, there is a list in Sch 2 of terms which 'may be unfair' (the 'grey list'; see para. **11.53**ff). It may provide very useful guidance as to which terms will be regarded as unfair, and was certainly so treated by the OFT (see the OFT Bulletins and Guidance, and now that of the CMA on Unfair Terms in Consumer Contracts where most of the terms regarded as unfair are classified by reference to the grey list). The list is derived from the Directive and, with some amendment and addition, it also appears in the Consumer Rights Act. It must, of course, be remembered that it is the basic fairness test which prevails. The list is a *grey* list, not a *black* list, so a term falling within it may be fair.

11.31 However, it is worth briefly re-emphasizing that the grey list is also significant in relation to the core exemption. If a term falls within the list, it is subject to the fairness test even though it would otherwise be covered by that exemption (s 64(6) CRA).

35 *Arpad Kasler* v *OTP Jelzabalogbank Zrt* Case C-26/13 (30th April, 2014), [2014] 2 All ER (Comm) 443, at [55]; *Matei* v *SC Volksbank Romania SA* Case C-143/13 (26th Feb, 2015) [2015] 1 WLR 2385 at [55].

36 *Director General of Fair Trading* v *First National Bank* (2001) per Lord Steyn at [36].

11.32 The second preliminary point to be made here on fairness is concerned with the factors identified as relevant to the test and, particularly, the identification of the 'time frame' of the assessment as that of the making of the contract. Section 62(5) states:

> Whether a term is fair is determined—
> (a) taking into account the nature of the subject matter of the contract, and
> (b) by reference to all the circumstances existing when the term was agreed and to all the other terms of the contract or of any other contract on which it depends.

The reference to the 'time frame' of the agreement is similar to the provision dealing with the requirement of reasonableness in the Unfair Contract Terms Act 1977 (s 11(1)), and a term may be unfair because of its potential coverage even though its operation would not be unfair in the particular case, just as under UCTA 1977 an exemption clause may operate reasonably in relation to the breach which has occurred, but fail to satisfy the requirement of reasonableness because of its potential coverage (*Stewart Gill Ltd* v *Horatio Myer & Co. Ltd* (1992)).

11.33 Obviously, when fairness is considered at the preventive, general level and there is no particular contract to refer to, the legislation 'must be made to work sensibly and effectively and this can be done taking into account the effect of contemplated or typical relationships between contracting parties' (*First National Bank* (2001) per Lord Steyn at [33]).

Significant imbalance

11.34 In *Aziz*,[37] the CJEU stated that in relation to significant imbalance it must 'in particular' be considered 'what rules of national law would apply in the absence of an agreement by the parties in that regard' (at [68]). The view was taken that (at [68]):

> Such a comparative analysis will enable the national court to evaluate whether and, as the case may be, to what extent, the contract places the consumer in a legal situation less favourable than that provided for by the national law in force.

This is looking for a significant imbalance in the rights and obligations of the parties, by considering the position of the consumer relative to what it would have been under the default position, had the term not been present.

11.35 Unfortunately, there will not always be a relevant default rule, and there is more likely to be one in a civil law system with a code, as is commonly the situation in other European countries. Further, when there is a default rule, it will not always represent a balance such that a departure from it, or a particular departure, shows a significant imbalance

37 *Aziz* v *Ciaxa d'Estalvis de Catalunya, Tarragona I Manresa* (C-226/12) March 2013 [2013] All ER (EC) 770.

between the parties.[38] In *First National Bank* there would have been no scope for the continuance of the interest charge, in the absence of the term which was being looked at (see para. **11.19**). Lord Bingham, having considered the development of the statutory background, concluded that he did not think that 'the term could be stigmatised as unfair on the ground that it violates or undermines a statutory regime enacted for the protection of consumers' (at [22]). Lord Steyn did not think that the argument could prevail 'in circumstances where the legislature has neither expressly nor by necessary implication barred a stipulation that interest may continue to accrue after judgment' (at [38]). This should be regarded as too broad a statement if taken generally, and Lord Millett, in considering fairness as a whole, said: 'It is obviously useful to assess the impact of an impugned term on the parties' rights and obligations by comparing the effect of the contract with the term and the effect it would have without it' (at [54]). In any event, the CJEU was not saying that looking at this was always determinative, just identifying it as something which should 'in particular' be considered, and in a common law system, such as English law, the idea may be less useful than in a codified, civil law system.

11.36 However, the basic idea of the CJEU in *Aziz* is comparison (or balancing) not simply by weighing the various elements of the contract against each other, but rather against a standard. Of course, where there is no relevant default term, there is no standard of the type envisaged by the CJEU. It has been proposed that 'reasonable expectations' be called into service[39] to provide a standard, as they do under s 3(2)(b)(i) of UCTA, but that is not a provision which the courts have found easy to use (see para. **10.36**), and frequent reference to it seems unlikely.

11.37 We should consider a different type of approach. In *First National Bank,* Lord Bingham said of significant imbalance:

> The requirement of significant imbalance is met if a term is so weighted in favour of the supplier as to tilt the parties' rights and obligations under the contract significantly in his favour. This may be by the granting to the supplier of a beneficial option or discretion or power, or by imposing on the consumer of a disadvantageous burden or risk or duty ... This involves looking at the contract as a whole.

This suggests some overall weighing of the rights and duties of the consumer against those of the trader as a whole, but it must not be forgotten that, subject to the requirements of 'transparency' and 'prominence', the assessment of the 'appropriateness of the price payable under the contract by comparison with the goods, digital content or services supplied under it' is excluded from the application of the fairness test by the core exemption (s 64(1)).

38 See the discussion of not every section of the BGB in German law embodying a value judgement which is the product of a balancing of the interests of the parties in a 'just and reasonable way'. P. Hellwege and L. Miller, 'Control of Standard Contract Terms' in G Dannemann and S Vogenauer eds, *The Common European Sales Law in Context: Interactions with Engish and German Law*, Oxford University Press, 2013, p. 442.

39 C. Willett, *Fairness in Consumer Contracts: The Case of Unfair Terms*, Ashgate Publishing, 2007, p. 49.

11.38 However, we should remember the reason put forward by the CJEU for that element of the core exemption. In *Kasler*, the CJEU saw that element of the exemption as reflecting the pragmatic difficulty that 'no legal scale or criterion exists that can provide a framework for, and guide, such a review'.[40] In *First National Bank* the House of Lords was effectively saying that the circumstances in which the interest was to be paid after default were not so different from those before default as to make any change in the balance between the rights and obligations of the parties. Of course, that is only a limited answer. A term prolonging a significant imbalance against the consumer is significantly imbalanced against the consumer. Albeit that the term in *First National Bank* could be seen as outside the core exemption, at least because it was dealing with payment after breach, nevertheless it can be seen as suggesting that the English courts do not see a relative weighing as infringing the core exemption—even though asking the next question, of whether there was significant imbalance in the initial interest rate, would have done so. This is not the brightest of lines, but such a relative weighing is much less impractical than weighing of rights and obligations at large. Further, the idea of a relative weighing as not infringing the core exemption can also be seen as suggested by the view of the CJEU that the 'exclusion does not apply to a term concerning a mechanism for amending the prices of the services provided to the consumer'.[41]

11.39 Another example of a relative weighing is provided by *Office of Fair Trading* v *Foxtons* (2009).[42] The case was concerned with a contract between property owners and letting agents. The contract provided for an 11 per cent commission for the agents when the property was initially let to a tenant and also for an 11 per cent commission on each renewal of it. The question arose as to the fairness of the renewal commission. The court decided that there was a significant imbalance and an unfair term. When the property was first let to a tenant the letting agents would have to undertake work in, for example, marketing the property. Such work did not have to be undertaken on a renewal. The judge took the line (at [90]):

> The commission amounts in question are significant, and operate adversely to the client the more time goes on. Commensurate services are not provided as time goes on.

Again, as in the *First National Bank* case, the term in question related to payment upon the happening of a specified event (which was, of course, in a post-breach situation in *First National Bank*). In both cases, the overall balance in the contractual rights could be considered relative to those at the commencement of the contract. The relative relevant benefits/burdens were largely unchanged in *First National Bank*, and had tipped considerably against the consumer in *Foxtons*, so whilst the initial benefits/burdens and the relative weighing in *First National Bank* clearly raised an unanswered question, the situation was less problematic in *Foxtons*. Unless, the initial payment was unbalanced against the estate agent (for example, as a 'loss leader' to get the landlord's initial business), it was clear that the renewal term was unbalanced against the consumer.

40 *Kasler* (2014) at [55]; *Matei* (2015) at [55].

41 *Kasler* at [56], referring to *Nemzeti Fogyasztovedelmi Hatosag* v *Invitel Tavkozlesi Zrt* (2012). Of course, such terms may be outside of the core exemption on the basis of a failure to meet the standard of 'plain intelligible language'.

42 However, as was pointed out in the Supreme Court in *Abbey National* (Lord Walker at [30]), the clause could, in any event, be seen as outside the core exemption because of a lack of plain intelligible language.

11.40 A broader, relative weighing across contracts is also suggested by the situation in *Office of Fair Trading* v *Abbey National* and the comment of Lord Phillips that (at [80]):

> It may be open to question whether it is fair to subsidise some customers by levies on others who experience contingencies that they did not foresee when entering into their contracts.

The fact that some consumers were paying an unduly high price for particular services allowed for the cross-subsidization of some customers by others. Of course, in that case, the banks acknowledged that there was a 'significant amount of cross subsidy' from the 12 million customers who regularly incurred unauthorized overdraft charges to the 42 million who did not (at [1]). However, again the point can be made that a relative weighing is much more impractical than looking at large at the adequacy or appropriateness of the price, as against the services supplied.

Good faith

11.41 Again, the judgment of the CJEU in *Aziz* is very significant here. The Court stated:[43]

> the national court must assess for those purposes whether the seller or supplier, dealing fairly and equitably with the consumer, could reasonably assume that the consumer would have agreed to such a term in individual contract negotiations.

The idea of what the consumer could reasonably have been thought to agree to, in this hypothetical situation, must be given much further consideration.

11.42 However, first we should also look at the line taken in relation to good faith by the House of Lords in *First National Bank*. Lord Bingham said (at [17]):

> The requirement of good faith in this context is one of fair and open dealing. Openness requires that the terms should be expressed fully, clearly and legibly, containing no concealed pitfalls or traps. Appropriate prominence should be given to terms which might operate disadvantageously to the customer. Fair dealing requires that a supplier should not, whether deliberately or unconsciously, take advantage of the consumer's necessity, indigence, lack of experience, unfamiliarity with the subject matter of the contract, weak bargaining position or any other factor listed in or analogous to those listed in Schedule 2 of the regulations.[44]

43 *Aziz* (2013) at [69].

44 Sched 2 of the 1994 Regulations had contained a list of factors that the court should consider in relation to good faith: the strength of the bargaining position of the parties; whether the consumer had an inducement to agree to the term; whether the goods or services were sold or supplied to the special order of the consumer; and the extent to which the seller or supplier has dealt fairly and equitably with the consumer. This was derived from recital 16 of the Directive, although without reproducing, arguably, the most important element ('whereas the requirement of good faith may be satisfied by the seller or supplier where he deals fairly and equitably with the other party whose legitimate interests he has to take into account'). However, the factors which referred to in sched 2 of the 1994 Regulations can be seen to reflect those in sched 2 of UCTA, relating to the requirement of reasonableness (see para. **10.54**).

Similarly, Lord Steyn saw good faith as importing 'the notion of open and fair dealing' (at [36]). Obviously, this relies on the setting of standards and, more broadly, Lord Bingham also recognized that good faith 'looks to good standards of commercial morality and practice' (at [17]); again, similarly, Lord Steyn saw the 'purpose of the provision of good faith and fair dealing' as being 'to enforce community standards of fairness and reasonableness'. On this view then, good faith broadly embodies certain 'standards' of dealing in relation to the two aspects of good faith—open dealing and fair dealing—which in turn seem to contain the ideas of (broadly) the sufficiency of notice of terms (including the clarity of their drafting) and advantage not being taken of a superior position by the seller or supplier. These two facets of good faith must be looked at further, particularly in relation to the line taken by the CJEU in *Aziz*.

11.43 First, we should consider the emphasis placed on 'open dealing' by the House of Lords in *First National Bank*. This is unsurprising in a system which places considerable emphasis on freedom of contract, as English law does, but, at first sight, it does not seem to appear in the approach taken by the CJEU in *Aziz*. However, the CJEU's reference to the hypothetical agreement of the consumer being in 'individual contract negotiations' should be emphasized here. In an idealized individual contract, the parties know exactly what they are each agreeing to, and there is, for example, no problem of 'small print' which is artificially incorporated, and of which the consumer does not know the contents. In addition, we have the reference, in the CJEU's hypothetical, to the trader who is dealing 'fairly and equitably' with the consumer. Scope can readily be found for the CJEU's approach to good faith to encompass the 'open dealing' seen as so important by the English courts.

11.44 Further, we should remember that it was emphasized in *Kasler* (at [39]) that the CJEU has

> consistently held that the system of protection introduced by Directive 93/13 is based on the idea that the consumer is in a position of weakness vis-à-vis the seller or supplier, as regards both his bargaining power and his level of knowledge, a situation that leads to his agreeing to terms drawn up in advance by the seller or supplier without being able to influence the content of those terms.

English law has dropped the restriction of the unfair terms regime to non-individually negotiated terms, but the underlying idea of the Directive still retains its importance, and 'open dealing' is a direct means of providing some diminution of the common relative knowledge imbalance, or 'weakness', of the consumer.

11.45 However, much as the English courts might like to place great emphasis on 'open dealing', that cannot be sufficient in itself when the unfair terms regime is also based on the idea of the relative weakness of bargaining power of consumers. A consumer could know very well that they are making a bad deal, but have no effective choice when their lack of bargaining power puts them in a 'take it or leave it' situation. Freedom of contract, and the market, are not operating to control the fairness of terms in such a situation. This means that good faith must look for more than 'open dealing', as was recognized in the reference to 'fair dealing' as well as in *First National Bank*.

11.46 Lord Bingham referred to fair dealing in terms of the idea of there not being any 'advantage taking' of the consumer. However, that does not provide a sufficiently high standard. The final part of recital 16 of the Directive, to which the CJEU referred in *Aziz* (at [69]) in arriving at their approach to good faith, states:

> whereas the requirement of good faith may be satisfied by the seller or supplier where he deals fairly and equitably with the other party whose legitimate interests he has to take into account.

Good faith may be seen as a matter of more than not taking advantage of the consumer's relative weakness, but rather of taking sufficient account of the legitimate interests of the consumer. In relation to the hypothetical question, which the CJEU set out as being the means to determine the presence or absence of good faith, this would seem to be relevant to it being the view of a reasonable trader 'dealing fairly and equitably' that is considered.

11.47 Good faith can be seen to be both a matter of there being sufficient 'openness' in relation to the terms, and of the terms being such that the reasonable trader, who has taken sufficient account of the legitimate interest of the consumer, would think that the consumer would agree to them. Again, we can see similarities with the factors referred to by Lord Millett in *First National Bank*. He identified as relevant in determining the fairness of a term (at [54]):

> whether if it were drawn to his attention the consumer would be likely to be surprised by it; whether the term is a standard term, not merely in similar non-negotiable consumer contracts, but in commercial contracts freely negotiated between parties acting on level terms and at arms' length; and whether, in such cases, the party adversely affected by the inclusion of the term or his lawyer might reasonably be expected to object to its inclusion and press for its deletion.

Fairness

11.48 Before leaving discussion of the fairness test, we should look at the decision of the Supreme Court in *ParkingEye Ltd v Beavis* (2015), and fairness as a whole. In that case, there was a car park which was attached to shopping units, with the entire site being owned by the same company. Two hours' free parking was provided. This was attractive to shoppers and, therefore, also to those who leased the shopping units. However, if a motorist overstayed they incurred a charge of £85 (reducible to £50 if paid within 14 days) for that breach of contract. The Supreme Court was asked to consider whether the clause was a penalty clause (see para. **20.70**), but also, more to the point here, whether the term was unfair under the Unfair Terms in Consumer Contracts Regulations 1999. The majority, with Lord Toulson dissenting, thought it was not unfair.

11.49 In comparison with the situation at common law, any damages in such a situation would have been minimal. That was not very helpful. The court made references to other external standards. They looked at Regulations[45] which set guidelines for similar charges levied by local authorities outside London, placing them at £50, reduced to £25 if paid within 14 days. They also referred to the Code of Practice of the accredited trade association, the British Parking Association (BPA), which stated that a car park operator 'must be able to justify the amount in advance' if their charge for such breaches was more than £100. The analogies were limited, but were generally seen as not indicating that the terms were unfair.

11.50 However, they were also seen as indicating that the term was not unfair in that the charge needed to be sufficient to generate the regular turnover of cars in the car park, which was a benefit to consumers (as well as shopkeepers and, therefore, also the owners of the car park). Lord Neuberger JSC and Lord Sumption JSC, delivering a joint judgment, stated: 'There is no reason to regard the amount of the charge as any higher than was [necessary] for that objective' (at [107]; see also Lord Mance JSC at [208]). Moreover, the court regarded the term as one which the reasonable consumer would have agreed to. They pointed out that the signs were very clear, and consumers generally could be seen as having accepted it. The court recognized that in relation to standard form contracts generally, that did not mean a great deal because of the take-it-or-leave-it factor, but thought that in this case there was every reason for consumers to accept it. They got two hours free parking, and the size of the overstaying charge was there to generate the desirable turnover of cars.

11.51 However, as has been indicated, Lord Toulson JSC dissented. It can be suggested that he may have gone beyond an appropriate perspective in looking at the level of the charge in relation to the 'basic state pension [of] £115 per week', and finding this comparison 'telling' (at [310]). Finding significant imbalance in such a way does raise the question of the proper remit for the court in relation to unfair terms. Ultimately, it would be looking at what goods or services the consumer should be able to afford.

11.52 However, it can also be suggested that the majority were too ready to accept that the level of charge for overstaying was fair. They did not question that it was necessary to generate sufficient turnover of cars, but they were told by ParkingEye that more than 99.5 per cent of those using the car park 'observed the rules' (at [113]), not becoming liable to pay the charge for breaching them. This suggests that sufficient compliance to achieve a sufficiently high turnover might have been achieved by a somewhat lower charge. Should that be the case, the relevant term was at least imbalanced, even when judged against ParkingEye's own justification for its size. It also suggests that the trader, dealing fairly and equitably, should not have been too readily seen as able to reasonably view the consumer as accepting. Certainly, that would be highly problematic if consumers knew that such a high charge was not necessary to achieve the desirable turnover— and should a trader acting fairly and equitably view it from that perspective? It would seem to be more in keeping with recognizing the legitimate interests of the consumer, and it can be suggested that the majority were here rather too focused on the legitimate interest

45 Civil Enforcement of Parking Contraventions (Guidelines on Levels of Charges) (England) Order 2007 (SI 2007/3487).

of the trader, which they had, rightly, concentrated on when looking at the question of whether the term was a penalty clause at common law.

The list and types of unfair terms

11.53 As has already been mentioned, the unfair terms regime contains a grey list of terms which 'may be unfair'. In the CRA this is in Sch 2. It largely reflects that in the Directive, although the language has been made clearer at points, and there are some additions to it which deal, broadly speaking, with terms providing for variations in the contract by the trader. The list in Sch 2 is set out at para. **11.55**, but a few preliminary points should first be made.

11.54 The first point to be emphasized is that in the CRA, the list is explicitly given a second level of importance. If a term falls within the listed terms, it cannot be ousted from the application of the fairness test by the core exemption. Of course, in relation to the fairness test the list does not even reverse the burden of proof, but it does, nevertheless, provide very helpful guidance on unfairness. Although it must always be remembered that, ultimately, it is the fairness test itself which prevails (*ParkingEye* at [105]), the other side of that is that the list is not exhaustive. Absence from it does not mean that a term is fair. There are, indeed, some difficulties in relation to its boundaries. First, the terms referred to in it are stated by reference to their 'object or effect', so that its content is not based simply on form. This has the benefit of helping to prevent it being avoided just by the form of a clause being changed, but does not help the certainty of its coverage. Secondly, the list often contains factors of assessment. Paragraph 2 relating to exemption clauses, for example, refers to terms which have the object or effect of '*inappropriately* excluding or limiting the legal rights of the consumer' (emphasis added). Of course, the need to make such an assessment to ascertain if a term falls within the scope of para. 2 should strengthen the argument that a term is unfair, if it clearly does. However, the additional significance of the list, in relation to the core exemption, may make such uncertainties points of significant dispute.

11.55 The grey list itself should now be considered. Part 1 of the schedule states the basic list, with some limitation on it in Part 2. Part 1 states:

> 1 A term which has the object or effect of excluding or limiting the trader's liability in the event of the death of or personal injury to the consumer resulting from an act or omission of the trader.
>
> 2 A term which has the object or effect of inappropriately excluding or limiting the legal rights of the consumer in relation to the trader or another party in the event of total or partial non-performance or inadequate performance by the trader of any of the contractual obligations, including the option of offsetting a debt owed to the trader against any claim which the consumer may have against the trader.
>
> 3 A term which has the object or effect of making an agreement binding on the consumer in a case where the provision of services by the trader is subject to a condition whose realisation depends on the trader's will alone.

4 A term which has the object or effect of permitting the trader to retain sums paid by the consumer where the consumer decides not to conclude or perform the contract, without providing for the consumer to receive compensation of an equivalent amount from the trader where the trader is the party cancelling the contract.

5 A term which has the object or effect of requiring that, where the consumer decides not to conclude or perform the contract, the consumer must pay the trader a disproportionately high sum in compensation or for services which have not been supplied.

6 A term which has the object or effect of requiring a consumer who fails to fulfil his obligations under the contract to pay a disproportionately high sum in compensation.

7 A term which has the object or effect of authorising the trader to dissolve the contract on a discretionary basis where the same facility is not granted to the consumer, or permitting the trader to retain the sums paid for services not yet supplied by the trader where it is the trader who dissolves the contract.

8 A term which has the object or effect of enabling the trader to terminate a contract of indeterminate duration without reasonable notice except where there are serious grounds for doing so.

9 A term which has the object or effect of automatically extending a contract of fixed duration where the consumer does not indicate otherwise, when the deadline fixed for the consumer to express a desire not to extend the contract is unreasonably early.

10 A term which has the object or effect of irrevocably binding the consumer to terms with which the consumer has had no real opportunity of becoming acquainted before the conclusion of the contract.

11 A term which has the object or effect of enabling the trader to alter the terms of the contract unilaterally without a valid reason which is specified in the contract.

12 A term which has the object or effect of permitting the trader to determine the characteristics of the subject matter of the contract after the consumer has become bound by it.

13 A term which has the object or effect of enabling the trader to alter unilaterally without a valid reason any characteristics of the goods, digital content or services to be provided.

14 A term which has the object or effect of giving the trader the discretion to decide the price payable under the contract after the consumer has become bound by it, where no price or method of determining the price is agreed when the consumer becomes bound.

15 A term which has the object or effect of permitting a trader to increase the price of goods, digital content or services without giving the consumer the right to cancel the contract if the final price is too high in relation to the price agreed when the contract was concluded.

16 A term which has the object or effect of giving the trader the right to determine whether the goods, digital content or services supplied are in conformity with the contract, or giving the trader the exclusive right to interpret any term of the contract.

17 A term which has the object or effect of limiting the trader's obligation to respect commitments undertaken by the trader's agents or making the trader's commitments subject to compliance with a particular formality.

> **18** A term which has the object or effect of obliging the consumer to fulfil all of the consumer's obligations where the trader does not perform the trader's obligations.
>
> **19** A term which has the object or effect of allowing the trader to transfer the trader's rights and obligations under the contract, where this may reduce the guarantees for the consumer, without the consumer's agreement.
>
> **20** A term which has the object or effect of excluding or hindering the consumer's right to take legal action or exercise any other legal remedy, in particular by—
>
> (a) requiring the consumer to take disputes exclusively to arbitration not covered by legal provisions, (b) unduly restricting the evidence available to the consumer, or (c) imposing on the consumer a burden of proof which, according to the applicable law, should lie with another party to the contract.

11.56 Certain groupings of types of terms can be identified in the list. Paragraphs 1, 2, and 20 of the list, for example, clearly encompass exemption clauses. There are also paragraphs which will encompass clauses falling within the common law rules dealing with penalty clauses or which raise related issues (paras 5 and 6—(see **20.70**)). In addition, several of the paragraphs can be identified as relating to clauses conferring an inappropriate discretion on the seller or supplier in relation to performance (for example, paras 11, 12, and 13).[46]

11.57 Probably the most novel elements of the grey list are those dealing with clauses conferring a discretion on the seller or supplier as to the performance of the contract. Some discretion may be appropriate, but what is shown by the line taken by the OFT is that it should be set within limited boundaries to be considered fair. For example, a roadside breakdown service originally used a clause which stated (OFT Bulletin 3 (Britannia Rescue Services)):

> We may cancel membership at any time by sending seven days' notice by recorded delivery to your last known address and in such event you will receive a pro rata refund of your subscription, unless the service has been used.

The OFT viewed that as 'potentially unfair ... since it allowed [the business] to cancel contracts on a discretionary basis and thus to get out of a bad bargain' (Bulletin 3 at p. 26). The clause was redrafted to allow the business to cancel in limited circumstances, where the service might be seen as being used inappropriately:

> If excessive use of the service has occurred through failure to seek permanent repair following any temporary repair effected by an agent or due to lack of routine vehicle maintenance, we may cancel membership by sending seven days' notice by recorded delivery to your last known address.

46 For a full consideration of the paragraphs of the list, as it stood under the 1999 Regulations, see E. Macdonald, *Exemption Clauses and Unfair Terms*, 2nd edn, Tottel, 2006, pp. 249–81.

11.58 Another example is provided by the contract of a supplier and installer of kitchens. In that contract, a clause was seen as 'of questionable fairness' in the light of para. 1(k) (OFT Bulletin 1 (Moben Kitchens)). The original clause stated:

> If, for any reason, the Company is unable to supply a particular item of furniture or a particular appliance, the Company will notify the Customer. The Company will normally replace it with an item of equivalent or superior standard and value.

The clause was revised to state:

> If, for any reason beyond the Company's control, the Company is unable to supply a particular item of furniture or a particular appliance, the Company will notify the Customer. With the agreement of the Customer the Company will replace it with an item of superior standard and value.

The revised clause was seen as an 'improvement' as it specified that the substitution must be for reasons 'beyond the company's reasonable control' and required the consumer's consent to the change. The former restriction should be emphasized. The OFT has stated that 'a term which would allow the supplier to vary what is supplied at will—rather than because of bona fide external circumstances—is unlikely to be fair even if customers have a right of cancellation and refund'.[47]

11.59 Some indication of the correctness of the OFT's basic approach to clauses conferring a wide discretion on the seller or supplier was provided in *Peabody Trust Governors* v *Reeve* (2008). The clause was one giving a 'social landlord' 'almost carte blanche in the field of variations apart from the areas of rent and statutory protection' (at [56]). The judge took the line (at [54]–[55]):

> 54. Although the Court is in no sense bound by the guidance provided by the Office of Fair Trading (OFT 356 'Guidance on unfair terms in tenancy agreements') ... that guidance does give landlords helpful commonsense indications of what is likely to be considered to be fair and should be carefully taken into account when drafting a variation clause in a tenancy agreement.
>
> 55. For example, the OFT must be right in saying (at para 3.89) that a term is likely to be objectionable if it 'gives the landlord a broad discretion that could be used to impose new restrictions, penalties or burdens unexpectedly on the tenant.' By contrast, a term allowing for variations is less likely to be thought unfair if 'its effect is narrowed, so that it can be used to vary terms to reflect changes in the law, for example, rather than be used to change the balance of advantage under the contract?'. (at para 3.92)

With such an extreme clause as the one in this case, the landlord could not use their status as a 'social landlord', whom it was argued could 'be trusted only to impose reasonable and proper

47 OFT, *Unfair Contract Terms Guidance* (February 2001) para. 11.7.

variations' (at [56]), to convince the court that the term was fair (although it was viewed as a relevant factor). Nor did it help the landlord to argue that if tenants did not like new terms, they could terminate their lease and go elsewhere. The point was made that 'in the case of relatively low cost housing operated by a registered social landlord, this is unrealistic. The tenant will typically have a strong necessity, will be of relatively limited means, may well lack experience and familiarity with contractual terms and will have a very weak bargaining position' (at [45], and see [57]).

11.60 In the *Invitel* case[48] the European Court of Justice (ECJ) considered a clause dealing with the mechanism for amending the price and, in the light of the grey list, stressed the importance to the fairness test of the term setting out 'the reason for, and the method of the variation of the price', and of the consumer having the right to cancel. Further, it was seen as of 'fundamental importance' to the fairness test whether it was possible for the 'consumer to foresee, on the basis of clear intelligible criteria, the amendments ... to the fees connected to the service' (at [24]–[28]).

Transparency and visibility of terms

The Directive

11.61 Article 5 of the Directive states:

> In the case of contracts where all or certain terms offered to the consumer are in writing, these terms must always be drafted in plain intelligible language. Where there is doubt about the written meaning of a term, the interpretation most favourable to the consumer shall prevail. This rule on interpretation shall not apply in the context of the procedures laid down in Article 7(2).

There are two elements to this: a requirement that written terms be drafted in plain, intelligible language, and rule of interpretation for ambiguous terms. Of course, plain, intelligible language is important more generally in the Directive (and the CRA) in relation to the core exemption and the fairness test.

11.62 The first of these aspects of art. 5 is now reflected in s 68(1), which requires that a written term of a consumer contract, or a consumer notice, be 'transparent'. A lack of transparency can be dealt with by the CMA or other enforcers seeking injunctions, for example. This deals with the question as to whether this aspect of art. 5 was truly to be viewed as a requirement, as no remedy was provided for in the Directive if terms were not in plain, intelligible language. The CMA and other enforcers can require that a lack of transparency is dealt with.

11.63 Plainly, the second element of art. 5 is a rule of construction. (Although in focusing on interpreting a term to determine its meaning to decide if what it actually does is fair, it should

48 *Nemzeti Fogyasztovedelmi Hatosag* v *Invitel Tavkozlezl ZRT* C-472/10 (2012).

not be forgotten that its lack of clarity may itself be indicative of unfairness.) The reference to 'art 7' in art. 5 is to the general rather than individual level of enforcement, so that the rule of construction in art. 5, and in its implementing domestic provision (s 69), is concerned with construction in the context of a dispute between a particular consumer and seller or supplier. In that context, it may simply be viewed as a version of the familiar common law contra proferentem rule: that any ambiguity in a clause will be construed against the person putting it forward (see para. **9.69**).

11.64 In relation to interpretation at the more general level, in *EC Commission* v *Spain* C-70/03 (2004), the ECJ envisaged an 'objective' interpretation. That seems to mean that neither a favourable nor unfavourable interpretation to the consumer is taken. Rather, it seems simply to envisage the objectively most likely interpretation being used.

Summary

- Part 2 of the Consumer Rights Act 2015 is basically derived from the European Directive on unfair terms. The Directive required there to be a fairness test of non-individually negotiated terms in contracts between consumers and sellers or suppliers ('traders' in the CRA). The CRA also looks at individually negotiated terms (and notices). We focused on terms.
- The fairness of terms can be challenged under the CRA by the individual consumer or at the general level by the CMA or other regulator. (The CMA has replaced the OFT as the primary general enforcer.)
- There was an overlap between the Regulations, which formerly implemented the unfair terms regime, and UCTA 1977, but also significant differences. The CRA provides a single unfair terms regime for consumers, and removes the consumer aspects from UCTA.
- Provided they are transparent and prominent, the 'core exemption' prevents the application of the fairness test in relation to terms defining the main subject matter of the contract, and also in relation to the question of the adequacy/appropriateness of the price in relation to the goods, services, or digital content supplied. This does not, however, apply to terms which fall within the grey list. The scope of the core exemption has proved to be highly controversial.
- A term is unfair if, contrary to the requirement of good faith, it causes a significant imbalance in the rights and obligations of the parties to the detriment of the consumer. There is also a 'grey list' of terms which may be unfair (Sch 2).

Further reading

H. Beale, 'Unfair Contracts in Britain and Europe' [1989] 42 CLP 197

H. Beale, 'Legislative Control of Fairness: The Directive on Unfair Terms in Consumer Contracts' in J. Beatson and D. Friedmann(eds), *Good Faith and Fault in Contract Law*, Oxford University Press, 1995, pp. 231–62

H. Beale, 'Unfair Terms in Contracts: Proposals for Reform in the UK' (2004) 27 Journal of Consumer Policy 289

S. Bright, 'Winning the Battle against Unfair Contract Terms' (2000) 20 LS 331

M. Chen-Wishart, 'Transparency and Fairness in Bank Charges' (2010) 126 LQR 157

H. Collins, 'Good Faith in European Contract Law' (1994) 14 OJLS 229

Law Commission and Scottish Law Commission, *Unfair Terms in Contracts*, Law Com Consultation Paper No 166, Scot Law Com Discussion Paper No 119

Law Commission and Scottish Law Commission, *Unfair Terms in Contracts*, Law Com No 292, Scot Law Com No 199

Law Commission and Scottish Law Commission, *Unfair Terms in Consumer Contracts: A New Approach?* Issues Paper (July 2012)

Law Commission and Scottish Law Commission, *Unfair Terms in Consumer Contracts: Advice to the Department for Business, Innovation and Skills* (March 2013)

E. Macdonald, 'Unifying Unfair Terms Legislation' (2004) 67 MLR 69

E. Macdonald, 'The "Core Exemption" from the Fairness Test in Unfair Terms Legislation' (2012) 29 JCL 121

P. Morgan, 'Bank Charges and the Unfair Terms in Consumer Contracts Regulations 1999: The End of the Road for Consumers?' [2010] LMCLQ 21

S. Whittaker, 'Unfair Contract Terms, Public Services and the Construction of a European Conception of Contract' (2000) 116 LQR 95

S. Whittaker, 'Unfair Terms, Unfair Prices and Bank Charges' (2011) 74 MLR 106

Chapter 12

Mistake

Introduction

12.1 There is much dispute about the scope and content of a chapter on the subject of mistake in the law of contract.[1] For this reason the reader will perhaps find more variety in the treatment of this topic than in any other area of contract law. One, or both, of the parties to a contract may enter into it under some misunderstanding or mistake. For example, S agrees to sell his car to B for £2,000. Unknown to both parties, the car, whilst parked in the street, has been totally wrecked by a bus colliding with it, shortly before the contract was made. This is traditionally known as 'common mistake'; both parties are under the same misapprehension. Alternatively, S offers to sell his 'surfing equipment' to B, who accepts. S intends to sell his surfboard, but B thinks the offer relates to S's windsurfboard. In this instance, where the parties are at cross-purposes, it is described as a case of 'mutual mistake', that is, each party wrongly believes that the other has agreed to his terms.

12.2 In contrast to the above examples, in which both parties are mistaken, there is also the category of 'unilateral mistake'. This occurs when one party enters into a contract under some mistake, but the other party is aware of this. For example, A intends to contract with B, but later discovers that the other party to the apparent agreement is, in fact, C. In cases of unilateral mistake, there is normally some misrepresentation or fraud involved, and this leads us to an important point. The subject of mistake in contract law cannot be easily divided off from other related subjects. So where parties are at cross-purposes, or where one party enters into a contract having mistaken the identity of the other party, these types of mistake relate to the formation of contracts: that is, have the parties reached a binding agreement? In short, such instances may be described as 'agreement mistakes'.

1 E.g., see C. J. Slade, 'Myth of Mistake in the English Law of Contract' (1954) 70 LQR 385; and P. Atiyah, *Introduction to the Law of Contract*, 5th edn, Oxford University Press, 1995, ch. 12. See also D. Friedmann, 'The Objective Principle and Mistake and Involuntariness in Contract and Restitution' (2003) 119 LQR 68 at 92–3.

12.3 Where the parties are both mistaken about the same fact, such as a contract for the sale of goods which no longer exist, there is no dispute about agreement. These cases involve the issue of 'performability'. This subject raises fundamental questions about the extent of contractual obligations (see *Great Peace Shipping Ltd* v *Tsavliris Salvage (International) Ltd* (2003)). In other words, are contractual obligations absolute or can a party escape liability if he or she is unable to perform through no fault of his or her own? As some writers have observed, the subjects of performability and the extent of contractual obligations suggest a close connection between mistake in the law of contract and the doctrine of frustration (see **Chapter 19**, and also the comments of Lord Phillips in *Great Peace Shipping Ltd* at [73]–[75]). In the hypothetical instance given earlier, if the car, which was the subject of the agreement, was destroyed immediately after the contract was concluded (through no fault of either party), would the parties be discharged from the contract? (For an interesting case which shows the sometimes arbitrary distinction between mistake and frustration, see *Amalgamated Investment & Property Co Ltd* v *John Walker & Sons Ltd* (1976).)

12.4 Although there are, traditionally, various subdivisions of mistake in the law of contract, the subject can be more helpfully divided into two broad categories: mistake relating to agreement, and mistake relating to the performability of the contract. The subject of mistake cannot be entirely separated from a number of related issues in the law of contract, as we have seen, but it is consistent with decisions of the courts and with the opinion of the majority of writers on the subject, to devote a separate chapter to this area of law. This is not to imply, however, that the case law and the traditional approach to the subject are not open to criticism.

Narrow view of mistake in contract law

12.5 The word 'mistake' has a narrower meaning in contract law than it does in everyday language. Parties will not be easily discharged from their contractual undertakings simply because they entered into the contract under some mistake or misunderstanding, or made a bad bargain (see *Clarion Ltd* v *National Provident Institution* (2000)). In the interests of certainty and commercial convenience, parties are bound by their apparent agreements. It will be remembered that the law takes a predominantly objective view of agreement. It is not, in general, the subjective intention of the parties with which the law is concerned, but rather what can be inferred from their conduct.[2] This principle is well illustrated in *Centrovincial Estates plc* v *Merchant Investors Assurance Co. Ltd* (1983):

> C had let several floors of an office building to the Food, Drink, and Tobacco Training Board, who underlet one floor to D at a rent of £68,320 per year. Under a rent review clause, it was provided that the rent paid by D should be increased at a later date (25 December 1982) to the current market rental value. On 22 June 1982 (by which date the Board was thinking of a

2 For a detailed discussion of intention in the law of contract, see A. De Moor, 'Intention in the Law of Contract: Elusive or Illusory?' (1990) 106 LQR 632. Also see D. Friedmann, 'The Objective Principle and Mistake and Involuntariness in Contract and Restitution' (2003) 119 LQR 68.

surrender to C of the lease), a firm of solicitors wrote to D, on behalf of C and the Board, inviting D to agree to a figure of £65,000 per year as the correct rental value at the review date. D accepted this proposal the following day. On 28 June, a partner in the firm of solicitors telephoned D to say that the letter of 22 June contained an error and that C had intended to propose a rent of £126,000 per year. D refused to agree to this corrected proposal and claimed that there was a binding contract concluded by the two letters of 22 and 23 June. C claimed that the parties had failed to reach agreement on the current rental value and that the matter should be referred to an independent surveyor, as provided for in the rent review clause. In other words, it was denied by C that the exchange of letters had resulted in a binding agreement. C argued that there was no meeting of the minds due to the error.

The Court of Appeal rejected C's contention and explained, *obiter*, the correct approach to such a mistake, stating:

> It was contrary to the well established principles in contract law to suggest that the offeror under a bilateral contract could withdraw an unambiguous offer, after it had been accepted in the manner contemplated by the offer, merely because he had made a mistake which the offeree neither knew nor could reasonably have known at the time when he accepted it.

Thus the law tends to uphold apparent agreements, even if one or both of the parties would not have entered into the contract if the true facts had been realized. Mistake, at common law, operates within strict limits. Where it is applicable, it operates in an inflexible way so as to render the whole transaction void from the start (ab initio). For example, if A sells goods to B and the contract is rendered void due to the doctrine of mistake, and B sells the goods to C, a bona fide purchaser for value, the goods can be recovered by A. This may cause hardship to C and will appear unfair, so the doctrine of mistake at common law cannot be invoked lightly. (Whether a separate, more flexible, equitable jurisdiction exists will be considered later in this chapter.)

Agreement mistake

Mistake as to identity

12.6 A difficult problem arises where S intends to sell goods to Y, but later discovers that the other party to the apparent agreement is, in fact, X. This situation is usually described as one of unilateral mistake: only one party is mistaken, as a result of some fraudulent misrepresentation by the other. In a typical example of this sort of case, S will have parted with goods in return for a cheque which turns out to be worthless. A contract can be set aside for such a fraudulent misrepresentation, but X, the 'rogue' (to use the time-honoured description), will normally have resold the goods to someone else (B) before the contract can be avoided by S.

12.7 What is the legal effect of such a mistake? The difficulty lies in deciding which of either S or B owns the goods. As long as B is a bona fide purchaser for value, and not a party to the rogue's fraud, there are two innocent people claiming ownership. Both have been duped by the rogue, who has normally disappeared by the time the fraud is discovered. The legal action which usually follows is in the law of tort, that is, S sues B for conversion in an attempt to recover the property.

12.8 To succeed in such a claim, S must show that there was no contract between himself and the rogue; that any apparent agreement was negatived by the mistake as to identity induced by the fraud. If S can show there was no contract whatsoever with the rogue, then title to the goods does not pass to the rogue and therefore B does not acquire title (ownership) from the rogue. Under s 21(1) of the Sale of Goods Act 1979 it is stated that where goods are sold by a person who is not their owner, and who does not have the owner's consent or authority to do so, the person buying from him will not (generally) acquire title to the goods. Thus S will attempt to prove that the apparent agreement with the rogue was void as a result of a mistake as to identity. As a consequence, an innocent purchaser buying from the rogue will not become the owner of the property.

12.9 On the other hand, B will assert that there was a valid contract between S and the rogue, which was merely voidable for fraud. If this view is accepted, then the rogue has a voidable title to the goods, and if the contract has not been avoided (set aside) at the time when B purchases the goods from the rogue, B will acquire title to them (see Sale of Goods Act 1979, s 23). The law has the difficult choice between protecting the owner of property, and upholding commercial transactions in the interests of certainty. (For further discussion, see A. Foster, 'Sale By a Non-Owner: Striking a Fair Balance between the Rights of the True Owner and a Buyer in Good Faith' (2004) 9 Cov LJ 1.) It might be thought that some apportionment of the loss, between the two innocent parties, would provide the fairest solution to the problem—this suggestion is considered later. It must be emphasized that it is no comfort to either S or B to know that they have a remedy against the rogue, for he will normally have disappeared. If he is found, he probably has no money with which to compensate the injured parties.

12.10 The case law on this subject is far from satisfactory, with decisions based on fine (even tenuous) distinctions. Some of the leading authorities are considered in the sections which follow, together with a discussion of the important House of Lords decision in *Shogun Finance Ltd v Hudson* (2003).

Identity or attributes?

12.11 Despite the fact that S has been tricked by the rogue into parting with the property, it can be recovered from a bona fide purchaser for value (B) only if S can show that he did not intend to deal with the rogue. The rogue must also be aware of S's mistake. But it may be difficult to say whether S's mistake is truly one as to the 'identity' of the person he is dealing with, or simply as to that person's 'attributes' (such as his creditworthiness). This fine distinction, and its practical importance, is well illustrated in the cases which follow. In the famous case of *Cundy v Lindsay* (1878) 3 App Cas 459:

> Lindsay & Co. (C) were linen manufacturers, who received an order for a large quantity of handkerchiefs from a rogue named Alfred Blenkarn. Blenkarn had business premises in the

same street as a reputable company, Blenkiron & Co., and he signed his letters to C in such a way that the name of his firm looked like 'Blenkiron' rather than 'Blenkarn'. C knew Blenkiron & Co. to be a reputable business, and sent the handkerchiefs to the rogue thinking that they were dealing with Blenkiron & Co. (the invoices were headed 'Messrs. Blenkiron and Co., London'). Before Blenkarn's fraud was discovered—he was later convicted of obtaining goods by deception—he sold 250 dozen handkerchiefs to Cundy (D), an innocent purchaser. C sued D for the return of the goods.

In order to succeed, Lindsay & Co. had to show that there was no contract between themselves and the rogue, Blenkarn. (For an interesting analysis of the case and its historical background, see C. MacMillan, 'Rogues, Swindlers and Cheats: The Development of Mistake of Identity in English Contract Law' (2005) 64 CLJ 711.) For if no contract existed, Blenkarn did not have title to the goods, and therefore none could be acquired by Cundy. In contrast, if there was a valid contract between C and the rogue, which was merely voidable for fraud, then title would pass to D as a bona fide purchaser for value. It was decided by the House of Lords that there was no contract between Lindsay and the rogue, as they intended to deal not with him, but with the respectable firm of Blenkiron & Co. The identity of the person they were dealing with was crucial to the claimants and there was clearly an important mistake in this respect. This mistake was known to the rogue. Lord Cairns stated (at 465):

> Of [Blenkarn] they knew nothing, and of him they never thought. With him they never intended to deal. Their minds never, even for an instant of time rested upon him, and as between him and them there was no consensus of mind which could lead to any agreement or any contract whatever. As between him and them there was merely the one side to a contract, where, in order to produce a contract, two sides would be required.

12.12 It must be remembered that the decision in *Cundy* v *Lindsay* (1878) protects the original owner of the property but places the loss (and considerable hardship) on the innocent purchaser for value. The mistake must be one of identity, where the identity of the other is regarded by the mistaken party as crucial at the time the contract is made. An interesting contrast is provided by *King's Norton Metal Co.* v *Edridge, Merrett & Co.* (1897):

King's Norton Metal (C), who were metal manufacturers, received a letter from 'Hallam & Co.' in Sheffield, ordering brass rivet wire. The letterhead on the order gave the appearance of a large and thriving company, depicting a large factory and listing a number of overseas depots. The goods were despatched to 'Hallam & Co.' but were never paid for. In fact, the impressive looking 'Hallam & Co.' was the fictitious creation of a rogue named Wallis. Before the fraud was discovered, Wallis had sold the goods to Edridge & Co. (D), who bought the metal in good faith. C sued D to recover damages for the conversion of these goods. In order to succeed, it had to be established that there was no contract between C and Wallis.

The Court of Appeal held that the contract was not void on the ground of mistake, but was merely voidable for fraud. Accordingly, title (albeit voidable) passed to Wallis, and D acquired a good title from him. C had intended to contract with the writer of the letter. Wallis and Hallam & Co. were, in fact, the same 'person' and therefore King's Norton Metal were not mistaken as to the identity of the person with whom they entered into a contract. They were mistaken only as to the creditworthiness or attributes of the person with whom they were dealing.

12.13 This distinction between a person's identity and his attributes is clearly a fine one. Some critics claim that the distinction is spurious. Lord Denning described it as 'a distinction without a difference' in *Lewis* v *Averay* (1972). More recently, in his dissenting opinion in *Shogun Finance Ltd* v *Hudson* (2003) at [5], Lord Nicholls stated that 'the distinction in outcome thus drawn between these two kinds of fraudulent misrepresentation, one as to "attributes" and the other as to "identity", is unconvincing. It has been described as a reproach to the law.' A person's name, as well as being the most important guide as to his identity, may also be one of his attributes. If a party to a contract gives a false name, and the other party regards the identity of the person he is dealing with as crucial, is this a mistake as to identity or as to attributes?

12.14 It is possible to distinguish the cases of *Cundy* v *Lindsay* (1878) and *King's Norton Metal* v *Edridge* (1897). In the former, there was a reputable company called Blenkiron & Co., of whom the claimant company had heard and with whom they clearly thought they were dealing. In the latter case, there was no 'Hallam & Co.', it being merely the fictitious creation of the rogue, Wallis. Had there actually been a company called Hallam & Co., and had this company been known by reputation to the claimants, then presumably the case would have been decided differently. But it is questionable whether the rights of an innocent purchaser for value, buying from the rogue, should depend on this rather tenuous distinction. It may well be difficult to say whether a particular mistake is one of identity or of attributes, and yet an innocent third party's rights turn on this assessment. In the other dissenting judgment in *Shogun Finance Ltd* v *Hudson* (2003) at [60], Lord Millett argued that the preferable solution should be to protect innocent third parties 'by treating the contract as voidable rather than void whether for fraud or for mistake'.

12.15 It might have been thought that there should be very few cases today where a person could successfully claim that his apparent contract with another is void due to a mistake as to the other's identity. (This is discussed further later in relation to *Shogun Finance Ltd* v *Hudson*.) In policy terms, it is a question as to which of the two innocent parties should bear the loss. It seems wholly wrong that the bona fide purchaser for value should suffer. (See C. Elliott, 'No Justice for Innocent Purchasers of Dishonestly Obtained Goods: *Shogun Finance* v *Hudson*' (2004) JBL 381 at 386.) The original owner of the goods can always take more care before parting with goods on credit, but there is little that an innocent purchaser from the rogue can do. (Although see Lord Walker's speech in *Shogun Finance Ltd* v *Hudson* (2003) at [182], where he disagrees with this assertion, arguing that 'it would not be right to make any general assumption as to one innocent party being more deserving than the other'.) Also, it serves the interest of commercial certainty if contracts are upheld despite the mistake made by the original owner in parting with the goods to the rogue. It seems correct that there should be a heavy burden to be discharged by the owner to show that he took reasonable steps to check the identity of the person he was dealing with. He must also regard that person's identity as crucial, a requirement which was discussed in *Citibank NA* v *Brown Shipley & Co. Ltd* [1991] 2 All ER 690. The facts were:

> By telephone, a rogue tricked a bank (the 'issuing bank') into preparing a banker's draft drawn on a client company's account, of which the rogue claimed (fraudulently) to be a signatory. The banker's draft was made in favour of another bank (the 'receiving bank') which, labouring under the same deception, had innocently agreed to supply large amounts of foreign currency to the rogue. The issuing bank handed the draft to the rogue, mistakenly believing him to be a messenger for the bona fide company. In return he gave the bank a forged letter which purported to confirm the company's earlier telephone instructions. The rogue then presented the draft to the receiving bank, which, after checking with the issuing bank that the draft was authentic, paid the money directly to the rogue. The receiving bank was then paid by the issuing bank on presentation of the draft. On discovering the fraud, the issuing bank sought to recover the value of the draft as damages in conversion by claiming that title in the draft had never passed to the receiving bank. In other words, it claimed that the rogue had never acquired good title to the draft and, therefore, neither had the receiving bank.

The issuing bank's claim was dismissed by Waller J, who held that the receiving bank did not convert the draft by presenting it for payment. He stated that the delivery of the authorized banker's draft from one bank to the other established a contract between the two banks. The fact that this delivery was brought about by the rogue did not affect the formation of a contract. (The rogue was merely a 'conduit pipe' through whom title did not need to pass.) Thus, the rogue's identity was not to be regarded as of fundamental importance in this situation. The judge stated (at 699–700):

> So far as authority is concerned, it will usually be very difficult for A to establish that it was of crucial importance to him who actually physically transported the draft to B. In this case, for example, delivery might have been done by post; it might have been done by one or other of the banks' messengers; it might have been done by some other messenger. It so happened that in this case that [sic] it was done by someone thought to be the customer or his messenger, but that was not of crucial importance. That being so, the authority, as it seems to me, albeit induced by fraud, would not be void; the authority would be actual, even if voidable.

Waller J went on to state (at 700) that in this area of law 'each case rests on its own facts'. It is likely that the judge, in finding against the issuing bank, thought that it (rather than the receiving bank) was in a better position to protect itself against the risk of dealing with a rogue.

Parties dealing face to face

12.16 Issues of mistake and fraud have also arisen in a series of cases in which the parties were dealing face to face with each other. When parties are not physically in each other's presence, for example where someone receives a letter ordering goods, it is possible to imagine, as a result of some deception, how they could be mistaken as to the identity of the person placing the order (although it must be acknowledged that the seller has more time in such circumstances to check the identity of this person). But when the contract is made *inter praesentes* it might seem more difficult for the seller to claim that he did not intend to contract with the person who was physically present (for example, in a shop), but with some other person who was not present. In *Phillips* v *Brooks Ltd* [1919] 2 KB 243:

> A man named North called in person at C's shop and asked to look at some jewellery, eventually selecting some pearls and a ring. He then made out a cheque for the total amount, stated 'You see who I am, I am Sir George Bullough', and gave an address in St James' Square. C had heard of Sir George Bullough and checked the address in a directory. Being satisfied, C allowed the man to take away the ring without the cheque (which was worthless) being cleared. North pledged the ring for £350 to the defendants, a firm of pawnbrokers, who were totally unaware of North's fraudulent conduct. C sued the pawnbrokers for the return of the ring, or alternatively its value, claiming that he intended to contract only with Sir George and not the man who came into his shop.

In the High Court, Horridge J rejected this argument and found in favour of the defendants. There was not a mistake as to identity so as to render the contract void. There was a passing of property and the defendants acquired a good title to the ring. But would it not be fair to say that the jeweller thought he was dealing with Sir George? He certainly hoped that he was doing so, but he did take the risk that the man was not Sir George. The jeweller did not make a careful check on his customer's identity. Horridge J (at 246) was surely correct in concluding that 'although [C] believed the person to whom he was handing the ring was Sir George Bullough, he in fact contracted to sell and deliver it to the person who came into his shop'.

12.17 When the parties deal with each other face to face, there is a strong presumption that the seller intends to contract with the person who is physically present, and not the person that the rogue is purporting to be. Another way of expressing this point is to say that the mistake is not as to identity at all but as to the attributes of the person with whom the seller is dealing. In the majority of these cases the owner of the goods parts with them on credit or in return for a worthless cheque. What concerns the seller, then, is the creditworthiness of the person with whom he is dealing. Despite this correct statement of the law in *Phillips* v *Brooks Ltd* (1919), the law became confused by some of the cases that were decided later. For example, in *Lake* v *Simmons* [1927] AC 487:

> A jeweller (C) was induced by a woman who came into his shop into letting her have possession of two pearl necklets on approval. She fraudulently represented that she was the wife of a person of some substance (namely that she was 'Mrs Van der Borgh'), and that she wanted the necklets for the purpose of showing them to her husband, and to a purely fictitious person, for their approval with a view to purchase by them. She then disposed of the necklets for her own benefit. C claimed on his insurance for loss of the necklets by theft or dishonesty; however, his policy excluded liability where the loss was incurred as a result of the dishonesty of a customer to whom the goods had been entrusted by the jeweller.

It was held that C's loss was covered by the insurance and that the exclusion clause did not defeat his claim. But the reasoning employed by the House of Lords is open to serious criticism (see the comments of Lord Phillips in *Shogun Finance Ltd* v *Hudson* (2003) at [141]). It was argued that C did not intend to deal with the woman who came into his shop and that there was no genuine consent by C to her obtaining possession of the necklets (see Viscount Haldane's speech at 500–1). The woman was not 'a customer' within the meaning of the exclusion clause, as C did not regard her as his customer; rather, he thought of the two men to whom she claimed she would show the necklets as his possible customers! Their Lordships concluded that there was no contract between C and the woman with whom he dealt face to face owing to a mistake as to her identity. (This is discussed further in *Citibank NA* v *Brown Shipley & Co Ltd* (1991)—see para. **12.15**.)

12.18 Another heavily criticized case, the facts of which are similar to *Phillips* v *Brooks Ltd* (1919), is *Ingram* v *Little* [1961] 1 QB 31:

> Elsie and Hilda Ingram were joint owners of a car, which they advertised for sale. A man, falsely calling himself 'Hutchinson', came to look at it and have a trial run. He then offered £717 to the women for their car, which they were willing to accept. However, he produced a cheque book to pay for the car, and it was then stated by Elsie Ingram that under no circumstances would they accept a cheque and that the proposed deal was off. The man told them he was P. G. M. Hutchinson, of Stanstead House, Caterham, and that he had business interests in Guildford. Hilda Ingram checked in the directory that there was indeed a P. G. M. Hutchinson residing at that address. The women then accepted the man's cheque in exchange for their car. The man was not P. G. M. Hutchinson and the cheque was dishonoured. The rogue, in the meantime, had sold the car to the innocent defendant (D). The women now sought to recover the car, or its value, from D.

The Court of Appeal decided that the apparent contract between the claimants and the man who called at their house was void due to the mistake as to identity. The car still belonged to the women and D did not acquire good title from the rogue. The majority argued (with Lord Devlin dissenting) that although the identity of the man would have been unimportant as long as he had paid cash for the car, it became of crucial importance once the man wished to pay by cheque. The women refused to accept a cheque initially and they verified that there was a P. G. M. Hutchinson listed at that address in the telephone directory. Therefore, their 'offer' was not addressed to the man who was in their presence, but to the real P. G. M. Hutchinson (whom they had never met).

It is submitted that, in certain exceptional circumstances, it might be possible to argue that an offer was not made to the person identified by sight and hearing, but *Ingram* v *Little* is some way from coming within this category. (The court's decision might have been more defensible if the women had gone to Stanstead House to deal with the genuine Hutchinson and then been deceived on the premises by someone falsely pretending to be that person.)[3] It is difficult to

3 Consider *Hardman* v *Booth* (1863), which Pearce LJ, in *Ingram* v *Little*, accepted was a clearer case of there being no contract than *Ingram* v *Little* itself.

escape the conclusion that the court allowed its sympathy for the women to cloud its judgment of the issues. In his dissenting speech, Lord Devlin correctly pointed out that what should have concerned the women was the creditworthiness of the person they were dealing with and not his identity. He stated (at 68):

> The fact that [the rogue] gave P.G.M. Hutchinson's address in the directory was no proof that he was P.G.M. Hutchinson; and if he had been, that fact alone was no proof that his cheque would be met. Identity, therefore, did not really matter.

It can hardly be claimed that the claimants took reasonable steps to check the identity of the person with whom they were dealing. But, more fundamentally, it can be argued that the material mistake in *Ingram* v *Little* was as to the man's attributes and not as to his identity. (This is not to deny that the women thought the man's identity was important.) In fact, there is little to distinguish the case from the earlier decision in *Phillips* v *Brooks*, which emphasized the need to protect the innocent purchaser for value who buys the goods from the rogue. *Ingram* v *Little* was perhaps too concerned with protecting the original owner of the goods. This is the dilemma which faces judges in cases of this sort. It has been cogently argued that the law should permit some division of the loss between the two innocent parties in such proportion as is just in all the circumstances (see Lord Devlin's comments in *Ingram* v *Little*). This solution did not find favour with the Law Reform Committee in 1966.[4] However, the Committee did recommend that 'where goods are sold under a mistake as to the buyer's identity, the contract should, so far as third parties are concerned, be voidable and not void'.

12.19 There is much sense in the Law Reform Committee's proposal, despite Parliament's failure to implement it. Further support for this view is provided by *Lewis* v *Averay* (1972). The facts, which closely resembled those of *Ingram* v *Little* (1961), were as follows:

> Lewis offered his car for sale at £450. A man arranged to see the car, tested it, and expressed interest in buying it. The man told Lewis that he was Richard Greene, a famous film and television actor,[5] and he wrote a cheque for the agreed price of £450, signed R. A. Green. As the purchaser wished to take away the car immediately, Lewis requested some means of identification, and was shown an admission pass to Pinewood Studios in the name of Richard A. Green, which bore the man's photograph. Lewis permitted the man to take the car and log book in exchange for the cheque. In fact the cheque had been taken from a stolen cheque book and was worthless; the man was not Richard Greene, the famous actor. The rogue sold the car to an innocent buyer, Averay, for £200. Lewis sued Averay for conversion.

The Court of Appeal did not allow Lewis to recover the car or its value, deciding that Averay acquired a good title to it. Lewis intended to deal with the man who called to see the car. Although the contract was voidable for fraud, Lewis was unable to recover the property from someone who

4 See 12th Report, *Transfer of Title to Chattels*, Cmnd 2958, 1966.

5 He was best known for his starring role in the television series *Robin Hood*.

bought in good faith from the rogue for value. The court disagreed with *Ingram* v *Little*, preferring to base its decision on *Phillips* v *Brooks* (1919). It is respectfully submitted that this is the correct conclusion to have reached. It has been argued that *Ingram* v *Little* is distinguishable on the ground that in that case the women would not conclude the agreement until they had looked in the telephone directory. But this is, to say the least, a tenuous argument. In *Shogun Finance Ltd* v *Hudson* (2003) the decision in *Ingram* v *Little* was heavily criticized in a number of the speeches, with Lord Millett stating (at [110]) that it should be overruled; this is discussed below.

12.20 The issue of mistake as to identity induced by fraudulent misrepresentation must now be considered in the light of the important decision of the House of Lords in *Shogun Finance Ltd* v *Hudson* (2003). The facts were:

> A rogue visited the showroom of a car dealer, having dishonestly acquired the driving licence of a Mr Durlabh Patel. He negotiated with the car dealer for the purchase of a Mitsubishi vehicle which was on display and agreed a price of £22,250, subject to getting hire purchase finance. The dealer produced a copy of the claimant Shogun's standard form hire purchase agreement, which was signed by the rogue to resemble the signature of Durlabh Patel; the customer details supplied by the rogue were those of Mr Patel. The real Mr Patel had no knowledge of this transaction. The dealer sent by fax the signed draft finance agreement, together with a copy of the driving licence, to Shogun Finance. Shogun, having checked the credit rating of Mr Patel, instructed the dealer to proceed with the hire purchase transaction. (Under such an arrangement, the finance company buys the car from the dealer and hires it to the customer under a hire purchase agreement, which enables the customer to purchase the vehicle when all the instalments have been paid.) After paying a deposit of 10 per cent, the rogue took possession of the vehicle and its documentation from the dealer, and then sold the car almost immediately for £17,000 to the defendant, Mr Hudson, who acted in good faith without knowledge of the hire purchase agreement or the rogue's fraudulent conduct. The rogue disappeared and Shogun, arguing that the vehicle belonged to them, claimed its return or its value from Hudson.

Mr Hudson contended that he acquired good title to the vehicle by virtue of s 27 of the Hire Purchase Act 1964. This states that where a vehicle has been hired under a hire purchase agreement and the debtor sells the vehicle to a private purchaser (P) who buys in good faith without notice of the hire purchase agreement, P can acquire title to the vehicle (even though the debtor was not the owner of it). Shogun argued that this statutory provision could not avail Mr Hudson, as the hire purchase agreement was a written document and the rogue was not the debtor under this agreement, since he was not the hirer named in the agreement. They claimed that they had intended to contract with the real Mr Patel, whose details they had checked (and therefore the issue of identity was crucial), rather than the rogue, and that the hire purchase agreement was void. Both the trial judge and a majority of the Court of Appeal (Sedley LJ dissenting) found in favour of the claimant—that the rogue, by entering into the written agreement fraudulently pretending to be someone else, was not the debtor under s 27 and, therefore, Mr Hudson could not rely on this provision to acquire title to the vehicle.

Mr Hudson appealed to the House of Lords, where his appeal was dismissed (with Lord Nicholls and Lord Millett dissenting). The majority in the House of Lords' decision relied on the fact that the case could not be subsumed under the general principle governing face-to-face transactions (discussed earlier), as it involved a written hire purchase agreement (see Lord Hobhouse at [51] and Lord Phillips at [178]). Shogun's standard hire purchase agreement contained essential information about the hirer and his identity. Shogun checked the particulars supplied to them relating to Durlabh Patel and it was with him that they agreed to contract. There was no intention to contract with the rogue and, therefore, there was no agreement with him and he was not to be regarded as the debtor. As a result, Mr Hudson could not rely upon the Hire Purchase Act 1964, s 27 and ownership remained with the claimant. The majority thought that the identity of the customer was of fundamental importance to the whole transaction and that the correct identification of the customer by the claimant was the sine qua non of Shogun's willingness to contract with him. (See more recently *TTMI Sarl* v *Statoil ASA, The Sibohelle* (2011), which followed *Shogun Finance Ltd*). Accordingly, the dealer's delivery of the vehicle to the rogue was without authority and it was not a delivery under a valid hire purchase agreement.

12.21 The decision in *Shogun Finance Ltd* v *Hudson* (2003) led to the unsatisfactory result that Mr Hudson, although buying in good faith from the rogue, suffered all of the loss. The dilemma of deciding which of two innocent parties should bear the loss in such cases of mistaken identity was referred to in a number of the judgments (for example, see Lord Nicholls at [13], Lord Millett at [60], and Lord Walker at [182]). However, the majority thought that it was inescapable that the contract in question was a written consumer credit transaction, not a face-to-face sale, and that commercial certainty dictated that the document was construed correctly. In so doing, they rejected the attempt of the minority (despite Lord Phillips being 'attracted to [their] solution' at [170]) to rationalize this area of the law by doing away with the distinction made between face-to-face transactions and those made where the parties are not in each other's presence. Under the solution proposed by the minority, this 'unprincipled distinction' (at [108]) between face-to-face and other types of transaction would be discarded, as 'the existence of physical immediacy in one case, and the absence of it in the other is immaterial' (at [28]). Moreover, the minority argued that *Cundy* v *Lindsay* (1878) should no longer be followed (see [36] and [110]).

12.22 The Law Reform Committee's 12th Report (discussed at para. **12.18**) recommended that where goods are sold under a mistake as to the buyer's identity the contract be regarded as voidable rather than void, thus protecting a third party (such as Mr Hudson) who buys in good faith. The majority thought that *Shogun Finance Ltd* v *Hudson* (2003), involving a written consumer credit agreement, was a different type of case (see Lord Hobhouse at [55]) and that, in this type of transaction, identity is of fundamental importance. But it is questionable whether the rights of someone who subsequently buys in good faith from the rogue should turn on technical distinctions of this kind. It might also be argued that what was of importance to the claimant finance company was the creditworthiness of the hirer rather than his identity (see Lord Nicholls at [35]) and that, in believing that the customer in the showroom and Durlabh Patel were one and the same, it 'not only took a credit risk, but also took the risk that the customer who was hiring the car was not Mr Durlabh Patel and that its credit enquiries had been fraudulently misdirected' (per Lord Millett at [107]). (One commentator has observed that 'although Shogun successfully argued that the identity of the customer was "absolutely crucial", their practice suggested that this was not in fact the case': see C. Elliott (2004) JBL 381 at 386.)

12.23 It is respectfully submitted that the majority in *Shogun Finance Ltd* v *Hudson* (2003) took too narrow a view of the problem. For example, Lord Hobhouse (with whom Lord Walker concurred) concluded by stating that the relevant principles of law 'are clear and sound and need no revision' and that 'to cast doubt on them can only be a disservice to English Law' (at [55]). It is difficult to agree with this statement in view of the considerable disquiet expressed about the present state of the law, with its technical distinctions and its lack of consistency in tackling the dilemma as to which of two innocent parties should bear the whole of the loss. It is submitted that the opinions of the dissenting law lords are more attractive, both in their recognition that the law needs to be 'coherent and rescued from its present unsatisfactory and unprincipled state' (per Lord Nicholls at [34]), and in asserting that 'the law should if at all possible favour a solution which protects innocent third parties by treating the contract as voidable rather than void' in this type of case (per Lord Millett at [60]). Similarly, both of the dissenting opinions are critical of the distinction between face-to-face and other transactions (see [24]–[25] and [66]–[70]). Lord Nicholls argued that there 'is no magic attaching to a misrepresentation made in writing rather than by word of mouth' (at [24]) and Lord Millett stated that 'the real objection to the present state of the law . . . is that the distinction between face to face and other contracts is unrealistic' (at [68]) and 'unsound' (at [70]). This led to a recognition in both dissenting judgments that the existing authorities cannot all be reconciled and that reform was necessary, even if that involved departing from a previous decision of the House of Lords. In the words of Lord Millett, 'the decision in *Cundy* v *Lindsay* stands in the way of a rational and coherent restatement of the law'. Lord Phillips summarized the approach of his dissenting colleagues with some clarity (at [169]) and confessed that he was strongly attracted by their approach. It is perhaps unfortunate that he found himself unable to adopt it. The decision of the House of Lords has missed a valuable opportunity to put the law on a clearer and more rational footing. (For further comment on this case, see C. Elliott (2004) JBL 381, A. Phang et al. (2004) 63 CLJ 24 and C. MacMillan (2004) 120 LQR 369.)

Mistake as to the terms or subject matter of a contract

12.24 Most of the cases considered in this section are instances of mutual mistake, where the parties are at cross-purposes as to the terms or subject matter of the contract. Once again, the issue is that there is no genuine agreement, despite appearances. Before looking at these decisions, a further case of unilateral mistake should be noted. In *Hartog* v *Colin & Shields* [1939] 3 All ER 566:

> D contracted to sell to C 3,000 Argentine hare skins. But by mistake he offered to sell them at a certain rate per 'pound' (weight), instead of per 'piece'. The price stated by D was extremely low—the price per piece was about one-third of that per pound. The negotiations leading up to the sale had been on the basis of the price per piece, and this was the accepted custom within the trade. C purported to accept this offer and sued D for non-delivery.

It was held that there was no contract. The apparent agreement was negatived as C must surely have known that D's offer was made due to a mistake. ('The [claimant] could not reasonably have supposed that the offer contained the offeror's real intention': per Singleton J at 568.) (See also *Chwee Kin Keong* v *Digilandmall.com Pte Ltd* (2006).) It is interesting to contrast the *Hartog* decision with the case of *Centrovincial Estates* v *Merchant Investors Assurance Co. Ltd* (1983), which was considered at para. **12.5**. In that case the offeror was bound by his apparent agreement with the defendant despite offering to rent premises to D for £65,000 per year, rather than at the intended rent of £126,000. The important distinction seems to be that in the *Centrovincial* case the offeree (D) did not know, and could not reasonably have known, of the mistake at the time of acceptance.

12.25 Generally, parties are bound by their apparent agreements in the interests of certainty and commercial convenience. As we have seen, the law takes a predominantly objective view of agreement. It is not usually the subjective intention of the parties with which the law is concerned,[6] but rather what can be inferred from their conduct: 'In contracts you do not look into the actual intent in a man's mind. You look at what he said and did' (per Lord Denning in *Storer* v *Manchester City Council* [1974] 3 All ER 824 at 828). If one party makes an offer, as in the *Centrovincial* case, that can be understood in only one reasonable way, and the other party understands and accepts the offer in that reasonable way, there will normally be a binding agreement even if the offeror intended some different meaning. There will also be a heavy burden falling on the party alleging a mistake to disprove the existence of a contract.

12.26 It is necessary to assess the extent of the objective principle, particularly in relation to parties at cross-purposes—for example, where one party intends to sell one thing and the other party intends to buy something different, or one party intends to contract on one set of terms and the other intends to deal on a different set of terms. In this type of situation (known as 'mutual mistake') the parties are mistaken as to each other's intention. In *Raffles* v *Wichelhaus* (1864), the facts were:

> D agreed to buy from C a cargo of 125 bales of Surat cotton 'to arrive ex *Peerless* from Bombay'. In fact, there were two ships called *Peerless* and both sailed from Bombay. D meant the *Peerless* which sailed in October, and C meant the *Peerless* which sailed in December. D refused to accept the cotton sent on the ship which sailed in December. C claimed that he was ready to deliver the goods which were shipped on the vessel named in the agreement and from the agreed port, and that D was liable for refusing to accept or pay for the goods.

It was accepted by the court that D was not liable due to the ambiguity inherent in the agreement. In fact, the court (for procedural reasons) did not have to decide whether there was a contract, but the most plausible inference from the decision is that there was no contract. It is possible that there was an agreement to ship the cotton on the 'October *Peerless*', but this is unlikely. Once it emerged that there were two ships of the same name, both due to sail from

6 But see De Moor (1990) 106 LQR 632 for a more detailed examination of the issue.

Bombay, it is impossible to say that the parties reached a genuine agreement. In terms of the objective approach, a reasonable person would not conclude that agreement had been reached. (For a recent case which distinguished *Raffles* v *Wichelhaus*, see *NBTY Europe Ltd* v *Nutricia International BV* (2005).)

12.27 A more difficult case involving ambiguity in an apparent agreement is *Scriven Bros* v *Hindley & Co.* (1913), in which the facts were as follows:

> C instructed an auctioneer to sell a number of bales of hemp and of tow by auction. (Tow is the coarse and broken part of flax or hemp.) The goods were described in the auctioneer's catalogue as a certain number of bales in two separate lots, with the same shipping mark, without disclosing the difference in the commodities; that is, it failed to state that one lot contained tow, not hemp. Before the sale, samples of the hemp and tow were available for inspection in a showroom. On the floor of the room the catalogue numbers of the lots of hemp and tow were marked in chalk opposite the respective samples. Having previously examined the hemp, and (mistakenly) believing both lots to contain hemp, D's manager did not inspect the samples which were on view. At the auction D's buyer, thinking that he was bidding for hemp, made an excessively high bid for the lot containing tow! His bid was successful. Expert witnesses stated that it was very unusual for Russian tow and Russian hemp to be landed from the same ship under the same shipping mark. C brought an action to recover the price.

Put simply, C intended to sell one thing, whilst D intended to buy something else. Neither was aware of the other party's misapprehension. It was held that there was no contract of sale as the parties had not reached agreement as to the subject matter of the proposed sale. This decision might seem rather favourable to the defendants, permitting them to escape a bad bargain. But the decision is probably sound. If we ask whether a reasonable person, taking an overview of the situation, would conclude that an agreement between the parties had been reached, the answer would probably be negative. Due to the ambiguities in the circumstances under which the auction took place, it is difficult to conclude that there was a contract for the sale of tow. But for the potentially misleading nature of the auction catalogue, however, the outcome of the case would surely have been different.

12.28 Interesting issues are raised by the famous case of *Smith* v *Hughes* (1871) LR 6 QB 597, but whether it can be accurately described as one of mutual mistake is debatable due to the disputed facts of the case. First, the facts:

> A farmer (C) offered to sell the manager of D, a race horse trainer, a quantity of oats and showed him a sample. The manager wrote to C accepting the offer. When the first delivery of oats was made, D discovered that the oats were 'green' (i.e. that season's oats) and of no use to him. He claimed that he thought he was buying 'old' oats and he refused to pay for that delivery or any subsequent delivery. C, who knew that the oats were new, refused

to take them back and sued D for the price. There was a dispute as to what was said in the exchange between C and D's manager; D claimed that C had described them as 'good old oats', whereas C denied using the word 'old'. After a finding in favour of D at the trial, C appealed.

If the word 'old' had in fact been used, then the finding for D was clearly correct. But if the word 'old' had not been used by the parties, then the situation was more complex. It was this problem that was dealt with by the appeal court. If D's manager believed the oats to be old and C was aware of his belief, without doing anything to encourage it (simply offering his goods and exhibiting his sample), was there a contract? As Cockburn CJ stated (at 603):

> The question is whether, under such circumstances, the passive acquiescence of the seller in the self-deception of the buyer will entitle the latter to avoid the contract. I am of the opinion that it will not.

In ordering a new trial the court agreed with his Lordship's conclusion. Assuming that the word 'old' was not used by the parties, D received the goods which he contracted to buy and which corresponded to the sample inspected by D's manager, and therefore he was bound by the contract. (For a detailed analysis, see D. Friedmann (2003) 119 LQR 68 at 71–4; see also *Statoil ASA* v *Louis Dreyfus Energy Services LP (The Harriette N)* (2009).) To quote Lord Cockburn once again (at 603):

> Here the defendant agreed to buy a specific parcel of oats. The oats were what they were sold as, namely, good oats according to the sample. The buyer persuaded himself they were old oats, when they were not so; but the seller neither said nor did anything to contribute to his deception. He has himself to blame. The question is not what a man of scrupulous morality or nice honour would do under such circumstances.

Agreement mistake in equity

12.29 It is understandable that the law should take a narrow view of mistake. This approach upholds the need to be able to rely on the apparent intention of the party with whom you are dealing, in the interests of certainty and commercial convenience. However, the equitable jurisdiction of the courts permits a more flexible approach.[7] A contract may be upheld as valid but, in the interests of justice, the court may still grant relief against the consequences of mistake. The most practical form of equitable relief is the discretion of the court to refuse specific performance even in cases where the contract is valid at law. In the case of *Malins* v *Freeman* (1837), for example, the defendant (due to his late arrival) mistakenly made a bid for one property at an auction thinking that he was bidding for another. The mistake was due to the defendant's

7 It does not, however, extend to relieving a party from a contract simply because he or she made a bad bargain. So a mistake as to the commercial consequences of an agreement, as opposed to its subject matter or terms, will not be sufficient: see *Clarion Ltd* v *National Provident Institution* (2000).

own carelessness, and the contract was clearly valid (contrast *Scriven Bros* v *Hindley* (1913), para. **12.27**). Although the claimant could have claimed damages, the court refused to order specific performance against the defendant. (See also *Wood* v *Scarth* (1855) for a further illustration of this flexible approach.) The court may exercise its discretion so as to avoid hardship to a defendant[8] and it 'will not be active in assisting one party to an agreement, who has always his remedy in damages, to take advantage of the mistake of the other so as to involve him in serious and unforeseen consequences' (*Stewart* v *Kennedy* (1890) 15 App Cas 75 at 105 per Lord MacNaghten).

12.30 In the interest of certainty, and to prevent fraud, the court will not allow a defendant to escape the performance of a contract simply because he made a mistake. In *Tamplin* v *James* (1879) 15 Ch D 215 the facts were:

> A certain inn, 'The Ship', and adjoining shop were to be sold by auction. The defendant knew the property for sale and he knew that certain gardens, which were hardly separated from the property to be sold, were occupied along with the inn and the shop. However, the gardens did not belong to the vendor and this was clear from the plans which were on display in the saleroom. The defendant did not look at the plans or at the particulars of sale, and he bought the land in the mistaken belief that he was buying the gardens along with the inn and shop.

The Court of Appeal ordered specific performance. There was no misrepresentation by the vendor; nor was there any ambiguity in the terms of the contract. (For an interesting contrast, see *Denny* v *Hancock* (1870), in which the vendor's plan of the property for sale was potentially misleading.) In the absence of these factors, a court will be justified in refusing specific performance only where 'hardship amounting to injustice' (per James LJ at 221) would be inflicted on the defendant by holding him to the agreement and where it would be unreasonable to do so. But in *Tamplin* v *James* it was the defendant's own carelessness that led to his mistake, and he bought the property which he intended to purchase; it was simply less extensive than he thought. It was not unreasonable or unjust for the court to hold him to his contract and grant the claimant specific performance.

12.31 Another equitable remedy which may be granted at the discretion of the court is that of rectification. The purpose here is to grant relief in relation to mistakes made in the recording of agreements. For instance, where A and B reach agreement on a certain set of terms and then a written agreement between them is subsequently drawn up which, by mistake, does not accurately reflect those terms, the court may rectify the document. In other words, the document is amended so as accurately to reflect either the terms agreed by A and B, or (where no actual agreement has been concluded) their prior common intention. This common intention has to be manifested in some objective way, and be continuing at the time the document in question was drawn up. (See *Joscelyne* v *Nissen* (1970) and *Chartbrook Ltd* v *Persimmon Homes Ltd* (2009) per Lord Hoffmann at [48] and [59]–[60]. Also, M. Smith, 'Rectification of Contracts

8 For an interesting, more modern example of this, see *Patel* v *Ali* (1984).

for Common Mistake, *Joscelyne* v *Nissen*, and Subjective States of Mind' (2007) 123 LQR 116; C. Nugee, 'Rectification after Chartbrook v Persimmon: Where Are We Now?' (2012) 26(2) Tru L I 76; and P. Davies, 'Rectification Versus Interpretation: The Nature and Scope of the Equitable Jurisdiction' (2016) 75(1) CLJ 62.)

The equitable remedy of rectification is not supposed, generally, to be available in cases of unilateral mistake (although exceptionally it may be; see *Roberts & Co. Ltd* v *Leicestershire County Council* (1961), and also D. McLauchlan, 'The "Drastic" Remedy of Rectification for Unilateral Mistake' (2008) 124 LQR 608). It is usually only where the document does not reflect the intention of both A and B that a claim for rectification will be granted. In the case of *Riverlate Properties Ltd* v *Paul* [1975] Ch 133, the facts were as follows:

> C, a landlord, granted a lease of a maisonette for 99 years to D at a price of £6,500, with a yearly ground rent of £25. It was C's intention that D should pay half the cost of structural and exterior repairs. But owing to a drafting error in the draft lease sent to D's solicitor, the lease which was executed did not reflect C's intention in this respect. Neither D nor her solicitor was aware of the mistake, and it was D's understanding that she was not responsible for these repairs. C's claim was to have the contract set aside, or, alternatively, rectified so as to include D's liability for sharing the cost of external repairs.

C's claim was rejected by both the trial and appeal courts. This is surely correct, as it would be contrary to the objective approach to agreement if a party could go back on an offer which he reasonably appears to have made and which has been accepted by the other party without any knowledge of the offeror's mistake. The matter was dealt with emphatically by Russell LJ (at 140–1):

> What is there in principle, or in authority, binding on this court, which requires a person who has acquired a leasehold interest on terms on which he intended to obtain it, and who thought when he obtained it that the lessor intended him to obtain it on those terms, either to lose the leasehold interest, or, if he wished to keep it, to submit to keep it only on the terms which the lessor meant to impose but did not? In point of principle, we cannot find that this should be so. If reference be made to principles of equity, it operates on conscience. If conscience is clear at the time of the transaction, why should equity disrupt the transaction?

But if one party is aware of the other's mistake and, by keeping quiet, unfairly derives some benefit from the error, there can be no objection to rectification in a case of unilateral mistake (see *Thomas Bates & Son Ltd* v *Wyndham's (Lingerie) Ltd* (1981)). Moreover, rectification may be available where one party is mistaken and the other both intends and suspects this, and behaves unconscionably so as to encourage the error (per Stuart-Smith LJ in *Commission for the New Towns* v *Cooper (GB) Ltd* (1995), and discussed in *Templiss Properties Ltd* v *Dean Hyams* (1999) and in *Hurst Stores & Interiors Ltd* v *ML Europe Property Ltd* (2004)). However, rectification will not be granted merely because one party has driven a hard bargain in the negotiations and the other party has not been sufficiently alert to the possible consequences of a particular provision of the agreement (see *Oceanic Village Ltd* v *Shirayama Shokusan Co. Ltd* (1999)). For a court to rectify on the ground of unilateral mistake, there needs to be clear evidence that the defendant has acted unconscionably and unfairly. (See *George Wimpey UK Ltd* v *VI Construction Ltd* (2005), where such a claim failed on the facts. The rectification argument was also unsuccessful in *Connolly Ltd* v *Bellway Homes Ltd* (2007), although the claimant company succeeded with its claim for damages based on misrepresentation. The strict limits on the application of rectification to cases of unilateral mistake are also illustrated by *Rowallan Group Ltd* v *Edgehill Portfolio No 1 Ltd* (2007).)

Common mistake

Performability mistake (or 'initial impossibility')

12.32 Where performability mistake is at issue, there is no dispute between the parties about the existence of an agreement. This type of mistake, often referred to as 'common mistake', arises where the parties share the same misapprehension about some underlying fact which renders the contract impossible to perform or devoid of purpose, and one party maintains that the agreement is nullified by the mistake. For example, A contracts to sell his bicycle to B but, unknown to both parties, the bicycle was wrecked beyond repair five minutes before their agreement. What is the legal position in cases of this type? Does such a mistake render the contract void as a matter of law; or could the seller be liable for failing to supply the bicycle as promised; or could the buyer be liable for the price of the bicycle?

12.33 It is true that problems of performability mistake are far from common in practice. But an analysis of them is crucial to an understanding of contract law, as it provides an important insight into the strength of contractual obligations. The general rule of contractual obligation is that a party is bound to perform the contract or else to provide a remedy for its breach. How strict is this rule? When will a party be excused from performance on the ground of 'impossibility'? The judgment in *Great Peace Shipping Ltd* v *Tsavliris Salvage (International) Ltd* (2003), discussed at para. **12.46**, is an important contribution to understanding these issues.

Mistake as to existence of subject matter

12.34 Usually this type of mistake has involved contracts for non-existent goods but, exceptionally, other factual situations can arise. For example, in *Galloway* v *Galloway* (1914), a man (D) and woman (C) entered into a separation deed by which D agreed to pay C the weekly amount of £1 for the support of their three children. D discovered that, contrary to his mistaken assumption, his first wife was not dead! Thus, the separation agreement between D and C was based on their common, but erroneous, assumption that they were in fact married to one another. D fell behind with his payments under the agreement and argued that the contract should be set aside. Ridley J held that there was no doubt that the agreement between the parties was void due to a common mistake of fact which was material to the existence of an agreement. (The case deals only with the validity of the agreement; presumably D was still under a legal duty to provide for the children.)

12.35 A more important line of cases deals with goods which have ceased to exist, physically or commercially, at the time the parties entered into a contract. In the leading case of *Couturier* v *Hastie* (1856) 5 HL Cas 673:

> There was a contract for the sale of a cargo of corn—of 'fair average quality when shipped'—which was thought to be in transit between Salonika and London. Unknown to the contracting parties, the corn had become badly overheated and had been sold at Tunis (by the master of the ship) shortly before the contract was made. The seller contended that the buyer was still liable for the price of the corn, namely that the buyer had purchased an interest in a 'maritime adventure' (including risks), represented by the shipping documents and insurance. The buyer argued that the contract was for the sale and purchase of goods, not for the sale of goods or the documents representing them, and therefore denied liability for the price.

Here we have an interesting dispute about the true interpretation, or construction, of the agreement between the parties. The House of Lords decided that the purchaser was not liable to pay for the corn. In an important speech, Lord Cranworth LC stated (at 681–2):

> [T]he whole question turns upon the construction of the contract . . . looking to the contract itself alone, it appears to me clearly that what the parties contemplated . . . was that there was an existing something to be sold and bought . . . The contract plainly imports that there was something which was to be sold at the time of the contract, and something to be purchased.

In other words, the contract was not void automatically because the goods no longer existed at the time of the contract. It was a question of construction: what did the parties contract about? Because the House of Lords interpreted the contract as one for the purchase of specific goods (and not the documents representing them as an alternative), the purchaser was not liable. It was never decided whether the seller would have been liable if an action for non-delivery of the goods had been brought by the purchaser against him. It is submitted that the seller would be liable in these circumstances only if, as a matter of construction, he assumed the risk of the goods' non-existence. This would perhaps be fairly unusual, but such a situation is well illustrated in the Australian High Court case of *McRae* v *Commonwealth Disposals Commission* (1951) 84 CLR 377. The facts were:

> The Commonwealth Disposals Commission (D) invited tenders 'for the purchase of an oil tanker lying on Jourmand Reef . . . the vessel is said to contain oil'. C's tender of £285 was accepted by the defendant Commission. C went to much expense in preparing for a salvage expedition only to discover, on arrival at the designated area, that there was no tanker to be found. (Nor was there any place known as 'Jourmand Reef'.)

The court held that this was not an example of a contract nullified by mistake. The defendants had made an implied promise that there was a tanker at a particular location. As there was no such tanker, this was a breach of contract and C was entitled to damages.[9] The court was clearly of the opinion that *Couturier* v *Hastie* (1856) did not establish a rule of law that a contract is void for mistake where the goods do not exist at the time the contract is made. It was stated (at 406–7):

> The truth is that the question whether the contract was void, or the vendor excused from performance by reason of the non-existence of the supposed subject matter, did not arise in *Couturier* v *Hastie*. It would have arisen if the purchaser had suffered loss through non-delivery of the corn and had sued the vendor for damages. If it had so arisen, we think that the real question would have been whether the contract was subject to an implied condition precedent that the goods were in existence.

12.36 The decision in the case of *McRae* v *Commonwealth Disposals Commission* (1951) is certainly in keeping with the approach taken in *Couturier* v *Hastie* (1856). However, *Couturier* v *Hastie* has received an interpretation in English law that perhaps is inconsistent with what was actually stated by the House of Lords in that case. Despite the fact that it was stressed that 'the whole question turns upon the construction of the contract', the decision led to the belief that in cases of non-existent goods the 'contract' will be void. This interpretation was encapsulated in s 6 of the Sale of Goods Act 1893 which purported to give effect to the decision in *Couturier* v *Hastie*. Section 6 of the Act (now the 1979 Act) provides that:

> Where there is a contract for the sale of specific goods, and the goods without the knowledge of the seller have perished at the time when the contract is made, the contract is void.

12.37 This raises a number of interesting issues. It appears to state as a rule of law something which was held to be a question of construction at common law. Therefore, it produces a more rigid approach than that favoured by the Australian High Court in *McRae* v *Commonwealth Disposals Commission* (1951). This can be illustrated by *Barrow, Lane & Ballard Ltd* v *Phillips & Co. Ltd* [1929] 1 KB 574, in which the facts were that C sold to D 700 bags of nuts, but at the time of making the contract there were not 700 bags in existence. In fact, there were only 591 bags, the remaining 109 having been stolen or misdirected (due to the actions of a third party). C claimed the price of the bags which were still in existence, but Wright J rejected this argument and held the contract to be void for mistake as to the existence of goods. This was stated as a matter of law under Sale of Goods Act, s 6. Apparently it made no difference that only some of the goods did not exist and that more than three-quarters of the bags were still there. Wright J stated (at 583):

> A contract for a parcel of 700 bags is something different from a contract for 591 bags, and the position appears to me to be in no way different from what it would have been if the whole 700 bags had ceased to exist.[10]

9 The damages awarded would include compensation for the money spent in reliance on the defendants' promise, i.e. in equipping a salvage expedition.

10 Had the contract been severable—i.e. an agreement for a number of separate lots which were to be paid for separately—then presumably the decision would have been different. The buyer would have been liable for the price of the remaining bags of nuts.

It is possible to distinguish *McRae* from the other cases we have considered on the basis that s 6 refers to goods that 'have perished' at the time of the contract, whereas in *McRae* the goods never existed.[11] But there is no reason, in principle, why this should make any material difference, and perhaps the wording of the Act is merely fortuitous. It might be pointed out that this discussion is rather academic; that in the modern age of instantaneous methods of communication, it is unlikely that there will be many problems relating to non-existent goods. But it might also be cogently argued that in view of these modern developments, it would be more realistic to hold that the seller of specific goods is usually understood to have promised that the goods exist.[12]

Mistake as to 'quality' of subject matter

12.38 In the cases which we have just considered, it is easy to understand why an apparent contract may be a nullity due to the non-existence of the subject matter. The contract may be emptied of all its content and, unless any other construction is possible, it may be regarded as void. But outside this category of cases involving non-existent goods, there are few clear instances of a contract being held void on the grounds of common mistake. Here we are concerned with cases where the parties are both mistaken as to some fundamental fact (such as the 'quality' of the thing contracted for) and whether an apparent contract can be nullified on these grounds. If the courts are willing to declare a contract void for this reason, there is perhaps an independent, albeit narrow, doctrine of common mistake recognized by the common law. (The relevant principles of this doctrine were considered in the Court of Appeal decision in *Great Peace Shipping Ltd* v *Tsavliris Salvage (International) Ltd* (2003) at [73]–[76].) It must be remembered that the courts will not permit a party to escape his or her contractual undertakings simply because he or she made what turned out to be a bad bargain (see *Great Peace Shipping Ltd*). But what if, for example, a person sells something at a tiny fraction of its true commercial value because both parties are mistaken as to its quality or its nature? Or, to pose a further question, if the subject matter lacks some essential quality which the parties thought it possessed, can it be argued that the object of the contract is impossible to achieve?

12.39 The leading case of *Bell* v *Lever Bros* [1932] AC 161 is difficult to interpret, but it illustrates the limitations of any general doctrine of common mistake. Generally, a mistake as to quality of the thing contracted for will not make a contract void. In *Bell* v *Lever Bros* the facts were:

> Lever Bros employed the appellants, Bell and Snelling, as chairman and vice-chairman (respectively) of the Niger Company—a company controlled by Lever Bros. Before the expiry of their five-year contracts, Lever Bros wished to terminate Bell's and Snelling's contracts,

11 A discussion of the meaning of 'perish' under the Sale of Goods Act is beyond the scope of this book. Briefly, it may be noted that some minor deterioration of goods will not amount to 'perishing'. However, goods may perish in a commercial sense, even though they physically still exist, when there is sufficient deterioration: see *Asfar* v *Blundell* (1896).

12 See Atiyah, *Introduction to the Law of Contract*, 5th edn, Clarendon, 1995, p. 222.

and under a further agreement Lever Bros promised to pay the men compensation of £30,000 and £20,000, respectively. After payment of the compensation, Lever Bros discovered that Bell and Snelling had committed certain breaches of duty during their employment, which would have entitled their employers to dismiss them without compensation. (In the course of their employment the men had secretly engaged in speculative transactions in cocoa on their own account.) It was found as a matter of fact that Bell and Snelling had forgotten about their breaches of duty at the time of entering into the compensation agreements with Lever Bros. Therefore, it was not a case either of fraud or of unilateral mistake. Lever Bros tried to recover the £50,000 on the ground that the compensation agreements with the two men were void due to common mistake.

Put simply, Lever Bros paid a total of £50,000 to terminate the contracts of two men who could have been dismissed for nothing. The trial judge and the Court of Appeal held that the compensation agreements were void due to a fundamental mistake. The House of Lords reversed this decision, with the majority holding that the contracts were valid and binding. It is worth considering the important and controversial words of one of the majority, Lord Atkin (at 223–4), in some detail. He stated:

> Is an agreement to terminate a broken contract different in kind from an agreement to terminate an unbroken contract, assuming that the breach has given the one party the right to declare the contract at an end? I feel the weight of the claimant's contention that a contract immediately determinable is a different thing from a contract for an unexpired term, and that the difference in kind can be illustrated by the immense price of release from the longer contract as compared with the shorter . . . But, on the whole, I have come to the conclusion that it would be wrong to decide that an agreement to terminate a definite specified contract is void if it turns out that the agreement had already been broken and could have been terminated otherwise. The contract released is the identical contract in both cases, and the party paying for release gets exactly what he bargains for. It seems immaterial that he could have got the same result in another way, or that if he had known of the true facts he would not have entered into the bargain.

Although it is difficult to agree that Lever Bros got 'exactly' what they bargained for, it must be accepted that it was in the company's interest, because of a corporate merger, to terminate the men's service contracts. Moreover, the compensation was a reward (at least in part) for the good work that the two men had done during their employment and it ensured their co-operation in carrying through the amalgamation. It might be contended that the value of this service was unaffected by the breach of contract committed by the two men. On the other hand, it might be argued that the basis of the compensation agreement was the termination of valid service contracts and that, accordingly, there was a common mistake as to a fundamental fact.

12.40 We have seen that a mistake as to the *existence* of the subject matter of an agreement can render the agreement void. But, in view of the actual decision in *Bell* v *Lever Bros* [1932] AC 161, are there any circumstances in which the courts will declare a contract void due to some fundamental mistake as to the *quality* of the thing contracted for? A narrow view, evident in some parts of the judgments given in *Lever Bros*, is that an agreement will be nullified only where the identity of the subject matter is in effect destroyed by the mistaken assumption; that is, 'does the state of the new facts destroy the identity of the subject matter as it was in the original state of facts?' (at 227 per Lord Atkin). In such a (rare) event, therefore, the mistake would be analogous to cases of non-existent goods and would nullify agreement.

12.41 A slightly wider view of the law, also expressed by Lord Atkin in *Bell* v *Lever Bros* [1932] AC 161 at 218, is that a common mistake will render a contract void where both parties are mistaken 'as to the existence of some quality which makes the thing without the quality essentially different from the thing as it was believed to be'.[13] This view of common mistake was approved in *Associated Japanese Bank (International)* v *Crédit du Nord SA* [1988] 3 All ER 902 (which is discussed later). In this case Steyn J stated, *obiter* (at 913), that this wider interpretation of *Bell* v *Lever Bros* is to be preferred. The test to be applied is that the mistake must render the subject matter of the contract essentially and radically different from the subject matter which the parties believed to exist.

12.42 However, there is still a distinct impression that much of this debate is merely abstract theorizing. If we look at the decision in *Bell* v *Lever Bros* (1932), and the decisions that have followed, it is apparent that 'cases where contracts have been found to be void in consequence of common mistake are few and far between' (per Lord Phillips in *Great Peace Shipping Ltd* v *Tsavliris Salvage (International) Ltd* (2003) at [85]; for cases which lend some support to the existence of such a doctrine, see *Scott* v *Coulson* [1903] 2 Ch 249 at 252, and also *Nicholson and Venn* v *Smith-Marriott* (1947)).[14] The doctrine is said to exist in theory, but in practice it is difficult to find examples of cases decided on this basis alone. This is not surprising in view of the outcome of *Lever Bros*. The company paid £50,000 to dismiss two men, when it could have dismissed them for nothing. If this was not sufficiently fundamental to come within a doctrine of common mistake, it is reasonable to question the existence of such a doctrine.

12.43 A further illustration of the very strict standard to be applied is the case of *Leaf* v *International Galleries* [1950] 2 KB 86. The facts were as follows:

> In 1944 the defendants sold a picture, entitled 'Salisbury Cathedral', to C for £85. The defendants represented that it was the work of John Constable. But when C tried to sell the painting, five years later, he discovered that it had not been painted by Constable. C sought rescission of the contract and repayment of £85 on the basis of the defendants' innocent misrepresentation. (C did not claim damages for breach of condition or warranty.)

13 Alternatively, in Lord Thankerton's words (at 235), the mistake must 'relate to something which both must necessarily have accepted in their minds as an essential and integral element of the subject matter'.

14 In a US case, *Sherwood* v *Walker* (1887), a contract for the sale of a cow believed by both parties to be barren was held to be void when it was discovered to be with calf, and worth considerably more than the price agreed by the parties.

The Court of Appeal held that C was not entitled to rescind the contract despite the defendants' innocent misrepresentation (see **Chapter 13**). In the opinion of Lord Denning, C had ample opportunity to examine the picture in the first few days after buying it, and as he had not rejected the painting within a reasonable period after its purchase, he lost the right to rescind. (For an interesting case on this point, see *Peco Arts* v *Hazlitt Gallery* (1983).) In his Lordship's opinion, a claim for damages for breach of contract might have succeeded, but C did not bring such a claim before the court. (But see *Harlingdon and Leinster Enterprises Ltd* v *Christopher Hull Fine Art Ltd* (1990).) Lord Denning also stated (at 89):

> There was a mistake about the quality of the subject-matter, because both parties believed the picture to be a Constable, and that mistake was in one sense essential or fundamental. Such a mistake, however, does not avoid the contract. There was no mistake about the subject-matter of the sale. It was a specific picture of 'Salisbury Cathedral'. The parties were agreed in the same terms on the same subject-matter, and that is sufficient to make a contract.

When a person buys the work of a famous artist it is, perhaps, rather perverse to suggest that he or she is buying merely 'a painting' (for example, of Salisbury Cathedral). There are perhaps two possible interpretations of *Leaf* in relation to common mistake. On the one hand, it could be argued that the relatively low price of the painting suggests a slightly speculative venture which includes the risk that the painting of Salisbury Cathedral was not 'a Constable'—in which case there is clearly no fundamental mistake. On the other hand, it could be asserted that the parties contracted for the sale of 'a Constable' and therefore there was a mistake as to an essential quality of the subject matter.

12.44 Lord Denning's statement (above) suggests therefore that a contract will rarely be void as a result of a common mistake as to some essential quality of the thing contracted for. Lord Denning's opinion echoes that of Lord Atkin in *Bell* v *Lever Bros* [1932] AC 161 at 224, in which the latter considered an example with facts similar to those which actually occurred in *Leaf* v *International Galleries* (1950). The apparent injustice suffered by the claimant in *Leaf* is overshadowed by the fact that, in the words of Lord Atkin (at 224), it is of 'paramount importance that contracts should be observed'.

12.45 But in the later case of *Associated Japanese Bank (International)* v *Crédit du Nord SA* [1988] 3 All ER 902, support was given for the existence of a doctrine of common mistake as to quality rendering a contract void ab initio at common law. It was not, in fact, necessary to decide the case on this particular basis, but Steyn J was at pains to explain the nature and scope of such a doctrine. The facts were:

The claimant bank (C) bought four specific microtextile compression packaging machines from Mr Jack Bennett (B) and then leased them back to him. B received £1,021,000 from C under the transaction. As a condition of the transaction, B's obligations under the 'leaseback' agreement were guaranteed by the defendant bank (D). At all times both banks believed that the four machines existed and were in B's possession. In fact, when B fell behind with his payments under the lease, it was discovered that the machines did not exist! (The transaction was a fraud perpetrated by B.) B was found to be bankrupt and therefore C's claim against him under the lease was fruitless. C sued the defendant bank on the guarantee.

In dismissing C's claim, Steyn J held that, on its construction, the guarantee was subject to an express condition precedent that there was a lease in respect of four existing machines. This was because both banks were informed and believed that the machines existed. (In any case, the learned judge thought that there was an implied condition precedent that the machines existed and so C's claim would have failed for this reason. In *Graves* v *Graves* [2007] EWCA Civ 660, the Court of Appeal implied a condition into a tenancy agreement to bring it to an end (at [38]–[41]), and held at [43] that it was 'therefore not necessary to consider whether the contract was frustrated or void for mistake'. On implied condition precedents and common mistake, see the subsequent case law of *Apvodedo NV* v *Collins* (2008) and *Butters* v *BBC Worldwide Ltd* (2009).)

Steyn J went on to explain, *obiter* (at 912–13), the principles relevant to common mistake as to quality of the subject matter: the law will normally uphold apparent contracts; the doctrine of mistake can be relied on only in unexpected and 'wholly exceptional' circumstances. It must be a mistake of both parties relating to facts as they existed at the time of contracting. A party seeking to rely on a common mistake must have had reasonable grounds for entertaining the belief on which the mistake was based. Applying the dicta of Lords Atkin and Thankerton in *Bell* v *Lever Bros* (1932), the learned judge stated that the mistake must render the subject matter of the contract 'essentially and radically different from that which the parties believed to exist'. (The Court of Appeal in *Great Peace Shipping Ltd* v *Tsavliris Salvage (International) Ltd* (2003) at [91]–[93] agreed with Steyn J's analysis and preferred it to Lord Denning's interpretation of *Bell* v *Lever Bros*. Steyn J's test was also applied in *Kyle Bay Ltd (t/a Astons Nightclub)* v *Underwriters* (2007) per Neuberger LJ at [24]–[27]. Here the Court of Appeal rejected a claim based on common mistake, observing that a 'significant' or even a 'substantial' mistake is not necessarily the same thing as one which renders the subject matter 'essentially and radically different' from what the parties believed it to be.)

Applying these principles to the facts of the case, Steyn J concluded (at 913) that 'the stringent test of common law mistake is satisfied; the guarantee is void ab initio'. For both parties, the guarantee of obligations under a lease with machines that did not exist was essentially and radically different from a guarantee of a lease with four machines that both parties thought were in existence at the time of contracting.[15]

15 For an interesting discussion of Steyn J's approach, see J. C. Smith, 'Contracts—Mistake, Frustration and Implied Terms' (1994) 110 LQR 400.

12.46 The scope of common mistake was also considered in the important case of *Great Peace Shipping Ltd* v *Tsavliris Salvage (International) Ltd* [2002] EWCA Civ 1407, [2003] QB 679, where the facts were:

> A vessel, the *Cape Providence*, was seriously damaged in the Indian Ocean and the defendants undertook to provide salvage services. A tug which they proposed to use was too far away, so the defendants entered into a hire contract for the claimants' vessel, the *Great Peace*, for a minimum of five days to escort and stand by the stricken *Cape Providence*, for the purpose of saving life. The contract gave the defendants the right to cancel on payment of five days' hire. At the time of contracting, the defendants thought that the *Great Peace* was 35 miles away and, therefore, could arrive within a short time. However, it turned out that the two vessels were about 400 miles apart. On discovering this, the defendants did not cancel the contract immediately, but they looked for a closer vessel to assist. They found an alternative within a few hours and cancelled the contract with the claimants, refusing to make any payment for the hire of the *Great Peace*. In defence of the claimants' action, the defendants argued that there had been a fundamental mistake of fact, that is, that the contract was based on the erroneous assumption that the two vessels were close together, and as a result the contract was either void at law or voidable in equity. The judge found in favour of the claimants.

The trial judge's decision was affirmed by the Court of Appeal and the appeal was dismissed. There is no doubt that it was a common assumption of both parties at the time of contracting that the two vessels were close enough to one another to enable the *Great Peace* to render the escort and stand-by services. But was the misapprehension of both parties so fundamental as to render the contract void? It was held that the common mistake which arose did not render the services essentially different from what the parties had agreed (at [165]). The court thought that it was significant that the defendants refrained from cancelling the agreement until they were certain they could obtain the services of a nearer vessel. It was also relevant that the *Great Peace* would still have been able to render several days of service, despite the longer journey, and the defendants would have wanted this if they had not been able to secure the services of an alternative vessel. In other words, 'the fact that the vessels were further apart than both parties had appreciated did not mean that it was impossible to perform the contractual adventure' (at [165]).

In delivering the judgment of the court, Lord Phillips (at [73]–[76]) explained the principles on which the doctrine of common mistake operates. He stated that where a contract is held to be void on the basis of common mistake, this results from a rule of law by which 'if it transpires that one or both of the parties have agreed to do something which it is impossible to perform, no obligation arises out of that agreement'. In considering the issue of impossibility, it is necessary to identify what it is that the parties actually agreed would be performed. Obviously this process involves considering any express provisions, but it also includes any implications arising from the circumstances of the agreement. The doctrine of common mistake (like that of frustration—see **Chapter 19**) applies only where a contract has no provision to cover the situation which has occurred. So 'if, on true construction of the contract, a party warrants that the subject matter of the contract exists, or that it will be possible to perform the contract, there will be no scope to hold the contract void on the ground of common mistake'. Lord Phillips acknowledged that the doctrine is narrow in scope and that (as the actual decision in *Bell* v *Lever Bros* (1932) illustrates) it will be rare that a mistake as to quality will make 'the thing without the quality essentially different from the thing as it was believed to be' and, therefore, void (at [86]). Such cases will arise less frequently than instances of frustration. This is because it is not uncommon for supervening events to occur which, without being the responsibility of either party, defeat the contractual adventure. But in cases where 'parties agree that something shall be done which is impossible at the time of making the agreement, it is much more likely that, on true construction of the agreement, one or other will have undertaken responsibility for the mistaken state of affairs' (at [85]).

12.47 The decision in *Brennan* v *Bolt Burden* (2005) provides a further illustration of the narrow scope of the doctrine of common mistake. (For a slightly less restrictive interpretation of the relevant test, see *Champion Investments Ltd* v *Ahmed* (2004) at [32].) The *Brennan* case involved C's claim for damages for personal injury (from exposure to carbon monoxide), which was settled on a mistaken legal basis. C had compromised her claim, believing that the claim form was served out of time, with the result that the claim was withdrawn with each side bearing its own costs. Due to the subsequent overruling of a relevant legal authority, it was later shown that the parties were mistaken about the claim form being served out of time. As a consequence, C argued that the compromise was void for mistake. The Court of Appeal rejected her argument by a majority. Maurice Kay LJ stated at [22]–[23]:

> [T]his is quite simply not a case of impossibility of performance. The compromise has at all times remained performable, albeit to [C's] disadvantage . . . that is in itself sufficient to put it beyond the reach of common mistake of law . . . the compromise was a matter of give-and-take which ought not lightly be set aside . . . and that, as a matter of construction, the risk of a future judicial decision affecting matters to [C's] advantage was impliedly accepted and bargained away by her solicitor.

Common mistake in equity

12.48 If the question of mistake as to quality is raised by one of the parties, the first task of the court will be to see (as a matter of construction) if either of the parties to the contract bears the risk of the relevant mistake. (For example, in *William Sindall plc* v *Cambridgeshire County Council* (1994), C argued that a contract to buy D's land should be rescinded for mistake when C discovered that a sewer ran across the land. The Court of Appeal, however, rejected C's argument as it was held that the agreement between the parties allocated the risk of this kind of mistake to C.) If the contract is silent on this point, then the doctrine of mistake may be considered.[16] (See *Great Peace Shipping Ltd* v *Tsavliris Salvage (International) Ltd* (2003), discussed earlier.)

16 See *Sheikh Bros* v *Ochsner* (1957), where a contract was held void after first deciding that neither party assumed the risk that the contract would be impossible to perform.

12.49 The opinion has been expressed by some writers and judges, most notably by Lord Denning (see *Solle* v *Butcher* [1950] 1 KB 671 at 691), that a common mistake, even of a fundamental nature, does not make the contract void at common law, but merely liable to be set aside in equity. (See also his Lordship's statement to the same effect in *Frederick Rose Ltd* v *William Pim Jnr Ltd* [1953] 2 QB 450 at 459–60.) However, this is inconsistent with what was stated in *Bell* v *Lever Bros* (1932) and with the most recent judicial pronouncements. In *Great Peace Shipping Ltd* v *Tsavliris Salvage (International) Ltd* (2003) at [118], the Court of Appeal said it was inconceivable that the House of Lords in *Bell* v *Lever Bros* 'overlooked an equitable right . . . to rescind the agreement, notwithstanding that the agreement was not void for mistake at common law'. It also stated that Lord Atkin's narrow test for common mistake 'broadly reflected the circumstances where equity had intervened to excuse performance of a contract assumed to be binding in law' (at [118]).

12.50 In *Solle* v *Butcher* [1950] 1 KB 671 the facts were:

> In 1947, D took a long lease of a building, which had previously been converted into five flats, with the intention of carrying out repairs caused by war damage and substantial alterations to the property. Although the flats were empty in 1947, one of them (Flat No 1) had been let before the war to a tenant at a rent of £140 per year. C and D were partners in an estate agents' business and they discussed the rent that could be charged for the flats once the improvements had been carried out. D relied on C in calculating the rents that could be charged, and C told D that he could charge £250 per year for the flat in question (Flat No 1), and that the rent was not controlled by the Rent Restriction Acts (as the flat had been altered extensively). In September 1947, D let Flat No 1 to C for seven years at an annual rent of £250; both parties were satisfied that the earlier rent of £140 did not apply as the 'standard rent'. In other words, they entered into the contract under the mistaken impression that the flat was not controlled by the Rent Restriction Acts. In fact, the maximum rent that could be charged was £140 and this could not be increased during the contractual tenancy (due to the relevant legislation) once the lease was executed. After nearly two years, C sought a declaration that the standard rent of the flat was £140 and tried to claim the amount that he had already overpaid to D under the lease. The trial court found that the standard rent was £140 per year. The defendant counterclaimed for rescission of the lease on the basis of common mistake of fact.

It was decided by the Court of Appeal that the contract was not void ab initio, once again illustrating the narrow view of common mistake at law. However, the court purported to exercise its equitable jurisdiction and ordered rescission of the lease, but on terms that would enable C 'to choose either to stay on at the proper rent [i.e. £250 per year] or to go out' (per Lord Denning at 696–7). In so doing, the court illustrated the flexibility of the equitable approach.[17] Not only did it relieve one party from the hardship caused by the mistake, but it also did justice to the other party. However, it was stated recently that the equitable jurisdiction which Lord Denning asserted 'was a significant extension of any jurisdiction exercised up to that point and one that was not readily reconcilable with the result in *Bell* v *Lever Bros*' (see *Great Peace Shipping Ltd* v *Tsavliris Salvage (International) Ltd* (2003) at [130]).

17 For a further example, see *AL and S Nutt* v *PE and Y Read* (1999).

12.51 A further example of the attempt to develop an equitable approach is provided by *Grist v Bailey* [1967] Ch 532:

> The defendant, Mrs Minnie Bailey, agreed to sell to the claimant, Frank Grist, a freehold house for £850, 'subject to the existing tenancy thereof'. At the time of contracting, both parties thought that the house was occupied by a protected tenant (under the Rent Acts) who was entitled to remain in the house, and the price reflected their belief. In fact, they were incorrect; the tenant left the house without making any claim to protection. The true value of the house with vacant possession was £2,250. Mrs Bailey refused to complete the contract and an action for specific performance was brought by the claimant. The defendant argued that the contract should be set aside on the ground of common mistake.

Goff J held that the common mistake as to the nature of the tenancy affecting the property was not sufficient to render the contract void at common law. (This is surely correct, for the subject matter was not fundamentally or essentially affected by the mistake.) But the considerable undervaluing of the house, due to the mistake, would have caused considerable hardship to the defendant. For this reason the judge upheld the defendant's claim for rescission. The contract was set aside in equity on the terms that the claimant was to have the option of entering into a fresh contract to buy the house at a proper vacant possession price (at 543).

12.52 It might be objected that the decision seems rather indulgent towards the vendor who made a bad bargain (which could presumably have been avoided if greater care had been exercised), and that it conflicts with the requirement of certainty in commercial dealings. But it could also be argued that it would have been extremely harsh to refuse to grant relief to the defendant in view of the material mistake. See further *Pitt* v *Holt* (2013), which serves as an example, in the context of trusts law, where the test for setting aside a voluntary disposition for mistake will centre on the gravity of the mistake and its consequences, and, moreover, the injustice of leaving a mistake disposition uncorrected is to be objectively evaluated.

12.53 A further example of the use of equity can be seen in *Magee* v *Pennine Insurance Co. Ltd* [1969] 2 QB 507, where the facts were:

> In 1961, C bought a car for his 18-year-old son to drive. C, who could not drive, signed a proposal form to insure the car with the defendant company, but the details of the form were completed by the person at the garage from whom he bought the car. Although there was no dishonesty on C's part, the information supplied on the form contained certain innocent misrepresentations. For example, it stated incorrectly that C held a provisional licence and that he and an elder son (who had a full licence) would drive the car as well as the younger son. (In signing the form, C promised that the information it contained was true and that this declaration was to be the basis of a contract of insurance with the defendant company.) The insurance policy on the car (and its replacement) was duly issued and renewed each year. In 1965, the younger son had a serious accident in the car which resulted in a claim on the

insurance. C claimed £600 under the policy as the value of the car, but he was offered £385 in settlement of his claim and he accepted this offer. On discovery of C's misrepresentations, the defendants refused to pay him £385 under the compromise agreement. C brought an action for this sum.

In the Court of Appeal, Lord Denning (at 514) accepted that this was a case of common mistake as 'both parties thought that the contract was good and binding'. However, he reiterated his opinion that a common mistake, even on a fundamental matter, does not make a contract void at law, but makes it liable to be set aside in equity. It was held (with Winn LJ dissenting) that the contract, despite being valid at law, would be set aside in equity. It was thought that it would be unfair to hold the insurance company to an agreement based on an invalid insurance policy. But it can be objected that justice was done to one party only. No terms were imposed by the court. The decision meant that C had paid insurance premiums for a number of years on an invalid policy and had totally wasted his money.

12.54 It is interesting that in *Magee* v *Pennine Insurance Co. Ltd* (1969), a case which closely resembles the facts of *Bell* v *Lever Bros* (1932), the contract was set aside, whereas in *Bell* the company was unable to recover its money from its ex-employees. Attempts have been made to distinguish between these two closely analogous cases by arguing that in *Bell* the money had already been paid to the men before discovery of the mistake, whilst in *Magee* the money had not been paid at the time the mistake was discovered. This may suggest therefore that it was not inequitable to set aside the agreement in *Magee*, but it might have been if the company had already paid out the £385 under the compromise agreement. However, there is nothing in the judgment to indicate that this was the basis of the decision.

12.55 In truth it is difficult to find any material difference between the facts of these two cases. The difference in outcome reflects the extent of the development of an equitable approach to common mistake since the time of the *Bell* v *Lever Bros* (1932) decision. Indeed, the Court of Appeal stated in *Great Peace Shipping Ltd* v *Tsavliris Salvage (International) Ltd* (2003) (at [153]) that the two cases can be reconciled 'only by postulating that there are two categories of mistake, one that renders a contract void at law and one that renders it voidable in equity'. The problem with this, as the court in *Great Peace Shipping Ltd* also pointed out (at [153]), is that it has not 'proved possible to define satisfactorily two different qualities of mistake, one operating in law and one in equity'. It could be argued that the resulting confusion tends to negate the purpose of a narrow approach to mistake at common law: that is, the need to uphold apparent contracts in the interest of certainty. The ambit of the equitable jurisdiction advocated by Lord Denning has been difficult to delineate.[18] In *Solle* v *Butcher* [1950] 1 KB 671 (at 693), he stated:

> A contract is . . . liable to be set aside if the parties were under a common misapprehension either as to facts or as to their relative and respective rights, provided that the misapprehension was fundamental and that the party seeking to set it aside was not himself at fault.

18 See *Great Peace Shipping Ltd* v *Tsavliris Salvage (International) Ltd* (2003) at [153]–[156].

The actual decision in *Solle* v *Butcher* may have achieved greater flexibility by extending the scope of the equitable jurisdiction, but in doing so it produced a lack of clarity. Lord Denning stated that the mistake has to be 'fundamental', but in what respect did this go beyond Lord Atkin's formulation of the common law test? (See *Great Peace Shipping Ltd* at [131] and [154].) Despite the efforts of later judges to provide some clarification,[19] this remained an insurmountable problem. In *Great Peace Shipping Ltd* (at [161]), the Court of Appeal expressed some understanding of Lord Denning's antipathy towards the decision in *Bell* v *Lever Bros* and thought that 'there is scope for legislation to give greater flexibility to our law of mistake than the common law allows'. However, it also stated (at [160]) that it had taken the opportunity for a 'full and mature consideration' of the decisions in *Bell* v *Lever Bros* and *Solle* v *Butcher* and concluded that there is 'no way that *Solle* v *Butcher* can stand with *Bell* v *Lever Bros*'. The court hesitated in holding that *Solle* v *Butcher* is 'not good law' but, in view of its critical comments, *Solle* v *Butcher* must now be regarded as being of dubious authority. (For further comment on the *Great Peace* decision, see A. Chandler et al., 'Common Mistake: Theoretical Justification and Remedial Inflexibility' (2004) (Jan) JBL 34; M. Doherty and H. James, 'The Law of Mistake in the 21st Century' (2003) 24 Business Law Review 59; C. Hare, 'Inequitable Mistake' (2003) 62 CLJ 29; and F. Reynolds, 'Reconsider the Contract Textbooks' (2003) 119 LQR 177.)

Documents signed by mistake

12.56 Generally the law takes a strict view of signed documents. In the absence of fraud or misrepresentation, a person who signs a document is bound by this, regardless of whether he has read or understood what he is signing (see *L'Estrange* v *Graucob* (1934)). This is a further illustration of the law's objective approach to agreement.[20] The signer of a document will, of course, be able to rescind a contract induced by the fraud of the other contracting party. But this will be of no avail if a bona fide third party has acquired rights under the contract, for value, before it is avoided. (The document in question may also bring the signer into a contractual relationship with someone other than the fraudulent person.) The only defence which is then of any assistance to the signer is to claim that the contract is void altogether and not merely voidable for fraud. This involves relying on the argument that his mind did not accompany the signing of the document and pleading non est factum ('it is not my deed').

12.57 This particular defence, as its name suggests, originated to protect a person who executed a deed after it had been incorrectly read over to him. It was a necessary development in an age when many people could not read. For example, in *Thoroughgood's Case* (1582):

> Thoroughgood (C), who could not read, was owed rent by a tenant. The tenant drew up a deed which was incorrectly read over to C by someone posing as a helpful bystander. Instead of merely releasing the tenant from his arrears of rent as he supposed, C in fact signed away his rights to the property. The tenant sold the land to an innocent purchaser; C sued in trespass for recovery of his land.

19 For an attempt to explain what is meant by a 'fundamental' mistake, both at common law and in equity, see *William Sindall plc* v *Cambridgeshire County Council* (1994).

20 For a critical view, see J. R. Spencer, 'Signature, Consent, and the Rule in *L'Estrange* v *Graucob*' (1973) 32(1) CLJ 104.

Thoroughgood succeeded in his action. He was not bound by his deed because it was misrepresented to him and he could not read it. In the context of its time, this was a fair and sensible exception to the general rule that deeds were regarded as absolutely binding. But, later, the defence of non est factum was extended to cover written documents not under seal, and to cases where the signer was not illiterate (see *Foster* v *Mackinnon* (1869) LR 4 CP 704 at 711). These developments were much more contentious, even though the defence did not cover a person who was simply negligent.

12.58 As the basis for the defence of non est factum is a lack of intent on the part of the signer, the result of a successful plea is that the contract is a complete nullity (i.e. void). In the interest of commercial certainty, and in view of the fact that most people today are able to read, the use of this plea should be strictly limited. Otherwise it can cause injustice to third parties. This restrictive approach was supported by the House of Lords in *Saunders* v *Anglia Building Society* (sometimes referred to as *Gallie* v *Lee*) (1971), which is the leading case on the scope of non est factum today. The facts were:

> Mrs Gallie (C) was a widow aged 78, who gave the deeds of her house to her nephew so that he (together with a business associate named Lee) could raise money by using the house as security. She stipulated that she should continue to live in the house until she died. Lee and her nephew asked C to sign a document which she was unable to read as she had broken her glasses. Lee told her, dishonestly, that it was a deed of gift to her nephew. In fact, it was a document (drawn up by a dishonest clerk) which transferred the house by sale to Lee for the price of £3,000. Lee failed to pay C any of the money; instead, he mortgaged the house to a building society for his own benefit, and nothing was paid by him to the nephew. Lee defaulted on the mortgage instalments and the building society claimed possession of the house. C sued Lee and the building society, seeking a declaration that the document that she signed was void on the ground of non est factum. Her claim was that she had not intended to sell the house to Lee, but rather she had intended to make a gift to her nephew.

The case is a good illustration of how a third party's rights may become involved where someone has mistakenly signed a document. The House of Lords (affirming the Court of Appeal's decision) held that the defence of non est factum could not be relied on by C in these circumstances. This was because, in the opinion of the judges, the document that she signed was not radically or totally different in character from the one that she thought she was signing. She intended that her nephew should be able to raise money by using the house as security, and it can be argued that this would have still been achieved under the document that she actually signed, but for Lee's dishonesty.[21] So this is the first limitation on the use of non est factum as a means of nullifying an apparent agreement.

12.59 The second limitation, and a further reason for C's claim being rejected, is that a party cannot rely on the defence where he or she has acted carelessly. The plea originated, as we have

21 Although this argument appears to overlook the fact that Mrs Gallie stipulated that she was to remain in occupation of the house during her lifetime.

seen, to protect those who could not read, at a time when illiteracy was widespread. Despite the subsequent development of the doctrine to cover a wider group of people, it is surely correct that someone who has been careless should not be able to rely on it as a means of escape from a document that they have signed. Otherwise it would be difficult for anyone to have confidence in the validity of a signature on a document and this would be extremely inconvenient in commercial matters. A person who has broken his glasses can usually delay signing a document until they have been repaired. Mrs Gallie was, regrettably, careless and the decision was therefore correct.

12.60 This point is also illustrated in *United Dominions Trust Ltd* v *Western* (1976), where D agreed to buy a car from dealers on hire purchase. In addition to the payment of a deposit, D signed a blank copy of a finance company's (C's) standard form agreement and left the dealers to fill in the relevant details. When the form was forwarded by the dealers to the finance company it contained inaccuracies about the price of the vehicle and the size of the deposit paid by D. The claimant company accepted the figures as correct and that the signed document formed a contract between themselves and D. D later found out that the figures did not represent what he had agreed with the dealers but he took no action to remedy the mistake. He paid no instalments under the agreement and the claimants claimed £750, which was the incorrect price stated on the form signed by D. The Court of Appeal found in favour of the claimants. It is clear that where a person signs a blank form and leaves someone else to fill in the details, he cannot argue that he failed to consent to the figures that are inserted. The signer of a blank document is careless, and no sensible distinction can be made between this situation and that where a person carelessly signs a completed document.[22]

12.61 We have seen the ways in which the scope of the defence of non est factum has been curtailed by decisions of the courts.[23] But, assuming that the signer has not been careless[24] (presumably to be judged by the standards of that person), and that the document signed was radically different from that which it was supposed to be, what types of people can rely on the plea? Those who have signed as a result of some deception will be able to; so too will those who are unable to understand the meaning of a document through no fault of their own, without having it explained to them, 'whether that be from defective education, illness or innate incapacity' (per Lord Reid in *Saunders* v *Anglia Building Society* [1971] AC 1004 at 1016).

12.62 The defence was successfully relied on in *Lloyds Bank plc* v *Waterhouse* (1990). This involved an illiterate defendant who signed a bank guarantee of his son's debt, without either reading the document or indicating that he was unable to read it. However, he had done his best, by asking questions, to ascertain the nature and extent of his liability, and the bank's employees had misrepresented the nature of the document to him. The Court of Appeal allowed the

22 Also note that the plea of non est factum is not open to a person who signs a document in the belief that it is 'just a form', having no precise idea as to its nature; see *Gillman* v *Gillman* (1946).

23 The restrictive approach of the courts is further illustrated by *Norwich and Peterborough Building Society* v *Steed (No 2)* (1993).

24 For further discussion, see *AL Factors Ltd* v *Pamela Morgan* (1999).

defendant's appeal; various reasons were given to support this decision, including the negligent misrepresentation of the bank. Woolf LJ did not deem it necessary to decide the issue of non est factum, but Purchas LJ had no doubts that the defence was successfully established by the defendant. He explained that the defendant's illiteracy was clearly a disability; that the signed document was different from that which he thought he was signing; and that the defendant was not careless, having 'energetically investigated the ambit of the guarantee from the outset'.

12.63 It might be safer, though, to regard the case as decided on the basis of negligent misrepresentation, rather than non est factum. It is surely questionable whether the defendant exercised proper care for his own protection. It might also be questioned whether the document actually signed by the defendant was radically or fundamentally different in character from the one that he thought he was signing.

Summary

- It is important to understand that some mistakes relate to whether the parties have reached *agreement*, whilst others involve questions of *performance*.
- In relation to 'performability', and the extent of contractual obligations, there is a connection between the subject of mistake and the doctrine of frustration (see **Chapter 19**).

Agreement mistake

- It will be remembered that the law takes a predominantly objective view of agreement (see **Chapter 2**).
- In cases of mistake as to identity, the law usually has to determine which of two innocent parties should bear the loss.
- The case law on mistake as to identity is unsatisfactory and the topic was considered by the House of Lords in *Shogun Finance Ltd* v *Hudson* (2003). Unfortunately, the majority in this case failed to take advantage of an opportunity to rationalize this area of law.
- Agreement mistake can also arise where the parties are at cross-purposes. Generally, parties are bound by their apparent agreements (judged objectively), but there may be situations where there is no contract due to inherent ambiguity.
- In the interest of justice, a court may grant relief against the consequences of mistake: for example, a court may exercise its discretion to refuse specific performance. Rectification is another equitable remedy.

Performability mistake

- Common mistake is where both parties share the same misapprehension about some underlying fact which makes the performance of the contract impossible or devoid of purpose.
- Where a contract is made for the sale of goods which have already ceased to exist, the outcome ought to turn on the construction of the agreement between the parties (see *Couturier* v *Hastie* (1856)).

- However, *Couturier* v *Hastie* led to a belief that in cases of non-existent goods the 'contract' will be void. (This interpretation was reflected in the Sale of Goods Act 1893 (now 1979), s 6.)
- Outside this category of cases involving non-existent goods, there are few instances of a contract being void for common mistake.
- The House of Lords in *Bell* v *Lever Bros* (1932) illustrates the fact that a mistake as to quality will not usually render a contract void.
- After *Solle* v *Butcher* (1950) it was thought that a court may set a contract aside in equity on the basis of a common mistake, although it was never clear how this more flexible approach could be reconciled with the decision in *Bell* v *Lever Bros*.
- The Court of Appeal in *Great Peace Shipping Ltd* v *Tsavliris* (2003) has concluded that *Solle* v *Butcher* cannot be regarded as good law, as it is inconsistent with *Bell* v *Lever Bros*.

Further reading

A. Chandler et al., 'Common Mistake: Theoretical Justification and Remedial Inflexibility' (2004) (Jan) JBL 34

P. Davies, 'Rectification versus Interpretation: The Nature and Scope of the Equitable Jurisdiction' (2016) 75(1) CLJ 62

A. De Moor, 'Intention in the Law of Contract: Elusive or Illusory?' (1990) 106 LQR 632

C. Elliott, 'No Justice for Innocent Purchasers of Dishonestly Obtained Goods: Shogun Finance v Hudson' (2004) (May) JBL 381

A. Foster, 'Sale by a Non-Owner: Striking a Fair Balance between the Rights of the True Owner and a Buyer in Good Faith' (2004) 9 Cov LJ 1

D. Friedmann, 'The Objective Principle and Mistake and Involuntariness in Contract and Restitution' (2003) 119 LQR 68

C. Hare, 'Identity Mistakes: A Missed Opportunity?' (2004) 67(6) MLR 993

C. MacMillan, 'How Temptation Led to Mistake: An Explanation of *Bell v Lever Bros Ltd*' (2003) 119 LQR 625

C. MacMillan, 'Mistake as to Identity Clarified' (2004) 120 LQR 369

C. MacMillan, 'Rogues, Swindlers and Cheats: The Development of Mistake of Identity in English Contract Law' (2005) 64 CLJ 711

C. MacMillan, *Mistakes in Contract Law*, Hart Publishing, 2010

D. McLauchlan, 'The "Drastic" Remedy of Rectification for Unilateral Mistake' (2008) 124 LQR 608

D. McLauchlan, 'Refining Rectification' (2014) 130 LQR 83

C. Nugee, 'Rectification after Chartbrook v Persimmon: Where Are We Now?' (2012) 26(2) Tr L I 76

A. Phang et al., 'Mistaken Identity in the House of Lords' (2004) 63 CLJ 24

C. Slade, 'Myth of Mistake in the English Law of Contract' (1954) 70 LQR 385

J. C. Smith, 'Contracts—Mistake, Frustration and Implied Terms' (1994) 110 LQR 400

M. Smith, 'Rectification of Contracts for Common Mistake, *Joscelyne v Nissen*, and Subjective States of Mind' (2007) 123 LQR 116

T. Yeo, 'Great Peace: A Distant Disturbance' (2005) 121 LQR 393

Chapter 13

Misrepresentation

Introduction

13.1 An operative misrepresentation (i.e. one which has legal effect) is basically a false statement of existing or past fact made by one party to the contract to the other, before, or at the time of, contracting, on which that other party relied in contracting. (Whether there is also a requirement that the misrepresentation should be material is considered later (see para. **13.39**).)

13.2 The person to whom a misrepresentation, or alleged misrepresentation, is made is referred to as the 'representee'. The person making the misrepresentation, or alleged misrepresentation, is the 'representor'.

13.3 Much discussion may occur before a contract is made. In the course of that discussion one party may make a statement to the other which subsequently proves to be untrue. The other party will feel aggrieved if he, or she, relied upon that statement in entering into the contract. What can be done? If that statement became a term of the contract, or of a collateral contract, then there is a breach of contract and the injured party can take action accordingly (see **Chapter 20**). If it did not become a term, there is no possibility of a remedy for breach. However, a remedy may lie for misrepresentation. This means that, when a dispute arises over a pre-contractual statement which has proved to be false, the injured party will often raise two arguments,[1] namely that:

1. the statement became a term;
2. the statement was an operative misrepresentation.

1 There might be the possibility of an action for mistake, but such an action lies within very narrow boundaries and has limited chances of success—see **Chapter 12**.

13.4 Misrepresentation is divided into different types; the classification is particularly important when the representee wishes to claim damages for the misrepresentation. Until the 1960s the classification was only twofold. Misrepresentations were either fraudulent or innocent (i.e. not fraudulent). There was no reason to separate negligent from wholly innocent misrepresentations because damages were available only for fraudulent misrepresentations (through the tort of deceit), and rescission was available for all misrepresentations. Because of the availability of damages we now differentiate four types of misrepresentation:

1. fraudulent misrepresentation—damages available under the tort of deceit;
2. a misrepresentation which is also a negligent misstatement, so that the damages are available for the tort of negligent misstatement;
3. a misrepresentation for which damages are available under s 2(1) of the Misrepresentation Act 1967 (i.e. the misrepresentor cannot prove that he or she believed the truth of what was misrepresented, and that there were reasonable grounds for doing so, up until the time the contract was made);
4. innocent misrepresentation, i.e. misrepresentations not falling within the above categories. No damages are available for innocent misrepresentation, as such, but s 2(2) allows the court to award damages in lieu of rescission where the misrepresentation is non-fraudulent.

The second and third categories are often both referred to as negligent misrepresentation,[2] but do need to be kept distinct.

13.5 However, even when the common law provided damages only for fraudulent misrepresentation, equity allowed rescission for all misrepresentations. If rescission occurs, the parties return to their pre-contractual positions. Rescission is the carrying into effect of the decision to treat a voidable contract as if it had never been made. It is a radical remedy and there are bars on its availability.

13.6 The topic of misrepresentation is difficult because of the involvement of the common law (including, frequently, tort), equity, and statute (Misrepresentation Act 1967 (MA 1967)). It is not an area which provides a ready means of redress for the consumer. The consumer organization Which? has commented:[3]

> The availability of existing remedies is patchy at best. Furthermore, where protection does exist, the remedies are too complex for consumers to understand and as a consequence are rarely used.

2 Obviously, within the third category it is not tortious negligence which is in question, and it is for the misrepresentor to establish his belief and its reasonableness. Nevertheless, as the action under MA 1967, s 2(1) is based upon the absence of reasonable belief—despite the fact that the absence of reasonable grounds for belief is not proven but merely not disproved—negligent misrepresentation is a more apt label than innocent misrepresentation for the third category, even though it has occasionally, confusingly, been referred to as innocent misrepresentation (e.g. *Royscott Trust Ltd* v *Rogerson* (1991) per Balcombe LJ).

3 Quoted in The Law Commissions, *Consumer Redress for Misleading and Aggressive Practices* (Law Com No 332, Scot Law Com No 226) para. S.18.

Against this background, the Law Commission proposed a simpler, more 'rough and ready' approach for consumers[4] and, with regard to misleading and aggressive practices, there are now the Consumer Protection (Amendment) Regulations 2014, amending the Consumer Protection from Unfair Trading Regulations 2008.

13.7 The Consumer Protection from Unfair Trading Regulations 2008 provide public enforcement by 'enforcers', primarily the Competition and Markets Authority (CMA),[5] to deal with misleading and aggressive commercial practices, and unfair commercial practices more broadly, through criminal sanctions and enforcement orders. The 2014 Regulations add to the 2008 Regulations, so that redress is now provided for the individual consumer, in relation to misleading and aggressive practices, to be able to 'unwind' contracts (which is similar to, but simpler, than rescinding) or receive a discount on the price and, in some cases, recover damages. The definition of consumer is 'an individual acting for purposes that are wholly or mainly outside that individual's business'.[6] A 'trader' is a 'person acting for purposes relating to that person's business, whether acting personally or through another person acting in the trader's name or on the trader's behalf'. Most contracts between such parties will be covered, but not those involving land transactions (other than residential leases)[7] or financial services.[8] (Land and financial services contracts were not generally regarded as suitable for the certain, but simple, 'rough and ready' remedies which were proposed, and they are also covered by other regulations.) Obviously, we are here concerned with 'misleading' commercial practices: aggressive practices are looked at in the chapter on duress and undue influence (**Chapter 14**).

What constitutes an operative misrepresentation?

13.8 As was stated earlier, an operative misrepresentation is, basically, a false statement of existing or past fact made by one party to the contract to the other, before or at the time of contracting, which induces the other party to contract. (Whether the misrepresentation must also be material is considered later (see para. **13.39**).)

13.9 As we shall see, the term 'statement' can be misleading because, although there is no general duty to disclose relevant facts in pre-contract negotiations, there are some circumstances in which a misrepresentation is found to have occurred because of something which the representor has omitted to say or write. In addition, it is possible to base a misrepresentation on physical appearance rather than on an oral or a written statement.

4 The Law Commissions, *Consumer Redress for Misleading and Aggressive Practices* (Law Com No 332, Scot Law Com No 226) para. S.18.

5 A list of relevant enforcers is provided under Sch 5 of the Consumer Rights Act 2015.

6 Regulation 2(1) Consumer Protection from Unfair Trading Regulations 2008 as amended by the Consumer Protection (Amendment) Regulations 2014.

7 Regulation 27C of the Consumer Protection from Unfair Trading Regulations 2008 (as amended by the Consumer Protection (Amendment) Regulations 2014).

8 Regulation 27D of the Consumer Protection from Unfair Trading Regulations 2008 (as amended by the Consumer Protection (Amendment) Regulations 2014).

13.10 There are two basic points to be considered when asking what constitutes an operative misrepresentation: (1) which 'statements' are capable of being misrepresentations, and (2) under what circumstances is the appropriate sort of 'statement' operative, that is, under what circumstances does it have legal effect as a misrepresentation? In simple terms, the first of these requirements is for a false statement of existing or past fact. For that statement then to constitute an operative misrepresentation, it must have been relied upon by the person to whom it was made in contracting with the person who made it. (It will be considered later whether in addition it must be material so that it would have been relied on by a reasonable person in making the decision to contract (at para. **13.39**).)

The misrepresentation

13.11 For a misrepresentation, there must be a false statement of existing or past fact. Statements of opinion or intention will not suffice in themselves, but they must be given careful consideration. A statement of fact may often be found where initially there appears to be only a statement of opinion, or intention. (In the past there was also an exclusion of statements of law, but it has now been held that these can found a restitutionary action for mistake (*Kleinwort Benson Ltd* v *Lincoln City Council* (1999)), and they should similarly be capable of constituting misrepresentations (*Pankhania* v *Hackney LBC* (2002)).)

Statements of intention

13.12 A statement of intention cannot, in itself, constitute a misrepresentation. A statement of fact is required. However, a statement of intention carries with it an implied statement of fact as to the state of mind of the representor. If someone falsely states their intention, then they have falsely misrepresented the fact that they hold that intention. In *Edgington* v *Fitzmaurice* (1885) 29 Ch D 459, Bowen LJ said (at 483):

> The state of a man's mind is as much a fact as the state of his digestion. It is true that it is very difficult to prove what the state of a man's mind at a particular time is, but if it can be ascertained it is as much a fact as anything else. A misrepresentation as to the state of a man's mind is, therefore, a misstatement of fact.

This is illustrated by the facts of *Edgington* v *Fitzmaurice*:

> The directors of a company issued a prospectus inviting subscriptions for debentures, that is, they were seeking to raise money. The prospectus stated that it was intended to use the money obtained to make improvements in the company's business by altering its buildings, purchasing horses and vans, and developing its trade. The real intention was to use the money obtained to pay off existing debts of the company.

It was held that a fact had been misrepresented because there was no intention to use the money in the manner stated.

Statements of opinion

13.13 In *Bisset* v *Wilkinson* [1927] AC 177 it was held that there was no misrepresentation. The statement made was only a statement of opinion and not fact. In that case:

> Mr Bisset wished to sell a piece of land in New Zealand. He told Mr Wilkinson that the land would support 2,000 sheep. No one had previously used the parcel of land in question as a sheep farm. Mr Wilkinson purchased the land. It failed to support 2,000 sheep.

The Privy Council held that the statement as to the capacity of the land did not constitute a misrepresentation. As that parcel of land had not previously been used for sheep farming, it was purely a statement of opinion and not one of fact.

13.14 Where an opinion is stated which is not held, however, the same reasoning applies as that used in *Edgington* v *Fitzmaurice* (1885). A misrepresentation of the representor's state of mind would have occurred (*Bisset* v *Wilkinson* [1927] AC 177 at 182). In such a situation, where there is a straightforward lie as to the opinion held by the representor, it is obvious where the misstated fact can be found but, even in the absence of such fraud, the line between opinion and fact has not proved to be as distinct as might at first be thought. The opinions of experts, or those in the best position to have ascertained the truth of the matter, create obvious difficulties when it is sought to distinguish between opinion and fact. An opinion given by such a person is likely to be treated as a statement of fact and, often quite reasonably, relied upon. In such circumstances, the courts have endeavoured to find that statements of fact have been made.

13.15 Despite an apparent statement of opinion, a misrepresentation was found in *Smith* v *Land and House Property Corpn* (1884) 28 Ch D 7.

> The claimant put a hotel up for sale. The particulars stated that it was 'let to Mr F. Fleck (a most desirable tenant), at a rental of £400 per annum, for an unexpired term of twenty-seven and a half years'. Mr Fleck was not a desirable tenant; he had not been paying his rent on time, and he was in arrears.

The court held that the statement as to Mr Fleck's suitability as a tenant was not merely a statement of opinion. The landlord was in a much better position than anyone else to know what sort of a tenant there was on the property. There was an implied misrepresentation. Bowen LJ said (at 15):

> [I]f the facts are not equally known to both sides, then a statement of opinion by the one who knows the facts best involves very often a statement of a material fact, for he impliedly states that he knows facts which justify his opinion.

The misrepresentation provided an answer to the claimant's claim for specific performance of the sale contract and the defendants were able to rescind.[9]

13.16 In *Brown* v *Raphael* (1958) the line was taken that, in this type of case, the fact which is being misrepresented is that the representor had reasonable grounds for his or her opinion or belief. Such a representation, that an opinion is based on reasonable grounds, will be found to have been made where the person stating his or her opinion is in a better position than the other party to know, or to find out, the truth. *Brown* v *Raphael* concerned the sale of a reversion. Its value depended upon the tax position of the person with the life interest. The buyer could not ascertain this and had to depend upon the statement of the seller indicating that the tax position was favourable. The question was whether this was a misrepresentation or merely a statement of opinion. It was held that it was a misrepresentation. One party knew the facts far better than the other could know them. The opinion on the tax position carried with it the implied statement of fact that the seller had reasonable grounds for that belief. There was a misrepresentation, as the seller had no such grounds.

13.17 The above argument should also apply in cases where the facts are accessible to either party but one party is an expert and he or she states an opinion on a matter within that area of expertise. The expert will impliedly state that he or she has reasonable grounds for that opinion. If the expert has not considered the question at all, or has been negligent in coming to a conclusion, then it would seem that the courts will be willing to find a misrepresentation. In *Esso Petroleum Co. Ltd* v *Mardon* (1976), an expert's assessment of the potential sales by a new petrol station was made negligently, without due consideration of all the facts. It was decided that there was a breach of an implied term that the expert would take due care in his assessment and also that there was a claim in tort for negligent misstatement. The point to note here is the court's obvious willingness to find a statement of fact in the statement of opinion by an expert, although the case was not decided on the basis of misrepresentation.

13.18 However, where the basic facts are best known to one party, but that party lacks the specialist knowledge or expertise needed to be able to draw reliable conclusions from them as to the matter stated, it would seem that no implied misrepresentation of fact will then be found. A statement by an ordinary consumer, with no specialist knowledge, as to the value of the contents of a flat containing his belongings and those of his parents did not imply that he had a reasonable basis for the value stated in making a contract of insurance (*Economides* v *Commercial Union Assurance Co. plc* (1997)).

No general duty to disclose

13.19 The law does not impose any general duty on a contracting party to disclose relevant facts to the other party and, in general, silence does not constitute a misrepresentation. In most cases the law allows a party to profit from his superior knowledge. It is possible to view this as

9 See also *Crédit Lyonnais Bank Nederland* v *Export Credits Guarantee Dept* (1996).

economically efficient, for otherwise the incentive to acquire information would be removed.[10] It is also the case that the lack of a general duty to disclose prevents the problems and uncertainties which would arise in determining what information should fall within the duty. However, there are exceptions to the general rule, which are considered below.[11]

13.20 *Turner* v *Green* (1895) provides an example of the operation of the general rule. In that case:

> Turner and Green were engaged in a legal dispute. Turner's solicitor, Fowler, reached a settlement with Green on behalf of his client. Before concluding that agreement, Fowler did not reveal to Green that other proceedings had taken place which made the settlement disadvantageous to Green.

When Turner claimed specific enforcement of the agreement, Green tried to rely upon the non-disclosure to resist the claim. The court held that mere non-disclosure of a material fact could not provide a basis for rescission or a denial of specific performance. It did not constitute a misrepresentation.[12]

Partial non-disclosure

13.21 The situation is different if there is not complete silence on a particular matter which is being dealt with, but partial disclosure. This occurs where what has been stated is literally true but is misleading because of other facts which have been omitted. In *Notts Patent Brick and Tile Co.* v *Butler* (1886):

> Butler wished to sell a piece of land which was subject to several restrictive covenants, one of which precluded its use as a brickyard. The claimant company, which manufactured bricks, wished to purchase the land to use in its business. The company inquired of Butler's solicitor whether the land was subject to any restrictive covenants. The solicitor stated that he was not aware of any but did not add that he had not inspected the relevant documents. The company contracted to purchase the land and paid a deposit.

The solicitor's reply was literally true, but misleading because he did not add that he had not inspected the relevant documents. There was a misrepresentation which entitled the purchaser to rescind the contract and recover the deposit. The same line was taken in *Dimmock* v *Hallett* (1866) where an estate was for sale. One of the farms on it was described as let to a certain tenant at £290 per year. It was not stated that the tenant had paid only £1 for the three months he leased the farm before his year's occupation, nor was it stated that he had left the farm and no

10 A. Kronman, 'Mistake, Disclosure, Information and the Law of Contracts' (1978) 7 JLS 1.

11 There are also other ways in which there may be liability if there has been no disclosure of defects in the goods or limitations on what they are fit to do, e.g. under the terms implied by s 14(2) (satisfactory quality) and s 14(3) (reasonable fitness for the buyer's particular purpose) of the Sale of Goods Act 1979.

12 See also *Keates* v *Cadogan* (1851); *Fletcher* v *Krell* (1872).

new tenant had been found for it, even at a lower rent. Again, what was said was literally true but, without the additional details, it constituted a misrepresentation.[13]

Change of circumstances

13.22 A statement of fact may be made which is true at the time it is made, but which has ceased to be true before the contract which it has induced is concluded. Under these circumstances, if the person making the representation knows of the change in the facts, there will be a misrepresentation if he fails to disclose it. In *With* v *O'Flanagan* (1936):

> O'Flanagan wished to sell his medical practice. In January he told With that the practice brought in about £2,000 a year. The contract for the sale of the practice was made in May. In the intervening months O'Flanagan was unwell and the practice became practically worthless. In the three weeks before the sale the takings of the practice averaged only £5 a week.

The change in the facts should have been revealed and failure to do so meant that the contract could be rescinded.[14] Two possible ways in which the misrepresentation could be seen to be occurring were identified. First, the misrepresentation could be the silence itself, on the basis that the initial statement had given rise to a duty to disclose the changes. Second, the misrepresentation could merely lie in the initial statement which is then seen as a continuing representation which becomes a misrepresentation with the change in the facts.[15] Whether there is a statement which can be regarded as a continuing representation and eventually a misrepresentation, or whether it is the silence itself which forms the basis of the right to rescind, is relevant to the question of whether or not the Misrepresentation Act 1967 can apply to the above situation. That Act applies where a misrepresentation is made and this is inapt to cover the situation where it is silence as such which is being dealt with.[16]

Fiduciary or confidential relationships

13.23 Where there is a fiduciary relationship, such as where the parties are principal and agent (*Armstrong* v *Jackson* (1917)), there will be a duty to disclose material facts. However, more than mere disclosure will be required if the relationship is one giving rise to the presumption of undue influence, such as solicitor and client or trustee and beneficiary. Such transactions may well be set aside unless the 'weaker party' has received independent advice (on undue influence, see **Chapter 14**).

13 See also *Atlantic Lines & Navigation* v *Hallam Ltd (The 'Lucy')* (1983) (see para. **13.38**); *Spice Girls* v *Aprilia* (2002) at [59].

14 See also *Davies* v *London and Provincial Marine Insurance Co.* (1878); *Reynell* v *Sprye* (1852) 1 De GM & G 660 at 708; *Shelley* v *United Artists Corpn* (1990). But see *Thomas Witter Ltd* v *TBP Industries Ltd* (1996).

15 *With* at 583–4 per Lord Wright MR; *Spice Girls* v *Aprilia* (2002) at [51].

16 *Banque Financière de la Cité SA* v *Westgate Insurance Co.* (1989).

Contracts uberrimae fidei

13.24 In relation to contracts uberrimae fidei (contracts of the utmost good faith), a duty to disclose material facts is imposed. In such contracts one party is usually in a far better position than the other to know or ascertain the relevant facts. Contracts of insurance form the main type of contracts uberrimae fidei. Contracts relating to family settlements are also contracts uberrimae fidei.[17] Other contracts are related to contracts uberrimae fidei and require more limited disclosure, for example, a surety contract.

Misrepresentation by conduct

13.25 A misrepresentation may stem from conduct. There are examples from the criminal law, which supply analogies in the context of misrepresentation. In *R* v *Barnard* (1837) the defendant wore the cap and gown of a university student to persuade an Oxford bootmaker to supply him with bootstraps. This form of dress was held to amount to a false pretence. A more up-to-date example is provided by the idea that in merely sitting down in a restaurant and ordering a meal there is an implied representation that the person concerned has the funds to pay for the meal (*Ray* v *Sempers* (1974)). In *R* v *Charles* (1977) it was held that the use of a cheque card carries with it a representation that the user has the bank's authority to use the card. In the context of misrepresentation itself, in *Spice Girls* v *Aprilia* (2002), attendance by all of the original Spice Girls at a commercial advertising shoot was part of the misrepresentation that the Spice Girls did not know, or have reasonable grounds to believe, that any of them intended to leave the group during the minimum term of the advertising agreement they were about to enter into. (Geri Halliwell had already told the other Spice Girls of her intention to leave before then.)

Misleading practices

13.26 It can be seen that the law on what constitutes a misrepresentation is complex, and would not be easy for the consumer to understand. The Consumer Protection from Unfair Trading Regulations (as amended by the 2014 Regulations) avoid the distinction between fact and opinion, and should be less difficult in relation to the situations where a failure to state something may be a misleading practice. The basic conception of the Law Commissions is that a commercial practice is misleading if it contains false information, or if it is likely to mislead the average consumer in its overall presentation.[18] There is no category of misleading omissions as

17 E.g. *Gordon* v *Gordon* (1821).

18 The 2008 Regulations contain a list of matters in relation to which the commercial practice must be misleading. The Law Commissions' proposals have simplified the situation in relation to enforcement by the consumer by omitting this list, but it is currently used for these purposes in Part 4A of the Consumer Protection from Unfair Trading Regulations (For the list see Regulations 5(4)–(7) of the Consumer Protection from Unfair Trading Regulations 2008). The Regulations also maintain the reference to 'deceiving', rather than 'misleading', the consumer. The Law Commissions preferred 'misleading' to 'deceiving' as '[t]he word "deceive" is ambiguous. Although it is often used to refer to deliberate dishonesty, we do not think that is what is meant in this context . . . The emphasis is on its effect on an average consumer, rather than the state of mind of the trader' (para. 7.23).

such, but the Law Commission felt that providing for the overall presentation to be misleading would deal with such omissions as could be dealt with without making the law too cumbersome, complex, or unclear to consumers, although they also thought that should be kept under review.[19]

13.27 The Law Commissions provided examples of omissions which they viewed as misleading through the overall presentation. For example:

> A consumer buys a lawnmower, which works satisfactorily, but the consumer is not aware that the mower requires an unusual and hard to obtain fuel.[20]

The Law Commission was of the view that:[21]

> The type of fuel would obviously be an important matter to the average consumer, as without the fuel the lawnmower would be useless. The average consumer would expect to be able to obtain appropriate fuel for a lawnmower they buy. If the trader fails to make the consumer aware that this will be very difficult, then we think the overall presentation is misleading.

When is a misrepresentation operative?

The parties to the contract

13.28 The person making the misrepresentation must become a party to the contract with the person to whom it was made (for example, *Hasan* v *Wilson* [1977] 1 Lloyd's Rep 431 at 431). However, agency can, of course, be as relevant here as elsewhere and it may suffice if the misrepresentation is conveyed by a third party to the misrepresentee, if the misrepresentor intended that to happen to induce the misrepresentee to contract.[22]

Reliance

13.29 In order for a misrepresentation to be operative, it must have been relied upon. It must have induced the contract. In *Smith* v *Chadwick* (1884), no remedy lay for a misrepresentation which had played no part in the claimant's decision to contract. There the prospectus of a company contained the false statement that a certain person of local importance, a Mr Grieve, was one of the directors. The claimant purchased shares in the company on the faith of the

19 The Law Commissions, *Consumer Redress for Misleading and Aggressive Practices* (Law Com No 332, Scot Law Com No 226) paras 7.3–7.61.

20 The Law Commissions, *Consumer Redress for Misleading and Aggressive Practices* (Law Com No 332, Scot Law Com No 226) para. 7.26, example from H. Collins, *A Private Right of Redress for Unfair Commercial Practices: A Report for Consumer Focus* (April 2009).

21 The Law Commissions, *Consumer Redress for Misleading and Aggressive Practices* (Law Com No 332, Scot Law Com No 226) para. 7.27.

22 E.g. *Pilmore* v *Hood* (1838); *Commercial Banking of Sydney* v *R H Brown & Co.* (1972).

prospectus but he had never heard of Grieve and he admitted that Grieve's name in the prospectus had not influenced him. The misrepresentation that Grieve was a director could not provide a basis for a claim in damages for fraud, as it had not been relied upon.

13.30 The requirement of reliance means that there are certain situations where there cannot be an operative misrepresentation. For example, there cannot be an operative misrepresentation where the misrepresentation is not known about, or the truth is known. Similarly, there will not be an operative misrepresentation where the representee decides not to rely upon the representor's statement but upon his, or her, own investigation of the facts.

13.31 *Horsfall* v *Thomas* (1862) 1 H & C 90 provides an example of a case where the misrepresentation was not known to the person whom it was meant to mislead.[23] That case concerned the sale of a defective gun. The defect, a soft spot in the metal, was concealed by a metal plug, but this did not constitute an operative misrepresentation. The gun had not been examined by the buyer and the metal plug could not have affected his judgment. Bramwell LJ said (at 99):

> If the plug, which it was said was put in to conceal the defect, had never been there, his position would have been the same; for as he did not examine the gun or form any opinion as to whether it was sound, its condition did not affect him.

Similarly, there will not be an operative misrepresentation where, although the misrepresentation is known about, it is corrected before the contract is made.[24]

13.32 The situation may be that the misrepresentation is not operative because, although it was known to the representee, it was not relied upon because the representee chose to rely upon his or her own investigation of the facts stated. In *Attwood* v *Small* (1838):

> Attwood was selling a mine. He made exaggerated and untrue statements as to its earning capacity. Before agreeing to buy the mine, Small sent his own experts to assess the mine's capacity. They concurred in Attwood's assessment.

When the true situation was discovered, the purchaser claimed to rescind for misrepresentation. The House of Lords held that the action for rescission failed. The purchaser had relied upon his own experts rather than the vendor.

13.33 Obviously, a misrepresentation cannot be held to have induced a contract where the representee knew it to be untrue before the contract was made. However, the misrepresentation

23 See also *Re Northumberland and Durham District Banking Co., ex p Bigge* (1859).

24 *Peekay Intermark Ltd* v *Australia and New Zealand Banking Group Ltd* (2006); *Cramaso LLP* v *Ogilvie-Grant* (2014) (SC) at [20].

will still be effective, provided it was relied upon, if there was merely an opportunity to discover the truth and that opportunity was not taken. In *Redgrave* v *Hurd* (1881):

> Mr Redgrave, a Birmingham solicitor, wished to sell his practice. Mr Hurd wished to establish himself in practice as a solicitor and agreed to make the purchase. Before Mr Hurd agreed, Mr Redgrave told him that the practice brought in £300–£400 a year. Mr Hurd was given an opportunity to examine the accounts but did not do so. Had he done so they would have revealed that the business was worth only about £200 a year.

The misrepresentation meant that Mr Hurd could rescind. The mere opportunity to discover the truth did not prevent rescission, provided the representee had relied upon the misrepresentation. (In relation to a claim for reduction in damages for non-fraudulent misrepresentation in this type of situation see para. **13.64** in relation to contributory negligence.)

Degree of reliance

13.34 Consideration now needs to be given to the degree of reliance required if a misrepresentation is to be operative. It would seem that a distinction needs to be drawn between fraudulent and non-fraudulent misrepresentations.

13.35 The first point to note is that it is clear that the misrepresentation need not have been the sole factor inducing the contract in order for it be operative. In *Edgington* v *Fitzmaurice* (1885):

> Revd Edgington was induced to take debentures in a company. He made the decision partly because of a misrepresentation in the prospectus (see para. **13.12**) and partly because of his own mistaken belief that the debenture holders would have a charge on the company's leasehold property. Revd Edgington admitted that he would not have become a debenture holder in the absence of his mistaken belief.

Revd Edgington was able to claim damages for deceit despite his mixed motives. It was not necessary to show that the misrepresentation was the sole cause of his contracting.

13.36 However, what is the level of reliance required in order for the misrepresentation to be operative? This problem was commented on by the Privy Council in *Barton* v *Armstrong* [1976] AC 104. In that case the Privy Council had to deal with a claim that a contract was affected by duress in the form of threats to the person, and the counter argument that the contract was valid because it would have been made even if the threats had not been uttered. Nevertheless, the situation in relation to misrepresentation was considered. It was said (at 118–19):

> Had Armstrong made a fraudulent misrepresentation to Barton for the purpose of inducing him to execute the deed . . . the answer to the problem would have been clear. If it were established that Barton did not allow the representation to affect his judgment then he could

> not make it a ground for relief even though the representation was designed . . . to affect his judgment. If on the other hand Barton relied on the misrepresentation Armstrong could not have defeated his claim to relief by showing that there were other more weighty causes which contributed to his decision to execute the deed . . . Their Lordships think that the same rule should apply in cases of duress and that if Armstrong's threats were a reason for Barton's executing the deed he is entitled to relief even though he might well have entered into the contract if Armstrong had uttered no threats to induce him to do so.

The Privy Council clearly envisaged that a misrepresentation could still be operative even though the contract might have been concluded had it not been made: they were not applying the 'but for' test (i.e. 'but for' the misrepresentation, would the contract have been made on those terms?). The decision to contract can be seen as a weighing process, and it is sufficient if the misrepresentation went into the scales on the side favouring the making of the contract.

13.37 However, *Barton* v *Armstrong* (1976) was a case of duress by threats of physical violence, and the analogy is with fraudulent misrepresentation rather than misrepresentation more generally; outside of fraudulent misrepresentation, the 'but for' test generally applies: the situation must have been such that 'but for' the misrepresentation, that contract would not have been made. The less stringent test in relation to fraud would seem to be a matter of deterrence.

13.38 A 'but for' approach was taken in *Atlantic Lines & Navigation* v *Hallam Ltd (The 'Lucy')* (1983), for example, with Mustill J taking the line that Hallam had failed to satisfy him that they would not have entered into a sub-charter of the ship, at the same rate of hire, had there not been a misrepresentation as to the restrictions on the voyages the ship could make under the head charter. The requirement has been expressed in different ways, such as whether the misrepresentation was a 'real and substantial part' of the claimant's decision to contract in *JEB Fasteners Ltd* v *Marks Bloom & Co. (a firm)* (1983), but in *Raiffeisen Zentralbank Österreich AG* v *Royal Bank of Scotland* (2010) it was made clear that this did require the 'but for' test to be satisfied in relation to the misrepresentation (at [170]): the misrepresentation does not have to be the only 'but for' factor relied upon, but it does have to be a 'but for' factor.[25]

Materiality

13.39 Materiality may assist the misrepresentee. A misrepresentation is 'material' if it would have induced the reasonable person to contract. If a misrepresentation is material then the court will infer that it did induce the contract, and it will be for the misrepresentor to prove otherwise (*Museprime* v *Adhill* (1990); *County Natwest* v *Barton* (2002)). The inference is particularly strong where the misrepresentation is fraudulent (*Ross River Ltd* v *Cambridge City Football Club* (2007) at [241]).

25 There will need to be some 'common sense relaxation' of this where the agreement was 'induced by two concurrent causes . . . so that it could not be said that, but for either the agreement would not have been made', as has been recognized in relation to economic duress (see *Huyton SA* v *Peter Cremer GmbH* [1999] CLC 230 at 250).

13.40 However, there is a question as to whether there is a requirement of materiality, that is, a requirement that a misrepresentation must have been such as to induce the reasonable person to contract. General statements as to the requirements of a misrepresentation are often found to include materiality (e.g. *Pan Atlantic Ins. Co. Ltd* v *Pine Top Ins. Co.* (1994)) and such a requirement is obviously necessary where silence as such can give rise to the right to rescind, for example, in relation to contracts uberrimae fidei, such as a contract of insurance. In that type of situation the question of materiality is referred to in order to determine which facts must be disclosed. The question is whether there is any broader requirement.

13.41 The fraudulent misrepresentor cannot rely upon a claim that his misrepresentation was not such as to have induced the reasonable person to contract (*Smith* v *Kay* (1859)). In addition, it is suggested that 'a remedy will be given where the representor knows or ought to know that the representee is likely to act on the representation' (*Chitty on Contracts*, 32nd edn, para. 7-041). The real area of dispute would seem to lie in relation to other negligent and purely innocent misrepresentations, with innocent misrepresentations obviously raising the strongest case for a requirement of materiality before the misrepresentee will have a remedy. In *MCI Worldcom* v *Primus* (2004), whilst allowing for the position to be different where fraud was present, Mance LJ indicated some requirement of materiality. He said (at [30]):

> whether there is a representation and what its true nature is must be judged objectively according to the impact that would have on a reasonable representee in the position and with the known characteristics of the actual representee.

Further, there may be some indication of a need for a requirement of materiality in *Avon Insurance* v *Swire Fraser* (2000) in the approach taken to the question of when a statement is untrue, introducing into that context the concept of inducement of the reasonable person. In that case the claim was based on s 2(1) of the Misrepresentation Act 1967 (so the representee did not have to establish negligence, but merely the existence of a misrepresentation, leaving it to the representor to disprove negligence—see para. **13.49**ff) and the court took the line that the inaccuracy of some incorrect representations is not sufficiently significant for them to be regarded as untrue and misrepresentations. Rix J said (at 579):

> a representation may be true without being entirely correct, provided that it is substantially correct and the difference between what is represented and what is actually correct would not have been likely to induce a reasonable person in the position of the claimants to enter into the contract.

The idea that mere 'puffs' are not misrepresentations (*Dimmock* v *Hallett* (1866)) may also, at least partly, be a reflection of a materiality requirement (*Chitty on Contracts,* 32nd edn, para. 7-041).

Misleading practices

13.42 The Law Commission took the view that in relation to the remedies provided to consumers against traders with regard to misleading practices, an objective test (akin to materiality) should be applied, and the misleading practice should be required to have been a 'significant factor' in the particular consumer's decision to contract.[26] Requiring it to be a 'significant factor' in relation to the particular consumer's decision to contract is obviously less strict than applying a 'but for' test. The Law Commissions thought 'it would be unrealistic to expect consumers to prove that without the commercial practice they would not have entered into the contract at all. Often there will be no way of telling why a consumer acted in that particular way following an aggressive or misleading practice. As behavioural science suggests, there are many unpredictable factors affecting consumers' decisions'.[27] Of course, the objective test has also to be satisfied so that the consumer will have to establish not only the significance of the misleading practice to them, but also that it would have been likely to have caused the average consumer to contract. This might seem particularly harsh in relation to the non-average, particularly vulnerable consumer. However, although generally the 'average consumer' is 'reasonably well informed, reasonably observant and circumspect', the 'average consumer' is the average member of a particular group where a clearly identifiable group of consumers is particularly vulnerable to the practice because of their mental or physical infirmity, age, or credulity in a way which the trader could reasonably be expected to foresee.[28]

Damages and types of misrepresentation

13.43 Rescission may be thought of as the primary remedy for misrepresentation. It is a very radical remedy and, unlike damages, it is available for all types of misrepresentation. Nevertheless, damages will be considered first. It is principally in the context of damages that it is necessary to distinguish the different types of misrepresentation, and it is convenient to classify misrepresentations when considering the issue of damages. The various types of misrepresentation are classified according to the state of mind of the misrepresentor.

13.44 It is, of course, possible to claim damages and to rescind the contract. For example, in *F & H Entertainments Ltd* v *Leisure Enterprises Ltd* (1970) the plaintiffs were able both to rescind and to recover damages under MA 1967, s 2(1). However, the courts will always strive to prevent a 'double recovery' and no damages should be available to cover a loss which has effectively been wiped out by rescission.

The types of misrepresentation which we must consider are:

1. fraudulent misrepresentations (damages are available through the tort of deceit);
2. misrepresentations which are also negligent misstatements (damages are available through the tort of negligent misstatement);

26 Regulation 27A(6) of the Consumer Protection from Unfair Trading Regulations 2008 (as amended by the Consumer Protection (Amendment) Regulations 2014) states: 'The third condition is that the prohibited practice is a significant factor in the consumer's decision to enter into the contract or make the payment.'

27 The Law Commissions, *Consumer Redress for Misleading and Aggressive Practices* (Law Com No 332, Scot Law Com No 226) para. 7.108.

28 See The Law Commissions, *Consumer Redress for Misleading and Aggressive Practices* (Law Com No 332, Scot Law Com No 226) para. 7.106; Regulation 2(5) of the Consumer Protection from Unfair Trading Regulations 2008.

3. misrepresentations coming within MA 1967, s 2(1);
4. wholly innocent misrepresentations, that is, misrepresentations not coming within any of the above categories.

However, Reg 5 of the Consumer Protection (Amendment) Regulations 2014 adds s 2(4) to the MA 1967, which prevents persons from bringing claims under s 2 MA 1967 'if the person has a right to redress under Part 4A of the Consumer Protection from Unfair Trading Regulations 2008 . . . in respect of the conduct constituting the misrepresentation'. As a result, s 2 does not apply to contracts between traders and consumers unless the subject matter of the contract is one which is not covered by the new regime, such as a land transaction (except a residential lease) or financial services transactions.

Fraudulent misrepresentations

13.45 The frequently cited definition of fraud is that of Lord Herschell in *Derry* v *Peek* (1889) 14 App Cas 337. He said (at 374):

> [F]raud is proved when it is shown that a false misrepresentation has been made, (1) knowingly, or (2) without belief in its truth, or (3) recklessly, careless whether it be true or false.

However, although this dictum is frequently cited, it must be treated with care if it is not to mislead. The essence of fraud is a lack of belief in the truth of the statement made. Despite the reference to carelessness, there is no fraud if the misrepresentor believes his statement to be true. Negligence and fraud are clearly distinct. 'The test for fraud is subjective and the question in the case of each defendant is whether he honestly believed to be true any representations that he intended to make.'[29] In *Derry* v *Peek*:

> The directors of a company issued a prospectus stating that it had the right to operate trams driven by steam power. The respondent purchased shares in the company on the faith of that statement. The company had the right to operate horse-drawn trams only. The use of steam-powered trams was conditional upon the company obtaining the consent of the Board of Trade. That consent was not given and the company was wound up.

The respondent sued the directors for damages in deceit. The trial judge had found that the directors honestly believed that their statements were true and, on that basis, the House of Lords found that there was no fraud and the action failed.

13.46 If the appropriate state of mind is present, the motive is not relevant to the question of fraud. It is irrelevant that there was no intention to cheat anyone or cause any loss by the untrue statement (*Polhill* v *Walter* (1832)). There is no requirement of 'dishonesty' in

29 *Maple Leaf* v *Rouvroy* (2009) per Andrew Smith J at [327].

the criminal law sense (*Standard Chartered Bank* v *Pakistan National Shipping Corpn (No 2)* (2000) at [27]).

13.47 Damages are available for a fraudulent misrepresentation by taking action in tort for deceit. Damages are measured according to tort principles rather than contractual principles.[30] In tort the aim is to give damages which will put the party back in the position he or she was in before the tort occurred (reliance loss). In the situation we are concerned with, tort damages will attempt to restore the representee to the position he or she would have been in had the misrepresentation not been made. They are not awarded to put the representee in the position he or she would have been in had the misrepresentation been true; that would be like awarding the contractual measure of damages. If we were dealing with an action for breach of contract, the aim of damages would be to put the injured party in the position he or she would have been in had the contract been fulfilled; that is, contract damages can cover the injured party's expectation loss, the benefit he or she would have derived from completion of the contract (see para. **20.2**ff).

13.48 However, in a sense it would oversimplify matters to say that contract damages can encompass lost profit whilst tort damages cannot. An action for damages for deceit (or under MA 1967, s 2(1), or for negligent misstatement) can encompass a claim for the 'opportunity cost' of reliance on the misrepresentation, that is, the representee cannot recover the profit he or she would have made had the misrepresentation been true (the contract measure of damages) but can recover for the profit he or she would have made had he or she not relied upon the misrepresentation, and used his or her resources in another way. In *East* v *Maurer* (1991), where the representee bought a hairdressing business on the basis of a fraudulent misrepresentation, the damages did not cover the profit that would have been made had the misrepresentation been true. But a sum was awarded for the profit which the representee would have made had he purchased a different hairdressing business in the area. A further example of tortious damages covering the 'opportunity cost' can be provided by the situation where a loan of £10,000 has been made on the basis of a negligent misrepresentation. The tortious measure of damages cannot provide for recovery of the interest which would have been paid under the particular contract, but they can encompass damages for the loss of the use of the £10,000 whilst it was locked up in that contract.[31]

13.49 It seems unlikely that the action for deceit will be much used now. Where the action for damages under MA 1967, s 2(1) is available, that will generally be preferable. Under s 2(1) the representee does not have to establish fraud or even negligence. Instead, it is for the representor to establish his or her reasonable belief in the truth of what was misrepresented, if he or she is to escape liability. Even the common law action for damages for negligent misstatement will often be preferable to the action for deceit. That action requires the representee to prove only negligence, and not fraud, on the part of the representor. However, there are a few ways in

30 *Doyle* v *Olby (Ironmongers) Ltd* (1969); *Smith Kline & French Laboratories Ltd* v *Long* [1989] 1 WLR 1 at 6.

31 See *Swingcastle* v *Alastair Gibson* (1991); see also *Clef Aquitaine* v *Laporte Materials* (2000) for a further example in relation to fraud.

which it may be beneficial to sue for deceit rather than for negligent misstatement. The test of remoteness may be less of a hurdle in relation to damages for deceit than for negligent misstatement. The normal tort test of remoteness, used in relation to a claim based on negligence, is that of 'reasonable foreseeability'. In *Doyle* v *Olby (Ironmongers) Ltd* [1969] 2 QB 158 the Court of Appeal indicated that all that is required in an action for deceit is that the damage 'flowed' from the deceit. Lord Denning said (at 167):

> [T]he defendant is bound to make reparation for all the actual damages flowing from the fraudulent inducement . . . it does not lie in the mouth of the fraudulent person to say that [the damage] could not reasonably have been foreseen.[32]

This may prove very significant in terms of the damages which are recoverable.[33]

13.50 However, on the current state of the law, a claim for damages under MA 1967, s 2(1) has the advantages of the claim for deceit which are denied in an action for negligent misstatement. In *Royscott Trust Ltd* v *Rogerson* (1991) the Court of Appeal stated that the test for remoteness of damage under s 2(1) was the laxer test used in deceit, rather than that used in relation to negligence test. The court came to that conclusion on the basis of the fiction of fraud in s 2(1) and, thus, on this reasoning any other advantages in the deceit action for damages could also apply to a claim for damages under s 2(1). This must be questioned, however, and some divergence of approach has already been indicated in relation to the issue of whether damages should be reduced for the injured party's contributory negligence.[34] More broadly, this equation of the treatment of damages for fraud and that under s 2(1), must be questioned in principle. Special treatment of fraud may be justified as deterrence and on the basis of morality. The same arguments do not apply when the misrepresentation falls under s 2(1) (see further at para. **13.63**). In any event, even without the advantages associated with the action for fraud, the damages claim under s 2(1) is usually preferable to a claim based on negligent misstatement at common law.

Negligent misstatements

13.51 The tort action for negligent misstatement was established in *Hedley Byrne & Co. Ltd* v *Heller & Partners Ltd* (1964). It requires not only proof of a lack of reasonable grounds for the representor's belief in the truth of what he, or she, asserted, but also that he or she owed the representee a duty of care.

13.52 As was indicated earlier, when damages are awarded in tort for negligent misstatement it will be on the tort basis of returning the injured party to the position he or she was in before the tort occurred (reliance loss). Unlike the contractual measure, it will not seek to put

32 See also Winn LJ at 168 and Sachs LJ at 171; G. Treitel, 'Damages for Misrepresentation' (1969) 32 MLR 556.

33 Contrast *Smith New Court Securities Ltd* v *Scrimgeour Vickers (Asset Management) Ltd* (1996) and *South Australia Asset Management Corpn* v *York Montague Ltd* (1996).

34 See *Alliance and Leicester Building Society* v *Edgestop Ltd* (1994) and *Gran Gelato Ltd* v *Richcliff (Group) Ltd* (1992)—see para. **13.64**.

the injured party in the position he or she would have been in had the statement been true, that is, the injured party will not be awarded his or her expectation loss. However, as we have seen, the possibility exists of claiming tort damages to cover the 'opportunity cost' of reliance on the misrepresentation, that is, the loss of the opportunity to use elsewhere resources committed to the contract. (See *Swingcastle* v *Gibson* (1991); *East* v *Maurer* (1991).)

13.53 Note that, in an action for negligent misstatement, not only must the representee establish the duty of care but it is also for the representee to prove that the representation was made negligently, and this contrasts with MA 1967, s 2(1).

Misrepresentation Act 1967, s 2(1)

13.54 The Misrepresentation Act 1967 resulted from the tenth report of the Law Reform Committee in 1962 (Cmnd 1782), which recommended that damages should be available for negligent misrepresentation. Of course, the courts did provide a damages remedy for negligent misstatement in *Hedley Byrne & Co. Ltd* v *Heller & Partners Ltd* (1964). Nevertheless, the Act provides for damages in s 2(1) and it is the statutory remedy which deserves the greater consideration here.

13.55 Section 2(1) states:

> Where a person has entered into a contract after a misrepresentation has been made to him by another party thereto and as a result thereof he has suffered loss, then, if the person making the misrepresentation would be liable to damages in respect thereof had the misrepresentation been made fraudulently, that person shall be so liable notwithstanding that the misrepresentation was not made fraudulently, unless he proves that he had reasonable grounds to believe and did believe up to the time the contract was made that the facts represented were true.

This deals with the situation where X falsely states a fact, Y enters into a contract in reliance upon it, and X cannot establish that he, or she, had reasonable grounds for believing that fact to be true. The reference to fraud imports the requirement that the 'misrepresentation' should be a misrepresentation within the definition given above, that is, a statement of existing or past fact. It can be strongly contended that it should go no further, but the current line is that it also affects the calculation of damages under s 2(1) (see para. **13.62**ff).

Advantages/disadvantages of an action under s 2(1)

13.56 Section 2(1) reverses the burden of proof from that which applies under the tort action for negligent misstatement. This is very important as it makes an action under s 2(1) a much easier way to obtain damages than an action which relies upon liability in tort for negligent misstatement. Under s 2(1) the representee has only to establish that he or she entered into a contract in reliance upon a misrepresentation made by the other party to the contract, and that he or she suffered loss thereby. It will then be for the representor to prove that, until the time the contract was made, he or she had reasonable grounds for his or her belief in the truth of the representation. If the representor cannot establish the reasonableness of his or her belief, the representor will be liable in damages.

13.57 Section 2(1) has a further advantage over the tort action for negligent misstatement. It does not require a duty of care to have existed between the parties. It merely requires that the misrepresentation should have led to a contract between representor and representee.

13.58 The importance of the burden of proof in s 2(1), and of the lack of any requirement of a duty of care, are both illustrated by the case of *Howard Marine & Dredging Co. Ltd* v *A Ogden & Sons (Excavations) Ltd* (1978):

> Ogden wished to hire barges from Howard Marine. During the negotiations Howard Marine told Ogden that the carrying capacity of their barges was 1,600 tonnes. Ogden and Howard Marine concluded a contract of hire. Ogden used the barges, and the work for which they were required fell behind schedule. Ogden discovered that the true carrying capacity was only 1,055 tonnes and refused to continue paying the hire charge.

Howard Marine sued Ogden for the hire charge. Ogden counterclaimed under s 2(1), and in tort for negligent misstatement. In the Court of Appeal, Ogden succeeded by a majority decision. Shaw LJ and Bridge LJ found for Ogden under s 2(1) on the basis that Howard Marine had not shown that they had reasonable grounds for their belief that the capacity was 1,600 tonnes. Lord Denning MR dissented as he thought that Howard Marine had established that their belief was reasonable. The importance of the distinctions between s 2(1) and the tort action for negligent misstatement is revealed in the fact that Howard Marine would have won had Ogden had to rely upon the tort action for negligent misstatement. Neither Lord Denning MR nor Bridge LJ thought that Howard Marine had owed a duty of care to Ogden. That prevented Ogden from succeeding in the tort action for negligent misstatement. In addition, even if there had been a duty of care, Bridge LJ thought that there was no evidence to establish that Howard Marine had been negligent and breached that duty. Shaw LJ was alone in thinking that Ogden could succeed in an action in tort for damages for negligent misstatement. If Ogden had not been able to make a claim under s 2(1), they would have lost by a majority decision in the Court of Appeal, rather than winning by one.[35]

13.59 However, s 2(1) can be used only where the negligent misrepresentation was made by one party to a contract to the other party before the contract was concluded. The tort claim for negligent misstatement is not linked to the making of a contract. For example, a claim can be made in tort for negligent misstatement against a third party to a contract. *Hedley Byrne & Co. Ltd* v *Heller & Partners Ltd* (1964) itself concerned a claim against a third party. The tort claim could relate to a statement made during pre-contractual negotiations which did not lead to a

35 R. Taylor, 'Expectation, Reliance and Misrepresentation' (1982) 45 MLR 139; J. Cartwright, 'Damages for Misrepresentation' [1987] Conv 243.

contract. In addition, the lack of any requirement for the existence of a contract means that the action could be used if a contract had apparently been made but was found to be void for mistake. An action under s 2(1) is doubtful if the contract is void. It should also be noted that a claim in tort for negligent misstatement is not dependent upon there being a misrepresentation in the sense indicated above.

Assessment of damages under s 2(1)

13.60 As has been indicated, the basis for the calculation of damages differs in contract and tort. It is more appropriate that damages under s 2(1) should be assessed on the basis of the rules in tort rather than contract, because s 2(1) is not dealing with a legally enforceable promise. Where there is a promise in the form of a contract term, it is apt that the damages for its non-fulfilment, its breach, should attempt to put the injured party in the position he or she would have been in had the promise been fulfilled (i.e. to compensate for the expectation loss). Section 2(1) does not relate to contract terms and promises, but to mere representations. The injured party has entered into a contract in reliance upon the representation and suffered loss thereby, but as he or she is not suing on a broken promise (a broken term), damages covering expectation loss would be inappropriate. It is apt to adopt the tort approach to damages, and undo the harm caused by the misrepresentation by putting the representee back in the position he or she was in before the misrepresentation (i.e. to compensate for the reliance loss).

13.61 Some of the earlier decisions dealing with damages under s 2(1) pointed towards the contract measure of damages,[36] but it is now clear that it is the tort measure of damages which is used under s 2(1) and the reference to fraud in s 2(1) is seen as providing a basis for this,[37] although it could simply be arrived at as a matter of principle. In *Chesneau* v *Interhome Ltd* (1983) counsel had argued that damages under s 2(1) should be assessed on the principles applied to damages in tort. Everleigh LJ said:

> For myself, I think that that is probably correct . . . The subsection itself says: '. . . if the person making the misrepresentation would be liable to damages in respect thereof had the misrepresentation been made fraudulently, that person shall be so liable. . .'. By 'so liable' I take it to mean liable as he would be if the misrepresentation had been made fraudulently.

13.62 Subsequently, the reference to fraud in s 2(1) was taken further, arguably well beyond its proper bounds. In *Royscott Trust Ltd* v *Rogerson* (1991), the Court of Appeal stated that damages under s 2(1) should be calculated as if they were damages for fraud, and applied the laxer remoteness test which is used in relation to deceit rather than that applied to negligent misstatement (see para. **13.49**). The court's conclusion was based upon the reference to fraud in s 2(1). *Royscott* concerned the hire purchase of a car (i.e. the dealer sells the car to the finance house, and the finance house contracts with the customer for its hire purchase). The car dealer

36 *Gosling* v *Anderson* (1972); *Jarvis* v *Swans Tours* (1973); *Watts* v *Spence* (1976).

37 *Chesneau* v *Interhome Ltd* (1983); *Sharneyford Supplies* v *Edge* [1987] 2 WLR 363 at 376 per Balcombe LJ (CA), [1985] 1 All ER 976 per Mervyn Davies J; *Naughton* v *O'Callaghan* (1990); *Royscott Trust Ltd* v *Rogerson* (1991).

and the customer misrepresented to the finance company that the customer was supplying a higher deposit than he was. They did so because the finance company did not undertake transactions unless the customer was supplying at least a 20 per cent deposit. The customer did not finish paying the instalments to the finance company before selling the car to a third party, who acquired good title to it. The finance house brought an action for damages under s 2(1) against the dealer. The Court of Appeal held that the loss through the sale of the car did not have to pass the remoteness test of reasonable foreseeability, which would be applied in the tort of negligent misstatement, but merely the laxer remoteness test applied to deceit. However, in dealing with a point relating to causation, the court also held that it was reasonably foreseeable that the customer would sell the car to a third party. The court's comments on the applicability of a remoteness test derived from deceit could be regarded as unnecessary to the decision.

13.63 The point should be made that the equation of s 2(1) and fraud is not easy to justify in principle and may be open to question in the future. In *Smith* v *Scrimgeour Vickers* [1996] 4 All ER 769, where the court was concerned with fraud, Lord Browne-Wilkinson made no comment as to the correctness of the decision in *Royscott Trust Ltd* v *Rogerson* (1991), but it is worth noting, in particular, Lord Steyn's consideration of the justification for the wider availability of damages for fraud than for negligence. He noted that deterrence may be in question and that 'in the battle against fraud civil remedies can play a useful role'. In addition, he noted 'moral considerations'. He said (at 790):

> That brings me to the question of policy whether there is a justification for differentiating between the extent of liability for civil wrongs depending on where in the sliding scale from strict liability to intentional wrongdoing the particular civil wrong fits in. It may be said that logical symmetry and a rule of not punishing wrongdoers by civil remedies may favour a uniform rule. On the other hand it is a rational and defensible strategy to impose wider liability on an intentional wrongdoer. As Hart and Honoré, *Causation in the Law* (2nd edn, 1985) at p. 304 observed: 'an innocent [claimant] may, not without reason, call on a morally reprehensible defendant to pay the whole of the loss he has caused'. The exclusion of heads of loss in the law of negligence, which reflects considerations of legal policy, does not necessarily avail the intentional wrongdoer.

Such arguments militate against the 'fiction of fraud' in s 2(1) being used to justify damages being awarded in exactly the same way as if the misrepresentor had been fraudulent, rather than as merely indicating a tortious measure, and *Royscott* has been criticized by other courts.[38]

13.64 Some divergence of approach between an action for deceit and an action under s 2(1) has been indicated in relation to the question of whether the injured party's damages will be reduced for contributory negligence.[39] The Law Reform (Contributory Negligence) Act 1945

38 E.g. *Avon Insurance* v *Swire Fraser* (2000) at 578–81; *Cheltenham BC* v *Laird* [2009] EWHC 1253 (QB), [2009] IRLR 621 at [524].

39 A. Oakley, 'Contributory Negligence of a Fraudulent Misrepresentee' [1994] CLJ 219.

applies where 'any person suffers damage as the result partly of his own fault and partly of the fault of any other person'. (Fault is defined in s 4—see para. **20.67**.) Where that is the situation, the damages recoverable shall be reduced to such an extent as the court thinks just and equitable having regard to the claimant's share in responsibility for the damage. It has been held that this does not apply to an action based on deceit,[40] but is the same approach taken in relation to a claim based on s 2(1)? *Royscott Trust Ltd* v *Rogerson* (1991), and its approach to the fiction of fraud, indicates that it would be, but the analogy made in *Gran Gelato Ltd* v *Richcliff (Group) Ltd* [1992] 1 All ER 865 was with an action for negligent misstatement. Where there was concurrent liability in tort and under s 2(1), it was held that contributory negligence was applicable to the claim under s 2(1). In *Gran Gelato*, liability under MA 1967, s 2(1) was seen (at 875) as 'essentially founded on negligence', and that being so it was seen as 'very odd if the defence of contributory negligence were not available as a defence to a claim under that Act'. However, having decided that the 1945 Act applied, Nicholls V-C then concluded that a reduction of the damages would not be 'just and equitable' for the claimant in *Gran Gelato*. He said (at 876):

> The essential feature of the present case is that Gran Gelato's claim, both at common law and under the 1967 Act, is based on misrepresentation. Richcliff intended, or is to be taken to have intended, that Gran Gelato should act in reliance on the accuracy of [its answers]. Gran Gelato did so act. In those circumstances it would need to be a very special case before carelessness by Gran Gelato, the representee, would make it just and equitable to reduce the damages payable . . . In principle, carelessness in not making other inquiries provides no answer to a claim when the [claimant] has done that which the representor intended he should do.

Thus, damages were not reduced in that case, and the reference to 'carelessness in not making other inquiries . . . where the [claimant] has done that which the representor intended him to do' might cover situations like that in *Redgrave* v *Hurd* (1881). However, the comments of Lord Hoffmann in *Standard Chartered Bank* v *Pakistan National Shipping Corpn* (2003) at [9]–[18] would indicate that the Law Reform (Contributory Negligence) Act 1945 might more readily be raised where the claimant's negligence lies not in a failure to discover the truth of the misrepresentation, but in concluding the contract because of a negligent misunderstanding of other factors. So, if the misrepresentation were negligent rather than fraudulent, the Act might more readily cover the type of situation which arose in *Edgington* v *Fitzmaurice* (1885) (see para. **13.35**) where the Reverend Edgington invested in debentures partly because of the misrepresentation and partly because he misunderstood the nature of debentures.[41]

40 *Alliance and Leicester Building Society* v *Edgestop Ltd* (1994); *Standard Chartered Bank* v *Pakistan National Shipping Corpn (No 2)* (2003).

41 The question of the applicability of contributory negligence to a claim based on breach of contract is dealt with at para. **20.66**ff.

Non-disclosure

13.65 Section 2(1) relates to misrepresentations which are 'made'. This language is inapt to cover silence, and it does not provide a right to damages where there is non-disclosure in circumstances where there is a duty to disclose. Section 2(1) does not apply to non-disclosure in contracts uberrimae fidei.[42] Given that, it is important whether cases such as *With* v *O'Flanagan* (1936) are regarded as continuing representations based on the statements made, which become misrepresentations with the change in circumstances, or as cases where what has been said has given rise to a duty to disclose further information and it is the non-disclosure itself which constitutes the misrepresentation. If the former is taken to be the mechanism by which a misrepresentation occurs, damages should be available under s 2(1) in such cases (A. Hudson, 'Making Misrepresentations' (1969) 85 LQR 524).

Damages in lieu of rescission (s 2(2))

13.66 Section 2(2) of the Misrepresentation Act 1967 is sometimes referred to as a statutory bar to rescission. In certain circumstances it permits the court to prevent rescission for non-fraudulent misrepresentation and award damages in lieu of rescission. This is considered further at para. **13.92**ff in relation to rescission.

Misleading practices

13.67 It should be remembered that s 2 of the Misrepresentation Act 1967 does not apply to situations falling within the scope of 'misleading and aggressive commercial practices'. Part 4A of the Consumer Protection from Unfair Trading Regulations 2008 (as amended by the Consumer Protection (Amendment) Regulations 2014) provides particular remedies for consumers in relation to misleading and aggressive commercial practices.[43] The primary remedies under the Regulations are 'unwinding' the transaction (which is similar to, but simpler than rescission) or a discount on the price. There will be scope for claims for damages for other losses—calculated on a reliance basis—including economic losses and damages for distress and inconvenience, but the consumer will have to establish those losses, and the trader will have a due diligence defence.

Innocent misrepresentation

13.68 Since the decision in *Hedley Byrne & Co. Ltd* v *Heller & Partners Ltd* (1964), and the Misrepresentation Act 1967, the category of innocent misrepresentations has ceased to encompass all non-fraudulent misrepresentations. Innocent misrepresentations are now simply those not covered by any of the categories just discussed. There is no damages remedy as such for

42 *Banque Financière de la Cité SA* v *Westgate (UK) Insurance Co.* (1989).

43 The Law Commissions, *Consumer Redress for Misleading and Aggressive Practices* (Law Com No 332, Scot Law Com No 226) para. 7.106; Consumer Protection from Unfair Trading Regulations 2008 (as amended by the Consumer Protection (Amendment) Regulations 2014).

innocent misrepresentation, although damages may be awarded in lieu of rescission under MA 1967, s 2(2).

Rescission

13.69 Although the common law allowed rescission where there was a fraudulent misrepresentation, it was equity which made it available for all types of misrepresentation. In addition, equity provided an action for rescission rather than merely recognizing the right, and was far more flexible than the common law when the contract was no longer entirely executory (see para. **13.77** on the bar of *restitutio in integrum*). In relation to misleading and aggressive practices under, or which led to, consumer contracts covered by Part 4A of the Consumer Protection From Unfair Trading Practices 2008 (as amended by the Consumer Protection (Amendment) Regulations 2014), the Regulations' primary remedy of 'unwinding' the transaction is similar to but more straightforward than rescission.

13.70 A misrepresentation renders a contract voidable at the option of the representee. This means that the contract can be rescinded and, in this context, rescission 'wipes out' the existence of the contract entirely and returns the parties to the positions they were in before the contract was made. It is *rescission ab initio* and must be distinguished from rescission for breach, which merely puts an end to the contract for the future. When a contract is rescinded for breach, its past existence is not disturbed. One effect of this is that, although damages may be available for misrepresentation as well as rescission, it should not be possible to rescind for misrepresentation and claim damages for breach. Once the contract has been rescinded for misrepresentation, there is no contract in relation to which damages for breach could be claimed. In contrast, termination for breach does not prevent any claim for damages for breach as the contract is only ended for the future. Some confusion can be avoided if the term 'rescission' is reserved for use in the context of voidable contracts, and 'termination' is used to describe the situation when a contract is ended after a breach.

13.71 Rescission may be a self-help remedy. It may be possible for the representee simply to tell the other party that he or she is electing to rescind. This is most obviously the case where the contract is still entirely executory and there has been no performance by either party. The right to rescind for misrepresentation will then serve to protect the representee if the representor tries to claim specific performance or sue for breach. Where the contract is not entirely executory, whether rescission requires the assistance of the court will depend on what has been done in performance of it. If, for example, the representee has received goods and handed over a cheque, he or she may still be able simply to return the goods and stop the cheque. However, if restoring the position before the contract was made requires the co-operation of the representor, it is likely that an appropriate order will have to be sought from the court. If, for example, the representor has received goods under the contract, the court may have to order their return. The situation is complicated where the subject matter of the contract has been altered in some way, and this problem will be considered later in relation to the bar upon rescission which occurs once the parties can no longer be returned to their pre-contract positions, that is, once *restitutio in integrum* is impossible.

13.72 In appropriate circumstances rescission can be achieved simply by notifying the representor of the election to rescind. In general, it is also necessary to inform the representor of the election to rescind. Merely coming to that decision and providing some evidence of it is usually insufficient. However, it seems that there is no need to inform the representor of the decision to rescind where the representee has simply retaken the property which he transferred under the voidable contract (*Re Eastgate, ex p Ward* (1905)). There is another, and more doubtful, exception to the need for communication in the case of *Car and Universal Finance Ltd* v *Caldwell* (1965). In that case:

> A Jaguar car was purchased from its original owner, Mr Caldwell, by Mr Norris, 'a rogue'. Norris paid by cheque and, when this proved to be worthless, Mr Caldwell wished to rescind but Norris and the car had disappeared. Mr Caldwell informed the police and the Automobile Association of the fraud and asked them to trace the car. Norris sold the car to a motor dealer with knowledge of the fraud, but it was eventually sold on to an innocent third party.

The question of ownership between Mr Caldwell, the original owner, and the innocent third party depended upon whether Mr Caldwell had rescinded before the sale to that innocent third party (see para. **13.85** on the bar to rescission where there has been a purchase by a bona fide third party). Norris had disappeared after the original sale, preventing the owner from communicating his election to rescind. Nevertheless, the Court of Appeal found that rescission had occurred. In informing the AA and the police, Mr Caldwell had done all he reasonably could, and he had clearly demonstrated his intention to rescind. In the circumstances, that was sufficient. The 'rogue', Norris, had intended to avoid actual communication of rescission when he had known that it would almost certainly be desired.

13.73 The decision in *Caldwell* is certainly beneficial to the original owner, but it means that the loss falls on the innocent third party purchaser. The court seems to have given too little consideration to the fact that it was, in effect, asked to determine which innocent party should bear the loss. In this situation one innocent party is bound to suffer a loss. Is it better that it falls on the party who was parting with money in return for goods, rather than on the party who was prepared to part with goods in return for a cheque? The decision seems unfortunate and has been criticized. There is every reason to confine it as much as possible, and it will probably not operate outside the sphere of fraudulent misrepresentations.[44]

Indemnity

13.74 There is a money remedy which may be used alongside rescission to help 'undo' the effects of the contract. It is called an 'indemnity' and it is available for all types of misrepresentation. It is a far more restricted money remedy than damages. It covers only the cost to the

44 See Law Reform Committee, 12th Report, Cmnd 2958, 1966, para. 16. In *Newtons of Wembley Ltd* v *Williams* (1965), where there was a direct sale from the rogue to the innocent third party, the innocent third party was held to acquire good title under Factors Act 1889, s 9. This limits the effect of *Caldwell* and makes an anomalous distinction between an innocent first purchaser directly from 'the rogue' and subsequent purchasers further down the chain.

representee of the obligations created by his contract with the representor. Given its restricted nature, an indemnity is unlikely to be appropriate where damages can be claimed. Its limited scope is illustrated by *Whittington* v *Seale-Hayne* (1900):

> The Whittingtons were breeders and exhibitors of prize poultry and wished to lease premises to carry on their business. The defendant assured them that his premises were in a sanitary condition, and the Whittingtons leased them on the basis of this innocent misrepresentation. In fact, the water supply was poisoned and Mr Cooper, the farm manager, fell ill and most of the poultry died. The local authority declared the premises unfit for habitation and required work to be done on the drains. Under the lease, the Whittingtons had to pay for that work. The Whittingtons rescinded the contract and also sought an indemnity. They claimed the cost of the rates and the repairs to the drains. In addition, they also claimed for their lost profit, their lost stock, their expenses in setting up the land as a poultry farm, and the medical bills of Mr Cooper, the farm manager.

The court held that only the rates and the repair bill could be covered by an indemnity. It could not extend beyond expenses which the lease had obliged the claimants to incur. Using the land as a poultry farm was their choice. The lease did not require them to spend money in that way, and the expenses connected with it could not be covered by an indemnity,[45] and, of course, lost profits would not even be covered by any damages claim for misrepresentation.

The bars to rescission

13.75 There are certain bars to rescission; once one of those bars comes into operation, the representee ceases to have the right to rescind the contract. The misrepresentee then has to be content with any remedy he or she may have in damages. The existence of a bar to rescission does not affect a claim to damages (*Production Technology Consultants Ltd* v *Bartlett* (1988)), except in relation to damages in lieu of rescission under s 2(2) (*Salt* v *Stratstone Specialist Ltd* (2015)). The common law bars can be listed:

1. *restitutio in integrum* is impossible;
2. third party rights;
3. affirmation;
4. lapse of time.

In addition, the courts' power to stop the representee from rescinding and to award him or her damages in lieu of rescission under MA 1967, s 2(2) is sometimes referred to as a 'statutory bar', and it is considered at para. **13.92**.

13.76 Section 1 of the Misrepresentation Act 1967 makes it clear that if the misrepresentation has also become a term, or if the contract has been performed, those events are not bars to rescission.

45 *Adam* v *Newbigging* (1886) per Bowen LJ, but see the judgments of Cotton and Fry LJJ.

Restitutio in integrum is impossible

13.77 Rescission takes both parties back to the position they were in before the contract was made. What if the contract is not wholly executory, but has been acted upon, so that it is not simply a matter of the representee informing the representor of his or her election? The court may order the return of property or money in order to restore the parties to their pre-contractual positions. The difficulties arise if property has been destroyed or altered and it is impossible to return the parties to their pre-contractual position. Representees cannot claim to be restored to their pre-contractual position if they cannot restore to the representor the property which was handed over by him or her under the contract. Under such circumstances, rescission is said to be barred because restitutio in integrum is impossible. (It is a matter of preventing the representee being unjustly enriched at the expense of the representor: *Halpern* v *Halpern (No 2)* (2007).) For example, where the representee bought shares in a partnership, he could not rescind on discovering the truth of the misrepresentation. The partnership had become a limited liability company in the meantime. The shares in the company were different in nature and status from those in the partnership. The representee could not give back what the representor had before the contract, that is, shares in a partnership (*Clarke* v *Dickson* (1858)).

13.78 However, in order for rescission to be possible, equity, unlike the common law, will not require that the parties be returned precisely to their pre-contractual positions. The courts

> can take account of profits and make allowances for deterioration. And I think the practice has always been for a court of equity to give this relief whenever, by the exercise of its powers, it can do what is practically just, though it cannot restore the parties precisely to the position they were in before the contract. (*Erlanger* v *New Sombrero Phosphate Co.* (1878) 3 App Cas 1218 at 1278–9)

13.79 Rescission in equity is possible on the basis of substantial restoration of the property and a payment to take account of the change. Where a company bought a phosphate mine and worked it, but did not exhaust it, the company was allowed to rescind on the basis that the mine could be substantially restored to the seller and the company would account to the seller for the profits obtained from working it (*Erlanger* v *New Sombrero Phosphate Co.* (1878)).

13.80 This type of approach was followed, quite recently, in *Salt* v *Stratstone* (2015). Mr Salt was a car enthusiast who purchased a Cadillac car, which had been stated to be 'brand new', from Stratstone in September 2007, at a price of £21,895. It manifested numerous defects, some of which were remedied by Stratstone, but in September 2008 Mr Salt had had enough and tried to return the car and get his money back. Stratstone refused, and in March 2009 Mr Salt commenced proceedings. He was initially claiming in relation to breach as to the quality of the car, but during the course of disclosure it came to light that the car was not 'brand new'. It had not had a registered owner prior to Mr Salt, but it was manufactured and delivered to Stratstone in 2005 and had undergone a series of repairs in 2005 and 2006, as well as being in a collision which damaged the front wheels. Obviously, at that point Mr Salt claimed on the basis of misrepresentation, as he would not have bought the car had it not been misrepresented as 'brand new'.

13.81 In the County Court the District Judge found that rescission was barred on the basis that *restitutio in integrum* was impossible, as the car had been registered and could not be returned as an unregistered car. He awarded damages of £3,250. Mr Salt appealed and the circuit judge found that rescission was not barred and ordered it. Stratstone appealed to the Court of Appeal.

13.82 The basic idea behind the bar because *restitutio in integrum* has become impossible was explained (at [2]):

> The remedy of rescission was . . . regarded as a mutual remedy; if a buyer wished to rescind the contract and recover the price which he has paid, he had to restore the article bought. If such restoration was impossible because the article had been consumed or changed in some way, the remedy of rescission was barred.

13.83 However, the Court of Appeal emphasized that rescission was the 'normal remedy' for misrepresentation, and should be awarded if possible, particularly in a case where the 'defendant makes no attempt to prove that he had reasonable grounds to believe his misrepresentation was true'. The Court found that although the car had been registered, and Mr Salt had had some use of it, rescission was not barred on the basis of the impossibility of *restitutio in integrum*. The 'registration' of the car was identified as a 'legal concept' which did 'not change the physical entity that a car is' (at [19]). There had been some depreciation of the car, and some use of it by Mr Salt, but the Court followed the line taken in *Erlanger* that rescission is prima facie available if 'practical justice' can be done. However, if 'practical justice' required the representor to be compensated for depreciation or the representee's benefit of the use of the car, it was for the representor to establish so, and in the instant case that had not occurred.

13.84 No precise rules have been formulated for the point at which equity will regard *restitutio in integrum* as impossible. The factors to be weighed in determining whether that point has been reached do not simply include the degree of change which the property has undergone. The fault of the representor will be considered. In *Spence* v *Crawford* [1939] 3 All ER 271, Lord Wright said (at 288):

> The court will be less ready to pull a transaction to pieces where the defendant is innocent, whereas in the case of fraud the court will exercise its jurisdiction to the full in order, if possible, to prevent the defendant from enjoying the benefits of his fraud at the expense of the innocent [claimant].

Further, as we have just seen, in *Salt* v *Stratstone* the Court of Appeal emphasized that the court would, in particular, try to find rescission possible where the misrepresentor had made no attempt to prove that he had reasonable grounds to believe his misrepresentation was true.

Third party rights—the bona fide third party purchaser

13.85 A contract is voidable for misrepresentation, and not void. We can illustrate the effect of this in relation to third party rights by reference to the sale of a car. Suppose that a 'rogue' purchases a car by means of a fraudulent misrepresentation. The contract for the sale of the car is valid until rescinded. Whilst the contract is valid the rogue has a voidable title to the car. If the rogue sells it to a bona fide third party before the contract is rescinded, the third party acquires a valid title which the original owner cannot defeat. This is why, in *Car and Universal Finance* v *Caldwell* (1965) (see para. **13.72**), Mr Caldwell was so anxious to convince the court that he had rescinded his contract with the rogue, Norris, before Norris sold the car to a bona fide third party. In that case Mr Caldwell recovered the car because the court, somewhat anomalously, accepted that rescission had occurred without communication to the rogue.

13.86 Where rescission has not occurred in time to prevent its being barred by a third party's rights, the argument is often raised that the contract is void for mistake, rather than merely voidable for misrepresentation (for example, *Lewis* v *Averay* (1972); *Phillips* v *Brooks* (1919)). In the rare cases where this is successful, it means that the contract never existed at all and that there was nothing to rescind—the rogue had no title to pass on to the third party, and the third party will not be able to use the above argument to defeat the original owner's claim to the car (for example, *Ingram* v *Little* (1961)).

Affirmation

13.87 As soon as the representee has learnt of the falsity of the misrepresentation, he or she can elect to affirm the contract or rescind it. Once the representee has affirmed, the right to rescind is lost. Affirmation may be express or implied. The representee may actually tell the representor of the decision not to rescind for misrepresentation, or affirmation may be implied from an act inconsistent with the representee having an intention to rescind. For example, the representee's continued use of the subject matter of the contract may amount to affirmation. Where a contract concerned the sale of shares, the right to rescind for misrepresentation was lost through delay and through continuing to act as a shareholder by attending, and participating in, a shareholder's meeting (*Sharpley* v *Louth and East Coast Railway* (1876)). An attempt to sell shares acquired on the basis of a misrepresentation may also constitute an affirmation (*Re Hop and Malt Exchange and Warehouse Co., ex p Briggs* (1866)). Similarly, where a misrepresentation induced the representee to lease machines from the representor, continued use of machines leased from the representor was held to amount to affirmation in *United Shoe Machinery Co of Canada* v *Brunet* (1909) (see also *Long* v *Lloyd* (1958)).

13.88 The possibility of affirmation arises only after the representee knows of the truth of the misrepresentation. In addition, it seems that there can be no affirmation if the representor did not know of the right to rescind even though he or she had discovered the truth of the misrepresentation. In *Peyman* v *Lanjani* (1985):

> Lanjani was the lessee of a restaurant. His title to the lease was defective as he had obtained the assignment of it to him by fraud. The fraud had involved M pretending to be Lanjani when dealing face to face with the landlord, as Lanjani was scruffy and spoke no English. Peyman agreed to purchase the lease from Lanjani. To obtain the landlord's consent to the

assignment, Lanjani again called upon M to impersonate him. Peyman learnt of that impersonation, and the earlier one which rendered Lanjani's title defective. Peyman had already become reluctant to continue with the sale but his solicitor, who was acting for both parties, advised him to continue. Before the landlord consented to an assignment to him, Peyman went into possession of the restaurant and paid £10,000 to Lanjani. A month later, Peyman went to another solicitor and was told that he had a right to rescind because of Lanjani's defective title.

Peyman gave notice of his decision to rescind. At first instance it was held that going into possession, and handing over payment, after he had discovered what had occurred meant that he had affirmed and could no longer rescind. The Court of Appeal held that Peyman had not lost his right to rescind. He had discovered the true facts, but he had acted without any knowledge that he had a legal right to rescind.[46]

13.89 However, the Court of Appeal in *Peyman* v *Lanjani* also considered the question of the representor being misled by an apparent, but not actual, affirmation into detrimentally relying upon the apparent affirmation. If an apparent affirmation occurs, the representee may be estopped from denying that he has affirmed the contract. No estoppel was found in that case, but such an estoppel will arise if the representor has relied upon the apparent affirmation to his detriment and there was nothing to indicate to the representor that the representee was acting in ignorance of either the truth, or the law.[47]

Lapse of time

13.90 Lapse of time can constitute evidence of affirmation,[48] but this relates to the situation where time has passed since the representee learnt the truth of the misrepresentation. Until the truth is known there can be no affirmation. However, in *Leaf* v *International Galleries* [1950] 2 KB 86 a five-year lapse between the making of the contract and the attempt to rescind barred rescission, although the representee attempted to rescind as soon as he discovered the truth. The lapse of time was held to constitute a bar in itself, at least in relation to an 'innocent' misrepresentation. (The case was decided before any distinction was made between the different types of non-fraudulent misrepresentation, and it would seem to relate to all non-fraudulent misrepresentations.) In *Leaf*:

In 1944, International Galleries represented to Mr Leaf that a painting they had for sale was by John Constable. Mr Leaf bought it for £85. In 1949, when he tried to sell the painting at Christie's, Mr Leaf discovered that it was not a Constable.

46 See also *Stevens & Cutting Ltd* v *Anderson* [1990] 1 EGLR 95 at 97; *Compagnia Tirrena di Assicurazioni SpA* v *Grand Union Insurance Co Ltd* (1991).

47 See also *Container Transport International Inc.* v *Oceanus Mutual Underwriting Association (Bermuda)* (1984).

48 *Clough* v *London and North Western Railway Co.* (1871) LR 7 Ex 26 at 35.

Mr Leaf tried to rescind the contract and obtain the return of the £85 from International Galleries. The Court of Appeal held that rescission was barred by lapse of time.[49] Jenkins LJ said (at 92):

> Contracts such as this cannot be kept open and subject to the possibility of rescission indefinitely . . . it behoves the purchaser either to verify or, as the case may be, to disprove the representation within a reasonable time.

13.91 However, in *Salt* v *Stratstone* (2015), in relation to lapse of time in itself, Roth J said (at [43]):

> it is something of a misnomer to say that rescission may be barred by lapse of time. It is only the lapse of a reasonable time such that it would be inequitable in all the circumstances to grant rescission which constitutes a bar to the remedy.

He emphasized that there had been no suggestion that Mr Salt could reasonably have discovered the true age of the car before seeing the documents disclosed during discovery related to the initial proceedings. It would seem that *Leaf* should be viewed as a case in which the misrepresentation should have been discovered much earlier by the misrepresentee.

Misrepresentation Act 1967, s 2(2)

13.92 As has already been indicated, s 2(2) is sometimes labelled as the statutory bar to rescission. It states:

> where a person has entered into a contract after a misrepresentation has been made to him otherwise than fraudulently, and he would be entitled, by reason of the misrepresentation, to rescind the contract, then if it is claimed in any proceedings arising out of the contract, that the contract ought to be or has been rescinded, the court or arbitrator may declare the contract subsisting and award damages in lieu of rescission, if of the opinion that it would be equitable to do so having regard to the nature of the misrepresentation and the loss that would be caused by it if the contract were upheld, as well as to the loss that rescission would cause to the other party.

Rescission is a very radical remedy. In relation to non-fraudulent misrepresentations, s 2(2) now gives the court a discretion to declare the contract subsisting and award damages in lieu of rescission where it 'would be equitable to do so'. This allows the court to substitute damages for rescission where the misrepresentation was fairly trivial and the radical nature of the remedy of rescission is not in keeping with the 'wrong' on which it was founded. The subsection requires account to be taken of 'the nature of the misrepresentation and the loss that would be caused by it if the contract were upheld, as well as the loss that rescission would cause to the other party'. This would seem to involve the weighing of these factors to decide if it would be

49 See also *Peco Arts* v *Hazlitt Gallery Ltd* [1983] 3 All ER 193 at 199–200.

'equitable' to deny rescission and award damages 'in lieu'. There are some examples of its use in the case law.

13.93 *William Sindall plc* v *Cambridgeshire County Council* (1994) indicates that rescission will be denied under s 2(2) where the misrepresentee is seeking it to escape from what has become a bad bargain for reasons unrelated to the misrepresentation. In that case:

> The builders, William Sindall plc, had purchased a piece of land from the council, to develop it. After that transaction was concluded, it took 18 months to obtain planning permission for their detailed development plans, and during that time the market slumped and the market value of the land was reduced from more than £5 million to £2 million. When the builders discovered a nine-inch sewer running through the land which had not been revealed by the council, they claimed that they had contracted with the council on the basis of a misrepresentation. The council had stated that, to its knowledge, there were no such incumbrances on the land. The builders claimed that there was effectively nothing which could be done to deal with the problem created for their development by the drain and claimed to be able to rescind the contract. The drain problem was remediable at a cost of approximately £18,000. At first instance, a misrepresentation was found and rescission was not denied under s 2(2).

The Court of Appeal concluded that there was no misrepresentation but, *obiter*, considered how s 2(2) of the Misrepresentation Act 1967 would have been dealt with had an operative misrepresentation been found. The court indicated that it would not have allowed the builders to make use of a relatively minor misrepresentation to rescind, and to escape from what had become a bad bargain because of a general fall in the value of land (which was not connected to the misrepresentation).

13.94 In *UCB Corporate Services* v *Thomason* [2005] 1 All ER (Comm) 601 rescission was denied in a situation in which the misrepresentation was viewed as not causing any loss to the representee. In that case:

> The misrepresentors had provided guarantees in relation to a loan made by the claimant misrepresentee to a company. The company was wound up and it was sought to enforce the guarantees, but the misrepresentors did not have the money. They sought to reach a compromise with their creditors and eventually did so. A waiver agreement was signed, releasing the misrepresentors from the rest of their indebtedness on payment of a small part of the money owed. However, before the waiver agreement was reached, the misrepresentors supplied details of their financial position to the claimants which were misleading. The judge characterized the misrepresentations as 'multiple, intentional (though not fraudulent) and fundamental'. He concluded that had the waiver agreements not been signed, the claimants would have quickly petitioned for bankruptcy, but thought there was no indication that there would have been a better recovery in bankruptcy than under the waiver agreement. He concluded that the claimants had suffered no loss because of the misrepresentation and so rescission was denied under s 2(2).

The Court of Appeal took the same line as the judge at first instance: rescission was not allowed under s 2(2). It thought that the judge had obviously been aware of the nature of the misrepresentation and he was right to conclude that the claimants had suffered no loss because of it. In addition, 'it was common ground that [the misrepresentors] would face a massive liability if the waiver was rescinded' (i.e. they would again be liable under the guarantees) (at [50]).

13.95 The issue arises as to the calculation of the sum to be paid 'in lieu' of rescission under s 2(2) when rescission is denied. In *Sindall* v *Cambridgeshire* the court indicated how it would have measured damages in lieu of rescission under s 2(2) had that been required. It took the line that just as rescission should not have been available to protect the builders from the slump in the market price of the land, s 2(2) also should not reallocate that market risk from the builders back to the council. This dismisses any simple idea of calculating damages in lieu of rescission merely on the basis that they are given to put the representee in the position he or she would have been in had rescission been allowed. It may be that the basic principle behind the calculation of damages under s 2(2) is that they should replace the remedy of rescission, but with account being taken of any 'over compensation' which rescission would have provided—such as coverage of a drop in market value which is unconnected with the misrepresentation.

13.96 It should be noted that if the misrepresentation is not wholly innocent, the representee may be claiming damages as well as rescission. MA 1967, s 2(3) deals with the possibility of a claim for damages under s 2(1) and the court also awarding damages under s 2(2). It aims to prevent a double recovery by providing that damages awarded under s 2(1) should take account of any damages awarded under s 2(2). The damages remedy in s 2(1) should cover only those losses not falling within damages in lieu of rescission under s 2(2).

13.97 Section 2(2) applies where the representee 'would be entitled . . . to rescind', and the question arises as to whether the court can still award damages in lieu of rescission if rescission itself would be prevented by one of the common law bars. There had been some doubt on this issue,[50] but in *Salt* v *Stratstone* (2015) the Court of Appeal looked at the earlier conflicting High Court decisions and, although speaking *obiter*, made it clear that the potential for damages to be awarded in lieu of rescission under s 2(2) depended upon the right to rescind still existing: once it is barred, damages are not available under s 2(2). The Court also noted that, in any event, if the representor could not establish reasonable grounds for believing in the truth of the misrepresentation, damages would be available under s 2(1).

Misleading practices

13.98 The Law Commissions recommended a simplified set of remedies for the consumer in relation to misleading and aggressive commercial practices. Under Part 4A of the Consumer Protection from Unfair Trading Regulations 2008 (as amended by the 2014 Regulations), the primary remedy is 'unwinding' the contract. Like rescission, the basic idea is to return the parties

50 *Atlantic Lines & Navigation* v *Hallam Ltd (The 'Lucy')* (1983); *Thomas Witter Ltd* v *TBP Industries Ltd* [1996] 2 All ER 573, 590: *Floods of Queenferry* v *Shand Construction* (2000); *Government of Zanzibar* v *British Aerospace* (2000); Beale (1995) 111 LQR 385.

to their pre-contractual positions, but with much less uncertainty and in a 'rough and ready' way. So, where the consumer has made a purchase of goods from the trader or contracted for services then, provided the consumer is able to reject some element of the goods or services within three months (90 days), it is simply a matter of the consumer getting a refund of the whole price. (The consumer must have indicated rejection within the relevant period. That does not have to be in writing. 'It may be by something said or done, but it must be clear.')[51] Of course, the remaining goods have to be made available to the trader, or returned. The bars to rescission, as such, do not arise. The consumer is not prevented from being able to unwind because he or she cannot make restitutio in integrum. If the consumer waits more than three months, or the goods or services have been fully consumed, the consumer will be able to claim a discount on the price. Except in relation to higher market value goods,[52] it will be simply a matter of an applicable discount band. Under the amended Consumer Protection from Unfair Trading Regulations 2008, bands of discount are set (25 per cent, 50 per cent, 75 per cent, or 100 per cent).[53] The applicable band depends upon the seriousness of the misleading practice, which will be a matter of the impact of the practice, the trader's behaviour, and any delay by the consumer. 'In the worst cases, the discount may be 100 per cent, and identical to a refund.'[54] Obviously, there is uncertainty in the level of discount, but the Law Commission viewed a discount as a 'simpler and more appropriate remedy than damages'. It was seen as avoiding the complexity of the law on damages, and the problem of establishing the amount by which the misrepresentation affected the value of the goods or services.[55] There will be scope for a claim for damages calculated on a reliance basis to cover financial loss which the consumer would not have incurred had the misleading practice not taken place, but it will not include a loss dealt with by any unwinding or discount which has been obtained. There is also recovery of damages for distress and inconvenience, but only if a significant purpose of the contract was to provide the consumer with pleasure, relaxation, or peace of mind.[56] In claiming damages, the consumer has to establish the losses, and the trader will have a due diligence defence. The Law Commission saw that as being in keeping with the line taken in s 2(1) of the Misrepresentation Act 1967, under which damages are available, once the misrepresentee has established the loss, unless the misrepresentor can prove reasonable grounds to believe in the truth of the misrepresentation. More generally, the Law Commissions commented in relation to their proposed remedies that, 'Overall [they] approximate the outcomes under the current law, but in a simplified way. It is a scheme which values certainty over flexibility'.[57] Apart

51 The Law Commissions, *Consumer Redress for Misleading and Aggressive Practices* (Law Com No 332, Scot Law Com No 226) para. 8.73; Reg 27E Consumer Protection from Unfair Trading Regulations 2008 (as amended by the Consumer Protection (Amendment) Regulations 2014).

52 £5,000 in Regulation 27I of the amended Regulations.

53 The Law Commissions proposed that there also be a 0 per cent band—paras 8.125–8.135.

54 The Law Commissions, *Consumer Redress for Misleading and Aggressive Practices* (Law Com No 332, Scot Law Com No 226) para. 8.78; Reg 27I of the amended Regulations.

55 The Law Commissions, *Consumer Redress for Misleading and Aggressive Practices* (Law Com No 332, Scot Law Com No 226) para. 8.119.

56 The Law Commissions, *Consumer Redress for Misleading and Aggressive Practices* (Law Com No 332, Scot Law Com No 226) para. 8.163; Reg 27J of the amended Regulations.

57 The Law Commissions, *Consumer Redress for Misleading and Aggressive Practices* (Law Com No 332, Scot Law Com No 226) para. 8.19.

from the disapplication of MA 1967, s 2 to situations covered by the Regulations, the consumer remains able to use other existing legal rules instead of the Regulations, but is not able to exercise a right, or be granted relief, under both.[58]

Exemption clauses and misrepresentations

13.99 Subject to the usual rules on incorporation and construction (see **Chapter 9**), an exemption clause may serve to exclude or restrict liability for non-fraudulent misrepresentation, but such clauses are ineffective in relation to a fraudulent misrepresentation.[59] In *S Pearson & Son Ltd* v *Dublin Corpn* (1907) the claimants contracted to construct sewage works for a price calculated in reliance upon a misrepresentation. It was said that liability for a fraudulent misrepresentation could not be affected by an exemption clause. More recently, in *HIH Casualty and General Insurance* v *Chase Manhattan Bank* (2003), Lord Bingham said: 'It is clear that the law, on public policy grounds, does not permit a contracting party to exclude liability for his own fraud' (at [16]).[60]

13.100 However, the Misrepresentation Act 1967, s 3 (as substituted by Unfair Contract Terms Act 1977 (UCTA), s 8) now renders an exemption clause ineffective, in relation to all types of misrepresentation, if the representor cannot establish that the clause satisfies the requirement of reasonableness in UCTA 1977, s 11. MA 1967, s 3 now states:

> If a contract contains a term which would exclude or restrict—
>
> (a) any liability to which a party to a contract may be subject by reason of any misrepresentation made by him before the contract was made; or
>
> (b) any remedy available to another party to the contract by reason of such a misrepresentation,
>
> that term shall be of no effect except in so far as it satisfies the requirement of reasonableness as stated in s 11(1) of the Unfair Contract Terms Act 1977; and it is for those claiming that the term satisfies the requirement of reasonableness to show that it does.

Section 3 deals with terms which exclude or restrict liability, or a remedy, for misrepresentation. It renders such a term ineffective unless the representor can establish that it satisfies the requirement of reasonableness.

13.101 The scope of MA 1967, s 3 presents difficulties in relation to clauses which appear to try to prevent a statement from being a misrepresentation at all, rather than merely excluding or restricting the liability or the remedies available for a misrepresentation. There may, for example, be a clause stating that the apparent facts are only matters of belief, or more commonly a 'non-reliance clause' stating that there was no reliance upon statements made. It is

58 Regulation 27L(2) of the Consumer Protection from Unfair Trading Regulations 2008 (as amended by the Consumer Protection (Amendment) Regulations 2014).

59 See further E. Macdonald, *Exemption Clauses and Unfair Terms*, 2nd edn, Tolley, 2005, ch. 6.

60 See also Lord Hoffmann at [76]. The question of whether an exemption clause can cover liability for the fraud of an agent is left open.

a similar problem to that which has to be considered in deciding whether a clause should be regarded as an exclusion clause in substance and subject to UCTA 1977, despite its form (see **Chapter 10**).

13.102 The courts have shown some willingness not to simply take such clauses at face value, but to look beyond their form, to determine whether they are exclusion clauses in substance. *Cremdean Properties Ltd* v *Nash* [1977] EGD 63 provides an early example. In that case:

> Nash contracted to sell to Cremdean Properties a block of properties in Bristol to be used as office space. The particulars of the properties had stated that the amount of office space available was 17,900 sq. ft but it was actually much less. A footnote to the special conditions of sale contained the following clause:
>
> > [The vendor's estate agents] for themselves and the vendors . . . give notice that (a) These particulars are prepared for the convenience of an intending purchaser . . . and although they are believed to be correct their accuracy is not guaranteed and any error, omission or misdescription shall not annul the sale or be grounds on which compensation may be claimed and neither do they constitute any part of an offer of a contract, (b) Any intending purchaser . . . must satisfy himself by inspection or otherwise as to the correctness of each of the statements contained in these particulars.

Cremdean sought rescission of the contract, or damages in the alternative, on the basis of a misrepresentation as to the amount of office space in the property. As a preliminary issue the effect of the footnote was considered. Nash argued that it prevented there being a representation at all, and that therefore it did not exclude or restrict liability and did not fall within MA 1967, s 3. The Court of Appeal held that the footnote came within the ambit of s 3 and that at the full trial of the action, the court would have to consider whether the footnote was 'reasonable' in order to decide if it was effective to exclude liability. Of interest here is the court's rejection of the argument that the clause fell outside the ambit of s 3. Bridge LJ thought that the clause was inappropriately worded to bring about the situation where no representation had been made, but he also said (at 71–2):

> [I]f the ingenuity of a draftsman could devise language which would have that effect, I am extremely doubtful whether the court would allow it to operate so as to defeat s 3. Supposing the vendor included a clause . . . in some such terms as 'notwithstanding any statement of fact included in these particulars the vendor shall be conclusively deemed to have made no representation within the meaning of the Misrepresentation Act 1967', I should have thought that *that was only a form of words the intended and actual effect of which was to exclude or restrict liability*, and I should not have thought that the courts would have been ready to allow such ingenuity in forms of language to defeat the plain purpose at which s 3 is aimed. (emphasis added)

Clearly, Bridge LJ was willing to look beyond the form of a clause, to its substance. Scarman LJ expressed the need to do so more graphically, stating (at 72):

> Humpty Dumpty would have fallen for this argument. If we were to fall for it, the Misrepresentation Act would be dashed to pieces which not all the King's Lawyers could put together again.

Buckley LJ agreed with both Bridge and Scarman LJJ.

13.103 However, determining when a clause should be viewed as an exclusion clause 'in substance' is a complex question, of which the courts have not provided a satisfactory analysis. It is clear, however, that they are more willing to take a clause at face value, as meaning that there was no representation made, when dealing with legally sophisticated parties who can be expected to have taken on board the impact of a non-reliance clause, for example, in a standard form contract. Indeed, between the large commercial enterprises, as in *Raiffeisen Zentralbank Österreich AG* v *Royal Bank of Scotland* (2010), representations were not found, and the clause was not viewed as an exemption clause. The judge did, however, contrast the situation with a very different one. He said (at [306]–[307]):

> Suppose . . . a car is sold. The dealer says 'I have serviced the car since it was new, it has had only one owner and the clock reading is accurate'. He is not fraudulent but mistaken, carelessly confusing one car for another, in relation to which the statement is true. Relying on his statement the buyer purchases the car. Without it he would not have done so. The car has had several owners, no known service history, and the clock reading is substantially inaccurate. The contract of sale provides (in one of many paragraphs on the back of the form which the buyer does not read and to which his attention is not directed) that the buyer is entering into the contract on the basis that no representations have been made to, or relied on by, the purchaser . . . In that example there has been a clear statement of fact, on a matter said to be within the representor's personal knowledge, which was in fact intended to induce the contract, upon which the purchaser in fact relied, which is false.

In that situation, Christopher Clarke J viewed the clause as one which would be viewed as an exclusion clause, and subject to MA, s 3. Of course, in relation to a consumer, it is the Consumer Rights Act 2015 which must now be looked at (see further **Chapter 13**), but the differentiation between legally sophisticated and unsophisticated traders still remains. Although simple in approach, this will generally be in keeping with the complex analysis which can be made to determine which clauses are exclusion clauses in substance.[61]

13.104 Of course, clauses which do fall within s 3 are then ineffective unless they satisfy the 'requirement of reasonableness' in s 11 of UCTA 1977. *Cleaver* v *Schyde Investments* (2011) emphasizes that, just as when it is applied in relation to a provision of UCTA itself, an appellate

61 E. Macdonald, 'Exception Clauses: Exclusionary or Definitional? It Depends!' (2012) 29 JCL 47. But see *Taberna Europe CDO II plc* v *Selskabet af 1 September 2008 A/S* (2016) [17]–[22].

court will be reluctant to overturn the decision of the judge at first instance on reasonableness, and that its application is a matter of the facts in each case. In *Cleaver* v *Schyde Investments* (2011):

> S contracted with C to buy a property, which S was going to develop into flats. C knew that his neighbour, a doctor, was applying for planning permission to turn part of the property into a medical centre. C did not disclose that in the standard enquiries answered in relation to a sale of land. When S found out about the planning application, it was concerned that it would detrimentally impact upon its application for a wholly residential development. (The doctor continued with his application even after the contract of sale had been made.)

It was accepted that C had made an innocent misrepresentation. S sought to rescind. The issue was whether C could rely upon the exemption clause, which was a term of the Law Society's standard conditions of sale, which allowed the buyer to rescind for misrepresentation only where the misrepresentation was fraudulent or reckless or where the property would differ substantially in quality, quantity, or tenure from what the buyer had been led to expect. At first instance, the judge found that the clause was not reasonable. It went to the Court of Appeal.

13.105 The Court of Appeal did not view it as generally unreasonable to restrict rescission as the clause did (at [54], [38]). Etherton LJ stated (at [38]):

> That is a perfectly rational and commercially justifiable apportionment of risk in the interests of certainty and the avoidance of litigation. While each case turns on its own particular facts, the argument in favour of upholding such a provision as a matter of the commercial autonomy of the contracting parties is particularly strong where, as here: (1) the term has a long history; (2) it is a well-established feature of property transactions; (3) it is endorsed by the leading professional body for qualified conveyancers; (4) both sides are represented by solicitors; and (5) the parties (through their solicitors) have negotiated variations of other provisions in the standard form.

The court noted the limited extent to which it was appropriate for an appellate court to interfere with the decision of the judge on reasonableness under s 11, and that every case depended on its particular facts. It concluded that it should not depart from the judge's view in this case. Longmore LJ stated (at [55]):

> But the question is not whether the clause is, in general, a reasonable clause. The question is whether it was a reasonable clause in the contract made between *this* vendor and *this* purchaser at the time when the contract was made. On the particular facts of this case both parties were aware of and wished (if possible) to exploit the development potential of the property. The planning position (and any change to it between the answer to enquiries and completion) was of obvious materiality. Yet the mere existence of an application for planning permission can hardly be said to make the property different in quantity, quality or tenure from what it had been represented to be.

The planning application did not affect the land in a way which would allow rescission under the clause, but as Etherton LJ said (at [52]), it 'changed the risk landscape' in relation to the crucial issue of planning permission for the way in which the representee's wished to develop the land.

13.106 Under the Consumer Rights Act 2015 (CRA) (see **Chapter 11**), the application of s 3 MA is now restricted to terms in non-consumer contracts. In relation to contracts between consumers and traders (i.e. consumer contracts with the CRA), it is now the fairness test, in s 62 CRA, which is applied to the term. Thus, in the consumer context, the question of whether a term is an exemption clause, or one preventing there being a misrepresentation, will not arise, as such. There could, however, be issues as to the whether the term is covered by the core exemption. The CRA also applies to consumer notices.

Summary

- An operative misrepresentation is basically a false statement of existing or past fact made by one party to the contract to the other, before or at the time of contracting, which the other relied upon in contracting.
- It is unclear to what extent there is a requirement of materiality, that is, that the misrepresentation would have induced a reasonable person to contract.
- Statements of opinion or intention are not statements of fact and so not misrepresentations, but implied statements of fact may be found behind them.
- Silence itself is not a misrepresentation, although there are exceptions, as with contracts of the utmost good faith (such as contracts of insurance). Partial non-disclosure may constitute a misrepresentation and one may also be found where a statement which was true when stated has become untrue by the time the contract is made, and the representor knew of this and did not disclose the change.
- The representee must have relied on the misrepresentation when entering into the contract.
- A less complex regime has been proposed by the Law Commissions in relation to misleading and aggressive practices which are likely to have caused the average consumer to contract with the trader, and were a significant element in the individual consumer's decision to contract.
- Damages are available for fraudulent misrepresentation under the tort of deceit. (The essence of fraud is the representor's lack of belief in what he or she stated.)
- Damages are available under the tort of negligent misstatement where there was a duty of care between the parties and the representor was negligent (i.e. the representor lacked reasonable grounds for believing in what he or she stated).
- Damages are available under s 2(1) of the Misrepresentation Act 1967. The burden of proof in relation to negligence is reversed, that is, the representee only needs to establish that an operative misrepresentation was made by the representor and it is then for the representor to prove that he or she had reasonable grounds to believe that what he or she said was true.

- No damages, as such, are available in relation to an innocent misrepresentation but an indemnity may accompany rescission and damages in lieu of rescission may be ordered by a court under s 2(2) of the Misrepresentation Act 1967 in relation to non-fraudulent misrepresentations.
- Under the amended Consumer Protection from Unfair Trading Regulations 2008, which provide remedies for consumers in relation to misleading and aggressive practices, s 2 of the Misrepresentation Act 1967 ceases to apply where that regime applies.
- The remedy of rescission is available in relation to all types of misrepresentation.
- There are bars to rescission:
  - where it is impossible to return the parties to their pre-contractual positions;
  - where a third party has acquired rights;
  - where the representee has affirmed the contract;
  - where there has been a sufficient lapse of time since the contract was made.
- Section 2(2) of the Misrepresentation Act 1967, giving the court power to award damages in lieu of rescission for a non-fraudulent misrepresentation, is sometimes referred to as the statutory bar, and is only available in absence of any common law bar to rescission.
- Under the amended Consumer Protection from Unfair Trading Regulations 2008, which provide remedies for consumers in relation to misleading and aggressive practices, consumers are provided with a right to 'unwind' the transaction for a period of 90 days, provided there is still some of the product/service to reject, and otherwise to a discount. The regime also encompasses damages claims on a reliance basis.
- An exemption clause is not effective in relation to liability for fraud.
- Under s 3 of the Misrepresentation Act 1967, exemption clauses dealing with misrepresentations are subject to 'the requirement of reasonableness' under UCTA.
- Under the Consumer Rights Act 2015, the application of s 3 MA is now restricted to terms in non-consumer contracts. In relation to contracts between consumers and traders (i.e. consumer contracts with the CRA), it is now the fairness test in s 62 CRA which is applied to the term.

Further reading

P. S. Atiyah and G. H. Treitel, 'Misrepresentation Act 1967' (1967) 30 MLR 369

H. Beale, 'Damages in Lieu of Rescission for Misrepresentation' (1995) 111 LQR 60

H. Beale, 'Points on Misrepresentation' (1995) 111 LQR 385

R. Hooley, 'Damages and the Misrepresentation Act 1967' (1991) 107 LQR 547

Law Commission and **Scottish Law Commission,** *Consumer Redress for Misleading and Aggressive Practices* Law Com No 332, Scot Law Com No 226 (2012)

Chapter 14

Duress and undue influence

Introduction

14.1

> In everyday life people constantly seek to influence the decisions of others. They seek to persuade those with whom they are dealing to enter into transactions, whether great or small. The law has set limits to the means properly employable for this purpose. (*Royal Bank of Scotland* v *Etridge (No 2)* (2001) per Lord Nicholls at [6].

Both duress and undue influence relate to the situation in which one party has distorted the other's decision to contract. Both concepts are used to deal with contracts made in unacceptable circumstances and, where a contract is made under duress or undue influence, it is voidable.[1] However, as influencing another's decision making is 'constantly' part of 'everyday life', it will become clear in the following discussion that identifying those circumstances which are unacceptable and amount to duress or undue influence requires the drawing of difficult borderlines. (The related but even more uncertain area of unconscionability is dealt with in **Chapter 16**.)

14.2 The uncertainty in the common law in this area, and the limitations of its coverage, mean that it is of little use in the more common type of situations of pressurized contracting which are encountered by the consumer—for example, where elderly consumers living by themselves encounter salesmen who will not leave their homes until they have signed a

1 It was said in *Barton* v *Armstrong* (1976) that threats to the person could render a contract void, but it is in keeping with the idea of an agreement made in unacceptable circumstances, rather than of a factually 'overborne will' (see para. 14.6), that a contract is voidable rather than being void. In any event, it is clear that all other types of duress and undue influence render contracts voidable.

contract.[2] The Consumer Protection from Unfair Trading Regulations 2008 provide public enforcement by 'enforcers', most importantly the Competition and Markets Authority (CMA),[3] to deal with misleading and aggressive commercial practices, and unfair commercial practices more broadly, through criminal sanctions and enforcement orders. Part 4A of the Consumer Protection from Unfair Trading Regulations 2008, as amended by the Consumer Protection (Amendment) Regulations 2014, now enable the individual consumer, in relation to aggressive and misleading practices, to 'unwind' contracts (which is similar to rescinding) or receive a discount on the price and recover damages. The Regulations have already been looked at in relation to misleading practices in the chapter on misrepresentation, and they will be addressed in relation to aggressive practices at the end of this chapter.

Duress

Introduction

14.3 If someone makes a contract whilst a gun is being held to his or her head, it is obvious that it was made in unacceptable circumstances (see *Barton* v *Armstrong* (1976)), but it is only in comparatively recent years that English law has clearly recognized any other type of duress. Even the legal effect of duress to goods was far from certain.[4] However, in *The Siboen and The Sibotre (Occidental Worldwide Investment Corpn* v *Skibs A/S Avanti)* (1976), Mocatta J recognized, *obiter*, that a contract could be voidable because economic duress had been present when it was made. 'Economic' duress simply refers to the fact that it is the economic interest of the individual which is being threatened, and the law now considers a very wide range of threats as constituting duress.

14.4 An example of a situation in which the plea of duress will commonly be raised is provided by *Atlas Express Ltd* v *Kafco (Importers and Distributors) Ltd* (1989). In that case:

> Kafco, a small company which imported and distributed basketware, had made a contract to supply Woolworths. Kafco needed to contract with a carrier for delivery to Woolworths. They concluded a contract with Atlas Express. Once the contract with Atlas had commenced, Atlas realized that they had miscalculated and that the rates specified in the contract made it a 'bad deal' from their point of view. Atlas told Kafco that they would cease to make the deliveries unless the contract pricing was changed. Kafco was heavily dependent upon the contract with

2 The period provided for consumers to cancel contracts made in their own homes (Regulation 30 of the Consumer Contracts (Information, Cancellation and Additional Payments) Regulations 2013 provide for a 'normal cancellation period' of 14 days for most types of contract) does not provide sufficient protection. Tactics are used by sellers to reduce the likelihood of consumers exercising this right and, in any event, it is often not a sufficient period for elderly, house-bound consumers who lack regular social contact and are embarrassed about what has happened, and reluctant to make a fuss (*Consumer Redress for Misleading and Aggressive Practices* Law Com No 332, Scot Law Com No 226 (2012) paras 3.52–3.54).

3 A list of relevant enforcers is provided under Sch 5 of the Consumer Rights Act 2015.

4 Contrast *Skeate* v *Beale* (1840) and *Astley* v *Reynolds* (1731); J. Beatson, 'Vitiating Factors in Contract' [1974] CL 97.

> Woolworths and knew that a failure to deliver the baskets would lead to its loss and an action for breach by Woolworths. At that time it was not possible for Kafco to find another carrier and Kafco felt that Atlas had them 'over a barrel'. Kafco agreed to the new contract, at the rates demanded by Atlas, but made it clear that they felt that they were acting under duress.

Atlas Express sued Kafco for non-payment of the new rate of carriage. Tucker J held that they could not succeed. The agreement to the new rates, in the new contract, had been made while Kafco were subject to economic duress. In any event, there had been no consideration for the new agreement.

14.5 *Atlas Express Ltd* v *Kafco (Importers and Distributors) Ltd* (1989) illustrates the situation in which a claim of duress will often arise. The parties have made a contract but, because of miscalculation, a misunderstanding as to their rights, a change in circumstances, or a desire to take advantage of the other's vulnerability which was created by reliance on the contract, one party decides to try to increase the contract price. He or she indicates to the other party that, unless the price is increased, there can or will be no performance.[5] The question is whether any new agreement will be voidable for economic duress, and that has become all the more important since the decision in *Williams* v *Roffey Bros & Nicholls (Contractors) Ltd* (1990) (see para. **4.42**ff) has thrown the emphasis onto the question of duress rather than consideration. In such cases, the important point would seem to be whether the new agreement was made improperly, in unacceptable circumstances, rather than whether it was remembered to include some 'technical' consideration, such as a stick of chewing gum, a chocolate bar, or the traditional peppercorn. However, it does place great significance on duress. It has been said:[6]

> The law of consideration is no longer used to protect a participant in such a variation. That role has passed to the law of economic duress, which provides a more refined control mechanism and renders the contract voidable rather than void.

We need to consider when the courts will find that a contract was made under duress.

The language of the courts

14.6 Before addressing the identification of duress, we should consider the language used by the courts in this context. At times, the courts have given the appearance of stating a clear test for duress whilst using language which, on closer examination, is obscure in its meaning.

5 We usually refer to 'threats' in this context, and we might become enmeshed in discussion of whether it is a threat if, for example, the one party simply says to the other, 'I want to perform, but I cannot do so at this price'. It is not helpful to try to decide whether this was a 'threat'. The type of factors to consider, and the tensions in the law which they represent, are set out below. Whether there is a 'threat' is a linguistic dead end, which could divert attention from them, particularly when it is borne in mind that the 'threat' may not even be expressed. One party may simply create a situation in which it is clear to the other party that there will be no performance unless the price is increased. The fact that the builders in *Williams* v *Roffey Bros & Nicholls (Contractors) Ltd* (1990) suggested the increased payment does not explain the assumption that there was no duress in that case.

6 *Adam Opel GmbH* v *Mitras Automotive (UK) Ltd* (2007) per David Donaldson QC at [42].

In particular, care must be taken with the use of terms such as 'voluntariness' and 'consent', and references to the 'overborne will'.[7] This use of language is superficially attractive. It seems to provide the perfect basis for interfering with an apparently valid contract. If individuals claiming duress were acting involuntarily, if they did not consent, then their agreement can be labelled as merely apparent, and dismissed. However, in considering whether they truly consented, in the sense of whether their agreements were given voluntarily, the test does not ask whether their actions were unwilled, as would be the case if they were in a state of automatism. It is clear from *DPP for Northern Ireland* v *Lynch* (1975) that truly unwilled actions, in the sense of automatism, are not what is considered by the courts in relation to duress. In *Lynch* this was acknowledged by the House of Lords in the context of a plea of duress in the criminal law, and Atiyah pointed out that the reasoning on that point should not be regarded as restricted to the criminal law.[8] When individuals under duress agree to contract because of the other party's threat, they do not do so 'involuntarily', because their will has been 'overborne', but rather because they choose to, albeit only because it is the least unattractive of the alternatives before them. It is not a question of individuals being made 'offers they could not refuse', merely one of being made offers which they were given very powerful reasons for accepting. In other words, there is no simple factual test of whether the person claiming duress has ceased to act 'voluntarily'. The real question in relation to duress is whether the decision to contract was made in unacceptable circumstances.[9]

Identifying duress

14.7 In *R* v *Attorney-General for England and Wales* (2003), Lord Hoffmann stated (at [15]) that there were 'two elements' in duress: first, 'pressure amounting to compulsion of the will of the victim' and, secondly, 'the illegitimacy of the pressure'. We have already seen that references, such as that to 'compulsion of the will of the victim', are not very helpful, but there are, nevertheless, two basic elements as to what constitutes duress: the threat must indeed be 'illegitimate', but instead of considering 'compulsion of the will of the victim', we must generally consider whether the situation was such that the party threatened had no reasonable alternative to agreeing. Indeed, before commencing his consideration of the 'illegitimacy' of the pressure, which was the significant point in *R* v *A-G*, Lord Hoffmann put aside examination of his first element, on the assumption that the pressure did cause 'compulsion of his will' as it left *R* with 'no practical alternative' (at [15]). Despite Lord Hoffmann's reference to 'compulsion of the will', it was nevertheless recognized that what is in question is a situation in which options have been curtailed, and unacceptably (illegitimately) so. Illegitimacy and lack of a reasonable alternative provide the basic test of whether appropriate pressure for duress is present, but there is, of course, an additional requirement if the law is to recognize duress in relation to the particular transaction: it must have been a sufficient cause of contract. This requirement is

7 E.g. *North Ocean Shipping Co. Ltd* v *Hyundai Construction Co. Ltd* [1978] 3 All ER 1170 at 1183; *Pao On* v *Lau Yiu Long* [1980] AC 614 at 636; *The Siboen and the Sibotre* [1976] 1 Lloyd's Rep 293 at 335; *Hennessy* v *Craigmyle & Co. Ltd* [1986] ICR 461 at 468.

8 See P. S. Atiyah, 'Economic Duress and the Overborne Will' (1982) 98 LQR 197.

9 *Dimskal Shipping Co. SA* v *International Transport Workers' Federation, The Evia Luck* [1992] 2 AC 152 at 165.

unsurprising, and it is assumed in Lord Hoffmann's statement of 'two elements'. His reference to 'compulsion of the will of the victim' also makes it clear that the duress must have caused the agreement. We should also note that, as duress makes a contract merely voidable, rescission may become barred by, for example, affirmation (as we have already seen may occur in relation to contracts which were voidable for misrepresentation). Each of these elements of an effective claim of duress should now be considered, although we should perhaps first note that there are dicta which do not correspond with this analytical division—indicating, for example, that whether there was a reasonable alternative is part of the consideration of illegitimacy,[10] or placing it within the question of causation[11]—but it is necessary to see the elements as distinct in this way to avoid confusion and fully understand the significance of each of them, and the tensions within the law.

Illegitimacy of the threat

14.8 It was established in *Universe Tankships Inc. of Monrovia* v *International Transport Workers' Federation and Laughton* [1983] 1 AC 366 that the threat must be 'illegitimate',[12] and this is important in distinguishing duress from hard bargaining:[13]

> [I]n life . . . many acts are done under pressure, sometimes overwhelming pressure, so that one can say that the actor had no choice but to act. Absence of choice in this sense does not negate consent in law: for this the pressure must be one of a kind which the law does not regard as legitimate.

'Generally speaking, the threat of any unlawful action will be illegitimate',[14] and unlawful here refers not just to threats to commit criminal acts, but also civil wrongs, such as torts and breaches of contract. Of course, it may be the demand itself rather than what is threatened which is unlawful, with blackmail providing the primary example: 'Blackmail is often a demand supported by a threat to do what is lawful, for example, to report criminal conduct to the police.'[15] For ease of reference, the phrase 'unlawful threats' will simply be used.

14.9 However, what must now be addressed are the two main issues which have arisen in relation to unlawfulness and illegitimacy. First, although a breach of contract is a civil wrong, it has been suggested that a threatened breach is not always illegitimate. Secondly, it has been recognized that there will be occasions when a lawful threat will be illegitimate, and the borderlines of that raise very difficult questions.

10 E.g. *DSND Subsea Ltd* v *Petroleum Geo Services ASA* (2000) at [131].

11 *Kolmar Group* v *Traxpo* (2010) at [92].

12 Lord Diplock at 384 and Lord Scarman at 400.

13 Lord Hoffmann in *R* v *Attorney-General for England and Wales* (2003) at [15], quoting Lord Wilberforce and Lord Simon of Glaisdale in *Barton* v *Armstrong* [1975] 2 All ER 465 at 476–7.

14 Lord Hoffmann in *R* v *Attorney-General for England and Wales* (2003) at [16].

15 *International Transport Workers Federation* v *Universe Tankships* [1983] 1 AC 366 at 401.

14.10 First, whether a threatened breach will always be illegitimate must be addressed. In *Huyton SA* v *Peter Cremer GmbH* [1999] CLC 230, Mance J said (at 251):

> Even in cases where the pressure relied on is an actual or threatened breach of duty, it seems to me better not to exclude the possibility that the state of mind of the person applying such pressure may in some circumstances be significant.

In *DSND Subsea Ltd* v *Petroleum Geo Services ASA* (2000), Dyson J expressed the view (at [134]) that a breach would not be 'illegitimate behaviour where it was reasonable behavior by a contractor acting bona fide', and in *Kolmar Group* v *Traxpo* (2010) Christopher Clarke J took the line that not all threatened breaches would be illegitimate but that 'generally' would be the case, 'particularly where the defendant must know that it would be a breach if the threat were implemented' (at [92]). The situation has been seen as one involving the question of 'bad faith', and that has been viewed as a more complex issue than simple knowledge. Peter Birks advocated an approach whereby a threatened breach would only be illegitimate when used in 'bad faith, being intended to exploit the [claimant's] weakness rather than solve financial or other problems of the defendant'.[16] Andrew Burrows would add two 'supplementary or clarificatory ideas' to this:[17]

> First, a threat should not be considered illegitimate (made in bad faith) if the threat is a reaction to circumstances that almost constitute frustration. And, secondly, a threat should not be considered illegitimate (made in bad faith) if it merely corrects what was clearly a bad bargain.

Such clarification does not reduce the considerable uncertainty in the concept of bad faith: what 'almost' constitutes frustration, or a sufficiently bad original bargain?

14.11 The problems of requiring bad faith to make a threatened breach illegitimate go beyond uncertainty. It would mean that, on occasion, no duress would be found even though the party threatened had no reasonable means of protecting their rights under the original contract, as, for example, where a legal remedy could not be procured quickly enough. A requirement of 'bad faith' will generate cases where rights under the original contract are left effectively unprotected, and there will then be a loss of discipline in the process of bidding for a contract: not as much care needs to be taken in providing an initial contract price, if it will be easy to obtain an enforceable renegotiation after the contract is underway. This puts the careful bidder at a disadvantage, and the other party does not see a true picture before accepting a bid. On the other hand, circumstances do change and, without the potential for effective renegotiation, initial mistakes may be penalized very heavily. A requirement of 'bad faith' might be seen as achieving a balance between protecting initial rights and encouraging the parties to renegotiate/compromise.

16 P. Birks, *An Introduction to the Law of Restitution*, Oxford University Press, 1989, p. 183.

17 A. Burrows, *The Law of Restitution*, 3rd edn, Oxford University Press, 2011, p. 175.

14.12 In addition, Burrows' 'clarificatory ideas' also suggest another type of balance, or re-balancing. They might be seen as helping to re-balance the situation where the law dealing with the original rights can be viewed as insufficiently confining them, because of a very narrow doctrine of frustration, or insufficiently policing their fairness in the first place, and allowing such a 'bad bargain'.

14.13 The basic tension between protecting initial rights, and thereby supporting discipline in the bargaining process, and encouraging renegotiation/compromise will be considered further later, in relation to the requirement of a lack of a reasonable alternative to agreeing. However, the issues are further illustrated here by considering, again, what happened in *Williams* v *Roffey Bros & Nicholls (Contractors) Ltd* (1990): the concept of 'bad faith' might provide a means of explaining why duress was assumed not to be present in that case. Clearly, if the carpenters had not completed under the original terms, it would have been a breach of contract. They were not going to breach, however, to 'exploit' the builders' 'weakness' in needing completion on time. They were going to breach because they had made a mistake, and a bad bargain in the first place, as well as running the job inefficiently. But the question then is whether we should be protecting the party who made a bad bargain through their own error, and then sought to escape it? And what of the difficulty of distinguishing the party who cynically made an apparently bad bargain to obtain the original contract, always intending to renegotiate something far more favourable once the other party was dependent upon his or her performance? The tension in the law is clear. The appropriate balance point is open to much argument. One thing which is clear is that the situation is a great deal more certain if a threatened breach is always illegitimate. A further means of explaining *Williams* v *Roffey Bros* is considered below (see para. **14.30**, and see also **n. 5**).

14.14 However, what must now be considered is the extension of what will amount to an illegitimate threat, beyond what is unlawful. Any extension of duress beyond the area of unlawful threats will be infringing upon freedom of contract without the obvious justification of 'unlawfulness'. It may be seen as the policing of contracts on the basis of inequality of bargaining power. Duress, even when confined to the unlawful, may be seen as rendering a contract voidable on the basis of inequality of bargaining power, but in an obviously restricted way. Other areas of the law indicate the unacceptability of the way in which the person making the threat has increased his or her bargaining power. Certainly, there are indications against any generalized doctrine of relief against inequality of bargaining power.[18]

14.15 However, in *CTN Cash and Carry Ltd* v *Gallaher* [1994] 4 All ER 714, the Court of Appeal took the view that it is possible for duress to be based on a lawful threat,[19] but, on the facts of the particular case, no duress was found. In that case:

18 See *Pao On* v *Lau Yiu Long* [1980] AC 614 at 634; *National Westminster Bank plc* v *Morgan* [1985] 1 All ER 821 at 830.

19 See also *Universe Tankships Inc of Monrovia* v *International Transport Workers Federation and Laughton* (1983).

> The claimant company ran a cash-and-carry business. The defendant supplied them with cigarettes (and was the only possible supplier of some brands) on a regular basis, on credit terms, but each transaction was covered by a separate contract. A dispute arose between them, and the defendants refused to continue to supply the claimants on credit unless the claimants paid the sum which the defendants were asserting was due to them. The claimants asserted that the sum was not due, but paid the defendants in order to continue to trade with them on credit terms. The claimants sued to recover the sum paid on the basis that it had been paid under economic duress.

The defendants had not been correct in thinking that the sums were due to them, but the threat was not unlawful. It did not involve a threatened breach of contract. It merely related to the terms of potential, unrelated future contracts. On this basis, the Court of Appeal rejected the claim of duress; nevertheless, the Court did recognize the possibility of duress being found without an unlawful threat, and consideration should be given to the factors indicated as relevant to that.

14.16 The dispute arose out of 'arm's-length' commercial dealings between two trading companies' (at 717). Such a situation was clearly not viewed as one which was fertile ground for such a claim of duress, and it did not matter that the defendants were the sole distributors of certain brands of cigarette and therefore were, in a sense, in a monopolistic position. The line was taken that:

> The control of monopolies is . . . a matter for Parliament. Moreover the common law does not recognise the doctrine of inequality of bargaining power in commercial dealings. (Steyn LJ at 717)

However, there are suggestions that it could make a difference if what was in question was a 'protected relationship' or transactions between a supplier and a consumer. (No explanation was given of what might be a 'protected relationship'.) It was also indicated that lack of bona fides by the party making the threat would be looked at. This is more easily accepted where what is threatened is not unlawful. Bad faith is looked at to identify a threat as wrongful, where the law does not otherwise do so, rather than bona fides being considered which could prevent a claim of duress being used to provide protection against an unlawful threat. 'That good or bad faith may be particularly relevant when considering whether a case might represent a rare example of "lawful act duress" is not difficult to accept' (*Huyton SA* v *Peter Cremer GmbH* [1999] CLC 230 at 251). In *CTN Cash & Carry*, the defendants believed they were entitled to the payment they were demanding.

14.17 It would seem that the relationship of the parties, and bad faith, will be relevant to deciding whether a lawful threat will be illegitimate. However, the clearest message from the court was that such illegitimacy will not easily be found. Steyn LJ said (at 719):

> The aim of commercial law ought to be to encourage fair dealings between the parties. But it is a mistake for the law to set its sights too highly when the critical inquiry is not whether the conduct is lawful but whether it is morally or socially unacceptable.

Subsequent cases indeed show that the courts take a restrictive approach to extending duress beyond threats which are clearly unlawful.

14.18 The lawful threat issue arose in *Alf Vaughan & Co Ltd* v *Royscot Trust plc* (1999). In that case:

> The claimants had vehicles, which they used in their business, on hire-purchase or similar terms from the defendants. The claimants went into receivership, and under the contracts that entitled the defendants to re-take possession of the vehicles. The receivers wanted to sell the business as a going concern, and therefore sought to stop the repossession by paying off the balance still due under the hire-purchase and similar agreements. They had found buyers for the business, and it was a matter of urgency to stop the repossession in order to be able to sell the business with the vehicles. The defendants refused to stop the repossession for payment of the sums due, but demanded about twice as much, and the receivers paid. The question was whether the excess payment could be recovered on the basis of duress.

The judge took the line that the threat to repossess the goods was not illegitimate. He emphasized that the threat was lawful. The defendants had a right to repossess the goods. The claimants could have sought relief from forfeiture, which would have made repossession unlawful, and would have been likely to have obtained such relief; however, they had not thought that there was time to do so, and had not done so. That proximity to the defendant's actions being unlawful was not viewed as sufficient to make their actions illegitimate. The judge thought that the claimants could have sought relief from forfeiture, even if it meant that they lost that sale. Further, the judge does not seem to have viewed the defendants as behaving 'unconscionably', in bad faith, despite the fact that there was certainly scope to view them as so acting: they were 'concerned to exploit the claimants' weakness rather than solving their own financial problems'.[20] The closeness of the defendants to unlawfulness, and the presence of a basis for finding bad faith, would indicate that it will, generally, be very difficult indeed to establish duress without unlawfulness.

14.19 However, care must be taken in drawing the line around unlawfulness and illegitimacy, where, although what is threatened is not unlawful, the threat draws its force from an unlawful act which has already occurred.[21] *Progress Bulk Carriers Ltd* v *Tube City IMS LLC (The*

20 Burrows, *The Law of Restitution*, 3rd edn, p. 179.

21 In *Borelli* v *Ting* (2010), the agreement in question was one by which the former chairman and chief executive of a company agreed not to block the scheme of arrangement which liquidators were seeking to implement, to gain money in order to pursue the liquidation and pay some of what was owed to the company's creditors. To obtain his agreement, the liquidators had to undertake not to investigate further in relation to his involvement in the company's defaults, and funds which had disappeared from the company. That ability to block was achieved by the use of forgery and false evidence, and the need for the agreement was because of his failure to comply with his duty under the winding up rules to co-operate with the liquidators. The agreement by which the liquidators promised not to pursue him was not allowed to stand: duress was found. The liquidators had been in a position where they had no real alternative to making the agreement if they were going to take further their attempts to recover any money for the company's creditors. The force of the threat derived from his earlier, unlawful actions.

Cenk Kaptanoglu) (2012) provides an example of a need to be cautious in saying that a breach is in the past, and that there is nothing unlawful in threatening not to make a new contract. Prudence is needed in drawing the lines around cases like *CTN Cash & Carry* v *Gallaher*, where there is a threat not to do what it was perfectly lawful not to do—a threat not to make a new, unrelated contract—and where the threat is not to make a contract which is related, in the sense that it involves the provision of an alternate performance for that not provided because of the breach, and a compromise of the breach. In *The Cenk K* the threat drew its force from the breach.

14.20 The facts of *The Cenk K* were:

> Charterers made a contract with the owners of *The Cenk K* to carry a cargo of shredded metal from Mississippi to China. The owners committed a repudiatory breach by chartering that ship elsewhere. The charterers were in a difficult position. They were under contract to B to deliver the cargo, using that ship, and any new shipping arrangements would have to be agreed by B. Use of a substitute vessel was discussed, and B was prepared to agree to one offered by the owners, but at a discount of $6 a metric ton. After the breach, the owners had told the charterers that they would provide a substitute and meet their losses from the failure to provide the Cenk K, but in the end they would only go as far as $2 a metric ton, and then only on the basis that the charterers gave up any claim in relation to the original breach. With the delays, and the situation in relation to B, the charterers had no reasonable alternative to agreeing. Arbitrators had found that the new agreement, providing the substitute vessel and compromising the charterer's claim for the original breach, was made under duress.

The owners claimed that the arbitrators had not used the correct test as there was nothing unlawful in refusing to make a contract, and therefore no duress. Cooke J took the line that it was 'clear from the authorities that "illegitimate pressure" can be constituted by conduct which is not in itself unlawful, although it will be an unusual case where that is so, particularly in the commercial context' (at [36]). This dealt with the owners claim, and the case may be viewed as one where a threat to do what was lawful—not make a new contract—was found to be illegitimate.

14.21 However, care must be taken with the case. It must be kept distinct from the situation in *CTN Cash & Carry* v *Gallaher*. Cooke J stated:

> [I]t would be very odd if pressure could be brought about by a threatened breach of contract, which did amount to an unlawful act but not by a past breach, coupled with conduct since that breach, which drove the victim of the breach into a position where it had no realistic alternative but to waive its rights in respect of that breach, in order to avoid further catastrophic loss.

In the situation in which the breach is what is creating the pressure, and the agreement is to provide a substitute performance and to compromise any claim arising from that breach, the threat should certainly be regarded as illegitimate—and could be viewed as unlawful—because of its relationship to the breach.[22] The line could be taken that a threat is unlawful where it draws its power from a past unlawful act, rather than from the lawful act which might be carried out in the future. However, whether the threat is regarded as unlawful or not, the situation is very distinct, and must be labelled as one involving duress if the other requirements are also satisfied. Further, it is a commercial situation, but it must not be allowed to create any difficulties by broadening illegitimacy in relation to commercial situations generally. In particular, the *CTN* type of case must be distinguished. In *CTN* the threat drew its force from the potential, future, lawful act, not from the past, unlawful one.

Lack of a reasonable alternative

14.22 The Privy Council recognized that economic duress could render a contract voidable in *Pao On* v *Lau Yiu Long* [1980] AC 614. Lord Scarman said that for duress to be found there must have been 'a coercion of the will which vitiates consent' and D's agreement must have been 'involuntary' (at 636). We have already seen how unhelpful such language is, but of greater interest is the list of factors which he regarded as relevant indicators of duress. He said (at 635):

> It is material to enquire whether the person alleged to have been coerced did or did not protest; whether at the time he was allegedly coerced into making the contract, he did or did not have an alternative course open to him such as an adequate legal remedy; whether he was independently advised; and whether after entering the contract he took steps to avoid it.

It is the reference to whether the person threatened 'did or did not have an alternative course open to him such as an adequate legal remedy' which is most significant, and which has subsequently come to the fore as generally required if duress is to be found. Thus, in *Universe Tankships Inc. of Monrovia* v *International Transport Workers' Federation* [1983] AC 366, after referring to the 'compulsion of the will of the victim', Lord Scarman said (at 400):

> There must be pressure, the practical effect of which is compulsion or the absence of choice . . . The classic case of duress is, however . . . the victim's intentional submission arising from the realisation that there is no practical choice open to him.

Lord Scarman's 'classic case' pointed to the true general limitation upon economic duress (alongside illegitimacy): the insufficiency of the alternative courses of action open to the person threatened. The 'classic case' actually shows the lack of reality in the idea that there is a test of voluntariness, referring to a situation where factually someone's will is overborne. It would be inconsistent to look for such lack of will and, at the same time, to acknowledge that the person concerned chose between alternatives. The explanation of this inconsistency is, as has been indicated (see para. **14.6**), partly due to the superficial justification for the court's interference with the parties' agreement, which is provided by a test which appears to be based,

22 Burrows asks the question: 'why could it not be said that the owners were threatening a continued breach of the charterparty?' (A. Burrows, *A Casebook on Contract*, 4th edn, Hart Publishing, 2013, p. 766). This may not provide a solution where the repudiation is accepted.

factually, upon a lack of willed action, but is also partly linguistic. In everyday speech the test of voluntariness is the question of whether the person threatened had 'no choice', and this, in turn, is understood as meaning 'did he, or she, have a "practical" or "reasonable" alternative?' This can be seen as reflected in Lord Scarman's movement from 'no choice' to the 'classic case' of 'intentional submission' in the face of 'no practical choice'.

14.23 The true nature of the test, as a matter of the availability of alternatives to agreeing[23] for the person threatened, is to be found in *B & S Contracts and Design Ltd* v *Victor Green Publications Ltd* [1984] ICR 419:

> B & S had agreed to erect stands for VG at Olympia to be used for a trade exhibition. B & S intended to use employees who were to be made redundant as soon as they had erected the stands, and they refused to work unless given £9,000 severance pay. B & S paid £4,500 but told VG to pay the rest, in addition to the contract price. It was clear that B & S would not be able to perform the contract unless those employees went back to work. If the stands were not erected, it would have had 'disastrous consequences' for VG and the exhibitors, and payment of the money was VG's only means of ensuring that the stands were erected.

It was held that VG had acted under duress. Griffiths LJ thought that the threatened breach placed VG (at 426):

> in the position envisaged by Lord Scarman in . . . *Pao On* v *Lau Yiu Long* in which they were faced with no alternative course of action but to pay the sum demanded of them.

Of course, it is not accurate to say that VG had 'no alternative' available. VG could have refused to pay and then sued for breach of contract. However, such an alternative was too damaging to VG, and Griffiths LJ clearly recognized that it was the acceptability of the alternatives which was being considered. He said that not having the stands 'would have clearly caused grave damage to [VG's] reputation and . . . might have exposed them to very heavy claims from the exhibitors' (at 426). Further, Kerr LJ, unequivocally stated (at 428) that a threat to break a contract will constitute duress if:

> the consequences of a refusal would be serious and immediate so that there is no reasonable alternative open such as legal redress.

There is generally a limitation upon duress, which is concerned with an assessment of the acceptability of the alternatives open to the person claiming duress. The test used by Kerr LJ is that of a 'reasonable alternative',[24] and that is the formulation adopted here, but others, such as 'practical

23 E. Macdonald, 'Duress by Threatened Breach of Contract' [1989] JBL 460.

24 See also, e.g., *North Ocean Shipping Co. Ltd* v *Hyundai Construction Co. Ltd, The Atlantic Baron* [1978] 3 All ER 1170 at 1182; *Vantage Navigation Corpn* v *Suhail and Saud Bahwan Building Materials, The Alev* [1989] 1 Lloyd's Rep 138 at 146–7.

alternative', have been used.[25] In fact, in *Borelli* v *Ting* (2010) the Privy Council referred to the party threatened as having no 'reasonable or practical alternative' (at [31]). There is some dispute as to how the lack of availability of alternatives should be described. The basic idea is, however, clear. It is not a matter of overborne wills, but of the curtailment of options.

14.24 The lack of a reasonable alternative for the party threatened is a separate requirement for duress, giving substance, alongside the need for subjective causation, to the references to the 'overborne will'. In *DSND Subsea Ltd* v *Petroleum Geo Services ASA* (2000), Dyson J stated (at [131]):

> The ingredients of actionable duress are that there must be pressure, (a) whose practical effect is that there is compulsion on, or a lack of practical choice for, the victim, (b) which is illegitimate, and (c) which is a significant cause inducing the claimant to enter into the contract.

However, it should be acknowledged that this is not universally recognized to be the case. Lack of a practical or reasonable choice for the party threatened has been seen merely as evidence that the illegitimate pressure was a sufficient cause of the contract. In *Kolmar Group* v *Traxpo* (2010), a case in which there clearly was no 'realistic' or reasonable alternative, Christopher Clarke J stated (at [92]):

> If there was no reasonable alternative, that may be very strong evidence in support of a conclusion that the victim of the duress was in fact influenced by the threat.

Nevertheless, it is a substantive requirement which is in question here, rather than merely evidence of causation. Why is that so?

14.25 In *Huyton SA* v *Peter Cremer GmbH & Co.* [1999] CLC 230, Mance J recognized that 'a simple [causal] enquiry whether the innocent party would have acted as he did "but for" an actual or threatened breach of contract' was not enough. He took the line that 'relief must, I think, depend on the court's assessment of the qualitative impact of the illegitimate pressure'. A reasonable or practical alternative test is another element in the law's striking of a balance between encouraging compromises and protecting initial rights (and discipline in the bidding process). It seemed to Mance J 'self-evident that relief may not be appropriate, if an innocent party decides, as a matter of choice, not to pursue an alternative remedy which any and possibly some other reasonable persons in his circumstances would have pursued' (at 252). If economic duress could be successfully claimed after any unlawful threat, it would undermine the security of any transaction caused by one party's announcement of his or her intention to breach his or her contract. The law has an interest in ensuring that many such transactions are regarded as binding, although they are founded on a wrong. The functioning of the legal system depends upon such compromises being made: not all such disputes could be litigated without overloading the legal system. Further, if the parties can reach agreement themselves, then it

25 E.g. *Enimont Overseas AG* v *RO Jugotanker Zader, The Olib* [1991] 2 Lloyd's Rep 108 at 114.

may increase their chances of being able to continue to do business with one another, both throughout that transaction and in the future. To make such compromises or renegotiations worthwhile, they must be transactions which cannot be reopened too easily. The alternatives test draws a line.

14.26 Nevertheless, Mance J also said in *Huyton SA* v *Peter Cremer GmbH & Co.* [1999] CLC 230 (at 252):

> It is not necessary to go as far as to say that it is an inflexible . . . essential ingredient of economic duress that there should be no, or no practical alternative course open for the innocent party.

There are situations in which it would be inappropriate to deny a claim of duress on the basis that the person threatened had a reasonable alternative to agreeing. First, the alternatives test should not be used where what is threatened (or the threat) is a criminal offence. There is no indication of it in *Barton* v *Armstrong* (1976), where the threats were of physical violence, and where a crime is involved, the law has no interest in the protection of a compromise. In relation to crimes, all that should be in question is illegitimacy, which is patently present, and causation.

14.27 Secondly, a question arises as to the protection of those less able to realize that there was a reasonable alternative, or to take advantage of it. Andrew Burrows asks:[26]

> [I]s it not objectionable to rule out [a claim of duress] on the ground that the claimant was weak or foolish to have given in?

Again, in *Huyton SA* v *Peter Cremer GmbH & Co.*, Mance J viewed the misconceptions of the party threatened being relevant to the question of available alternatives, if the other party was in some sense responsible for them, or could have foreseen the other party arriving at them (at 252). It is possible to have a general test of whether there was a reasonable alternative to agreeing, but not to apply it to the full extent in every case. The concept of good faith might be called upon. Again, it is essentially a matter of how far the law goes in protecting compromises, but, for example, the exploitation of known weakness should not be permitted simply on the basis that there was a reasonable alternative. An analogy can be made with the clear acceptance that a fraudulent misrepresentor cannot rely upon a claim that the misrepresentation was not such as to have induced the reasonable person to contract (*Smith* v *Kay* (1859)—see para. **13.41**).[27]

Causation

14.28 The further question which must be asked is the degree to which the 'threat' must have induced the contract. Similar points could be made here as in relation to the question of the degree of reliance required for a misrepresentation to be operative (see para. **14.34**ff). Following *Barton* v *Armstrong* (1976), it would seem that in cases of threats to the person it is

26 Burrows, *The Law of Restitution*, 3rd edn, p. 272.

27 There are issues about the appropriate borderlines between duress, undue influence, and unconscionability.

sufficient if the threat can be viewed as 'a' cause of the contract—and the 'but for' test need not be satisfied. However, outside of that type of duress, it has been said that 'the minimum basic test of subjective causation in economic duress' ought to be a 'but for' test (*Huyton SA* v *Peter Cremer GmbH* [1999] CLC 230 at 250). One exceptional situation where the 'but for' test should not be required is where there are two concurrent causes of the decision to contract, neither in themselves sufficient, so that if the 'but for' test was applied, the contract would be found to have no cause. In that situation a 'common sense relaxation, even of a "but for" requirement is necessary' (*Huyton SA* at 250).

14.29 However, it should be recognized that there may be cases in which it is insufficient that the threat satisfies a 'but for' test, and there are references to it being necessary for the threat to be a 'significant' cause.[28] There may be cases in which the new contract would not have occurred without the threat, but the threat has become merely the background to the making of the new contract. The threatened claimant may have agreed for positive reasons, such as the maintenance of a long term relationship with the defendant, particularly if it is plain that the defendant did not realize that what they were threatening was a breach. Alternatively, the party threatened may have agreed because they think the new terms demanded will have little impact, or carry little risk for them, and so they see no point in doing anything other than accepting.

14.30 The idea of a threat which, although it is a 'but for' cause, should not be regarded as a sufficient cause for a successful claim of duress, as it was merely part of the background to the new agreement, provides another possible explanation of the assumption that the new agreement was not affected by duress in *Williams* v *Roffey Bros & Nicholls* (1990). It would seem that 'but for' the likelihood of the carpenters' breaching, the builders would never have considered offering them additional payment to complete on time, but the situation might be seen as one in which that 'threat' could be regarded as merely the background to the promise to pay more, with the foreground factor being the recognition that the carpenters had underpriced the job in the first place. Such a line would be difficult to draw, but causation issues, explored beyond the basic 'but for' criterion, usually are.

Rescission

14.31 It was made clear in relation to misrepresentation that the right to rescind a voidable contract may be lost (see para. **13.85**), and the same applies here. In *The Atlantic Baron (North Ocean Shipping* v *Hyundai Construction Co. Ltd)* (1978) the right to rescind was lost through affirmation.[29] There, a contract had been made for the building of a ship. When the dollar was devalued the builders threatened to cease work unless the price was increased to take account

28 E.g. *The Evia Luck* [1992] 2 AC 152 at 165.

29 In *Halpern* v *Halpern* (2007) it was recognized that rescission would also be barred by restitutio in integrum becoming impossible, but the court did indicate an unwillingness to see it preventing there being any remedy for the duress, and a money equivalent might be recognized as being able to be used to prevent such impossibility. It is clear, however, that where the unlawful act precedes the threat, and is related to it, and is the source of the threat's power (as in *Progress Bulk Carriers Ltd* v *Tube City IMS LLC (The Cenk Kaptanoglu)* (2012)), there can be no bar through the party who made the threat not being returned to the position which was brought about by the unlawful act (*Borelli* v *Ting* (2010) at [38]–[39]).

of that. There was no legal basis to the builders' claim, but the purchasers agreed to it. They had already chartered out the ship to Shell and would not have been able to obtain a suitable alternative. Mocatta J found that the agreement to pay the increased price was made under duress, but the purchasers could not rely upon it. They were found to have affirmed the contract. By the time the final payments had to be made, the market had changed to such an extent that the purchasers could have refused to pay the increase without any risk of non-delivery, but they made no protest. The ship was delivered in November 1974. No indication of any intention to claim duress was given until the end of July 1975.

Undue influence

Introduction

14.32 Whilst the common law delayed in developing duress beyond duress to the person, equity provided a more extensive remedy through undue influence. Although there has been an overlap with what will now constitute duress, with illegitimate pressure constituting undue influence,[30] it would be better now to see such cases as matters of duress, and for the latter doctrine to be confined to what it has chiefly been concerned with: influence based on the relationship of the parties. The necessary relationship has proved difficult to describe.

> Several expressions have been used in an endeavour to encapsulate the essence: trust and confidence, reliance, dependence or vulnerability on the one hand and ascendancy, domination or control on the other. None of these descriptions is perfect. None is all embracing. Each has its proper place. (*Royal Bank of Scotland* v *Etridge (No 2)* (2001) at [11])

This multifaceted description is hardly surprising. However, the basic idea is that one party has ceased to decide upon such a transaction on the basis of his or her consideration of the transaction as such, but because of the advice, or orders, of the other party; and that surrender of decision making has occurred because of the relationship of, for example, trust or domination which exists between them. Undue influence renders a contract voidable, and also allows for the recovery of gifts. (Obviously the bars to rescission will apply here as elsewhere, so that, for example, a contract cannot be rescinded for undue influence once it has been affirmed.)

14.33 *Allcard* v *Skinner* (1887) is one of the classic cases of undue influence, and it was concerned with a gift made by a nun, A, to the mother superior, for the purposes of the sisterhood. The rules of the sisterhood, reflected in the vows which she had taken, required poverty, complete and unquestioning obedience to the mother superior, and no advice outside of the sisterhood without the mother superior's approval. A subsequently left the convent, and eventually sought the return of her gift. The court would have ordered it, on the basis of undue influence, but did not do so because of the six-year delay between her leaving the convent and seeking its return.

30 E.g. *Williams* v *Bayley* (1866).

14.34 *Allcard* v *Skinner*, however, was not a case where undue influence was established. It was presumed, and whilst there are cases of 'actual' (i.e. proven) undue influence, the situation is more commonly that the facts are such as to have brought about its presumption. Presumed undue influence developed because the courts were asked to deal with 'insidious forms of spiritual tyranny' and 'protect persons from the exercise of such influence under circumstances which render proof of it impossible' (*Allcard* v *Skinner* (1887) 36 Ch D 145 at 183–4). In *Barclays Bank plc* v *O'Brien* [1993] 4 All ER 417 (at 423) the House of Lords recognized a subdivision within presumed undue influence, which can be referred to as types A and B; the House of Lords in *Royal Bank of Scotland* v *Etridge (No 2)* (2001) further clarified this. In some cases, there are in fact two different presumptions of different types. The first type of situation (type A), where there is a double presumption, involves a presumption of law that the relationship is one in which there is relevant influence, and an evidential presumption that undue influence has been exercised. The second type of situation (type B) merely involves the evidential presumption that undue influence has been exercised: the necessary relationship of influence, does, first, have to be established. Importantly, though, it should be emphasized that in both situations (A and B), for the evidential presumption that undue influence was used, to arise, the transaction must be one which 'calls for an explanation' or which is 'not readily explicable by the relationship of the parties' (*Royal Bank of Scotland* v *Etridge (No 2)* (2001) at [14], [21], [24]). The usual way in which the evidential presumption of exercise of undue influence is rebutted (the legal one cannot be) is by showing that the party claiming to have been subject to it received independent advice.

14.35 In considering undue influence, then, it is necessary to look at whether it can actually be proved to have been exercised to produce the transaction ('actual undue influence'), or whether it is a type A situation, giving rise to the double presumption, or a type B situation, giving rise to the single presumption. However, although the structure through which the court approaches a claim of undue influence has become more defined, it remains unclear as to exactly what is required for undue influence, and also, therefore, as to what is being presumed. In short, it is not clear what makes the influence 'undue': is it simply its extent (i.e. that it is excessive), or that it has been exercised in some sense 'wrongfully'? In broad terms, the question is: is it just about the claimant's 'consent', or does it require wrongfulness by the defendant?

14.36 It was strongly contended that it was simply a matter of impaired 'consent'—and that nothing wrongful was required on the part of the other party—by Birks and Chin,[31] but this view has met with considerable opposition.[32] On the whole, the courts lean towards the idea of

31 P. Birks and Chin Nyuk Yin, 'On the Nature of Undue Influence' in J. Beatson and D. Friedmann (eds), *Good Faith and Fault in Contract Law*, Oxford University Press, 1995.

32 R. Bigwood, 'Undue Influence: "Impaired Consent" or "Wicked Exploitation"' (1996) 16 OJLS 503; D. Capper, 'Unconscionable Bargain in the Common Law World' (2010) 126 LQR 403; M. Chen-Wishart, 'Undue Influence: Beyond Impaired Consent and Wrongdoing to a Relational Analysis' in A. Burrows and Lord Rodger (eds), *Mapping the Law: Essays in Memory of Peter Birks*, Oxford University Press, 2006.

some wrongfulness being required. In *Royal Bank of Scotland* v *Etridge (No 2)* (2001), for example, Lord Nicholls said (at [8]) of undue influence that it arises out 'of a relationship between two persons where one has acquired over another a measure of influence, or ascendancy, of which the ascendant person then takes unfair advantage'. Similarly, in *R* v *Attorney General for England and Wales* (2003), where undue influence was considered, as well as duress, Lord Hoffmann said (at [21]):[33]

> Like duress at common law, undue influence is based upon the principle that a transaction to which consent has been obtained by unacceptable means should not be allowed to stand. Undue influence has concentrated in particular upon the unfair exploitation by one party of a relationship which gives him ascendancy or influence over the other.

14.37 However, in *Niersmans* v *Pesticcio* (2004), Mummery LJ said (at [20]):[34]

> Although undue influence is sometimes described as an 'equitable wrong' or even as a species of equitable fraud, the basis of the court's intervention is not the commission of a dishonest or wrongful act by the defendant, but that, as a matter of public policy, the presumed influence arising from the relationship of trust and confidence should not operate to the disadvantage of the victim, if the transaction is not satisfactorily explained by ordinary motives: *Allcard v. Skinner* (1887) 36 Ch D 145 at 171. The court scrutinises the circumstances in which the transaction, under which benefits were conferred on the recipient, took place and the nature of the continuing relationship between the parties, rather than any specific act or conduct on the part of the recipient. A transaction may be set aside by the court, even though the actions and conduct of the person who benefits from it could not be criticised as wrongful.

Further, in *Macklin* v *Dowsett* (2004) Auld LJ emphasized that undue influence was concerned with the 'protection of the vulnerable', and 'misconduct' by the other did not have to be established (at [10]). Indeed, in *Allcard* v *Skinner* (1887), Bowen LJ said, of the mother superior (at 190–1):

> I acquit her most entirely of all selfish feeling in the matter. I can see no sort of wrongful desire to appropriate to herself any worldly benefit from the gift; but, nevertheless, she was a person who benefited by it so far as the disposition of the property was concerned, although, no doubt, she meant to use it in conformity with the rules of the institution, and did so use it.

It may be that the wrongfulness which is required in addition to the claimant's impaired decision making may be no more than that, in the light of the relationship, the defendant should

33 See also Lord Millett in *National Commercial Bank (Jamaica) Ltd* v *Hew* (2003) at [29]–[31].

34 See also *Hammond* v *Osborn* (2002); *Forde* v *Birmingham City Council* (2009) at [103].

have, and did not, ensure that the claimant was liberated from their influence in relation to the relevant transaction (for example, by independent advice).[35]

14.38 A further introductory point should be made here as to the modern context of many cases concerned with undue influence. The issue tends to arise in cases in which a wife has guaranteed a loan by a bank to the husband's business and charged the matrimonial home as security. When the business runs into difficulties, the wife claims that she provided the guarantee and executed the charge under the undue influence of her husband, and that the bank is affected by that, and cannot enforce its security against her. Given this common context, although the problem is not confined to the relationship of husband and wife—or even unmarried partners—the basic problem has sometimes been labelled as one of 'sexually transmitted debt'. Although we are chiefly concerned here with what these cases tell us about undue influence, as such, the question does arise as to when a third party to the undue influence is affected by it. There is a question of balancing the protection of the wife with the need not to stultify the family home as an asset which small businesses can use to raise money. Banks will not lend money on the basis of security which is too likely not to be available to them.

Actual undue influence

14.39 In *Bank of Credit and Commerce International SA* v *Aboody* [1992] 4 All ER 955, Slade LJ said (at 976) that actual undue influence requires:

> (a) that the other party to the transaction . . . had the capacity to influence the complainant; (b) that the influence was exercised; (c) that its exercise was undue; (d) that its exercise brought about the transaction.

Obviously, this raises again the issue of the meaning of 'undue'. A further requirement of 'manifest disadvantage' was dismissed in *CIBC Mortgages* v *Pitt* (1994), and it was not applied to actual undue influence as a requirement in *Etridge*, when 'manifest disadvantage' was reconceived as the need for the transaction to be one 'calling for an explanation', for the generation of the presumption of the exercise of undue influence. However, Lord Nicholls also made the point, in *Etridge* (at [12]):

> It is not essential that the transaction should be disadvantageous to the pressurised or influenced person, either in financial terms or in any other way. However, in the nature of things, questions of undue influence will not usually arise, and the exercise of undue influence is unlikely to occur, where the transaction is innocuous. The issue is likely to arise only when, in some respect, the transaction was disadvantageous either from the outset or as matters turned out.

Obviously, it is generally presumed undue influence which is in question. Someone claiming influence will normally use the easier route, requiring them merely to establish what will give rise to the presumption, or presumptions, rather than actually prove that undue influence has occurred.

35 R. Bigwood, 'Undue Influence: "Impaired Consent" or "Wicked Exploitation"' (1996) 16 OJLS 503.

Presumed undue influence—the double presumption—type A

14.40 Equity took the approach that there were some categories of relationship where the vulnerability or dependence of one party would normally be such that the existence of influence did not need to be established but was presumed as a matter of law (not just evidentially), and so could not be rebutted. This means that when the relationship between the relevant parties falls within one of these identified categories, the necessary influence for a claim of undue influence is presumed to exist and the alleged wielder of the influence cannot prove otherwise. Examples of these relationships are 'parent and child, guardian and ward, trustee and beneficiary, solicitor and client, medical advisor and patient' (*Royal Bank of Scotland* v *Etridge (No 2)* (2001)). It should be noted that the relationship of husband and wife is not one of those encompassed within the presumption of the existence of relevant influence.[36]

14.41 However, in *Etridge* it was made clear that the above automatic presumption of law is only as to the existence of relevant influence between the parties. It is only if another factor is present that there is a second, evidential presumption that undue influence was exercised, and that factor relates to the transaction. As has been indicated, the transaction must be one which 'calls for an explanation' or which is 'not readily explicable by the relationship of the parties' (*Etridge* at [14] and [21]). Lord Nicholls said (at [24]):

> The second prerequisite . . . is good sense. It is a necessary limitation upon the width of the first prerequisite. It would be absurd for the law to presume that every gift by a child to a parent, or every transaction between a client and his solicitor or between a patient and his doctor, was brought about by undue influence unless the contrary is affirmatively proved . . . The law would be rightly open to ridicule, for transactions such as these are unexceptionable. They do not suggest that something may be amiss. So something more is needed before the law reverses the burden of proof, something which calls for an explanation.

This further factor will be considered at para. **14.49**ff. Here, it should be emphasized that, unlike the first presumption, this second presumption is merely evidential, so that it can be rebutted. All that the triggering of this second presumption means is that the evidential burden shifts to the person who allegedly exercised undue influence, that is, he or she will be found to have exercised undue influence unless they adduce sufficient evidence to the contrary. Rebutting the presumption will also be returned to later.

Presumed undue influence—the single presumption—type B

14.42 The second situation in which it is said that there is presumed undue influence only involves a single presumption, and that merely the evidential one. Before that can come into play it must be established not only that the transaction is one calling for an

36 *Bank of Montreal* v *Stuart* (1911); *Midland Bank plc* v *Shephard* [1988] 3 All ER 17 at 21; *National Westminster Bank plc* v *Morgan* [1985] 1 All ER at 821 at 826.

explanation, but also, first, that the relationship between the parties involved relevant influence (*Royal Bank of Scotland* v *Etridge (No 2)*(2001) at [21]), and it is here, perhaps, that the case law provides most consideration of the relevant influence. In general, discussion of the requirements of a relationship of influence has been quite limited. There is a tendency merely to rely upon labelling a relevant relationship as 'confidential' or 'fiduciary'. However, as has been indicated, what is required is a relationship in which one party has surrendered relevant decision making. It may be through 'domination' and 'control', but most commonly what is in question is a relationship of trust and confidence: the type of trust and confidence which leads one party, A, to rely upon the other party, B, to act in A's interests rather than B's own interests. It is reliance upon, and trust in, disinterested advice. The cases illuminating the type of trust and confidence required will now be considered. However, whilst the focus in the discussion of the cases below is on the relationship required, sight must not be lost of the fact that *Etridge* made it clear that the evidential presumption that undue influence has been exercised will only arise if the transaction is also one which 'calls for an explanation'.

14.43 In *Lloyds Bank Ltd* v *Bundy* [1974] 3 All ER 757 a relevant relationship was found, and the situation was distinguished from the trust which can exist in a business relationship between parties dealing at arm's length. In that case, the facts were as follows:

Mr Bundy charged his home to guarantee his son's business debts to the bank. Both father and son used the same bank. The father's relationship with the bank was longstanding, and he relied upon it for advice. When the assistant manager brought the charge to Mr Bundy's home to be signed he realized that Mr Bundy looked to him for advice. The assistant manager not only explained the legal effect of the charge but also discussed the situation of the son's company. Mr Bundy 'was seeking and being given advice on the viability of the company as a factor to be taken into account' in his decision to sign the charge. The charge was not to enable the son to borrow more money from the bank, but merely to secure his existing loans. The execution of the charge meant that the bank was not demanding repayment immediately, but it did not guarantee a period within which it would not do so. Very little was gained by Mr Bundy, or his son, in return for the execution of the charge, but the bank gained security for existing debts. The assistant manager had not perceived any conflict of interest, and had not advised Mr Bundy to obtain independent advice.

When the bank claimed possession of Mr Bundy's home, he argued that the charge should be set aside for undue influence. The Court of Appeal concluded that Mr Bundy's reliance upon the bank to give general advice on the wisdom of the transaction was a relevant relationship. (As is plain, it was also a transaction which called for an explanation—the father gained little from it.) In the absence of independent advice for Mr Bundy, the presumption of the exercise of undue influence was not rebutted. Sir Eric Sachs considered the usual type of relevant relationship (at 767):

> [T]here must of course be shown to exist a vital element which in this judgement will be referred to as confidentiality. It is this element which is so impossible to define and which is a matter for the judgment of the court on the facts of any particular case . . . It imports some quality beyond that inherent in the confidence that can well exist between trustworthy persons who in business affairs deal with each other at arm's length. It is one of the features of this element that once it exists, influence naturally grows out of it.

Despite his reluctance to regard the 'vital element' of 'confidentiality' as definable, Sir Eric Sachs' distinction between the situation in which a relevant relationship exists and that of business dealings at arm's length between trustworthy persons makes it clear that he is referring to the situation where one party is expected to give disinterested advice to the other. The question in relation to this usual type of relevant relationship is: Is the person concerned trusted to the extent that he or she is relied upon to act in the interests of the other party, and not his or her own? It is that degree of trust, reliance, or confidence which can give rise to undue influence.

14.44 The relationship of banker and customer was again considered in *National Westminster Bank plc* v *Morgan* (1985), and the House of Lords distinguished the case from *Lloyds Bank Ltd* v *Bundy* (1974). In *Morgan*, the facts were as follows:

> A husband and wife were in danger of losing their home because the building society was seeking possession for non-payment of the mortgage. The bank agreed to a refinancing of the house purchase on the basis of a bridging loan to cover the few weeks until the husband expected to have the money. His business was then looking prosperous, although it had been through hard times. However, the bank required a charge on the house for the loan. The bank manager called at the house to obtain the wife's signature on the legal charge. He mistakenly assured the wife that the charge would not extend to her husband's business liabilities to the bank. In fact, the charge was sufficiently widely worded to cover those business liabilities, but it was not the intention of the bank that it should be so used and it never was so used. The husband died and the bank sought possession of the house.

The wife did not raise the issue of innocent misrepresentation, but merely claimed that the charge should be set aside for undue influence. The House of Lords held that there was no relevant relationship. The manager had explained the charge to her, but the wife had not looked to the manager for general advice on the wisdom of the transaction. She executed the charge because that was how she and her husband planned to preserve the family home, and she knew that it was the only way to do so. In *Bundy* the bank had discussed with Mr Bundy the position of his son's business. In addition, in *Morgan* the transaction was 'readily explicable'—it was a normal commercial loan taken as the only hope the couple had of preserving the matrimonial home—and so no presumption of undue influence could arise, in any event. (At the time, the House of Lords put this in terms of the transaction not involving a 'manifest disadvantage' to the wife, but that test was clarified in *Royal Bank of Scotland* v *Etridge (No 2)* (2001)—on this second requirement, see para. **14.49**.)

14.45 We should give brief consideration to the use by Lord Scarman, in *National Westminster Bank plc* v *Morgan* (1985), of the term 'dominating influence' to indicate the situation in which a relevant relationship of influence exists. Although the existence of a dominating influence would undoubtedly suffice (where decision making has been surrendered to the dominant person), it was made clear in *Goldsworthy* v *Brickell* [1987] 1 All ER 853 that there is no requirement that the relationship be a dominating one. The facts there were as follows:

> Mr Goldsworthy owned a farm which, from 1970 to 1976, he had run with his son as his sole employee. He had little faith in his son's abilities, relations between them were strained, and the farm was in a run-down condition. The son did not live in the farmhouse with his father. From the end of 1976, Mr Brickell, a neighbouring farmer, gave Mr Goldsworthy help and advice in the running of his farm. Mr Brickell's employees worked on Mr Goldsworthy's farm at no cost to him. One of Mr Brickell's female employees cleaned Mr Goldsworthy's house and did his shopping for him. Mr Goldsworthy's reliance upon Mr Brickell and his employees was such that, by early 1977, Mr Brickell was effectively managing Mr Goldsworthy's farm. In April 1977, Mr Goldsworthy, who was then 85, whilst keeping the right to live on the farm, granted Mr Brickell a tenancy of his farm with an option to purchase it on his death. Both were on terms very disadvantageous to Mr Goldsworthy.

The Court of Appeal set aside the tenancy agreement. There was a relevant relationship between Mr Brickell and Mr Goldsworthy and the presumption of undue influence was raised. The court made it clear that the relationship was sufficient even though it fell short of domination. It was enough that the appropriate trust and confidence existed between the parties.

14.46 *Goldsworthy* also contains further indication that the essence of the 'trust and confidence' relationship in which the required 'influence' will be found is that of reliance, not merely upon someone's judgement but also upon their advice being totally disinterested, that is, not tainted by their own interests. Nourse LJ explained why the relationships of solicitor and client, and doctor and patient, are regarded as giving rise to the legal presumption that the relationship is one of influence. He said (at 868):

> [D]octors and solicitors are trusted and confided in by their patients and clients to give them conscientious and disinterested advice on matters which profoundly affect, in the one case their physical and mental and, in the other, their material wellbeing. It is natural to presume that out of trust and confidence grows influence.

He also explained why the banker–customer relationship is not one which gives rise to this legal presumption:

> [A] banker, being a person having a pre-existing and conflicting interest in any loan transaction with a customer, cannot ordinarily be trusted and confided in so as to come under a duty to take care of the customer and give him disinterested advice.

Again the emphasis is upon it being the expectation of disinterested advice, which is significant in the relationship of influence.[37]

14.47 Although it seems necessary to identify the relevant 'influence', Lord Scarman's warning in *National Westminster Bank plc* v *Morgan* [1985] 1 All ER 821 must be borne in mind. He said (at 877):

> There is no precisely defined law setting the limits to the equitable jurisdiction of a court to relieve against undue influence. This is the world of doctrine, not of neat and tidy rules.

14.48 Again it should be emphasized that *Royal Bank of Scotland* v *Etridge (No 2)* (2001) has made clear that establishing a relevant relationship of influence is not sufficient to generate the evidential presumption that undue influence was exercised. That also requires the transaction to be one which 'calls for an explanation'.

Transactions 'calling for an explanation'

14.49 As has been indicated, the evidential presumption of the exercise of undue influence does not arise unless the transaction is one which 'calls for an explanation' or is 'not readily explicable by the relationship of the parties' (*Royal Bank of Scotland* v *Etridge (No 2)* (2001) at [14] and [21]). This derives from the judgment of Lindley LJ in *Allcard* v *Skinner* (1887) 36 Ch D 145. Making the point that the existence of a relationship of influence is not sufficient but that, coupled with it, the nature of the transaction may raise the presumption, Lindley LJ said (at 185):

> But if the gift is so large as not to be reasonably accounted for on the ground of friendship, relationship, charity, or other ordinary motives on which ordinary men act, the burden is on the donee to support the gift.

It was a gift which was in question in that case, but the point applies to transactions more generally.

14.50 In *National Westminster Bank plc* v *Morgan* (1985) this requirement was restated in terms of 'manifest disadvantage', that is, that the transaction must be one sufficiently disadvantageous to the person claiming undue influence to require evidence to rebut the presumption of the exercise of undue influence. However, in *Etridge* the view was taken that seeing this requirement in terms of 'manifest disadvantage' had caused difficulties, particularly in the situation of the wife providing a guarantee to support the husband's business borrowing. The line was taken that there should be a return to a requirement more closely reflecting the original statement of Lindley LJ in *Allcard* v *Skinner* (1887) and hence the references earlier to a transaction 'calling for an explanation' or one which 'is not readily

37 See also *Elton John* v *James* [1991] FSR 397 at 449–51.

explicable by the relationship of the parties' (*Royal Bank of Scotland* v *Etridge (No 2)* (2001) at [14] and [21]).

14.51 The situation in which a wife provides a guarantee to the bank of the husband's business borrowing having proved troublesome in this context, it is worth some further consideration. It would seem that finding the requisite trust and confidence between husband and wife may be very easy. Lord Scott took the line in *Etridge* (at [189]) that:

> I would assume in every case in which a wife and husband are living together that there is a reciprocal trust and confidence between them. In the fairly common circumstance that the financial and business decisions of the family are primarily taken by the husband, I would assume that the wife would have trust and confidence in his ability to do so and would support his decisions.

Nevertheless, it would also seem that it will be difficult for the presumption to be generated in the husband-and-wife guarantee type of case. It was indicated that 'in the ordinary course' such a situation would not trigger the evidential presumption (at [30]). It was recognized that 'in a narrow sense' such a transaction is disadvantageous to the wife: 'she undertakes a serious financial obligation and in return she personally receives nothing' (at [28]) (hence the difficulties with the *National Westminster Bank plc* v *Morgan* (1985) approach). However, the further point was made that:

> Ordinarily, the fortunes of husband and wife are bound up together. If the husband's business is the source of the family income, the wife has a lively interest in doing what she can to support the business. A wife's affection and self-interest run hand-in-hand in inclining her to join with her husband in charging the matrimonial home, usually a jointly-owned asset, to obtain the financial facilities needed by the business. (at [28])

So, the 'ordinary' situations of that type were seen as not generating the presumption. Lord Nicholls said (at [30]):

> Wives frequently enter into such transactions. There are good and sufficient reasons why they are willing to do so, despite the risks involved for them and their families. They may be enthusiastic. They may not. They may be less optimistic than their husbands about the prospects of the husbands' businesses. They may be anxious, perhaps exceedingly so. But this is a far cry from saying that such transactions as a class are to be regarded as prima facie evidence of the exercise of undue influence by husbands.

So, although finding the requisite trust and confidence between husband and wife may be very easy, *Etridge* indicates that it will be difficult for the presumption to be generated in the husband-and-wife guarantee type of case.

14.52 However, Lord Nicholls also provided some indication of the circumstances in which a husband-and-wife guarantee case might not be 'ordinary', but would be one in which the court should intervene. He said:

> In the eye of the law, undue influence means that influence has been misused. Statements or conduct by a husband which do not pass beyond the bounds of what may be expected of a reasonable husband in the circumstances should not, without more, be castigated as undue influence. Similarly, when a husband is forecasting the future of his business, and expressing his hopes or fears, a degree of hyperbole may be only natural. Courts should not too readily treat such exaggerations as misstatements. Inaccurate explanations of a proposed transaction are a different matter. So are cases where a husband, in whom a wife has reposed trust and confidence for the management of their financial affairs, prefers his interests to hers and makes a choice for both of them on that footing. Such a husband abuses the influence he has. He fails to discharge the obligation of candour and fairness he owes a wife who is looking to him to make the major financial decisions. (*Royal Bank of Scotland* v *Etridge (No 2)* (2001) at [32])

Rebutting the presumption

14.53 The evidential presumption of the exercise of undue influence may be rebutted by showing that the transaction was entered into 'only after full, free and informed thought about it' (*Zamet* v *Hyman* [1961] 3 All ER 933 at 938). In *Inche Noriah* v *Shaik Allie Bin Omar* [1929] AC 127 (at 135)—in the context of a gift, but the point is more generally applicable—it was said:

> It is necessary for the donee to prove that the gift was the result of the free exercise of independent will. The most obvious way to prove this is by establishing that the gift was made after the nature of the transaction had been fully explained to the donor by some independent and qualified person so completely as to satisfy the Court that the donor was acting independently of any influence from the donee and with full appreciation of what he was doing.

However, 'the weight, or importance, to be attached to such advice depends on all the circumstances . . . [A] person may understand fully the implications of a proposed transaction . . . and yet still be acting under the influence of another' (*Etridge* at [20] per Lord Nicholls). There may, for example, be occasions when a transaction is so disadvantageous that no one taking due account of proper advice could enter into it. Clearly, at such times, independent advice will not rebut the presumption.

Undue influence and third parties

14.54 Although our primary interest is in the elements of actual or presumed undue influence, some consideration will now be given to when a third party will be affected by undue influence: actual or presumed. As has been indicated, the context in which undue influence has often been raised in recent years is that of a wife claiming that she was acting under the undue influence of her husband when she became a surety for a loan to the husband, or the husband's business, and secured it by a charge on the matrimonial home. Under such circumstances, if the transaction is to be set aside for undue influence, the bank (or other creditor) to which the surety was given will have to be affected by the undue influence. What is in issue is a question of balance. There is a need to protect wives from undue influence but the family home is an important asset for small businesses to use to raise money. In *Royal Bank of Scotland* v *Etridge (No 2)* (2001), Lord Nicholls noted at [37] that what was needed was to achieve a balance point between competing interests:

> On the one side there is the need to protect a wife against a husband's undue influence. On the other side there is the need for the bank to be able to have reasonable confidence in the strength of its security. Otherwise it would not provide the required money.

This question of the balance point will be given some brief consideration here. (The discussion will basically take place in terms of the common situation of the husband/wife/bank/guarantee transaction, but the issue is not restricted to the husband and wife relationship, or the situation in which the transaction is a guarantee.)

14.55 After a series of decisions by the lower courts, the House of Lords first considered the question of when third parties are affected by undue influence in *Barclays Bank plc* v *O'Brien* [1993] 4 All ER 417. The case was concerned with the surety, charged on the matrimonial home, which a wife had given in relation to the overdraft of her husband's business. She claimed that she had executed it whilst acting under the undue influence of her husband and that he had misrepresented the extent and duration of the borrowing covered by it. By the time the case reached the House of Lords the claim was restricted to misrepresentation, but it is clear that the test of the impact upon the bank is the same whether the wife acted under undue influence or misrepresentation.

14.56 The House of Lords said that there were basically two ways in which a bank's surety could be affected by a husband's undue influence and a charge set aside. That would occur if either (a) the husband had acted as the bank's agent to obtain the execution of the charge, or (b) the bank had actual or constructive notice of the facts giving rise to the wife's claim (at 428). As has been indicated, although stated in relation to husband and wife, this is of more general application. The first possibility, involving a finding of an agency relationship between creditor and debtor, is unlikely to occur. It is 'notice' which is significant, and, in particular, 'constructive notice'. In effect, through addressing two issues, 'constructive notice' provides the balance point. The two issues are, first, the point at which the creditor is 'put on inquiry' and second, the steps which the House of Lords, in *O'Brien* and subsequently in *Etridge*, stated:

> [A] bank should take to ensure that it is not affected by any claim the wife may have that her signature . . . was procured by the undue influence or other wrong of her husband. (*Royal Bank of Scotland* v *Etridge (No 2)* (2001) at [37])

Once factors in the situation put the creditor 'on inquiry' as to the potential for undue influence, the creditor would, absent further action, be fixed with constructive notice of any undue influence found, but it has become clear what steps should be taken by the creditor that will normally prevent that occurring. Those steps will limit the possibility that there has been undue influence, but they 'will not guarantee that . . . wives will not be subjected to undue influence or misled when standing as sureties'. However, as has been indicated, what is necessary is a balance between protecting the vulnerable and not stultifying the matrimonial home as potential security for the borrowing of small businesses.

'Put on inquiry'

14.57 In *Barclays Bank plc* v *O'Brien*, Lord Browne-Wilkinson, with whom the other members of the court agreed, said ([1993] 4 All ER 417 at 429):

> A creditor is put on inquiry when a wife offers to stand surety for her husband's debts by the combination of two factors: (a) the transaction is on its face not to the financial advantage of the wife; and (b) there is a substantial risk in transactions of that kind that, in procuring the wife to act as surety, the husband has committed a legal or equitable wrong that entitles the wife to set aside the transaction.

This, in effect, indicates a focus on two factors to determine if the bank has been 'put on inquiry': first, the relationship between the parties; second, the nature of the transaction. In *Royal Bank of Scotland* v *Etridge (No 2)* (2001), the above passage was seen as meaning 'quite simply, that a bank is put on inquiry whenever a wife offers to stand surety for her husband's debts' (per Lord Nicholls at [44]). Outside of the husband and wife situation, the difficulty is that 'the reality of life is that relationships in which undue influence can be exercised are infinitely various' (at [86]) and certainty is needed as to when a creditor will be 'put on inquiry'. It would be too uncertain and too difficult for the creditor to investigate the details of the relationship between a wide range of potential borrowers and sureties. To achieve the necessary certainty, the line was taken that the creditor should be 'put on inquiry' whenever the 'relationship between the debtor and the surety is non-commercial' (at [87]). That was viewed as setting a low but very clear trigger point for the bank to take the necessary steps to limit the possibility of undue influence and protect itself from constructive notice of any that remained. The clarity of the trigger point is very desirable and the taking of the steps then required of the creditor was seen as 'a modest burden' and 'no more than is to be reasonably expected of a creditor who is taking a guarantee from an individual' (at [87]).

14.58 Putting a creditor on inquiry is not, then, confined to particular relationships between a guarantor and debtor. Of course, neither is it confined to the debtor–guarantor situation. Joint loans to husbands and wives were distinguished from the surety situation as they would not normally put the creditor 'on inquiry'. However, they would do so if the creditor was aware the loan was actually being taken for the husband's purposes alone, rather than their joint purposes (at [48]). This emphasizes the additional important point: it is not the actual relationship between the parties which is in question, nor the actual transaction, but the relationship and transaction as they reasonably appear to the creditor, or of which the creditor has actual knowledge. Constructive notice was not found where what was involved was a mortgage of the family home and the mortgage application stated that it was to buy a holiday home, even though its purpose was actually to allow the husband to speculate on the stock exchange (*CIBC Mortgages* v *Pitt* (1993)).

What can the third party do to prevent itself being fixed with constructive notice?

14.59 If a low point is set for the creditor to be put on inquiry, what must the creditor do to prevent it being found to have constructive notice of any undue influence between husband and wife (or other parties)? In *Barclays Bank plc* v *O'Brien*, guidelines were provided. It was indicated that, in the ordinary case, the creditor can avoid being found to have constructive notice of any undue influence ([1993] 4 All ER 417 at 429–30):

> if it insists that the wife attend a private meeting (in the absence of the husband) with a representative of the [creditor] at which she is told of the extent of her liability as surety, warned of the risk she is running and urged to take independent legal advice.

Nothing of the sort had occurred in *O'Brien* and the bank had constructive notice of the husband's wrong. However, in the main, since *O'Brien*, creditors have shown themselves reluctant to take exactly the approach indicated there. Creditors did not want to run the risk of claims based on assurances alleged to have been given to wives (e.g. that the creditor would not call in the relevant loan) at any such meetings (*Royal Bank of Scotland* v *Etridge (No 2)* (2001) at [55]). Creditors have instead preferred to ensure that they obtain confirmation from a solicitor that the solicitor has advised the wife appropriately. The acceptability of such a practice as a means of preventing the creditor from being affected by undue influence between husband and wife was recognized in *Etridge*. The line was taken that:

> Ordinarily it will be reasonable that a bank should be able to rely upon confirmation from a solicitor, acting for the wife, that he has advised the wife appropriately. (at [56])

As was emphasized in *Etridge*, it will not be sufficient merely for the creditor to know, or have confirmation, that a solicitor is acting for the wife:

> Knowledge by a bank that a solicitor is acting for a surety wife does not, without more, justify the bank in assuming that the solicitor's instructions extend to advising her about the nature and effect of the transaction. (*Etridge* at [168])

A solicitor's role may be no more than executing an agreed transaction. What is required by the creditor is confirmation that she has received 'appropriate advice'.

14.60 Of course, as has been indicated, the approach taken by the House of Lords in *Etridge* does not generally seek to make the creditor ensure that there is no undue influence operating. In general, what was seen as required were steps to ensure that her decision was an informed one:

> The furthest a bank can be expected to go is to take reasonable steps to satisfy itself that the wife has had brought home to her, in a meaningful way, the practical implications of the proposed transaction. This does not wholly eliminate the risk of undue influence or

> misrepresentation. But it does mean that a wife enters into a transaction with her eyes open so far as the basic elements of the transaction are concerned. (per Lord Nicholls at [54]; but see Lord Hobhouse at [111])

In other words, the procedures indicated by the House of Lords should ensure that the wife is informed but they will not necessarily mean that she is liberated from any undue influence. Nevertheless, the court recognized that there is a point at which the solicitor should decline to act and refuse to supply confirmation of advice to the bank. That will occur in 'exceptional circumstances where it is glaringly obvious that the wife is being grievously wronged' (at [62]).

Aggressive trade practices

Introduction

14.61 The Consumer Protection from Unfair Trading Regulations 2008 have provided public enforcement mechanisms to deal with misleading and aggressive trade practices, and more broadly with unfair commercial practices. The Law Commissions recommended that redress should be provided for the individual consumer in relation to misleading and aggressive practices, and the 2008 Regulations were amended by the Consumer Protection (Amendment) Regulations 2014 to bring that about. Obviously, here we are concerned with aggressive practices. (Misleading practices were considered in **Chapter 13**, on misrepresentation.) The aim is to provide a straightforward legal structure to afford consumers a remedy in situations where there is none, or where it is inadequate, or too complex, or uncertain.

14.62 The Law Commissions provided examples of the sort of situations which consumers had encountered:[38]

> **Example: pressure doorstep-selling**
> An elderly housebound man was sold a £3,000 bed. The salesman stayed for three hours, giving the impression that he would only leave if the consumer agreed to buy.
> The trader offered a 14-day cancellation period, but the next day the salesman returned, unpacked the bed and took a cheque for the full amount.
>
> **Example: pressure-selling a car**
> A consumer was subjected to four hours of pressure-selling and felt unable to leave the dealer's showroom. The salesperson added that if the consumer did not buy the car, the salesperson would be sacked. The consumer was worn down and agreed to buy the car.
>
> **Example: pressure-selling a holiday club**
> A couple agreed to attend a two-hour presentation about a holiday club. In fact the presentation lasted six hours and, feeling under considerable pressure, the couple eventually agreed to become club members. The next day they returned to try to cancel the contract. The company threatened to call the police if they did not leave.

38 *Consumer Redress for Misleading and Aggressive Practices* Law Com No 332, Scot Law Com No 226 (2012) para. 1.15.

Basic scope

14.63 The idea is that where a consumer has been subject to an aggressive commercial practice by a trader, and made a contract for a product, the consumer should have a remedy. The definition of 'consumer' reflects that now commonly used in relation to European-derived legislation, so that a consumer means 'an individual acting for purposes that are wholly or mainly outside that individual's business'.[39] A 'trader' is a 'person acting for purposes relating to that person's business, whether acting personally or through another person acting in the trader's name or on the trader's behalf'. The contract must be for a product but that definition is intentionally kept very broad, including goods, services, digital content, rights, or obligations,[40] but not dealing with land other than a residential lease, and not financial services.[41] The consumer needs to show that the trader carried out an aggressive commercial practice, which was likely to cause the average consumer to make a decision to enter into a contract for a product which they would not otherwise have taken and which was a 'significant factor' in the particular consumer's own decision to contract. A practice is aggressive 'if, in its factual context, taking account of all its features and circumstances, (a) it significantly impairs or is likely significantly to impair the average consumer's freedom of choice or conduct in relation to the product concerned through the use of harassment, coercion or undue influence, and (b) it thereby causes or is likely to cause him to take a transactional decision he would not have taken otherwise.'[42] Coercion 'includes the use of physical force'.[43] 'Undue influence' means 'exploiting a position of power in relation to the consumer so as to apply pressure, even without using or threatening to use physical force, in a way which significantly limits the consumer's ability to make an informed decision'.[44] There is a list of factors to be taken into account in deciding if a commercial practice is aggressive, including its 'timing, location, nature or persistence', the 'use of threatening or abusive language or behaviour', the 'exploitation by the trader of any specific misfortune or circumstance of such gravity as to impair the consumer's judgment, of which the trader is aware, to influence the consumer's decision', and 'any threat to take any action which cannot legally be taken'.[45]

14.64 The aggressive trade practice must have impacted significantly upon the consumer's own decision to contract, but also be such as to be likely to have done so in relation to the average consumer. Thus, it is not merely a matter of subjective decision making; rather, a standard of expected resistance to aggressive commercial practices is generally set. The 'average consumer' is generally

39 Regulation 2(1) Consumer Protection from Unfair Trading Regulations 2008 (as amended by the Consumer Protection (Amendment) Regulations 2014).

40 Regulation 2(1) of the Consumer Protection from Unfair Trading Regulations (as amended by the Consumer Protection (Amendment) Regulations 2014).

41 Regulation 27C & 27D of the Consumer Protection from Unfair Trading Regulations (as amended by the Consumer Protection (Amendment) Regulations 2014).

42 Regulation 7(1) of the Consumer Protection from Unfair Trading Regulations 2008.

43 Regulation 7(3)(a) of the Consumer Protection from Unfair Trading Regulations 2008.

44 Regulation 7(3)(b) of the Consumer Protection from Unfair Trading Regulations 2008.

45 Regulation 7(2) of the Consumer Protection from Unfair Trading Regulations 2008.

'reasonably well informed, reasonably observant and circumspect'. Obviously, if it was left there, questions would arise as to the efficacy of the protection which would be afforded to the elderly, or other consumers who are more vulnerable than the 'average consumer'. However, the idea is that it should be the average member of a particular group of consumers who is referred to where

1. the commercial practice is directed to a particular group of consumers; or
2. a clearly identifiable group of consumers is particularly vulnerable to the practice because of their mental or physical infirmity, age, or credulity in a way which the trader could reasonably be expected to foresee.

Remedies

14.65 The primary remedy is the right to 'unwind' the contract. This is obviously akin to rescission, and the idea is to restore the consumer to the position before the aggressive practice took place, but it is to be less complex. So, for example, where the consumer has made a purchase from the trader or contracted for services, then, provided the consumer is able to reject some element of the goods or services within three months (90 days), it is simply a matter of the consumer getting a refund of the whole price. The bars to rescission, as such, do not arise. The consumer is not prevented from being able to unwind because he or she cannot make restitutio in integrum. If the consumer waits more than three months, or the goods or services have been fully consumed, the consumer is able to claim a discount on the price. Bands of discount are set (25 per cent, 50 per cent, 75 per cent, or 100 per cent in the amended Regulations) and which one is applicable depends upon the impact of the practice, the trader's behaviour, and any delay by the consumer. There is also scope for claims for damages for other losses, calculated on a reliance basis, but the consumer must establish those losses and the trader has a due diligence defence. Obviously, this is intended to be quite a 'rough and ready' system, but a fuller and simpler one, in comparison with common law rules. Common law rights and remedies remain in place, but the legislation should provide more effective and extensive means of dealing with the high-pressure selling techniques which are commonly the problems encountered by consumers, rather than only dealing with something which the common law would label as duress or undue influence.

Summary

Duress

- English law was slow to recognize duress beyond duress to the person, but it is now clear that economic duress can render a contract voidable.
- This recognition enabled the court in *Williams* v *Roffey Bros* (1990) to make it plain that the real issue when a contract is varied (so that more is paid for the same performance) is not whether there is technical consideration but whether there is duress.
- In finding a test for economic duress, the language of the courts has not always been helpful. References to the 'overborne will' and voluntariness do not provide a real test—plainly, the person under duress does exercise his or her will and make a choice.

- There is, basically, a two-stage test:
  1. the illegitimacy of the threat;
  2. the lack of a reasonable alternative to agreeing, for the person threatened.
- Illegitimate threats include threatened criminal and civil wrongs, but it is questioned whether a threatened breach is always sufficient.
- It has been envisaged that a threat may be illegitimate without the law otherwise regarding it as wrongful. In that situation, the question of the bona fides of the person making the threat may be relevant.
- Only the first stage of the test is needed if what is threatened is a criminal wrong.
- In addition, the duress must be a sufficient cause of the new contract.
- As with misrepresentation, rescission for duress may be barred.

Undue influence

- Both actual and presumed undue influence will render a contract voidable.
- The influence in question is such that one party has abdicated their relevant decision making to the other. Actual undue influence is where it is established that undue influence brought about the transaction in question.
- Presumed undue influence arises in two ways:
  - First, the relationship falls within one of the categories of relationship which gives rise to the legal presumption of the existence of relevant influence (for example, parent and child, guardian and ward, trustee and beneficiary, solicitor and client, medical adviser and patient). The exercise of undue influence will then be presumed evidentially if the transaction is one 'calling for an explanation'. The latter presumption can be rebutted. The former cannot.
  - Second, the existence of relevant influence is established between the parties. The exercise of undue influence will be presumed, evidentially, if the transaction is one 'calling for an explanation'. This presumption can be rebutted.
- The evidential presumption of the exercise of undue influence can be rebutted by showing that it was only entered into after 'full free and informed thought about it' by the relevant party. This may be achieved by showing independent advice was received.
- Third parties to the influence may be affected by it.
  - If A enters into a transaction with B because of (actual or presumed) undue influence by C, the transaction may be voidable.
  - It will be voidable if either C was acting as B's agent to procure the transaction or B has actual or constructive notice of the facts giving rise to the undue influence claim.

Aggressive practices

- The Consumer Protection from Unfair Trading Regulations (as amended by the Consumer Protection (Amendment) Regulations 2014)) provide consumers with remedies (unwinding the contract, refund, damages) in relation to aggressive commercial practices.

Further reading

P. S. Atiyah, 'Economic Duress and the Overborne Will' (1982) 98 LQR 197

J. Beatson, 'Duress as a Vitiating Factor in Contract' (1974) 33 CLJ 97

J. Beatson, 'Duress, Restitution and Contract Modification' in J. Beatson, *The Use and Abuse of Unjust Enrichment*, Oxford University Press, 1990, pp. 95–114

R. Bigwood, 'Undue Influence: "Impaired Consent" or "Wicked Exploitation"' (1996) 16 OJLS 503

P. Birks, 'The Travails of Duress' [1990] LMCLQ 342

P. Birks, 'Undue Influence as Wrongful Exploitation' (2004) 120 LQR 34

P. Birks and Chin Nyuk Yin, 'On the Nature of Undue Influence' in J. Beatson and D. Friedmann (eds), *Good Faith and Fault in Contract Law*, Oxford University Press, 1995, pp. 57–98

A. Burrows, *The Law of Restitution*, 3rd edn, Oxford University Press, 2011, chapter 10 (Duress), chapter 11 (Undue influence)

D. Capper, 'Unconscionable Bargain in the Common Law World' (2010) 126 LQR 403

M. Chen-Wishart, 'Undue Influence: Beyond Impaired Consent and Wrongdoing to a Relational Analysis' in A. Burrows and Lord Rodger (eds), *Mapping the Law: Essays in Memory of Peter Birks*, Oxford University Press, 2006, pp. 201–22

Law Commission and the Scottish Law Commission, *Consumer Redress for Misleading and Aggressive Practices* Law Com No 332, Scot Law Com No 226 (2012)

E. McKendrick, 'The Further Travails of Duress' in A. Burrows and Lord Rodger (eds), *Mapping the Law: Essays in Memory of Peter Birks*, Oxford University Press, 2006, pp. 181–200

D. O'Sullivan, 'Developing O'Brien' (2002) 118 LQR 337

S. Smith, 'Contracting under Pressure: A Theory of Duress' (1997) 56 CLJ 343

Chapter 15

Illegality

Introduction

15.1 An agreement may possess all the requisite elements of a valid contract, such as offer and acceptance and consideration, but it may nevertheless contravene a legal rule or be regarded as contrary to public policy. Such a contract can be regarded as 'improper', or 'illegal' in a very general sense, or at least tainted with illegality. Since there are many and disparate reasons for statutory and judicial intervention on the basis of illegality or impropriety, it is not always easy to categorize these reasons.

15.2 It is conventional to subdivide illegal contracts on the basis of the legal consequences of those contracts. Accordingly, contracts are described as being either 'void' or 'illegal'. The problem with such a classification is that there is no general agreement as to which category each type of improper contract falls into. Such a division also fails to reflect the fact that the nature of the illegality which may taint a contract can vary considerably in its seriousness.[1] It is also possible to classify the different types of illegality according to either the nature of the objectionable conduct, or the source of the rule which invalidates it. None of the attempts at classification is wholly convincing.

15.3 It must be emphasized that the traditional approach to the subject is of only limited value as an analytical device. However, for the purpose of clear exposition, it is proposed to adhere to the now favoured distinction between void and illegal contracts. But first, a warning: the following sections are not intended as an exhaustive list of all the different types of illegality. Furthermore, the detailed discussion is focused on those areas of greater commercial and practical significance, particularly in relation to restraint of trade.

1 See G. H. Treitel, *Law of Contract*, 11th edn, Sweet & Maxwell, 2003, p. 430.

Void contracts

15.4 A variety of contracts are rendered void as a result of some statutory provision. For example, a wagering contract was formerly rendered void by the Gaming Act 1845, s 18, which stated:

> All contracts or agreements, whether by parole or in writing, by way of gaming or wagering, shall be null and void; and no suit shall be brought or maintained in any court of law or equity for recovering any sum of money or valuable thing alleged to be won upon any wager, or which shall have been deposited in the hands of any person to abide the event on which any wager shall have been made.

It should be emphasized that this provision did not declare such a contract to be illegal but simply void, that is, no rights were conferred on either party.[2] However, this provision was repealed by the Gambling Act 2005 (s 334), as part of a major legislative reform of the law on gambling. Section 335(1) of the new Act now states that 'the fact that a contract relates to gambling shall not prevent its enforcement'. (Of course, this does not preclude such an agreement being held unlawful on some other ground: see s 335(2).)

Contracts in restraint of trade

15.5 A contract in restraint of trade is one by which a person promises another that his or her future freedom to trade, or to conduct his or her profession, with whomsoever he or she wishes will be curtailed in some way. The restriction may be geographical, for instance covering a particular town or area, and usually it will also cover a specific period of time. The basic rule is that such restraints are prima facie void, but they may become valid if they can be justified as being reasonable between the parties and not inimical to the public interest.

15.6 The doctrine of restraint of trade is largely associated with two particular classes of agreement. (The ambit of the doctrine and its application to other types of agreement are considered later.) These are: (a) an agreement by a person selling the 'goodwill' of a business that he or she will not start another business in direct competition with the buyer; and (b) an agreement between employer and employee by which the latter promises that he or she will not, on leaving his or her present employment, work for a rival of his or her employer, or start a business in competition with his or her employer. There are two major reasons for the legal regulation of such contracts. First, it is thought to be in the public interest that competition should not be unnecessarily restricted. Secondly, without such a doctrine, one party could exploit the weaker bargaining position of the other in an unfair manner.[3] (For an interesting example, see *Schroeder Music Publishing Co.* v *Macaulay* (1974) and more recently the case of *Proactive Sports Management Ltd* v *Rooney* (2011).)

2 Although the winner could not sue the loser, the loser could not recover his money if he had paid up.

3 The relevance of the respective bargaining strengths of the parties was illustrated in *Dawnay Day & Co. Ltd* v *Frederick de Braconier d'Alphen* (1998).

15.7 Although restraint of trade agreements appear to be anti-competitive, it should be pointed out that they can serve more desirable purposes. For example, where the goodwill of a business is being sold, the purchaser will wish to protect his or her legitimate interest in receiving value for the price that he or she has paid. If the seller were permitted to set up a rival business immediately in direct competition with the purchaser, then potential purchasers would in future be deterred from buying businesses. In turn, this would affect a future vendor, as he or she would not receive full value for the business that he or she has built up. Also, in the case of employers, they should be able to protect themselves, in a reasonable way, from employees going to work for rival firms and taking with them secret or confidential information, or the customers or clientele of their former employer. These are illustrations of how restraint of trade agreements may indeed be reasonable and commercially necessary. On the other hand, it must be ensured that the restraint imposed by such an agreement is not wider in scope than it need be to achieve its intended purpose.

15.8 A useful starting point for our discussion of agreements in restraint of trade is the case of *Nordenfelt* v *Maxim Nordenfelt Guns and Ammunition Co. Ltd* [1894] AC 535. The facts were as follows:

> N was a manufacturer and inventor of guns and ammunition. Although his customers were fairly few, his trade was worldwide. He sold his business to a company for £287,500 and entered into an agreement restricting his future commercial activities. When the company was amalgamated with another, two years later, N's agreement to the restraint of his activities was repeated in a contract of service he entered into with the amalgamated (respondent) company. (It was accepted by the court that the covenant N entered into with the respondents could be regarded as a covenant made on the occasion of selling a business and could therefore be assessed according to the principles relating to such a case.) The restriction was that N should not, for a period of 25 years, 'engage except on behalf of the company either directly or indirectly in the trade or business of a manufacturer of guns ... or ammunition ... (or in any business competing or liable to compete in any way with that for the time being carried on by the company)'.

The latter part of the covenant, contained within the brackets, was clearly too wide in its scope, as it extended to all competing businesses. But this clause was severable from the rest of the agreement. The question for the House of Lords to decide was whether the rest of the covenant was too wide or whether it was a reasonable restriction on N's future activities. Although the restraint was not restricted to any particular geographical area, their Lordships dismissed N's appeal and held that the covenant was necessary for the protection of the respondents' commercial interests. As the company's trade was worldwide, a commensurate restraint was reasonable. The restraint was upheld as valid. In a famous statement, Lord Macnaghten explained (at 565) the basic approach to such cases in the following authoritative way:

> The public have an interest in every person's carrying on his trade freely: so has the individual. All interference with individual liberty of action in trading, and all restraints of trade of themselves, if there is nothing more, are contrary to public policy, and therefore void. That is the general rule. But there are exceptions: restraints of trade and interference with individual liberty of action may be justified by the special circumstances of a particular case. It is a sufficient justification, and indeed it is the only justification, if the restriction is reasonable—reasonable, that is, in reference to the interests of the parties concerned and reasonable in reference to the interests of the public, so framed and so guarded as to afford adequate protection to the party in whose favour it is imposed, while at the same time it is in no way injurious to the public.[4]

It should be appreciated that the facts of *Nordenfelt* were unusual. Most restraints need to be narrower in both duration and geographical area in order to be valid. But the judgments in the case still provide a useful foundation for our study of contracts in restraint of trade (as acknowledged in *Man Financial (S) Pte Ltd* v *Wong Bark Chuan David* (2007) at [69]–[73]). The judicial approach involves a balancing of interests between an individual's freedom to carry on his or her chosen trade or profession without restraint and the protection of certain legitimate commercial interests of those buying the goodwill of a business, or of employers. It is not in the public interest for restraint of trade agreements to operate simply to reduce competition, and for this reason there is a presumption that such agreements are void. But if the purchaser of a business or an employer can show that he or she is trying to protect a genuine proprietary interest, and that the clause in question is both reasonable and not contrary to the public interest, then it may be adjudged as valid. The courts are better placed to judge the reasonableness of an agreement as between the two parties than they are the question of the public interest.

Sale of a business

15.9 *Nordenfelt* v *Maxim Nordenfelt Guns and Ammunition Co. Ltd* (1894) is a good illustration of a valid restraint contained in a contract for the sale of a business. The purchaser gave value for the goodwill by paying a fair amount for the vendor's business. It was reasonable, as between the contracting parties, that the purchaser's proprietary interest was to be protected by restricting the vendor's freedom to trade in the same goods in the future. The courts are more willing to uphold restraints in contracts for the sale of a business than they are in contracts between employer and employee. In contracts of service there is more likely to be an inequality of bargaining strength between the parties; restrictions on an employee's future activities may well be unconscionable. In addition, it may be difficult for an employer to claim that he is protecting a genuine proprietary interest rather than merely guarding against future competition (but see *Leeds Rugby Ltd* v *Harris* (2005)).

15.10 For a restraint to be valid in an agreement to sell a business, the first requirement is that there is a genuine sale of a business from one party to the other (see *Vancouver Malt and Sake*

4 The agreement was not contrary to the public interest, as it strengthened the position of an English company in its manufacturing of guns to be sold worldwide!

Brewing Co. Ltd v *Vancouver Breweries Co. Ltd* (1934)). Without this there will be no transfer of an intangible asset, namely the goodwill, from the vendor to the purchaser. Second, the clause must not be too wide in its scope. The restraint will not be valid if it purports to confer protection on the purchaser that goes beyond the actual business sold by the vendor. For example, in *British Reinforced Concrete Engineering Co. Ltd* v *Schelff* (1921), the facts were:

> The claimant company manufactured and sold 'BRC' road reinforcements throughout the country. The defendant had a smaller, more local business, selling 'Loop' road reinforcements, but he was not involved in manufacturing these products. The claimant company bought the defendant's business, and the defendant covenanted that he would not enter into competition with them (either in business or in the employment of a rival) in the manufacture or sale of road reinforcements. The defendant was later employed by a road reinforcement company and was sued by the claimant company for breach of his agreement with them.

The court held that the restraint of trade clause in the sale of the business was too wide, and was void. The clause sought to restrain the defendant in general terms from competing with the claimant company. The claimants were entitled to the protection of their proprietary interest in the defendant's business, which they had just bought, but they were not entitled to protection in respect of their wider business interests. The defendant's business was concerned with the sale, not the manufacture, of a particular type of road reinforcement. It was not reasonable to restrict the defendant's future activities in such an extensive way.

15.11 Restraints may be unreasonable because they purport to cover too long a period or too wide an area. It must be emphasized that *Nordenfelt* v *Maxim Nordenfelt Guns and Ammunition Co. Ltd* (1894) was unusual—the clientele of the business sold was small in number, but spread throughout the world. An unusually extensive restraint, in both time and area, was adjudged to be reasonable in the circumstances. What amounts to a reasonable period of time for a restraint to operate will, naturally, depend on the nature of the business being sold. A purchaser of a business who pays for the goodwill is entitled to contract for the benefit of protection against competition for a limited period. This period can be long enough to allow for the goodwill or 'know-how' which has been bought to be fully transferred to the purchaser. But it should not be excessive in either time or area.[5]

15.12 *Nordenfelt* v *Maxim Nordenfelt Guns and Ammunition Co. Ltd* (1894) illustrates the fact that if part of the restraint clause is too wide but the remainder of it is reasonable, the court may sever the offending part from the rest of the clause, which may then be upheld. The extent of the court's power, and its willingness, to do this is considered later. But a further example of this approach can be found in *Goldsoll* v *Goldman* (1915):

> The claimant (C) and the defendant (D) each carried on a similar business as a dealer in imitation jewellery in London. In order to avoid competition, D sold his business to C and agreed that he would not, for a period of two years, 'either solely or jointly with or as agent or employee for any

5 See also art. 81 (ex art. 85) of the Treaty establishing the EEC (1957).

> other person or persons or company directly or indirectly carry on or be engaged concerned or interested in or render services ... to the business of a vendor of or dealer in real or imitation jewellery in ... London, or any part of the UK, Ireland, the Isle of Man, France, United States, Russia, or Spain'. C sought an injunction when D committed breaches of the agreement.

The Court of Appeal held that the agreement was too wide in area, but that the unreasonable parts of the restraint were capable of being severed from the rest of it. Accordingly, D's promise not to carry on business in the UK and the Isle of Man was a reasonable restraint, and therefore enforceable against him. The commercial activities covered by the covenant (namely, 'real or imitation jewellery') were also too wide, but it was reasonable to restrain the defendant from dealing in imitation jewellery. Thus, the court undertook a certain amount of rewriting of the agreement for the parties in order to reduce the excessive restraint to one of reasonable scope. It should be added that the court may be less willing to apply the idea of severance in cases between employer and employee (see *Attwood* v *Lamont* (1920), discussed at para. **15.22**) as there is less likely to be parity in terms of the bargaining strength of the parties. In the sale of a business, the court will wish to ensure that the purchaser does receive value for the price paid for the goodwill.

Restraints in a contract of employment

15.13 A restraint of trade in a contract of employment is prima facie void. It will be valid only if it protects a genuine proprietary interest of the employer, such as trade secrets or freedom from solicitation of his or her customers, and so long as it is a reasonable restraint, and not against the public interest. (For further discussion, see *Leeds Rugby Ltd* v *Harris* (2005) at [50]–[56].)The clause will not be valid if it merely attempts to protect the employer from competition. Obviously, an employee may gain experience and expertise in the course of his or her employment which may equip him or her to be a future competitor of his or her employer. The employer cannot prevent this. It is in the public interest that employees acquire skills and are able to use them and pass them on to others. However, an employee would have an unfair advantage in his or her future activities if he or she were able to utilize confidential or secret information obtained from his or her employer. He or she may also be able to gain a personal knowledge of, and influence over, his or her employer's customers. In these situations, it is appropriate that an employer is able to restrain his or her employee's future activities in order to protect his or her proprietary interests. (For a useful discussion, see Lord Parker's judgment in *Herbert Morris Ltd* v *Saxelby* [1916] 1 AC 688 at 709; and also Lord Atkinson's speech in the same case at 704. See also *Norbrook Laboratories (GB) Ltd* v *Adair* (2008).)

Trade secrets and confidential information[6]

15.14 It is not always easy to distinguish between those situations where an employee has access to highly confidential information and those where he or she has simply developed an

6 For a discussion of the relevance of the distinction between the terms 'trade secrets' and 'confidential information', see *Faccenda Chicken Ltd* v *Fowler* (1987). Here it was explained that an employee, after his employment has terminated, may use confidential information unless this is expressly forbidden. However, he is not entitled to use or disclose 'trade secrets' either during or after his employment, regardless of whether there is an express stipulation to this effect. (Presumably, a trade secret is something of a highly confidential nature.) The ambit of any implied term imposing restrictions on an employee after the employment comes to an end was considered in *Peter Brooks* v *Olyslager OMS (UK) Ltd* (1998).

expertise or skill during the course of his or her employment. (For a recent discussion, see *FSS Travel & Leisure Systems Ltd* v *Johnson* (1998).) The employer is entitled to protect him or herself in the former situation, but not the latter (see Lord Atkinson's judgment in *Herbert Morris Ltd* v *Saxelby* [1916] 1 AC 688 at 704–5). So the first question to be decided is 'what constitutes trade secrets?' This was the issue in *Forster & Sons Ltd* v *Suggett* (1918), where the facts were:

> The claimant company (C) and the defendant (D) entered into an agreement under which D was to be employed as works engineer at C's works and was not to divulge any trade secret during his employment or afterwards. The company made glass bottles and glass-making machinery. There was also a covenant in D's contract which prevented him, at the end of his employment with C, from going to work in the UK for a rival glass-making firm or being involved in glass bottle manufacture for a period of five years. In the course of his employment with the claimant company, D had been instructed in certain confidential methods which were of economic value. D wished to be released from his promise and the company sought an injunction to enforce the agreed restraint.

Sargant J granted an injunction to the company to restrain D from divulging any trade secrets or manufacturing processes to potential rivals of the claimant company. He did not think that the restraint was unreasonable in the circumstances of the case. The time restraint of five years was upheld. The fact that the restraint covered the whole of the UK was also reasonable. But it must be emphasized that much depends on the particular circumstances of the case in deciding whether a restraint is reasonable. In other cases, a five-year restraint covering the whole country may well be unreasonable.

15.15 In some cases the courts have experienced greater difficulty in deciding whether an employee is in a position to pass on trade secrets to one of his employer's rivals. In *Herbert Morris Ltd* v *Saxelby* (1916), the claimants were the leading manufacturers of hoisting machinery in the UK and the defendant was employed by them as a draughtsman under a contract which restrained him, on leaving the company, from working in the same field for a period of seven years. The House of Lords held that the covenant was void as a result of being too wide; seven years was too long a period. But some doubts were also expressed as to whether the defendant was in a position to pass on trade secrets. The same issue was discussed (and *Saxelby* was distinguished) in *Commercial Plastics Ltd* v *Vincent* [1965] 1 QB 623. The facts were:

> The claimant company (CP) were manufacturers of thin PVC calendered plastic sheeting, a rapidly developing section of the plastics industry, in which new discoveries were being frequently made. CP had five principal UK competitors, with whom they shared most of the market, but CP's pre-eminence was in the field of manufacturing thin PVC calendered sheeting for adhesive tape. This was a particularly difficult process and CP had

spent considerable amounts of money, time, and effort on research into this process. As a result, they had a very large share of this particular market. CP employed Vincent (V), a plastics technologist, to coordinate research and development in the production of thin PVC calendered sheeting for adhesive tape. His work gave V access to the company's mixing specifications recorded in code, but it was not possible for him to remember these details without the help of documents. It was a condition of V's employment that he would not seek employment with any of CP's rivals in the PVC calendered sheeting field for one year after leaving CP's employment. V wanted to disregard this condition and CP sought an injunction.

CP's action failed because the clause in restraint of trade was too wide. The clause was worldwide, whereas CP did not require protection outside the UK. Moreover, it extended to their competitors in the whole PVC calendering field, when CP required protection from V only in relation to competitors in the plastics/adhesive tape industry. Accordingly, the Court of Appeal thought that the clause was unreasonable and therefore void. The court expressed some regret at this finding, as it thought that a suitably drafted restraint would have been enforceable against V. However, it was decided that severance of the offending parts of the clause was not possible in this case, as the restraint was contained in just one provision which was too wide.

15.16 It is relevant to note that, in spite of the decision in *Commercial Plastics* v *Vincent* (1965), the court was of the opinion that the claimant company did have confidential information which it was entitled, by a suitably worded covenant, to restrain the defendant from divulging (per Pearson LJ, delivering the judgment of the court, at 642). Given the circumstances of the case this must surely be correct: there was identifiable objective knowledge which could be regarded as the employer's 'trade secrets'. The outcome of the case was, therefore, unfortunate. But similar issues were raised by the later case of *Littlewoods Organisation Ltd* v *Harris* [1978] 1 All ER 1026. The facts were as follows:

Littlewoods ran a retail chain store business and a mail order business in the UK. Their main competitor in the mail order field was Great Universal Stores Ltd (GUS) which had a large number of subsidiaries carrying on various businesses throughout the world. Littlewoods and GUS, between them, enjoyed two-thirds of the mail order trade in the UK. Littlewoods' mail order business centred on a twice-yearly catalogue. These catalogues required considerable advance planning and business skill, especially in relation to the price, quantity, and type of goods which were to be sold. Paul Harris was employed by Littlewoods and, having been rapidly promoted due to his considerable ability, he became executive director of their mail order business. As a result, he was responsible for planning and compiling Littlewoods' catalogues. A clause in his contract restrained Harris's future activities by providing that, in the event of the determination of his contract, he should not at any time within 12 months enter into a contract of service with GUS Ltd or any of its subsidiary companies, or be involved in the trading or business of GUS

> or its subsidiaries. Harris resigned from his job with Littlewoods, informing them that he had accepted an offer of employment from GUS. Littlewoods sought an assurance from him that he did not intend to infringe the restraint clause by going to work for GUS within 12 months of leaving their employment. Harris refused to give this, and Littlewoods sought an injunction.

There was no doubt that Harris knew a great deal about Littlewoods' mail order sales trends, the percentage and identity of the returns, sources of manufacture, findings of market research, and the company's plans for the foreseeable future. But did this amount to confidential information which they were entitled to protect by a covenant in restraint of trade? The Court of Appeal held that the claimants were entitled to the protection of a reasonable covenant restraining Harris from going to work for a rival in the mail order business within a limited period of leaving their employment. (See also *Rock Refrigeration Ltd* v *Jones* (1997), and *Thomas* v *Farr Plc* (2007).)

In *Littlewoods*, Lord Denning considered at some length the question of an employer's protection of confidential information. He explained the difficulty of drawing a line between information which is confidential and that which is not. Where information is of a type that an employee can carry it away in his head, it is particularly hard to prove a breach of a covenant which restrains an employee from divulging confidential information. In practice, the only effective restraint is to stipulate that an employee must not work for a rival firm for a limited (and reasonable) period of time. His Lordship concluded (at 1034):

> It seems to me . . . [that] this really was a case where Littlewoods had a great deal of confidential information which Paul Harris had acquired in the course of his service with them and which they were entitled to protect by a reasonable covenant against his going away and taking it to their rivals in trade . . . [namely, GUS].

There was the further question in *Littlewoods* of whether the restraint on Harris was too wide. (See *Commercial Plastics* v *Vincent* (1965) (para. **15.15**), where the facts were very similar.) The covenant prevented Harris from being concerned in businesses of GUS and its subsidiaries. Yet these businesses were extremely varied and worldwide, whereas the interests of Littlewoods were restricted to the UK and to only two commercial areas. Was the fact that the clause was too widely drawn fatal to its enforceability against Harris? Lord Denning was critical of the outcome of *Commercial Plastics* and he explained the need to construe the restraint clause in relation to its intended purpose. Such a clause should not be rendered ineffective simply because of unskilful drafting and the inclusion of words that were too wide in scope. He argued (at 1035) that a court is able to limit a wide restraint so as to ensure that the clause is reasonable and enforceable. In the present case, he stated that the clause should be restricted to the UK and to the mail order business, but that an injunction would be granted to Littlewoods. Thus the restraint was enforceable. But in the later case of *Wincanton Ltd* v *Cranny* (2000), distinguishing *Littlewoods*, it was held that where a non-competition clause in a contract of employment has been made wide intentionally in an attempt to cover all possible situations, it will be found to be unenforceable. Here, the employer had not attempted to 'focus on the particular restraint necessary in respect of a particular employee'.

15.17 So far, we have considered cases where the employer has stipulated some restraint on an employee in a contract of service. A slightly different situation occurred in *Kores Manufacturing Co. Ltd* v *Kolok Manufacturing Co. Ltd* [1959] Ch 108, where two companies agreed that neither would, without the other's consent, employ a person who had worked for the other company during the previous five years. Both companies were involved in the manufacture of similar products involving chemical processes. An action was brought by one of the companies against the other to enforce the agreement by restraining the defendants from employing a former employee of the claimants. The Court of Appeal held that the agreement did not satisfy the essential requirement for a restraint of trade to be enforceable, as it was unreasonable in the circumstances. If either company had tried to enforce a similar restraint contained in a covenant given by an employee they would not have succeeded. This was because the companies were merely trying to prevent competition and were not protecting a genuine proprietary interest. Furthermore, the agreement between the companies failed to distinguish between employees who were in possession of trade secrets and those who were not (and were not even likely to be): 'The five year ban was equally applicable to an unskilled manual labourer who had been for a single day in the employment of the claimants, and to a chief chemist with many years' service' (per Jenkins LJ at 124). It did not make any difference that the parties dealt on equal terms in reaching their restraint of trade agreement. It was still open to the court to hold that the restraint was both unreasonable and too wide. It also appears to be contrary to the public interest for the labour force to be restricted in such a way.

Clauses restraining solicitation of customers

15.18 An employer is entitled to protect his or her trade connections, otherwise it would be possible for a former employee to entice away his or her customers. A distinction must be made, however, between an employee who has acquired some influence over his or her employer's customers, and one who merely has knowledge of such customers. Obviously much will depend on the type of business in question and the type of work carried out by the employee. But if the employee has enjoyed a position in which customers have relied on his or her individual skill or judgement, and are likely to take their trade to him or her if he or she starts his or her own business, or goes to work elsewhere, then the employer is entitled to reasonable protection from this potential loss of trading connection.

15.19 In *Fitch* v *Dewes* (1921), a restraint was held by the House of Lords to be enforceable against a solicitor's managing clerk. Whilst working in Tamworth, he had agreed with his employer that he would not practise within seven miles of Tamworth town hall after leaving his employment. This covenant was enforceable, despite the fact that the restriction was of unlimited duration. It was adjudged reasonable, given the nature of the profession concerned. The defendant would have acquired an influence over his employer's clientele and a limited time restraint would not have afforded the required protection to the employer. However, in other circumstances, a restraint may well be void for covering too wide an area or too long a period. In many trades, an employee's influence over his ex-employer's clients or customers will diminish as time passes. (See also *M & S Drapers* v *Reynolds* (1957).)

15.20 Restraints against damaging an employer's trading connection are not limited to particular professions or to senior personnel (although greater protection may be reasonable against senior employees). For example, in *Marion White Ltd* v *Francis* (1972), the defendant, Ann Francis, worked as a hairdresser in the claimant's salon. She covenanted not to work as a hairdresser within a half-mile radius of C's premises for 12 months after leaving C's salon. On her dismissal, Ann Francis went to work at a salon merely 150 yards from C's premises. It was held that the covenant was not too wide in those particular circumstances and was enforceable. (In fact, a declaration was granted to C. An injunction was not possible as the time limit in the covenant had elapsed by the time the case was resolved.)

The scope of restraint clauses and severance

15.21 We have seen that clauses in restraint of trade, in employment contracts, have been enforceable even where the restraint was unlimited in time (as in *Fitch* v *Dewes* (1921)) or covered the whole country (see *Forster* v *Suggett* (1918), discussed at para. **15.14**). However, the restraint must not be unreasonably wide in area or long in duration; what is reasonable will depend on the circumstances of the case and the business in question (as in *Proactive Sports Management Ltd* v *Rooney* (2011) discussed at para. **15.28**). The restraint must be to protect the employer's business and not simply to inconvenience the employee. In *Mason* v *Provident Clothing & Supply Co. Ltd* [1913] AC 724, for example:

> Provident Clothing Limited employed Mason as a local canvasser in its Islington branch in London. His job was to obtain members and collect their instalments; he had no duties outside his assigned district. Mason covenanted not to enter into similar employment within 25 miles of London for a period of three years.

The House of Lords, allowing Mason's appeal, held that the clause covered an area which was much greater than was reasonably required for the protection of his former employers. Provident Clothing were entitled to protect themselves against the danger of a former employee canvassing or collecting for a rival firm in the district in which he had been employed. But the restraint which the company was trying to enforce was too wide. The possibility of enforcing a more limited (and reasonable) restraint was considered by the court. It was stated that this could be done where severance was possible, and where the excessive part of the clause was merely technical, or of trivial importance, and not part of the main substance of the clause. Their Lordships did not favour such an approach where the employer, having deliberately framed a clause in unreasonably wide terms, now asked the court in effect to rewrite the clause to make it reasonable and enforceable. In the circumstances of the case, this was undoubtedly a fair conclusion. (But contrast *T Lucas & Co. Ltd* v *Mitchell* (1974).) In the *Mason* case, the company's argument was dealt with convincingly by Lord Moulton (at 746):

> It is evident that those who drafted this covenant aimed at making it a penal rather than a protective covenant, and that they hoped by means of it to paralyse the earning capacities of the man if and when he left their service, and were not thinking of what would be a reasonable protection to their business, and having so acted they must take the consequences.

15.22 The question of severance was also considered in *Attwood* v *Lamont* (1920). The facts were:

> The claimant, Harry Attwood, owned a general outfitter's business, which comprised several departments. James Lamont was employed by Attwood as head of the tailoring department, but he was not directly concerned with any of the other departments. In his employment contract he had bound himself, after the termination of his contract, not to be involved in 'the trade or business of a tailor, dressmaker, general draper, milliner, hatter, haberdasher, gentlemen's, ladies' or children's outfitter, at any place within a radius of ten miles of the employer's place of business' in Kidderminster. Lamont left Attwood's and started his own business outside the ten-mile radius. He did business with several of his former employer's customers, however, and took orders from them within the ten-mile radius. Attwood sought an injunction to restrain Lamont from disregarding the covenant. Lamont claimed that the clause was too wide in its terms to be reasonable.

Although the clause was wider than was reasonably necessary for the protection of Attwood's business, the Divisional Court had been willing to permit severance, that is, to reject the illegal part of the clause and to enforce the part relating to the tailoring business. However, the Court of Appeal held that not only was the covenant too wide, but it was also not susceptible to severance. It would have been possible, by deleting the offending words in the clause, to reduce its scope to reasonable proportions, but the Court of Appeal refused to do so. Although the court would not have been rewriting the agreement for the parties, it would have radically altered the scope and purpose of that agreement to have permitted severance. Moreover, their Lordships thought that there were strong public policy grounds for refusing severance so that employers would be encouraged to keep such restraint clauses within the bounds of reasonableness. Otherwise employers could impose unreasonably wide restraints in employment contracts and then rely on the court, through the process of severance, to give effect to part of the offending clause.

15.23 Severance will be permitted in certain instances, but it is not very clear what the requirements are. We saw earlier in *Goldsoll* v *Goldman* (1915) that, although a covenant was too wide in both the area and the commercial activity to be covered, the court permitted severance of the offending parts and enforced the remainder, which was then a reasonable restraint. (See also *Kall Kwik Printing (UK) Ltd* v *Rush (Frank Clarence)* (1996).) But it should be remembered that in *Goldsoll* the covenant was between the vendor and purchaser of a business. In this context, the policy grounds for refusing severance are not so strong. The court is happy to permit the purchaser to get full value for the price he has paid for the proprietary interest in the business. But, in relation to covenants between employer and employee, a court may be more reluctant to enforce a restraint of trade clause.

15.24 A good example of the differing views about the ability of a court in effect to rewrite a restraint clause for the parties can be seen in *Littlewoods Organisation* v *Harris* [1978] 1 All ER 1026. It will be recalled that Harris's agreement with Littlewoods prevented him from going to work, within 12 months, for their main mail order rival (GUS) or its subsidiaries. Although Littlewoods' interests were limited to the UK and to two commercial areas, the clause was worldwide in scope and not restricted to the mail order business. Lord Denning argued that unskilful drafting should not prevent the clause from being construed more narrowly so as to limit its scope to preventing Harris from working for GUS's mail order business in the UK. Megaw LJ shared Lord Denning's view and insisted (at 1043) that, in using the principles of construction available to the court to limit the scope of the clause, he was not rewriting the covenant. However, there was a strong dissenting judgment from Browne LJ. He stated (at 1046):

> With all deference to Lord Denning MR and Megaw LJ, I think this is rewriting the clause, and rewriting it so as to make enforceable that which would otherwise be unenforceable ... I think that is something which this court cannot do. I do not think that severance has any relevance to this part of the contract.

Although the outcome of the *Littlewoods* case is obviously defensible, it must be acknowledged that this dissenting judgment is a valid criticism of the majority's approach. Severance permits the illegal part of a covenant to be separated from the rest by deleting it, leaving the remainder in force. In theory at least, it does not permit a rewriting of the covenant for the parties. (For an illustration of this distinction, see *Scully UK Ltd* v *Anthony Lee* (1998).) The majority in *Littlewoods* thought that the principles of construction enabled the court to restrict the scope of an unreasonably wide clause, but this approach comes very close to a rewriting of the agreement by the court.[7]

Restraints protecting other interests

15.25 Restraint clauses may also be used in circumstances which do not fit neatly into the categories that we have just considered. For example, in *Eastham* v *Newcastle United Football Club Ltd* [1964] Ch 413, the facts were:

> The claimant, George Eastham, was a highly rated footballer who played for Newcastle United, the defendant club. Under the rules (at that time) of the Football Association and the Football League, his employment with the club was subject to a retain-and-transfer system. This system prevented a player who was employed by one club from being employed by another. His transfer to another club could be effected only with the consent of both clubs. Eastham wanted to join another club, Arsenal, and sought a declaration against his present club and the football authorities.

It is clear that the defendant club was not using the restraint clause, namely the retain-and-transfer system, to protect either of the two established proprietary interests (discussed earlier). But this did not automatically mean that the club had no further interests capable of protection (see Wilberforce J's comments at 432). However, it was decided that, on the facts of the case, the

7 Lord Denning stated at 1037: 'I think that limiting words ought to be read into the clause so as to limit it to the part of the business for which Littlewoods are reasonably entitled to protection.'

retain-and-transfer system was invalid and was unnecessary for the protection of the club's proprietary interests. Eastham was granted a declaration not only against his employer, but also against the football authorities whose rules led to the unjustifiable restraint on his freedom of employment. (The rules relating to the transfer system were altered as a result of this case.) But the case does, at least, suggest that the interests that can be protected are not strictly limited, and this point was also acknowledged in *Leeds Rugby Ltd* v *Harris* (2005) (per Gray J at [50]).

15.26 In other instances a covenant may be used to restrict a person's commercial freedom even though the parties are not, strictly speaking, bound by a contract of employment. A good example is provided by *Schroeder Music Publishing Co. Ltd* v *Macaulay* [1974] 3 All ER 616. The facts were as follows:

> Tony Macaulay, a young and unknown songwriter, entered into an agreement with the defendant music publishing company, whereby the defendants engaged his exclusive services. Under this agreement, Macaulay gave the company the copyright of all his compositions for the next five years (with a further five-year option), and in return was to receive royalty payments. The company could end the contract by giving Macaulay one month's written notice, but there was no corresponding provision to allow Macaulay to do the same. The company was not even under any obligation to publish any of Macaulay's songs. Although this agreement was not a contract of employment as such, Macaulay sought a declaration that it was contrary to public policy, as being in unreasonable restraint of trade, and void. The company argued that the doctrine of restraint of trade was inapplicable to its standard form agreement.

The House of Lords held that the restrictions in the agreement between Macaulay and the publishing company were not fair and reasonable in that they combined a lack of obligation on the company's part with a total commitment on the part of Macaulay. If the company chose not to publish his work, for instance, he would be unable to earn his living as a songwriter. Thus the contract was an unreasonable restraint of trade and Macaulay was entitled to a declaration.[8] Lord Reid stated (at 622):

> Any contract by which a person engages to give his exclusive services to another for a period necessarily involves extensive restriction during that period of the common law right to exercise any lawful activity he chooses in such manner as he thinks best. Normally the doctrine of restraint of trade has no application to such restrictions: they require no justification. But if contractual restrictions appear to be unnecessary or to be reasonably capable of enforcement in an oppressive manner, then they must be justified before they can be enforced.

15.27 Similar issues arose in *Silvertone Records* v *Mountfield* (1993), which concerned a dispute between a record company and the members of a pop group in relation to their recording and publishing contracts. The agreements (made when the group was comparatively unknown)

8 The case is also of considerable interest on the subject of unconscionability and is discussed further in Chapter 16.

gave the company, inter alia, the option of the group's services for six further periods beyond the duration of the original contract. The group claimed that the agreements were one-sided and represented an unreasonable restraint of trade. The company claimed that it had been made clear to the group that the agreements were a package and that the group members had waived their objections to it. Accordingly, the company sought a declaration that the agreements were enforceable against the group. Humphries J held that the whole agreement was objectionable, as there was a large inequality of bargaining power between the parties at the time it was entered into. (In a situation like this one, it was held to be a restraint of trade if a performer was prevented from reaching the public with his or her work for a prolonged period.) The judge stated that the members of the group had not waived their objections to the enforceability of the agreements. (See also *Zang Tumb Tuum Records* v *Johnson* (1993) for a further example of a one-sided and unenforceable contract between a record company and a pop group.)

15.28 The doctrine of restraint of trade has also been successfully relied upon in an agreement covering matters which do not form the main occupation of an individual but rather are ancillary to it. The case of *Proactive Sports Management Ltd* v *Rooney* (2011) related to an agreement entered into by a professional footballer under which he assigned his image rights to Proactive, granting exclusive rights to his name for use in all promotional activity in return for a commission rate of 20 per cent of his earnings. In considering the question of a possible restraint of trade, the court recognized that the exploitation of image rights was almost always going to be an activity which was ancillary to another occupation, concluding that this was just as capable of protection as any other occupation. Thus, although the ancillary nature of an activity might lead to the restriction on trading being insubstantial and therefore justifiable, this was not seen to be an adequate reason to not apply the doctrine. A number of factors were examined to test the restrictions of the contract, including duration (the agreement was for eight years and this was found to be a very lengthy period over which the restraints were imposed); the circumstances surrounding execution (when he had entered into the contract Rooney was only 17 years old and had not taken independent legal advice); and the practical difficulties of termination. Citing earlier authorities of *Schroeder Music Publishing Co. Ltd* v *Macaulay* (1974) discussed at para. **15.26** and *Esso Petroleum Co. Ltd* v *Harper's Garage (Stourport) Ltd* (1968) (see para. **15.29**), the court found that the contract was in restraint of trade and, in line with the well-established effect of such a finding, from the time at which a party had withdrawn from the contract, the contract was deemed unenforceable.

Are the categories of restraint closed?

15.29 The two main types of contract in which restraint clauses are prima facie unenforceable are those between employer and employee, and those between the buyer and seller of a business. Does the doctrine also apply to other types of agreement or are the categories of restraint of trade closed? This issue has arisen in relation to 'solus' trading agreements, for example, where garage proprietors agree with an oil company not to sell the products of rival companies. Such arrangements can benefit both parties, as the garage or filling station operator may receive a rebate on the price of petrol or a loan (at favourable rates) to help with the development of his or her business. The advantage to the oil company is obvious. This type of agreement was the subject of the important case of *Esso Petroleum Co. Ltd* v *Harper's Garage (Stourport) Ltd* (1968). The facts were:

> H owned two garages (H1 and H2) which were both subject to solus agreements with Esso. Under the terms of these agreements H agreed to buy all his petrol from Esso and, in turn, was to receive a small rebate on the price of petrol. The agreement in relation to H1 was for four and a half years; it stipulated that H should buy Esso's petrol and no other and it laid down certain other conditions. In relation to H2, there was a similar solus agreement, but in addition Esso had a mortgage over the premises to secure a sum of £7,000 lent to H. The H2 agreement was for the duration of the mortgage repayments, that is, 21 years. The mortgage provisions also stipulated that H was to buy his petrol exclusively from Esso. H later started to sell another brand of petrol, and Esso sought an injunction to prevent him from doing so. Were the ties in the agreements in restraint of trade and unenforceable?

The House of Lords held that both agreements were within the scope of the restraint of trade doctrine. (Per Lord Reid: 'In the present case the respondents before they made this agreement were entitled to use this land in any lawful way they chose, and by making this agreement they agreed to restrict their right by giving up their right to sell there petrol not supplied by the appellants.') This meant that the agreements would not be enforced by the court unless they were reasonable. Their Lordships held that the restriction on H1 was reasonable, but that the restriction relating to H2 was not. The principal reason for distinguishing between the two agreements was the difference in their respective lengths. A restriction lasting 21 years was an unreasonable one in the circumstances (but contrast *Alec Lobb Garages Ltd* v *Total Oil (Great Britain) Ltd* (1985)). The restriction should not have been longer than was reasonably necessary to protect the legitimate interests of the oil company, that is, to maintain a stable system of distribution. A much shorter restriction would have sufficed to achieve this end. Duration of the restriction is a relevant factor to consider when questioning whether an agreement is unfair or oppressive and operating in restraint of trade. (See *Proactive Sports Management Ltd* v *Rooney* (2011).)

Further regulation of restraint of trade

15.30 We have seen that contracts in restraint of trade are unenforceable, unless the restriction is reasonable as between the parties to the agreement and is not against the public interest. The courts have been more adept at judging the first of these requirements than the second. Consideration of the public interest necessitates more wide-ranging enquiry than the courts have traditionally been prepared to undertake. (For a classic example, see *Mogul Steamship Co. Ltd* v *McGregor, Gow & Co. Ltd* (1892).) Whereas the reasonableness of a restraint clause from the point of view of the parties will be fully explored in court by the litigants, the public interest will not be directly represented. Judges may be better equipped, by both outlook and training, to weigh the relative interests of the parties to an agreement than to consider the broader economic issues raised by restraint agreements.

15.31 Although there has been some indication of a greater willingness to take account of the public interest in restraint of trade cases,[9] the failure of judges to do so in the past is one of the factors which inhibited the development of a comprehensive common law doctrine to regulate anti-competitive behaviour. Other factors include the uncertainty about the ambit of the common law doctrine of restraint of trade, and its inability (until recently) to protect third parties who were adversely affected. For these reasons, domestic competition policy has been delineated largely by legislative provisions, which have been substantially changed by the Competition Act 1998. It is not necessary in a book on the general principles of contract law to enter into a detailed discussion of these legislative provisions; those requiring further information should consult a specialist work on UK competition law.[10]

Other contracts void at common law on grounds of public policy

Contracts to oust the jurisdiction of the courts

15.32 We have seen in **Chapter 6** that it is possible for the parties to an agreement to stipulate that their agreement shall not be legally enforceable. Thus, in *Jones* v *Vernons Pools* (1938) it was a condition of entry that the arrangements of the 'football pool' were binding in honour only: a so-called 'gentlemen's agreement'. The company could not be sued successfully by the claimant as the agreement carried with it no legal obligations on either side, and conferred no legal rights. (See also *Rose and Frank Co.* v *JR Crompton & Bros Ltd* (1925).) It is not, however, open to the parties to a contract to stipulate that their agreement will have legal consequences but will not be susceptible to the supervision of the courts.

15.33 An agreement which purports to prevent the parties to it from submitting questions of law to the courts is contrary to public policy and void. (Only the offending part of the agreement is void; the rest of the contract may be valid and enforceable.) Contractual freedom is, therefore, limited in this way, as it is thought to be in the public interest that parties should not be free to oust the jurisdiction of the courts.

15.34 The parties may, however, provide that no cause of action will arise until an arbitrator has made an award. This type of arbitration clause is not regarded as contrary to public policy. This was established in *Scott* v *Avery* (1855) 5 HL Cas 811, where a contract between a shipowner and the underwriters made it clear that no action should be brought against the insurers until the arbitrators had dealt with any dispute arising between the parties. It was held that it is permissible for the parties to agree that no right of action shall accrue until an arbitrator has

9 For instance, see *Esso Petroleum Ltd* v *Harper's Garage Ltd* (1968) and *Schroeder Music Publishing* v *Macaulay* (1974).

10 E.g., see S. Singleton, *Competition Act 1998*, Blackstone Press, 1999.

decided on any difference which may arise between them. Lord Campbell (at 851) explained the matter as follows:

> What pretence can there be for saying that there is anything contrary to public policy in allowing parties to contract, that they shall not be liable to any action until their liability has been ascertained by a domestic and private tribunal, upon which they themselves agree? Can the public be injured by it? It seems to me that it would be a most inexpedient encroachment upon the liberty of the subject if he were not allowed to enter into such a contract.

The important point is that such an arbitration clause does not oust the jurisdiction of the courts. Within our legal system there will always tend to be a conflict between two distinct approaches to dispute settling: that is, the 'ideal' principle of justice which wants justice no matter what the cost, and the 'pragmatic' principle which seeks to limit litigation and its concomitant costs. Although it is the right of the citizen to have his or her legal position decided by the ordinary courts, it is desirable that many disputes should first be heard by an arbitrator. There has to be some compromise between these two approaches, so it is permissible for contracting parties to provide that any disagreement that arises will be referred to arbitration.

15.35 The general rule, that an agreement which purports to oust the jurisdiction of the courts is void, is well illustrated in *Baker* v *Jones* [1954] 1 WLR 1005. The facts were:

> An association, which controlled the sport of weightlifting in the UK, by its rules vested the government of the association in a central council consisting of the officers and a number of members. The association empowered its central council to be the sole interpreters of the rules and to act on behalf of the association regarding any matter not dealt with by the rules. In all circumstances, the decision of the council was to be regarded as final. As a result of disagreements between the members, two libel actions were brought against certain officers and council members. The central council authorized the payment of two sums of £100 to solicitors, out of the association's funds, towards the defendants' legal costs. A member of the association challenged this decision of the council by seeking a declaration that this use of the association's funds was improper.

Lynskey J held that the provision in the rules giving the central council the sole right to interpret the rules was contrary to public policy and void. (It should also be noted that there was no power under the association's rules for the central council to authorize the use of funds for the proposed purpose.) The contract in these circumstances was contained in the association's rules, so the relationship between its various members was indeed contractual. The judge explained (at 1010) that although, in theory, the parties to a contract may make any contract they like, this is subject to certain limitations imposed by public policy. One of these limitations is that the jurisdiction of the courts cannot be ousted by the agreement of the parties. He cited with approval the statement of Lord Denning in *Lee* v *Showmen's Guild of Great Britain* [1952] 2 QB 329 at 342:

> If parties should seek, by agreement, to take the law out of the hands of the courts and put it into the hands of a private tribunal, without any recourse at all to the courts in case of error of law, then the agreement is to that extent contrary to public policy and void.

15.36 A further example of a situation where an agreement to oust the jurisdiction of the courts may arise is that of a maintenance agreement between husband and wife. As part of a separation agreement, a husband may promise his wife an allowance in exchange for which she agrees not to apply to the courts for maintenance. This issue arose in *Hyman* v *Hyman* (1929), where it was held that a wife cannot, by her own agreement, preclude herself from invoking the jurisdiction of the court. (See also *Sutton* v *Sutton* (1984); *Hyman* v *Hyman* was distinguished by the Court of Appeal in the case of *Soulsbury* v *Soulsbury* (2007).) The main disadvantage of this common law rule was that if the husband did not pay the promised allowance, his wife was not able to sue him to enforce payment. But under the present statutory provisions (see Matrimonial Causes Act 1973, s 34), a wife can successfully sue her husband, if the agreement is written, to enforce payment of the promised allowance.

Contracts undermining the status of marriage

15.37 In the public interest, the law seeks to uphold the sanctity of marriage. Accordingly, certain types of agreement which tend to undermine or damage the institution of marriage are invalidated. One example of this is a contract which purports to restrict a person's freedom to marry whomsoever he or she wishes. In *Lowe* v *Peers* (1768), for instance, a man promised the claimant, under seal, that he would not marry any other person except her. He stated that if he broke this promise to her, he would pay her £2,000. His promise was held to be void, as it restricted his freedom of choice without there being any reciprocal promise from the claimant. (Until the abolition of an action for breach of promise in 1970, a couple's engagement to marry—involving reciprocal promises—was a valid contract. This was not the situation in *Lowe* v *Peers*, where the parties did not directly promise to marry each other.)

15.38 Another type of agreement which is thought to undermine the status of marriage is the so-called 'marriage brokage' contract, that is, ¡an agreement for reward for the procurement of marriage. Such agreements are regarded as contrary to public policy and therefore void. The rather outmoded reasoning behind this rule is that these agreements tend to promote unsuitable marriages and, for this reason, are harmful to the public! (Given the current rate of matrimonial breakdown, such a moral stance might appear particularly quaint.) The invalidity of such agreements appears to extend to those between matrimonial agencies and their clients where the latter are introduced to a number of people of the opposite sex with a view to marriage.

In *Hermann* v *Charlesworth* (1905), the facts were:

> Miss Hermann saw an advertisement in the defendant's paper, *The Matrimonial Post and Fashionable Marriage Advertiser*, and later signed an agreement with the defendant in the following terms: 'In consideration of being introduced to or put in correspondence with a gentleman through the influence of the proprietor of the paper entitled "The Matrimonial

> Post and Fashionable Marriage Advertiser", and in the event of a marriage taking place between such gentleman and myself, I hereby agree to pay to the said proprietor the sum of £250 on the date of my said marriage.' Miss Charlesworth also paid the defendant a 'special client's fee' of £52. She was introduced to several men by the defendant, who also interviewed and wrote to others on her behalf, but no marriage or engagement followed. She sued the defendant to recover the £52.

The Court of Appeal held that it made no difference that the agreement was not intended to bring about Miss Charlesworth's marriage with a particular individual. It was still to be regarded as a marriage brokage agreement, despite the fact that she was introduced to a number of men and therefore had some degree of choice. It was decided that the transaction in this case came within the rule which invalidates marriage brokage contracts. Accordingly, the claimant was entitled to recover the money paid under this contract, even though the defendant had brought about introductions and incurred expense in doing so.

15.39 A distinction between pre-nuptial and post-nuptial agreements was drawn in *MacLeod* v *MacLeod* (2008), where it was considered that a post-nuptial agreement, although remaining subject to the court's discretionary power of variation, could be valid and enforceable under the Matrimonial Causes Act 1973. In respect of pre-nuptial agreements, the court advised these should be declared void in accordance with the traditional rule unless and until Parliament decided to change the law. More recently, however, in *Granatino* v *Radmacher (formerly Granatino)* (2010), the majority in the Supreme Court, with Baroness Hale dissenting, rejected the previously drawn distinction between the two types of agreement. Here, both pre-nuptial and post-nuptial agreements were considered to be capable of being effective, providing it was fair to hold the parties to their agreement and providing the arrangement had been freely entered into by the parties with full awareness of its consequences.

Illegal contracts

15.40 It should be borne in mind that the distinction between illegal and void contracts is not universally accepted. The terminology employed both by academics and by the courts is far from consistent. The distinction is maintained here largely for expository purposes and it is conceded that other categorizations are equally acceptable. A contract may be improper for such a variety of reasons, ranging from the serious to the trivial, that the subject does not always lend itself to analysis by categorization. But whereas the vitiating aspect of a 'void' contract (as described earlier) will be apparent on the face of the agreement, the 'illegal' contract may or may not be improper at face value. If the vitiating aspect is not apparent on the surface, the agreement may be rendered unlawful by some ulterior purpose of one or both of the parties.[11]

11 This distinction is well explained in J. C. Smith and J. A. C. Thomas, *Casebook on Contract*, 11th edn, Sweet & Maxwell, 2000, p. 684.

Policy factors and the illegality defence

15.41 Contracts may be illegal at common law on grounds of public policy. (See *Patel* v *Mirza* (2016), discussed at paras **15.83–15.87**.) The maxim *ex turpi causa non oritur actio* means that no action can arise from a bad cause. This applies with the effect that the courts will not enforce a contract which involves a legal wrong (other than the breach of contract itself), whether this arises in its formation or its purpose of performance, or if it involves conduct which is contrary to public policy. (See further Law Commission Consultation Paper, No 154, *Illegal Transactions: The Effect of Illegality on Contracts and Trusts*, 1999, para. 7.70.) Consequently, a person may not benefit from his or her own crime, tort, or fraud.

15.42 Therefore, the doctrine is seen to have general application beyond the law of contract and has been relied upon in other areas of law. For example, in *Stone & Rolls Ltd (in Liquidation)* v *Moore Stephens (a firm)* (2009) the defence was successfully relied upon to prevent a company which engaged in serious fraud from claiming its auditors were in breach of their duty of care in failing to detect the fraud. Although the application of the maxim relies on the claimant being 'personally' liable, this can also extend to the activities of a company whose acts may be found to be 'personal'. (See *Safeway Stores Ltd* v *Twigger* (2010).)

15.43 The policy precludes a person from recovering compensation for losses suffered as a result of his or her own criminal act or for damage arising from a sentence imposed on him or her for carrying out a criminal act. This is well illustrated by the House of Lords decision in *Gray* v *Thames Trains Ltd* (2009) in which the claimant, who had committed manslaughter as a result of psychological problems caused by the negligence of the rail company, was precluded from recovering general damages for his conviction and detention, for damage to his reputation, and also for special damages for his loss of earnings.

15.44 *Gray* v *Thames Trains Ltd* (2009) demonstrates that a person will not recover compensation where his or her cause of action is based on his or her criminal or immoral act, and the test for determining liability here focused on causation. This was followed in *Delaney* v *Pickett* (2011) and showed how the causation principle can also apply whether the criminal is acting alone or as a partner in crime as part of a joint criminal enterprise. Here, at first instance, Delaney was not allowed to claim for damages for injuries sustained in a car accident caused by Pickett's negligence. The purpose of their journey together was to supply illegal drugs and reliance was placed on the *ex turpi causa* defence. However, the Court of Appeal ruled that the illegal acts were incidental: the damage had been caused by Pickett's tortious act in the negligent manner in which he had driven the car and consequently the defence would not be upheld. The causation principle developed earlier in *Gray* v *Thames Trains Ltd* (2009) was followed, and later in *Joyce* v *O'Brien* (2013) the court ruled that this principle should apply in circumstances when a criminal was acting alone or as part of joint enterprise. The facts of *Joyce* v *O'Brien* (2013) were as follows:

Joyce (J) fell from the footplate of a van driven by O'Brien (O) and was seriously injured. O pleaded guilty to dangerous driving. J claimed damages for personal injury on the basis of O's negligence. However, the insurance company (T) asserted that O and J had been making their escape after stealing a set of ladders and for this reason O, and therefore T, was not liable; J and O had been engaged in a joint criminal enterprise.

Joyce and O'Brien had been involved in joint criminal activity and the public policy reflected in the principle *ex turpi causa* was applicable. Although the case offered some much needed clarity in this area of the law, by highlighting the flexibility of the doctrine, the scope for potential uncertainty in the operation of this public policy rule becomes equally apparent.

15.45 As illustrated above, the doctrine of *ex turpi causa* is an aspect of public policy which continues to influence and shape the operation of the illegality defence. The position of the law on illegality, including the final recommendations of the Law Commission Report No 320, *The Illegality Defence* (2010), is discussed further at paras. **15.81–15.83**. Recent case law, culminating in the highly significant Supreme Court ruling in *Patel* v *Mirza* (2016), is discussed further at paras **15.83–15.87**. But before that, what follows is a broader consideration of the subject and a series of case examples where the issues of illegality or impropriety have been raised. It is by no means an exhaustive guide to the subject of illegality but it does offer useful illustrations of how the issues have previously been dealt with by the courts.

Contracts to commit an unlawful act

15.46 If the purpose of an agreement between the parties is to commit a crime, or a tort, or a fraud against another party, then it can be said that such a contract is illegal and unenforceable. (See further *Patel* v *Mirza* (2016) discussed at paras **15.83–15.87**.) A contract will be unenforceable if at the time of its formation, one of the parties had the intention of performing it in an unlawful manner; the intention must be present at the time of the execution of the contract (*ParkingEye Ltd* v *Somerfield Stores Ltd* (2012)). It is not surprising that the courts refuse to assist those whose purpose is to achieve an unlawful or an illegal end. (For a discussion of evidential issues where illegality is claimed, see *Pickering* v *McConville* (2003), and also *Colen* v *Cebrian (UK) Ltd* (2003) at [19].) Even where an agreement is of a type which is commonly made in certain commercial contexts, it will still be unenforceable if it is based on an unlawful transaction. For example, if a shipowner carries X's goods and, in return for a promise of an indemnity from X, certifies that the goods are shipped 'in good condition', despite his knowledge that they are not, he would not be able to enforce the indemnity. The purpose of such an arrangement is to defraud a third party, and the fact that such a practice is widespread does not excuse the unlawful nature of the agreement (see *Brown Jenkinson & Co. Ltd* v *Percy Dalton Ltd* (1957)).

15.47 The situation becomes more complex where there is a lawful contract between the parties but it is performed by one of them in an unlawful manner, for example, in breach of a statutory provision. The party who is in breach of the law may be unable to enforce any claim (for example, to recover the price of goods) as a result of his or her own illegal performance. (See *Anderson Ltd* v *Daniel* (1924).) Of course, this principle will not apply to the innocent party under the transaction unless in some way he or she participated in the other party's illegal performance. (This subject is discussed in more detail later.) However, even the guilty party may be able to enforce the contract in some circumstances. Much may depend on the purpose of the statute in question. In *St John Shipping Corpn* v *Joseph Rank Ltd* [1956] 3 All ER 683, for example:

> Under a contract of carriage, the claimants conveyed a cargo of wheat from America to England in their ship, which was overloaded and thus contravened the Merchant Shipping (Safety and Load Line Conventions) Act 1932. A fine of £1,200 was imposed on the master of the ship in respect of this offence, but the freight earned by the excess wheat carried was £2,295. The defendants, who were to receive about one-third of the cargo of wheat, paid part of the freight for their share, but withheld £2,000 of the agreed sum in view of the overloading. (It should be noted that the wheat was delivered safely to them.) The claimants claimed the balance of the freight and the defendants argued that the contract was unenforceable by the claimants by reason of illegality.

Devlin J explained that, although a contract which is entered into with the object of committing an illegal act is unenforceable, this principle was not applicable in the present case. He stated (at 687) that 'whether or not the overloading was deliberate when it was done, there is no proof that it was contemplated when the contract of carriage was made'. Accordingly, the judge held that the claimants were entitled to the balance of the freight; they were not barred from recovering it by the fact that the overloading was a crime. It is important to note that the statutory provision in question did not make the contract of carriage unlawful; it merely penalized overloading. As this infringement of the legislation was not contemplated by the contract, there was nothing to prevent even the guilty party from enforcing that contract. The goods were safely delivered and no part of the claim for freight could be identified clearly as being the excess illegally earned. The purpose of the Act was achieved by the fine imposed on the master of the ship for the offence. (See also *Hughes* v *Asset Managers plc* (1995), and the Law Commission Consultation Paper, No 189, *The Illegality Defence: A Consultative Report*, 2009, which discusses both cases, at paras 3.4–3.11.)

15.48 Devlin J's remarks in *St John Shipping Corpn* v *Joseph Rank Ltd* (1956) were applied in *Shaw* v *Groom* (1970). In this case a landlord failed to provide his tenant with a rent book, in contravention of the relevant landlord and tenant legislation. The Court of Appeal held that this omission did not disentitle the landlord from recovering the rent of the premises from the tenant. The purpose of the legislation was not to preclude the landlord from recovering rent, but merely to penalize him for the breach of the statutory provision. This is a sensible approach in view of the scope and purpose of the statute. If this purpose is to be achieved by the imposition of a fine on the offender, it may well be unfair and unnecessary to go further and make the contract unenforceable by the party who is in breach of the law. Otherwise, even a minor transgression by the offender might excuse the 'innocent' party from performing his contractual obligations.

15.49 In contrast to the unlawful performance of an otherwise lawful contract, we should also consider a contract which is illegal in itself. (See further *Patel* v *Mirza* (2016), discussed at paras **15.83–15.87**). For example, in *Re Mahmoud and Ispahani* (1921) the claimant, who had a licence to sell linseed oil, sold some to the defendant in contravention of the Seed, Oils, and Fats Order 1919. This statute made it an offence to buy or sell linseed oil without a licence; the defendant was unlicensed—he had induced the claimant to sell him the oil by a fraudulent representation that he was licensed. The defendant later refused to accept delivery of the oil and was sued for damages by the claimant. The Court of Appeal held that the claimant's claim failed because of the illegality of the contract. Despite the fact that the claimant was the innocent party, the legislation specifically prohibited any sale of oil to unlicensed persons.

Contracts promoting sexual immorality

15.50 An agreement which tends to promote sexual immorality may be found to be illegal as a principle of common law. This is certainly the case where the agreement in some way involves or encourages prostitution. In the rather old case of *Pearce* v *Brooks* (1866) LR 1 Ex 213, for instance, the claimant agreed to hire a horse and carriage to a prostitute, knowing that it would be used, in some way, to assist her in her enterprise. It was held that the claimant could not recover the hire charge when the defendant refused to pay it. Lord Pollock explained (at 218):

> I have always considered it as settled law that any person who contributes to the performance of an illegal act by supplying a thing with the knowledge that it is going to be used for that purpose, cannot recover the price of the thing so supplied . . . Nor can any distinction be made between an illegal and an immoral purpose; the rule which is applicable to the matter is ex turpi causa non oritur actio, and whether it is an immoral or an illegal purpose in which the [claimant] has participated, it comes equally within the terms of that maxim, and the effect is the same; no cause of action can arise out of either the one or the other.

Such a conclusion may not be surprising, and the statement of Lord Pollock was later applied in *Upfill* v *Wright* (1911), a case involving rent paid for an immoral purpose of keeping a mistress. It is, however, debatable how widely the notion of 'sexual immorality' should be interpreted. Societal attitudes to such questions are constantly changing and behaviour that is regarded as shocking to one generation may not seem so outrageous to a later generation. (For example, see *Armhouse Lee Ltd* v *Chappell* (1996).)

Contracts prejudicial to the interests of the state

15.51 This is a very general heading and is susceptible to a number of interpretations. One obvious instance is a trading contract concluded in time of war between someone in the UK and a foreign enemy. Such an agreement is, not surprisingly, illegal. If the contract predates the outbreak of hostilities it will still be dissolved, but rights and obligations which existed before the outbreak of war may be enforced after its conclusion.

15.52 There is also a prohibition against contracts which tend to injure the UK's friendly relations with another state (i.e. one with which we are not at war). If an agreement promotes action which is inimical to a friendly foreign country it will be regarded as unlawful and unenforceable by our courts (see *De Wutz* v *Hendricks* (1824)). An interesting example of the application of this prohibition is provided by *Regazzoni* v *KC Sethia Ltd* [1957] 3 All ER 286. The facts were as follows:

> An ordinance issued by the government of India prohibited the taking of goods out of India if they were destined for any part of South Africa, or were intended to be taken to South Africa despite being initially destined for another country. An English company, KC Sethia Ltd, agreed to sell and deliver to Polissino Regazzoni 500,000 bags of jute. To the knowledge of both contracting parties, the jute was to be shipped from India to Genoa so that it might there be resold to a South African buying agency in contravention of the Indian ordinance. Sethia failed to deliver the jute and Regazzoni claimed damages in an English court for breach of contract. Sethia defended the action by claiming that the contract was, to Regazzoni's knowledge, an illegal contract and therefore unenforceable, as its breach of the Indian ordinance was harmful to the interests of the state.

The House of Lords held that, as a matter of public policy, the contract was unenforceable in England. Its performance would have involved—as the parties were well aware—doing an act in a friendly foreign country which violated the law of that country. Lord Reid explained the reasoning of the court as follows (at 293):

> The real question is one of public policy in English law; but, in considering this question, we must have in mind the background of . . . the comity of nations. This is not a case of a contract being made in good faith but one party thereafter finding that he cannot perform his part of the contract without committing a breach of foreign law in the territory of the foreign country. If this contract is held to be unenforceable it should, in my opinion, be because from the beginning the contract was tainted so that the courts of this country will not assist either party to enforce it.[12]

It was stressed by Lord Reid (at 294–5) that in deciding that the contract was unenforceable for breach of Indian law, the court was not necessarily implying its approval of that particular law. On the other hand, there was no express disapproval of that law. But, in a different situation, if our courts regarded a particular foreign law as positively distasteful for some reason, they might not refuse to enforce a contract which was in breach of such a law.

Contracts prejudicial to the administration of justice

15.53 Under this heading we can include agreements to interfere with or suppress a prosecution. The validity of such an agreement may, however, depend upon the nature of the unlawful act which raised the possibility of the criminal proceedings. If the harm caused by the act was

12 See also *United City Merchants* v *Royal Bank of Canada* (1981), in which dicta of Viscount Simmonds and Lord Reid in *Regazzoni* were applied.

of an essentially private nature (such as criminal libel or common assault) then an agreement not to prosecute might well be permissible. On the other hand, it would not be valid to agree to suppress a prosecution for an act which was more overtly injurious to the public interest—in any case, it is a substantive crime to conceal an arrestable offence. It should also be noted that an agreement to interfere with the due course of a criminal investigation or prosecution might well be unlawful on the ground that it constitutes an attempt or conspiracy to pervert the course of justice. In *R* v *Andrews* (1973), for example:

> D witnessed a traffic accident between a motor car and a moped, as a result of which criminal proceedings against the car driver were contemplated. D invited the car driver to pay him to give false evidence at the prospective prosecution, and the driver offered him a sum of money, but no bargain was in fact struck. D was convicted on a charge of inciting the motorist to pervert the course of justice.

The Court of Appeal dismissed the defendant's appeal against the conviction. It stated that to produce false evidence in order to mislead the court and to pervert the course of justice was a substantive offence, that inciting someone to act in this way was also an offence, and that therefore the conviction was justified. The case was concerned with the defendant's culpability rather than the question of illegality of contracts, but it is obvious that had the defendant and the motorist reached an agreement, it would have been both illegal and unenforceable on the ground of public policy. (For another discussion of agreements which interfere with the course of justice, see *Farhad Faryab* v *Phillip Ross & Co.* (2002).)

15.54 Another example of agreements which may be prejudicial to the administration of justice are those between a husband and wife where they collude in order to facilitate divorce proceedings. Whether such collusion invalidates an agreement today will depend on whether or not it is a corrupt agreement, that is, one that is designed to practise a deception on the court.[13]

Contracts promoting corruption in public life

15.55 It would be contrary to the public interest if public offices or honours could be bought and sold. Such practices encourage corruption and result in the public not being served by the most able public officials. Consequently, agreements for the sale or purchase of such offices are unlawful. A good example of the scope of this principle is provided by *Parkinson* v *College of Ambulance Ltd and Harrison* (1925). The facts were:

> Colonel Parkinson was told by Harrison, the secretary of the defendant charity, that the charity would arrange for him to be granted a knighthood if he made a substantial donation. Harrison had told Parkinson of the charity's royal patronage. Parkinson paid £3,000 to the College of Ambulance on the understanding that he would receive a knighthood, and he

13 See *Nash* v *Nash* (1965).

> also promised further payment to the charity in the future. When Parkinson did not receive a knighthood and realized that he had been duped, he brought an action against the charity to recover back the money that he had paid.

Lush J held that as the contract was for the purchase of a title, it was contrary to public policy and was an illegal contract. Despite the fact that the claimant had been defrauded, he knew that he was entering into an improper agreement and he could not recover the money he had paid to the charity; nor could he recover damages from the charity or its secretary. In this case, the attempt to buy influence was clearly improper. However, in commercial situations the use of 'intermediaries' to lobby for contracts is a common practice, and it may be difficult to decide at precisely which point legitimate business practices cross the line and become contrary to public policy. (See the case of *Tekron Resources Ltd* v *Guinea Investment Co. Ltd* (2003) at [93]–[101], where this point was considered.)

The effects of impropriety and illegality

15.56 We have seen that there are numerous types of impropriety which can affect a contract and that these involve varying degrees of unlawfulness. For this reason it is difficult to generalize about their consequences. We have considered the effects of impropriety on some types of contract in earlier parts of this chapter. What follows is intended only as an outline of some of the main principles that have been developed by the courts for dealing with problems of impropriety.

Void contracts

15.57 In the case of contracts that are void due to some statutory provision (discussed at para. **15.4**), it is necessary to look closely at the particular statute in question to assess the effects of impropriety. In contracts void at common law on the grounds of public policy, it will be remembered that it may be possible to separate the offending part of the agreement from the rest of it. For example, where an agreement purports to prevent the parties to it from submitting questions of law to the courts, although such a clause will be void, the rest of the contract may be enforceable.

15.58 In the section on contracts in restraint of trade, we considered the doctrine of severance. This permits the unreasonable part of a clause or covenant to be separated from the rest of it, by deleting it, leaving the remainder in force. For example, in *Goldsoll* v *Goldman* (1915), the restraint imposed on the vendor of a jewellery business was too wide in the geographical area that it purported to cover. However, the Court of Appeal held that the unreasonable parts of the restraint were capable of being severed from the rest of it. The restraint that was permitted by the court was the one covering the UK, as this was reasonable in the circumstances. It should be borne in mind that courts may be less willing to apply the idea of severance in cases between employer and employee, as the parties are unlikely to possess equal bargaining strength.

15.59 A party to an agreement which is void for being contrary to public policy may have paid money to the other party under that 'contract'. It seems likely that the party who has paid the money will be able to recover it from the other. For example, in *Hermann* v *Charlesworth* (1905), the claimant paid a special client's fee of £52 to the defendant under a so-called 'marriage brokage' contract. Despite being introduced to several men by the defendant, the claimant did not become engaged or married to any of them. The Court of Appeal decided that this contract was invalid, as it was contrary to public policy to enforce marriage brokage contracts. Yet the claimant was entitled to recover the money paid under the contract, even though the defendant had brought about the introductions as promised. It should be noted that some of the reasoning employed by their Lordships in this case was far from convincing.

Illegal contracts

15.60 It is difficult to generalize about the effects of illegality, as much depends upon the circumstances of each case, such as the nature and seriousness of the illegality in question, and the state of mind of the contracting parties. (See *Vakante* v *Addey & Stanhope School* (2004) at [7]–[9].) Although we have concentrated so far on contracts which are illegal at common law on the grounds of public policy, it must be emphasized that the making of certain agreements may also be prohibited by statute. (See further *Patel* v *Mirza* (2016), discussed at paras **15.64** and **15.83–15.87**.) It is an instructive starting point to consider certain cases involving illegality arising out of a statutory prohibition. In *Re Mahmoud and Ispahani* (1921) (discussed earlier), the facts were that C sold linseed oil to D, in contravention of a statutory provision. C was misled by D into thinking that D possessed a licence to deal in linseed oil, when in fact he had no such licence. Subsequently, D refused to accept delivery of the oil and claimed that the contract was illegal. C claimed damages.

The Court of Appeal held that as D was unlicensed, the contract in question was prohibited by the Seed, Oils, and Fats Order of 1919 and was, therefore, illegal. Despite the innocence of the claimant, his claim was unsuccessful. The statutory prohibition was in the public interest and no claim could be made under the contract. It seems that the state of mind of the parties did not make any difference to the outcome where there was such an unequivocal statutory prohibition of this type of contract. Their agreement was illegal from the outset.

15.61 The situation in *Re Mahmoud and Ispahani* (1921) can be contrasted with that where an innocent party sues on a contract which is not ex facie illegal, but which is performed by the other party in an illegal manner. For example, in *Archbold's (Freightage) Ltd* v *Spanglett Ltd* (1961):

> The defendants agreed to carry a load of whisky by road, from Leeds to London, for Archbold's. Archbold's were unaware that the vehicle to be used by the defendants did not have the correct licence in order to comply with the Road and Rail Traffic Act 1933, s 1(1). The defendants, however, were aware of this fact. Somewhere on the route to London the goods were stolen as a result of the negligence of the defendants' driver. The defendants argued that they were not liable for damages, because the contract was illegal by reason of the Road and Rail Traffic Act.

It was held that Archbold's were not debarred from recovering damages by the illegality of the defendants' use of their vehicle. Archbold's were innocent, but that fact had not helped the claimant in *Mahmoud*'s case (para. **15.49**). The reason why *Mahmoud* was distinguishable from the present case was due to the nature of the statutory prohibition. In *Mahmoud*, the contract of sale to an unlicensed person was expressly forbidden (see also *J Dennis and Co. Ltd* v *Munn* (1949)), whereas in *Archbold's (Freightage) Ltd* the carriage of Archbold's whisky was not as such prohibited. The legislation in question merely regulated the manner in which carriers should transport goods. The contract was not, therefore, expressly forbidden by the statute and the claimants were entitled to damages. It is worth noting that if both parties to the contract had known that the vehicle did not have an appropriate licence, the contract would have been unenforceable, as they would have known that it could not be carried out without breaking the law.

15.62 It must be emphasized that it is important to look at the language, scope, and purpose of the relevant statute in considering the effects of any illegality arising out of the contravention of its provisions. (For example, see *Hughes* v *Asset Managers plc* (1995).) In certain circumstances, it may even be possible for an 'illegal' contract to be enforced by both the innocent and the guilty party. If we reconsider the case of *St John Shipping Corpn* v *Joseph Rank Ltd* (1956), where the claimants carried a cargo of wheat from America to England in an overloaded ship, the question arose whether they could sue for the balance of freight owing to them under the contract of carriage. The claimants had infringed the Merchant Shipping Act 1932 and the master of the ship was, accordingly, fined. But it was held that this did not prevent them from recovering the freight from the defendants. The relevant statutory provision did not intend to make such a contract of carriage unlawful: it simply aimed to penalize overloading. Thus, the purpose of the statute was achieved adequately by the imposition of a fine on the master of the ship. In reaching this conclusion, Devlin J had to contend with the following observation of Lord Atkin in *Beresford* v *Royal Insurance Co. Ltd* [1938] 2 All ER 602 at 605: 'No system of jurisprudence can with reason include amongst the rights which it enforces rights directly resulting to the person asserting them from the crime of that person.' Devlin J explained that the relevant prohibition in *St John Shipping* imposed a penalty under the criminal law which was designed to deprive the offender of the benefits of his crime. This being so, it would be unfair if the civil law imposed a further penalty by denying the claimants the freight which was owed under the contract. He added (at 693) that 'it would be curious, too, if in a case in which the magistrates had thought fit to impose only a nominal fine their decision could in effect be overridden in a civil action'.

15.63 The fact that the guilty party was not prevented from succeeding in the above case serves as a useful warning that general rules about the effects of illegality are difficult to detect. (For a discussion of the relevant principles, see *Colen* v *Cebrian (UK) Ltd* (2003) at [23].) This is inevitable in view of the differing degrees of seriousness which can arise in illegality cases. (See Law Commission Consultation Paper, No 189, *The Illegality Defence: A Consultative Report*, 2009, at para. 3.52: 'to expect one set of detailed and ostensibly rigid rules to cater for all circumstances that may be encountered is overly ambitious.') It is unlikely that the courts will apply a consistent set of rules regardless of how they view the impropriety in question. An interesting contrast to *St John Shipping Corpn* v *Joseph Rank Ltd* (1956) is provided by *Ashmore, Benson, Pease, & Co.* v *AV Dawson Ltd* (1973). The facts were:

> Ashmores wished to have a 25-ton 'tube-bank', which they had manufactured, transported from their works to a port for shipment. Ashmores' transport manager arranged for Dawsons, a small road haulage firm, to carry the tube-bank. He was also present when it was loaded on to one of Dawsons' vehicles, and he was familiar with the statutory regulations governing the transporting of loads on vehicles. Dawsons overloaded their vehicle in contravention of s 64(2) of the Road Traffic Act 1960, but Ashmores' manager raised no objection to their use of an inappropriate vehicle—the goods should have been carried on a 'low loader', but Dawsons did not have one. On the journey to the port, the vehicle toppled over, causing more than £2,000 of damage to the tube-bank. Ashmores brought an action for damages against Dawsons.

At the trial the claimants gained judgment as the contract was lawful when made. But the Court of Appeal held that even if the contract was lawful at its inception, its performance was unlawful. Ashmores, through their manager, had participated in the illegality, since he had permitted the excessive loading of the vehicle. As a result of this participation, the claimants were debarred from claiming damages in respect of the accident which occurred.

A 'new era' for the defence of illegality

15.64 In the landmark case of *Patel* v *Mirza* [2016] UKSC 42, nine Justices sitting in the Supreme Court took the opportunity to re-examine the law of illegality, deciding unanimously in favour of a restitutionary award in response to an unjust enrichment, despite the illegal transaction on which that enrichment was based.[14] The ruling has triggered significant implications for the future scope and application of the doctrine, marking a 'new era' for the defence of illegality (per Lord Mance at [206]), and is discussed in detail at paras **15.83–15.87**. However, before examining the facts of the case and the judicial reasoning which has brought about such a momentous development in this field of law, it is appropriate to explore some of the decisions reached in earlier cases which, until the *Patel* v *Mirza* decision, represented the confused state of the law of illegality.

15.65 In 2009, the Law Commission reported that the present law is 'unnecessarily complex, uncertain, arbitrary and lacks transparency' (see Law Commission Consultation Paper, No 189, 2009, at para. 3.52). As can be seen from a review of a few general principles relating to the effects of illegality in contracts which are illegal from the outset, such cases offer ample evidence of these criticisms. It should be noted also how reliance on matters of public interest and public policy, or alternatively the application of legal technicalities, has justified the variety of conclusions reached—factors which, as we will later learn, have proved of pivotal importance in the *Patel* v *Mirza* Supreme Court ruling.

An illegal contract is unenforceable by either party

15.66 It is generally accepted that where both parties participate equally in a transaction which is illegal in itself, then neither can enforce the agreement against the other. In a famous statement in *Holman* v *Johnson* (1775) 1 Cowp 341 at 343, Lord Mansfield stated

14 See S. Green and A. Bogg (eds) *Illegality after Patel v Mirza*, Hart Publishing, 2018.

that 'no court will lend its aid to a man who founds his cause of action upon an immoral or an illegal act'. This is a principle based on public policy and, as a result (somewhat oddly), it may enable the defendant to rely on the illegality or the immorality as a means of escaping liability under an agreement. It will be remembered from *Pearce* v *Brooks* (1866) that the claimant who hired a carriage to a prostitute, in the knowledge that it would in some way assist with her occupation, was unable to recover the hire charge when the defendant refused to pay. No cause of action could arise out of an illegal transaction of this type to which the claimant had contributed. (But see *Howard* v *Shirlstar Container Transport* (1990), in which the claimant was permitted to benefit from his illegal act—a breach of Nigerian air traffic control regulations—as such an outcome was held not to be an affront to public conscience.)

15.67 A slightly different problem arises where both parties are aware of a prohibition, but one of them can be regarded as more blameworthy than the other. If the purpose of the prohibition in question is to protect the public, the court may still decide that even the less culpable party is unable to enforce the illegal agreement. For example, in *Mohamed* v *Alaga & Co. (a firm)* [1999] 3 All ER 699, M claimed that he had an agreement with the defendant solicitors, under which he would introduce Somali asylum seekers to the solicitors and assist the solicitors (as a translator) in preparing their clients' cases. In return, the solicitors were to pay him a share of any fees received from the Legal Aid Board for acting on behalf of these clients. M's claim to enforce the agreement, which was contrary to r 7 of the Solicitors' Practice Rules 1990, was rejected by the Court of Appeal, as it was an attempt to enforce an illegal contract. The court reached this conclusion despite the fact that the prohibition in question was imposed on solicitors, and it was they who faced professional penalties for breach of the rules. It was held that the public interest would not be protected if a non-solicitor could enforce such an agreement. However, the Court of Appeal held that M could succeed with his claim for a reasonable price for the work he carried out at the solicitors' request. The court thought it was relevant here that, if the alleged agreement had been made, M's conduct was less blameworthy than that of the solicitors. (See the comments of Lord Bingham CJ at 707; see also the interesting discussion of both this and subsequent decisions by the Law Commission: Law Commission Consultation Paper, No 189, *The Illegality Defence: A Consultative Report*, 2009, paras 4.21–4.28.)

Money or property transferred is not recoverable

15.68 A further general principle relates to property which is transferred under an illegal transaction. For example, in *Parkinson* v *College of Ambulance Ltd and Harrison* (1925) the claimant gave money to the defendant charity after receiving assurances from its secretary that it could arrange a knighthood for him. Having failed to receive the promised honour, the claimant tried to recover his money. Due to the illegality of the transaction, it was held that he was not entitled to the return of his money despite having been defrauded. There can be little surprise at such a result, for this seems to follow logically from the principle considered earlier. Both parties were equally involved in a transaction, which was illegal in itself, and therefore neither could enforce the agreement against the other.

15.69 But a slightly different problem occurred in *Belvoir Finance Co. Ltd* v *Stapleton* [1971] 1 QB 210. The facts were as follows:

> The claimant finance company (BF) were supplied with cars by a dealer which they in turn let on hire-purchase terms to the Belgravia Car (BC) hire company. All three parties were (to their knowledge) involved in an illegal transaction, as the contracts of sale and of hire were in breach of certain statutory regulations. BC fraudulently sold the cars to innocent buyers and then went into liquidation. BF sued the defendant, who was an assistant manager of BC and who had actually sold the cars, in conversion. His defence to this action was based on the argument that BF could not recover because of their own participation in the illegal transactions. For their part, BF needed to show that they were the owners of the cars at the time of the defendant's fraudulent disposal of them.

The Court of Appeal held, perhaps surprisingly, that the defendant was liable. It appeared to be prepared to overlook the illegality of the original contract under which BF bought the cars from the dealer, and it found that the cars belonged to the finance company. This conclusion was reached in spite of the fact that the cars had never been delivered to BF—the cars went directly from the dealer to the car hire company. In allowing the claimants to recover damages against the defendant it does seem that, despite protestations to the contrary (at 218), the Court of Appeal enforced an illegal contract.

Exceptions

15.70 It should be noted that there are early case examples of exceptions to the general rule that money or other property transferred under an illegal transaction cannot be recovered. For example, if a party can make out his or her case quite independently of the illegal contract (i.e. based on some lawful ground), then he or she will be able to recover his or her money or property because, in so doing, he or she is not forced to rely on the illegality in question. (See *Amar Singh* v *Kulubya* (1964) for a neat illustration of this point.) For another, rather questionable example, it is instructive to consider *Bowmakers Ltd* v *Barnet Instruments Ltd* (1945). The facts were:

> The claimant company, Bowmakers, supplied certain machine tools to the defendants, Barnet Ltd, under three hire-purchase contracts. These contracts were illegal (or at least this was assumed by the court), as they were in breach of wartime ministerial regulations. The defendants, having failed to make all the hire-purchase payments which were due under the contracts, sold the tools which they had acquired under two of the contracts. In addition, they refused to return the remaining tools, which they held under the third contract, to the claimants. The defendants argued that the claimants had no remedy against them, because of the illegality of the three agreements.

The Court of Appeal held that the claimants' action for conversion (of all the goods) was successful despite the illegality of the transactions. It was argued that the claimants' action did not rely on the illegal hire-purchase contracts, but on the independent cause of action that they were the owners of the goods. This certainly explains why the claimants' action could succeed in relation to the goods which were sold by the defendants, but it is far from convincing in relation to the goods which were merely retained. In respect of these goods, which were not sold by the defendants, the court was surely allowing the claimants to succeed in an action which was based on an illegal transaction. The claimants' right to recovery of these goods was clearly based on the defendants' failure to make the payments that were agreed under an illegal hire-purchase contract. It might be argued, by way of defence of the court's decision, that it would have been unfair if the defendants had been able to hide behind the mere breach of a ministerial order as a means of escaping liability.[15]

15.71 The *Bowmakers Ltd* v *Barnet Instruments Ltd* (1945) approach was followed by the House of Lords in *Tinsley* v *Milligan* (1993), where the facts were:

> Two women, T and M, lived together in a house for which they jointly provided the money to buy. They agreed for the house to be in T's name only, so that M could make false claims for social security payments (from which they both benefited). They later quarreled, and T claimed possession of the house. M argued that T held the house on trust for both of them in equal shares, but was her claim barred by her own illegal conduct?

The House of Lords, by a narrow majority, upheld the Court of Appeal's decision—that T held the property on trust for both of the parties in equal shares—but it relied on different reasoning. The majority held that M did not need to rely on the illegality to support her claim. She needed only to show that she had contributed to the purchase price of the house and that there was an understanding between the parties that the house was jointly owned, that is, that there was a resulting trust. In reaching their decision, the majority applied the principle established in *Bowmakers* v *Barnet*, enabling M's claim to succeed on what appear to be rather technical grounds. The judgment seems to take little account of the illegality of the claimant's conduct. (*Quaere*: Would a claimant whose conduct involved more serious offences than M's be allowed to succeed under similar circumstances—on a technicality—or would the court be forced to consider the public policy issues involved? See Lord Goff's dissenting views in *Tinsley* v *Milligan* at 79.)

The approach of the House of Lords has been criticized,[16] and the judgment of the Court of Appeal in *Tinsley* v *Milligan* is to be preferred. (See further *Patel v Mirza* (2016), discussed at paras **15.83–15.87**.) The Court of Appeal was prepared to assess the conduct of M to see whether it was so serious as to merit the penalty which would be incurred by the loss of her interest in the house, and, if it was not, whether the public conscience would be affronted by the success of her claim. It can be appreciated why the House of Lords had reservations about this

15 See also *Saunders* v *Edwards* (1987).

16 E.g., see N. Enonchong, 'Illegality: The Fading Flame of Public Policy' (1994) 14 OJLS 295.

more discretionary approach, with the uncertainty which would inevitably accompany it. Calls for reform to the illegality defence in trusts arose out of the 1964 House of Lords decision. (See further Law Commission Report No 320, *The Illegality Defence* (2010), paras 1.15–1.33.)

15.72 Similar issues were raised in *Tribe* v *Tribe* (1995).

> In this case, C owned 459 out of 500 shares in a family company and was the tenant of two leasehold properties which the company occupied as licensee. The landlord of the properties claimed against C for repairs and, if the claims were successful, C would be faced with having to sell the company. In order to prevent this, C transferred his shares to one of his sons (D), a director of the company. It was never intended that the proposed price for the transfer should actually be paid and, indeed, D did not pay. Eventually, after satisfactory resolution of the disputes over the lease, C wanted to revert to the position which had existed before he was faced with claims for repair. However, D now refused to transfer the shares back to C, and C took action to recover them.

The judge found that the illegal purpose of the transfer (i.e. to deceive C's creditors into thinking he was no longer the owner of the shares) had not been carried into effect in any way. As the claims over repairs were resolved, no deception of creditors was needed by C. The judge upheld C's claim for return of the shares and the Court of Appeal dismissed D's appeal. It appears that it was sufficient for C to withdraw voluntarily from the illegal transaction when it was no longer necessary, without any need to repent his illegal purpose (per Millet LJ in the Court of Appeal).

15.73 Another exception to the general rule about the irrecoverability of property transferred under an illegal contract is where the parties are not in pari delicto, that is, where they are not equally guilty. In certain circumstances it may be possible for the court to allow the less culpable party to recover property that he has transferred to the other, more guilty party. If, for example, one party has entered into an unlawful agreement, having been defrauded by the other (or as a result of oppression), it is eminently sensible that the 'victim' should not be debarred from recovering property which has been transferred. It may not always be quite so easy, however, to decide whether one party is more culpable than the other. In *Kiriri Cotton Ltd* v *Dewani* (1960), for example:

> KC Ltd let a flat in Uganda for a term of seven years to Dewani, who paid a premium of Shs10,000. Although neither party realized they were breaking the law, the taking of a premium was, in fact, a breach of a government ordinance. This ordinance did not make any express provision that an illegal premium was recoverable by the tenant (in contrast to the analogous legislation in England). Dewani brought an action to recover the premium.

The Privy Council held that the premium was recoverable by the tenant, despite the lack of an express provision in the ordinance permitting this. It was clear that the statute was aimed at protecting a particular class of person from another, namely prospective tenants from landlords. So although both parties were unaware that they were breaking the law, the court was of the opinion that the duty of observing the law fell more heavily on the landlord than the tenant. Thus, despite appearances to the contrary, they were not in pari delicto. (Of course, some statutes make express provision to achieve this effect, in which case there is no need to rely on the common law principle.) The approach of the law was summed up by Lord Mansfield, in *Browning* v *Morris* (1778) 2 Cowp 790 at 792, in the following way:

> But, where contracts or transactions are prohibited by positive statutes, for the sake of protecting one set of men from another set of men; the one, from their situation and condition, being liable to be oppressed or imposed upon by the other; there, the parties are not in pari delicto; and in furtherance of these statutes, the person injured, after the transaction is finished and completed, may bring his action and defeat the contract.

15.74 The scope of this principle was discussed in *Green* v *Portsmouth Stadium Ltd* [1953] 2 QB 190. The facts were:

> Frederick Green, a bookmaker, claimed that he had been overcharged by the defendants over a period of years, contrary to the provisions of s 13(1) of the Betting and Lotteries Act 1934. The defendants owned the Portsmouth Stadium greyhound racing track. Green alleged that although the highest charge which the defendants were authorized to make under s 13(1) was 11s 3d, he had been charged £2 each time he went on to the course. He now claimed from the defendants the excess fees which he had paid to them. He based his argument on the fact that he was not in pari delicto with the defendants and sought to rely on the dictum of Lord Mansfield.

The Court of Appeal held that the claimant was not able to recover the amounts that he had been overcharged by the defendants as the obligation imposed by the relevant statute was enforceable only by criminal proceedings. (The Act did not expressly provide for the recovery of any overcharge—it stated only that the person responsible for it was guilty of an offence.) This reasoning is not entirely convincing, but the court went on to reject Green's argument that he was not in pari delicto with the defendants. Lord Hodson (at 197) observed that the claimant had not proved that he was less guilty. He stated that, as far as the evidence went, Green seemed to have been 'as much a party to breaking [the law]' as the defendants.

15.75 A further exception to the general rule is where a party repents or withdraws before the contract has been substantially performed. (See *Tribe* v *Tribe* (1995), discussed earlier, and also the Law Commission Consultation Paper, No 189, *The Illegality Defence: A Consultative Report*, 2009, paras 4.45–4.59.) So where a party takes proceedings before the illegal purpose has been achieved, he may be allowed to recover property which he has transferred under the contract (for example, see *Taylor* v *Bowers* (1876)). But this raises the obvious problem of deciding whether the repentance has taken place at an early enough stage to allow recovery. How will a court decide whether matters have progressed too far? The first requirement, if the claimant is to succeed, is to show that it is a genuine case of repentance, that is, that he has chosen to abandon the illegal purpose. If he has no choice in the matter due to the other party's failure to perform, he will not be allowed to recover (see *Bigos* v *Bousted* (1951)). The second requirement relates to the time at which the repentance takes place in relation to the progress of the illegal purpose (see *Ouston* v *Zurowski* (1985)).[17] Where the illegal purpose has been accomplished it is obvious that recovery will not be allowed. But it also appears that even where the illegal agreement has been only partly performed, recovery will not be permitted if the illegal purpose has been substantially achieved. For example, in *Kearley* v *Thomson* (1890) 24 QBD 742:

> The defendant firm of solicitors was to act on behalf of a petitioning creditor against a bankrupt named Clarke. The claimant, a friend of Clarke's, agreed to pay the defendants their costs, in return for which they would neither appear at the public examination of Clarke, nor oppose his order of discharge. The solicitors, on receiving the promised payment, did not appear at Clarke's public examination, in accordance with their illegal agreement with the claimant. But the claimant changed his mind before any application was made for the bankrupt's discharge, and he tried to recover the money which he had paid to the defendants.

It was held by the Court of Appeal that he could not recover the money. The illegality of the agreement was that it was aimed at interfering with the course of justice. As this purpose had already been substantially achieved, the repentance came too late. In the words of Fry LJ (at 747):

> [W]here there has been a partial carrying into effect of an illegal purpose in a substantial manner, it is impossible, though there remains something not performed, that the money paid under that illegal contract can be recovered back.

Related transactions between the parties

15.76 The parties to an illegal contract may also enter into a subsequent agreement which is based on the illegal transaction. In this case, the later agreement will also be tainted by the illegal purpose of the original contract. So if one party owes another money under an illegal contract, and he gives some security in respect of the money which is due, this will be unenforceable against him by the other party. In *Fisher* v *Bridges* (1854), for example, C agreed to sell, and subsequently conveyed, land to D for a purpose which was illegal. The defendant still owed some money to C under the transaction and he executed a deed by which he promised payment of the outstanding sum. It was held that such a deed was unenforceable as it was tainted by the illegality of the main transaction. This is hardly surprising, for if the law refuses to enforce the original contract, it follows that any subsequent agreement which springs from this should be treated in the same way.

15.77 A separate issue (not to be confused with the above rule) is where the courts allow one party a remedy against the other, despite the illegality of their contract, under a 'collateral'

17 *Ouston* v *Zurowski* (1985). In this Canadian case one party was entitled to recover under an illegal contract because he repented before performance of the contract, that is, by not carrying into effect the illegal purpose (a 'pyramid' scheme) in a substantial manner before abandoning the scheme.

contract. We have seen, in other areas of contract law, how this device is sometimes used by the courts to enable a fair solution to be reached when it would otherwise be precluded by some substantive principle of law. Here it is used so as to enable the innocent party to sue the guilty party under an illegal transaction without relying on the transaction itself. An instructive case is *Strongman (1945) Ltd* v *Sincock* (1955):

> The claimant building company contracted with the defendant, an architect, to modernize some houses. An appropriate licence was required from the Ministry of Works so that the refurbishment did not contravene statutory regulations; without such a licence the contract was illegal. The defendant promised the claimants, before the contract was made, that he would take responsibility for securing the necessary licences. The claimants carried out work which exceeded £6,000 in value. But the defendant had obtained licences for only £2,150. The defendant paid only £2,900 to the builders and he argued that the performance of the contract was illegal. The builders sued for the unpaid sum.

The Court of Appeal held that, despite the illegality of the main transaction, the builders could succeed on the basis of the collateral promise made by the defendant that he would obtain the necessary licences for the work. Presumably it was thought that the work was carried out by the builders on the understanding that he had in fact done as he promised. Although the conclusion reached by the court was desirable, there is, in truth, some difficulty in distinguishing this case from *Re Mahmoud and Ispahani* (1921) (discussed at para. **15.49**). It should be added that this judicial device will be used to assist the 'innocent' party in very limited circumstances.

Inconsistencies and complexities

15.78 It is clear from the previous sections that the courts are not always consistent in their application of the common law principles relating to the enforcement of illegal agreements, resulting in a body of case law which is complex and far from satisfactory. The House of Lords' decision in *Tinsley* v *Milligan* (1993) (see the discussion at para. **15.71**) illustrates the way in which technical legal arguments may lead to an avoidance of the consideration of wider issues of policy and justice. Furthermore, a recurring problem faced by the court is how to signify its disapproval of an illegal agreement without allowing one party to be unjustly enriched or advantaged at the expense of the other. (See the discussion at para. **15.67** of *Mohamed* v *Alaga & Co. (a firm)* (1999).)

15.79 In 2010, following on from earlier Consultation Papers, the Law Commission published its final recommendations (see *The Illegality Defence*, Report No 320, 2010).[18] The first Consultation Paper, in 1999, concluded that there is a need for legislative reform of this area of law and recommended, provisionally, that the existing rules relating to the effects of illegality

18 Law Commission Consultation Paper, No 154, *Illegal Transactions: The Effect of Illegality on Contracts and Trusts*, 1999 and Law Commission Consultation Paper, No 189, *The Illegality Defence: A Consultative Report*, 2009.

should be replaced by a discretion.[19] Such a discretion would enable a court to decide whether to enforce an illegal agreement, to recognize that property rights have been transferred or created by it, or to hold that benefits conferred under the agreement are recoverable.[20] In this Paper, the Law Commission favoured a structured discretion, in the interests of greater certainty and to provide guidance to the courts. It provisionally recommended that, in the exercise of its discretion, the court should have regard to:

> (i) the seriousness of the illegality involved;
> (ii) the knowledge and intention of the party seeking to enforce the illegal transaction, seeking the recognition of legal or equitable rights under it, or seeking to recover benefits conferred under it;
> (iii) whether refusing to allow standard rights and remedies would deter illegality;
> (iv) whether refusing to allow standard rights and remedies would further the purpose of the rule which renders the transaction illegal; and
> (v) whether refusing to allow standard rights and remedies would be proportionate to the illegality involved.[21]

15.80 However, in its more recent Consultation Paper, in 2009, the Law Commission concluded that legislation was not needed (Consultation Paper, No 189, 2009, para. 3.122), and that in most areas the 'courts could reach the desired result through development of the case law' (Consultation Paper, No 189, paras 1.5 and 3.108. For a critique of its proposals, see P. Davies, 'The Illegality Defence—Two Steps Forward, One Step Back?' (2009) Conv & PL 182). In relation to contract, unjust enrichment, and tort claims it was thought that the courts would be able to rationalize and develop the law in a satisfactory way (paras 1.6 and 3.123), and that any reform which is necessary 'can be safely left to incremental case law development' (para. 3.124). The Paper argued that, despite the complexity of the relevant legal rules, the courts have generally managed to reach a just conclusion in the majority of cases (para. 3.125). In assessing how the courts have achieved this, the Law Commission thought that judges, despite the so-called rules, 'do in fact take into consideration a whole variety of factors which ensure that relief is only denied where it is a fair and proportionate response to the claimant's conduct' (para. 3.125). It thought that these 'factors', which relate to the policies underpinning the illegality doctrine, should be given greater prominence and be 'openly weighed and considered' (para. 3.125; some of these factors are discussed at paras 3.126–3.135). It stated that the present legal rules in this area are sometimes circumvented, 'so as to give better effect to the underlying policies as they apply to the facts' of each case, and that it would be preferable if this was explained more openly by the courts in their judgments (para. 3.140). The Consultation Paper recommended (at para. 3.142):

---

19 Law Com No 154, para. 9.1.

20 Law Com No 154, para. 1.18 and paras 7.2–7.26.

21 Law Com No 154, para. 1.19 and paras 7.27–7.43. Note that this proposed discretion was not to apply where there were express statutory provisions relating to the effect of illegality on a transaction. The Law Commission also made it clear in its 2009 Report that it did not recommend any legislative reform in relation to 'statutory illegality' (Law Commission Consultation Paper, No 189, para. 3.102).

> that the courts should consider in each case whether the application of the illegality defence can be justified on the basis of the policies that underlie that defence. These include: (a) furthering the purpose of the rule which the illegal conduct has infringed; (b) consistency; (c) that the claimant should not profit from his or her own wrong; (d) deterrence; and (e) maintaining the integrity of the legal system. Against those policies must be weighed the legitimate expectation of the claimant that his or her legal rights will be protected. Ultimately a balancing exercise is called for which weighs up the application of the various policies at stake. Only when depriving the claimant of his or her rights is a proportionate response based on the relevant illegality policies, should the defence succeed. The judgment should explain the basis on which it has done so.

15.81 The final recommendations of the Law Commission (Report No 320, 2010) follow the provisional recommendations set out in the 2009 Consultation Paper. It notes that the two recent House of Lords cases involving the illegality defence, namely *Gray* v *Thames Trains* (2009) and *Stone & Rolls* v *Moore Stephens* (2009), 'show that the law is developing in the way we had hoped' (para. 1.11). It concludes that 'the recent case law shows that the courts have become more open in explaining the policy reasons behind the illegality defence' and for this reason, 'in most areas of law, think that the illegality defence should be left to developments in common law' (para. 1.8). The final Report therefore does 'not recommend legislative reform in relation to the illegality defence as it applies to claims for breach of contract, tort or unjust enrichment' (para. 3.41).

15.82 However, the Law Commission concludes that statutory reform is required in one area: that is, to deal with cases where a trust has been set up in order to conceal the true ownership for unlawful purposes, because of the binding authority of the House of Lords' decision in *Tinsley* v *Milligan* (discussed earlier). The Law Commission referred to the widespread criticism of *Tinsley* v *Milligan*, but felt that it was not possible for the lower courts to evade this decision. For this reason, the Law Commission prepared a draft Bill 'to provide the courts with a discretion to determine the effect of illegality on a limited class of trust' (para. 4.2). (For further discussion, see P. Davies, 'The Illegality Defence: Turning Back the Clock' (2010) Conv & PL 282.) The Draft Trusts (Concealment of Interests) Bill was attached to the Final Report of 2010, but in its 2012 Report on the implementation of Law Commission proposals the government announced that 'reform of this area of the law cannot be considered a pressing priority for the Government at present' and therefore they 'are minded not to implement the Commission's proposals'. Reform has since been brought about by virtue of the Supreme Court hearing of *Patel* v *Mirza* (2016), and it is to this significant judgment that we now turn.

15.83 In *Patel* v *Mirza* (2016) the facts of the case were:

> Mr Patel paid Mr Mirza £620,000 to bet on shares in RBS using insider information. If this act had been carried out it would have constituted a crime under s 52 of the Criminal Justice Act 1993. However, the inside information did not come through and therefore the agreement was not carried out. When Mr Mirza refused to return the £620,000 to Mr Patel, Mr Patel sued Mr Mirza for recovery of the payment on the basis of unjust enrichment.

In the court of first instance, although Mr Mirza did not plead illegality, Donaldson QC dismissed the claim on that basis, relying on the authority of *Tinsley* v *Milligan* (1994) and the principle that such a claim was unenforceable as Mr Patel would have to rely on his own illegality to establish it. The majority in the Court of Appeal upheld the conclusions based on the reliance principle but also held that Mr Patel's appeal could succeed on the grounds that the agreement had not been executed. Gloster LJ, however, focused on the policy implications underlying the defence of illegality, and consideration of this subsequently formed the basis of the judgments of the majority of the Justices in the Supreme Court.

15.84 The most recent cases on the defence of illegality had already started to reveal differences of opinion developing amongst the judiciary. Lord Toulson, in *ParkingEye* v *Somerfield Stores* (2012), had promoted a policy-based approach towards the defence, but this had been a minority view. Lord Wilson in *Hounga* v *Allen* (2014) had led support for a policy-based approach but was similarly in a minority position, with the majority favouring an orthodox, rule-based view. The orthodox approach dominated again in *Les Laboratoires Servier* v *Apotex* (2015) and Etherton LJ in particular, expressed criticism of the alternative, policy-based approach. In *Jetivia v Bilta* [2015] UKSC 23 with divergent views highly evident, Lord Neuberger [at 15] proposed resolution by a court of seven or nine Justices as soon as possible—*Patel* v *Mirza* (2016) offered such an opportunity and a panel of nine judges sat to hear the case.

15.85 The Supreme Court unanimously dismissed the appeal, upholding the Court of Appeal's decision that Mr Patel should be entitled to restitution of the £620,000 that he paid to Mr Mirza on the basis that otherwise Mr Mirza would be unjustly enriched. The reliance principle from *Tinsley* v *Milligan* (1994) was overruled, as was the rule from *Parkinson v College of Ambulance Ltd* (1925). What is highly significant is that although the Justices were unanimous in their decision, the reasoning behind that decision was reached from divergent perspectives, revealing a distinct division in the Supreme Court. Lord Toulson, Lady Hale, Lord Kerr, Lord Wilson, Lord Hodge, and Lord Neuberger favoured a discretionary policy-based approach. In contrast, Lord Sumption, with whom Lord Mance and Lord Clarke broadly agreed, favoured a more rule-based means of dealing with the issue. (See further S. Green and A. Bogg eds, *Illegality after Patel* v *Mirza*, Hart Publishing, 2018.)

15.86 Support for the discretionary approach was explained as being founded on justice to secure a fair result which could be reached following careful consideration of the factual context of the case. To reach the best result in terms of policy, Lord Toulson referred to Professor Burrows' recent formulation (*Restatement of the English Law of Contract*, Oxford University Press, 2016, pp. 229–30) recommending that judges need to have the flexibility to consider and weigh a range of factors in the light of the facts of the particular case before them [see paras 82–94 of the judgment]. The 'range of factors' listed are as follows [at 93]:

> If the formation, purpose or performance of a contract involves conduct that is illegal (such as a crime) or contrary to public policy (such as a restraint of trade), the contract is unenforceable by one or either party if to deny enforcement would be an appropriate response to that conduct, taking into account where relevant—

(a) how seriously illegal or contrary to public policy the conduct was;
(b) whether the party seeking enforcement knew of, or intended, the conduct;
(c) how central to the contract or its performance the conduct was;
(d) how serious a sanction the denial of enforcement is for the party seeking enforcement;
(e) whether denying enforcement will further the purpose of the rule which the conduct has infringed;
(f) whether denying enforcement will act as a deterrent to conduct that is illegal or contrary to public policy;
(g) whether denying enforcement will ensure that the party seeking enforcement does not profit from the conduct;
(h) whether denying enforcement will avoid inconsistency in the law thereby maintaining the integrity of the legal system.

It was noted that the final factor is capable of a wider or narrower approach, depending on what one understands by inconsistency. While finding the list 'helpful', Lord Toulson warned however against attempts to 'lay down a prescriptive or definitive list because of the infinite possible variety of cases', adding that 'potentially relevant factors include the seriousness of the conduct, its centrality to the contract, whether it was intentional and whether there was marked disparity in the parties' respective culpability' [at 107].

15.87 The effect of the Supreme Court hearing in *Patel* v *Mirza* (2016) is such that the earlier, confusing and difficult rules have undoubtedly been overtaken. Yet, with its basis in discretion, this new and controversial approach to the defence of illegality is by its very nature unlikely to deliver the much needed certainty in this area of law. A 'new era' in illegality has indeed begun.

Summary

- An otherwise valid agreement may contravene a legal rule or be deemed contrary to public policy.
- There is a variety of reasons for statutory and judicial intervention on the basis of 'illegality'.
- It is conventional to make a distinction between 'void' and 'illegal' contracts (i.e. on the basis of the legal consequences of the contract).
- Contracts in restraint of trade are void prima facie, but may become valid if they can be justified as reasonable between the parties and not against the public interest.
- Other contracts that are void at common law on the grounds of public policy include contracts to oust the jurisdiction of the courts, and contracts undermining the status of marriage.
- Examples of agreements where issues of 'illegality' have been raised include: contracts to commit an unlawful act; contracts promoting sexual immorality; contracts that prejudice the interests of the state; contracts prejudicial to the administration of justice; and contracts promoting corruption in public life.

- It is difficult to generalize about the legal consequences of illegality as much depends on the nature of the illegal agreement and the state of mind of the contracting parties.
- Despite the difficulty in formulating precise rules about the effects of illegality, there are some general principles that may be applied by the courts.
- There have been two Law Commission Consultation Papers on this subject. The first (in 1999) concluded that legislative reform is necessary in this area of law. However, the more recent one (2009) concluded that legislation was not needed as 'the courts could reach the desired result through the development of the case law'. This position was confirmed in the 2010 Final Report.
- The recent case of *Patel* v *Mirza* (2016) has granted the judiciary an opportunity to re-examine the law of illegality and the majority of the Justices in the Supreme Court hearing favoured a discretionary, policy-based approach.

Further reading

R. Buckley, *Illegality and Public Policy*, Sweet & Maxwell, 4th ed, 2017

R. Buckley, 'Illegal Transactions: Chaos or Discretion?' (2000) 20 LS 155

A. Burrows, 'Illegality after *Patel v Mirza*' (2017) 70 (1) Current Legal Problems 55

P. Creighton, 'The Recovery of Property Transferred for Illegal Purposes' (1997) 60 MLR 102

P. Davies, 'The Illegality Defence: Turning Back the Clock' (2010) 4 Conv & PL 282

P. Davies, 'The Illegality Defence—Two Steps Forward, One Step Back?' (2009) 73 Conv & PL 182

N. Enonchong, 'Illegality: The Fading Flame of Public Policy' (1994) 14 OJLS 295

S. Green & A. Bogg (eds), *Illegality after Patel v Mirza*, Hart Publishing, 2018

Law Commission Consultation Paper, No 154, 'Illegal Transactions: The Effect of Illegality on Contracts and Trusts', 1999

Law Commission Consultation Paper, No 189, 'The Illegality Defence: A Consultative Report', 2009

Law Commission Final Report, No 320, The Illegality Defence, 2010

R. Nolan, 'When Principles Collide' (2009) 125 LQR 374

S. Smith, 'Reconstructing Restraint of Trade' (1995) 15 OJLS 565

P. Watts, 'Illegality and Agency Law: Authorising Illegal Action' (2011) 3 JBL 213

Chapter 16

Unconscionability and unfairness

Introduction

16.1 The law of contract has to tread a delicate path between two distinct and often opposing ideas. On the one hand, the law supports the freedom on the part of the individual to enter into a contract of his or her choosing without unnecessary judicial or statutory interference. On the other, the law does not wish to see one party to a contract take unfair advantage of the other by virtue of either his or her own superior bargaining strength, or the other's weakness. It is often stated that our law does not possess a general doctrine of 'unconscionability',[1] and that such a doctrine would be injurious to predictability and certainty. As we have seen in earlier chapters, the law seeks stability in matters of commercial activity, and it does not favour general doctrines which offer too wide a basis for judicial interference with the bargains reached by the parties.[2] The 'classical' view of contract law has fostered the idea of freedom of contract and the law has taken an essentially objective view of agreement. In other words, it is not primarily concerned with the fairness of exchange between the parties so long as they have, to outward appearances, reached agreement. It is not for the courts to intervene simply because one party has made a poor bargain. To this extent it is true to say that (formally) the law of contract has not been concerned, traditionally, with the substantive fairness of a transaction.[3]

16.2 The law is, of course, concerned with procedural fairness. Therefore, a contract may be set aside for such reasons as fraud, misrepresentation, duress, or undue influence. This approach has been likened to the conduct of a game, in that the law ensures that the rules are

1 E.g. see *Thames Trains Ltd* v *Adams* (2006) at [31].

2 For an illustration, see *Union Eagle Ltd* v *Golden Achievement Ltd* [1997] 2 All ER 215 (and the comments of Lord Hoffmann at 218).

3 But see S. Smith, 'In Defence of Substantive Fairness' (1996) 112 LQR 138.

fair but it does not try to interfere with the outcome (or result) once the basic rules have been followed. This may well represent the theory behind the law, but it is difficult to accept that it is a reflection of reality—for, in reality, judges have used a variety of techniques to ensure a fair outcome when one party appears to have exploited some unfair advantage.[4] We should not be misled by what judges say they are doing. It is what they actually do which is important.

16.3 In practice, in some cases, in order to achieve a fair result, a judge may rely on equitable doctrines, or on techniques of construction and interpretation of contracts; he or she may imply terms, or may refuse certain remedies. It is misleading to argue that issues of unconscionability or unfairness will form no part of judicial thinking when contemplating the use of such powers and doctrines. Judges may even make overt reference to the issue of unconscionability as a factor in reaching a particular conclusion.[5] 'Despite lip service to the notion of absolute freedom of contract, relief is every day given against agreements that are unfair, inequitable, unreasonable, or oppressive.'[6] This vigilance on the part of judges using their common law and equitable powers helps to ensure that freedom of contract and 'objectivity' are not seriously abused.

16.4 Such intervention is, of its very nature, both piecemeal and unpredictable. In some areas where the problem of unfairness was especially pressing, such as in relation to the use of unfair exemption clauses, judicial attempts at 'policing' have been augmented and largely superseded by statutory change. Thus the Unfair Contract Terms Act 1977 represented a significant move towards controlling the fairness of certain types of contractual terms, followed by the EC Directive on Unfair Terms in Consumer Contracts which was also introduced to regulate unfair terms in non-negotiated contracts between consumers and businesses, and, of course, more recently the introduction of the Consumer Rights Act 2015 (see earlier discussion in **Chapters 10 and 11**). But such legislative developments, whilst very important in themselves, have not brought to an end the need for common law and equitable principles which promote fairness and prevent unconscionable bargains.

16.5 This introduction would not be complete without a warning about judicial pronouncements on the existence, or absence, of some general principle relating to unconscionable contracts. Our law of contract stresses certainty and stability, so it tends to discourage statements of general (and uncertain) application to the effect that the courts have a general power to 'police' agreements on the ground of unconscionability. (This is in contrast to such general statements as are contained in the USA's Uniform Commercial Code, s 2–302, for example.) Although attempts have been made to assert a general principle, most notably by Lord Denning in *Lloyds Bank Ltd* v *Bundy* [1974] 3 All ER 757 (at 765), these have tended to encounter opposition from other senior judges. So Lord Denning's assertion of such a principle was criticized in the House of Lords by Lord Scarman in *National Westminster Bank plc* v *Morgan* [1985] 1 All ER 821 at 830. (We shall return to this later.)

4 E.g. see *Silvertone Records* v *Mountfield* (1993).

5 E.g. see *Backhouse* v *Backhouse* (1978); *Cresswell* v *Potter* (1978); *Watkin* v *Watson-Smith* (1986); *Boustany* v *Pigott* (1993); and *Commission for the New Towns* v *Cooper (GB) Ltd* (1995).

6 S. Waddams, 'Unconscionability in Contracts' (1976) 39 MLR 369 at 390.

Examples of judicial intervention to prevent unfairness

16.6 This section contains a brief account of some of the areas in which questions of unfairness and unconscionability have influenced the courts.

16.7 We saw in **Chapter 4** that the courts are not supposed to be concerned with the adequacy of consideration so long as the consideration is 'sufficient' in a legal sense. The theory is that it is not for the courts to make bargains for the parties, who are free to agree to whatever exchange they wish, no matter how one-sided, so long as there is no procedural unfairness (such as fraud or duress). This may be a perfectly reasonable approach where the parties, knowing of the technical requirement of consideration, agree to some nominal consideration, or where the apparent inadequacy of the consideration is offset by some other benefit which the parties were presumably aware of when contracting (see *Mountford* v *Scott* (1975)). It is also true to say that the courts will not intervene simply because someone has paid a higher price for goods than they need have done; the courts are not regarded as the appropriate place for controlling prices or fair exchange. But the fact that the courts are not concerned (formally) with the adequacy of the consideration does not mean they will take no interest in a case where the exchange between the parties is extremely unfair. The courts share the ordinary person's intuitive dislike of injustice and judges will use whatever techniques are available to avoid an unconscionable result.[7] For example, in *Boustany* v *Pigott* (1993), P (who was elderly) granted B a renewal of a lease on terms which were very favourable to B. It appeared that B took advantage of P in a number of ways, before and at the time of the agreement, and with full knowledge that her behaviour was unconscionable. The Privy Council set aside the lease because of B's unconscionable conduct. It was held that B had clearly abused her position in relation to P, by exploiting P's incapacity.

16.8 A good illustration of judicial flexibility is provided by *Backhouse* v *Backhouse* [1978] 1 All ER 1158, where the facts were:

> A husband (H) and wife (W) bought a house in their joint names with the help of a mortgage. W left the matrimonial home and went to live with another man. H persuaded his wife to sign an agreement which transferred the house into his sole name. Although no duress was used, H did not advise his wife to seek independent legal advice. In exchange for signing the document of transfer, W received only a release from her liability under the mortgage. (She signed because of a sense of guilt towards H.) The couple was divorced and both of them remarried. As a result of an increase in property values, the house was soon worth much more than when they bought it. W applied, inter alia, for a lump sum order and a property transfer order in respect of the former matrimonial home.

7 In *Watkin* v *Watson-Smith* (1986) Times, 3 July, a contract for the sale of a house at a serious undervalue was set aside on the grounds of mistake. The judge held that he would have set the contract aside as an unconscionable bargain, had it been necessary to do so. (In this case it was the old age and lack of judgement of the vendor, together with his desire for a quick sale, which produced the unconscionable agreement.)

This is an interesting case. In a strict (or objective) sense, the contract was freely entered into; it is not a case of procedural unfairness. The exchange also met the technical requirement of consideration provided by both parties. But looking at the case from a more realistic point of view it is immediately obvious that the whole transaction was extremely unfair. Due to a sense of guilt, or emotional strain, the wife entered into an agreement (without legal advice) from which she derived very little material value. The indemnity against liability on the mortgage was virtually worthless in practice, as the value of the house was rising considerably. If the Family Division of the High Court had adopted the traditional view, there could be little reason for granting the wife relief from her very bad bargain. However, Balcombe J held that having regard to the wife's contribution to the purchase of the house, it would be repugnant to justice to deprive her of all interest in it. Accordingly, she was granted a share in the capital asset (the house) which she had helped to create, but she was not to benefit from any increase in value in the house occurring after her departure. The husband was ordered to pay her a lump sum of £3,500.

16.9 In *Backhouse* v *Backhouse* the judge specifically asked whether the agreement was unconscionable.[8] In answering that question, he was prepared to consider the inadequacy of the consideration and subjective factors about the parties. He said (at 1165–6):

> [The wife] was given no value for her transfer, merely the release from her liability on the mortgage, and she received no independent advice . . . When a marriage has broken down, both parties are liable to be in an emotional state. The party remaining in the matrimonial home, as the husband did in this case, has an advantage.

16.10 Despite the general rule about the courts' lack of interest in the adequacy of the consideration, there are other well-known examples of the courts intervening for this very reason. Some of these decisions can also be rationalized on other grounds which do less violence to traditional theory, but this should not mean that sight is lost of questions of unfair exchange being to the fore. In *Lloyds Bank Ltd* v *Bundy* [1974] 3 All ER 757:

> Herbert Bundy was an elderly farmer. His only financial asset was his farmhouse. His son, Michael, ran a company which had run into financial difficulty; its account at Lloyds Bank was overdrawn. Herbert Bundy, who also banked at Lloyds, guaranteed his son's company's overdraft by charging his house to the bank. The son's plant-hire business deteriorated further, and the bank was not prepared to maintain Michael Bundy's overdraft without additional security. The new assistant bank manager, together with Michael Bundy, went to see Herbert Bundy to explain that the bank's financial support of the son's company would be withdrawn unless he was prepared to extend his guarantee of the son's overdraft. In effect, the old man would have to increase the charge on his farmhouse to £11,000, which was slightly more than its value, in return for which the bank merely promised not to withdraw the son's overdraft facilities for the time being. The bank manager gave Herbert Bundy a partial explanation of

8 He also referred to the similar case of *Cresswell* v *Potter* (1978), where an agreement between a husband and wife was set aside, largely on the basis of its unconscionability.

> what was wrong with the son's company, but was unable to go into detail. Herbert Bundy, who was not independently advised at the meeting, signed the relevant documents there and then. Six months later the bank withdrew its support of the company, which was still in trouble, and proceeded to enforce the charge and guarantee against Herbert Bundy. The bank sought to evict the old man from his farmhouse.

The Court of Appeal set aside the guarantee and charge signed by Herbert Bundy, allowing his appeal against the trial judge's decision. Although his colleagues preferred to base their decision on the narrower ground of undue influence, Lord Denning asserted a much wider principle to justify a finding in favour of Herbert Bundy. The general principle which he outlined is considered later, together with the views of his critics, but it is significant that he referred specifically (at 765) to the fact that 'the consideration moving from the bank was grossly inadequate'. He observed that although the agreement conferred a considerable benefit on the bank, there was a marked absence of corresponding benefit to either the old man or his son's company: 'All that the company gained was a short respite from impending doom.' In short, it was an unconscionable agreement.

16.11 Similarly, in *Schroeder Music Publishing Co. Ltd* v *Macaulay* [1974] 3 All ER 616, the House of Lords held an agreement to be unenforceable, as an unreasonable restraint of trade, when a music publishing company engaged the exclusive services of a young songwriter. The claimant gave the company the copyright of all his compositions for the next five years, but on terms that were extremely disadvantageous to him. The restrictions in the agreement combined a lack of obligation on the company's part with a total commitment on the claimant's part. In reaching their conclusion, the judges were clearly mindful of the inadequacy of the consideration provided by the company. Lord Diplock went further than the other judges by observing that what was in issue was not some nineteenth-century economic theory about the public interest in freedom of trade, but 'the protection of those whose bargaining power is weak against being forced by those whose bargaining power is stronger to enter into bargains that are unconscionable' (at 623).[9]

16.12 Although the restraint of trade doctrine is traditionally discussed in terms of the public interest (see **Chapter 15**), it is evident that the issue of fairness will frequently be influential in courts' decisions on this subject. The requirement that the restraint clause must be reasonable between the parties gives a judge the opportunity to assess the unconscionability of a particular agreement. Obviously the fairness of the exchange—that is, the adequacy or generosity of the consideration—may determine whether a particular restraint is reasonable in the circumstances. Therefore, if one party has agreed not to compete with the other, but has received little material advantage in return for such an undertaking, then the court may be more disposed towards holding the restraint to be unreasonable and unenforceable.

9 See also *Silvertone Records* v *Mountfield* (1993) and *Zang Tumb Tuum Records* v *Johnson* (1993).

16.13 To take a different example, an agreement might appear fair but may be capable of operating in an unfair or oppressive way. In *Shell UK v Lostock Garage Ltd* [1977] 1 All ER 481, for instance, the facts were as follows:

> L Ltd was a small garage which was tied to Shell under the terms of a solus agreement made in 1955. This required L to sell only Shell's petrol. The agreement, which could be terminated by 12 months' notice, worked well until the oil crisis in the mid-1970s, when there occurred a petrol 'price war'. L had to compete with four neighbouring garages—two were Shell garages and two were 'free'. The two garages not tied to Shell cut their prices and Shell then introduced a support scheme which effectively subsidized the other two garages. L's garage was excluded from the scheme and was forced to trade at a loss, since it was unable to compete with the neighbouring garages. To meet the competition, L obtained petrol from another supplier, M. Shell threatened M with proceedings for inducing breach of contract and M stopped supplying L, which was then forced to resume taking its petrol from Shell. In the resulting legal action, L claimed that it was no longer tied to Shell under the solus agreement. Shell brought an action against L claiming, inter alia, damages for breach by L of the agreement because L took petrol from another supplier. L defended this claim by arguing that the agreement was unenforceable as being an unreasonable restraint of trade; alternatively, that the agreement was subject to an implied term by Shell that they would not discriminate against L in favour of competing and neighbouring garages.

The case gave rise to widely differing judicial views about the relevant issues, and it is not possible to consider all aspects of the decision here. It was held by the majority that Shell were not in breach of the solus agreement by operating the support scheme, there being no implied term that Shell should not discriminate against L. But Shell's claim for an injunction restraining L from breaking the tie provision was refused, with a variety of reasons being offered by the judges. For example, it would not have been just or equitable to grant Shell an injunction restraining L from breaking the tie provision whilst Shell were operating the support scheme and excluding L from it, as the scheme operated to L's prejudice. Therefore Shell could not enforce the tie provision whilst the support scheme was operating. Lord Denning commented (at 490):

> [The tie] appeared superficially to be fair and reasonable at the time of the contract . . . but, at the end of 1975, Shell started to subsidise two neighbouring Shell garages to such an extent that they were able to, and did, undercut Lostock . . . To insist on the tie in these circumstances . . . was most unfair and unreasonable. So much that I think the courts should decline to enforce it. At any rate, they should not enforce it so long as Shell operated their support scheme to the prejudice of Lostock.

16.14 A further example of the relevance of unconscionable behaviour can be found in *Foley v Classique Coaches* [1934] 2 KB 1. C agreed to sell a piece of land to D, but this contract was conditional upon D (who ran a motor coach business) entering into a separate agreement under which C would supply all of D's petrol 'at a price to be agreed by the parties . . . from time to time'. An arbitration clause in the 'petrol' contract provided for the resolution of any disputes which might arise in the performance of the petrol agreement. After the conveyance of the land, D bought petrol from C for three years but then tried to argue that he was not bound because the agreement was too uncertain and that, furthermore, it was an unreasonable restraint of trade. The Court of Appeal rejected D's arguments and held that there was a binding contract. Scrutton LJ was clearly influenced by D's conduct, which appeared to have been unconscionable. It would have been unfair to allow D to escape from his contractual obligation to buy C's petrol, having obtained a good deal on the purchase of the land in the first place. Scrutton LJ stated (at 7) that he was glad to decide the case in C's favour as he did 'not regard [D's] contention as an honest one'.

16.15 The discretion of a court to grant the equitable remedy of rectification in cases of mistake in the recording of agreements may also be influenced by the unconscionable behaviour of one of the parties (see **Chapter 12**). In *Commission for the New Towns* v *Cooper (GB) Ltd* (1995) the unconscionable conduct of the defendant was a vital issue in the Court of Appeal holding that rectification can be granted in cases of unilateral mistake.

16.16 Another area of contract law where the courts have taken a close interest in questions of fairness is in relation to the use of exemption or exclusion clauses. This topic has been discussed in detail in **Chapters 9 and 10**, but a few brief points need to be made here. It will be remembered that a party will use an exemption clause to exclude or limit his or her liability for, inter alia, breach of contract. This may be an entirely reasonable practice between two equal parties and it may simply be a means of allocating risk and indicating which of them should take out insurance cover. By limiting liability, one party may be able to provide cheaper services as a result, and for this reason the other party may choose to contract with him or her. (See, for example, *Photo Production Ltd* v *Securicor Transport Ltd* (1980)).[10]

16.17 But there are other situations where the exemption clauses may be very unreasonable. The stronger party imposes his or her terms on the weaker one, and unreasonably, and unfairly, limits or excludes liability. As we have seen, the courts were willing to 'strain' construction to prevent such exclusion clauses protecting the party in breach, and also to inhibit the incorporation of unusual or unreasonable clauses by means of the 'red hand' rule (see **Chapter 9**).

16.18 Of course, since the enactment of the Unfair Contract Terms Act 1977, the courts have not needed to draw on the common law so much to deal with unreasonable exemption clauses, but this should not obscure the general point which is being made here that the courts, faced with unjust or unconscionable agreements (or terms), may develop techniques to help them prevent an unfair outcome.

16.19 Further, although we have tended to refer to unconscionability, we should also give some thought to the idea of good faith. In *Interfoto Picture Library Ltd* v *Stiletto Visual Programmes Ltd*

10 See generally the test of reasonableness under the Unfair Contract Terms Act 1977 in Chapter 10.

[1989] 2 QB 433, Bingham LJ did not view the 'red hand' rule in terms of unconscionability, as such, but rather in line with the similar idea of good faith. He said (at 439):

> In many civil law systems, and perhaps in most legal systems outside the common law world, the law of obligations recognises and enforces an overriding principle that in making and carrying out contracts parties should act in good faith . . . English law has, characteristically, committed itself to no such overriding principle but has developed piecemeal solutions in response to demonstrated problems of unfairness.

Cases such as *Errington* v *Errington and Woods* (1952) (see para. **2.67**), *Blackpool and Fylde Aero Club Ltd* v *Blackpool Borough Council* (1990) (see para. **2.16**), and *Harvela Investments Ltd* v *Royal Trust Co. of Canada* (1984) (see para. **2.15**) have been seen as explicable in terms of good faith.[11]

16.20 Of course, if those three cases are viewed as examples of the common law covertly policing good faith, then it is pre-contractual good faith which is in question, and it must be conceded that that is an idea which the House of Lords has found itself particularly at odds with, in relation to both uncertainty and the undermining of the boundary between negotiation and contract. In *Walford* v *Miles* [1992] 2 AC 128 at 138, Lord Atkin said:

> [T]he concept of a duty to carry on negotiations in good faith is inherently repugnant to the adversarial position of the parties when involved in negotiations. Each party to the negotiations is entitled to pursue his (or her) own interest, so long as he avoids making misrepresentations. To advance that interest he must be entitled, if he thinks it appropriate, to threaten to withdraw from further negotiations or to withdraw in fact, in the hope that the opposite party may seek to reopen the negotiations by offering him improved terms.

Again, the concerns about certainty are seen to stand in the way of a general doctrine, but, as has been indicated, specific examples which may best be explained by such an underlying idea can be found.[12]

16.21 However, as Bingham LJ's dictum indicated, good faith is not just about pre-contract, but also about performance, and in that situation there is at least no concern about the boundary between negotiation and obligation. There will of course still be major concerns about uncertainty, but again examples can be found from cases already mentioned in this chapter, and others, and it should be noted that recently, in *Yam Seng Pte Ltd* v *International Trade Corporation Ltd* (2013), the court was prepared to imply a term explicitly requiring good faith in relation to an aspect of the performance. This will be returned to below in relation to trends towards a general principle.[13]

11 See, e.g., M. Furmston and G. J. Tolhurst, *Contract Formation—Law and Practice*, Oxford University Press, chapter 12.

12 See, e.g., the consideration of the postal rule in E. Macdonald, 'Dispatching the Dispatch Rule? The Postal Rule, E-Mail, Revocation and Implied Terms' [2013] Web Journal of Current Legal Issues (2).

13 Of course, at much the same time, an express term dealing with good faith was being narrowly construed in *Mid Essex Hospital Services NHS Trust* v *Compass Group UK and Ireland t/a Medirest* [2013] EWCA Civ 200.

A general doctrine?

16.22 In a commercial context, between parties who contract on an equal footing, the classical (or laissez-faire) approach has the obvious advantage of certainty, and the courts will be wary of introducing a general discretion to relieve against hardship. This is well illustrated in the case of *Union Eagle Ltd* v *Golden Achievement Ltd* [1997] 2 All ER 215. The case involved a written contract in which the appellant purchaser (P) agreed to buy a flat in Hong Kong from the respondent vendor (V) and paid a 10 per cent deposit to V. It was a term of the agreement that completion was to be effected before 5.00pm on 30 September 1991, and that time was of the essence in this respect. The agreement provided that P would forfeit the deposit in the event of failure to comply with any term or condition of the contract. P was ten minutes late in attempting to complete the transaction and was told by V that the contract would be rescinded and the deposit forfeited. P's action for specific performance was dismissed by the Hong Kong Court of Appeal, but P appealed to the Privy Council, arguing that P was entitled to relief against forfeiture of the deposit. The Privy Council dismissed the appeal. It stated that it was important to uphold V's right to rescind, in view of P's breach of an essential condition as to time. This right to rescind allowed V to know his position with certainty and that he was entitled to resell the flat. In delivering the judgment of the court, Lord Hoffmann (at 218) rejected the suggestion that there was an unlimited discretion to relieve against hardship by imposing a fair solution in this type of case. The stipulation as to time was of great importance and P was, regrettably, late. The court held that it was irrelevant that he was only slightly late. Lord Hoffmann stated (at 218):

> The principle that equity will restrain the enforcement of legal rights when it would be unconscionable to insist upon them has an attractive breadth. But the reasons why the courts have rejected such generalisations are founded not merely upon authority . . . but also upon practical considerations of business. These are, in summary, that in many forms of transaction it is of great importance that if something happens for which the contract has made express provision, the parties should know with certainty that the terms of the contract will be enforced. The existence of an undefined discretion to refuse to enforce the contract on the ground that this would be 'unconscionable' is sufficient to create uncertainty.

16.23 The above case illustrates the traditional view that a general doctrine of unconscionability is undesirable, as its precise scope would be difficult to formulate and it would be inimical to certainty and stability in a commercial context. But the problem with the absence of any general principle is the development of unrelated rules, or even lone instances of unfairness being dealt with, and this can create anomalies.

16.24 In *Lloyds Bank Ltd* v *Bundy* [1974] 3 All ER 757 (discussed earlier), Lord Denning was keen to postulate a general principle. He made a connection between the (hitherto) distinct areas of duress, unconscionable transactions, undue influence, undue pressure, and salvage agreements. He stated (at 763) that despite the fact that our law does not, in general, interfere with freedom of contract, nevertheless:

> There are cases in our books in which the courts will set aside a contract, or a transfer of property, when the parties have not met on equal terms, when the one is so strong in bargaining power and the other so weak that, as a matter of common fairness, it is not right that the strong should be allowed to push the weaker to the wall. Hitherto those exceptional cases have been treated each as a separate category in itself. But I think the time has come when we should seek to find a principle to unite them. I put on one side contracts or transactions which are voidable for fraud or misrepresentation or mistake. All those are governed by settled principles. I go only to those where there has been inequality of bargaining power, such as to merit the intervention of the court.

This approach shows a willingness to break down doctrinal barriers in the interest of a more interventionist role for the courts. He went on (at 765) to propose the following general principle:

> Gathering all together, I would suggest that through all these instances there runs a single thread. They rest on 'inequality of bargaining power'. By virtue of it, the English law gives relief to one who, without independent advice, enters into a contract on terms which are very unfair or transfers property for a consideration which is grossly inadequate, when his bargaining power is grievously impaired by reason of his own needs or desires, or by his own ignorance or infirmity, coupled with undue influences or pressures brought to bear on him by or for the benefit of the other. When I use the word 'undue' I do not mean to suggest that the principle depends on proof of any wrongdoing.

Although the Court of Appeal was unanimous in allowing Mr Bundy's appeal, the other two judges did not find it necessary to base their judgments on such a wide principle as that suggested by Lord Denning. The novelty of the Denning principle was his emphasis on the need to protect the weaker party where there was a clear disparity in bargaining strength between the parties.

16.25 It should not be thought that Lord Denning's was a lone voice. In *Schroeder Music Publishing Co.* v *Macaulay* [1974] 3 All ER 616 it was not necessary to go beyond the restraint of trade doctrine to release the young songwriter from his contract with a music publishing company. But Lord Diplock went further (at 623):

> Because this can be classed as a contract in restraint of trade the restrictions that [Macaulay] accepted fell within one of those limited categories of contractual promises in respect of which the courts still retain the power to relieve the promisor of his legal duty to fulfil them. In order to determine whether this case is one in which that power ought to be exercised, what your lordships have been doing has been to assess the relative bargaining power of the publisher and the songwriter at the time the contract was made and to decide whether the publisher had used his superior bargaining power to exact from the songwriter promises that were unfairly onerous to him.

Thus his Lordship stressed that the important consideration for the court was the protection of the weaker or vulnerable party against being forced by a much stronger party to enter into a very bad bargain. The important question to be answered, according to Lord Diplock, is: 'was the bargain fair?' (at 623). In deciding that it was not fair, the court took into account the fact that the terms of the contract had not been the subject of negotiation between the parties; on the contrary, they had been dictated by the publishing company, who had been able to do this as a result of greatly superior bargaining power.[14]

16.26 The danger with terms like 'inequality of bargaining power', 'unconscionability', and good faith is that they can become rather trite through indiscriminate use. Certainly, inequality of bargaining power, for example, is inherent in a great number of commercial transactions, but obviously not all of these are to be regarded as situations in which the court should intervene. What matters is the use (or misuse) to which such disparity is put. The case of *Alec Lobb Garages Ltd* v *Total Oil (Great Britain) Ltd* (1985) provides a useful illustration. The facts were:

> The claimant company, Alec Lobb Ltd, owned premises from which it ran a garage and filling station. (The company comprised a mother and son who were the shareholders and directors.) The company was in serious financial difficulties. It was not possible for the claimants to approach any other petrol company for finance, as they were already 'tied' to the defendants under a previous loan agreement. Further negotiations took place between the claimants and the defendants during the course of which the claimants were independently advised by solicitors and accountants. The defendants agreed to put further capital into the claimant company by means of a lease and lease-back transaction. This consisted of a lease of the garage to the defendants for 51 years in return for the payment of a fair premium of £35,000 and an immediate lease-back of the premises to the son, personally, for a term of 21 years at a rent of £2,250. This underlease to the son also contained a petrol 'tie': he was to buy his petrol exclusively from the defendants. The transaction did not succeed in rescuing the claimant company from its lack of working capital. Nearly ten years after making this agreement, the claimants sought to have the transaction set aside on the grounds, inter alia, that the bargain was harsh and unconscionable or, alternatively, that the 'tie' covenant was void as being an unreasonable restraint of trade.

It is the first of these two grounds that is of interest to our present discussion, but it may be stated briefly that the Court of Appeal held that the petrol supply restraint was not unreasonable in view of all the circumstances. (It is worth noting that the adequacy of the consideration was one of the factors that the court took into account in reaching this conclusion.) The court went on to state that where one party had acted oppressively, coercively, or extortionately towards the other, such a transaction would be set aside. An agreement was not rendered unconscionable merely because the parties to it were of unequal bargaining strength and the stronger party had not shown that the terms were fair and reasonable. Furthermore, a contract was not

14 See also *Silvertone Records* v *Mountfield* (1993).

unconscionable merely because a party was forced to enter into it from economic necessity. It was important, on the facts of *Alec Lobb*, that no pressure had been exerted on the claimants by the defendant oil company. The claimants had received independent advice (which they had disregarded) and they had sought the defendants' assistance to escape their financial difficulties. The fact that the claimants had little realistic alternative, and that they had made a bad bargain, was not sufficient to render the defendants' conduct unconscionable.

16.27 This is a necessary restriction on the use of 'inequality of bargaining power': it does not, itself, establish that there was anything wrong with the transaction. It is the unfair or coercive exploitation of the superior bargaining strength of one party against the other which is the reason for judicial intervention. This was not present in the instant case. However, it should be pointed out that Lord Denning's statement in *Lloyds Bank Ltd* v *Bundy* [1974] 3 All ER 757 at 765 makes this restriction abundantly clear. He did not state that inequality of bargaining strength alone constitutes a sufficient ground for interfering with freedom of contract. This point was recognized by Dillon LJ (at 313):

> Inequality of bargaining power must anyhow be a relative concept. It is seldom in any negotiation that the bargaining powers of the parties are absolutely equal. Any individual wanting to borrow money from a bank, building society or other financial institution . . . will have virtually no bargaining power; he will have to take or leave the terms offered to him . . . But Lord Denning did not envisage that any contract entered into in such circumstances would, without more, be reviewed by the courts by the objective criterion of what was reasonable. The courts would only interfere in exceptional cases where as a matter of common fairness it was not right that the strong should be allowed to push the weak to the wall. The concepts of unconscionable conduct and of the exercise by the stronger of coercive power are thus brought in, and in the present case they are negatived by the [findings of fact].

16.28 However, such limitations on Lord Denning's general principle were not brought to the fore in its dismissal in *National Westminster Bank plc* v *Morgan* [1985] 1 All ER 821 (see generally para. **14.44**). Lord Scarman (at 830) observed that Lord Denning's general principle was not the ground for the majority's decision in *Lloyds Bank Ltd* v *Bundy* (1974), and continued:

> Nor has counsel for the wife sought to rely on Lord Denning's general principle; and, in my view, he was right not to do so . . . The fact of an unequal bargain will, of course, be a relevant feature in some cases of undue influence. But it can never become an appropriate basis of principle of [this] doctrine . . . I question whether there is any need in the modern law to erect a general principle of relief against inequality of bargaining power. Parliament has undertaken the task (and it is essentially a legislative task) of enacting such restrictions on freedom of contract as are in its judgment necessary to relieve against the mischief . . . I doubt whether the courts should assume the burden of formulating further restrictions.

Thus the House of Lords issued its rebuke to Lord Denning for venturing to construct a more general principle. A number of observations can be made about Lord Scarman's speech. By his own concession, the wife's counsel, in *Morgan,* did not try to rely on the Denning principle. If this had been attempted, it would have been evident that the Denning principle did not apply to instances of mere inequality of bargaining power.

16.29 Another aspect of Lord Scarman's attack on Lord Denning's approach should be considered. He argued that the task of restricting freedom of contract, in order to give relief against inequality of bargaining power, is 'essentially a legislative task'. Therefore, he 'questioned' the need for such a general principle. Is a general common law doctrine otiose?

16.30 One commentator shrewdly observed on an earlier occasion:[15]

> Legislation, like judicial decisions, reflects the needs of a society, and the fact that the need for control of agreements has become so pressing in particular cases as to prompt legislative intervention argues . . . in favour, rather than against the need for general control.

A general principle could co-exist with specific statutory intervention. Even the considerable protection provided by the Unfair Contract Terms Act 1977, the Unfair Terms in Consumer Contracts Directive, and the Consumer Rights Act 2015 does not cover all situations. There could still be a place for a general principle or doctrine.

16.31 Of course, the idea of any such general principle as 'inequality of bargaining power' will be criticized on the basis of the generation of uncertainty. However, although the law goes through periods in its history when the need for certainty and predictability appear to dominate judicial thought, such times may be followed by periods of greater flexibility. The idea of a doctrine of good faith tends to raise the spectre of 'visceral justice',[16] where 'judges react impressionistically to the merits of a situation and dispose of cases accordingly', but even if it would generate uncertainty, 'visceral justice' does not present a credible picture of what is likely to occur,[17] and in *Yam Seng Pte Ltd* v *International Trade Corporation Ltd* (2013) the judge noted that, in its lack of any general acceptance of a doctrine of good faith, English law was 'swimming against a tide' of both European law and that of other common law jurisdictions (at [124]). Certainly, we are becoming accustomed to the idea of good faith in the fairness test in the Unfair Terms in Consumer Contracts Directive, and also in our ever increasing awareness of its use in the contract law of other European countries. There is an impetus towards the recognition of such a doctrine in English law from such external influences.[18] Since *Yam Seng Pte Ltd* v *International Trade Corporation Ltd* (2013) there has been a notable increase in parties relying on terms of good faith and this opens up the debate of good faith more generally. For example, see *Greenclose Ltd* v *National Westminster Bank Plc* (2014), where the court rejected a

15 S. Waddams (1976) 39 MLR 369 at 390.

16 M. Bridge, 'Good Faith in Commercial Contracts' in R. Brownsword, N. J. Hird, and G. Howells, *Good Faith in Contract: Concept and Context*, Dartmouth, 1999, p. 140.

17 R. Brownsword, *Contract Law: Themes for the Twenty-First Century*, 2nd edn, Oxford University Press, 2006, pp. 130–4.

18 E.g. M. Furmston and G. J. Tolhurst, *Contract Formation—Law and Practice*, Oxford University Press, 2010, chapter 12.

general doctrine, and *Emirates Trading Agency LLC* v *Prime Mineral Exports Private Ltd* (2014), where it was held that there was an implied term to act in good faith. Also see *D&G Cars Ltd* v *Essex Police Authority* (2015), where the parties agreed there was an express term to act with honesty and integrity. Although recognizing that 'integrity' was different from 'good faith', Dove J confirmed that this required fair dealing and transparency and, given that the case concerned acting on behalf of a law enforcement agency, on the facts it was found that an identical term would have been implied at law. Undoubtedly this is an area of change and the treading of a delicate path between freedom and superior bargaining strength remains a challenge for the law of contract in this respect. Issues of uncertainty will still be forcefully put forward but the climate may be somewhat less hostile to a general doctrine than was the case when Lord Denning talked of 'inequality of bargaining power'.

Summary

- There is a tension in the law between supporting 'freedom of contract', and attempting to ensure that one party does not take unfair advantage of the other by exploiting his or her superior bargaining strength.
- It is not, in general, a matter for judicial intervention simply because one party has made a poor bargain.
- But, in practice, the courts will often try to achieve a fair result by means of a variety of techniques and doctrines, so as to ensure that freedom of contract is not seriously abused.
- The courts have been wary of claiming a general discretion to relieve against hardship by imposing a fair solution. The classical approach has the obvious advantage of certainty.
- However, in the absence of any general principle which permits intervention, there has developed a number of unrelated rules and doctrines for dealing with unfairness. (This can cause anomalies.)
- An attempt was made by Lord Denning to provide a more general principle which would allow a more interventionist approach by the courts (see *Lloyds Bank* v *Bundy* (1974)).
- But this approach was rejected by the House of Lords (see *National Westminster Bank* v *Morgan* (1985)). It was argued that the restriction of freedom of contract, so as to provide relief against unfairness, should be left to Parliament.
- Particularly with the impetus from Europe and elsewhere, it might be argued that there are signs of a movement towards a doctrine of good faith.

Further reading

N. Bamforth, 'Unconscionability as a Vitiating Factor' [1995] LMCLQ 538

M. Bridge, 'Good Faith in Commercial Contracts' in R. Brownsword, N. J. Hird, and G. Howells (eds), *Good Faith in Contract: Concept and Context*, Dartmouth, 1999, pp. 139–64

S. Bright, 'Winning the Battle against Unfair Contract Terms' (2000) 20 LS 331

R. Brownsword, *Contract Law—Themes for the Twenty-First Century*, 2nd edn, Oxford University Press, 2006

D. Campbell, 'Good Faith and the Ubiquity of the "Relational' Contract" (2014) 77(3) MLR 475

J. Devenney and A. Chandler, 'Unconscionability and the Taxonomy of Undue Influence' [2007] JBL 541

M. Furmston and G. J. Tolhurst, *Contract Formation—Law and Practice*, Oxford University Press, 2010, chapter 12

A. Mason, 'Contract, Good Faith and Equitable Standards in Fair Dealing' (2000) 116 LQR 66

E. Peel, 'Reasonable Exemption Clauses' (2001) 117 LQR 545

S. Smith, 'In Defence of Substantive Fairness' (1996) 112 LQR 138

S. Waddams, 'Unconscionability in Contracts' (1976) 39 MLR 369

C. Willett (ed.), *Aspects of Fairness in Contract*, Blackstone, 1996

R. Zimmermann and S. Whittaker (eds), *Good Faith in European Contract Law*, Cambridge University Press, 2000

Chapter 17

Privity and third party rights

Introduction

17.1 The doctrine of privity of contract has been a long-established, yet controversial, principle of English law. The Contracts (Rights of Third Parties) Act 1999 has led to important reform of the doctrine and it will be considered in detail later in the chapter. However, it is appropriate to start with an explanation of what is meant by the term 'privity of contract'. It represents the principle that only a party to a contract can enforce rights, or have duties enforced against him or her, under that contract (for example, see *Price* v *Easton* (1833)). The doctrine was referred to briefly in **Chapter 4**, in connection with the rule that consideration must move from the promisee. A party to a contract is one to whom a promise is made and who, in exchange for the promise, gives consideration for it. The traditional view has been that a promisee who is promised some benefit, but gives nothing in return, cannot enforce the promise; similarly, that a beneficiary of a promise, who is not the promisee, and who provides no consideration, cannot sue on that promise. Thus, the traditional approach gave precedence to the notion of bargain, rather than to the intention of the contracting parties. It is easy to understand why someone who is not a party to a contract should not have burdens imposed upon him or her and this facet of the doctrine has not been subject to criticism, nor has it been affected by the 1999 legislation. But the idea that a 'stranger' to a contract should not be able to enforce a provision which was intended for his or her benefit has been much more controversial.

17.2 In *Tweddle* v *Atkinson* (1861) two fathers, by an agreement, promised one another that they would each pay a sum of money to William Tweddle, the son of one of them, who was to marry the other's daughter. William Tweddle sued his father-in-law's executors to enforce this promise, as his father-in-law died without having paid the promised sum. Despite the fact that the contract was for his benefit, his action failed as he did not provide consideration for the promise. An alternative explanation for the decision is that William Tweddle was not a party to the contract and, therefore, he could not enforce any benefit under a contract to which he was a stranger.

17.3 The privity rule, despite its uncertain origins and its potential for unfairness, was even more firmly established in English law by the House of Lords in *Dunlop Pneumatic Tyre Co Ltd* v *Selfridge & Co. Ltd* [1915] AC 847. The facts were as follows:

> Dunlop sold some tyres to Dew & Co., on the terms that Dew & Co. would not resell them for less than Dunlop's list prices, and that when Dew & Co. resold them to trade buyers, they (Dew & Co.) would insist on the same undertaking from the trade buyers. Dew & Co. sold the tyres to Selfridge, who agreed to conform with this restriction and, in the event of breaking the agreement, to pay Dunlop £5 for each tyre sold (in breach of it). Selfridge later sold tyres to customers for less than the list price and Dunlop sued Selfridge for damages.

The House of Lords gave judgment for Selfridge and dismissed the action. Lord Haldane LC affirmed the doctrine of privity authoritatively, by stating (at 853):

> In the law of England certain principles are fundamental. One is that only a person who is a party to a contract can sue on it. Our law knows nothing of a jus quaesitum tertio arising by way of contract. Such a right may be conferred by way of property, as, for example, under a trust, but it cannot be conferred on a stranger to a contract as a right to enforce the contract in personam. A second principle is that if a person with whom a contract not under seal has been made is to be able to enforce it consideration must have been given by him to the promisor or to some other person at the promisor's request.

17.4 The doctrine, despite its evident unpopularity with the judiciary, survived and even developed (see *Scruttons Ltd* v *Midland Silicones Ltd* (1962), discussed later). It has been subjected to the scrutiny of law reform bodies for more than 60 years. For example, in 1937 the Law Revision Committee recommended in its sixth Interim Report that a third party should be able to enforce a contractual promise received by another for his benefit.[1] In 1991, a Law Commission Consultation Paper supported the argument for reform of the privity rule, stating:

> Over 50 years ago, the Law Revision Committee recommended the abolition of the third party rule . . . Nothing has happened since [its] Report to suggest that its recommendations were misguided. Indeed, the greater complexity of the law as further exceptions and circumventions have developed, and the experience of statutory reform elsewhere, reinforce its conclusions. (Law Commission Consultation Paper, No 121, 'Privity of Contract: Contracts for the Benefit of Third Parties', 1991, at p. 95)

These arguments were supported by Steyn LJ's criticisms of the doctrine in *Darlington Borough Council* v *Wiltshier Northern Ltd* [1995] 1 WLR 68 at 76, where he stated:

1 Cmnd 5449, 1937, at p. 30. Paragraph 48 states: 'We therefore recommend that where a contract by its express terms purports to confer a benefit directly on a third party, the third party shall be entitled to enforce the provision in his own name, provided that the promisor shall be entitled to raise as against the third party any defence that would have been valid against the promisee. The rights of the third party shall be subject to cancellation of the contract by the mutual consent of the contracting parties at any time before the third party has adopted it either expressly or by conduct.'

> The case for recognising a contract for the benefit of a third party is simple and straightforward. The autonomy of the will of the parties should be respected. The law of contract should give effect to the reasonable expectations of contracting parties. Principle certainly requires that a burden should not be imposed on a third party without his consent. But there is no doctrinal, logical or policy reason why the law should deny effectiveness to a contract for the benefit of a third party where that is the expressed intention of the parties.

17.5 The above statements, and many more like them from judges and academic critics, illustrated the unpopularity of the privity rule and the need for its reform.[2] Furthermore, English law was out of step with that of many European countries, which do not prevent third parties from enforcing contractual provisions.[3] In addition to hindering the closer harmonization of the laws of European Union member states, the English doctrine of privity was capable of disappointing various reasonable commercial and consumer expectations. The resulting unfairness of a strict application of the doctrine necessitated a series of, often complex, exceptions to it (discussed later). Before examining the legislative reform, it is important to understand the ambit of the privity rule prior to the Contracts (Rights of Third Parties) Act 1999, as the common law doctrine was reformed, not abolished, by the Act.

Further development of the doctrine

17.6 Despite challenges to its validity, the House of Lords affirmed the doctrine once again in *Scruttons Ltd* v *Midland Silicones Ltd* [1962] AC 446 (at 467 and 473). The scope of the doctrine was considered in a slightly different form in this case as the stranger to the contract was not suing to enforce a positive right, but instead was seeking the protection of a term of the contract as a defence to an action by one of the contracting parties under a separate cause of action. In other words, the case was concerned with whether a third party can use a term of a contract as a shield, despite not being able to use a term intended for his benefit as a sword. The facts were:

> A drum containing chemicals was shipped from America to London. The bill of lading, under which it was shipped, limited to $500 (£179) per package the liability of the carrier in the event of loss, damage, or delay. Scruttons, who were the stevedores engaged by the carrier (under a separate contract), negligently dropped and damaged the drum whilst delivering it to the consignees, Midland Silicones. Midland Silicones sued Scruttons in tort, claiming the value of the lost contents (£593). Scruttons (the stevedores) argued that under the bill of lading their liability was limited to £179.

2 See R. Flannigan, 'Privity—The End of an Era (Error)' (1987) 103 LQR 564. But for a contrasting view, see R. Stevens, 'The Contracts (Rights of Third Parties) Act 1999' (2004) 120 LQR 292, who argues (at 322) that 'the illness diagnosed was not as serious as it was thought and the operation may have caused more problems than it solved'.

3 See Law Commission Report, No 242, *Privity of Contract: Contracts for the Benefit of Third Parties*, Cm 3329, 1996, at para. 3.8. For a discussion of Irish law reform proposals in this area, see C. Kelly, 'Privity of Contract: the Benefits of Reform' (2008) 8 JSIJ 145.

The House of Lords held that the stevedores were not entitled to rely on the limitation of liability contained in the bill of lading. Reference to the 'carrier' in the bill of lading (which incorporated relevant American legislative provisions for the carriage of goods by sea) did not include the stevedores. Moreover, there was nothing in the bill of lading which implied that the parties to it intended the limitation of liability to extend to the stevedores. The court stated that, as it is a fundamental principle that only a party to a contract can take advantage of the provisions of that contract, the stevedores could not rely on a contract to which they were not a party in defending the action against them. It made no difference that the stevedores were attempting to use the contract as a shield and not as a sword. It was decided that the rule precluded a third party from taking an advantage from the contract (per Lord Reid at 373), despite the inconvenience of this conclusion to the commercial world.

17.7 A party to a contract is a person to whom a promise is made, in return for which he or she provides consideration. If it could be shown, in circumstances like those of *Scruttons* v *Midland Silicones Ltd*, that the stevedore was a party to the contract and had provided consideration, he would then be able to rely on a clause in a bill of lading limiting the liability of the carrier. It did not matter that a rather strained and artificial interpretation of the facts was required to achieve this result. In *Scruttons* v *Midland Silicones Ltd*, one of the arguments advanced (unsuccessfully) by the stevedores was that they were the undisclosed principals of the carrier who acted as their agent and, therefore, the stevedores had a contractual relationship with the claimants through the agency of the carrier. This contention was rejected by the court, but Lord Reid explained (at 474) the conditions which would need to be satisfied for this agency argument to succeed. He stated, inter alia, that the bill of lading must make it clear that the stevedore is intended to be protected by its provisions which limit liability. The contract must also make it clear that the carrier, as well as contracting for these provisions on his own behalf, is also contracting as agent for the stevedore, who will in turn be protected by the provisions. Moreover, the carrier would need the stevedore's authority to act in this way. Lastly, any difficulties about consideration moving from the stevedore would need to be overcome.

17.8 The matter was considered again in *New Zealand Shipping Co. Ltd* v *Satterthwaite (AM) & Co.* [1975] AC 154, where the facts were similar to those of *Scruttons* v *Midland Silicones Ltd* (1962):

> Cargo was shipped from Liverpool to the claimant (consignee) in New Zealand, under a bill of lading which conferred certain exemptions and immunities on the carrier. A clause in the bill of lading specifically provided that no servant or agent of the carrier (including independent contractors employed by the carrier) would be liable to the claimant for any loss or damage resulting from that person's negligence or default in carrying out the work. The clause also made it clear that the carrier was deemed to be acting as agent or trustee on behalf of those persons who were to be employed in handling the cargo, and that such persons were to be regarded as parties to the contract (i.e. the bill of lading). The defendants were stevedores in New Zealand, employed by the carrier (as independent contractors) to unload the cargo. The cargo was damaged as a result of the defendants' negligence whilst unloading. The

claimant brought an action against the stevedores and argued that they could not rely on the exemptions and immunities contained in the bill of lading because they were not a party to the contract.

A majority of the Privy Council held that the stevedores were entitled to claim exemption from liability under the contract (see also *Port Jackson Stevedoring Pty* v *Salmond & Spraggon (Australia) Pty (The New York Star)* (1980)). It should be noted that, in contrast to *Scruttons* v *Midland Silicones Ltd*, the bill of lading provided that the exemptions of liability should apply to independent contractors such as stevedores. Applying Lord Reid's dictum in *Midland Silicones*, the court held that the exemption in the bill of lading was designed to cover the whole carriage of the goods by whomsoever it was performed. The solutions offered by the court to the problems of privity and consideration, whilst no doubt reflecting commercial realism and judicial ingenuity, were far from convincing from the perspective of legal doctrine.

17.9 The court held in *Satterthwaite* that the bill of lading was not simply a contract (or evidence of a contract) between the owners of the goods and the carrier. It also represented a contract between the owners and the stevedores, made through the carrier as agent. This was further explained by the idea of the owners making a unilateral offer, to those involved in unloading the goods, of exemption from liability in exchange for performing the requested services. The stevedores provided consideration by unloading the goods, despite the fact that they were already under an existing contractual obligation (owed to the carrier) to do precisely this. Although the stevedores were bound to unload the goods under a contract with the carrier, it will be remembered that the performance of an existing contractual duty owed to a third party can amount to good consideration (see **Chapter 4**). It was evident from Lord Wilberforce's judgment on behalf of the majority that he was determined to give effect to the clear purpose of a contractual document and not to allow this purpose to be defeated by technical difficulties. He explained the need for the law to take a practical approach to everyday commercial transactions, rather than to be confined by the technical and schematic rules of contract law.

17.10 There is no denying that this solution is commercially desirable—allowing the benefit of an exclusion clause, which is clearly intended to benefit a third party, to be relied on by that third party—but it is artificial and not entirely convincing. It was held that the stevedore entered into a contractual relationship with the owner (either shipper or consignee) by performance of the act of unloading which the owner requested in exchange for his promise. In other words, the contract is formed at a later date than the main contract (between the shipper and the carrier), that is, when the stevedore performs the requested service. The decision in *New Zealand Shipping Co. Ltd* v *Satterthwaite* (1974) was supported by the Privy Council case of *Port Jackson Stevedoring Pty* v *Salmond & Spraggon (Australia) Pty* (1980), where the facts were similar to those of *Satterthwaite*. In *Port Jackson Stevedoring* the defendant stevedores, who were employed by the carrier, did not take proper care of a consignment of razor blades, which were stolen from a wharf after being unloaded by the stevedores from the ship. Once again, the court had to decide whether the defendants could rely on the defences and immunities contained in the bill of lading and the Privy Council held that they could do so. It was stated that all the parties concerned (i.e. the shipper, the carrier, and the stevedore) knew that this immunity was intended, and that the law should give effect to commercial practice in this respect.

17.11 This solution reflects commercial realism, but it was achieved only by some rather unconvincing reasoning, which was necessary to get around the doctrine of privity. It was also uncertain to which cases the solution could be applied. (See, for example, *The Mahkutai* (1996), in which the Privy Council held that the *Satterthwaite* approach should not be extended so as to apply to an exclusive jurisdiction clause in a bill of lading.) It is clear that a simpler and more predictable solution was required.

17.12 A further illustration of the practical problems caused by the doctrine, and of the need for rather artificial and technical solutions, is provided by the famous case of *Beswick* v *Beswick* (1968). The facts were:

> John Beswick helped his uncle, Peter Beswick, who ran a coal merchant business. As Peter was in poor health, he agreed to let John have the business. In return, John was to pay a weekly sum of £6 10s to Peter and, after Peter's death, he was to pay £5 per week to Peter's widow. John made the agreed payments to Peter until the latter's death, but he made only one payment of £5 to Peter's widow and then refused to pay any more. Peter's widow sued John for the arrears under the agreement and asked for specific performance of the contract. She sued both in her capacity as administratrix of her husband's estate, and in her personal capacity.

The House of Lords held that, as she was not a party to the contract, the widow could not succeed in her own right. However, it was decided that she should be granted an order for specific performance as administratrix (personal representative) of her husband's estate. In this capacity there was no problem of privity, as she was suing on behalf of her deceased husband, whose rights she was entitled to enforce. In effect, she was able to enforce the defendant's promise for her own benefit and so the outcome was a fair one. But this was achieved only because she was administratrix of the estate; in her personal capacity, she would have been unable to enforce the defendant's promise due to the obstacle provided by the doctrine of privity.

Reform of the law and C(RTP)A 1999

17.13 As has been illustrated, the privity doctrine was capable of disappointing reasonable contractual and commercial expectations. The fact that a series of ingenious (if contrived) devices were resorted to by the courts, together with a number of established common law and statutory exceptions to the doctrine, to avoid injustice in many cases, did not negate the case for reform. The various exceptions to, and evasions of, the basic rule merely served to demonstrate how impracticable and unpopular the doctrine of privity had become, and this was reflected in the strictures of the judiciary. For example, in *Woodar Investment Development Ltd* v *Wimpey Construction UK Ltd* [1980] 1 All ER 571 at 591, Lord Scarman expressed the wish that the House of Lords would, in the future, 'reconsider *Tweddle* v *Atkinson* and other cases which stand guard over this unjust rule'. Despite critical remarks such as these, the judiciary (with the notable exception of Lord Denning) showed a disinclination to directly challenge the basic rule and to overturn the doctrine of privity. The courts were probably correct in insisting that such a fundamental change was more appropriately to be undertaken by Parliament.

17.14 The Law Commission considered the case for reform of the general rule which prevented a person from enforcing a right under a contract to which he or she is not a party (the 'third party rule') in its Report, *Privity of Contract: Contracts for the Benefit of Third Parties* (Law Commission Report, No 242, Cm 3329, 1996). This Report supported the case for reform of the third party rule and stated that its recommendations would allow contracting parties to provide for enforceable third party rights without resorting to the various evasions and exceptions which had developed to circumvent the privity rule. The Report argued that this reform should be brought about in the form of detailed legislation, this strategy being favoured because of the certainty it would bring to the law. It observed that, despite the repeated criticism levelled at the privity doctrine in appellate cases, little progress had been made in actually overturning the third party rule. The legislative process offered the prospect of more detailed reform of the law and it was not dependent upon the vagaries of litigation.

17.15 The Contracts (Rights of Third Parties) Act 1999, based largely on the Law Commission's 1996 Report (see above), brought about a significant reform of the doctrine of privity of contract.[4] The Act does not affect the existing exceptions to, and circumventions of, the doctrine, but it introduces an important new (and more general) exception into the law. The Act deals with the conferral of rights on third parties, but naturally it does not alter the rule which prevents liabilities being imposed on a third party. It must be emphasized that the doctrine of privity was not abolished by the Act; it creates a general and relatively simple exception to the doctrine. In doing so, the Act brings English law more closely into line with that of most of the other members of the European Union and of many common law jurisdictions. The Act was passed on 11 November 1999, but it applies only to those contracts concluded on or after 11 May 2000 (i.e. six months after the new Act received Royal Assent). However, the parties to a contract concluded during the six-month period after the Act was passed were able expressly to provide for it to apply (see s 10(2) and (3)).

Conferring a third party right

17.16 Section 1(1) of C(RTP)A 1999 states that a 'third party' is able to enforce a term of a contract in his or her own right if:

> **(a)** the contract expressly provides that he may, or
> **(b)** subject to subsection (2), the term purports to confer a benefit on him.

4 For further discussion of the Act, see M. Dean, 'Removing a Blot on the Landscape—The Reform of the Doctrine of Privity' [2000] JBL 143; P. Kincaid, 'Privity Reform in England' (2000) 116 LQR 43; C. MacMillan, 'A Birthday Present for Lord Denning: The Contracts (Rights of Third Parties) Act 1999' (2000) 63 MLR 721; N. Andrews, 'Strangers to Justice No Longer: The Reversal of the Privity Rule under the Contracts (Rights of Third Parties) Act 1999' (2001) 60 CLJ 353; R. Stevens, 'The Contracts (Rights of Third Parties) Act 1999' (2004) 120 LQR 292; and H. Beale, 'A Review of the Contracts (Rights of Third Parties) Act 1999' in Burrows and Peel (eds) Contract Formation and Parties.

Section 1(2) provides that s 1(1)(b) will not apply if, on the proper construction of the contract, 'it appears that the parties did not intend the term to be enforceable by the third party'. The third party does not have to be in existence when the contract is made; a contractual provision might seek to benefit the future offspring of the contracting parties, or a company which is yet to be incorporated. But the third party must be expressly identified in the contract by name, or as a member of a class, or as answering a particular description (s 1(3)). (In *Avraamides* v *Colwill* (2006), the Court of Appeal, per Waller LJ at [19], emphasized that under s 1(3) the third party must be *expressly* identified, and that this requirement 'does not allow a process of construction or implication'). References in the Act to a third party enforcing a contractual term are to be understood as including the right to rely on an exclusion or limitation clause; such references, therefore, are not restricted to a third party suing to enforce a positive right (s 1(6)). If a third party comes within the provisions of this new exception to the privity doctrine, he or she can exercise his or her right to enforce the contractual term in the same way as if he or she were a party to the contract, and the rules relating to damages, injunctions, and specific performance apply equally to him or her (s 1(5)). However, any rights which are conferred on a third party are subject to any other relevant terms of the contract (s 1(4)); for example, where third party rights are created, the contracting parties might choose to limit those rights expressly by some other term of the contract.

17.17 What is the ambit of this new and wide-ranging exception to the doctrine of privity? The right of a third party, under C(RTP)A 1999, s 1(1) (above), to enforce a term of a contract is based on the intention of the contracting parties. This right may be conferred expressly by the contract, under the first limb, which is relatively straightforward. Alternatively, under the second limb, the third party may enforce a contractual term which purports to confer a benefit on him or her, subject to the proviso that this will not apply if, on a proper construction of the contract, the parties did not intend the term to be enforceable by the third party. The Law Commission used certain well-known past cases to illustrate the scope of the new third party right, especially in relation to the second limb of the test (Law Com No 242, paras **7.45–7.51**). Applying the new law to *Beswick* v *Beswick* (1968) (discussed earlier), for example, the first limb of the test would not confer a right on the uncle's widow, as there was no express provision to that effect in the contract. (Examples of such a provision would include words like 'and C shall have the right to enforce the contract'; see Law Com No 242, para. 7.10.) However, under the second limb, she would now almost certainly be able to enforce the nephew's promise in her own right. This is because the contract between the nephew and the uncle purported to confer a benefit on her and she was expressly identified in that contract. It is extremely unlikely that the presumption could be rebutted, as the nephew would be unable to demonstrate that, on a proper construction, the contracting parties did not intend the term to be enforceable by her.

17.18 It might be questioned whether the second (and more complicated) limb was necessary, especially in view of its potential to introduce uncertainty into the law, and whether the first limb might have been better standing alone. However, the view of the Law Commission was that, on its own, the first limb would have been too restrictive an approach to reforming the law. This is because it would have failed to give rights to a third party in situations where, although no express right of enforceability had been conferred by the contracting parties, it had been intended that the third party should have such a right (Law Com No 242, para. 7.11). Moreover, the Law Commission argued that with the inclusion of the 'proviso' (i.e. C(RTP)A 1999, s 1(2)), the second limb represents a workable solution to the problem of giving effect to the contracting parties' intentions without the introduction of too much uncertainty into the law. It is possible that there may be problems for the courts in deciding whether on a 'proper construction' the parties intended, on conferring a benefit on a third party, for it to be enforceable by the third party. But these problems are not insurmountable to judges used to taking an objective approach to contractual intention and, in the longer term, difficulties may be avoided by the more careful drafting of contracts by the parties. If the parties to a contract do not wish to confer an enforceable right on a third party, they should state this in clear terms, otherwise there may well be a strong presumption that the third party has the right to enforce the term in question. In *Nisshin Shipping Co. Ltd* v *Cleaves Ltd* (2003), the first reported case involving the interpretation of the 1999 Act, it was held at [23] that if a contract is 'neutral' (i.e. silent) as to the parties' intention, s 1(2) will not 'disapply' s 1(1)(b). This is because the wording of the subsection creates a rebuttable presumption: that is, that the parties *do* intend to confer rights on a third party to enforce a term, where they have included a term which purports to confer a benefit on an expressly identified third party (even though they have not expressly conferred such a right). Of course, the presumption may be disproved if there is evidence that the parties did not intend an enforceable right to be bestowed on the third party (see A. Burrows, 'The Contracts (Rights of Third Parties) Act and its Implications for Commercial Contracts' [2000] LMCLQ 540 at 544). In the *Nisshin Shipping* case, Colman J at [23] explained:

> Whether the contract does express a mutual intention that the third party should not be entitled to enforce the benefit conferred on him or is merely neutral is a matter of construction having regard to all the relevant circumstances.

17.19 The *Nisshin Shipping* approach received confirmation by the Court of Appeal in *Laemthong International Lines Co. Ltd* v *Artis (The Laemthong Glory) (No 2)* (2005). The case involved the delivery of a large quantity of sugar from Brazil to Aden. The claimant owners chartered their ship (*The Laemthong Glory*) for the carriage of this cargo. A clause of the charter party provided that if the original bills of lading (i.e. documents of title which represent the goods) were not available on the ship's arrival at the discharge port, the master of the ship could release the cargo to the receivers (the second defendants) on receipt of a letter of indemnity (LOI). The LOI was to be issued by the charterers of the vessel, who were the first defendants in the case. Before the ship arrived in Aden, the receivers notified the charterers that the bills of lading had not arrived. They asked the charterers to issue their LOI to the owners, and to instruct that the cargo be delivered without production of the bills of lading. The charterers agreed to this request on condition that, in turn, the receivers issued their own LOI to the charterers (which they did). The charterers then sent the receivers' LOI, together with their own, to the owners, and asked them to instruct the master to deliver the cargo. This was done, but the ship was then arrested by the Yemen Bank, which alleged that it held all the original bills of lading for the cargo and claimed for the value of the goods. The owners brought an action against the charterers and the receivers.

17.20 It was clear that the owners could enforce the charterers' LOI, as it was addressed to them. But they also wanted to enforce the receivers' LOI; the problem here was that this was not addressed to them, but to the charterers. Accordingly, the owners sought to rely on s 1 of the C(RTP)A 1999. At the trial, it was held (by Cooke J) that the owners could enforce the receivers' LOI against the receivers, and that the owners were entitled to an order that both the charterers and the receivers provide the necessary security to secure the release of the ship. The receivers appealed, arguing that the terms of the LOI, on which the owners relied, did not purport to confer a benefit on the owners and that, on the proper construction of the contract, the parties did not intend the terms of the receivers' LOI to be enforceable by the owners. These arguments were rejected by the Court of Appeal. Clarke LJ, delivering the judgment of the court, stated at [48] and [54] that the relevant terms of the receivers' LOI (addressed to the charterers) purported to confer a benefit on the owners. The owners were entitled to enforce these terms in their own name, because there was nothing in the receivers' LOI to suggest that the parties did not intend the relevant terms to be enforceable by the owners (i.e. the third party). Clarke LJ stated at [54] that if the court was correct in holding that the relevant terms in the receivers' LOI were intended to be for the benefit of the owners, 'it makes no sense to hold that it was nevertheless intended that the receivers' liability should not be directly to the owners'. He continued:

> The whole purpose of the receivers' LOI was on the one hand to ensure that the receivers received the cargo from the ship without production of the original bills of lading and on the other hand to ensure that the owners were fully protected from the consequences of arrest or other action which might be taken by the holders of the original bills of lading.

An attempt to rely on s 1(1)(b) appeared to have succeeded in a further case, but the decision of Lindsay J was reversed by the Court of Appeal in *Prudential Assurance Co Ltd* v *Ayres* (2008). Here, the claimant insurance company (C) entered into a sub-lease of office premises with the defendant law firm (Ds). Ds later assigned the lease to an American law firm (F), and were required under their licence to assign to provide C with a guarantee of F; that is, that if F were to default with the rent, Ds would be liable to pay. Subsequently, C and F entered into a further agreement (a 'supplemental deed') to the effect that the liability of the tenant under the lease was to be limited to the partnership, and therefore did not extend to the assets of individual partners: thus any action by C against the tenant or 'any previous tenant' under the lease for non-payment of rent was restricted to partnership assets. F later became bankrupt, with rent unpaid, and C tried to recover this from Ds as F's guarantors. Ds argued that the supplemental deed agreed between C and F excused them from their liability to pay. At the trial, the judge held that the supplemental deed purported to confer a benefit on Ds within s 1(1)(b) of the Act; therefore Ds could enforce the relevant provision against C in refusing to pay. However, the Court of Appeal allowed C's appeal, deciding that on its proper construction the supplemental deed did not purport to confer any benefit on Ds (per Moore-Bick LJ at [42]). Accordingly, it provided no defence to C's claim, as the court found it 'impossible to accept that the parties intended to alter in a significant way the nature of the relationship between [C] and [Ds] that had been established' under the licence to assign (at [40]). The case was in fact decided on the basis of the construction of the supplemental deed, and therefore has little to contribute to our understanding of the ambit of s 1(1)(b) (at [41]–[42]). (For another recent case in which an attempt to rely on s 1(1)(b) failed, see *Dolphin Maritime and Aviation Ltd* v *Sveriges Angfartygs Assurans Forening* (2009).)

17.21 Following a successful reliance on s 1 of the C(RTP)A 1999 in *Laemthong International Lines Co. Ltd* v *Artis (The Laemthong Glory) (No 2)* (2005), the legislative provisions have been applied once again to assist a shipowner in the enforcement of a LOI. In the case of *Great Eastern Shipping Co Ltd* v *Far East Chartering Ltd (The Jag Ravi)* (2012), an LOI was found capable of being accepted by a shipowner as the charterer's agent. Delivering the judgment of the Court of Appeal, Tomlinson LJ stated that:

> the words 'The Owners/Disponent Owners/Charterers' could not, or could not properly, in the context be construed as a compendious way of describing a single offeree . . . It was more natural to regard the phrase as comprising a descending hierarchy, progressing from the owners through time charterers down to voyage charterers . . . the natural and proper meaning of the letter of indemnity is that it is addressed to both the owners and the charterers. (at 41 and 42)

The LOI was read as being addressed to both the owners and the charterers and therefore capable of acceptance by the charterer. The acceptance had taken place through the shipowner's conduct in delivering the cargo. The court also emphasized that there was no reason of public policy which precluded enforcement of the LOI (see 50–52) and the owners were entitled to enforce the indemnity under the C(RTP) Act 1999. A further example of a successful reliance on s 1 of the C(RTP)A 1999 is presented by the case of *Cavanagh* v *Secretary of State for Work and Pensions* (2016). Here a claim was brought against the defendant by two of its employees and by their trade union. The court held that the employees, having opted to have their subscriptions to the union deducted from their salary and paid by the defendant Secretary of State to the union, had a contractual right to insist that he continued with that arrangement. Moreover, the union could enforce that right under the 1999 Act.

Varying or cancelling the agreement

17.22 Where a third party has a right conferred on him or her under a contract, should the contracting parties have the freedom to vary, or even cancel, the third party's right? It could be argued that without such a freedom there would be an unacceptable interference with the rights of the contracting parties, who would usually have the right to vary their agreement. However, the recognition of third party rights naturally involves some restriction on the contracting parties' freedom to modify the original contract, otherwise the reform of the third party rule (described earlier) would lack utility. The Law Commission sought to establish an appropriate test to determine the 'crystallization' of the third party's rights, i.e. the point beyond which the contracting parties would lose the right to vary or cancel the contract. It favoured a test of reliance or acceptance by recommending that 'the contracting parties' right to vary or cancel the contract or, as the case may be, the contractual provision should be lost once the third party has relied on it or has accepted it' (see Law Com No 242, 1996, para. 9.26). However, it stated also that 'the contracting parties may expressly reserve the right to vary or cancel the third party's right irrespective of reliance or acceptance by the third party' (para. 9.40). In other words, the Law Commission recommended a compromise between the conflicting interests referred to above, by allowing the contracting parties expressly to reserve the right to vary or cancel the right of the third party.

17.23 Accordingly, C(RTP)A 1999, s 2(3) provides that the restriction on the right of the contracting parties to vary or cancel a third party's right, set out in s 2(1), is subject to any express term of the contract under which the contracting parties may: (a) by agreement rescind or vary the contract without the third party's consent, or (b) alter the circumstances for the third party's consent to be given from those set out in s 2(1). If the contracting parties do not include such an express provision in their agreement, their freedom to vary or cancel the third party's right is controlled by s 2(1). This states that where a third party has a right conferred on him or her (see s 1, earlier), the contracting parties are not permitted to agree to cancel or alter the agreement in such a way as to extinguish or alter the third party's right, without his or her consent, if:

(1) the third party has communicated his or her assent (by words or conduct) to the term to the promisor,
(2) the promisor is aware that the third party has relied on the term, or
(3) the promisor can reasonably be expected to have foreseen that the third party would rely on the term and the third party has in fact relied on it.

Therefore, once a third party right has been conferred (under s 1), there are general restrictions (under s 2(1)) on the freedom of the contracting parties to vary or cancel their agreement subsequently, in the absence of any express provision in the contract (s 2(3)). In s 2(1), it should be noted that the word 'reliance' is not restricted to where a third party has relied on the term to his or her detriment; the third party's conduct need not have left him or her in a worse position than before the promise was made. This distinction was made by the Law Commission, which defined reliance on a promise as 'conduct induced by the belief (or expectation) that the promise will be performed or, at least, that one is legally entitled to performance of the promise' (Law Com No 242, para. 9.14). This approach is consistent with one of the major reasons for reforming the privity doctrine, that is, that it can disappoint the reasonable expectations of the third party. If the third party has relied on the promise, this demonstrates that expectations have been created, even if no detriment has been suffered (see Law Com No 242, para. 9.19).

17.24 It should be noted that, under C(RTP)A 1999, s 2(1), the promisor (i.e. the contracting party against whom the term is enforceable by the third party) actually has to be aware of the third party's reliance or, alternatively, can reasonably be expected to foresee that the third party would rely on the term and has in fact done so. Normally, where a promisor has contracted to confer a right on a third party, he or she should be aware that there is likely to be reliance on the contract by the third party. So, as a general rule, the promisor should check with the third party, where this is possible, before cancelling or varying the contractual provision in question. As an alternative to the reliance test, s 2(1) also provides a test of acceptance. The rationale is that where a third party communicates his or her assent effectively, this allows the promisor to know where he or she stands, and the third party should be able to enforce his or her right without having to show reliance (see Law Com No 242, para. 9.20). Therefore, to avoid any uncertainty, a third party may make certain of performance of the promise by communicating his or her assent to the promisor. It should be noted that communication in this context does not include the posting of a letter; the Act states that the assent may be by words or conduct, but if it is sent by post it will not be regarded as communicated until it is received by the promisor (s 2(2)(b)).

Defences

17.25 The Law Commission recommended that the right of the third party to enforce a term of the contract 'should be subject to all defences and set-offs that would have been available to the promisor in an action by the promisee and which arise out of or in connection with the contract' (Law Com No 242, para. 10.12). Accordingly, C(RTP)A 1999, s 3 deals with the defences available to a promisor where a claim is made by a third party in reliance on s 1. Section 3(2) provides that, subject to any express term of the contract to the contrary (s 3(5)), the promisor can rely on any defence or set-off which:

(1) arises from the contract and is relevant to the term in question, and
(2) would have been available to him or her if the action had been brought by the promisee (i.e. the party to the contract by whom the term is enforceable against the promisor).

In addition, the promisor is able to rely on (a) by way of defence or set-off any matter, and (b) by way of counterclaim any matter not arising from the contract, 'that would have been available to him or her by way of defence or set-off or, as the case may be, by way of counterclaim against the third party if the third party had been a party to the contract' (s 3(4)).

Other provisions of C(RTP)A 1999

17.26 Section 4 makes it clear that the conferral of an enforceable right on a third party does not affect the right of the promisee to enforce any contractual term (discussed later in this chapter). This section is consistent with the view expressed by the Law Commission (Law Com No 242, paras 11.3–11.4), which argued that the promisee (a contracting party who has provided consideration) should not lose the right to enforce a contractual right simply because the contract has conferred an enforceable right on a third party. It might be objected that this could raise the prospect of a double liability for the promisor, that is, to pay damages to both the third party and the promisee for the same loss. Section 5 aims to prevent this by providing that, where a contractual term has conferred an enforceable right on a third party and the promisee has recovered damages in respect of the third party's loss, this will be taken into account in any proceedings brought by the third party. In other words, any sum awarded to the third party will be lowered appropriately to take account of the sum recovered by the promisee. This section does not deal explicitly with the reverse situation, in which the third party has already recovered damages from the promisor; but the logic of s 5 would suggest that, in such a case, there will be a similar restriction on the damages recoverable by the promisee. (However, in this situation, it is unlikely that the promisee will have suffered any loss and that is presumably why no express provision was included in the Act.)

17.27 C(RTP)A 1999, s 6 sets out the types of contract which do not fall within the ambit of the Act. For example, s 6(1) provides that s 1 does not confer a third party right 'in the case of a contract on a bill of exchange, promissory note or other negotiable instrument'. This exclusion follows the recommendation of the Law Commission (Law Com No 242, para. 12.17), which was of the opinion that it would cause considerable uncertainty in the law if a more general third party right were created in relation to bills of exchange, promissory notes, and other negotiable instruments, in addition to the one which is provided by the Bills of Exchange Act 1882. Under the 1882 Act, third party rights of enforceability are conferred only on holders of those instruments. If the 1999 Act had applied, it would have extended this right to third parties who were not holders and, in so doing, have undermined the policy of the 1882 Act and led to confusion.

17.28 The Law Commission recommended also that third party rights of enforceability should not be conferred in relation to contracts for the carriage of goods by sea, and contracts for the international carriage of goods by road, rail, or air (Law Com No 242, para. 12.6). Once again, the reasoning was that such a general right might be inconsistent with the policy of existing legislation, which is more attuned to the needs of a particular industry (such as shipping), and that the resulting conflict would produce uncertainty in the commercial world. (For the relevant legislation in relation to the carriage of goods by sea, see the Carriage of Goods by Sea Act 1992, s 2(1); contracts for the international carriage of goods by road or rail, or the carriage of cargo by air, are regulated by international conventions which are given force in English law by various implementing statutes.) For this reason, C(RTP)A 1999, s 6(5) states that no third party right of enforceability (under s 1) is conferred in relation to (a) contracts for the carriage of goods by sea, or (b) contracts for the carriage of goods by rail or road, or cargo by air. However, s 6(5) expressly states that this does not prevent a third party from enforcing exclusion or limitation of liability clauses in these two types of contract.

17.29 The Contracts (Rights of Third Parties) Act 1999 confers no third party right in the case of any contract binding on any company and its members under s 14 of the Companies Act 1985 (see s 6(2)). Also, s 6(3) provides for the exclusion of employment contracts from the ambit of the new third party right. Accordingly, s 1 confers no third party right to enforce (a) any term of a contract against an employee, (b) any term of a worker's contract against a worker, or (c) any term of a relevant contract against an agency worker. This provision ensures that, for example, a customer of an employer will not be able to use the Act to bring an action against an employee for a breach of his or her contract of employment.

17.30 The Contracts (Rights of Third Parties) Act 1999 does ensure that the provisions of the Arbitration Act 1996 apply in relation to third party rights. This addition was introduced slightly later, at the Report stage in the House of Commons. The accompanying Explanatory Notes advise that s 8 of the Act provides that, where appropriate, the provisions of the Arbitration Act 1996 shall apply in relation to third party rights. Without the addition of s 8, the main provisions of the Arbitration Act 1996 would not apply because a third party is not a party to an arbitration agreement between the promisor and the promise (see further A. Burrows, 'The Contracts (Rights of Third Parties) Act and Its Implications for Commercial Contracts' (2000) LMCLQ 540). Section 8 was analysed in detail in the case of *Nisshin Shipping Co. Ltd* v *Cleaves Ltd* (2003) (discussed at para. **17.18**). More recently, in *Fortress Value Recovery Fund I LLC* v *Blue Skye Special Opportunities Fund LP* (2013), its scope and application was once again considered, with the Court of Appeal emphasizing the distinction between substantive and procedural rights, as provided for in s 8(1) and 8(2) respectively. Here the court noted, as matters of interpretation and construction, that if contracting parties wish to grant to a third party an enforceable procedural right to have a dispute referred to arbitration, s 8(2) provides the means to do so (see Toulson LJ at [45] and [56]).

17.31 It is apparent that the Law Commission's aim was not to confer upon a third party the identical rights as would be enjoyed by a contracting party; for example, it did not support the argument in favour of amending the Unfair Contract Terms Act 1977 (see **Chapter 10**) so as to restrict the promisor's ability to exclude liability to third parties. The Commission argued that its test of enforceability was based on giving effect to the intentions of the parties to a contract to bestow legal rights on a third party, and that to apply UCTA 1977 to claims by third parties 'would cut across the essential basis' of the proposed reform (Law Com No 242, para. 13.10). The Commission considered s 2(2) of the 1977 Act more specifically, which it felt needed to be the subject of an express provision. Therefore, it recommended that UCTA 1977, s 2(2) should not apply in respect of a claim by a third party under the new law. (It will be remembered that s 2(2) states that a person cannot limit or exclude liability for negligently caused loss or damage, other than personal injury or death, unless the contract term or notice in question satisfies the requirement of reasonableness.) Section 7(2) of C(RTP)A 1999 reflects the Law Commission's view by providing that UCTA 1977, s 2(2) will 'not apply where the negligence consists of the breach of an obligation arising from a term of a contract and the person seeking to enforce it is a third party acting in reliance on section 1'.

17.32 Finally, it should be noted that C(RTP)A 1999, s 7(1) makes it clear that the right of enforceability under s 1 'does not affect any right or remedy of a third party that exists or is available apart from this Act'. This provision reflects the view of the Law Commission (Law Com No 242, paras 12.1–12.2), which argued for the retention of other existing statutory exceptions and found 'no merit' in attempting to abolish the common law exceptions to the doctrine. Moreover, it acknowledged that some of the common law exceptions give third parties more certain rights than those conferred under the new Act. But the Commission observed that some of these common law exceptions to the doctrine 'have developed through somewhat artificial and forced use of existing concepts' (para. 12.1) and that such exceptions might 'wither away', as a consequence of the new law, as they become redundant.

17.33 It is clear also, from C(RTP)A 1999, s 4 (see earlier), that the conferral of an enforceable right on a third party does not affect the right of the promisee to enforce any contractual term and, in some instances, the promisee may be able to assist the third party. Therefore, it is necessary in this chapter to consider the other main exceptions to the privity doctrine, including a discussion of the right of the promisee to bring an action, although it should be emphasized that some of these exceptions will become less important as a consequence of the 1999 Act. (Also, it should be remembered that the Act does not apply to all types of contract.)

Other statutory exceptions

17.34 In contrast to the more general exception to the doctrine provided by the Contracts (Rights of Third Parties) Act 1999, there are other, narrower statutory exceptions which were introduced to avoid the commercial inconvenience caused by the privity rule. A good example is that of contracts of insurance, where various Acts confer rights on third parties. A car owner, for instance, may require insurance cover not only for his or her own use of his or her vehicle, but also for other people who drive his or her car with his or her permission. In theory, the contract of insurance which he or she takes out for the benefit of third parties would not be enforceable by them. However, to avoid this result, specific legislation was introduced to permit a third party to benefit from such an insurance policy. For example, Road Traffic Act 1988, s 148(7) states that a person issuing an insurance policy is liable to indemnify not just the person taking out the policy, but also 'the persons or classes of persons specified in the policy in respect of any liability which the policy purports to cover'. In another statutory exception to the privity rule, it is provided that a person can effect an insurance on his or her life for the benefit of his or her spouse or children (see Married Women's Property Act 1882, s 11). Such a life insurance creates a trust in favour of the named beneficiaries, rather than becoming part of the insured person's estate.

17.35 For a fuller list of statutory exceptions, see the Law Commission's report (Law Com No 242, pp. 31–5). It is worth noting, in this context, the Package Travel, Package Holidays and Package Tours Regulations 1992 (SI 1992/3288), which implemented Council Directive 90/314/EEC on package travel, package holidays, and package tours. The problem for the consumer that was posed by the doctrine of privity was that the services comprising a package holiday may not be performed directly by the organizer or retailer with whom the contract was made. In order to get around this difficulty, the Regulations confer direct rights on consumers (see Regulation 2(2)) against the organizer or retailer with whom they contracted (see Regulation 15). (See further *Titshall* v *Qwerty Travel Ltd* (2011).)

Action brought by the promisee

17.36 The conferral of an enforceable right on a third party by the Contracts (Rights of Third Parties) Act 1999 does not affect the right of a promisee to enforce any term of the contract (see s 4). As explained at the start of this chapter, a contract between A and B, under which A promises to confer some benefit on C, was not enforceable by C due to the privity doctrine. However, the promisee (B) is able to bring an action against A, as a party to a binding contract. One possible remedy for B is to seek an order for specific performance against A to force him or her to confer the promised benefit on C. An order for specific performance has the effect of ordering a contracting party to do what he or she has undertaken to do (see **Chapter 21**). If we return to the case of *Beswick* v *Beswick* (1968) (discussed earlier), it was held that although the widow could not succeed in her own right, she should be granted an order for specific performance as administratrix of her husband's estate. In this capacity, as his personal representative, there was no problem of privity, as she was suing on behalf of the promisee (her deceased husband), whose rights she was entitled to enforce. The contract in *Beswick* v *Beswick* was of a type that may be specifically enforced, but this would not have been the case if, for example, the contract had been for personal services—as such contracts are not normally specifically enforceable. The remedy of specific performance is not one which is widely available and such an order will not be made where damages are an adequate remedy. It could be argued that, as the 1999 Act has given the third party an enforceable right to claim damages in a case such as *Beswick* v *Beswick*, it is less likely that specific performance would be either sought by the promisee, or granted, if similar facts occurred today.

17.37 Where the promisee sues for damages as a result of the promisor failing to confer a benefit on the third party, the question arises as to how such damages are to be assessed. Of course, the promisee can sue for his or her own loss (if he or she has suffered any) but, in general, he or she cannot recover damages for the loss of the third party. The promisee is not able to recover anything other than nominal damages where he or she has not suffered any direct loss. The rule was challenged in *Jackson* v *Horizon Holidays* [1975] 3 All ER 92, where the facts were:

> Mr Jackson (C) booked a holiday with the defendant company for himself, his wife, and his two small children. The price of the holiday (in Sri Lanka) was £1,200, which covered air fares and luxury hotel accommodation. When booking the holiday, C made various stipulations about the accommodation and meals that he and his family were to receive. He was assured that the hotel in question would be up to his expectations. In fact, C and his family were greatly dissatisfied with the hotel, its facilities, and the meals that were served. C brought an action against the defendants for breach of contract, claiming damages in respect of disappointment and distress for himself, his wife, and his children. The defendants did not contest their liability, but they appealed against the amount of damages (£1,100) awarded by the deputy High Court judge.

The Court of Appeal dismissed the appeal and held that the damages awarded by the judge were not excessive. The majority stated that the amount would have been excessive if it had been awarded only for the loss suffered by Mr Jackson himself. (In this respect, the trial judge's decision was reversed by the majority in the Court of Appeal.) But, in these circumstances, where one party makes a contract for the benefit of himself and others, the court held that he should be able to claim on behalf of the whole party. Mr Jackson could, therefore, recover damages not only for his own dissatisfaction with the holiday, but also for that of his family. Lord Denning stated (at 95):

> In this case it was a husband making a contract for the benefit of himself, his wife and children. Other cases readily come to mind. A host makes a contract with a restaurant for a dinner for himself and his friends . . . It would be a fiction to say that the contract was made by all the family, or all the guests . . . The real truth is that in each instance, the father, the host . . . was making a contract himself for the benefit of the whole party. In short, a contract by one for the benefit of third persons.

17.38 The approach adopted by the majority in *Jackson* v *Horizon Holidays* (1975) was potentially an attractive one, but it was based heavily on Lord Denning's view of what the law should be, rather than on any convincing authority. This circumvention of the privity rule was not without its critics, and it is not surprising that the matter was considered once again by the House of Lords in *Woodar Investment Development Ltd* v *Wimpey Construction UK Ltd* [1980] 1 All ER 571. The facts were as follows:

> A contract for the sale of 14 acres of land for development, for a price of £850,000, included a provision that on completion the purchasers should also pay a further £150,000 to a third party who had no legal connection with the vendors. The contract gave the purchasers the right to rescind the contract if, before completion, a statutory authority 'shall have commenced' to acquire the property by compulsory acquisition. In fact, compulsory purchase proceedings had been started for part of the property at the time the contract was completed, but it later became clear that there was a prospect of planning permission being granted for most of the land. Nevertheless, the purchasers wished to rescind the contract. The vendors claimed damages on the basis that the purchasers had wrongfully repudiated the contract. They included in their claim the loss suffered by the third party.

A majority of the House of Lords held that the purchasers had not wrongfully repudiated the contract and their appeal was allowed. The question of damages was not, therefore, relevant to the actual decision. But the court went on to consider the state of the law regarding the recovery of damages for the benefit of third parties and it disapproved of Lord Denning's broad statements in *Jackson* v *Horizon Holidays Ltd* [1975] 3 All ER 92 at 95–6. This does not mean that the actual decision in *Jackson* was incorrect, but the House of Lords would not endorse Lord Denning's interpretation of the relevant legal authorities. The actual decision in *Jackson* could still be supported on the basis that the claimant recovered solely for his own loss (see the rather terse judgment of James LJ in *Jackson*, at 96), or alternatively that the case belonged to a special type of contract (for example, where a person contracts for a family holiday, or books a restaurant meal for a party) which requires 'special treatment' (per Lords Wilberforce and Keith in *Woodar*, at 576 and 588, respectively).

However, in *Woodar* it was clear that the promisee (the vendors) would have suffered no loss in relation to the promisor's failure to pay the money to the third party. The House of Lords suggested that the vendors would not have been able to recover substantial damages for the third party's loss (see, e.g., the statement of Lord Wilberforce at 577). But, if the *Woodar* facts were to occur today, the third party would be able to claim the promised sum directly under C(RTP) A 1999. This is because the contract purported to confer a benefit on the third party, who was expressly identified, and the promisor would surely not be able to rebut the presumption that the third party was intended to have an enforceable right.

17.39 In spite of the House of Lords' decision in *Woodar Investment Development Ltd* v *Wimpey Construction UK Ltd* (1980), which rejected the idea that a contracting party could generally recover the third party's loss, later cases have considered this matter in different circumstances. For example, in *Linden Gardens Trust Ltd* v *Lenesta Sludge Disposals Ltd* (1993), the House of

Lords considered whether a building owner can recover substantial damages for breach of a building contract if he has parted with the property to a third party. In one appeal, a company (A) contracted with B for the removal of blue asbestos from its property. But, in breach of the agreement, not all the asbestos was removed by B, whilst A in the meantime had sold the property to C. A had attempted to assign its contractual rights to C, but this transaction was invalid and C was thus prevented from succeeding in its action against B for breach of contract. A was not in fact a party to the action in one appeal, but was in the other case which was considered at the same time by the House of Lords. Their Lordships discussed whether A could recover anything other than nominal damages if it brought an action against B as a result of the loss suffered by C. It was decided that A should be permitted to recover substantial damages, as it was in the contemplation of both contracting parties that the property was likely to be bought by a third party before B's breach occurred, and that A should be regarded as having entered into the contract for C's benefit, as C's loss was foreseeable to B. (Their Lordships relied on *Albacruz (Cargo Owners)* v *Albazero (Owners), The Albazero* [1977] AC 774 per Lord Diplock at 847.) Accordingly, A could recover for C's loss in these commercial circumstances, as C had no direct remedy. The *Linden Gardens* decision was then applied, and extended, by the Court of Appeal in *Darlington Borough Council* v *Wiltshier Northern Ltd* (1995).

17.40 *Linden Gardens Trust Ltd* v *Lenesta Sludge Disposals Ltd* (1993) was distinguished in the House of Lords case of *Panatown Ltd* v *Alfred McAlpine Construction Ltd* (2000), as on the facts of the latter case the third party had been given a direct cause of action against the contractor. In these circumstances, the necessity for the *Linden Gardens Trust* approach was not present, as the third party had a right to recover substantial damages by suing the contractor directly. Therefore, in arbitration proceedings brought by the claimant employer against the defendant contractor, seeking the recovery of substantial damages, a majority of the House of Lords decided against the employer and allowed the contractor's appeal. (For further discussion of this case, see M. Reynolds, 'When Principle and Precedent Collide: Panatown' (2003) Con & Eng Law 8(1) 13–34, which expresses the view that the decision in *Panatown Ltd* v *Alfred McAlpine Construction Ltd* (2000) creates uncertainty in this area, leaving the fundamental principles concerning privity and recovery by a third party unresolved.) Although there is uncertainty over the ambit of the *Linden Gardens Trust* exception, this may well be resolved by a stricter adherence to the general rule in future, in view of the third party right which can now be conferred directly under C(RTP)A 1999.

17.41 Finally, there is another situation in which the promisee may be able to enforce a promise on behalf of a third party. This is where A makes a promise (expressly or impliedly) to B that he will not sue C. If an action is brought by A against C, B may be able to prevent A from succeeding with such an action. For example, in *Snelling* v *John G Snelling Ltd* (1972), the facts were:

> Three brothers were co-directors of a family business, a building company. The business expanded, but disputes arose between the brothers and relations between them worsened. The three brothers made loans to the company to provide additional finance. The three of them contracted that in the event of any one of them voluntarily resigning his directorship,

he would forfeit the money owed to him by the company. The agreement stated that if this occurred, the remaining directors could use the money, not for their personal benefit, but to repay a loan made to their business by a finance company. Three months later, Brian Snelling (the claimant) voluntarily resigned as a director and claimed payment from the defendant company of the sum which he had loaned to it. The company was joined by the other two brothers, Peter and Barrie, as co-defendants, who claimed that the sum due to the claimant had been forfeited by his resignation. Could the defendant company rely on a term in the agreement (between the brothers) which was for the company's benefit, when it was not a party to that agreement?

It was held by Ormrod J that the co-defendants, Peter and Barrie Snelling, were entitled to a declaration that the terms of the agreement were binding on Brian, the claimant. The company, on the other hand, was not a party to the agreement and could not, therefore, rely directly on its terms. However, the judge achieved a fair outcome by granting a declaration that the claimant was not able to call upon the defendant company to repay the loan and his action against the company was dismissed. The judge stated that this course of action was possible as the co-defendant brothers had made out a clear case and succeeded on their counterclaim, and because all the relevant parties were before the court, it would have been a proper case for a stay of all further proceedings. But as the judge thought that the claimant's claim had failed, he dismissed the claim rather than merely ordering a stay of further proceedings. In this way, the claimant was prevented from obtaining a judgment against the company in defiance of the clear agreement made with his brothers, which was intended to put the family company on a secure business footing. It should be noted that the claimant did not actually promise not to sue the company, but such a promise was a necessary implication of the agreement which he made. (This decision can be contrasted with *Gore* v *Van der Lann* (1967).)

Circumventions of, and exceptions to, the doctrine

17.42 A number of devices and ingenious arguments have been used in the past to avoid the inconvenience or unfairness caused by a strict application of the privity doctrine. In view of the Contracts (Rights of Third Parties) Act 1999, such devices may be of less practical significance in the future, but they were not abolished by the new legislation (see s 7(1)) and therefore need to be considered in the sections which follow.

Collateral contracts

17.43 A good example of judicial ingenuity in avoiding the problem of privity is the use of the concept of a collateral contract. This concept was discussed in detail in **Chapter 7**, and it was considered also in **Chapter 4** in relation to the practice of manufacturers of goods providing guarantees to the consumer whose contract is with the retailer (now see Regulation 15 of the Sale and Supply of Goods to Consumers Regulations 2002 (SI 2002/3045)). The manufacturer is not, of course, a party to the main contract between the retailer and the consumer, and it might appear that such guarantees are unenforceable, as the consumer provides no consideration for the manufacturer's promise. In a rather artificial way, however, it could be argued that, where the consumer is invited to fill in a card or form and send it off to the manufacturer within a specified period, the performance of such an act by the consumer is an acceptance of the manufacturer's (unilateral) offer of a guarantee. Another way of examining such transactions is to say that the guarantee is the subject of a collateral contract, that is, one that exists alongside the main contract between the retailer and the consumer. The collateral contract represents a judicial device aimed at avoiding an unfair outcome which would otherwise be caused by an established rule of law. This is illustrated by the case *Shanklin Pier* v *Detel Products Ltd* (1951), where the facts were:

> The claimants (the pier owners) employed contractors to paint their pier under a contract which enabled the claimants to specify the paint to be used. The defendant company, wishing to secure the contract for supplying the paint, told the claimants that their paint (known as DMU) would last for at least seven years. On the strength of this representation (or 'guarantee'), the claimants instructed the contractors to buy and use the defendants' paint for painting the pier. In fact, the paint was unsatisfactory and lasted for a mere three months! The claimants brought an action against the defendants, but they had to get around the problem that the paint was bought from the defendants by the contractors. Could the claimants enforce the defendants' guarantee that the paint would last for at least seven years?

The court found in favour of the claimants. Although the main contract was between the defendants and the contractors for the sale of the paint, there was also a collateral contract between the defendants and the claimants which guaranteed the durability of the paint known as DMU. It must be presumed that the claimants gave consideration for the defendants' guarantee of their paint by instructing the contractors to buy DMU rather than any other paint. (For a further, and more questionable, example of the use of the collateral contract device in relation to guarantees, see *Wells (Merstham) Ltd* v *Buckland Sand and Silica Co. Ltd* (1965).) As the 1999 Act now permits an enforceable right to be conferred directly on a third party, there will be less need to use the collateral contract device to avoid the privity doctrine in future.

Trust of a promise

17.44 In affirming the common law rule of privity in *Dunlop Pneumatic Tyre Co.* v *Selfridge* [1915] AC 847 (at 853), Lord Haldane stated that although a third party cannot acquire rights by way of a contract, such a right may be conferred by way of property, for example, under a trust. The idea of a trust, as developed in equity, is that of B (the trustee) having rights over property (for example, land or a fund), which he or she is bound by agreement with A, from whom he or she received the property, to exercise on behalf of C, the beneficiary. To put this another way, B holds the property on trust for the benefit of C. Under such an arrangement, C acquires an equitable interest in the property and he or she can enforce his or her rights against the trustee. When the trust is set up, C becomes the beneficial owner of the property and, accordingly, his or her rights are not a result merely of a promise in his or her favour.

17.45 The concept of a trust had some potential as a means of circumventing the privity rule. To take the familiar situation: A makes a promise to B, in exchange for consideration supplied by B, to confer some benefit on C. If it could be argued that B was a trustee for C, then C's rights would be enforceable. One difficulty is the limitation that, for there to be a valid trust, there must (inter alia) be property which is capable of being held on trust and in which the third party has an equitable interest. The question arose as to the circumstances in which the courts were prepared to find that a trust of a contractual right had been created. In other words, when could a promisee under a contract legitimately claim that he or she was a trustee of the benefit of that promise on behalf of a 'stranger' to the contract? Initially the courts showed a willingness to rely on the trust idea in this way (see *Tomlinson* v *Gill* (1756); also *Gregory and Parker* v *Williams* (1817); and *Lloyd's* v *Harper* (1880)). The best-known example is *Les Affréteurs Réunis SA* v *Leopold Walford Ltd* [1919] AC 801, where the facts were:

> The appellants (the shipowners) entered into a contract to charter a ship to a company (the charterers) for a specific period. Under the contract, the appellants promised to pay a sum of money to the respondent brokers, Leopold Walford Ltd (LW), who had negotiated the contract. Clause 29 of the contract stated: 'A commission of 3 per cent on the estimated gross amount of hire is due to Leopold Walford Ltd on signing this charter (ship lost or not lost).' The ship was requisitioned by the French government and the shipowners refused to pay any commission to LW. It should be noted that LW was not a party to the agreement, although clause 29 was included for its benefit. Although the action was brought by LW, with the consent of the appellants it was treated as if the charterers had been added as claimants.

The House of Lords held that Leopold Walford Ltd was entitled to recover the commission from the shipowners. The charterers, who were the promisees, were able to enforce the appellants' promise made for the benefit of a third party. The charterers were trustees for LW, who were the beneficiaries of the promise. It was stated by Lord Birkenhead (at 806–7):

> It appears to me that for convenience, and under long-established practice, the broker in such cases, in effect, nominates the charterer to contract on his behalf, influenced probably by the circumstance that there is always a contract between charterer and owner in which this stipulation, which is to enure to the benefit of the broker, may very conveniently be inserted. In these cases the broker, on ultimate analysis, appoints the charterer to contract on his behalf. I agree with the conclusion . . . that in such cases charterers can sue as trustees on behalf of the broker.

17.46 This approach of implying a trust of a contractual right appeared to offer a convenient solution to a third party trying to enforce a promise made for his or her benefit. However, the solution raised certain difficulties. Principally, it was objected that the contracting parties will rarely, in fact, intend to create a trust. This is because if they do so, it would mean that they were not free to vary the terms of their agreement in the future, as this would interfere with the beneficiary's rights. As they are unlikely to intend such a restriction on their own contractual rights, it meant that the trust device was of limited utility. The courts now insist on clear evidence that the parties intended to create a trust, and this explains why the trust of a contractual right idea is of little value to third parties today. (For example, in *Vandepitte* v *Preferred Accident Insurance Corpn of New York* (1933), the Privy Council held that there will be a trust only if it can be definitely proved that there was an intention to create one, and in this case no such intention to constitute a trust was proved.) The courts' reluctance to imply a trust is further illustrated by *Re Schebsman* [1944] Ch 83. The facts were:

> Mr Schebsman was employed by both a Swiss company and its English subsidiary. On the termination of Schebsman's employment with the two companies, the English company agreed to pay him £5,500 in six annual instalments. The agreement also specified that the payments would be made to Schebsman's widow, if he died, and to his daughter, if his widow also died. During the period in which the payments were to be made to him by the company (and two years after the agreement was made), Schebsman was declared bankrupt and then died. His trustee in bankruptcy sought a declaration that the outstanding sums still to be paid by the English company formed part of the debtor's (i.e. Schebsman's) estate; if this claim succeeded, the money payable by the company would have been available for Schebsman's creditors. The claim failed: the company was entitled to go ahead and make the agreed payments to Schebsman's widow.

The trustee in bankruptcy's appeal was dismissed by the Court of Appeal. The company was, in fact, willing to make the payments to the widow and such payment was held by the court to be due performance of the contract. (The court refused to imply a term into the agreement entitling the trustee in bankruptcy to intercept the sums which were to be paid to the wife and daughter.) This had the effect of preventing the trustee in bankruptcy's claim. However, the court also made it clear that under the agreement between the company and Schebsman, the latter was neither a trustee nor an agent for his wife and daughter. Du Parcq LJ stated (at 104) that unless the parties, by their language and by the circumstances of the case, show a clear intention to create a trust, the court should not be quick to imply such an intention. As the parties to the agreement in *Schebsman* would almost certainly have wished to retain their right at common law to vary the terms of that agreement, his Lordship did not think that a trust had been created. (For instance, Schebsman might have wanted the money to be paid to someone other than his widow.)

17.47 Thus, the courts are reluctant to 'disregard the dividing line between the case of a trust and the simple case of a contract made between two persons for the benefit of a third' (per Lord Greene MR in *Re Schebsman* [1944] Ch 83 at 89). (See also *Green* v *Russell* (1959) in which it was held that the mere intention, under a contract, to provide benefits for a third party was insufficient to create a trust.) For these reasons, it is clear that the idea of a trust of a contractual right is not a very useful means of evading the privity rule, although it is still theoretically available in cases which come within its narrow ambit. In view of the 1999 legislation offering a more straightforward method of conferring an enforceable right on a third party, it is unlikely that the trust argument will be of much practical significance in the future. (For an unsuccessful attempt to rely on the trust argument, see *Rolls Royce Power Engineering plc* v *Ricardo Consulting Engineers Ltd* (2003) at [104]–[117].)

Assignment

17.48 The idea of assignment of contractual rights represents another limit on the doctrine of privity. A party to a contract may, in certain circumstances, assign (transfer) his or her existing contractual rights to a third party. For example, a creditor (A) may assign his or her rights against a debtor (B) to a third party (C). By means of such a transaction, C acquires rights against B, as a result of standing in the place of A. The consent of the debtor (B) to such an assignment is not required, although he or she must normally be notified of the transaction. It is argued that B is not at a disadvantage under this type of transaction, as the identity of the creditor usually does not matter to B. In its Consultation Paper on the doctrine of privity, the Law Commission stated that 'the practical importance of assignment is considerable; the whole industry of debt collection and credit factoring depends upon it' (see Law Commission Paper 121, 1991, p. 51).

17.49 Although the law generally permits the assignment of contractual rights, this is subject to the provisos that such transactions must not be unfair to the debtor and must not be contrary to the public interest. In particular, it should be noted that rights arising out of 'personal' contracts are incapable of assignment. For example, where A employs B to perform certain services, it would be unfair to permit A to assign his or her contractual rights to C. So an employer is not entitled to transfer the benefit of his or her employee's services to a third party. In view of the willingness of the law to allow the assignment of existing contractual rights to a third party, it made the inflexibility of the privity doctrine, prior to 1999, difficult to understand. In the words of the Law Commission (Law Com 242, 1996, para. 2.17): 'If an immediate assignment is valid, there can hardly be fundamental objections to allowing the third party to sue without an assignment.'

Agency

17.50 Another important limit on the ambit of the privity rule is provided by the doctrine of agency. Under the law of agency, when an agent (B) makes a contract with a third party (C) on behalf of his or her principal (A), this is treated by the law as if the principal had himself made the contract. A and C may sue one another for breach of that contract. However, this 'exception' to the doctrine of privity is perhaps more apparent than real. The law is simply treating A and B as one person. The agent, acting on behalf of his or her principal, makes a contract between his or her principal and a third party.

17.51 However, the law goes further by permitting A to enforce a contract made on his behalf by B, despite the fact that C was unaware that B was acting on A's behalf. (Of course, A must prove that B did in fact have his or her authority to make the contract with C.) This idea of the 'undisclosed principal' appears to be at variance with the doctrine of privity and it can, perhaps, be justified only on the basis of commercial convenience. The third party is contractually bound to a person with whom he or she did not intend to contract and of whose existence he or she was unaware. (For discussion of whether the doctrine of the undisclosed principal can be reconciled with the privity rule, see Tan Cheng-Han, 'Undisclosed Principals and Contract' (2004) 120 LQR 480.)

17.52 Despite the obvious potential for evading the doctrine of privity through the idea of agency, the courts have been reluctant to imply an agency simply for this purpose. A person has to do more than merely claim that a contract was made on his or her behalf. For there to be an agency, one person has to acquire the authority to be the representative of another (see *Southern Water Authority* v *Carey* (1985)). For example, an agent may have the express authority of his or her principal to act as his or her representative, or such authority may be implied as a result of the relationship between the parties. In either case, it is said that the agent has 'actual' authority. Agency may also arise in other circumstances. For example, unless a third party is notified to the contrary, he or she is entitled to rely on an agent's 'apparent' authority to represent another. So where A represents to C that he or she has given B authority to act as his or her representative, C is entitled to assume that B has the authority which he or she appears to have. (For a discussion of the scope of this doctrine, see *First Energy (UK) Ltd* v *Hungarian International Bank Ltd* (1993).)

17.53 The extent of the courts' willingness to accept an agency argument, as a means of circumventing the privity doctrine, was discussed at the start of this chapter in relation to attempts by third parties to rely on an exclusion clause. Here the issue is whether a third party can claim the benefit of an exclusion clause as a defence to an action by one of the contracting parties under a separate cause of action (usually negligence). It will be remembered that in *Scruttons Ltd* v *Midland Silicones Ltd* [1962] AC 446, the House of Lords held that the stevedores (third party) were not entitled to rely on the limitation of liability contained in the bill of lading, when sued in tort for their negligence in unloading the goods. The doctrine of privity prevented the stevedores from relying on a contract to which they were not a party in defending the action. The argument of the stevedores that they were the undisclosed principals of one of the contracting parties (the carrier), who acted as their agent, was also unsuccessful. Lord Reid set out (at 474) the conditions which needed to be satisfied for the agency argument to succeed. He explained that the bill of lading must make it clear that the stevedore is intended to be protected by its provisions which limit liability. The bill of lading must make it clear that the carrier, as well as contracting for these provisions on his or her own behalf, is also contracting as an agent for the stevedore, who will in turn be protected by the provisions. The carrier needs the stevedore's authority to act in this way, and any problems of consideration must be overcome.

17.54 Although the stevedores were unsuccessful with this agency argument in *Scruttons Ltd* v *Midland Silicones Ltd* (1962), it will be recalled that the Privy Council, in *New Zealand Shipping Co. Ltd* v *Satterthwaite* (1974), allowed the stevedores the protection of an exemption clause. In *Satterthwaite*, the court held (inter alia) that the bill of lading was not simply a contract between the owners of the goods and the carrier. It also represented a contract between the owners and the stevedores, made through the carrier as agent. (See also *Port Jackson Stevedoring Pty* v *Salmond & Spraggon (Australia) Pty* (1980).) Despite the success of the agency argument in these cases, it provides a rather technical and uncertain solution to the problem. (For example, see *The Mahkutai* (1996).) The courts naturally wish to take a practical approach to everyday commercial transactions, but a simpler solution is preferable to the one offered by the agency approach. A more convenient way of conferring such a benefit on a third party is now available under the new legislation (see earlier discussion). In C(RTP)A 1999, references to a third party enforcing a contractual term are to be understood as including the right to rely on an exclusion or limitation clause (see s 1(6)).

Privity and the doctrine of consideration

17.55 In *Dunlop Pneumatic Tyre Co. Ltd* v *Selfridge & Co. Ltd* [1915] AC 847, Lord Haldane LC (at 853) referred to the fundamental principles in English law that 'only a person who is a party to a contract can sue on it . . . [and] that if a person with whom a contract not under seal has been made is to be able to enforce it consideration must have been given by him to the promisor or to some other person at the promisor's request'. If we reconsider *Tweddle* v *Atkinson* (1861) (discussed at the start of this chapter), the decision could be explained in terms of either lack of privity, or lack of consideration provided by the son-in-law. However, there has been much debate as to whether the privity doctrine is distinct and independent from the rule that consideration must move from the promisee, with academic opinion being quite divided on the subject.[5]

17.56 The phrase 'consideration must move from the promisee' is a little enigmatic, but it is generally accepted as meaning that a person can enforce a contractual promise only if he himself provided the consideration for that promise; that is, consideration must have been provided by the claimant. When the phrase is understood in this sense, it is clear that it is not possible to 'reform the privity doctrine while leaving untouched the rule that consideration must move from the promisee' (see Law Commission Report, No 242, Privity of Contract: Contracts for the Benefit of Third Parties', 1996, para. 6.5), because the two doctrines are very closely linked. Accordingly, the Law Commission recommended that the legislation reforming the privity doctrine 'should ensure that the rule that consideration must move from the promisee is reformed to the extent necessary to avoid nullifying [the] proposed reform of the doctrine of privity' (para. 6.8). In the event, it was realized that a specific provision to this effect was unnecessary. It would be achieved by the central provision of the new law (i.e. C(RTP)A 1999, s 1) conferring a third party right to enforce a contractual term, as such a provision could only be interpreted as also reforming the rule that consideration must move from the promisee.

17.57 The Law Commission also addressed the wider policy implications, for the doctrine of consideration,[6] of reforming the privity rule (Law Com No 242, paras **6.13–6.17**). It was concerned, in particular, with the argument that a third party's right to enforce a contractual term puts him or her in a better position than a gratuitous promisee. However, by permitting an identified third party to enforce a contractual term, under C(RTP)A 1999, s 1, the law is giving effect to the intentions of the contracting parties, who have provided consideration; the bargain is being enforced, albeit by the third party. It can be argued that this situation is

5 See Law Commission Report, No 242, *Privity of Contract: Contracts for the Benefit of Third Parties*, Cm 3329, 1996, para. 6.1.

6 See also C. Mitchell, 'Privity Reform and the Nature of Contractual Obligations' (1999) 19 LS 229.

distinguishable from the one in which no consideration is given by a promisee in exchange for a promise (i.e. the gratuitous promisee); here, there is no bargain to be enforced, as no consideration was present.

17.58 The specific problem of whether a 'joint promisee' who has provided none of the consideration under a contract can sue, is one which requires some discussion. Where a promise is made in favour of A and B, in circumstances where they can be regarded as joint promisees but only A provides any consideration, can B enforce the promise? This problem was raised in the Australian case of *Coulls* v *Bagot's Executor and Trustee Co. Ltd* [1967] ALR 385, where the facts were:

> Arthur Coulls agreed to give to the O'Neil Construction Co. the sole right to quarry and remove stone from his land. The agreement continued: 'O'Neil Construction Ltd agrees to pay at the rate of 3d per ton for all stone quarried and sold, also a fixed minimum royalty of £12 per week for a period of ten years with an option of another ten years [at the same rate] . . . I [Arthur Coulls] authorise the above Company to pay all money connected with this agreement to my wife, Doris Coulls and myself, Arthur Coulls as joint tenants.' This written agreement (not under seal) was signed by Arthur Coulls, Doris Coulls, and O'Neil. After the death of Arthur Coulls, the O'Neil Company paid the royalty to Doris Coulls as agreed. The action involved a dispute between Arthur Coulls's executors and his wife as to who should receive the royalty payments.

It was held by a majority of the High Court of Australia that after Arthur Coulls's death, the O'Neil Company was bound to pay the royalties to his estate and not to his wife. Three of the judges thought that Doris Coulls was not a party to the agreement and that the authority given by her husband to the company under the agreement, to make payments to her, lapsed on his death (i.e. she was not a promisee). It was thought significant that the husband had 'authorized' payment to his wife; she was not entitled to payment in her own right. However, Barwick CJ and Windeyer J dissented, as they considered Doris Coulls to be a joint promisee. (The majority of the court were of the opinion that a joint promisee could sue even though he or she had provided no consideration.) In his judgment, Barwick CJ argued (at 395) that the agreement was one in respect of which there was privity between the company and both the husband and wife, as joint promisees. Windeyer J (at 403) thought that the promise of the company was to pay for the stone at the agreed rate, with 'such payments to be made to the husband and wife jointly during their lives and thereafter to the survivor'. Windeyer J went on to consider her apparent lack of consideration for the promise (at 405):

> Still, it was said, no consideration moved from her. But that, I consider, mistakes the nature of a contract made with two or more persons jointly. The promise is made to them collectively. It must, of course, be supported by consideration, but that does not mean by considerations furnished by them separately. It means a consideration given on behalf of them all, and therefore moving from all of them. In such a case the promise of the promisor is not gratuitous: and, as between him and the joint promisees, it matters not how they were able to provide the price of his promise to them.

17.59 The Law Commission (Law Com No 242, para. 6.10) argued that a joint promisee should have the right to sue despite not having provided the consideration. (See also *McEvoy* v *Belfast Banking Co. Ltd* [1935] AC 24 at 43 per Lord Atkin.) However, the Commission did not include such joint promisees within its reform proposals, for a variety of reasons which need not be considered here. It thought it preferable to leave the matter to the courts to develop 'in the confident expectation' that, especially in view of the statutory reform of the privity doctrine, they will accept the joint promisee argument 'so that a joint promisee who has not provided consideration will not be left without a basic right to enforce the contract' (at para. 6.11). In the words of one recent commentator on C(RTP)A 1999, an 'acceptable source of judicial creativity might be development of the existing joint promisee doctrine. Perhaps that rule is elastic enough to allow the court to fill any gaps in the legislative scheme' (see N. Andrews, 'Strangers to Justice No Longer: The Reversal of the Privity Rule under the Contracts (Rights of Third Parties) Act 1999' (2001) 60 CLJ 353 at 379).

Conclusion

17.60 The doctrine of privity has traditionally represented the principle that only a party to a contract can enforce a benefit, or have burdens imposed on him or her, under that contract. The restriction on a third party being able to enforce a provision which was intended for his or her benefit meant that the intentions of the contracting parties could be thwarted, and the reasonable expectations of the third party denied, by the doctrine. This necessitated a series of technical, and sometimes artificial, methods of evading the strict application of the privity rule. Also, a number of statutory exceptions were required to circumvent the doctrine in areas of commercial practice where its application was extremely inconvenient.

17.61 After repeated judicial and academic criticism over many years, and a detailed Law Commission report on the subject, the law was finally reformed by means of the important Contracts (Rights of Third Parties) Act 1999. However, the Act does not apply to all types of contract; nor does it directly affect the existing exceptions to, and circumventions of, the doctrine. It introduces a new, and more general, exception into the law, but the doctrine of privity was not abolished by the Act. The Law Commission (Law Com No 242, para. 5.10) also expressed the view that the new Act should not be interpreted as preventing the future development of third party rights through the common law. (For example, see *London Drugs Ltd* v *Kuehne & Nagel International Ltd* (1992); for further discussion of the *London Drugs* case, and the role of the courts in making 'incremental changes to the common law necessary to address emerging needs and values in society', see *Fraser River Pile and Dredge Ltd* v *Can-Drive Services Ltd* (2000) per Iacobucci J at 208–9.[7])

17.62 Finally, the aspect of the privity rule which states that a third party cannot have burdens imposed upon him or her by the contracting parties has not been affected by the 1999

7 For a discussion of this and other Canadian Supreme Court decisions, see M. Ogilvie, 'Privity of Contract in the Supreme Court of Canada: Fare Thee Well or Welcome Back?' (2002) JBL 163.

legislation. It should be noted, however, that certain contractual restrictions on the use of land are said to 'run with the land' and can therefore burden people other than the original contracting parties. (The debate as to whether this principle has a wider application, beyond the boundaries of land law, requires no further elaboration here.)

Summary

- Privity of contract, that is, that only a party to a contract can enforce a right under that contract (the 'third party rule') or have obligations imposed on him or her by the contract, is a long-established principle of English law.
- The third party rule was capable of disappointing reasonable contractual and commercial expectations.
- Judicial and academic opinion supported reform of the third party rule, despite the many exceptions to and circumventions of the rule which are available.
- The common law privity doctrine has been reformed, not abolished, by the Contracts (Rights of Third Parties) Act 1999, which was based largely on a Law Commission Report (1996).
- The Act does not affect the existing exceptions to (or evasions of) the privity doctrine, but it introduced a new and more general exception to the doctrine.
- Under the Act (s 1(1)), a third party can enforce a term of a contract in his or her own right if (a) the contract expressly provides for this, or (b) the term purports to confer on him or her a benefit (unless it appears that the contracting parties did not intend the term to be enforceable by the third party).
- Where a third party right has been conferred, there are general restrictions (under s 2(1)) on the freedom of the contracting parties to vary or cancel their agreement subsequently, in the absence of any express provision in the contract (s 2(3)).
- The third party's right to enforce a term is subject to the defences that would have been available to the promisor in an action by the promisee, unless there is an express term to the contrary (s 3).
- The conferral of an enforceable right on a third party does not affect the right of the promisee to enforce any contractual term (s 4), with suitable protection for the promisor against 'double liability' (s 5).
- Certain types of contract remain outside the scope of the Act (s 6), although the provisions of the Arbitration Act 1996 may apply to a third party (s 8).
- The right of enforceability under s 1 does not affect any right (or remedy) of a third party which is available to him or her elsewhere than in the Act (s 7).
- The Act has not affected the aspect of the privity rule which states that a third party cannot have burdens imposed on him or her (subject to certain exceptions) by the contracting parties.

Further reading

N. Andrews, 'Strangers to Justice No Longer: The Reversal of the Privity Rule under the Contracts (Rights of Third Parties) Act 1999' (2001) 60 CLJ 353

H. Beale, 'A Review of the Contracts (Rights of Third Parties) Act 1999' in A. Burrows and E. Peel (eds) *Contract Formation and Parties*, Oxford University Press, 2010, pp. 225–50

A. Burrows, 'The Contracts (Rights of Third Parties) Act and Its Implications for Commercial Contracts' (2000) 4 LMCLQ 540

T. Cheng-Han, 'Undisclosed Principals and Contract' (2004) 120 LQR 480

M. Dean, 'Removing a Blot on the Landscape—The Reform of the Doctrine of Privity' [2000] JBL 143

R. Flannigan, 'Privity—The End of an Era (Error)' (1987) 103 LQR 564

P. Kincaid, 'Privity Reform in England' (2000) 116 LQR 43

Law Commission Report, No 242, 'Privity of Contract: Contracts for the Benefit of Third Parties', Cm 3329, 1996

C. MacMillan, 'A Birthday Present for Lord Denning: The Contracts (Rights of Third Parties) Act 1999' (2000) 63 MLR 721

C. Mitchell, 'Privity Reform and the Nature of Contractual Obligations' (1999) 19 LS 229

P. Rawlings, 'Third Party Rights in Contract' (2006) 7 LMCLQ 7

M. Reynolds, 'When Principle and Precedent Collide: Panatown' (2003) 8(1) Con & Eng Law 13

R. Stevens, 'The Contracts (Rights of Third Parties) Act 1999' (2004) 120 LQR 292

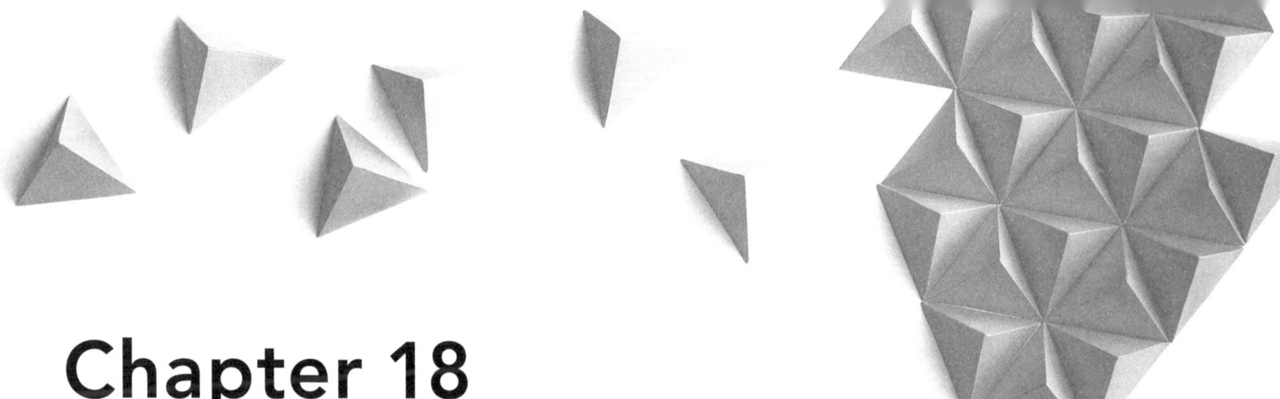

Chapter 18

Performance and breach

Performance

Discharge by performance and agreement

18.1 Although we are often considering the situation where something has gone wrong with a contract, most contracts are performed without any problems arising. The usual way in which a party to a contract ceases to have any obligations under the contract is by doing what the contract requires. Where performance has been completed, and liability has ceased, the situation is referred to as 'discharge by performance'.

18.2 What is required for performance of the contract will depend upon its express and implied terms and their construction (see **Chapter 7**). Often no fault will be required for a breach to occur, that is, contractual obligations are often a matter of strict liability. For example, the terms implied by ss 12–15 of the Sale of Goods Act 1979, dealing with the title and the quality of the goods, impose strict liability. They can be breached without any fault on the part of the seller. In contrast, terms requiring the exercise of a particular skill or expertise will normally require only that due care be taken in the exercise of the skill or expertise (see, e.g., Supply of Goods and Services Act 1982, s 13; *Thake* v *Maurice* (1986)—see para. **7.7**).

18.3 A breach will arise if there is disparity between what was promised and what has occurred, or not occurred, and there is no lawful excuse. The burden of proving that a breach has occurred lies on the party alleging that it has. Frustration (see **Chapter 19**) provides an example of 'lawful excuse' for non-performance. It discharges both parties from further performance of the contract.

18.4 The parties may provide that the contract itself, or some of the obligations under it, are not to be immediately effective. A condition precedent may suspend entirely the formation of the contract, or it may not delay formation itself but merely the operation of some, or all, of the obligations under the contract. Obviously there can be no breach as long as the contract, or the particular obligation, has not become operative. In *Pym* v *Campbell* (1856) the situation was perceived as one where prior to the fulfilment of the contingency there was no contract in existence. In that case, the facts were:

> The claimant wished to sell to the defendant a share in an invention of the claimant. A written document appeared to contain an agreement for the purchase. The claimant sought to rely upon it, but the defendant established that the parties had further agreed that the written document was to be the agreement only if the claimant's invention was approved of by a third party, Abernethie. Abernethie had not given his approval of the invention.

The court concluded that there was no contract at all. Abernethie's approval was a condition precedent to the existence of the contract. There was no contract and no breach by the defendant. However, it may be that a condition precedent merely suspends some of the obligations until it is fulfilled and other obligations may be operative prior to the contingency being fulfilled, including subsidiary obligations in relation to the contingency. So, for example, in *Marten* v *Whale* (1917) where the obligation to sell land was subject to the purchaser's solicitor's approval of the title, the obligation to make the sale was suspended until the contingency was fulfilled (which it was not), but prior to that the purchaser had to ensure that it was possible for that approval to be given.

18.5 The parties may have provided that the contract is to end upon the occurrence of a certain circumstance—a condition subsequent. A condition subsequent is a condition upon the fulfilment of which an existing contract is extinguished. *Head* v *Tattersall* (1871) is the case usually quoted in this context:

> A horse was sold on the basis that it had been hunted with the Bicester hounds. It was expressly stated by the seller that if it had not been so hunted the buyer could return it by 5 pm on the following Wednesday. Before that time arrived the horse was injured and the buyer discovered that it had not been hunted with the Bicester hounds. The buyer had not been at fault with regard to the injury to the horse.

It was held that the buyer could return the horse, despite its injury, because it had not been hunted with the Bicester hounds.

18.6 The contract may also provide one party with an option to end the contract under certain circumstances. Those circumstances could include a breach by the other party which would not otherwise give rise to the right to terminate (i.e. the breach is not a breach of condition or a sufficiently serious breach of an innominate term). When that occurs, the damages awarded for the breach will not cover the loss of the rest of the contract, as they would do if the breach itself gave rise to the right to terminate.[1]

1 See para. **8.35** and *Financings Ltd* v *Baldock* (1963). But see also *Lombard North Central plc* v *Butterworth* (1987), para. **8.35**.

18.7 The original contract may not provide for its termination but the parties may make a new agreement to end the original contract, that is, a contract may be discharged by agreement. Any such fresh agreement raises the issue of consideration unless it is contained in a deed (see **Chapter 4**). There is no problem where it is decided to end a contract which is still executory, when both parties still have obligations to perform. The giving up of rights on each side will furnish the necessary consideration. The situation is more difficult where only one party still has to perform. That party should then supply fresh consideration for the agreement to end the original contract, but the decision in *Williams* v *Roffey Bros & Nicholls (Contractors) Ltd* (1990) (see para. **4.39**ff) on what can constitute consideration should be borne in mind—as should the possibilities of waiver or promissory estoppel (see **Chapter 5**). The same consideration problems arise where the parties agree to change their agreement rather than end it. In addition, formality issues may arise where the original contract was one requiring formalities.

Order of performance and independent obligations

18.8 The order of performance may be indicated by contingent conditions. For example, the fulfilment by A of an obligation under the contract he has made with B may be a condition precedent to B's performance. If the performance of an obligation of one party, A, is a condition precedent to the other party's, B's, liability to perform, then the contract is safer for B than for A: B will not be left in the situation where he has performed and A refuses to do so. The same, of course, does not apply to A. Whether the contract makes A's performance a condition precedent to B's liability may depend upon B's superior bargaining power, or the practicalities of the situation, or simply what is usual in a particular type of contract. In *Trans Trust SPRL* v *Danubian Trading Co. Ltd* (1952) there was a contract for the sale of 1,000 tons of rolled steel. There was an obligation on the buyer to open a confirmed letter of credit to pay for the steel. It was necessary that the buyer should open the letter of credit before the seller became liable to deliver. It was known to both parties that the seller could not obtain the goods until the letter of credit was opened. The obligation to open the letter of credit was construed as a condition precedent to the seller's obligation to deliver. The seller did not have to perform until the buyer had done so.

18.9 Concurrent conditions also indicate the order of performance. For example, in sale of goods contracts, in the absence of contrary intention, Sale of Goods Act 1979, s 28 makes the seller's obligation to deliver, and the buyer's obligation to pay, concurrent conditions. Each party must be willing to perform his or her obligation in order to claim that the other should do so. The concurrent condition provides some security for each party's performance.

18.10 However, many contractual obligations are independent of each other. Their performance is not linked to that of the other party and non-performance may not provide an excuse for the other's failure to perform. For example, the landlord's obligation to repair and the tenant's to pay rent were held to be independent of each other and the landlord's failure to repair did not justify the tenant in refusing to pay the rent (*Taylor* v *Webb* (1937)).

Entire contracts

18.11 We have already seen that contingent promissory conditions may set the order of performance. The performance of an obligation of one party may be a condition precedent to the other party becoming obliged to perform. This can lead to cases where the situation is that of an 'entire contract' and one party is obliged to perform his or her side of the contract before the other party becomes obliged to pay him or her. The harsh result which can be achieved in such cases is illustrated by *Cutter* v *Powell* (1795):

> Mr Cutter had signed on as second mate on the Governor Parry for a voyage from Jamaica to Liverpool. It was stated that he would receive 30 guineas 'provided he proceeds, continues and does his duty' from Jamaica to Liverpool. The ship sailed on 2 August and arrived at Liverpool on 9 October. Unfortunately, Mr Cutter died on 20 September, before the ship reached Liverpool. His widow was suing for payment for the work he had done before his death. The usual rate of pay was £4 per month. The voyage was one which should have taken about two months.

The court held that the contract was entire. There was no obligation to pay for any work done unless the voyage was completed and, as Mr Cutter did not complete the voyage, his widow could not claim any payment. Mr Cutter's completion of the voyage was a condition precedent to the obligation to pay for the work he had done. This seems harsh, but the court was obviously influenced in its conclusion by the fact that 30 guineas was much greater than the sum which he would have expected to earn under a contract based on payment by the month rather than for the whole voyage. Lord Kenyon CJ said:

> He stipulated to receive the larger sum if the whole duty were performed, and nothing unless the whole of that duty were performed; it was a kind of insurance.

In other words, there was good reason, in the amount contracted for, to regard Mr Cutter's completion of the voyage as a condition precedent to any obligation to pay him. The conclusion reached in *Cutter* v *Powell* (1795) would have been otherwise if the contract had not been entire but severable, that is, if the obligation to act as second mate from Jamaica to Liverpool had been divided up so that the corresponding obligation was to pay so much for each month of the voyage. Finding that a contract is severable rather than entire is one way of avoiding the sort of result that was reached in *Cutter* v *Powell*.[2]

18.12 *Sumpter* v *Hedges* [1898] 1 QB 673 provides another example of the operation of the rule on entire contracts. In that case:

2 In relation to salaries or wages the common law is assisted by Apportionment Act 1870, s 2 which states that 'all rents, annuities, dividends, and other periodical payments in the nature of income . . . shall . . . be considered as accruing from day to day'.

Mr Hedges contracted with Mr Sumpter for Mr Sumpter to build two houses on his land for the sum of £565. Mr Sumpter did part of the work, to the value of £333, but his financial circumstances were such that he could not complete the work. Mr Hedges finished the houses himself. In doing so he made use of unused materials which belonged to Mr Sumpter and which he had left on Mr Hedges' land.

The question was whether Mr Sumpter could recover payment in relation to the work which he had carried out in erecting the houses. The court said that he could not. The contract was for a lump sum to be paid upon completion of the houses and he could not succeed in his claim when he had not done that.

18.13 Some mitigation of the entire contracts rule occurs when the work done by one party is adopted by the other party, whom it has benefited. The benefiting party will then have to pay for the work done. (The action is then one for quantum meruit—a restitutionary action: see **web chapter 2**.) On the same basis, Mr Hedges paid Mr Sumpter the value of Mr Sumpter's materials which he, Mr Hedges, had used on the houses after Mr Sumpter stopped work. He did not have to pay for the work Mr Sumpter had done on the houses because it could not be said that his adoption of the work was a matter on which he could act 'voluntarily'. He did not have sufficient choice in the matter. He either had to finish the houses himself or have the nuisance of incomplete buildings on his land. In contrast, he had a fully effective range of choices open to him when he decided to use Mr Sumpter's materials in the completion of the houses.

18.14 However, the greater mitigation of the entire contracts rule came with the idea of 'substantial performance'. In *Hoenig* v *Isaacs* [1952] 2 All ER 176:

Mr Isaacs contracted with Mr Hoenig for the decoration and furnishing of his flat for £750. Mr Hoenig fulfilled the contract except in relation to some defects in a bookcase and a wardrobe, costing about £55 to rectify.

Mr Hoenig was able to recover the sum due under the contract, less the sum Mr Isaacs could claim in damages for the defects (the cost of putting them right). Mr Hoenig had 'substantially performed'.

'Substantial performance' may simply be a matter of correctly identifying what is required for fulfilment of the condition precedent. Somervell LJ distinguished the case before him from that of *Cutter* v *Powell* (1795). He said (at 178):

> [*Cutter* v *Powell*] clearly decided that his continuing as mate during the whole of the voyage was a condition precedent to payment. It did not decide that if he had completed the main purpose of the contract, namely serving as mate for the whole voyage, the defendant could have repudiated his liability by establishing that in the course of the voyage, the sailor had, possibly through inadvertence, failed on some occasion in his duty as mate whereby some damage had been caused.

He continued (at 179):

> The question here is whether in a contract for work and labour for a lump sum payable on completion the defendant can repudiate liability under the contract on the ground that the work though 'finished' or 'done' is in some respects not in accordance with the contract.

18.15 As Somervell LJ indicated in *Hoenig* v *Isaacs* (1952), the idea of 'substantial performance' depends upon asking whether the work has been 'done', albeit with defects. In *Bolton* v *Mahadeva* [1972] 2 All ER 1322, the idea of 'substantial performance' did not entitle the contractor to recover. In that case:

> Mr Mahadeva had contracted with Mr Bolton for the installation of a central heating system for £560. The system was defective and it would have cost about £175 to make it function correctly. There were fumes in the living room and, on average, the house was 10 per cent less warm than it should have been, although in some rooms it was as much as 30 per cent colder.

Mr Bolton had not 'substantially performed' and could not recover the contract price with damages for the defects set off against it. Here the judgments indicate a general assessment of the extent to which the performance carried out differs from that required by the contract. Cairns LJ said (at 1324):

> The main question in the case is whether the defects in workmanship . . . were of such character and amount that the claimant could not be said to have substantially performed his contract. That is, in my view, clearly the legal principle which has to be applied in cases of this kind.

The explanation of substantial performance being sufficient to enable a claim to payment to be made may be that:

> it is frequently correct to say that absolutely exact and complete performance by the claimant is not a condition precedent to the duty of the defendant. If substantial performance by the claimant was sufficient to charge the defendant, then such substantial performance was the only condition and the requirement has been exactly fulfilled. (Corbin, 'Conditions in the Law of Contract' (1919) 28 Yale LJ 739 at 759)

18.16 The Law Commission has criticized cases such as *Bolton* v *Mahadeva* (1972) and recommended that the party whose performance is not in keeping with the contract, and whom the entire contracts rule deprives of payment, should receive some payment for the benefit he or she has conferred on the other party (Law Com Report, No 121, *Pecuniary Restitution for Breach of Contract*, 1983). But there has been no move to implement that recommendation and Brian Davenport QC added a strong note of dissent to the report. He concluded that, in almost all contracts of any substance, provision is now made for staged payment (i.e. payment as and when a stage of the work is completed), thus avoiding the problem posed by the entire contracts rule.

However, he thought that the rule served a useful purpose which the majority's recommendation would undermine. He stated:

> The so-called mischief which the report is intended to correct is therefore likely only to exist in relation to small, informal contracts of which the normal example will be a contract between a householder and a jobbing builder to carry out a particular item of work. Experience has shown that it is all too common for such builders not to complete one job of work before moving on to the next. The effect of the report is to remove from the householder almost the only effective sanction he has against the builder not completing the job. In short he is prevented from saying with any legal effect, 'Unless you come back and finish the job I shan't pay you a penny'.

Breach

18.17 A breach of contract may provide the injured party with a right to damages (see **Chapter 20**), or he or she may be able to sue for the contract price if it has become due. On occasion, equity may provide specific enforcement of the whole or part of the other party's obligations. In addition, the question may arise of using a restitutionary remedy to recover sums paid or the value of goods or services supplied (see **web chapter 2**). Consideration may also need to be given to relief from forfeiture for the party in breach.

18.18 However, one of the often disputed consequences of breach is that of the right to terminate the contract. In addition to a common law right to terminate, the parties may accrue a contractual right to terminate, if for example, the agreement between them includes a notice of termination (See further *Phones 4U Ltd (In Administration)* v *EE Ltd* (2018).) When certain breaches occur, the injured party has a choice whether to terminate the contract.

Termination for breach

18.19 An injured party has a right to damages for any breach. However, we have also seen that the injured party occasionally also has the right to terminate the contract because of the other party's breach. So, for example, there is a right to terminate if there is a breach of condition or if there is a sufficiently serious breach of an innominate term (i.e. a breach which substantially deprives the injured party of all the benefit which he or she was intended to derive from the contract—*Hong Kong Fir Shipping Co. Ltd* v *Kawasaki Kisen Kaisha Ltd* (1962): see **Chapter 8**). Such terms are labelled according to the intention of the parties at the time of contracting (*Bunge Corpn* v *Tradax Export SA* (1981)—see para. **8.5**). (Although the main focus here is on commercial agreements, note the amendments to consumer contracts which have been brought about by the Consumer Rights Act 2015 such that different remedies are available (see e.g. ss 20–24); that the consumer no longer has the common law right to treat a contract to supply goods as at an end where the breach is of a term required by the Act to be treated as included in the contract (see e.g. s 19); and further that this is the new terminology which is applied in a consumer context (see para. **8.4**)).

18.20 However, one party may repudiate the contract. He or she may indicate that he or she no longer intends to be bound by it, and that may be done in the context of an actual breach or an anticipatory breach (see para. **18.21**). The injured party will have the right to terminate where the other party gives 'an intimation of an intention to abandon and altogether refuse performance of the contract . . . [or of] an intention no longer to be bound by the contract' (*Freeth* v *Burr* (1874) LR 9 CP 208 at 213 per Lord Coleridge). If the injured party elects to accept the repudiation, the contract will be terminated (*Geys* v *Société Générale* (2012)). Yet, determining whether the contract has been repudiated may be difficult. It can occur as a consequence of the party stating that he or she will not perform or, more problematically, by the parties' actions. For example, one party may allege that the other has rendered it impossible for him or her to perform the instant contract because that party has undertaken other obligations. It will then be a matter of finding whether those other obligations are 'of such a nature or have such an effect that it can truly be said that the party in question has put it out of his power to perform' (*Alfred C Toepfer International GmbH* v *Itex Itagrani Export SA* [1993] 1 Lloyd's Rep 360 at 362). Another example of an area where difficulties arise is that of instalment contracts to be performed over a period of time. In *Decro-Wall International SA* v *Practitioners Marketing Ltd* (1971), the facts were:

> The claimants, a French manufacturing company, made a contract with the defendants giving the defendants the sole right to sell their products in the United Kingdom. The defendants undertook to develop the UK market for the claimants' goods and were very successful in doing so. However, the defendants were obliged to pay for a batch of goods within 90 days of receiving it and they were often late in paying. Despite the successful market development by the defendants, the claimants chose to terminate the contract for late payment by the defendants. The claimants never doubted that they would receive payment for goods delivered, even though it might often be late. The lateness of the payments caused them little damage.

The question for the Court of Appeal was 'whether these past failures to pay on the due date, coupled with the likelihood of similar failures, constituted a repudiation of the contract' which entitled the claimants to terminate. The Court of Appeal held that the termination had not been justified. The breaches which had occurred, and what was likely to happen in the future, did not go to the root of the contract.

18.21 The intention of the party in breach is relevant in this situation as it is in relation to an anticipatory breach; a mistake as to the requirements of the contract may be relevant here as with anticipatory breach, that is, the party in breach may think that what he or she intends to do in the future will amount to performance, whereas it will in fact amount to breach. There is difficulty with the court's treatment of such intention (see para. **18.32**ff).

18.22 When a breach occurs which could lead to termination, the injured party has a choice (*Decro-Wall International SA* v *Practitioners in Marketing Ltd* (1971); *Geys* v *Société Générale* (2012)). He or she can terminate or he or she can decide to continue with the contract, to affirm it, in which case he or she is simply left with his or her remedy in damages. The injured party does have time to decide whether to affirm or terminate, but doing nothing for too long may be seen as affirmation (*Stocznia Gdanska SA* v *Latvian Shipping (No 3)* (2002) per Rix LJ). Once affirmation has occurred, the injured party can no longer terminate for that breach, but if the breach is continuing or fresh breaches occur then the possibility of terminating is again present (*Stocznia Gdanska*). As has been indicated, if the injured party behaves as if he or she has decided to continue with the contract, then that can amount to affirmation provided that the injured party knew, or should have known, of the facts giving rise to the right to terminate, and possibly of the existence of that right. However, if he or she does not have such knowledge, and has not been in a position where he or she should have had such knowledge, actions indicating the continuance of the contract will not constitute affirmation, but the injured party may be estopped from terminating if the party in breach has acted in reliance on the representation of affirmation created by the injured party's actions (*The Kanchenjunga* (1990)).

18.23 Termination for breach is sometimes referred to as 'rescission' of the contract, and this can be confusing. It is better to confine the use of the word 'rescission' to the context of voidable contracts, for example where the contract has been made on the basis of a misrepresentation. In that context rescission is 'rescission ab initio': it is as if the contract had never existed. In the context of breach, rescission merely relates to the future.

> [R]escission [for breach] is quite different from rescission ab initio, such as may arise for example in cases of mistake, fraud or lack of consent. In those cases the contract is treated in law as never having come into existence . . . In the cases of an accepted repudiatory breach the contract has come into existence but has been put an end to or discharged . . . acceptance of a repudiatory breach does not bring about rescission ab initio. (*Johnson* v *Agnew* [1979] 1 All ER 883 at 889 per Lord Wilberforce)

18.24 It is easier not to confuse the two situations if we refer to termination, rather than rescission, in relation to breach. What occurs on termination for breach can be more easily understood if we think of the contract in terms of primary and secondary obligations. The division is between the basic promised performance (primary obligations) and the obligations which arise on breach (secondary obligations). When X and Y have made a contract under which X is to build a wall for Y, and Y is to pay X for doing so, then the primary obligations relate to the building of the wall and the payment of money. When X refuses to build the wall, or builds a defective wall, there is a breach of X's primary obligations and the secondary obligation on X to pay damages arises. If the breach is merely a minor defect in the wall, Y will be able to claim damages from X for the breach and X and Y will still be liable to perform any further primary obligations. However, when X's breach is such as to entitle Y to terminate the contract, and he or she chooses to do so, the primary obligations cease, but damages are still calculated in relation to the promised performance. There is no question of the situation becoming one where the contract is treated as if it had never existed. In *Photo Production Ltd* v *Securicor Transport Ltd* [1980] 1 All ER 556 Lord Diplock analysed the situation in relation to the unperformed obligations, in terms of primary and secondary obligations, and made the continuing role of the contract clear. He said (at 567):

> [W]here such an election [to terminate] is made (a) there is substituted by implication of law for the primary obligations of the party in default which remain unperformed a secondary obligation to pay monetary compensation to the other party for the loss sustained by him in consequence of their non-performance in the future and (b) the unperformed primary obligations of that other party are discharged.

When there is a breach which gives rise to termination, the party in breach must pay damages for the immediate consequences of the breach and, in addition, for the loss caused by the non-performance of the rest of his or her primary obligations. In the secondary obligations the continued life of the contract is clear, as is the distinction between termination for breach and rescission ab initio.

18.25 A situation may arise in which one party claims to be able to terminate, because of the breach of the other, but he or she gives a reason which does not in fact justify termination. If, at the time of termination, there is another, unstated reason which would justify that termination, then it can usually be relied upon by the party who is terminating to prevent his or her actions from themselves being a repudiatory breach. In *The Mihalis Angelos* (1971) the charterers had purported to cancel the charter on the basis of a force majeure clause. In fact, the charterers had no right to cancel on that basis. However, they were subsequently held not to be in breach because the owners had been in breach of a condition of the contract. That breach of condition had given the charterers the right to terminate when they had claimed to do so. It did not matter that they had not stated the correct justification for their termination at the time.

18.26 However, a party who initially states an invalid reason for terminating will not be able to rely upon an effective reason, which is only subsequently brought to the other party's attention, 'if the point which was not taken could have been put right', that is, where not stating the correct justification has prevented the other party from dealing with it (*Heisler* v *Anglo-Dal Ltd* [1954] 1 WLR 1273 at 1278). It may also be that the party who claimed to be able to terminate will be estopped from asserting a true basis of termination, or will be taken to have waived it (*Glencore Grain* v *Lebanese Organization for International Commerce* (1997)).

Anticipatory breach

18.27 We now need to consider the question of anticipatory breach. This involves looking at the situation when X and Y have made a contract and, before the time for performance arrives, X declares that he no longer intends to perform. X is said to repudiate the contract and Y has the option to terminate the contract and claim damages at that point.

Anticipatory breach, therefore, refers to the situation, before the time for performance, when one party has indicated to the other that he does not intend to perform the contract. He or she may have done so expressly, or his or her actions may have shown that to be the situation. He or she may, for example, sell to Z the goods which the contract already requires him or her to deliver to Y. What is required is 'an intimation of an intention to abandon and altogether to refuse performance of the contract . . . [or of] an intention no longer to be bound by the contract' (*Freeth* v *Burr* (1874) LR 9 CP 208 at 213 per Lord Coleridge). This encompasses the situation where one party may wish to perform, but his or her act or default has made it impossible for him or her to do so (*Universal Cargo Carriers Corpn* v *Citati* (1957)). The 'impossibility situation' then has to be distinguished from frustration which occurs when the impossibility is not self-induced (see **Chapter 19**).

18.28 On the occurrence of X's anticipatory breach of his contract with Y, Y has a choice. Y can either keep the contract alive or he can accept X's repudiation and terminate it. If Y decides to keep the contract alive, he has no immediate right to damages. He will be able to claim damages only if X persists in his attitude and does not perform at the appointed time. In that case Y is simply suing for a breach because X has not performed at the time when performance became due. However, if Y accepts the repudiation and terminates the contract, he can sue for damages immediately, on the basis of X's anticipatory breach. Even if he does not accept the repudiation, and cannot therefore sue for damages at that point, he may still be granted, immediately, an order for specific performance compelling X to perform when performance becomes due (*Hasham* v *Zenab* (1960)).

18.29 Termination, or acceptance of repudiation, does not require a particular form of communication.

> An act of acceptance of a repudiation requires no particular form; a communication does not have to be couched in the language of acceptance. It is sufficient that the communication or conduct clearly and unequivocally conveys to the repudiating party that the aggrieved party is treating the contract as at an end. (*Vitol SA* v *Norelf Ltd* [1996] 3 All ER 193 at 200 per Lord Steyn)

It may be possible for the injured or aggrieved party to be seen as having accepted a repudiatory breach, simply through not performing their further obligations under the contract, although a failure to act will often be equivocal (*Vitol SA* v *Norelf Ltd*). In the more recent case of *Masri* v *Consolidated Contractors International UK Ltd* (2006), it was argued that *Vitol SA* v *Norelf Ltd* could be relied upon to conclude that acceptance of repudiation required no communication on the facts and could occur through conduct. The High Court clarified the position, stating that the relevant issue was whether the conduct would have clearly and unequivocally conveyed to a reasonable person in the position of the repudiating party that the aggrieved party is treating the contract as an end.

18.30 The injured party does have time to decide whether to affirm or terminate, but doing nothing for too long may be seen as affirmation (*Stocznia Gdanska SA* v *Latvian Shipping (No 3)* (2002), Rix LJ). Once affirmation has occurred, the injured party can no longer terminate for that anticipatory breach and may then have to wait for a fresh anticipatory breach or breach at the time for performance. However, if the repudiation is continuing or fresh repudiation occurs, then the possibility of terminating is again present, without the need to wait for breach at the time of performance (*Stocznia Gdanska SA*).

18.31 *Hochster* v *De La Tour* (1853) made it clear that damages can be claimed immediately on the basis of an accepted anticipatory breach, without any need to wait for the time of performance. In that case:

> In April 1852 the defendant made a contract with the claimant for the claimant to act as a courier for him from 1 June. On 11 May the defendant told the claimant that he had changed his mind, and that the claimant's services would not be required. On 22 May the claimant commenced an action against the defendant.

The court had to consider the defendant's claim that he could not be in breach of contract, and an action could not be commenced, before 1 June. The court rejected this and held that the claimant could sue successfully before the date for performance. A similar result was reached in *Frost* v *Knight* (1872). In that case the defendant had promised the claimant that he would marry her when his father died. Subsequently the defendant broke off his engagement to the claimant. She took action while the defendant's father was still alive and was successful in her claim.

18.32 The basic requirement for an anticipatory breach is an intention not to perform. That is quite simple where one party is aware that what he or she intends will mean that the contract will be broken when it is time for performance. The situation is more complicated where one party mistakenly believes that what he or she intends is in keeping with the contractual requirements. It would seem that the actions and statements of the mistaken party must be considered to see if, objectively, an intention is shown to abandon the contract or refuse future performance. A comparison can be made between *Woodar Investment Development Ltd* v *Wimpey Construction* (1980) and *Federal Commerce and Navigation Co. Ltd* v *Molena Alpha Inc* [1979] 1 All ER 307. In the latter case:

> The charterers and owners had made a time charter of a ship. The charterers deducted certain sums from their periodic hire payments. The owners disputed their right to do so and told the master not to issue freight pre-paid bills of lading. The owners thought that they were entitled to take that line. Effectively, the charterers could not make use of the ship if such bills of lading could not be issued.

The charterers claimed that the owners' instructions to their ship's master amounted to a wrongful repudiation of the contract. The House of Lords found for the charterers, despite the fact that the owners had believed that they were acting within their rights and did not want to lose the charter. The owners' actions deprived the charterers of substantially the whole benefit of the charters.

Lord Wilberforce said (at 315):

> If a party's conduct is such as to amount to a threatened repudiatory breach, his subjective desire to maintain the contract cannot prevent the other party from drawing the consequences of his actions.

18.33 However, a mere mistaken claim to a right to terminate may not show an intention to abandon the contract or refuse future performance. *Woodar Investment Development Ltd* v *Wimpey Construction UK Ltd* [1980] 1 WLR 277 should be considered. The facts were:

> There was a contract for the sale of land. The contract stated that in certain circumstances the buyer, Wimpey, would be entitled to terminate. Wimpey honestly misconstrued the contract and wrongly thought that circumstances giving rise to the express right to terminate were present. Changes in the market made the contract uneconomic for Wimpey, and Wimpey wrongly claimed to be entitled to terminate. The seller, Woodar, argued that this amounted to a repudiation of the contract.

A majority of the House of Lords held that the seller, Woodar, could not claim damages for a repudiatory breach of contract. Wimpey mistakenly believed that it was exercising a contractual right, and it was seeking to act within the contract and not to repudiate it. Communications between Woodar and Wimpey showed that they were seeking to resolve which one of them had correctly interpreted the contract and their actions were not inconsistent with the continuance of the contract once that had been resolved.

18.34 The question of mistaken demands, which were in breach of contract, was also considered by the Privy Council in *Vaswani* v *Italian Motors (Sales and Services) Ltd* [1996] 1 WLR 270. The case was concerned with a contract for the sale of a Ferrari Testarossa. A deposit was paid, but when the delivery time arrived, the sellers mistakenly demanded a higher price than that contracted for (the contract allowed for an increase in the price for some reasons but not others). There was a clause allowing for forfeit of the deposit if, once the car was ready for delivery, the buyer failed to pay the outstanding amount within seven days. When the buyer failed to make payment, the sellers forfeited the deposit. Applying both *Federal Commerce and Navigation Co. Ltd* v *Molena Alpha Inc.* (1979) and *Woodar Investment Development Ltd* v *Wimpey Construction UK Ltd* (1980),[3] the court held that the mistaken

3 See also *Gulf Agri Trade FZCO* v *Aston Agro Industrial AG* [2008] EWHC 1252 (Comm), [2009] 1 All ER (Comm) 991.

demand for a sum as payment was not, by itself, sufficient to amount to a repudiatory breach. Lord Woolf said (at 276):

> While therefore here the request for the payment of an excessive price would not in itself amount to a repudiation, if the conduct relied on went beyond the assertion of a genuinely held view of the effect of the contract the conduct could amount to repudiation. This is the position if the conduct is inconsistent with the continuance of the contract.

In the instant case the conduct was not seen as inconsistent with the continuance of the contract and, in the view of the court, was not repudiatory. This was explained further. It was said (at 277):

> In this case while the sellers did indicate to the buyer that he should pay a sum which was excessive or the deposit would be forfeited they never went so far as to indicate to the buyer that it would be purposeless to pay the correct sum required . . . All they had done was to put forward their calculation which had gone unchallenged. There was nothing to prevent the buyer paying the sum he calculated was due. Until he at least tendered the sum he considered was due the sellers were not required to deliver the vehicle . . . The sellers did not threaten a 'breach of the contract with serious consequences' as in *Federal Commerce and Navigation Co. Ltd* v *Molena Alpha Inc.*, and there was no conduct by them which was totally inconsistent with the continuance of the contract.

18.35 A more recent example of a mistaken claim to treat the contract as terminated was considered by the Court of Appeal in *Eminence Property Developments Ltd* v *Heaney* (2011). Here, the court applied the ruling in *Woodar Investment Development Ltd* v *Wimpey Construction UK Ltd* (1980), and similar to the earlier case, *Eminence Property Developments Ltd* v *Heaney* (2011) also concerned a contract for the sale of land. The issue on appeal was whether a vendor, who had served notices of rescission on the buyer before the final date for complying with notices to complete had been reached and then mistakenly treated the contract as ended, was acting in repudiatory breach of contract. Whilst emphasizing the individuality of all cases, Lord Justice Etherton stated (at 242) that the legal test for repudiatory conduct is:

> whether, looking at all the circumstances objectively, that is from the perspective of a reasonable person in the position of the innocent party, the contract-breaker has shown a clear intention to abandon and altogether refuse to perform the contract.

Although the relative simplicity of this test was noted, the actual difficulties in applying the test to the facts of any particular case were also highlighted, with *Woodar Investment Development Ltd* v *Wimpey Construction UK Ltd* (1980) serving as a good example of this. Determining whether or not there has been a repudiatory breach was found to be a highly fact-sensitive exercise, requiring consideration of all of the circumstances in forming an objective assessment of the contract-breaker's intentions. These intentions could also be informed by motive, normally a subjective matter, if this threw light on the way the act would be viewed by a reasonable person. In *Eminence Property Developments Ltd* v *Heaney* (2011) itself, the vendor had not shown a clear intention to abandon and altogether refuse to perform the contract (indeed, the contract was advantageous to him), and consequently the rescission notices which he had served did not constitute a repudiatory breach of contract.

18.36 When an anticipatory breach occurs, the injured party may decide to keep the contract alive. What are the consequences of that decision? In *Avery* v *Bowden* (1856), the court considered the situation where the innocent party had elected not to accept the defendant's repudiation of the contract. He had kept the contract alive in the hope that performance would ensue. In that case:

> The defendant had chartered the claimant's ship to load a cargo at Odessa within 45 days. The ship was ready to load, but the defendant repeatedly told the ship's captain that he could not obtain a cargo. Before the 45 days were up, the Crimean War started and the contract was frustrated. The outbreak of war had made it illegal to load a cargo at an enemy port.

It was held that the claimant could not recover damages. In the first place, the court did not think that what the defendant had done was sufficient to amount to a repudiatory breach. However, even if it had been sufficient, the claimant still did not have a cause of action. The court thought that such an anticipatory breach could not found a cause of action until it was accepted by the claimant. In this case the claimant had not accepted the repudiation. He had continued to ask for performance until war was declared and the contract was frustrated.

18.37 In *Avery* v *Bowden* (1856) the contract was kept alive only to be frustrated. However, keeping the contract alive may also provide the party who had evinced an intention to repudiate with an opportunity to terminate because of the other party's breach. If the contract is kept alive, it is kept alive for the benefit of both parties. The party who would have been the injured party, had he accepted the repudiation, may himself subsequently commit a breach and be liable for the consequences of so doing. In *Fercometal SARL* v *MSC Mediterranean Shipping Co. SA* (1988):

> A charter-party contained a clause enabling the charterer to cancel if the ship was not ready to load by 9 July. Before 9 July, the charterer wrongfully purported to cancel the charter. The owner could have accepted that purported termination as a repudiation but chose to continue with the contract. The ship was not ready to load on 9 July. The charterer claimed to cancel on the basis of the express provision for cancellation.

The House of Lords held that the charterer could take advantage of the express right to cancel. The owner had chosen to continue the contract, and that kept the contract alive for the benefit of both parties. The charterer's earlier conduct did not prevent the charterer from taking action on a subsequent breach by the owner. The earlier case of *Braithwaite* v *Foreign Hardwood Co. Ltd*

(1905) can no longer be regarded as establishing that if X repudiates a contract with Y, and Y does not accept the repudiation, Y is nevertheless excused his subsequent non-performance of his obligations. However, Y's non-performance of a particular obligation might not be actionable by X if X was estopped from such a claim, that is, if X had indicated that he would no longer require Y to perform a particular obligation and Y had relied upon that in not making himself ready to perform.

18.38 The above cases illustrate the danger in deciding to keep the contract alive, rather than accepting the repudiation and terminating the contract. However, even where the repudiation is accepted, events subsequent to that which would have impacted upon the performance may still be relevant to the question of damages. In *The Mihalis Angelos* (1971) what was in question was a right for the repudiating party to cancel, which would inevitably have arisen:

> There was a charter-party which stated that the ship was 'expected ready to load' at Haiphong about 1 July. Clause 11 provided that if the ship was not ready to load by 20 July the charterers had an option to cancel the charter-party. The charterers purported to cancel on 17 July, and the owners accepted that as a repudiation of the contract.

It was held that, although it was clear on 17 July that the ship would not be ready to load by 20 July, the charterers could not exercise the option before 20 July. Nevertheless, the charterers had been entitled to cancel because the owners were in breach of a condition. The owners had stated that the ship was 'expected ready to load' on 1 July without having any reasonable grounds for such an expectation. The owners were in breach of a condition and, on that basis, the charterers could terminate the contract. However, the Court of Appeal also stated that, even had that not been the case, the owners would have recovered only nominal damages—and that is the important point in this context, that is, had there been no breach of condition by the owners, the Court of Appeal would have been prepared to award them only nominal damages for what would then have been a repudiatory breach by the charterers on 17 July. Only nominal damages would have been available because, on 17 July, it was inevitable that the ship would not arrive by 20 July and, on 20 July, the charterers would have been able to exercise the option to terminate the contract without breaching it. In other words, the owners would not have received performance anyway, even had there been no breach on 17 July, and they would not have suffered a substantial loss through a repudiatory breach on 17 July.

18.39 Events subsequent to the accepted repudiation also reduced the damages awarded in *Golden Strait Corpn* v *Nippon Yusen Kubishika Kaisha* (2007). In that case:

> In 1998 the parties entered into a seven-year charter-party. In December 2001 the charterers repudiated the contract and the owners accepted the repudiation. In March 2003 the second Gulf War broke out and the war clause in the charter-party would have given the charterers the right to cancel. The question arose as to whether the owners' damages for the charterers' repudiatory breach in 2001 should encompass the entirety of the time then remaining under the charter-party or whether they should be limited by the outbreak of the Gulf War, when the charterers would have had a right to cancel.

Normally damages are awarded by reference to the circumstances at the time of the breach, that is, here, the time of the repudiation. This is seen to create certainty for both parties. However, such calculation is usually in keeping with the basic principle on which damages are awarded (placing the injured party in the position he or she would have been had the contract been performed) and the injured party's duty to mitigate. The duty to mitigate means that the injured party will not recover for any loss which he or she would not have suffered had they behaved reasonably on the breach occurring. So, for example, if the breach is the non-delivery of goods for which there is a market, the injured party can purchase replacement goods in the market when the breach occurs and the damages awarded will cover the excess of the contract price over the market price at the time of the breach. If the injured party delays, and the market price increases, the damages paid will not increase. It was reasonable to buy replacement goods when the breach occurred. However, *The Golden Strait* was not a case where awarding damages based on the time of the breach would comply with basic principle. At the time of the breach there was the prospect of the contract continuing for the rest of its whole seven-year duration. By the time the case came to court, it was clear it would have been lawfully cancelled in 2003. Awarding damages based on the full duration of the contract would have put the injured party in a better position than if the contract had been performed. It would seem that the damages will not be calculated according to the circumstances at the date of the breach when there is a temporal element in the injured party's loss (i.e. where it is a loss over time, or a loss which only accrues after the breach) and the temporal element would not be nullified by acting in accordance with the duty to mitigate, that is, procuring a substitute contract at the time of the breach. In *The Golden Strait* case any substitute contract would have contained the same cancellation right, and also not have run for the remainder of the full contract duration (see Lord Brown at [82]).

Mitigation

18.40 There is a further difficult problem to be considered in the relationship between the injured party's choice in respect of the other party's anticipatory breach and the duty to mitigate. The duty to mitigate means that the injured party will not receive damages to cover any loss which the injured party would not have incurred had he behaved reasonably on breach (see **Chapter 20**). The problem is that if the injured party chooses not to accept the repudiation, then there is no breach at that point and no duty to mitigate. Of course, in most cases, the injured party will not be able to perform if the other party will not co-operate, but what of the exceptional cases? In exceptional cases the injured party will be able to perform without the co-operation of the other party and will then be able to put him or herself into the position where he or she can claim in debt for the money due under the contract, rather than having to sue for damages for breach. (Very exceptionally the injured party may be able to claim in debt without performing, where the money falls due under the contract independently of the injured party's performance—*Ministry of Sound (Ireland) Ltd* v *World Online Ltd* (2003).) If the injured party can sue for the debt, he or she will not be concerned with the rules restricting recovery of damages, including the duty to mitigate. This can lead to the injured party claiming payment for an unwanted and 'wasted' performance, which contrasts awkwardly with the mitigation rule's limitation on recovery.

The point arises from the decision in *White and Carter (Councils) Ltd* v *McGregor* [1962] AC 413. In that case:

> The claimants supplied litter bins to local councils and then made money by selling advertising on them. The defendants contracted for three years of advertisements of their garage business but, that same day, they repudiated the contract. The claimants refused to accept the repudiation and went ahead with the advertisements.

Eventually the claimants claimed the sum owed to them under the contract in return for their performance and, by a bare majority, the House of Lords allowed the claim. Obviously the claimants could have simply accepted the repudiation and claimed damages at that point. Instead they chose to expend more money to carry out a performance which was no longer wanted. The case sits uneasily alongside the mitigation rule. However, Lord Reid suggested a qualification upon the injured party's right to choose not to accept the repudiation, to continue to perform, and to claim the sum due under the contract. He thought that if it could be shown that the injured party had 'no legitimate interest' in performing, rather than accepting the repudiation and claiming damages, he ought not to be able to 'saddle the other party with an additional burden with no benefit to himself' (at 431).

18.41 It is clear that there is general acceptance of Lord Reid's limitation on the general right of the injured party to choose whether to accept the repudiation, but it has been stated in different ways in subsequent case law.[4] So, for example, in *The Odenfeld* (1978), Kerr J said that:

> any fetter on the innocent party's right of election whether or not to accept a repudiation will only be applied in extreme cases, viz. where damages would be an adequate remedy and where an election to keep the contract would be wholly unreasonable.

18.42 *Reichman* v *Beveridge* (2006) provides an example of a case where damages were viewed as not providing an adequate remedy and not accepting the repudiation was not 'wholly unreasonable'. The case was one in which tenants under a five-year lease left the premises when there were almost two years of the lease still to run. The issue was whether the landlord could claim the rent which they should have continued to pay, or whether the landlord should have accepted their repudiation by forfeiting the lease and mitigated his loss. The court took the line that the landlord's conduct was not 'wholly unreasonable' in not taking steps to find a new tenant, rather than leaving it to the tenants to propose one. Further, the law not being wholly certain, there was, at least, a significant risk that damages would not be available to cover loss of future rent if the landlord forfeited the lease and they would lose money if they could only re-let the property at a lower rent. Damages would not provide an adequate remedy. It was emphasized that it is 'for the party in breach to establish that the innocent party's conduct is wholly unreasonable and that damages would be an adequate remedy' (at [41]). The burden lies on the repudiating party to establish that the case is one in which the innocent party's choice is restricted (see further *The Dynamic* (2003)).

4 See further *The Puerto Buitrago (Attica Sea Carriers Corpn v Ferrostaal Poseidon Bulk Reederei GmbH)* (1976); *The Odenfeld (Gator Shipping Corpn v Trans-Asiatic Occidental Shipping Establishment)* (1978); *The Alaskan Trader (Clea Shipping Corpn v Bulk Oil International Ltd)* (1984); *The Dynamic (Ocean Marine Navigation v Koch Carbon Inc)* (2003); *Reichman v Beveridge* (2006); *Isabella Shipowner SA v Shagang Shipping Co Ltd* (2012).

18.43 In the recent case of *Isabella Shipowner SA* v *Shagang Shipping Co Ltd* (2012), Justice Cooke usefully summarized the effect of the authorities, stating that:

> an innocent party will have no legitimate interest in maintaining the contract if damages are an adequate remedy and his insistence on maintaining the contract can be described as 'wholly unreasonable', 'extremely unreasonable' or, perhaps, in my words, 'perverse' (at [44]).

Whichever words are used to describe the actions of the innocent party and whatever the formulation, as Lloyd J acknowledged in *The Alaskan Trader* [1984] 1 All ER 129, there is a point at which the 'injured party cannot enforce his contract according to its strict legal terms' (at 136). As noted before, however, such circumstances are exceptional and *The Alaskan Trader*, a case in which the innocent party was viewed as not having had a legitimate interest in not accepting repudiation, aptly illustrates this point. In that case:

> The charterers had repudiated a charter-party when the ship required repairs because of a serious problem with the engines. The owners would not accept the repudiation but repaired the ship and kept it ready, fully crewed, for the charterers for seven months until the end of the charter period.

The question, then, was whether the owners could recover the hire for that period. Lloyd J upheld the decision of the arbitrator that they could not. They had no legitimate interest in doing so rather than claiming damages. If a replacement charter could not be found, it would have been less costly if they had not kept the ship with a full crew, ready to sail, for that period. Maintaining the time charter had led to a commercial absurdity. Also, in *The Puerto Buitrago* (1976), the cost of repair was double the value of the ship when repaired and four times as much as its scrap value. In these circumstances, to refuse to accept a premature redelivery of the vessel in order for the repairs to be carried out would have been 'truly perverse' and repair would have been 'an exercise in futility' (*Isabella Shipowner SA* v *Shagang Shipping Co Ltd* (2012) per Justice Cooke at [44]).

Summary

Performance

- Parties usually cease to have obligations under the contract because they have performed—discharge by performance.
- What is required for performance depends upon the contract terms.
- The parties may provide that the contract, or some of the obligations under it, are not immediately effective. A condition precedent may suspend the formation of the contract or the operation of some of the obligations.
- The parties may have provided that the contract is to end upon the occurrence of certain circumstances—a condition subsequent.
- The order of performance may be provided for by contingent conditions.

Entire contracts

- One party is obliged to perform his or her side of the contract before the other becomes obliged to pay.

- The injured party will have to pay for any work or materials which he or she voluntarily chooses to adopt.
- Where there has been 'substantial performance' the party in breach can recover the contract price and pay damages to cover defects.

Breach

- The jured party can choose to terminate the contract for breaches of conditions and for sufficient breaches of innominate terms (see **Chapter 8**).
- The injured party can also terminate for a repudiatory breach where the other party indicates that he or she no longer intends to be bound by the contract.
- A party may claim to terminate for a reason which does not justify termination. If at the time he or she claims to terminate there is another, then unstated, reason which would justify termination, he or she can usually rely upon that to prevent the claimed termination from subsequently being found to be a repudiatory breach.
- Where repudiation relates to performance which is not yet due it is anticipatory breach.
- On the occurrence of an anticipatory breach, the injured party can elect to keep the contract alive or accept the repudiation and terminate the contract.
- If the choice is to keep the contract alive after an anticipatory breach then there is no breach at that point and no claim to damages.
- If the choice is to terminate after an anticipatory breach, there is an immediate right to damages.
- If the choice is to keep the contract alive after an anticipatory breach, and it is subsequently frustrated, no claim to damages exists from the prior anticipatory breach.
- If the choice is to terminate the contract after an anticipatory breach, the amount of damages recovered may be affected by subsequent events such as those which would have provided the party in breach with legitimate reasons for cancellation of the contract.
- Even where there is a repudiation by one party, the injured party may sometimes be able to perform their side of the contract without the cooperation of the other party. Under those circumstances the injured party may be able to choose to continue with the contract, perform their obligations, and claim the contract price from the other party. In keeping with the duty to mitigate, which arises on breach, the injured party will not be able to do that where the injured party had no legitimate interest in performing, rather than claiming damages.

Further reading

D. Capper, 'A Golden Victory for Freedom of Contract' (2008) 24 JCL 176

J. W. Carter and E. Peden, 'Damages following Termination for Repudiation: Taking Account of Later Events' (2008) 24 JCL 145

Q. Lui, 'The White & Carter Principle: A Restatement' (2011) 74 MLR 17

G. Treitel, 'Assessment of Damages for Wrongful Repudiation' (2007) 123 LQR 9

Chapter 19

The doctrine of frustration

Introduction: initial and subsequent impossibility

19.1 After the parties have concluded a contract, events beyond their control may occur which 'frustrate' the purpose of their agreement, or render it very difficult, or impossible, or even illegal, to perform. An example of this is where a hall which has been booked for the performance of a play is destroyed by fire, after the contract has been concluded, but before the date of performance of the play. Some writers have seen a close resemblance between this type of 'subsequent impossibility' and the subject of common mistake (also referred to as 'initial impossibility'). Indeed, there are similarities between the two subjects. (See, e.g., *Dany Lions Ltd* v *Bristol Cars Ltd* (2013).) In *Great Peace Shipping Ltd* v *Tsavliris Salvage (International) Ltd* (2003) at [61], it was stated that 'consideration of the development of the law of frustration assists with the analysis of the law of common mistake'. Both provide an important opportunity to define the strength of contractual obligations. How absolute are they? Under what circumstances will a party be excused from performing his or her contractual undertakings or from having to provide a remedy to the other? There are close similarities in some of the factual situations to which the two types of 'impossibility' apply. (For example, contrast *Griffith* v *Brymer* (1903) and *Krell* v *Henry* (1903). The former was decided on the basis of mistake and the latter on the basis of frustration.)

19.2 In certain circumstances, it may be a fine, almost tenuous, dividing line between these two different branches of contract law. In *Amalgamated Investment & Property Co. Ltd* v *John Walker & Sons Ltd* [1976] 3 All ER 509, for example, the facts were:

> The defendants owned a commercial property which they advertised for sale as being suitable for occupation or redevelopment. In July 1973 the claimants agreed, subject to contract, to buy the property for £1,710,000. The defendants knew that the claimants' purpose in

purchasing the property was to redevelop it and that they would require planning permission to do so. In their enquiries before entering into a binding contract, the claimants asked the defendants whether the property was designated (i.e. 'listed') as a building of special architectural or historic interest. The defendants replied, on 14 August, that it was not. This was correct at the time. But in January 1973, unknown to the parties, officials at the Department of the Environment had included the property in a provisional list of buildings to be listed as being of architectural or historic interest. On 25 September, the parties signed the contract of sale. On 26 September, the Department of the Environment wrote to the defendants and informed them that the property had been included in the statutory list of buildings of special interest. (The list was given legal effect the following day.) It transpired that the property had been unconditionally selected for inclusion in the list on 22 August. The value of the building without redevelopment potential was one and a half million pounds less than the contract price! The claimants claimed rescission of the agreement on the basis of common mistake, or alternatively, they sought a declaration that the agreement was void or voidable and an order rescinding the agreement.

The claimants' action was unsuccessful and specific performance was ordered against them. The case could not be treated as one of common mistake as the mistake did not exist at the time the contract was concluded. It was after the contract was made that the property was actually listed. (In the opinion of the court, the earlier inclusion of the property in the list of buildings of special interest was merely an administrative step towards listing.) The alternative argument put forward by the claimants was that the contract was frustrated; that is, they had paid a high price for a property on the basis of its redevelopment potential and subsequently found that this objective was not possible to achieve. This contention was also rejected by the Court of Appeal, as the claimants were assumed to have taken the risk that the building may have been listed at some time after the contract was concluded. They were very unlucky that it was listed so soon after purchase, but this was an inherent risk in the ownership of buildings (per Buckley J at 517). In other words, it was foreseeable that the obtaining of planning permission, which was crucial to the claimants, might be thwarted by the listing of the building.

Although the claimants' action failed, and they could claim neither common mistake nor frustration, the case is instructive with regard to the distinction between these two separate branches of contract law. The difference between initial and subsequent impossibility turned on the precise time at which the building was listed. Yet it is clear from the evidence that this 'listing' was more of a process than a single decision or event. Is there any logical or practical reason why this factual situation should not be treated as one of mistake rather than one of frustration? The law seems rather rigid in its approach to these two related areas of impossibility when much may depend on a matter of days or even hours. The traditional justification for a rigid distinction between the two subjects is that mistake is concerned with the formation of contracts, whereas frustration deals with the discharge of contracts that have already been concluded. This explanation tends to ignore the difficulties posed by cases such as *Amalgamated Investment & Property Co. Ltd* v *John Walker & Sons Ltd*.

19.3 In the Court of Appeal decision in *Great Peace Shipping Ltd* v *Tsavliris Salvage (International) Ltd* (2003) (discussed in **Chapter 12**), Lord Phillips, having examined the development of the doctrine of frustration (at [62]–[72]), compared frustration to common mistake and stated (at [85]):

> Circumstances where a contract is void as a result of common mistake are likely to be less common than instances of frustration. Supervening events which defeat the contractual adventure will frequently not be the responsibility of either party. Where, however, the parties agree that something shall be done which is impossible at the time of making the agreement, it is much more likely that, on true construction of the agreement, one or other will have undertaken responsibility for the mistaken state of affairs.

However, by comparing the two doctrines in some detail, the court in the *Tsavliris* case has helped to explain the principles which they have in common.

Development of the doctrine of frustration

19.4 The doctrine of frustration is a means of dealing with situations where events occur, after the contract has been concluded, which render the agreement illegal, or impossible to perform, or even commercially sterile. The frustrating event must also not be the fault of either party, or have been foreseeable. (On the latter issue, see *Walkden* v *Walkden* (2009) at [53]; and for a detailed discussion of the relevance to the doctrine of the foreseeability of a risk, see *Edwinton Commercial Corporation* v *Tsavliris Russ Ltd, The 'Sea Angel'* (2007) at [102]–[104] and [127]–[128].) Of course, the parties might expressly provide for the consequences of a frustrating event by what is known as a force majeure clause. For example, a building contract might provide for what will happen in the event of a strike. In this way the parties themselves deal with the consequences of future events which might affect performance, and the doctrine of frustration will not usually apply. Certain types of agreement—for example, export sales, shipping, building, or engineering contracts—are particularly susceptible to disruption by unforeseen events. But, in the absence of express provision by the parties, the doctrine of frustration is a legal recognition of the fact that in some instances it is just to excuse a party from his or her contractual obligations.

19.5 Until a little more than a hundred years ago, the law was reluctant to excuse a party his or her performance of a contract even in cases where supervening events rendered that performance difficult or impossible. The rationale of this rule was that a party could always make express provision for unforeseen events and, if he or she did not do so, he or she should be bound by his or her contractual obligations. This is known as the 'absolute contracts' rule, which was clearly stated in the seventeenth-century case of *Paradine* v *Jane* (1647). In this case, C brought an action against D for the rent due on a lease. D argued that he had been dispossessed of the land by force by an 'alien born, enemy to the king and kingdom [who] had invaded the realm with an hostile army of men'. D claimed that due to events beyond his control he had lost the profits from the land and, therefore, that he was not liable for the rent. This plea was rejected by the court. D had undertaken an obligation to pay rent under a contract and he was bound to fulfil this despite the supervening events. He could always have expressly covered this contingency in his contract with C.

19.6 This rigid approach has been mitigated, to some extent, by the gradual development of the doctrine of frustration. However, it must be emphasized that the doctrine operates within strict limits and does not provide an easy means of escape for those who have simply made a bad bargain (see *Amalgamated Investment & Property Co. Ltd* v *John Walker & Sons Ltd* (1976) at para. **19.2**). The famous case which marks the recognition of the doctrine is *Taylor* v *Caldwell* (1863) 3 B & S 826. The facts were as follows:

> On 27 May 1861, Taylor entered into a contract with Caldwell which gave T the use of the Surrey Gardens and music hall on four separate days later that summer. T was to use the premises for a series of four concerts, and for holding day and night fêtes on the days in question, and he was to pay £100 for each day. After the contract was concluded, but before the date of the first concert, the music hall was destroyed by fire. The fire was not the fault of either party and it made the performance of the concerts impossible. No express provision had been made by the parties to cover this contingency. T claimed damages for the money he had wasted in advertising the concerts.

It was held that the defendants were not liable and T's claim for damages did not succeed. This seems a fair decision, but how did the court circumvent the general rule that in a contract to do a positive thing, a person must perform it or pay damages for failure to do so? Blackburn J stated that this rule applies only where the contract is not subject to any condition, either express or implied. He continued (at 833):

> [T]here are authorities which, as we think, establish the principle that where, from the nature of the contract, it appears that the parties must from the beginning have known that it could not be fulfilled unless when the time for the fulfilment of the contract arrived some particular specified thing continued to exist, so that, when entering into the contract, they must have contemplated such continuing existence as the foundation of what was to be done; there, in the absence of any express or implied warranty that the thing shall exist, the contract is not to be construed as a positive contract, but as subject to an implied condition that the parties shall be excused in case, before breach, performance becomes impossible from the perishing of the thing without default of the contractor.

The judge held that the continued existence of the music hall was essential to the performance of the contract and the parties contracted on this basis. Although there was no express provision to this effect, the court implied one as a matter of construction. If the parties had thought about it when making the contract, they would have agreed to such a condition. In other words, the doctrine of frustration, as established in *Taylor* v *Caldwell*, was based on an effort to give effect to the presumed intention of the parties.

The importance of the case is that it established the doctrine of frustration and made deep inroads into the notion of absolute contractual obligations. But, as we shall see, there is some debate about the theoretical basis of the doctrine. For example, in *Shell UK Ltd* v *Lostock Garage Ltd* [1977] 1 All ER 481 at 487, Lord Denning stated (*obiter*) that 'the legal effect of frustration does not depend on an implied term. It does not depend on the presumed intention of the parties, nor on what they would have answered, if asked, but simply on what the court itself declares to amount to a frustration.' In other words, the court is imposing a fair solution, in the event of unforeseen circumstances, rather than giving effect to the presumed contractual intention of the parties. (More recently, Lord Phillips stated in *Great Peace Shipping Ltd* v *Tsavliris Salvage (International) Ltd* (2003) [70] that 'the doctrine of frustration was patently judge-made law'.)

19.7 Once the doctrine of frustration had been established, its scope had to be determined. *Taylor* v *Caldwell* (1863) dealt with the physical destruction of the subject matter of a contract, and its result was unexceptionable. Similarly, where a contract is made to do something which subsequently becomes illegal (for example, trading with a country against which war is later declared), there is no difficulty in treating the contract as frustrated. But a more common and problematic type of case is where the commercial purpose of a contract is drastically affected by unforeseen events, whilst the performance of the contract remains physically and legally possible. A good example is the famous case of *Krell* v *Henry* [1903] 2 KB 740, where the facts were:

> Henry (D) agreed to hire a flat in Pall Mall from Krell (C) for the days of 26 and 27 June. These were the days that the coronation processions of Edward VII were to take place and the windows in the flat afforded good views of the procession route. D agreed in writing, on 20 June, to pay £75 for the exclusive use of the flat on the two days of the processions. The contract made no express reference to the coronation procession or to any other purpose. A deposit of £25 was paid by D at the time of contracting and the balance was to be paid the day before the processions took place. Due to the King's illness, the processions did not take place on the proposed days. Krell claimed £50 from Henry, who in turn counterclaimed for the return of the £25 which he had already paid under the contract.

The Court of Appeal decided that the contract was frustrated despite the fact that its performance was still physically possible. The doctrine is not strictly limited to 'cases in which the event causing the impossibility of performance is the destruction or non-existence of some thing which is the subject-matter of the contract or of some condition or state of things expressly specified as a condition of it' (per Vaughan Williams LJ at 749). Accordingly, the doctrine was applied in circumstances where some event, which must reasonably be regarded as the basis of the contract, failed to take place. The flat in Pall Mall could still have been used on the days in question, but the true purpose of the contract was frustrated by the postponement of the processions. Vaughan Williams LJ stated (at 750):

> In my judgment, the use of the rooms was let and taken for the purpose of seeing the royal processions . . . It was a licence to use rooms for a particular purpose and none other. And in my judgment the taking place of those processions on the days proclaimed along the proclaimed route, which passed 56A, Pall Mall, was regarded by both contracting parties as the foundation of the contract. I think that it cannot reasonably be supposed to have been in the

> contemplation of the contracting parties, when the contract was made, that the coronation would not be held on the proclaimed days, or the processions not take place on those days along the proclaimed route; and I think that the words imposing on the defendant the obligation to accept and pay for the use of the rooms for the named days, although general and unconditional, were not used with reference to the possibility of the particular contingency which afterwards occurred.

This was a potentially far-reaching and controversial decision. It extended the doctrine to cases where the commercial object or purpose of the contract was frustrated. It raises problems as to what exactly is the 'foundation' of a particular contract (for instance, contrast the decision in *Krell* v *Henry* with that in *Herne Bay Steam Boat Co.* v *Hutton* (1903), para. **19.9**). Although the outcome of *Krell* v *Henry* seems fair, the courts have to be careful not to allow a party a convenient means of escape from a contract simply because it turns out to be a bad bargain. *Krell* v *Henry* represents, perhaps, the furthest development of the doctrine of frustration, and subsequent cases have suggested a rather narrower view. It is unlikely that any further extension of this authority will be permitted by the courts.[1]

A narrower interpretation of frustration

19.8 In *Krell* v *Henry* (1903) it was clear that the foundation of the contract was the taking place of the coronation processions on the planned dates. A suite of rooms in Pall Mall would not normally be hired on a daily basis and the high price clearly indicated that the contracting parties had a specific and common purpose or object in entering into the agreement. For these reasons, it was a very unusual case indeed. More typically, where a party hires or leases property from another it may be less obvious whether they share a common object. Their individual motives for contracting may be different and it may be difficult to say whether the common purpose is frustrated. The property which is to be hired may be susceptible to different types of use and enjoyment. Therefore, some restriction on the use of the subject matter of the contract, due to supervening events, will not necessarily result in the contract being discharged under the doctrine of frustration.

19.9 An interesting contrast to *Krell* v *Henry* (1903) is provided by *Herne Bay Steam Boat Co.* v *Hutton* (1903). The facts were that D agreed to hire the steamboat *Cynthia* from C for £250, on 28 and 29 June 1902, 'for the purpose of viewing the naval review and for a day's cruise round the fleet'. A deposit of £50 was paid in advance. The royal naval review, which was intended as part of the coronation festivities, was subsequently cancelled due to the King's illness. However, the fleet was still anchored at Spithead on 28 June. D did not use the *Cynthia* on either of the agreed days and C sued for the balance of the hire charge. It was held that C could recover the £200 from D and that the contract was not discharged on the ground of frustration.

At first sight it might be difficult to see why the case was decided differently from *Krell* v *Henry*. But on closer examination it is possible to distinguish it and to emphasize the limited application of *Krell* v *Henry*. It was held by the Court of Appeal, in *Herne Bay*, that the taking place of the

1 See *Maritime National Fish Co.* v *Ocean Trawlers* [1935] AC 524 at 529 per Lord Wright.

royal review was not the foundation of the contract, despite the reference made to this event in the contract. It was still possible to cruise around the fleet and therefore the whole purpose of the contract was not frustrated. It is also significant that the contract was for the hire of a boat—something which is frequently hired for a variety of purposes, whereas in *Krell* v *Henry* it was highly unusual for rooms in Pall Mall to be let by the day. It seems that the contract in *Herne Bay* was for the hiring of a boat by D to make a certain voyage which it was still possible to make. The hirer had a particular object in mind, but this object was not the concern of C as owners of the boat. The contract was not physically impossible to perform, nor was the common purpose of both parties totally defeated. For these reasons the case can be distinguished from *Krell* v *Henry*, but it is clearly a very fine distinction.

19.10 The strict limits of the doctrine of frustration can be further illustrated by *Tsakiroglou & Co. Ltd* v *Noblee Thorl GmbH* (1962). The facts were as follows:

> The appellants contracted to sell groundnuts to the respondents at a price which included the carriage of the goods from the Sudan to Hamburg. Although no reference was made to this in the contract, it was assumed that shipment of the goods would be via the Suez Canal. The price of the nuts was calculated on this basis. After the contract was made, but before its performance, the Suez Canal was closed to commercial traffic owing to political events. The alternative route, via the Cape of Good Hope, would have taken the appellants more than twice as long to ship the goods and would have doubled the cost of carriage. The appellants did not make the shipment and claimed that the contract had been frustrated by the closure of the Suez Canal.

The House of Lords rejected this argument. It was still possible to ship the goods, albeit at greater expense, and the contract was not discharged. The court refused to imply a term that the goods were to be shipped by the most direct route. The fact that the appellants had made what turned out to be a bad bargain did not by itself lead to the doctrine of frustration being applied. (*Amalgamated Investment & Property Co. Ltd* v *John Walker & Sons Ltd* (1976), discussed earlier, is another vivid illustration of this point.) A court should not rewrite the contract for the parties. The appellants were under a contractual obligation to ship the goods to Hamburg by any reasonable route that was available.

19.11 In *British Movietonews Ltd* v *London and District Cinemas* [1952] AC 166, another decision which shows the limited application of the doctrine, the contract in question related to the supply of films during the Second World War. The dispute occurred over the arrangements for termination of the contract. In 1943 a government order imposed certain restrictions on film supplies and, in a second agreement, the parties altered their termination arrangements until 'such time as the Order is cancelled'. It was presumably the parties' intention that this later (second) agreement should prevail only for the duration of wartime conditions.

The Court of Appeal was willing to hold that the contract was frustrated when the Order continued after 1945 for reasons other than national safety, and to depart from the literal words of the agreement by giving effect to the presumed intentions of the parties. However, its decision was reversed by the House of Lords and the narrower approach to frustration was upheld. The House of Lords, as in *Tsakiroglou & Co. Ltd* v *Noblee Thorl GmbH* (1962), was not prepared to rewrite the agreement for the contracting parties on the basis of what they were presumed to have intended at the time the contract was made. The parties were not to be discharged lightly from their contractual obligations despite the obvious hardship to one of them. In the words of Lord Simon (at 185):

> The parties to an executory contract are often faced, in the course of carrying it out, with a turn of events which they did not at all anticipate—a wholly abnormal rise or fall in prices, a sudden depreciation of currency, an unexpected obstacle to the execution, or the like. Yet this does not in itself affect the bargain which they have made.

19.12 It is well established that financial hardship alone is no reason for allowing a party to a contract to rely on the doctrine of frustration. A clear statement to this effect was made by the House of Lords in *Davis Contractors Ltd* v *Fareham UDC* [1956] AC 696. The facts were:

> Davis Contractors agreed to build 78 houses for a local council, for the sum of £92,425, within an eight-month period. Due to serious shortages of skilled labour and materials, the work took 22 months to complete and cost Davis Contractors approximately £18,000 more than they had estimated. The contractors argued that the contract with Fareham Council was frustrated due to the long delay, which was the fault of neither party. They attempted to claim a larger sum than the agreed contract price as a fair reward for the services they had performed for the council (i.e. they claimed on a quantum meruit basis).

The House of Lords rejected the argument of Davis Contractors; the contract was not frustrated. The parties had contracted for a specific number of houses which had now been built as agreed. There was no change in the basic obligations under the contract. Mere hardship or inconvenience to one of the contracting parties was not enough to frustrate a contract. Given the uncertainty in the supply of materials and labour at that time, the contractors could have made some express stipulation about this in the contract, yet they failed to do so. They were not allowed to escape from a bad bargain by simply arguing that the contract was frustrated. In Lord Radcliffe's words (at 727), frustration could not be 'lightly invoked as the dissolvent of a contract'. (See also a statement to this effect by Lord Roskill in *Pioneer Shipping* v *BTP Tioxide (The Nema)* [1982] AC 724 at 752, which was recently cited with approval by Lord Clarke in *Armchair Answercall Ltd* v *People in Mind Ltd* [2016] EWCA Civ 1039 at 29, discussed at para. **19.39**.)

19.13 For a recent illustration of the principle that a party cannot escape his or her contractual obligations merely because the contract has become more expensive to perform, see *Thames Valley Power Ltd* v *Total Gas & Power Ltd* (2006). In this case, a sharp increase in the market price of gas made a contract significantly less profitable for the supplier, but this did not render its performance impossible. A further example of the strict limits of the doctrine is provided by the Court of Appeal in *CTI Group Inc* v *Transclear SA (The Mary Nour)* (2008). Here the sellers (T) agreed to deliver a large quantity of cement to the buyers (C), but failed to do so when T's own proposed suppliers withdrew their willingness to provide the cargo. (T did not have a legally binding agreement with the suppliers.) T was aware of the commercial background to the case, that is, that another company was putting pressure on suppliers not to deal with them. The trial court held that the contract between T and C was not frustrated, as T had assumed the risk of failing to secure the cargo from its intended source of supply. The Court of Appeal upheld this decision, and Moore-Bick LJ stated (at [27]):

> In my view it is impossible to hold that the contract in this case was frustrated ... the fact that a supplier chooses not to make goods available for shipment, thus rendering performance by the seller impossible, is not of itself sufficient to frustrate a contract of this kind. In order to rely on the doctrine of frustration it is necessary for there to have been a supervening event which renders the performance of the seller's obligations impossible or fundamentally different in nature from that which was envisaged when the contract was made ... for the reasons given earlier the sellers bore the risk of a refusal on the part of the supplier to make goods available.

19.14 This narrow view of frustration adopted by the courts has meant that the doctrine will rarely succeed where performance of the contract is still possible, but where it has merely become more difficult or disadvantageous for one of the parties to perform. (See also *Armchair Answercall Ltd* v *People in Mind Ltd* [2016] EWCA Civ 1039, discussed at para. **19.39**.) Of course, where performance is actually prevented by supervening events beyond the contemplation and control of the parties, a contract may be frustrated. For example, in *International Sea Tankers of Liberia Inc.* v *Hemisphere Shipping Co. of Hong Kong Ltd (The Wenjiang)* (1982) a tanker, which was chartered to carry a cargo of oil from Basrah, was trapped (along with 60 other ships) on the Shatt-al-Arab river when war broke out in 1980 between Iran and Iraq. The parties agreed that in such circumstances the charter-party[2] was frustrated. The point of contention in this and similar cases was the precise date on which the contract was frustrated, as this determined when the hire charge ceased to be payable by the charterers.[3]

19.15 The important subject of who bears the loss when a contract is frustrated is dealt with in detail later. But it should be remembered that the parties may, and frequently do, include some express provision which deals with the allocation of risk in relation to supervening events. In this way the possible application of the doctrine of frustration is avoided by means of a relevant clause in the contract.

Scope of the doctrine

Leases

19.16 It used to be argued that the doctrine of frustration could not apply to leases. This is because a lease is not simply a contract enabling a tenant to make use of the land in question; it creates a legal estate in the land. The argument ran that this legal estate survives despite

2 That is, a contract for the hire of a ship and the delivery of cargo.

3 See also *Kodros Shipping Corpn of Monrovia* v *Empresa Cubana de Fletes, The Evia* (1982).

supervening events which may prevent the use or enjoyment of the land (e.g., see *London & Northern Estates Co.* v *Schlesinger* (1916)). This is a rather technical view which ignores the commercial reality of some leases, especially where the lease is short term and the tenant is concerned with the use of the land for a specific purpose rather than in the creation of any legal estate. After some judicial uncertainty on the subject (see *Cricklewood Property and Investment Trust Ltd* v *Leighton Investment Trust Ltd* (1945)), the leading case is now *National Carriers Ltd* v *Panalpina (Northern) Ltd* (1981). The facts were as follows:

> The appellants had a ten-year lease of a warehouse from the respondents. After five and a half years of the lease, the local authority closed the only access road to the warehouse for a period of about 18 months. This closure of the road prevented the appellants from using the warehouse for their business. As a result, the appellants stopped their payment of rent to the respondents and claimed that the lease was frustrated.

The House of Lords decided that the closure of the access road was not a sufficiently serious interruption to amount to a frustrating event. (This was in spite of the harm to the appellants' business caused by the closure.) There were still a further three years of the lease remaining when the road was opened again. The appellants were still liable for the rent under the lease. But although the frustration claim in fact failed, the House of Lords held that the doctrine is capable of applying to a lease. Their Lordships could see no reason why, in principle, the doctrine should not apply to all types of contract. However, in practice, it will be quite rare for a lease to be frustrated. (*Quaere*: If the access road had been closed for most of the period of the lease, would the contract then have been frustrated in the *National Carriers* case?) It seems that the circumstances in which a lease will most likely be held to be frustrated are where the lease is short term and it is obvious that it is for a specific purpose. If that purpose is thwarted by supervening events beyond the control of both parties, the lease may well be frustrated. (For further discussion of the limited application of the doctrine to leases, see M. Pawlowski, 'Mistake, Frustration and Implied Conditions in Leases' (2007) 11 L&T Review 158. This article also comments on *Graves* v *Graves* (2007), in which the Court of Appeal (at [41]) implied a condition into an assured shorthold tenancy agreement that it would come to an end if housing benefit was not available to the tenant. Both parties to the agreement were mistaken about the availability of housing benefit. Thomas LJ stated (at [43]) that in this case it was 'not necessary to consider whether the contract was frustrated or void for mistake'. The case is also discussed in J. Brown, 'A New Way of Terminating Leases?' (2008) Conv and PL 70.)

Illegality

19.17 The doctrine of frustration will apply in circumstances where the performance of a contract is contrary to some law passed after the contract is made. (If the illegality exists before the contract is made, the doctrine is not relevant—but see **Chapter 15**.) This is often described as a case of 'supervening illegality'. In such circumstances the contract is not impossible to perform, nor have the obligations under the contract (necessarily) been radically altered. It is more a question of public policy in ensuring that the law is not broken. For this reason it is not possible for the parties to exclude the operation of the doctrine, in relation to certain types of supervening illegality (such as trading with the enemy), by express agreement.[4]

19.18 An obvious example of a contract's frustration due to supervening illegality is where its performance would involve trading with an enemy country at a time of war. In *Fibrosa Spolka Akcyjna* v *Fairbairn Lawson Combe Barbour Ltd* (1943), which is discussed in detail later, there was a contract for the sale of machinery to a Polish company. The machinery was to be manufactured in England and delivered to Gdynia. Subsequently, Germany invaded Poland and occupied Gdynia. The contract was held to be frustrated despite a clause in the contract which expressly dealt with the consequences of delay due to 'any cause whatsoever ... including war'. Trading with a country occupied by the enemy would have been contrary to the public interest. (For a further example of a contract frustrated by war, see *Avery* v *Bowden* (1856).)

19.19 A similar example is presented by the insurance case of *Islamic Republic of Iran Shipping Lines* v *Steamship Mutual Underwriting Association (Bermuda) Ltd* (2010). This serves as a recent illustration of an attempt to claim that a contract of insurance was discharged by frustration and/or supervening illegality. Here, a contract of insurance between the claimant and the defendant concerning liability in respect of bunker oil pollution was affected by measures implemented by the UK government pursuant to the Counter-Terrorism Act 2008. The Financial Restrictions (Iran) Order 2009 prohibited transactions between persons operating in the financial sector and two designated Iranian entities, one of which was the claimant, IRISL. The defendant, a protection and indemnity club, chose to terminate the insurance cover it provided in respect of IRISL's ships even though HM Treasury had issued a licence under the 2008 Act, permitting it to continue with this insurance cover. An IRISL ship, the ZOORIK, was involved in an accident which caused bunker oil pollution and the question of liability for loss arose. The court held that the Order and the licence did not frustrate the contract of insurance between the parties. The reason for this was that although the scope of the permitted cover was narrower than before, its nature was not different as it remained indemnity insurance. Distinguishing from the earlier authority of *Denny Mott & Dickinson* v *James Fraser & Co.* (1944), the Commercial Court held that the purpose of this contract was to provide indemnity insurance and part of that purpose remained lawful.

19.20 In *Islamic Republic of Iran Shipping Lines* v *Steamship Mutual Underwriting Association (Bermuda) Ltd* (2010), Beatson J offered a useful summary of the case law on the doctrine of frustration (see in particular [99]–[130] of the judgment). He made reference to Lord Radcliffe's 'classic test' in *Davis Contractors Ltd* v *Fareham UDC* [1956] AC 696 at 729: 'frustration occurs whenever the law recognises that without default of either party a contractual obligation has become incapable of being performed because the circumstances in which performance is called for would make it a thing radically different from that which was undertaken by the contract', and also to Lord Simon's statement in *National Carriers Ltd* v *Panalpina (Northern) Ltd* [1981] AC 675 at 700:

4 It will be remembered that, normally, the parties can avoid the operation of the doctrine by express stipulation in the contract relating to supervening events.

> frustration of a contract takes places when there supervenes an event (without default of either party and for which the contract makes no sufficient provision) which so significantly changes the nature (not merely the expense or onerousness) of the outstanding contractual rights and/or obligations from what the parties could reasonably have contemplated at the time of its execution that it would be unjust to hold them to the literal sense of its stipulations in the new circumstances.

(See also Lord Clarke's references in *Armchair Answercall Ltd v People in Mind Ltd* [2016] EWCA Civ 1039 at [28]–[30].)

Beatson J explained that in considering the facts and claims made in the *IRISL* case, he acknowledged and similarly adopted the 'multi-factorial' approach to the application of the doctrine of frustration as presented by Rix LJ in *Edwinton Commercial Corporation* v *Tsavliris Russ Ltd, The 'Sea Angel'* (2007)—by including ex ante factors (i.e. factors existing at the time of the contract) and post-contractual factors. By considering the elements through this 'multi-factorial' approach, the conclusion was reached that the contract of insurance in the instant case was not discharged by reason of frustration.

19.21 Other examples of supervening illegality are where new licensing regulations are introduced after the parties have contracted, or where restrictions on the import or export of certain goods are subsequently introduced. A problem may arise where the supervening illegality affects just part of the contract, such as in *Cricklewood Property and Investment Trust Ltd* v *Leighton Investment Trust Ltd* (1945):

> In 1936, Cricklewood Property obtained a building lease for 99 years for the purpose of building a shopping centre on a residential estate. With the outbreak of war in 1939, restrictions on the supply of building materials were introduced, and Cricklewood Property were unable to build on the land. As building on the land was a term of the lease, Cricklewood Property claimed that the contract was frustrated. The landlord, Leighton's Investment Ltd, brought an action for the rent. (Whether the doctrine of frustration can apply to a lease is discussed earlier and will not be considered here.)

It was decided that the contract was not frustrated and that Cricklewood Property were still liable for the rent under the lease. The reasoning was that it was a long lease, and 90 years of it were still unexpired. It was most unlikely that wartime regulations would last for a substantial part of the duration of the lease and there would be plenty of time for building once they had ended. There was no frustration, therefore, as the illegality did not destroy the main purpose of the lease. For a contrasting case, in which the main purpose of the contract was frustrated due to supervening illegality (restrictions on trading in timber), see *Denny, Mott, & Dickson* v *James Fraser & Co.* [1944] AC 265.[5]

5 See Lord MacMillan's statement in *Denny, Mott, & Dickson* (at 272): 'It is plain that a contract to do what it has become illegal to do cannot be legally enforceable. There cannot be default in not doing what the law forbids to be done.'

Impossibility: destruction of subject matter

19.22 We have seen in *Taylor* v *Caldwell* (1863) a clear instance of 'impossibility', namely the destruction of the subject matter of the contract. The contract was held to be frustrated by the fire which destroyed the music hall. The fire was not the fault of either party, nor was there any express stipulation to cover such a contingency. The main purpose of the contract was for the hirer of the hall to hold a series of concerts, and this became impossible as a result of the fire. It did not matter that the whole of the subject matter of the contract—which included the use of the Surrey Gardens—was not destroyed.

19.23 A similar approach can be seen in *Appleby* v *Myers* (1867), where C contracted to erect machinery on D's premises. When the work was well under way, but before it was completed, an accidental fire destroyed D's premises and the machinery that had been erected so far. C's claim to recover damages for the work already done and the cost of materials failed as the destruction of D's premises discharged both parties from their obligations under the contract. (The application of the Law Reform (Frustrated Contracts) Act 1943 to these facts is considered later.) The court's view was that the contract did not include an absolute undertaking by D that his premises would remain unaltered so as to permit C to complete the work contracted for. D had not assumed the risk of the accidental destruction of the premises. Of course, *Appleby* v *Myers* differs slightly from *Taylor* v *Caldwell* (1863) in that the premises were not the subject matter of the contract in *Appleby* v *Myers*. However, the existence of the premises was clearly essential for the performance of the contract and their destruction was rightly held to be a frustrating event.

19.24 Cases can occur where the subject matter of the contract is badly damaged by accident, but not totally destroyed. For example, in *Asfar* v *Blundell* [1896] 1 QB 123, a ship with a cargo of dates sank and was refloated after a few days. On arrival, it was found that the cargo was badly affected by the accident. It was held that the cargo owner was not liable to pay freight as the goods, in a commercial sense, had perished. It did not matter that the goods could still be put to some other commercial use, such as distillation into spirit; their nature had changed to such a degree that they could no longer be classified as dates. They were transformed into a 'mass of pulpy matter impregnated with sewage and in a state of fermentation' (per Lord Esher at 127).[6]

Impossibility: sale of goods

19.25 Where a contract involves the sale of goods, we have to look at the particular rules relating to this subject in addition to the common law principles. A contract for the sale of goods may be frustrated for reasons that we have already considered, such as supervening illegality (see *Avery* v *Bowden* (1856)). But reference should also be made to the relevant provisions of the Sale of Goods Act 1979. Section 7 states:

6 Contrast the decision in *Horn* v *Minister of Food* (1948). See also I. Brown, 'Perished Goods and the Sale of Goods Act 1979 s.6' (2000) LMCLQ 12.

> Where there is an agreement to sell specific goods, and subsequently the goods, without any fault on the part of the seller or buyer, perish before the risk passes to the buyer, the agreement is avoided.

So if S agrees to sell to B goods which are identified at the time the contract is made, and those goods subsequently perish before the risk passes to B, the contract is frustrated (or 'avoided'). As with the common law, the contract will be frustrated only if neither of the parties is at fault. If the goods are not 'specific', however, the section will not apply. If, for example, S agrees to supply B with 100kg of 'Golden Delicious' apples, but no particular source is specified, the contract will not be frustrated if the apples that S intended to use are subsequently destroyed. This is a contract for generic rather than for specific goods. S would be liable for non-delivery of the goods if he could not find another supply in order to fulfil his contractual obligations. (But contrast *Howell* v *Coupland* (1876).)[7]

19.26 Under a contract for the sale of goods it is well established (see Sale of Goods Act 1979, s 20(1)) that risk passes with ownership. (The Act uses the word 'property' to mean ownership.) Therefore, the risk of theft or damage to goods, unless otherwise agreed, falls on the owner, and not necessarily on the person who is in possession of them at the time. If the risk has passed to the buyer, and the goods are then damaged, the buyer will still be liable if he or she refuses to accept or pay for the goods. The contract will not be frustrated. If the property in the goods has not passed, and remains with the seller at the time of the loss or damage, the seller will have to carry out his or her contractual obligations, unless the contract is frustrated. (For an interesting illustration in a shipping context, contrast the two cases *DGM Commodities Corp* v *Sea Metropolitan SA (The Andra)* (2012) and *Adelfamar SA* v *Silos e Mangimi Martini SpA (The Adelfa)* (1988), which show that responsibility for discharging the cargo by the receiver can influence whether there has been a frustrating event to relieve the obligation to pay demurrage—the charge paid by the charterer to the owner for detaining the ship for loading and unloading, beyond the time agreed.)

19.27 It should be noted that, under the Sale and Supply of Goods to Consumers Regulations 2002, Regulation 4, there is an amendment to the rule on passing of risk where the buyer deals as a consumer. In such cases 'the goods remain at the seller's risk until they are delivered to the consumer' (now Sale of Goods Act 1979, s 20(4)).

Impossibility: death or illness

19.28 Most commercial contracts do not require performance by a particular person and no other. Therefore, death or illness does not normally prevent performance of the contract. But where a contract is for some personal service, to be rendered by a party to the contract,

---

7 If, to take the same example, the sale of 100kg of 'Golden Delicious' apples is stated to be 'from the seller's existing stock' (which exceeds 100kg), and the entire stock is then destroyed before the property passes, the contract would probably be frustrated, even though the goods were not 'specific'. This would be in accordance with common law principles.

the death or incapacity of that party will make performance impossible. In *Whincup* v *Hughes* (1871), for example, the claimant's son was apprenticed to a watchmaker for a six-year period at a premium of £25, but the watchmaker died after just one year. The contract, which was for a skilled and personal service, was obviously frustrated. However, at that time, C could not claim back any of the premium (for reasons which are explained later).[8] In *Robinson* v *Davison* (1871) a contract was held to be frustrated when a person who had been engaged to play the piano at a concert, on a particular day, was unable to do so because of illness. Also, in *Notcutt* v *Universal Equipment Co. (London) Ltd* (1986), a contract of employment was brought to an end, under the doctrine, as a result of the employee's chronic illness and his inability ever again to perform his contractual obligations. (For an interesting case involving a slightly different set of facts, see *Shepherd* v *Jerrom* (1987); and contrast *Jones* v *Friction Dynamics Ltd* (2007).) Since the *Notcutt* decision, there can be no doubt that the doctrine of frustration does apply to contracts of employment. However, there are sound policy reasons for the courts being cautious about the extent of such an application. (For a discussion, see D. Brodie, 'Performance Issues and Frustration of Contract' (2006) 71 Employment Law Bulletin 4.)

Impossibility: due to unavailability

19.29 In some circumstances the subject matter of a contract, whilst still in existence, may simply not be available for the purpose that was contracted for. We have seen, in *The Wenjiang (International Sea Tankers of Liberia Inc.* v *Hemisphere Shipping Co. of Hong Kong)* (1982) for instance, how an oil tanker which was trapped on the Shatt-al-Arab river at the outbreak of war in 1980 was thus unavailable to fulfil a contract to carry oil from Basrah. In this, and in a number of similar cases, the charter-parties were frustrated due to the unavailability of the subject matter. The dispute in these cases related to the precise date on which the contracts were frustrated. (A charter-party may also be frustrated where a ship is requisitioned for such a period as to substantially affect the obligations under the contract—see *Bank Line Ltd* v *Arthur Capel & Co.* (1919).)

19.30 In many cases the unavailability of the subject matter will only be temporary. If the contract specifies performance within a particular time, or on a certain date, then the unavailability of the subject matter at the crucial time will frustrate the contract (see *Robinson* v *Davison* (1871), para. **19.28**). But it may not always be obvious whether there is a time limit on performance of the contract. In *Jackson* v *Union Marine Insurance Co. Ltd* (1874) LR 10 CP 125 the facts were as follows:

> Jackson's ship was chartered to go, in January 1872, directly from Liverpool to Newport, and there to load a cargo of iron rails to be shipped to San Francisco. Jackson took out insurance on the chartered freight for the voyage. On the way to Newport, on 2 January, the ship ran aground in Caernarfon Bay. It took a month to free the ship and a further six months for repairs to be carried out. Meanwhile, the charterers had chartered another ship as a replacement.

8 The situation is now covered by s 1(2) of the Law Reform (Frustrated Contracts) Act 1943.

> Jackson claimed against the defendant insurance company for a total loss of the freight to be earned under the contract, by perils at sea. To succeed with such a claim, it was essential to decide whether the contract between Jackson and the charterer was frustrated, or whether he could have successfully sued the charterer for not loading the goods. In other words, did the charterer have the right to treat the contract with Jackson as discharged?

It was held that a voyage undertaken after the ship had been repaired would have been a very different adventure from the one which the parties had contracted for. A condition could be implied that the ship would arrive in Newport in time for the particular voyage. Its failure to do so within a reasonable time put an end to the contract. The long delay for repairs meant that the contract was frustrated: 'The adventure was frustrated by perils of the seas, both parties were discharged, and a loading of cargo in August would have been a new adventure, a new agreement' (per Lord Bramwell at 148).

19.31 In *Olympic Airlines SA (in Special Liquidation)* v *ACG Acquisition XX LLC* (2013), however, a lease for an aircraft which had defects including corrosion was not found to be frustrated by the Greek aviation authorities' withdrawal of the certificate of airworthiness, or by their refusal to renew it ((2012) at [173]). At appeal, Tomlinson LJ highlighted the contractual differences between an operating lease for a passenger aircraft and a time charter-party for a ship, stating that '[u]nder an operating lease the position is very different. The lessee takes possession of the aircraft and becomes responsible for its maintenance and insurance. After delivery the aircraft, engines and every part are at the sole risk of the lessee, who therefore bears the risk of loss, theft, damage, destruction and unexpected mechanical problems' ((2013) at [40]). The parties had been reminded that the need to rely upon the doctrine of frustration would only arise in the event that Olympic was unable to allege a breach of the lease by ACG (per Teare J (2012) at [177]). With reference to the guidance given by Rix LJ in *Edwinton Commercial Corp.* v *Tsavliris Russ, The 'Sea Angel'* (2007), which, it will be remembered, recommended that the application of the doctrine requires a 'multi-factorial approach' (at [111]–[112]), Teare J stated that he was 'not persuaded that the demands of justice favour frustration of the contract' ([184]), referring to matters of the length of the lease and a normal allocation of risk. He concluded that 'to hold that the lease was frustrated would reverse the allocation of risk on which the parties (absent any question of breach) had agreed' ([184]–[186]) and thus the court found in favour of ACG.

19.32 The courts will sometimes have to decide whether a contract covering a lengthy period is frustrated by supervening events which cover part of that period. Typical examples of this include the effects of a strike on a shipping contract (see *The Nema (Pioneer Shipping* v *BTP Tioxide)* (1982)), or the requisition of a commercial ship by the government at a time of war. Delay will frustrate a contract if it defeats the commercial venture, but this can be a difficult question to decide upon. In such instances the court must look at, and compare, both the length of the contract and the length of the interference which causes the unavailability of the subject matter, although this deliberation will not be the sole determinant of whether a contract is frustrated. (The Court of Appeal stated recently that while these factors are 'an important consideration', they are 'only a starting point ... the development of the law shows that such a single-factored approach is too blunt an instrument': see *Edwinton Commercial Corporation* v *Tsavliris Russ, The 'Sea Angel'* (2007) per Rix LJ at [118].)

It should also be noted that the courts are supposed to judge the situation as at the date of the frustrating event and not with the benefit of hindsight. This can lead to odd results. For example, in *Tamplin Steamship Co. Ltd* v *Anglo-Mexican Petroleum Products Co.* (1916):

> A tanker was chartered from December 1912 for a five-year period. In February 1915, the vessel was requisitioned as a troop ship. The owners of the ship claimed that the contract was frustrated by this supervening event.

The House of Lords decided that the commercial object of the contract was not frustrated as, at the time of the event in question, it appeared likely that the ship would still be available to fulfil a substantial part of the contract after the war ended. As it turned out, the House of Lords was wrong in its assumption, because the war did not end until 1918. But the case illustrates the difficulty in judging the likely effect on a contract of some event which causes the temporary unavailability of the subject matter. (In contrast to the above case, see *Metropolitan Water Board* v *Dick, Kerr, & Co.* (1918). A contract, made in 1914, to build a reservoir within six years was interrupted in 1916 by a government Order, as a result of war. The contract was frustrated because the delay caused by the Order was likely to cause a radical change to the nature of the contract, if it was later resumed.)

Impossibility: not just financial hardship

19.33 We have seen that the doctrine of frustration operates within strict limits. This is to prevent a party from trying to escape from a bad bargain on the grounds of financial hardship caused by subsequent events. The decision in *Krell* v *Henry* (1903) (discussed at para. **19.7**) is not without its critics, but it was a very unusual case and probably correct in those particular circumstances. More typically, *Amalgamated Investment & Property Co. Ltd* v *John Walker & Sons Ltd* (1976) illustrates the fact that financial hardship alone, suffered by one of the parties as a result of supervening events, will not normally frustrate a contract. It was stated by Lord Radcliffe in *Davis Contractors Ltd* v *Fareham UDC* [1956] AC 696 at 729:

> [I]t is not hardship or inconvenience or material loss itself which calls the principle of frustration into play. There must be such a change in the significance of the obligation that the thing undertaken would, if performed, be a different thing from that contracted for.

19.34 In the example of *Tsakiroglou & Co. Ltd* v *Noblee Thorl GmbH* (1962) (see para. **19.10**), performance of the contract, for the shipment of groundnuts from the Sudan to Hamburg, was made much more difficult and expensive by the subsequent closure of the Suez Canal. It was still possible for the nuts to be shipped via the Cape of Good Hope, but this alternative route would have taken over twice as long and doubled the cost of carriage. The price of the shipment was calculated on the basis that the route would be via the Suez Canal, but the contract did not specify the route; nor did it specify a date for delivery. The House of Lords held that the contract was not frustrated. Performance of the contract was more difficult and expensive for the appellants, but it was not impossible. The court refused to imply a term that the goods were to be shipped by the customary and cheapest route. (See further *Ocean Tramp Tankers Corpn* v *V/O Sofracht, The Eugenia* (1964) and *Bunge SA* v *Kyla Shipping Co Ltd, The Kyla* (2013).)

Effect of express provision for frustrating event

19.35 The doctrine of frustration has developed as a means of dealing with subsequent, unforeseen events which render performance of a contract impossible or illegal, or which fundamentally change the nature of the contractual obligations undertaken by the parties. However, the parties may make express provision dealing with certain supervening events and, in so doing, effectively preclude the operation of the doctrine. The original theory behind the doctrine, as explained in *Taylor* v *Caldwell* (1863), was that it was based on an effort to give effect to the presumed intention of the parties. In other words, it could not operate if the parties had dealt with a particular contingency by express provision. (But see *Jackson* v *Union Marine Insurance Co. Ltd* (1874), para. **19.37**.)

19.36 One obvious exception, as we have seen, is that frustration on the ground that the contract involves trading with an enemy country cannot be excluded by express provision (see *Ertel Bieber & Co.* v *Rio Tinto Co. Ltd* (1918)). This is for reasons of public policy and is not exceptionable. But, generally, the parties may make express provision for other types of supervening event, such as strikes, closure of shipping routes, illness, floods, fires, and other disasters. Thus the parties can allocate the risk of such events as they see fit. They may, for example, expressly provide for an extension to the period of performance of the contractual obligations. They may further provide that should the interference with the contract continue beyond a specified period, then either party is entitled to terminate the contract. The parties can expressly decide that neither party is entitled to compensation in the event of these contingencies. Such forward planning is particularly useful for those involved in international trade, where the threat of disruption is more likely. (See, e.g., *Olympic Airlines SA (in Special Liquidation)* v *ACG Acquisition XX LLC* (2013), discussed at para. **19.31**.)

19.37 Although the doctrine of frustration is limited to supervening events which are not expressly provided for in the contract, the courts might interpret an express provision in such a way that the doctrine may still operate. In *Jackson* v *Union Marine Insurance Co. Ltd* (1874) a contract for the hire of a ship stated that the vessel was to proceed with all possible speed (dangers and accidents of navigation excepted) from Liverpool to Newport, in order to load a cargo of iron for San Francisco. The ship ran aground, not far from Liverpool, and was delayed for eight months. It was held that, notwithstanding the express exception of dangers and accidents of navigation, the contract was frustrated. The words of exception appeared to cover the contingency which in fact occurred, but the court found a way of limiting their application because it clearly felt that a voyage undertaken after the repair to the ship would have been a different 'adventure' altogether. Accordingly, the express provision was given a restrictive interpretation by the court; it would excuse the owner of the ship and protect him from an action for breach of contract, but it would not deprive the charterer of the right to treat his contractual undertakings as discharged. For a further example of a restrictive interpretation of an express provision, see *Metropolitan Water Board* v *Dick, Kerr, & Co.* (1918).

Frustration does not apply to foreseeable events

19.38 The doctrine of frustration does not generally apply to situations where the supervening event was foreseen or foreseeable. (Once again, trading with the enemy is an obvious exception for public policy reasons. Even if war was foreseeable, it would not prevent the doctrine from being applied.) If the parties foresee that a particular event might occur which may affect their performance of the contract, it will be assumed that they contracted in accordance with that risk. For example, in *Davis Contractors Ltd* v *Fareham UDC* [1956] AC 696, the House of Lords rejected the company's claim that the contract, for the construction of 78 houses within a period of eight months for a fixed price, was frustrated by shortages of labour and materials which increased the cost of the work. The basic obligations under the agreement remained unchanged and financial hardship to one of the parties was not a sufficient reason for invoking the doctrine.

The *Davis Contractors* decision can be defended on the basis that the risk of increased costs, due to various shortages, was clearly foreseen by the company. It must therefore be assumed that it accepted that risk at the time of contracting. (The company had in fact sent a letter along with the original tender stating that the tender was subject to the availability of adequate supplies of labour and building materials. This letter was not incorporated into the contract, nor was such a provision expressly included in the contract.) Lord Radcliffe stated (at 731):

> Two things seem to me to prevent the application of the principle of frustration to this case. One is that the cause of the delay was not any new state of things which the parties could not reasonably be thought to have foreseen. On the contrary, the possibility of enough labour and materials not being available was before their eyes and could have been the subject of special contractual stipulation. It was not made so.[9]

19.39 However, the significance of foreseeability of risk has been considered recently in two decisions handed down by the Court of Appeal. The first was in *Edwinton Commercial Corporation* v *Tsavliris Russ Ltd, The 'Sea Angel'* (2007) at [102]–[104]. Here, Rix LJ explained that there was no absolute rule to the effect that foreseeability precluded the application of the doctrine of frustration in all circumstances, and went on to state (at [127]):

> In a sense, most events are to a greater or lesser degree foreseeable. That does not mean that they cannot lead to frustration … However … the less that an event, in its type and impact, is foreseeable, the more likely it is to be a factor which, depending on other factors in the case, may lead on to frustration.

9 Whether the doctrine can apply to events which were foreseen or contemplated by the parties is also discussed in *The Eugenia* (1964). See also the more recent case of *Globe Master Management Ltd* v *Boulas-Gad Ltd* (2002).

The case of *Armchair Answercall Ltd v People in Mind Ltd* (2016) also afforded the Court of Appeal an opportunity to consider the scope and application of the doctrine of frustration. The decision illustrates the relevance of foreseeability in determining whether the doctrine should apply and serves as a recent reminder that—with a test which can prove difficult to satisfy—a finding of frustration is rare. The facts were:

> People In Mind (PIM) took over the management of a company which provided call centre services. Their clients were managed by franchisees. To accommodate the change, PIM retained the services of the managing director of the former company to transition the existing franchisees to the new structure. This contract was for 12 months and services were provided through a nominee company—Armchair Answercall (AA). When the transition went poorly, the franchisees all left the company and set up a competing business. The franchise agreements were terminated. PIM then refused to pay the monthly fee to the consultant AA. They argued that AA's contract had been frustrated when all the franchisees left.

The Court of Appeal considered that the definition of transition under the contract with AA included more than PIM thought it did. When all the franchisees left, PIM could recruit new franchisees and customers and use AA's services in that process. Also, the treatment of a franchisee during the transition negotiations had contributed to the departure of the franchisees as a whole. The supposed frustrating event was, at least in part, the results of the act of AA, whether or not they would be said to amount to fault. The agreement taken in its context must be taken to have contemplated that the franchisees might not be persuaded to transition to the new business. For this reason, their departure was foreseeable and the court therefore held that the contract was not frustrated.

Frustration cannot be 'self-induced'

19.40 The doctrine of frustration applies only in circumstances where the supervening event is beyond the control of the parties to the contract. It follows that, where the alleged frustrating event is caused by the deliberate act or decision of one of the parties, or by his or her negligence, the doctrine will not apply. Whichever theory lies behind the doctrine—whether it is based on the presumed contractual intention of the parties, or whether it is simply a fair solution imposed by the courts—it is not possible to justify its application to subsequent events which are 'self-induced'. An example of this rule is provided by *Ocean Tramp Tankers Corpn* v *V/O Sofracht, The Eugenia* (1964), where the facts were:

> The Eugenia was let out to the charterers to go from Genoa to the Black Sea to load cargo, and thence to India to unload cargo. Having loaded, the ship proceeded on its route to India, which took it via Suez. In breach of contract, the charterers allowed the ship to enter a war zone. (The contract contained a 'war clause' which prohibited the charterers from sailing the ship into a dangerous zone without the owner's permission.) The ship entered the Suez Canal and was trapped when the canal was closed. The charterers tried to rely on the detention of the ship as a frustrating event.

The Court of Appeal held that the charterers could not rely on the fact that the ship was trapped in the canal, as this was their own fault. They were in breach of contract by allowing the ship to enter a war zone and, therefore, the alleged frustrating event was self-induced. A different case, illustrating the same basic rule, is *Maritime National Fish Ltd* v *Ocean Trawlers Ltd* (1935), where:

> Maritime National Fish (MNF) chartered a steam trawler, fitted with an otter trawl, from Ocean Trawlers (OT). The parties expressly agreed that the trawler should be used only in the fishing industry. Both parties knew, at the time of the agreement, that it was illegal to use an otter trawl without a licence from the Canadian government. A few months after the contract was made, MNF applied for five licences for the five trawlers which they were operating, but they were granted only three by the government. MNF were, therefore, forced to name the three ships which they wished to license, and the three which they chose did not include the one chartered from OT. OT brought an action for the hire, and MNF argued that the contract was frustrated by the refusal of the government to grant more than three licences to them.

One of the reasons given by the Canadian appeal court for rejecting MNF's contention was that the risk of not obtaining a licence was foreseeable, and MNF could have insisted that some express provision be made for this contingency. Having failed to do so, MNF accepted the risk of not obtaining a licence to fish with OT's trawler. The Privy Council did not disagree with this ruling, but their Lordships thought that it was unnecessary to hear detailed argument on this point. They held that the Canadian court's other reason for dismissing MNF's contention was correct and was a sufficient basis for dismissing MNF's appeal: namely, that the alleged frustrating event arose from the deliberate act or choice of MNF. The doctrine of frustration could not be relied upon where the supervening event in question was 'self-induced'.

19.41 *Maritime National Fish Ltd* v *Ocean Trawlers Ltd* (1935) was applied by the Court of Appeal in *J Lauritzen A/S* v *Wijsmuller BV, The Super Servant Two* [1990] 1 Lloyd's Rep 1. The facts were:

> The defendants agreed to transport the claimants' drilling rig from Japan to Rotterdam. The contract specified that the rig was to be delivered between 20 June and 20 August (in 1981) and was to be carried by what was described as the 'transportation unit'. This unit was defined as meaning either *Super Servant One* or *Super Servant Two*. Before performance of the contract was due, the defendants decided to use *Super Servant Two* for transporting the claimants' rig, and they entered into contracts with other parties for which they planned to use *Super Servant One*. On 29 January 1981, *Super Servant Two* sank whilst being used on another job and, shortly afterwards, the defendants told the claimants that they would not be carrying out their obligations under the contract, as *Super Servant One* was unavailable due to use in other contracts. Under a 'without prejudice' agreement, the defendants eventually transported the claimants' rig on a barge towed by a tug. The claimants later claimed for the losses they had suffered.

The Court of Appeal held that the defendants could not rely on the doctrine of frustration as it was their own choice that they decided not to use *Super Servant One* for this purpose. (Also see *Bunge SA* v *Kyla Shipping Co Ltd, The Kyla* (2013).) The sinking of *Super Servant Two* did not bring the contract to an end automatically, as the defendants had an alternative. In other words, if it had been foreseen at the time of contracting that one of the vessels might become unavailable to transport the rig, the parties would not have been concerned as there was another vessel which could perform the same task. It would have been different if the defendants owned only one 'transportation unit' and that had sunk through no fault of their own. Bingham LJ stated (at 9):

> The doctrine [of frustration] must avail a party who contracts to perform a contract of carriage with a vessel which, through no fault of his, no longer exists. But that is not this case. The contract [with the claimants] did provide an alternative ... [T]he present case does not fall within the very limited class of cases in which the law will relieve one party from an absolute promise he has chosen to make.

19.42 Similar issues were raised in the House of Lords in *Paal Wilson & Co. A/S* v *Partenreederei Hannah Blumenthal, The Hannah Blumenthal* [1983] 1 All ER 34. The case concerned the sale of a ship under a contract which provided that any dispute arising out of the sale was to be settled by arbitration. Disputes arose about the vessel, and the buyers commenced arbitration proceedings. As originally agreed, both parties appointed an arbitrator, but a third arbitrator (as provided for in the contract) was never appointed. In all, there was a period of more than seven years' delay in the arbitration. The question arose whether the arbitration agreement was frustrated as a result of the long delay, which was the fault of both parties. The House of Lords held that, in such circumstances, the fact that the parties were under a mutual obligation to keep the arbitration process moving meant that neither party could rely on the delay of the other as a ground for claiming frustration of the agreement to arbitrate. Lord Brandon stated (at 44):

> [T]here are two essential factors which must be present in order to frustrate a contract. The first essential factor is that there must be some outside event or extraneous change of situation, not foreseen or provided for by the parties at the time of contracting, which either makes it impossible for the contract to be performed at all, or at least renders its performance something radically different from what the parties contemplated when they entered into it. The second essential factor is that the outside event or extraneous change of situation concerned, and the consequences of either in relation to the performance of the contract, must have occurred without either the fault or default of either party to the contract.[10]

In *The Flying Music Co Ltd* v *Theater Entertainment SA* (2017), a contract to put on a performance in Greece had been agreed during a time of civil unrest and economic upheaval. As the continuation of the country's state of affairs did not amount to circumstances which were 'radically different' from those which were contemplated by the parties when they entered into the agreement, this did not constitute a frustrating event.

10 See also Griffiths LJ's useful summary of the relevant authorities in his dissenting judgment in the Court of Appeal in the same case: [1982] 3 All ER 394 at 406–7.

19.43 However, if the 'fault' of a party to a contract is merely of a minor nature, he or she may still be able to rely on the doctrine. It will be a question of degree as to whether the particular 'fault' or 'default' amounts to self-induced frustration. Where a person acts in a deliberate way (as in *The Eugenia* (1964)), or makes a deliberate choice (as in *Maritime National Fish* (1935)), so as to bring about the frustrating event, he or she will be precluded from relying on the doctrine. But, for example, would a contract for some personal performance be frustrated if the person concerned became incapacitated by his or her own carelessness—such as a professional acrobat who sustains injury on a private skiing expedition and, as a result, is unable to perform his or her act? This type of problem was acknowledged, without being resolved, in *Joseph Constantine Steamship Line Ltd* v *Imperial Smelting Corpn Ltd* [1941] 2 All ER 165 (per Viscount Simon LC at 173). There seems to be no reason, in principle, why events brought about by a party's own negligence should not be regarded as self-induced and thus preclude the application of the doctrine.

It should be noted that, where self-induced frustration is alleged, the onus of proof falls on the party making the allegation. In *Joseph Constantine*, the owners of a steamship (*The Kingswood*) chartered the vessel to the respondents, to go to Australia and load a cargo there. Before the cargo was loaded, an explosion occurred in the boiler of the ship, preventing the contract from being carried out. The respondents sued the owners for damages and the owners claimed that the contract was frustrated by the explosion. The respondents argued that the onus of proof rested on the owners to show that the explosion was not their fault. The House of Lords held that the contract was frustrated. The cause of the explosion was not clear, but the respondents had failed to prove that the frustrating event was the owner's fault. The burden of proof was not on the owners to disprove negligence on their part.

Effects of the doctrine

19.44 So far in this chapter we have been concerned with the issue of whether a contract is frustrated. We must now consider the practical consequences that arise when the parties are discharged under the doctrine. Unless the law provides for a fair distribution of the loss resulting from the supervening event, it may not be satisfactory simply to hold that the contract is frustrated. For example, a party may have incurred considerable expenditure in reliance upon the contract before the frustrating event occurred. The common law rules governing this type of situation have now been improved upon by the Law Reform (Frustrated Contracts) Act 1943. Both are considered in turn below.

19.45 It is well settled that frustration automatically brings the contract to an end at the time of the frustrating event. This is in contrast to discharge by breach of contract where the innocent party can choose whether to treat the contract as repudiated. Moreover, a contract which is discharged by frustration is clearly different from one which is void for mistake. A frustrated contract is valid until the time of the supervening event but is automatically ended thereafter, whereas a contract void on the grounds of mistake is a complete nullity from the beginning. A clear statement about the legal effect of frustration on a contract can be found in *Hirji Mulji* v *Cheong Yue Steamship Co. Ltd* [1926] AC 497, where the facts were:

> The respondent owners of a ship, *The Singaporean*, agreed by a charter-party of November 1916 to hire out their vessel to the appellants from 1 March 1917. The appellants agreed to use the ship for ten months from the date of delivery. Before 1 March 1917, the ship was requisitioned by the government and not released until February 1919. When the ship was requisitioned, the owners, thinking that she would soon be released, asked the appellants if they were still willing to take up the charter (i.e. a little later). The appellants said that they would do so, but when the ship was finally released (later than expected) in February 1919, they refused to accept it. The owners argued that the appellants could not rely on the doctrine of frustration, despite the supervening event, as they had chosen to affirm the contract.

On appeal from the Supreme Court of Hong Kong, the Privy Council held that the contract was frustrated in 1917. This meant that the obligations under the contract were brought to an end immediately and automatically at the time of the frustrating event. The application of the doctrine did not rely upon the election of the parties. So even where the parties continue to treat the contract as subsisting for a period of time after the supervening event, the court may declare it to be frustrated. In reference to the delay caused by the requisitioning of the ship, Lord Sumner said (at 501) that it was immaterial that the parties thought at first that the delay would not frustrate the contract. He went on (at 509–10) to explain that whereas repudiation (or rescission) for breach is 'a right to treat the contract as at an end if [the victim] chooses', frustration operates independently of the choice of the parties. Frustration operates, he added, 'irrespective of the individuals concerned, their temperaments and failings, their interest and circumstances'.

19.46 As a consequence of the rule that a contract is valid until the time of the frustrating event, and is determined automatically thereafter, certain other rules were said to follow. The common law position was encapsulated in the slightly enigmatic expression that 'the loss lies where it falls'. For example, where money was paid under a contract which was later frustrated, it was not recoverable. This was because parties remained liable for contractual obligations which fell due before the supervening event. On the other hand, the parties escaped from performing those obligations which had not yet fallen due at the time of frustration. The potential for unfairness under this common law approach can best be understood by looking at the relevant decisions. In *Chandler* v *Webster* [1904] 1 KB 493 the facts were:

> The claimant contracted to hire a room in Pall Mall from the defendant for the purpose of watching the coronation procession on 26 June 1902. The price for the hire of the room was £141 15s and it was payable immediately. The claimant paid £100, but before he paid the balance the procession was cancelled due to the illness of the King. The claimant sought to recover the money he had paid.

The Court of Appeal held that his claim could not succeed. Moreover, he was liable for the remaining £41 15s, as this obligation had fallen due before the frustrating event occurred. Despite receiving no actual benefit whatsoever, the claimant was still liable for the hire of the room. Lord Collins MR explained the justification for this outcome (at 499):

> If the effect [of a frustrating event] were that the contract were wiped out altogether, no doubt the result would be that the money paid under it would have to be repaid as on a failure of consideration. But that is not the effect of the doctrine; it only releases the parties from further performance of the contract. Therefore the doctrine of failure of consideration does not apply.

19.47 The harsh results of this rule as laid down by *Chandler* v *Webster* (1904) were, not surprisingly, subjected to considerable criticism. The Law Revision Committee[11] suggested that the rule should be changed but, before any implementation of this Report took place, *Chandler* v *Webster* was overruled by *Fibrosa Spolka Akcyjna* v *Fairbairn Lawson Combe Barbour Ltd* [1943] AC 32 ('the *Fibrosa* case'). The case involved a contract under which the respondents, an English company, were to manufacture certain machinery for the appellants, a Polish company, and deliver it to Gdynia. The appellants were to pay £4,800 for the machinery, a third of which (i.e. £1,600) was to be paid with the order. In fact, only £1,000 was paid with the order. Subsequently, Germany invaded Poland and occupied Gdynia. At this time, none of the machinery had been delivered. For reasons which we have considered earlier, the contract was frustrated and the appellants sued for the return of the £1,000.

The Court of Appeal followed the rule in *Chandler* v *Webster* and held that the money was irrecoverable. But the House of Lords decided that there had been a total failure of consideration and that the appellants were entitled to recover £1,000 from the respondents. Viscount Simon stated (at 46–7):

> To claim the return of money paid on the ground of total failure of consideration is not to vary the terms of the contract in any way. The claim arises not because the right to be repaid is one of the stipulated conditions of the contract, but because, in the circumstances that have happened, the law gives the remedy . . . [I]t does not follow that because the [claimant] cannot sue 'on the contract' he cannot sue dehors [or outside] the contract for the recovery of a payment in respect of which consideration has failed.[12]

The decision in the *Fibrosa* case was an improvement on the harshness of *Chandler* v *Webster*, but it was not a complete solution to the problem of money paid under a contract which was then frustrated. This was freely acknowledged by their Lordships in the course of their judgments (see [1943] AC 32 at 49–50, 54–5, and 71–2). Recovery of money paid depended on there having been a total failure of consideration; the performance of just a part of the consideration would thus prevent such a claim from succeeding. (For example, consider *Whincup* v *Hughes* (1871).) So if the English company had delivered part of the machinery before the discharge of the contract, failure of consideration would not have been total, and the advance payment would have been irrecoverable.

11 Seventh Interim Report, Cmnd 6009, 1939.

12 The term 'consideration' is used here in a different sense from that which we saw in Chapter 4. There it meant the promise given in exchange for some act or promise, whereas in this context it denotes the actual performance of the promise. See the comments of Viscount Simon in the *Fibrosa* case [1943] AC 32.

Furthermore, the decision in the *Fibrosa* case made no allowance for the expenses which were incurred under the contract by the payee. In other words, it was not really a fair solution to both parties; it provided for the return of the prepayment, but it did not compensate the recipient for the expenditure that it had incurred whilst partially carrying out the contract. In the *Fibrosa* case itself, the £1,000 was recoverable, but the English company received nothing for the considerable amount of work it had done on the machinery before the frustrating event. The common law did not allow the apportionment of the prepaid sum in this situation. To deal with these obvious defects in the law, the Law Reform (Frustrated Contracts) Act 1943 was enacted soon after the *Fibrosa* case.

The Law Reform (Frustrated Contracts) Act 1943

General

19.48 The Law Reform (Frustrated Contracts) Act 1943 (LR(FC)A 1943) was introduced in an attempt to provide for a fair solution between the parties when their contract has been frustrated. (See also *Great Peace Shipping Ltd* v *Tsavliris Salvage (International) Ltd* (2003) at [161].) It aimed at preventing the unjust enrichment of either party to the contract at the expense of the other. It deals only with situations where contracts have 'become impossible of performance or been otherwise frustrated' and the parties have consequently been discharged from further performance (s 1(1)). It should be noted that the Act does not lay down the general principles under which the doctrine will be invoked and this question is still dealt with under the common law rules that we have considered earlier in this chapter. Also, the parties may themselves have made express provision for the frustrating event which has occurred, in which case, under s 2(3), the court is to give effect to the parties' intentions and the Act is excluded by their contrary agreement.

19.49 LR(FC)A 1943 does not apply to all types of contract. Section 2(5) states that the Act is not applicable to the following:

> (a) any charterparty, except a time charterparty ... or to any contract (other than a charterparty) for the carriage of goods by sea; or
> (b) any contract of insurance ...
> (c) any contract to which section 7 of the Sale of Goods Act (now 1979) applies, or to any other contract for the sale, or for the sale and delivery, of specific goods, where the contract is frustrated by reason of the fact that the goods have perished.

The main changes introduced by the Act

19.50 LR(FC)A 1943, s 1(2) provides that:

> All sums paid or payable to any party in pursuance of the contract before the time when the parties were so discharged (in this Act referred to as 'the time of discharge') shall, in the case of sums so paid, be recoverable from him as money received by him for the use of the party by whom the sums were paid, and, in the case of sums so payable, cease to be so payable.

In other words, this subsection enacts that advance payments made in pursuance of the contract before the supervening event are recoverable. This provision goes further than *Fibrosa Spolka Akcyjna* v *Fairbairn Lawson Combe Barbour Ltd* (1943), in that claims under s 1(2) are not restricted to cases where the consideration for the payment has totally failed. It also provides that money which is payable under the contract before the frustrating event, but not yet paid, ceases to be payable. Of course, there will be cases where the recipient of the advance payment has incurred expenses before the contract was frustrated. It may well be that the parties agreed on some advance payment for this very reason. If the whole sum is recoverable on discharge, then this can be as unfair to the payee as the old rule in *Chandler* v *Webster* (1904) was to the payer. For this reason, the new provisions are subject to the following important proviso which is appended to s 1(2):

> Provided that, if the party to whom the sums were so paid or payable incurred expenses before the time of discharge in, or for the purpose of, the performance of the contract, the court may, if it considers it just to do so having regard to all the circumstances of the case, allow him to retain or, as the case may be, recover the whole or any part of the sums so paid or payable, not being an amount in excess of the expenses so incurred.

It should be emphasized that this award of expenses can be made only where an advance sum was either paid or payable before the frustrating event. Thus LR(FC)A 1943, s 1(2) represents an improvement upon the common law decision in the *Fibrosa* case. In that case the English company had incurred considerable expenditure and received nothing in return. As we have seen, the common law did not permit the apportionment of an advance payment in circumstances such as these, and the legislature acted promptly in response to criticism of this lack of flexibility.

19.51 Under LR(FC)A 1943, s 1(2), a party who has incurred expenses in the performance of the contract may be awarded expenses up to a limit of the sums paid or payable to him or her under the contract before the frustrating event. Such an award will be made where the court 'considers it just to do so having regard to all the circumstances of the case'—in other words, any award is at the discretion of the court. To return to the facts of *Fibrosa Spolka Akcyjna* v *Fairbairn Lawson Combe Barbour Ltd* (1943), for example: the English company might, under the new provision, have been compensated for its expenses incurred before the supervening event. But it will be remembered that only £1,600 was to be paid by the Polish company with the order for the machinery. Therefore that amount (£1,600) would be the maximum that could have been awarded to the English company for expenses. In considering an award for expenses, in circumstances such as those of the *Fibrosa* case, the court will take account of whether the goods are of any commercial value to the sellers. If they can be sold to another buyer, then the expenses incurred under the original contract (before frustration) will not have been wasted.

19.52 The case of *Gamerco SA* v *ICM/Fair Warning (Agency) Ltd* [1995] 1 WLR 1226 provides a rare judicial discussion of the application of LR(FC)A 1943, s 1(2). The facts were that, in 1992, the claimant concert promoters (C) agreed to promote a pop group's (D's) concert at a football stadium in Madrid on a specific date, as part of that group's European tour. Shortly before the date of the concert, but after the contract was made by the parties, engineers discovered that the stadium was unsafe and its use was subsequently prohibited by the local authorities. Thus, C's permit to hold the concert was withdrawn and, as no other suitable venue was available at this time, the concert was cancelled. C had paid $412,500 to D in advance, and both parties had incurred some expenditure in preparing for the concert. The action involved C's claim to recover the advance payment under s 1(2) of the Act, and D's counterclaim for breach of contract by C for failing to secure the required permit for the performance.

The judge, Garland J, in the High Court held that the contract was frustrated due to the stadium being unsafe and its use for the concert being banned. D's counterclaim was unsuccessful as C was not required to ensure that the permit, once obtained, would remain in force. More significantly, it was decided to allow C's claim in its entirety, with the judge ordering the repayment of the whole sum paid in advance to D; that is, there was no deduction (or 'set off') to compensate D. The judge felt that, despite the fact that D had incurred some expenditure in advance of the proposed performance, justice would be done by making no deduction from the ordered repayment under the proviso. It seems that the precise nature of D's expenses was not very clear and the judge found it impossible to determine an accurate amount: 'the best I can do is to accept that [D] did incur some expenses, but the extent of them is wholly unproven' (per Garland J at 1235). Presumably it was felt that C's expenses were heavier and more calculable than those of the defendant pop group.

19.53 Another important innovation introduced by LR(FC)A 1943 is contained in s 1(3), which states:

> Where any party to the contract has, by reason of anything done by any other party thereto in, or for the purpose of, the performance of the contract, obtained a valuable benefit (other than a payment of money to which ... [section 1(2)] ... applies) before the time of discharge, there shall be recoverable from him by the said other party such sum (if any), not exceeding the value of the said benefit to the party obtaining it, as the court considers just, having regard to all the circumstances of the case and, in particular—
>
> (a) the amount of any expenses incurred before the time of discharge by the benefited party in, or for the purpose of, the performance of the contract, including any sums paid or payable by him to any other party in pursuance of the contract and retained or recoverable by that party under ... [section 1(2)], and
>
> (b) the effect, in relation to the said benefit, of the circumstances giving rise to the frustration of the contract.

19.54 Under the common law, a party escaped the performance of those obligations which had not yet fallen due at the time of frustration. So if (hypothetically), in *Fibrosa Spolka Akcyjna* v *Fairbairn Lawson Combe Barbour Ltd* (1943), the contract had been for the English company to manufacture the machinery at a price of £4,800, to be paid on delivery, it would have received nothing when the contract was frustrated before completion of the work. This is supported by *Appleby* v *Myers* (1867), where the claimant claimed damages for the work already done in erecting machinery on the defendant's premises before the contract was frustrated by an accidental fire which destroyed both the machinery and the premises. This claim was unsuccessful, as the supervening event discharged both parties from their obligations under the contract and gave no cause of action to either of them. (The contract did not provide for any advance payment and the court interpreted the agreement as one for payment on completion of the work.)

19.55 The ponderously worded LR(FC)A 1943, s 1(3) was introduced to improve upon the rather unjust position at common law. Where a party has obtained a 'valuable benefit' under the contract, before the supervening event, the court may order him or her to pay a fair sum for it, having regard to all the circumstances. To return to the facts of *Appleby* v *Myers* (1867), the court would now have to consider whether the defendants did in fact obtain a valuable benefit from the claimant's work. Before the fire took place, the machinery (albeit unfinished) possibly constituted a benefit; but after the fire, such benefit as had been obtained was rendered worthless to the defendant (see s 1(3)(b), earlier). It is therefore far from clear that the Act would improve the claimant's position in such a case. (*Quaere*: Should the court assess the value of the alleged benefit on the basis of how things stood immediately before the frustrating event?)

19.56 An illustration of the potential usefulness of LR(FC)A 1943, s 1(3) is provided by the old case of *Cutter* v *Powell* (1795). The second mate of a ship, the *Governor Parry*, was promised 30 guineas for the completion of a voyage from Kingston (Jamaica) to Liverpool. (The basic rate of pay per month was £4, but the contract in question provided for a much higher rate; this was payable only where the sailor served for the whole of the voyage.) The sailor died after seven weeks of the voyage and his widow (the executrix) claimed a proportion of his wages, on a quantum meruit basis, for the work he had done on the voyage before his death. The court rejected the widow's claim, as the contract stipulated that the voyage had to be completed. This is sometimes referred to as the 'doctrine of strict performance'.

It is possible that the outcome of *Cutter* v *Powell* would be different today under s 1(3) and that the widow could recover from the defendant for the valuable benefit which he had obtained from the sailor's labour (although the work would presumably be compensated at the basic rate only). But it is also possible that the Act would have been excluded by the contrary agreement of the parties, as provided for by s 2(3).[13] This might depend on the construction of their agreement. Did they agree, for example, that there was to be no payment whatsoever unless the entire voyage was completed by the sailor?

19.57 The first major case to be decided on the LR(FC)A 1943 was *BP Exploration Co. (Libya) Ltd* v *Hunt (No 2)* [1982] 1 All ER 925. (The judgments of the Queen's Bench Division, the Court of Appeal, and the House of Lords can all be found under this reference.) The facts were as follows:

13 But consider *BP Exploration Co. (Libya)* v *Hunt (No 2)* (1982), where the House of Lords took a narrow view of s 2(3), refusing to hold that it defeated the claimant's claim for an award of a just sum.

Nelson Hunt had been granted an oil concession in Libya by the government of that country. He entered into an agreement with a large oil company, BP, to exploit the oil concession, as he lacked the resources to go ahead on his own. BP were to do the exploratory work, which they would finance, and in return they would get a half share of Hunt's concession. They also had to make certain 'farm-in' payments to Hunt in cash and oil. As soon as the oil field became productive, BP were to receive half of all the oil produced from it, together with 'reimbursement oil' (taken from Hunt's share) to meet the cost of the company's 'farm-in' payments and to cover Hunt's share of the development expenses. Thus BP were to bear the principal risk of failure in their combined venture. After much expenditure, a large oil field was discovered, which became productive in 1967. But in 1971 BP's half share in the concession was expropriated by the new Libyan government, following a revolution in that country. The same fate befell Hunt's half share in 1973. At the time of the frustrating event, BP had received about one-third of the reimbursement oil to which they were entitled. The company brought a claim under s 1(3) of the Act for an award of a just sum.

The claim was allowed by Robert Goff J and he awarded BP a just sum under s 1(3) of the Act. The precise calculation of the amount is a complex matter which will not be elaborated here. Hunt's appeals to both the Court of Appeal and the House of Lords were unsuccessful. The main judgment on the scope of s 1(3) is that of the trial judge. (In the House of Lords, their Lordships dealt with fairly minor, technical issues.) Robert Goff J (at 950) explained that Hunt's benefit was the increase in the value of the oil concession as a result of BP's work. It should be noted, however, that the value of this benefit was substantially reduced by the circumstances giving rise to the frustration of the contract, namely the expropriation of the parties' interests in the oil field.

Summary

- The doctrine of frustration developed to deal with cases where events occur after a contract is made which render the agreement illegal or impossible to perform, or which fundamentally change the nature of the obligations undertaken by the parties.
- A frustrating event must not be the result of any fault of either of the contracting parties.
- The doctrine of frustration does not generally apply to situations where the supervening event was foreseen or foreseeable.
- If the parties have made express provision for how they will deal with the consequences of future events which may affect performance, the doctrine of frustration will not usually be applicable.
- The doctrine operates within strict limits and cannot be used simply to escape the consequences of what has turned out to be a bad bargain.
- The doctrine of frustration may apply where the subject matter of the contract is destroyed, or where a contract is made to perform an act which subsequently becomes illegal.

- The use of the doctrine is very restricted in cases where, although the commercial purpose of the contract has been drastically affected by unforeseen events, the performance of the contract is still possible.
- Frustration brings a contract to an end, automatically, at the time of the frustrating event.
- The common law held that the 'loss lies where it falls' (for example, money paid under a contract which was later frustrated was not recoverable).
- Despite improvements to the common law position on the effects of frustration, there was still a lack of flexibility for the courts to provide a fair solution between the parties.
- The Law Reform (Frustrated Contracts) Act 1943 was enacted to improve upon the common law, by preventing the unjust enrichment of either party to the contract at the expense of the other. (It should be noted that the 1943 Act does not set out the general principles under which the doctrine may be invoked; this is still a matter for the common law.)
- Under s 1(2) of the 1943 Act, advance payments made before the frustrating event are recoverable, subject to an entitlement of the payee to an award of expenses up to a limit of the amount paid (or payable) to him or her before the frustrating event. Such an award is at the court's discretion.
- The award of expenses is available only where an advance sum was either paid or payable before the frustrating event.
- Under s 1(3) of the 1943 Act, where a party has obtained a 'valuable benefit' under the contract prior to the frustrating event, the court may order him to pay a fair sum for it, having regard to all the circumstances.

Further reading

D. Brodie, 'Performance Issues and Frustration of Contract' (2006) 71 Employment Law Bulletin 4

P. Clark, 'Frustration, Restitution and the Law Reform (Frustrated Contracts) Act 1943' [1996] 2 LMCLQ 170

C. Hall, 'Frustration and the Question of Foresight' (1984) 4 LS 300

E. McKendrick, 'The Construction of Force Majeure Clauses and Self-Induced Frustration' [1990] 2 LMCLQ 153

M. Pawlowski, 'Mistake, Frustration and Implied Conditions in Leases' (2007) 11 (5) L&T Review 158

J. C. Smith, 'Contracts—Mistake, Frustration and Implied Terms' (1994) 110 LQR 400

L. Trakman, 'Frustrated Contracts and Legal Fictions' (1983) 46 MLR 39

Chapter 20

Damages

Introduction

20.1 Although it is common to speak of 'enforcing the contract', the primary remedy for breach of contract is not specific performance but damages, and damages will form the subject matter of this chapter, whilst specific enforcement will be covered in the next. However, many disputes will be settled without the assistance of the courts.[1] The parties may reach an agreement which resolves their dispute. The contract itself may have been drafted to deal with difficulties. It might contain a liquidated damages clause (see para. **20.69**ff), stating how much is to be paid by one party in the event of a particular breach. The other party may then simply be able to deduct that sum from his or her contractual payments. In addition, the order of performance may have been fixed so that one party, X, can withhold his or her performance until the other party, Y, performs. Y then has an incentive to perform in order to trigger X's obligation (see para. 18.8). In this context the right to terminate for breach should not be forgotten. The threat to exercise that right may induce the other party to comply with the contract, and the actual exercise of it enables an injured party to extract themselves from the contract. (Note that in relation to consumers, remedies have changed through the introduction of the Consumer Rights Act 2015 (see ss 20–24) and the consumer no longer has the common law right to treat a contract to supply goods as at an end where the breach is of a term required by the Act to be treated as included in the contract (see s 19).) However, here we are concerned primarily with contractual damages, with specific performance and injunctions being considered in Chapter 21.

1 S. Macauley, 'Non-Contractual Relations in Business' (1963) 28 Am Soc Rev 55; H. Beale and A. Dugdale, 'Contracts between Businessmen: Planning and the Use of Contractual Remedies' (1975) 2 Br J Law and Soc 45.

Basic principle and the claims

Expectation loss

20.2 In general, the sum awarded for breach of contract will be calculated so as to compensate the injured party rather than to recover any profit made by the party in breach. This means generally, if the 'injured' party has suffered no loss, the damages awarded will be nominal—merely marking the contractual right. However, the House of Lords has indicated that, very exceptionally, recovery of the profit of the party in breach is possible (*A-G* v *Blake* (2000)). This is dealt with at para. **20.18**ff. However, what must be emphasized here is the ordinary recovery of damages for breach of contract and compensating the injured party's loss.

20.3 The loss claimed will often relate to damage to the injured party's economic interest, such as the loss of profit, but it may also include personal injury or damage to property. In addition, in limited cases it will be possible to recover damages for mental distress occasioned by the breach and, more broadly, there has been some recognition that damages must be available to cover the 'consumer surplus', the non-financial benefit which the injured party was to derive from the contract. Such claims will be looked at in the final section of this chapter. Here we should consider the basic principle, without addressing those complications.

20.4 The basic principle behind an award of contractual damages is that the injured party should be put in the position he or she would have been in had the contract been performed. This was stated by Parke B in *Robinson* v *Harman* (1848) 1 Ex 850. He said (at 855):

> The rule of the common law is that where a party sustains a loss by reason of a breach of contract he is, so far as money can do it, to be placed in the same situation with respect to damages as if the contract had been performed.

This basic principle means that contractual damages cover the injured party's expectation loss—the loss of what he or she would have received had the contract been performed.[2] This means that damages cover the profit which the injured party would have derived from the contractual performance. This can be simply explained by an example: X contracted with Y for the purchase of some goods from Y for £500 and, when the time came for delivery, Y refused to deliver. By that time the market price of the goods had risen to £600. X can claim £100, the profit he or she would have made on the contract. Had Y performed, X would have had goods worth £600 by the time of delivery (and it will cost him or her £100 more than the contract price to buy substitute goods in the market). £100 will put X in the position he or she would have been in had Y performed.[3] In appropriate circumstances, however, instead of expectation loss the injured party may claim for his or her reliance loss (see para. **20.9**ff).

2 But see Fuller and Perdue, 46 Yale LJ 52.

3 See Sale of Goods Act 1979, s 51.

20.5 Nominal damages are awarded where there is no loss. Such a situation should be distinguished from the case where the loss is difficult to quantify, for example where the injured party has been deprived of an opportunity of participating in the final round of a beauty competition (*Chaplin* v *Hicks* (1911)). Under such circumstances, the court will not leave the injured party with nominal damages even though quantification is difficult. However, where the benefit to be derived from the contract, the expectation loss, is uncertain, it may be better for the injured party to claim for wasted expenditure, that is, reliance loss.[4]

20.6 Although it is simple to state the basic principle on which contractual damages are awarded, in some cases questions arise as to how that should be measured and converted into money terms. Here we shall briefly consider some of the cases in which there is a basic established measure of damages.

20.7 There are, of course, many situations in which an established rule for measuring damages can be followed. In the context of sale of goods, for example, the basic situations are covered by statute. Section 51(3) of the Sale of Goods Act 1979 provides a prima facie basis for calculating damages when the buyer fails to deliver. Section 51(3) states:

> Where there is an available market for the goods in question the measure of damages is prima facie to be ascertained by the difference between the contract price and the market or current price of the goods at the time or times when they ought to have been delivered or (if no time was fixed) at the time of refusal to deliver.

As has been indicated, where there is a market for the goods in question, this will put the buyer in the position he or she would have been in had the contract been performed. His or her damages cover the difference between the contract price and what he or she would have had to pay to buy substitute goods in the market when the seller breached. Of course, he or she might not have bought substitute goods on that day, but the duty to mitigate will normally confine damages to that sum even where he or she delays purchasing and the market price rises further. The duty to mitigate, which is dealt with later, does not allow the injured party to recover damages for a loss which could have been avoided by behaving reasonably after the breach (see para. **20.53**ff). In other words, the injured party will normally be assumed to have taken the risk of any change in the market if that party delays purchasing substitute goods.

20.8 There is a similar prima facie rule for the situation in which the seller has delivered defective goods. SGA 1979, s 53(3) states that the prima facie loss is the 'difference between the value of the goods at the time of delivery to the buyer and the value they would have had if they had' not been defective. This may provide an appropriate answer whether the goods are wanted for use or for resale.

---

4 See para. 20.9ff. See also *McRae v Commonwealth Disposals Commission* (1951); *Commonwealth of Australia v Amann Aviation Pty Ltd* (1991).

Reliance loss

20.9 Although the basic principle on which contractual damages are awarded is that of putting an injured party in the position they would have been in had the contract been performed, and obviously that provides for recovery of the expectation interest, there are nevertheless cases in which an injured party may not attempt to claim the 'profit' they should have derived from the contract, but merely the expenses they incurred in reliance upon the contract. This is referred to as 'reliance loss', and a claim for reliance loss may well occur because an injured party finds it difficult to establish what profit, if any, they would have made on the contract. That was the situation in *Anglia Television Ltd* v *Reed* [1971] 3 All ER 690 when Robert Reed broke his contract with Anglia to be the leading man in a film to be made for television entitled *The Man in the Wood*. His breach meant that the film could not be made. Anglia sued for damages, but did not claim for lost profit as they could 'not say what their profit on this contract would have been if Mr Reed had come here and performed it'. Anglia sued for their wasted expenditure and recovered it. Lord Denning MR said (at 692):

> [A claimant] in such a case as this has an election: he can either claim for his loss of profits; or for his wasted expenditure. But he must elect between them. He cannot claim both. If he has not suffered any loss of profits—or if he cannot prove what his loss of profits would have been—he can claim in the alternative the expenditure which has been thrown away, that is, wasted, by reason of the breach.

Two points in that dictum deserve comment. First, we must look at the question of whether the injured party can always claim his or her reliance loss rather than his or her expectation loss. Secondly, some consideration needs to be given to whether there is a bar upon claiming both expectation and reliance loss.

20.10 The first point to consider is whether an injured party can always claim their reliance loss. The question becomes important if the contract is one on which the injured party would have made a loss, that is, their expectation loss is less than their reliance loss, because they made a bad bargain. The answer is that an injured party is free to make whichever claim they choose, but they will not recover a greater sum in a reliance claim than they would have done if they had claimed their expectation loss. The basic contractual principle is that of putting the injured party in the position they would have been in hawd the contract been fulfilled. That is not overridden by the claim being merely for reliance loss. The 'expectation loss principle underpins the award of damages in wasted expenditure cases'.[5] This can be made more intelligible by consideration of two cases, *C and P Haulage* v *Middleton* (1983) and *CCC Films (London) Ltd* v *Impact Quadrant Films Ltd* (1984).

5 *Omak Maritime Ltd* v *Mamola Challenger Shipping Co* (2010) at [47].

20.11 In *C and P Haulage* v *Middleton* (1983):

> Mr Middleton was a self-employed engineer. C & P granted him a six-monthly renewable licence to occupy certain premises. He spent money making the premises suitable for his work—a wall had to be built, a telephone moved, and electricity laid on. It was an express term of the licence that fixtures put in by Mr Middleton were not to be removed at the expiry of the licence. Ten weeks before the end of a six-month term, he was wrongfully ejected from the premises by C & P. As a temporary measure, he worked from home until well after the six-month period would have expired.

Mr Middleton claimed the cost of the improvements he had made to the premises. The court held that C & P had been in breach of contract in ejecting him from the premises before the expiry of the six-month term, but he had not suffered any loss and was entitled only to nominal damages. He had not had to pay for other premises, as he had used his home, and he had not had to shut down his business and lose profits thereby. He would have lost the money spent on improving the premises even if C & P had waited until the end of the six months to eject him, and he could not succeed in a claim for that expenditure. The court was being asked to put Mr Middleton back in the position he would have been in had he not made the contract. The Court of Appeal refused to do that. Contract damages are to put the injured party in the position he or she would have been in had the contract been performed. Mr Middleton would have lost the money he had spent if the licence had simply not been renewed at the end of the contract period, with no breach by C & P. Basically Mr Middleton had made a bad bargain, and contract damages are not to compensate for that.

20.12 The line taken by the Court of Appeal in *C and P Haulage* v *Middleton* (1983) was followed by Hutchinson J in *CCC Films (London) Ltd* v *Impact Quadrant Films Ltd* [1984] 3 All ER 298, but in the latter case it was not obvious that what the court had to deal with was a bad bargain, and the judge had to consider the question of the burden of proof. In *CCC Films*:

> IQ owned the rights to certain films. IQ granted CCC a licence to exploit, distribute, and exhibit three films (*Dead of Night*, *Children Shouldn't Play with Dead Things*, and *Blue Blood*). CCC paid IQ $12,000 for the licence. IQ delivered the films but they then undertook their safe delivery to Munich, to a potential purchaser who might help CCC exploit their licence. In breach of contract, IQ failed to ensure the safe delivery of the films to Munich. CCC could not establish any lost profits from the breach but claimed the $12,000 from IQ as wasted expenditure. Neither party produced evidence of whether it would or would not have been possible for CCC to recoup that expenditure had the contract been performed.

Hutchinson J held that an injured party had an unfettered choice whether to claim for reliance or expectation loss. If they claimed for reliance loss, then it was for the party in breach to establish that the injured party's expenditure would not have been recouped had the contract been performed, that is, it was for the party in breach to establish that the injured party had made a bad bargain.[6] In coming to this conclusion Hutchinson J quoted from, and adopted, the reasoning of Learned Hand CJ in *L Albert & Son* v *Armstrong Rubber Co.* 178 F 2d 189 (1949). Hutchinson J quoted (at 311):

> In cases where the venture would have proved profitable to the promisee there is no reason why he should not recover his expenses. On the other hand, on those occasions in which the performance would not have covered the promisee's outlay, such a result imposes the risk of the promisee's contract upon the promisor. We cannot agree that the promisor's default in performance should under this guise make him an insurer of the promisee's venture; yet it does not follow that the breach should not throw upon him the duty of showing that the value of the performance would in fact have been less than the promisee's outlay. It is often very hard to learn what the value of the performance would have been; and it is a common expedient, and a just one, in such situations to put the peril of the answer upon the party who by his wrong has made the issue relevant to the rights of the other. On principle, therefore, the proper solution would seem to be that the promisee may recover this outlay in preparation for the performance, subject to the privilege of the promisor to reduce it by as much as he can show that the promisee would have lost, if the contract had been performed.

In the instant case CCC recovered. IQ could not establish that CCC would not have recouped the sum claimed had the contract been performed.[7]

20.13 The second point which should be considered is whether both expectation and reliance loss can be claimed. In order to consider that question, certain terminological problems need to be noted and avoided. In the earlier discussion the term 'profit' has been used to encompass the entire sum which the injured party would have derived from the contractual performance, that is, the gross profit. When used in this loose way, as it was for example in *Anglia Television Ltd* v *Reed* (1971), the terminology can lead to confusion. The term could be made more explicit by referring to the 'gross' profit because it encompasses two elements: the net profit after deduction of expenses, and the expenses. Once this terminological problem is recognized it helps to explain what should be meant when it is stated that it is not possible to recover for both lost profits and wasted expenditure.[8] It certainly should not be possible to recover twice for the same loss, and this must be the true limitation. If the claim for profits was, as it normally would be, a claim for the gross profits, then clearly the injured party could not recover both gross profit and expenses. If the injured party could do that, he or she would be recovering the expenses twice because, in addition to being recovered separately, the expenses would also be encompassed within the sum awarded for the lost gross profit.

6 See also *Omak Maritime Ltd* v *Mamola Challenger Shipping Co* (2010).

7 See also *Commonwealth of Australia* v *Amann Aviation Pty Ltd* (1991).

8 See Lord Denning MR (para. 20.9) in *Anglia Television Ltd* v *Reed* and *Cullinane* v *British 'Rema' Manufacturing Co. Ltd* (1954).

However, that should not prevent the success of claims to both net profit and expenses. If the injured party limited the claim for lost profits to net profit, then he or she should additionally be able to claim expenses. Together they would make up only the gross profit and the full extent of his loss. There would be no double recovery. Statements as to the mutual exclusion of claims for expectation and reliance loss must be viewed with caution against the background of the terminological difficulties. The basic prohibition must simply be against allowing the injured party to recover the same loss twice (see J. Macleod, 'Damages, Reliance and Expectancy Interest' [1970] JBL 19).

Pre-contract expenditure

20.14 On a slightly different point, it is necessary to give some further consideration to the damages awarded in *Anglia Television Ltd* v *Reed* (1971). In that case the main part of the expenditure wasted had been incurred before the contract with Reed was concluded. Before contracting with Reed, Anglia Television had arranged a place to film and had employed a director, a designer, and a stage manager. Under the contract Reed was to be available to Anglia between 9 September and 11 October. However, Reed's agent had double-booked him, and on 3 September Anglia were informed that he would not be making their film. Anglia tried hard but could not find a substitute and they abandoned the proposed film. However, when Anglia sued, Reed argued that he was liable for only part of the expenditure that they were trying to recover. He claimed he was liable only for the £854.65 spent after he contracted with Anglia. The Court of Appeal awarded Anglia the whole £2,750 they were claiming, despite the fact that most of it was incurred before Reed contracted. Obviously the pre-contract expenditure had not been incurred in reliance on the contract, but it had been wasted because of such reliance and the court thought that it was simply a matter of whether or not the loss was too remote; it held that it was not (on remoteness, see para. **20.28**ff). Obviously, recovery of pre-contract expenditure should similarly be limited by the question of what the injured party would have recouped had the contract been performed.

Restitution

20.15 Restitution is generally concerned with the unjust enrichment of one party at another's expense, and we should give some consideration here to pursuing D's profits from his or her breach of the contract he or she had with C.[9] As has been indicated, the line generally taken has been that damages for breach of contract are compensatory, and if C has suffered no loss as a result of a breach of contract, the award of damages will be purely nominal and D's profit from his or her breach is irrelevant. Indeed, it is argued that D should breach where it is economically efficient for him or her to do so, and that it is economically efficient when D can make a greater profit through breaching than performing, even after compensating C for any loss due to the breach (see para. **20.65**). If C's damages relate not merely

9 For an outline of the law of restitution see web chapter 2.

to C's losses but also to D's profits, then the possibility of economically efficient breach is removed or impaired (depending on whether all the profits are awarded) (see D. Campbell and D. Harris, 'In Defence of Breach: A Critique of Restitution and the Performance Interest' (2002) 22 LS 208).

20.16 However, building generally on cases such as those in which a property right has been infringed and a sum awarded relating to D's gain rather than C's loss, and those cases in which an account of profits has been ordered from a fiduciary (for example, *Boardman* v *Phipps* (1967)), or on the disclosure of confidential information (for example, *A-G* v *Guardian Newspapers (No 2)* (1990)), in *A-G* v *Blake* (2000) the House of Lords recognized that, in exceptional cases, C may be awarded the profits of D's breach of contract.

20.17 In *A-G* v *Blake* (2000) the more specific foundation of recovery based on a breach of contract and D's profits from the breach was *Wrotham Park Estate Co.* v *Parkside Homes Ltd* (1974). That case was seen as 'a solitary beacon, showing that in contract, as well as tort, damages are not always narrowly confined to recoupment of financial loss' but that in a suitable case, recovery for breach of contract 'may be measured by the benefit gained by the wrongdoer from the breach' (*Blake* at 396). The facts of *Wrotham Park Estate Co.* were:

> In 1971 land was sold to D with a covenant restricting building on that land in favour of C's land. Without knowledge of the covenant and in breach of it, D began building on the land. In early 1972, C issued a writ claiming an injunction to prevent further building in breach of the covenant and to order the demolition of such building as had occurred. The action came for trial in 1973, by which time 14 homes had been built.

Unsurprisingly, Brightman J refused to order the wasteful destruction of 14 houses. However, despite the lack of any loss to C through the breach, he granted damages in lieu of an injunction under the Chancery Amendment Act 1858 (Lord Cairns's Act). It was held that D should pay C the hypothetical sum which C might have obtained through bargaining for the release of the covenant, although it was clear that C would not have entered into such a bargain (the 'hypothetical release' approach). The sum to be awarded was arrived at as a proportion of the profit which D obtained from the breach.

20.18 However, in *A-G* v *Blake* (2000) the House of Lords was asked to go further and, in effect, give C an account of profits to cover all of D's gain. In *Blake*:

> Blake had been employed as a member of the Secret Intelligence Service from 1944 to 1961, at which point it was discovered that he had been betraying secrets to the Soviet Union since 1951. He was convicted and sentenced to 42 years' imprisonment, but he escaped to Moscow in 1966. In 1989 he wrote his autobiography and it was published in 1990. The action arose out of the amount he was to be paid by the publishers in this country.

By the time Blake wrote his autobiography, the information contained in it had ceased to be confidential, and recovery of his profits was not available on the basis of breach of confidentiality. However, when he joined the Secret Intelligence Service, Blake had signed a contractually binding undertaking that he would not disclose official information in the press or in book form. He had therefore breached a contract in making some of the disclosures in the book. On that basis, the House of Lords (Lord Hobhouse dissenting) held that the Attorney-General was entitled to succeed in recovering the profits of Blake's autobiography. It was made clear that such an award would only be made in exceptional cases. Lord Steyn emphasized the close relationship of the case to those in which there is disclosure of confidential information. In addition, Blake's position could be seen as analogous to that of a fiduciary. Lord Nicholls, with whom Lord Goff and Lord Browne-Wilkinson agreed, saw no reason why, in practice, 'the availability of the account of profits need disturb settled expectations in the commercial or consumer world'. He emphasized that 'normally the remedies of damages, specific performance and injunction, coupled with the characterisation of some contractual obligations as fiduciary, will provide an adequate response to breach of contract'. He made it clear that it would only be in exceptional cases, where those remedies are not adequate, that 'any question of an account of profits will arise'. He identified three factors, none of which, by itself, he regarded as a good reason for ordering an account of profits. Those factors were:

> the fact that the breach was cynical and deliberate; the fact that the breach enabled the defendant to enter into a more profitable contract elsewhere; and the fact that by entering into a new and more profitable contract the defendant put it out of his power to perform his contract with [C].

The exclusion of such factors as sufficient to allow for an account of profits is in keeping with the idea that 'efficient breach' is desirable (see para. **20.65**), that is, the idea that if D can breach, compensate C for C's loss, and still make a greater profit elsewhere, then D should do so. However, Lord Nicholls did give some indication of what might make a case sufficiently exceptional. He said (at 398):

> No fixed rules can be prescribed. The court will have regard to all the circumstances, including the subject matter of the contract, the purpose of the contractual provision which has been breached, the circumstances in which the breach occurred, the consequences of the breach and the circumstances in which relief is being sought. A useful general guide, although not exhaustive, is whether the [claimant] had a legitimate interest in preventing the defendant's profit-making activity and, hence, in depriving him of his profit.

In the particular case, Lord Nicholls took the view that the 'Crown had and has a legitimate interest in preventing Blake profiting from the disclosure of official information, whether classified or not, while a member of the service and thereafter' (at 399). He emphasized that members of the security services should not have any incentive to reveal information. He viewed it as of 'paramount importance that members of the service should have complete confidence in all their dealings with each other, and that those recruited as informers should have the like confidence' (at 399). On that basis an 'absolute rule against disclosure, visible to all, [made] good sense' (at 400).

20.19 It can be seen that the facts of *A-G* v *Blake* (2000) were very unusual and the line could have been taken that the factors making it exceptional enough to justify an account of profits were so exceptional that such a restitutionary approach to breach would seldom occur. Certainly, as has been indicated, Lord Nicholls saw no reason why, in practice, 'the availability of the account of profits need disturb settled expectations in the commercial or consumer world'. However, in his dissenting judgment, Lord Hobhouse took the view that if there were attempts to extend the award of non-compensatory damages for breach further into commercial law, 'the consequences [would] be very far reaching and disruptive'. The approach taken since *Blake* must now be considered.

20.20 In *AB Corpn* v *CD Co., The Sine Nomine* (2002) (an award of arbitrators amongst whom was Sir Christopher Staughton), there was a refusal to apply the approach taken in *A-G* v *Blake* (2000). The line was taken that the case was concerned with a marketable commodity—the services of a ship. The wrongful withdrawal of the ship would be dealt with by ordinary compensatory contract damages. The injured party could get a replacement from the market and damages based on that course would then be sufficient. The view was expressed that 'The commercial law of this country should not make moral judgments, or seek to punish contract breakers'. However, *Blake* and, in particular, the 'hypothetical release' approach taken in *Wrotham Park Estate Co.* v *Parkside Homes Ltd* (1974) has been followed. They should, however, only be turned to when the other contractual remedies are inadequate.[10]

20.21 In *Esso Petroleum Co. Ltd* v *Niad Ltd* (2001) the court was concerned with a contract under which a garage was supplied with petrol by Esso. Esso sought to operate a 'pricewatch' scheme under which it would regulate pump prices so as to be competitive in each particular area. It reduced its prices to garages where that was required to maintain that competitive pricing. Niad paid the reduced prices to Esso but failed to maintain the required prices, charging its customers more. Sir Andrew Morritt V-C was prepared to give Esso an account of profits. First, he did not view damages as an adequate remedy as they could not realistically be assessed. It was 'almost impossible' to attribute lost sales to particular breaches by a particular garage. Secondly, the breaches gave 'the lie to the advertising campaign' publicizing the pricewatch scheme and undermined its effectiveness to achieve benefits for Esso and other garages. Finally, he concluded that Esso 'undoubtedly had an interest in preventing Niad from profiting from its breach of obligation'.

20.22 In *Experience Hendrix LLC* v *PPX Enterprises Inc* (2003), following a dispute, there had been an agreement that D would not license certain recordings in which Jimi Hendrix merely featured as sideman to another artiste. That agreement was breached. C, the Hendrix estate, sought an injunction to prevent future breaches and an account of profits in relation to the money D had already made out of wrongfully exploiting those recordings. Evidence was given

10 *Devenish Nutrition Ltd* v *Sanofi-Aventis SA* (2008) at [58].

on behalf of C that 'the way those recordings had been brought onto the market had confused and alienated potential buyers' of Jimi Hendrix's own work with the Jimi Hendrix Experience band. Evidence was given (at [14]) that:

> Such buyers may mistakenly purchase sideman recordings, instead of Experience Hendrix featured recordings, and then become disappointed and frustrated, avoiding further purchases of Jimi Hendrix music. The space available for Jimi Hendrix albums in retail record stores is generally limited, and the presence of numerous sideman recordings poses the risk of displacing featured recordings. Thus the sideman recordings both divert and discourage potential purchasers of featured recordings.

An injunction was granted to prevent future exploitation of the relevant recordings; the question was as to an account of profits in relation to the profits made prior to the injunction. The court recognized that *A-G* v *Blake* (2000) had stated that the account of profits for a breach of contract should only be available in exceptional circumstances (at [24]) and 'obvious distinctions' were drawn between the instant case and *Blake*. Mance LJ said (at [37]):

> First we are not concerned with a subject anything like as special or sensitive as national security. The state's special interest in preventing a spy benefiting by breaches of his contractual duty of secrecy and so removing at least part of the financial attraction of such breaches has no parallel in this case. Second the notoriety which accounted for the magnitude of Blake's royalty-earning capacity derived from his prior breaches of secrecy and that too has no present parallel. Third there is no direct analogy between PPX's position and that of a fiduciary [as had been made in *Blake*].

20.23 However, although the instant case was not as exceptional as *Blake*, that was not seen as preventing the court from providing any money remedy based on D's profits. Rather, although an account of profits was regarded as inappropriate, the view was taken that there could be an award based on D's profits of the 'hypothetical release' type, as in *Wrotham Park Estate Co.* v *Parkside Homes Ltd* (1974). Peter Gibson LJ saw the case as suitable for such an award as:

> (1) there has been a deliberate breach by PPX of its contractual obligations for its own reward, (2) the claimant would have difficulty establishing contractual loss therefrom, and (3) the claimant has a legitimate interest in preventing PPX's profit making activity carried out in breach of PPX's contractual obligations.

Plainly, the legitimate interest envisaged here is of a different order from that in *A-G* v *Blake* (2000) and, despite *Esso Petroleum* v *Niad*, the distinction drawn between *Hendrix* and *Blake* would indicate that an account of profits rather than 'hypothetical release' damages will very seldom be available. It is more likely that the 'hypothetical release' approach will be taken, rather than an account of profits being ordered,[11] but it should not be forgotten that both are

11 *Vercoe* v *Rutland Fund Management Ltd* (2010) at [341].

exceptional. Certainly, it should not be enough that C's ordinary contractual damages for breach would be nominal.[12]

20.24 A major outstanding question is the basis of these awards. Are they truly restitutionary or is it that we have not yet been able to satisfactorily identify the loss, and the awards are compensatory? Is the basis of the award in *Blake* different to those situations in which part of the profits are recovered?[13]

Timing

20.25 The final point to be made in this section is the time frame against which damages are assessed. Damages are usually assessed in accordance with the circumstances existing at the time of the breach. This is normally in keeping with the basic principle that the injured party should be put in the position he or she would have been in had the contract been performed. However, that will not always be the case, and it has been said that assessment at the time of the breach 'is not an absolute rule; if to follow it would give rise to injustice, the court has power to fix such other date as may be appropriate in the circumstances' (*Johnson* v *Agnew* [1979] 1 All ER 883 at 896). The determination of the appropriateness of some other date will often depend upon the rule as to mitigation of damages. The duty to mitigate means that the injured party will not be compensated for any loss which he or she could have avoided by taking reasonable steps after the breach. If the mitigation rule does not indicate that he or she should have acted to limit his or her loss immediately upon the breach occurring, then the time for the calculation of damages may similarly be delayed. In *Suleman* v *Shahsavari* [1989] 2 All ER 460 the duty to mitigate indicated that damages were not to be calculated in accordance with the circumstances at the time of the breach but at the time of judgment. In that case:

> Mr Suleman thought that he had contracted to buy a house. Unfortunately for him it was eventually decided that the solicitor of the vendor had not had authority to sign the contract of sale on the vendor's behalf. When there was no completion of the supposed contract of sale, Mr Suleman initially sought specific performance against the vendor. Specific performance was eventually denied and it was determined that the solicitor's lack of authority meant that there was no contract of sale. On that basis, Mr Suleman claimed damages from the vendor's solicitor for breach of warranty of his authority.

Mr Suleman succeeded in his action against the solicitor. The court had to determine the damages to be paid. The difference between the market price of the house and the 'contract' price on the supposed date of completion of the sale was £9,500. The difference with reference to the date of judgment was £29,500. Mr Suleman was awarded £29,500 on the basis that it had been reasonable for him to delay seeking such damages while trying to claim specific performance

12 D. Campbell and P. Wylie, 'Ain't No Telling which Circumstances Are Exceptional' (2003) 63 CLJ 605.

13 J. Edelman, *Gain Based Damages: Contract, Tort, Equity and Intellectual Property*, Hart Publishing, 2002.

against the vendors. His actions were not contrary to the duty to mitigate. Andrew Park QC (sitting as a deputy judge of the High Court) said (at 463):

> [Mr Suleman] has conducted himself entirely reasonably in seeking to obtain specific performance . . . He has been in no way dilatory over his claim and cannot be accused of having unreasonably failed to mitigate his damage.

20.26 More recently the House of Lords departed from calculating damages according to the circumstances at the time of the breach in *Golden Strait Corpn* v *Nippon Yusen Kubishika Kaisha* (2007). They opted instead for an approach in keeping with both basic principle and the duty to mitigate. In that case:

> In 1998 the parties entered into a seven-year charter-party. In December 2001 the charterers repudiated the contract and the owners accepted the repudiation. In March 2003 the second Gulf War broke out and the war clause in the charter-party would have given the charterers the right to cancel. The question arose as to whether the owners' damages for the charterers' repudiatory breach in 2001 should encompass the entirety of the time then remaining under the charter-party or whether they should be limited by the outbreak of the Gulf War, when the charterers would have had a right to cancel.

As has been indicated, damages are usually awarded by reference to the circumstances at the time of the breach, in this case the time of the repudiation. This is seen to create certainty for both parties. However, it is also usually in keeping with the basic principle on which damages are awarded (placing the injured party in the position he or she would have been in had the contract been performed) and the injured party's duty to mitigate. *The Golden Strait* was not a case where awarding damages based on the time of the breach would comply with basic principle, however. At the time of the breach there was the prospect of the contract continuing for the rest of its whole seven-year duration. By the time the case came to court, it was clear it would have been lawfully cancelled in 2003. Awarding damages based on the full duration of the contract would have put the injured party in a better position than if the contract had been performed. It would seem that the damages will not be calculated according to the circumstances at the date of the breach when there is a temporal element in the injured party's loss (i.e. where it is a loss over time, or a loss which only accrues after the breach) and the temporal element would not be nullified by acting in accordance with the duty to mitigate, that is, procuring a substitute contract at the time of the breach. In this case any substitute contract would have contained the same cancellation right and also not run for the remainder of the full contract duration (see Lord Brown at [82]).

Restrictions on recovery

20.27 We have seen the basic principle on which damages are awarded: putting the injured party in the position he or she would have been in had the contract been performed. This provides for the recovery of expectation loss. Sometimes the injured party may instead choose to claim reliance loss, but such a claim will still be subject to the basic principle, and the injured party cannot be better off than if the contract had been performed. (Reliance loss cannot be claimed as a means of escaping the effects of a bad bargain.) However, what we must now consider is that there are further rules which mean that the injured party will not always recover the full amount needed to put him or her in the position he or she would have been in had the contract been performed. We need to consider such rules as those about remoteness and mitigation of damages.

Remoteness of damage

20.28 There is a need for some restriction upon the liability of the party in breach for losses which he or she has caused. A breach may lead to extremely unlikely loss or damage. Some limitation must be put upon the damage for which the party in breach can be liable. The rule as to remoteness of damage serves this purpose. It prevents recovery for a loss which is too remote. However, the issue of the basis of this restriction, and of its extent, has come to the fore recently. In *Transfield Shipping Inc* v *Mercator Shipping Inc, The Achilleas* (2008), Lord Hoffmann said (at [9]):

> The case therefore raises a fundamental point of principle in the law of contractual damages: is the rule that a party may recover losses which were foreseeable ('not unlikely') an external rule of law, imposed upon the parties to every contract in default of express provision to the contrary, or is it a prima facie assumption about what the parties may be taken to have intended, no doubt applicable in the great majority of cases but capable of rebuttal in cases in which the context, surrounding circumstances or general understanding in the relevant market shows that a party would not reasonably have been regarded as assuming responsibility for such losses?

The question has become whether the traditional remoteness rule is used, or whether we have to look for an 'assumption of responsibility'. Traditionally, the approach has been taken that remoteness has simply been a matter of what, at the time of contracting, the parties could reasonably contemplate as being liable to result from the breach. However, in *The Achilleas* the House of Lords may have introduced the assumption of responsibility approach, with the 'reasonable contemplation' approach being departed from where the defendants could not reasonably be regarded as having assumed responsibility for some, or all, of those reasonably contemplatable losses, or where they could reasonably be regarded as having assumed more.[14] This will be returned to later after the traditional approach has been considered. However, it would seem that most cases will continue to be determined by the traditional rules—in most cases they will embody the parties' presumed intentions.[15]

14 The test is 'inclusionary' as well as 'exclusionary'—*Supershield Ltd* v *Siemens Buillding Technologies FE Ltd* (2010) at [43].

15 See *The Achilleas* at [11]; *John Grimes Partnership* v *Gubbins* (2013); *Sylvia Shipping Co Ltd* v *Progress Bulk Carriers Ltd (The Sylvia)* (2010).

20.29 The basic rule embodied in the traditional approach to remoteness stems from the case of *Hadley* v *Baxendale* (1854) 9 Exch 341. In that case, the facts were as follows:

> The claimants were millers. They owned and occupied the City Steam Mills, Gloucester. The crankshaft of their steam engine was broken so that the mill could not function. They arranged with the defendant carriers for the shaft to be taken to W Joyce & Co. of Greenwich, who had agreed to make a new shaft, using the old one as a model. The defendant carriers broke their contract by delaying delivery. The new shaft was not received for several days after it should have been. The claimants lost profits because of the delay in the return to work of the mill. The defendants argued that such loss of profits was too remote for them to be liable.

Alderson B set out the test for remoteness. He said (at 355):

> Where two parties have made a contract which one of them has broken the damages which the other party ought to receive in respect of such a breach of contract should be such as may fairly and reasonably be considered as either arising naturally, i.e. according to the usual course of things, from such breach of the contract itself, or such as may reasonably be supposed to have been in the contemplation of both parties at the time they made the contract as the probable result of the breach of it.

This is commonly known as the rule in *Hadley* v *Baxendale* and it can be broken down into two parts. The party in breach will be liable for losses either:

(1) arising naturally, that is, according to the usual course of things; or
(2) such as may reasonably be supposed to have been in the contemplation of the parties, at the time they made the contract, as a probable result of the breach.

20.30 In effect, although the remoteness rule is often stated in this dual form, both parts relate to what the parties could reasonably contemplate as liable to result from the breach (see *Heron II* (1969) at para. **20.34**). The only difference between the two parts of the rule is the degree of knowledge attributable to the party in breach, as a reasonable person, at the time of contracting. The first part of the rule deals with what any reasonable person should contemplate, because that is what would 'usually' occur. The second part of the rule deals with the more extensive reasonable contemplation which should be produced by knowledge of special circumstances extending the complainant's loss beyond the 'usual'. In effect, the question almost inevitably is 'what could have been contemplated by the party in breach, as a reasonable person?' (The injured party should know of the special circumstances which may add to his or her losses on a breach occurring.) In *Hadley* v *Baxendale*, the prolonged closure of the mill, and the loss of profits thereby, was not viewed as a 'natural' result of the breach. It was thought that the millers might have had a spare crankshaft. In addition, such loss could not be brought within the second part of the rule. All that had been made known to the carriers at the time of contracting was that they were transporting a broken crankshaft for millers. They were given no special knowledge of the situation to bring the loss within their reasonable contemplation as liable to result of the breach. It was not made known that the millers did not possess a spare shaft.

20.31 It should be emphasized that the point in time at which the loss must be within the reasonable contemplation of the parties is when the contract was made (*Jackson* v *Royal Bank of Scotland* (2005)).

20.32 Viewing the two parts of the rule as simply making up one rule was fully explained by Asquith LJ in *Victoria Laundry (Windsor) Ltd* v *Newman Industries Ltd* (1949). In addition, the case well illustrates the difference between the 'usual' type of loss, and that for which additional knowledge, at the time of contracting, is required. In that case:

> Victoria Laundry wished to expand their business, and they ordered a larger boiler from Newman Industries. Delivery was to take place on 5 June. The boiler was damaged before delivery, and delivery was delayed until 8 November. Newman were aware of the nature of Victoria Laundry's business and had been informed that Victoria Laundry intended to put the boiler into use in the shortest possible time.

Victoria Laundry claimed for the profit they would have earned with the boiler in the time between 5 June and 8 November. In particular, Victoria Laundry claimed for the loss of, first, the extra laundry business they could have taken on, there being a shortage of laundries at the time, and, secondly, the loss of a number of highly lucrative dyeing contracts which they could and would have accepted from the Ministry of Supply. The Court of Appeal allowed recovery for the former but not the latter, although the court envisaged recovery of a sum to cover the loss of 'ordinary' dyeing business.

20.33 Newman knew before contracting that Victoria Laundry was in the business of laundering and dyeing, and that the boiler was wanted for immediate use in that business. They were supplying a boiler in accordance with strict technical specifications, and could be taken to know more about the use or purposes to which boilers were put than the uninformed layman. They did not know whether the boiler was to replace a unit of equal or inferior capacity. The court thought that reasonable persons in their shoes must be taken to foresee that a laundry which wanted a boiler for immediate use, at a time when there was a shortage of laundry facilities, would be liable to suffer a loss if delivery was delayed for five months. That was the case whether they wanted the boiler in order to extend their business, to maintain it, or to reduce a loss. In other words, Victoria Laundry could recover for the ordinary extra laundry business they would have taken on. They could not recover for the loss of the special dyeing contracts. In the absence of additional information, the reasonable person, in Newman's position, could not foresee that loss as liable to result from the breach. No notice had been given of the possible highly lucrative dyeing contracts and their loss was too remote.

20.34 It was indicated earlier that the two parts of the rule in *Hadley* could be reformulated as a single rule, capable of encompassing the different levels of knowledge to be attributed, in different circumstances, to the parties. In delivering the judgment of the Court of Appeal in *Victoria*

Laundry (Windsor) Ltd v *Newman Industries Ltd* (1949), Asquith LJ reformulated the rule in *Hadley* in this way. He re-stated it as entitling the injured party to recover such part of his loss 'as was at the time of the contract reasonably foreseeable as liable to result from the breach', and this is reflected in the earlier discussion of the case. However, in *Heron II (Koufos* v *Czarnikow Ltd)* [1969] 1 AC 350 the House of Lords criticized the *Victoria Laundry* formulation. It was seen as not sufficiently indicating the degree of probability with which the loss must be foreseen. In particular, their Lordships felt that the test of remoteness in contract must be kept distinct from the lesser requirement in tort. They thought that the tort test encompassed any type of damage which was reasonably foreseeable, even though it might happen only 'in the most unusual case'. The contract test required a loss to be reasonably foreseen with a much greater degree of probability. Lord Reid (at 386) thought there was a good reason for the difference:

> In contract, if one party wishes to protect himself against a risk which to the other party would appear unusual, he can direct the other party's attention to it before the contract is made.

(See also Lord Pearce at 413, and Lord Upjohn at 423.) In contrast, in tort the parties could well be strangers.

20.35 To distinguish the two tests, their Lordships favoured referring to 'reasonable contemplation' in contract, rather than 'reasonable foreseeability'. In addition, there was much discussion of how the degree of probability necessary in contract should be expressed. It was seen as something less than an even chance, but greater than what is required in tort. Various phrases were thought to encompass the requisite degree of probability—'not unlikely', 'substantial probability', 'likely', 'liable to result', 'serious possibility', 'real danger'. The extensive search for a way to express the requisite degree of probability is not very helpful. The main point to note is that the House of Lords wished to keep the contract and tort tests distinct, and required a higher degree of probability in contract than in tort.

20.36 In *Heron II (Koufos* v *Czarnikow Ltd)* (1969), the facts were as follows:

> A vessel was chartered to take a cargo of sugar from Constanza to Basrah, where there was a sugar market. It was the intention of the charterers to sell the sugar in the market immediately upon arrival there. In breach of contract the vessel arrived nine days late in Basrah. The market price had dropped in the intervening nine days and the charterers claimed the difference in the price from the owners of the ship.

The House of Lords held that the charterer was entitled to recover the difference in price of the sugar because of the nine-day delay. The owner of the vessel had not known that the intention was to sell the sugar on arrival, but he had known that there was a sugar market in Basrah. That being the case, he had to be taken to have realized that it was not unlikely that the sugar would be sold on arrival and he had to be taken to know that, in a market, prices fluctuate from day to day. The charterer's loss was not too remote. It should have been reasonably contemplated as liable to result from the delay.

20.37 The traditional contract test for remoteness can be stated as being whether the loss was such that, at the time of contracting, the parties would have reasonably contemplated it as liable to result from a breach. A number of general points must be emphasized in relation to this test.

20.38 It should be emphasized that the parties need not have considered the possibility of a breach, or its consequences, at all. 'Parties at the time of contracting contemplate not the breach of the contract but its performance.' What matters is the conclusion of reasonable people, in the position of the parties, had they considered the question (*Victoria Laundry (Windsor) Ltd* v *Newman Industries Ltd* [1949] 2 KB 528). It should also be noted that the usual formulation of the rule refers to the contemplation of the parties and it must be emphasized that what might reasonably be contemplated by the injured party alone, because of his or her more extensive knowledge of any loss he or she might suffer, is irrelevant. The original two-part statement of the rule in *Hadley* emphasizes that point. The remoteness test is really about what could be contemplated by the reasonable person in the position of the party in breach. However, as was made clear in *Victoria Laundry*, although the assessment is based on the reasonable person, what he or she may reasonably contemplate as liable to result may be affected not only by actual knowledge of special circumstances but also, more generally, by his or her position and the circumstances of the contract. If the party in breach is a businessperson, then more may be taken to be within his or her reasonable contemplation as likely to result than if he or she is a consumer. In *Victoria Laundry* it was pointed out that the general knowledge of the business of those it contracts with may be taken to be more extensive in the case of a supplier than a carrier (distinguishing *Victoria Laundry* and *Hadley* v *Baxendale* (1854)). However:

> it must always be a question of circumstances what one contracting party is presumed to know about the business activities of the other. No doubt the simpler the activity of the one, the more readily can it be inferred that the other would have reasonable knowledge thereof. However, when the activity of A involves complicated construction or manufacturing techniques, I see no reason why B who supplies a commodity that A intends to use in the course of those techniques should be assumed, merely because of the order for the commodity, to be aware of the details of all the techniques undertaken by A and the effect thereupon of any failure of or deficiency in that commodity. (*Balfour Beatty Construction (Scotland) Ltd* v *Scottish Power plc* 1994 SLT 807 at 810 per Lord Jauncey)

Type/degree of loss

20.39 Some refinement of the basic test must be considered in relation to a distinction between type of loss and degree of loss. The issue was raised by the case of *H Parsons (Livestock) Ltd* v *Uttley Ingham & Co. Ltd* (1978). In that case:

> Mr Parsons was a pig farmer. He ordered from the defendants a hopper to store pig nuts. The defendants were manufacturers of bulk food storage hoppers. The defendants knew

> the purpose for which the hopper was required. The contract described the hopper as 'fitted with a ventilated top'. The ventilator was sealed for transport to the pig farm and when the defendants installed the hopper they forgot to open the ventilator. The hopper was 28 feet high, and it was not possible to see that the ventilator was closed from the ground. Because of the lack of ventilation some of the pig nuts stored in the hopper became mouldy. The farmer continued to feed them to the pigs until the pigs became ill. An outbreak of E Coli ensued, and 254 pigs died.

The question was whether the defendants were liable, in damages, for the death of the pigs. The Court of Appeal held that they were: the losses were not too remote. Scarman LJ, with Orr LJ agreeing, found that the remoteness test from *Heron II* was satisfied. The degree of loss did not have to come within the test, provided the type of loss did; 'no more than common sense was needed for them to appreciate that food affected by bad storage conditions might well cause illness in the pigs fed on it' and the pigs becoming ill was regarded as only a different degree of loss and not a different type of loss from them dying.

20.40 However, the distinction between extent of loss and type of loss is not without difficulty. What constitutes a type of loss? Was the lost profit on the ordinary laundry business really a different type of loss from the lost profit on the highly lucrative dyeing contracts in *Victoria Laundry (Windsor) Ltd* v *Newman Industries Ltd* (1949)? A distinction has, however, been made. In *Brown* v *KMR Services Ltd* [1995] 4 All ER 598 the losses of Lloyd's names were unforeseeable in their extent, due to the unanticipated size and frequency of the various disasters that occurred between 1987 and 1990. The agent who had misadvised them could not, however, claim that the losses were too remote. They were of the type which were clearly liable to result. The point to note in this context is the dictum of Stuart Smith LJ (at 621):

> I accept that difficulty in practice may arise in categorisation of loss into types or kinds, especially where financial loss is involved. But I do not see any difficulty in holding that loss of ordinary business profits is different in kind from that flowing from a particular contract which gives rise to very high profits, the existence of which is unknown to the contracting party who therefore does not accept the risk of such loss occurring.

Of course, losses will often stem from 'particular contracts', but the point has also been made that:

> loss of profits claimed by reference to an extravagant or unusual bargain are not of the same type as damages referable to bargains that are usual. (*North Sea Energy* v *PTT* [1997] 2 Lloyd's Rep 418 at 438)

20.41 However, the point should be made that under the 'assumption of responsibility' approach from *The Achilleas* a more easily explicable (if not more easily applicable) approach will be taken to distinguishing different types of loss, because it will depend on the (objective) views of the parties. Lord Hoffmann said (at [22]):

> What is the basis for deciding whether loss is of the same type or a different type? It is not a question of Platonist metaphysics. The distinction must rest upon some principle of the law of contract. In my opinion, the only rational basis for the distinction is that it reflects what would have been regarded by the contracting party as significant for the purposes of the risk he was undertaking. In *Victoria Laundry (Windsor) Ltd* v *Newman Industries Ltd* [1949] 2 KB 528, where the [claimants] claimed for loss of the profits from their laundry business because of late delivery of a boiler, the Court of Appeal did not regard 'loss of profits from the laundry business' as a single type of loss. They distinguished (at p 543) losses from 'particularly lucrative dyeing contracts' as a different type of loss which would only be recoverable if the defendant had sufficient knowledge of them to make it reasonable to attribute to him acceptance of liability for such losses. The vendor of the boilers would have regarded the profits on these contracts as a different and higher form of risk than the general risk of loss of profits by the laundry.

Economic justification

20.42 The remoteness test has been perceived as economically efficient (R. Posner, *Economic Analysis of Law*, 2nd edn, Aspen, pp. 94–5). The remoteness rule:

> induces the party with knowledge of the risk either to take any appropriate precautions himself or, if he believes that the other party might be the more efficient loss avoider, to disclose the risk to the other party and pay him to assume it.[16]

The remoteness rule therefore means that the party supplying goods or a service does not always have to increase his or her prices to protect him or herself against unusual losses by the other party if the supplier breaches. The other party has an incentive to protect him or herself until the situation reaches the point at which it is cheaper for him or her to inform the supplier, and make a contract which is priced to take into account the risk of those losses.

The Achilleas

20.43 As has been indicated, *The Achilleas* may indicate a different basis to remoteness than has traditionally been seen to be the case, and modification of the approach taken. The issue is whether recoverable losses should be restricted, or extended, to those in relation to which the breaching party, as a reasonable person, can be regarded as having accepted the risk. An example of a problem can quickly make obvious why the question is raised.

16 See also D. Harris, D. Campbell, and R. Halson, *Remedies in Contract and Tort*, 2nd edn, Butterworths, 2002, ch. 6.

> [C] rings up his local taxi driver and books a taxi to drive him to the airport at 7am the next day. He tells the driver that it is most important as he is flying to New York to sign a multi-million dollar contract. The taxi driver oversleeps, [C] misses his flight and loses his deal. Is the taxi driver liable? (H. Beale, W. Bishop, and M. Furmston, *Contract Cases and Materials*, 2nd edn, Oxford University Press, 1990, p. 478)

It is this type of question which tends to lead to the reaction that the traditional remoteness test is not sufficient—that there must be some different test, or further element—and that was the question considered in *The Achilleas*.

20.44 The facts of *Transfield Shipping Inc* v *Mercator Shipping Inc, The Achilleas* (2008) can be briefly stated.[17]

> The case was concerned with a charter of the ship *The Achilleas*. The rate of hire was at the daily rate of $16,750. Under the charter the latest date for redelivery of the ship was 2 May 2004. The charterers gave notice that the ship would be redelivered between 30 April and 2 May 2004. The owners then made a contract for a new four- to six-month hire of the ship to a third party at a daily rate of $39,500. (The market rate had considerably increased since the previous charter had been made.) The latest date by which it could be delivered to the third party was 8 May 2004 and after that they were entitled to cancel. Because of a delay during their final subcharter, the charterers were late redelivering the vessel. By 5 May it was clear that the vessel would not be redelivered in time for the owners to provide it to the third party by 8 May. There was an unusual, 'extremely volatile', market at the time and the market rate had fallen again. The owners renegotiated with the third party for delivery to take place by 11 May, with the daily rate of hire reduced to $31,500 a day.

The issue was the amount of damages the owners should recover for the charterers' breach in late redelivery of the vessel. The general understanding of the shipping market had been that the damages recoverable in such cases were the difference between the charter rate and the market rate for the period of the delay in redelivery, and that was what the charterers were arguing was due. However, the owners were claiming the loss of the higher rate of the new charter, with the third party, for the entirety of the new charter (i.e. the difference between a daily rate of $39,500 and a daily rate of $31,500 for the period of the hire to the third party).

20.45 A majority of arbitrators, the judge at first instance, and the Court of Appeal found in favour of the amount contended for by the owners. They found that the loss was not too remote: it was within the parties' reasonable contemplation that late redelivery would cause the loss of a new charter. However, the House of Lords followed the conclusion of the dissenting arbitrator and found in favour of the charterers' contention that they were only liable for the difference in

17 For contrasting views of the case see E. Peel, 'Remoteness Revisited' (2009) LQR 6 and A. Kramer, 'The new Test of Remoteness in Contract' (2009) LQR 408.

the charter rate and the market rate for the period of the delay in redelivery. The difficulty lies in the diverse reasoning which was used to reach this conclusion.

20.46 Lord Rogers and Baroness Hale took the traditional approach, simply applying the *Hadley* v *Baxendale* rule and finding that the loss of the higher rate of the new charter for its entirety was not a 'type' of loss the parties could have reasonably contemplated as liable to result from the breach, as it was due to an 'extremely volatile' market. Plainly, this takes a narrow, and difficult to explain, approach to what amounts to a 'type of loss'.

20.47 However, as has been indicated, Lord Hoffmann (with Lord Hope basically agreeing) took a very different approach. He took the line that the traditional remoteness rule is merely an expression of what the parties would normally be taken to intend (objectively), and that it will thus be departed from when their objective intentions are shown to be different. According to Lord Hoffmann, what is in issue 'is the interpretation as a whole, construed in its commercial setting' (at [11]). It is a matter of what the parties 'contracting against the background of market expectations . . . would reasonably have considered the extent of the liability they were undertaking' (at [22]). In this case the line was taken that the charterers could not reasonably be regarded as having assumed responsibility for losses on the new contract because of the general understanding of the shipping market of the recoverable damages in these circumstances, and the fact that the charterers could have no knowledge of or control of any such new contract.

20.48 The judgments in the House of Lords leave the law on remoteness in some uncertainty. Lord Walker basically agreed with both approaches.[18] Lord Hoffmann's approach solves the taxi driver problem, referred to at para. **20.43**, without any need to strain the concept of type of loss. It also connects the remoteness test to the creation of the contract in the parties' voluntary undertaking of liability. He said (at [12]):

> It seems to me logical to found liability for damages upon the intention of the parties (objectively ascertained) because all contractual liability is voluntarily undertaken. It must be in principle wrong to hold someone liable for risks for which the people entering into such a contract in their particular market, would not reasonably be considered to have undertaken.

However, the line which should now be taken on remoteness has been a matter of much debate.[19] Lord Hoffmann's approach had the potential for great uncertainty.[20] In giving judgment in *The Achilleas* Baroness Hale expressed considerable unease. She said at [93]:

18 Although see *Sylvia Shipping Co Ltd* v *Progress Bulk Carriers Ltd (The Sylvia)* (2010) at [39].

19 E.g. A. Kramer, 'An Agreement-Centred Approach to Remoteness and Contract Damages' in N. Cohen and E. McKendrick (eds), *Comparative Remedies for Breach of Contract*, Hart Publishing, 2004; A. Tettenborn, '*Hadley* v *Baxendale* Foreseeability: A Principle beyond Its Sell By Date' (2007) 23 JCL 120; A. Robertson, 'The Basis of the Remoteness Rule in Contract' (2008) 28 LS 172; A. Kramer, 'Remoteness: New Problems with the Old Test' in R. Cunnington and D. Saidov, *Contract Damages: Domestic and International Perspectives*, Hart Publishing, 2008.

20 *MFM Restaurants Pte Ltd* v *Fish & Co Restaurants Pte Ltd* (2010).

> I am not immediately attracted to the idea of introducing into the law of contract the concept of the scope of duty which has perforce had to be developed in the law of negligence. The rule in *Hadley* v *Baxendale* asks what the parties must be taken to have had in their contemplation, rather than what they actually had in their contemplation, but the criterion by which this is judged is a factual one. Questions of assumption of risk depend upon a wider range of factors and value judgments. This type of reasoning is, as Lord Steyn put it in *Aneco Reinsurance Underwriting Ltd* v *Johnson & Higgins Ltd* [2002] 1 Lloyd's Rep 157, para 186, a 'deus ex machina'. Although its result in this case may be to bring about certainty and clarity in this particular market, such an imposed limit on liability could easily be at the expense of justice in some future case. It could also introduce much room for argument in other contractual contexts. Therefore, if this appeal is to be allowed, as to which I continue to have doubts, I would prefer it to be allowed on the narrower ground identified by Lord Rodger, leaving the wider ground to be fully explored in another case and another context.

20.49 However, it would seem that we are arriving at a position in which there should be not great uncertainty, but greater flexibility than existed under the traditional approach. In *John Grimes Partnership* v *Gubbins* (2013) the court had to consider whether a consulting engineering firm was liable for the drop in value of a property development which its breach had caused to be delayed by 15 months (the actual sum had not been determined, but figures of around £400,000 were discussed). At first instance, the judge took the line that the *Achilleas* had not effected a major change. His approach was that the traditional approach should be applied, and was only to be displaced if the commercial background showed that would not reflect the expectation or intention reasonably to be imputed to the parties. He found that there was no such displacement. The Court of Appeal agreed. Sir David Keene stated (at [24]):

> It seems to me to be right to bear in mind, as Lord Hoffmann emphasised in *The Achilleas*, that one is dealing with the law of contract, where the situation is governed by what has been agreed between the parties. If there is no express term dealing with what types of losses a party is accepting potential liability for if he breaks the contract, then the law in effect implies a term to determine the answer. Normally, there is an implied term accepting responsibility for the types of losses which can reasonably be foreseen at the time of contract to be not unlikely to result if the contract is broken. But if there is evidence in a particular case that the nature of the contract and the commercial background, or indeed other relevant special circumstances, render that implied assumption of responsibility inappropriate for a type of loss, then the contract-breaker escapes liability. Such was the case in *The Achilleas*.

In the instant case, there was no evidence 'to show that there was some general understanding or expectation in the property world', to lead to a contrary conclusion to that of the traditional test, as there had been in the commercial context of *Achilleas* (at [26]). Further, the difference between the level of the engineer's fee (£15,000) and that of the loss did not take the case out of the ordinary situation. The line was taken that 'such contrast is merely one possible pointer towards a contracting party not having undertaken a potential liability which is reasonably foreseeable and by itself would not normally suffice to establish such an absence of responsibility' (at [30]). It would seem then that the traditional approach to remoteness normally stands, and will only be displaced where the commercial background or 'other relevant special circumstances' show that the parties did not contract on that basis, rendering inappropriate the usual assumption that they did so.

Causation

20.50 The party in breach will not be liable for the injured party's loss if his or her breach is not regarded as a sufficient cause of it. It has to be an effective cause (*County Ltd* v *Girozentrale Securities* (1996)). Problems arise from intervening acts and events. In *Monarch Steamship Co. Ltd* v *A/B Karlshamns Oljefabriker* [1949] AC 196 the defendants contracted to carry goods for the claimants from Manchuria to Sweden. In breach of contract, sailing was delayed. The ship did not reach Sweden before the outbreak of the Second World War. The ship was stopped and the claimants incurred extra expense as a result of the goods continuing the voyage in a neutral ship. The defendants argued that they were not liable for the expense because it was not due to their breach but to the outbreak of war. It was held that the outbreak of war was not an intervening cause which broke the chain of causation. At the time of contracting, it had been foreseeable that delay might result in such problems being encountered. The situation would have been different had the claimants' loss been caused by the ship being struck by a typhoon. That might have happened at any time and the loss would not then have been regarded as caused by the defendants' delay (at 215).

20.51 An intervening act will not break the chain of causation where it is an act which the party in breach is under an obligation to guard against. It is an implied term of the contract between banker and customer that the customer will draw his or her cheques with due care so that he or she does not facilitate fraud. When a customer made out a cheque in such a way that the amount could be readily altered, he was liable to the bank for the full amount paid out on a cheque which had been fraudulently increased by a third party (*London Joint Stock Bank* v *Macmillan* (1918)).

20.52 The injured party may break the chain of causation with his or her own negligence. That was the situation in *Quinn* v *Burch Bros (Builders) Ltd* (1966), where the defendants breached their contract with the claimant plasterer by failing to provide him with a stepladder. The claimant was injured when he tried to use an unsecured trestle instead of a stepladder. Paull J held that his negligence had broken the chain of causation (see also *Lambert* v *Lewis* (1982)).

20.53 The actions of the injured party, and their effect upon his or her claim to damages, are also considered in the context of the duty to mitigate and the problem of contributory negligence (see later).

Mitigation

20.54

> [Mitigation] imposes on a [claimant] the duty of taking all reasonable steps to mitigate the loss consequent on the breach; and debars him from claiming any part of the damage which is due to his neglect to take such steps. (*British Westinghouse Electric and Manufacturing Co. Ltd* v *Underground Electric Railways Co. of London* [1912] AC 673 at 689 per Lord Haldane)

Mitigation is frequently discussed in terms of a 'duty' to mitigate, as it is in the quotation, but this can be misleading. There is no 'duty' as such, but merely a limitation upon recoverable damages.[21] The question of what steps are reasonable is one of fact (*Payzu Ltd* v *Saunders* [1919] 2 KB 581 at 586). The burden of showing a failure to mitigate is on the party in breach (*James Finlay & Co.* v *NV Kwik Hoo Tong HM* [1928] 2 KB 604 at 614).

20.55 Three aspects to mitigation can be identified. First, if there are reasonable steps which the injured party could take to reduce his or her loss, and if he or she does not take those steps, then the damages awarded to him or her will be limited to what he or she would have lost had he or she acted reasonably. Secondly, the expenses reasonably incurred in dealing with the breach will be recoverable. Thirdly, if the injured party takes action which in fact reduces his or her loss, then the damages payable will be reduced accordingly.

Reasonable steps to limit loss

20.56 The 'duty' to mitigate means that the injured party cannot recover damages for any loss which he or she could have avoided by taking reasonable steps. There was no failure to mitigate in *James Finlay & Co.* v *NV Kwik Hoo Tong HM* (1928), where the steps suggested by the party in breach would have damaged the injured party's commercial reputation. In that case, the facts were as follows:

> The claimants contracted to purchase sugar from the defendants. The contract stated that it was to be shipped in September. It was shipped in October but, wrongly, the bill of lading stated that it had been shipped in September. Being unaware of the breach, the claimants contracted with sub-buyers for the sale on of the sugar. The contract with the sub-buyers stated that the bill of lading should provide 'conclusive evidence' of the date of shipment. The sub-buyers rejected the goods because of the inaccuracy of the bill of lading.

The claimants sued the defendants. The defendants contended that the claimants were entitled to only nominal damages, as the claimants should have mitigated by enforcing the subsale, on the basis of the 'conclusive evidence' clause. It was held that the claimants did not have to mitigate in that way. Once they knew the truth, enforcing the sub-contract would not have been in the ordinary course of business, and would have damaged their business reputation.[22]

20.57 In *Pilkington* v *Wood* (1953), again there was no failure to mitigate. The steps to reduce loss suggested by the party in breach were not reasonable. There the injured party had purchased land with a defective title because of his solicitor's negligence. When he sued his solicitor the court held that the injured party was not expected to have undertaken 'a complicated and difficult piece of litigation' against the vendor of the land, to try to mitigate his loss. That was the case even though the solicitor was prepared to indemnify him in respect of the cost of that litigation.

21 *Sotiros Shipping Inc.* v *Sameiet Solholt, The Solholt* [1983] 1 Lloyd's Rep 605 at 608.

22 See also *London and South of England Building Society* v *Stone* (1983).

20.58 The duty to mitigate was not satisfied in *Brace* v *Calder* (1985). There it was considered that it would have been reasonable to accept another contract from the party in breach as a means of reducing loss. In that case, the facts were as follows:

> The four defendants carried on business in partnership as Scotch whisky merchants. They contracted with the claimant for him to manage their office business for two years. Before the expiry of the two years the partnership was dissolved on the retirement of two of the partners. The other two partners carried on the business. The claimant stated that the dissolution of the partnership had terminated his contract. He claimed the salary that he would have earned during the remainder of the two years. The remaining partners wished to employ him on the same terms as the original agreement.

The Court of Appeal accepted that there had been a wrongful termination of the claimant's contract, but held that he was entitled only to nominal damages. He could have mitigated his loss. It would have been reasonable to accept the alternative employment with the two partners. The situation would have been different had the claimant's technical dismissal, on the termination of the original contract, been more than that—if, for example, he had been dismissed in humiliating circumstances.

> It is plain that the question of what it is reasonable for a person to do in mitigation of his damages cannot be a question of law but must be one of fact in the circumstances of each case. There may be cases where as a matter of fact it would be unreasonable to expect a [claimant] to consider any offer made in view of the treatment he has received from the defendant. If he had been rendering personal services and had been dismissed after being accused in the presence of others of being a thief, and if after that his employer had offered to take him back into his service, most persons would think he was justified in refusing the offer, and that it would be unreasonable to ask him in this way to mitigate the damages in an action for wrongful dismissal. (*Payzu* v *Saunders* [1919] 2 KB 581 (see below) per Bankes LJ at 586)

20.59 The duty to mitigate was held to cover the new contract offered by the party in breach in *Payzu Ltd* v *Saunders* [1919] 2 KB 581. In that case, the facts were as follows:

> The claimant had contracted to purchase crêpe de Chine from the defendant. The defendant was to supply it, as required, over a nine-month period. The claimant was to have the goods on credit, payment to be made within one month of each delivery. Owing to a cheque going astray, the first payment was late and the defendant wrongly claimed to be able to terminate the contract. The defendant offered to continue to supply the claimant under a new contract on the same terms, except for the single change that payment was to be made on delivery. The claimant was in a position to pay on delivery but he refused the offer. The market price of the goods had risen.

The claimant contended that the wrongful termination of the original contract entitled him to damages to cover the rise in the market price above the contract price. It was held that the claimant should have mitigated the loss by accepting the defendant's offer of a 'cash on delivery' contract at the original price. Had the claimant accepted that offer, he would have obtained the goods at the original contract price but not on credit terms. In other words, he would have avoided having to pay the increased market price and, on that basis, the court held that he was entitled to recover only for the loss of a month's credit on each order—that is, the only loss he would have made had he accepted the defendant's offer. The court thought that there was nothing to make this a case in which it was not reasonable to avoid the increased market price by accepting the new offer from the party in breach. Scrutton LJ thought that 'in commercial contracts it is generally reasonable to accept an offer from the party in default' (at 589).[23]

20.60 However, there has been criticism of the approach taken in *Payzu Ltd* v *Saunders* to the claim to damages based on the rise in the market value of the goods between contract and delivery date. The effect of the court's decision was to transfer the benefit of that rise in the market from the injured party to the party in breach. The claimant's refusal of the defendant's offer meant that the defendant could realize the rise in value of the goods in the market. If the court had decided differently on the mitigation point, that rise in value would have been paid in damages to the claimant: the original contractual allocation of the market risk would have been maintained. As the court decided that the mitigation rule prevented the claimant from recovering that sum, the rise in market price of the goods was left with the defendant, who had lost it under the original contract allocation of the market risk (see Bridge (1989) 105 LQR 398).

Expenses incurred

20.61 The above cases concern the argument that the injured party has failed to act as the reasonable person would have done to reduce his loss. In addition, where the injured party has incurred expenses in reacting to the breach, the party in breach may argue that those expenses are not recoverable because they were unreasonably incurred. *Banco de Portugal* v *Waterlow & Sons Ltd* [1932] AC 452 provides an example of a case where the expenditure was held to have been reasonable, and Lord Macmillan stated that the injured party's actions 'ought not to be weighed in nice scales at the instance of the party whose breach of contract has occasioned the difficulty' (at 506). In that case, the facts were as follows:

> Waterlow contracted to print a series of 'Vasco da Gama' 500 escudo bank notes for the bank. In breach of contract they printed and delivered a second batch to Marang, in the mistaken belief that he had the bank's authority. Marang and his associates formed the Banco de Angola e Metropole in Portugal to put the notes into circulation. When the Banco de Portugal discovered what had occurred, they called in all 'Vasco da Gama' 500 escudo notes and redeemed both the authorized and unauthorized notes.

23 See also *The Solholt (Sotiros Shipping Inc.* v *Schmeiet Solholt)* (1983).

The Banco de Portugal claimed the cost of printing the notes and also the cost of redeeming the unauthorized notes. Waterlow contended that, as the authorized and unauthorized notes could be distinguished, the bank need not have paid out on the unauthorized notes. The House of Lords held that the bank could recover that sum. It had acted reasonably to maintain confidence in the currency.

20.62 Expenditure which is not reasonably incurred cannot be recovered. If the injured party takes out a loan to obtain the release of his ship, which has been detained in breach of contract, and the loan is at a very high rate of interest, the interest charge will not be recovered where it is unreasonably incurred (*The Borag (Compania Financiera 'Soleada' SA* v *Hamoor Tanker Corpn Inc)* (1981)).

Benefit gained

20.63 There is said to be one further aspect of mitigation, namely that the injured party cannot recover for a loss which he or she has avoided. A benefit stemming directly from the breach is taken into account in calculating the loss caused (*British Westinghouse Electric and Manufacturing Co. Ltd* v *Underground Electric Railways Co. of London Ltd* (1912)), although there must be a direct connection between the breach of contract and the benefit enjoyed by the innocent party (*Globalia Business Travel S.A.U. (formerly TravelPlan S.A.U.) of Spain* v *Fulton Shipping Inc of Panama* (2017)).

Anticipatory breach

20.64 The further difficulty occasioned in relation to anticipatory breach was considered at para. **18.40**.

Economic efficiency

20.65 Mitigation has obvious links with the issue of causation. However, in not including in the injured party's damages a loss which he or she would not have incurred had he or she acted reasonably, the mitigation rule can be seen as a means of preventing resources from being wasted. In that context it can also be viewed as an incentive to breach: it is not a disincentive to do so. It can be seen as part of the promotion of the 'efficient breach' which it has been argued is economically desirable.

> In some cases a party would be tempted to breach the contract simply because his profit from breach would exceed his expected profit from completion of the contract, and if damages are limited to loss of expected profit, there will be an incentive to commit a breach. There should be. The opportunity cost of completion to the breaching party is the profit he would make from the breach, and if it is greater than his profit from completion, then completion will involve a loss to him. If that loss is greater than the gain to the other party from completion, breach would be value maximising and should be encouraged. (Posner, *Economic Analysis of Law*, 2nd edn, pp. 89–90)

The rationale is that the injured party is satisfied because damages provide him or her with the benefit he or she would have derived from the contract. If the party who breached can pay those damages and, after doing so, make a profit in excess of that which he or she would have derived from the contract, then it is economically efficient to encourage the breach. A greater benefit has been derived from the breach than would have followed from performance. The mitigation rule can be seen as part of the encouragement to efficient breach.[24]

Contributory negligence

20.66 The injured party may have contributed to his or her injury through his or her own negligence. One question which needs to be considered is whether damages can be reduced in contract, as in tort, on the basis of the injured party's contributory negligence. In tort, reduction of damages—on the basis of the injured party's negligent contribution to his own injury—is dealt with by the Law Reform (Contributory Negligence) Act 1945 (LR(CN)A 1945). The question here concerns the applicability of that Act to an action in contract.

20.67 The Law Reform (Contributory Negligence) Act 1945 applies where 'any person suffers damage as the result partly of his own fault and partly of the fault of any other person'. Where that is the situation, the damages recoverable 'shall be reduced to such an extent as the court thinks just and equitable having regard to the claimant's share in the responsibility for the damage' (s 1). 'Fault' is defined in s 4, which states that it 'means negligence, breach of statutory duty or other act or omission which gives rise to a liability in tort or would, apart from this Act, give rise to the defence of contributory negligence'.

20.68 The current law, on the applicability of LR(CN)A 1945 in relation to a breach of contract, basically requires a threefold division of the cases (*Forsikringsaktieselskapet Vesta* v *Butcher* [1986] 2 All ER 488 at 508 per Hobhouse J):

1. Where the defendant's liability arises from some contractual provision which does not depend on negligence on the part of the defendant.
2. Where the defendant's liability arises from some contractual obligation which is expressed in terms of taking care (or its equivalent) but does not correspond to a common law duty to take care which would exist in the given case independently of contract.
3. Where the defendant's liability in contract is the same as his liability in the tort of negligence independently of the existence of any contract.

With the definition of fault in LR(CN)A 1945, s 4, the Act clearly seems inappropriately worded to cover cases in the first category; *Vesta* indicated that it would only be applied to the third

24 But see Harris, Campbell and Halson, *Remedies in Contract and Tort*, 2nd edn, 2002, chapter 7. Bridge (1989) 105 LQR 398 at 408 states that the mitigation rule is based on 'several impulses that mollify the strictness of contractual obligation and that are hard, perhaps impossible to rationalize in their totality. The rules of mitigation may well express the law's concern to avoid economic waste, but it would be a mistake to believe that this represents entirely the law's concern in the matter.'

category, and that is the line that has been taken.[25] The Law Commission has recommended that contributory negligence should be applicable in both categories 2 and 3 (Law Com Rep No 219 (1993)). Of course, since the decision in *Henderson* v *Merrett Syndicates* (1995), concurrent liability, bringing the situation within category 3, is more likely to be found and the problem diminished. However, the point has been made that 'the ebbing and flowing of the tort of negligence should not be affecting the ambit of contributory negligence in contract' and that it would be sensible to amend the law, as the Law Commission suggested, to make it simpler and fairer.[26]

Penalties and liquidated damages

20.69 Given the complexity of the rules just described, it is hardly surprising that the parties should sometimes choose to include a term in their contract stating what damages are to be available upon the occurrence of a particular breach or breaches. Such a clause is known as a 'liquidated damages' clause. The fixing of liability by such a clause has the benefit of introducing certainty into the question of damages. It makes it easier for the parties to calculate the risks involved in the contract and to insure appropriately. It may even help to avoid a dispute reaching the point where it is litigated. There is much to be said for such clauses and the courts will enforce them.

20.70 However, the courts have had to deal with the question of whether a clause fixing a sum to be paid on breach is a liquidated damages clause or a penalty clause. The classic statement differentiating the two is that of Lord Dunedin in *Dunlop Pneumatic Tyre Co. Ltd* v *New Garage and Motor Co. Ltd* [1915] AC 79 at 86: 'The essence of a penalty is a payment of money stipulated as *in terrorem* of the offending party; the essence of damages is a genuine covenanted pre-estimate of damage.' In other words, a penalty clause is an attempt to coerce performance by setting an excessive sum to be paid on breach. However, this conflicts with the view generally taken by English law that damages merely compensate the injured party and do not punish the party in breach. Moreover, the Supreme Court has recently confirmed that the true question to be asked is whether the clause is penal, not whether it is a pre-estimate of loss. (See further the combined cases *Cavendish Square Holding BV* v *Talal El Makdessi* and *ParkingEye Ltd* v *Beavis* [2015] UKSC 67 discussed at paras **20.79–20.86**.) An injured party will not recover the sum specified in the penalty clause, but will be limited to recovering his or her actual loss. The clause is not struck out of the contract, but will not be enforced beyond the sum which represents the actual loss of the injured party.[27]

20.71 The EC Directive on Unfair Terms in Consumer Contracts should be noted in the context of this discussion of penalty and other clauses. In the consumer context, using the unfair terms in consumer contracts regime may avoid some of the difficulties in the borderlines of the applications of the rules on penalty clauses.

25 E.g. *Barclays Bank plc* v *Fairclough Building Ltd* (1995); *Raflatac* v *Eade* (1999); *Barclays Bank plc* v *Fairclough Building Ltd (No 2)* (1995).

26 A. Burrows, *Understanding the Law of Obligations*, Hart Publishing, 1998, p. 150.

27 *Jobson* v *Johnson* [1989] 1 All ER 621 at 633.

Distinguishing penalty and liquidated damages clauses

20.72 An obvious problem created for the courts in this area is to distinguish penalty clauses and liquidated damages clauses. They may take the same form and an express label, placed upon them by the parties, by no means determines the issue. Apart from attempts to avoid the rule about penalty clauses, any such label may simply not have been used in its technical sense. 'Though the parties to a contract who use the words "penalty" or "liquidated damages" may prima facie be supposed to mean what they say, yet the expression used is not conclusive. The court must find out whether the payment stipulated is in truth a penalty or liquidated damages.'[28]

20.73 It is a matter of construing the contract to determine the classification of the clause on the basis of the circumstances known, or which should have been known, at the time of contracting. The traditional view is to be found in *Dunlop Pneumatic Tyre Co. Ltd* v *New Garage and Motor Co. Ltd* [1915] AC 79. Lord Dunedin set out four 'tests' to help with this question. He said (at 87–8):

> (a) It will be held to be a penalty if the sum stipulated for is extravagant and unconscionable in amount in comparison with the greatest loss that could conceivably be proved to have followed from the breach.
>
> (b) It will be held to be a penalty if the breach consists only in not paying a sum of money, and the sum stipulated is a sum greater than the sum which ought to have been paid
>
> . . .
>
> (c) There is a presumption (but no more) that it is a penalty when a single lump sum is made payable by way of compensation, on the occurrence of one or more or all of several events, some of which may occasion serious and others but trifling damage.
>
> On the other hand:
>
> (d) It is no obstacle to the sum stipulated being a genuine pre-estimate of damages, that the consequences of the breach are such as to make precise pre-estimation almost an impossibility. On the contrary that is just the situation when it is probable that pre-estimated damage was the bargain between the parties.

In that case Dunlop sold motor car tyres to dealers who in turn sold them on. In return for a discount, the dealers had undertaken not to tamper with the marks on the goods, not to sell the tyres to private customers below Dunlop's list price, not to sell to anyone whose supply Dunlop had suspended, and not to exhibit or export any of the tyres. It was stated that they were to pay £5 as 'liquidated damages' for a breach. The dealers sold a tyre below list price. Dunlop's business was carried on through sales to dealers, and all the dealers to whom they sold were required to sign the agreement. There was evidence that if a dealer undersold, it had the effect

28 *Dunlop Pneumatic Tyre Co. Ltd* v *New Garage and Motor Co. Ltd* [1915] AC 79 at 86. See also *Clydebank Engineering and Shipbuilding Co. Ltd* v *Castaneda* (1905).

of forcing other dealers to buy elsewhere, thereby reducing the number of outlets for Dunlop's goods.

20.74 The House of Lords decided that the clause requiring £5 'liquidated damages' was indeed a liquidated damages clause and not a penalty. This was largely on the basis of (d) above. There was evidence that failure to maintain the price would cause the manufacturers damage on a broad scale, through reduction of their retail outlets, but it was not clear how much loss would result from one specific underpriced sale. It was regarded as reasonable for the parties to estimate that loss, and the clause was upheld, as the figure was not extravagant. In addition, the fact that the same sum was payable in relation to different breaches did not mean that it had to be labelled as a penalty. The test in (c) above did not mean that the clause in the particular case was a penalty clause. All the prohibitions on dealers related to the same type of broad potential damage to Dunlop. In addition, the loss from breach of any one was uncertain and such things 'could not be weighed nicely in a chemical balance'. The court thought that it was a matter of whether the loss from one particular breach could clearly never reach the specified sum, and that was not the case.

20.75 The loss arising from a particular breach may vary according to a particular factor. If the clause indicating the sum to be paid on breach is one which varies the amount appropriately in accordance with this factor, that may indicate that the clause is a liquidated damages clause. It may be, for example, that the breach is one which can continue for a period of time and the loss will increase as the time passes. A clause increasing the sum to be paid with the increasing period of time may well be found to be a liquidated damages clause (*Clydebank Engineering and Shipbuilding Co. Ltd* v *Castaneda* (1905)). On the other hand, it may be that the variation of the sum payable does not relate to likely variations in the loss suffered, but is an arbitrary variation in relation to likely loss. Such arbitrary variation indicates that the clause was not a genuine pre-estimate of damage (*Public Works Comr* v *Hills* (1906)). The situation is even more extreme, and more clearly indicative that the clause is a penalty, where the loss varies in exactly the opposite way to the variation in the clause: a penalty clause is indicated where there is 'a sliding scale of compensation but a scale that slides in the wrong direction' (*Bridge* v *Campbell Discount Co. Ltd* [1962] AC 600 at 623).

20.76 A further point should be made here as to the trend in relation to the basic approach to the construction of a clause which states the amount of damages to be paid upon a breach or breaches occurring. In *Philips Hong Kong Ltd* v *A-G of Hong Kong* (1993) the Privy Council emphasized the usefulness of the liquidated damages clause because of the certainty it creates for both parties and, against that background, the point was made that the courts' power to deal with penalty clauses was one which 'was always recognised as being subject to fairly narrow constraints' and not one giving a general jurisdiction to rewrite the parties' bargain.[29] In particular, the point was made that although the nature of the clause had to be assessed against what could be foreseen at the time of contracting, the courts would not find a clause to be a penalty

29 See also *AMEV-UDC Finance Ltd* v *Austin* (1987); *Robophone Facilities Ltd* v *Blank* [1966] 1 WLR 1428 at 1447.

clause just because some hypothetical examples of its use could be found in which there would be a gap between the sum specified under the clause and the loss suffered. The likelihood of the losses in question had to be considered as well. Lord Woolf, delivering the judgment of the court, said:

> Arguments of this nature should not be allowed to divert attention from the correct test as to what is a penalty clause provision—namely is it a genuine pre-estimate of *what the loss is likely to be*?—to the different question, namely are there possible circumstances where a lesser loss would be suffered? (emphasis added)

20.77 The Court of Appeal has adopted Colman J's 'recasting' in 'more modern terms' of the 'classic test'.[30] Coleman J said in *Lordsvale* v *Bank of Zambia* [1996] QB 752 at 762:

> [W]hether a provision is to be treated as a penalty is a matter of construction to be resolved by asking whether at the time the contract was entered into the predominant contractual function of the provision was to deter a party from breaking the contract or to compensate the innocent party for the breach. That the contractual function is deterrent rather than compensatory can be deduced by comparing the amount that would be payable on breach with the loss that might be sustained if the loss occurred.

Importantly, it was also made plain that a clause would not be seen as penal simply because of a comparison of those amounts. The amount stated would not be struck down as a penalty 'if it could in the circumstances be explained as commercially justifiable provided always that the dominant purpose was not to deter the other party from breach' (Colman J at 763–4).[31]

20.78 In *Murray* v *Leisureplay* (2005) what was in issue was a clause stating that the chief executive was to receive one year's gross salary and benefits on wrongful termination of his contract. At first instance that was held to be penal because, inter alia, it did not take account of the fact that an injured party has a duty to mitigate and the loss of the contract in question would give the ex-chief executive the possibility of taking up other opportunities during that year. The Court of Appeal concluded that the clause was not penal. Buxton LJ said (at [115]):

> An entrepreneurial company . . . promoting a product conceived by one man, will often place high value on retaining the services, and the loyalty and attention of that one man as its chief executive: to the extent of including in his 'package' generous reassurance against the eventuality of dismissal. That such reassurance exceeds the likely amount of contractual damages on dismissal does not render the terms penal unless the party seeking to avoid the terms can demonstrate that they meet the test of extravagance posited by Lord Dunedin.

30 *Murray* v *Leisureplay* (2005); *Euro London Appointments* v *Claessens International* (2006); *Cine Bes Filmcilik ve Yapimcilik* v *United International Pictures* (2003).

31 See also *Euro London Appointments* v *Claessens International* (2006) at [30].

20.79 The significance of matters of construction and surrounding commercial context to determine the penal character of a clause were emphasized in the recent Supreme Court ruling on the conjoined cases *Cavendish Square Holding BV* v *Talal El Makdessi* and *ParkingEye Ltd* v *Beavis* [2015] UKSC 67. This delivered a landmark restatement of the law relating to penalty clauses and shall now be considered.

20.80 The facts of each case were as follows:

In *Cavendish Square Holding BV* v *Talal El Makdessi*:

> Mr Makdessi agreed to sell Cavendish Square Holding BV a controlling stake in the holding company of a large advertising and marketing communications group in the Middle East. The agreement between the parties contained two clauses which provided that if he breached certain restrictive covenants, Mr Makdessi (a) would not be entitled to receive the final two instalments of the sale price (at clause 5.1); and (b) may be obliged to sell his remaining shares to Cavendish at asset value, that is, a price that excluded the value of the goodwill of the business (clause 5.6). When Mr Makdessi breached the restrictive covenants, he argued that the two clauses were unenforceable penalties. The Court of Appeal overturned the decision at first instance, and agreed with Mr Makdessi.

In *ParkingEye Ltd* v *Beavis*:

> There was a car park which was attached to shopping units, with the entire site being owned by the same company. Two hours' free parking was available to users of the car park, which was attractive to shoppers and, therefore, also to those who leased the shopping units. However, if a motorist overstayed they incurred a charge of £85 (reducible to £50 if paid within 14 days) for that breach of contract. When Mr Barry Beavis overstayed the two-hour limit by almost one hour, he argued that the charge was a penalty at common law and therefore unenforceable, and/or that the charge was unfair and unenforceable by virtue of the Unfair Terms in Consumer Contracts Regulations (SI 1999/2083). The court of first instance held it not to be so and the Court of Appeal upheld that decision.

20.81 Both Cavendish and Mr Beavis appealed to the Supreme Court and the two appeals were heard together. Cavendish's appeal was allowed on the basis that the clauses were not penalties. Mr Beavis's appeal was dismissed on the basis that the charges were nevertheless enforceable. What is most significant regarding the hearing is how the Court chose to take a different approach to the traditional view as laid down in *Dunlop Pneumatic Tyres* (1915). Instead, an approach was promoted which allows for a sum in excess of a genuine pre-estimate of loss not to be regarded as penal, if it is not out of all proportion to a legitimate interest of the promisee which extends beyond his or her interest in recovery of that loss. This test was found to be satisfied in relation to the non-competition clause in Cavendish and the time limit on parking in ParkingEye.

20.82 The fact that a clause is not a pre-estimate of loss does not automatically mean it will be regarded as a penalty. It was stated [at 32]:

> The true test [of a penalty] is whether the [clause] imposes a detriment on the contract-breaker out of all proportion to any legitimate interest of the innocent party in the enforcement of the primary obligation. The innocent party can have no proper interest in simply punishing the defaulter. His interest is in performance or in some appropriate alternative to performance. In the case of a straightforward damages clause, that interest will rarely extend beyond compensation for the breach, and we therefore expect that Lord Dunedin's four tests would usually be perfectly adequate to determine its validity. But compensation is not necessarily the only legitimate interest that the innocent party may have in the performance of the defaulter's primary obligations.

20.83 Lord Neuberger and Lord Sumption affirmed that the law relating to penalties only applies to secondary obligations which arise on the occurrence of a breach, and not to primary ones (at 32). The penal character of a clause is a matter of construction and evidence of the commercial background is relevant (at 28). Therefore, although there is a possibility that clever drafting may be used to avoid the rule (at 130), the court will look to the substance of the clause and not its form (at 39) to decide if what has occurred has brought about a breach. Lord Mance agreed with this, stating [at 152]:

> What is necessary in each case is to consider, first, whether any (and if so what) legitimate business interest is served and protected by the clause, and, second, whether, assuming such an interest to exist, the provision made for the interest is nevertheless in the circumstances extravagant, exorbitant or unconscionable.

Lord Hodge also agreed, reaffirming that the test was whether the remedy was 'exorbitant or unconscionable', having regard to the 'innocent party's interest in performing the contract' [at 255] and not whether it was a genuine pre-estimate of loss [at 246–7] or intended as deterrence [at 248]. Lord Toulson agreed with Lord Hodge's formulation of the test, and with Lord Mance and Lord Hodge on the approach to be taken toward penalty clauses and forfeiture clauses (at 294).

20.84 Applying the principles to the cases under appeal, the Supreme Court found in respect of Cavendish that both clauses were primary obligations and not subject to the penalty rule. Clauses 5.1 and 5.6 were price adjustment clauses which served a legitimate function relating to Cavendish's commercial objective of acquiring the business and protecting its goodwill.

20.85 In the hearing of the issues specific to ParkingEye, the majority in the Court found that although the penalty rule was engaged, the charge to Mr Beavis was not a penalty and therefore not unfair. (Lord Toulson dissented on the basis that the clause would have fallen foul of the

1999 Regulations.) Here, though, we are concerned with the penal nature of the clause. For further discussion on the unfairness aspect of the case, see para. **11.49**) The charge was deemed to protect two legitimate business interests: (a) to manage the efficient use of the car park; and (b) to generate income to meet the costs of operating the scheme at a profit (see [98]).

20.86 The findings in *Cavendish* and *ParkingEye* demonstrate a significant relaxation of the rules relating to penalty clauses. The dichotomy between a genuine pre-estimate of loss and a penalty or deterrent has been removed and it will be more difficult to successfully argue that a clause is an unenforceable penalty. Moreover, this new approach has widened the courts' involvement in commercial arrangements: they are now tasked with establishing the nature and extent of the interests of the parties and determining whether those interests are legitimate. It is likely such changes will introduce more uncertainty into an already complex area.

Avoidance of the rule on penalties

20.87 The first point to emphasize is that the rule about penalty clauses only applies where the sum specified in the clause in question becomes payable on breach. The courts have had to decide whether payment is due upon breach or other circumstances. If the sum specified becomes payable under circumstances which are not a breach, then the rule as to penalty clauses does not apply. An example is provided by *Alder* v *Moore* (1961):

> The Association Football Players' and Trainers' Union took out an insurance policy on behalf of their members. It provided for payment of £500 if a player suffered permanent disablement preventing him from playing professional football. Brian Moore was a professional footballer with West Ham. He received an injury which permanently deprived him of 90 per cent of his vision in one eye. It was thought that he would never be able to play professional football again and the insurance company paid him £500. The policy required him to sign a declaration on receiving such a payment. The declaration stated that 'in consideration of the [£500] I hereby declare and agree that I will take no part as a playing member of any form of professional football and that in the event of infringement of this condition I will be subject to a penalty of [£500]'. Mr Moore's sight did not return, but he started to play professional football again, on a part-time basis, with Cambridge United. The insurance company claimed the £500.

The Court of Appeal (with Devlin LJ dissenting) held that he had not committed a breach by playing professional football again. The insurance company was entitled to the £500 as it was merely payable upon the resumption of professional football. The clause was not subject to the rule on penalties.

20.88 Specifying a condition upon which a payment must be made, and ensuring that it is not a breach, may provide a means of evading the operation of the rules on penalties. This can be seen more clearly in the case of *Bridge* v *Campbell Discount Co. Ltd* [1962] AC 600, where Lord Denning said (at 629): 'equity commits itself to this absurd paradox: it will grant relief to a man who breaks his contract but will penalise the man who keeps it'. In that case, the facts were as follows:

> Mr Bridge had obtained a car on a hire purchase basis. The contract contained an option for him to give notice to terminate the hiring and return the car at any time. However, it also contained a clause requiring him to pay 'compensation' for 'depreciation' upon termination of the contract. The clause was effectively one to ensure a minimum payment. It required a payment to make up two-thirds of the hire purchase price when combined with the money already paid. Mr Bridge returned the car after he had made only one of the required 36 monthly payments.

The Court of Appeal found that returning the car did not involve a breach, as Mr Bridge had merely exercised the option and, on that basis, the requirement as to the payment of compensation could not be subject to the rule on penalty clauses. The House of Lords avoided this conclusion by construing the return of the car not as an exercise of the option, but as a breach. It was then able to find that the clause was a penalty clause. A decreasing sum could not be genuine compensation for depreciation. The depreciation would increase as the amount payable under the clause decreased. The hire purchase company was not able to recover the amount specified in the penalty clause, but only its actual loss.[32] (Very controversially, the High Court of Australia has recently turned away from restricting the application of the rules on penalty clauses to payments on breach in *Andrews* v *Australia and New Zealand Banking Group Ltd* (2012). See J. W. Carter, W. Courtney, E. Peden, A. Stewart, and G. J. Tolhurst, 'Contractual Penalties: Resurrecting the Equitable Jurisdiction' (2013) 30 JCL 99.) Although the Supreme Court in *Cavendish* and *ParkingEye* (2015) regarded this as holding 'strong persuasive force', it was not accepted that 'English law should take the same path' [at 42].)

20.89 There are other means of achieving much the same result as would follow from a penalty clause if it was allowed to take effect. In other words, there are other ways of avoiding the rule on penalty clauses. (Although note the direction of the Supreme Court in *Cavendish* and *ParkingEye* (2015) to look to the substance of the clause and not its form (at 39), which may bring about further changes in this respect.) The contract may, for example, provide a discount for prompt payment rather than a penalty for late payment. Where the contract requires payment in instalments, there is the possibility of using an acceleration clause which provides that if one payment is not made on time then all the instalments immediately become due.[33] In addition, the position of deposits must be considered.

Deposits

20.90 The rules governing penalties now need to be compared with the approach taken by the courts to deposits. The basic rule in relation to an advance payment is that it has to be determined

32 See also *Export Credit Guarantee Department* v *Universal Oil Products Co* (1983); *Transag Haulage Ltd* v *Leyland DAF Finance plc* (1994).

33 *Proctor Loan Co.* v *Grise* (1880), but see *O'Dea* v *Allstates Leasing Systems (WA) Pty Ltd* (1983).

whether it is a deposit or a part payment. Was it meant to secure performance or merely partly to discharge the contract price? Basically, a part payment will be recoverable if there is a total failure of consideration by the seller,[34] but, until recently, a deposit was not recoverable as it was required to secure performance.[35] The fact that a deposit could not be recovered, no matter how little relationship it had to any loss caused by the failure to perform, made an uneasy contrast with the rules in relation to penalties. In effect, the law's treatment of deposits provided a means of avoiding the rules on penalties. However, this anomaly was noted and mitigated by the Privy Council in *Worker's Trust and Merchant Bank Ltd* v *Dojap Investments Ltd* (1993). The approach taken there was that it was anomalous that the rules on penalties did not apply to deposits, and that that should only be the case if the sum specified was 'reasonable'. However, the assessment of whether the sum was 'reasonable' was carried out on an admittedly illogical basis. The simple line taken was that the long-standing, customarily required deposit was 10 per cent of the purchase price, and anything in excess of that would be regarded as 'unreasonable' unless it could be shown to be justified by special circumstances. In the instant case, the sum demanded had been 25 per cent of the purchase price, and the vendor claimed to be entitled to retain it when the buyer failed to complete the purchase within the time specified. The Privy Council ordered that, subject to the vendor's claim for damages, the entire sum should be returned by the vendor. As the entire sum was not to be viewed as a deposit, but as a penalty, the vendor could not even retain 10 per cent.

Unfair Terms in Consumer Contracts Directive

20.91 The point was made earlier that there is considerable scope for avoiding the rules as to penalty clauses by setting out to achieve the same end (a disincentive to non-performance) by a different form of clause, and this can produce anomalies. However, in the consumer context there is considerable potential to mitigate that problem through the use of the regime for consumer protection which derives from the Unfair Terms in Consumer Contracts Directive. The application of the fairness test under that regime is not limited to particular types of clause. The only concern is the exclusion from the fairness test of terms falling within the core exemption.

A particular kind of loss: mental distress and the consumer surplus

20.92 We have until now been considering examples of financial loss, and these are the classic types of claim which the law of contract has had to deal with, and which its rules were elaborated around. However, with the development of the consumer culture in particular, the question has been raised as to the recovery of a loss when the contract was not made to make a money profit, but was wholly or partly concerned with some enjoyment, pleasure, or the relief of distress. If contract damages are not awarded to protect such expected gains from the contract, then contract rights are actually far more limited than the basic ideas and rules would

34 *Dies* v *British and International Mining and Finance Corpn Ltd* (1939); *Hyundai Heavy Industries Co. Ltd* v *Papadopoulos* (1980); *Rover International Ltd* v *Cannon Film Sales Ltd* (1989).

35 *Howe* v *Smith* (1884). A statutory discretion is provided in relation to a contract for the sale of land—Law of Property Act 1925, s 49(2).

suggest, and they do not adequately protect consumers. We should now consider this question, and we will start by considering the cases which have focused on recovery for damages for mental distress, before considering another line of authority concerned with the basis of calculation of damages.

Damages for mental distress

20.93 The usual contractual damages claim will relate to damage to the injured party's economic interest, but it may also cover personal injury or damage to property. However, with exceptions, contract damages do not encompass, on a general basis, damages for mental distress, that is, damages for vexation, frustration, anxiety, and disappointment. The basic restriction was established in *Addis* v *Gramophone Co. Ltd* (1909). In that case:

> Mr Addis was employed as manager of G Co.'s business in Calcutta. His contract entitled him to six months' notice of dismissal. G Co. gave him six months' notice but immediately appointed his successor and ensured that Mr Addis could no longer act as manager.

The manner of his dismissal injured Mr Addis' feelings but the House of Lords would not allow him to recover a sum in damages for that injury.

20.94 However, damages for mental distress have now been recognized as exceptionally available, and the starting point for considering that is the judgment of Bingham LJ in *Watts* v *Morrow* [1991] 4 All ER 937. He first stated the general non-availability of damages for mental distress. He said (at 959):

> A contract-breaker is not in general liable for any distress, frustration, anxiety, displeasure, vexation, tension or aggravation which his breach of contract may cause to the innocent party. This rule is not, I think, founded on the assumption that such reactions are not foreseeable, which they surely are or may be, but on considerations of policy.

This states the general rule and emphasizes that the general non-availability of damages for mental distress is a matter of policy. The question of the 'policy' behind the general non-availability of damages for mental distress will be returned to later. Here what must now be considered is Bingham LJ's statement of the exceptional situations in which such damages are available. First, he said (at 959):

> But the rule is not absolute. Where the very object of a contract is to provide pleasure, relaxation, peace of mind or freedom from molestation, damages will be awarded if the fruit of the contract is not provided or if the contrary result is procured instead. If the law did not cater for this exceptional category of case it would be defective.

This requires the 'very object of the contract' to be of an appropriate type, that is, 'pleasure, relaxation, peace of mind or freedom from molestation'. Plainly, as the point (object) of such contracts is not to provide a profit but some mental benefit, it would be very obvious that an award of contract damages was not protecting the injured party's contractual 'rights', if damages for mental distress were not available in these cases. Hence Bingham LJ's reference to the law being 'defective' if it did not 'cater for this exceptional category of case'. However, this exception has now been extended by the House of Lords in *Farley* v *Skinner* (2001), and this will be returned to later. Here Bingham LJ's second exception should now be set out. He said (at 960):

> In cases not falling within this exceptional category, damages are in my view recoverable for physical inconvenience and discomfort caused by the breach and any mental suffering directly related to that inconvenience and discomfort.

These exceptions will now be considered, although the latter will be looked at first.

Mental distress consequent on physical inconvenience

20.95 As has been indicated, the second exception which Bingham LJ identified in *Watts* v *Morrow* (1991) provides for the recovery of damages for mental distress where it is a consequence of the physical inconvenience caused by the breach. This can be illustrated by, for example, *Perry* v *Sidney Phillips & Son* [1982] 3 All ER 705. In that case:

> Ivan Perry purchased a house on the faith of a survey carried out by the defendant surveyors which stated that the house was in good order. After moving in, Mr Perry discovered that the roof leaked and was in poor condition, and that the septic tank was inefficient and 'gave off an offensive odour'. These defects caused him distress, worry, and inconvenience.

In addition to damages for the reduced value of the property, because of the defects, the Court of Appeal agreed with the judge at first instance that Mr Perry was entitled to damages for his mental distress. Kerr LJ said (at 712):

> So far as the question of damages for vexation and inconvenience is concerned, it should be noted that the deputy judge awarded these . . . because of the physical consequences of the breach.

20.96 Similarly, in *Watts* v *Morrow* (1991) itself, although C could not recover more generally for their mental distress, they did recover for that consequent on the physical inconvenience caused by the breach. The case was concerned with a survey of property which, in breach of contract, the defendant surveyor had performed negligently. C were busy people who wished to purchase a second home to relax in at weekends. The survey report indicated that the house they had decided upon had no major defects. That was inaccurate, and C had to expend considerable time and money in having it repaired. They recovered the difference between what they paid for the property and what it was worth because of the defects.[36] In addition, following

36 They did not recover the larger sum which represented the cost of the repairs—see A. Dugdale, '*Watts* v *Morrow*: Penalising the House Purchaser' (1992) 8 Professional Negligence 152.

Perry v *Sidney Phillips & Son* (1982), they recovered for the mental distress consequent upon the physical inconvenience they had suffered, although, as has been indicated, they did not recover more generally for their mental distress.

20.97 This limited exception to the general non-availability of damages for mental distress was also seen as providing an alternative basis to the recovery of such damages in *Farley* v *Skinner* (2001), which we shall return to later, and some extension of the exception may be indicated. All of the judges, in that case, viewed the case as being one qualifying under the second exception. Lord Steyn made the point that noise (of aircraft flying overhead) can produce a physical reaction and made reference to it being capable of constituting a nuisance. He regarded it as a matter of degree whether it passed the threshold to constitute inconvenience and discomfort within Bingham LJ's test (at [30]). Lord Hutton and Lord Scott regarded the injured party as having suffered physical inconvenience and discomfort as the aircraft noise had a physical effect upon him through his hearing (at [85]). Lord Clyde can be viewed as going further, if somewhat uncertainly, taking the view that there was no 'particular magic' in the word 'physical' and regarding it as sufficient if what was in question was 'inconvenience' rather than merely 'matters purely sentimental' (at [35]).

'Objects' exception

20.98 As has been indicated, in *Watts* v *Morrow* (1991) Bingham LJ set out the, more significant, 'objects' exception to the general non-availability of damages for mental distress. It was, however, extended by the House of Lords in *Farley* v *Skinner* (2001), and that will be considered later. First, some understanding of the exception as Bingham LJ set it out can be gleaned from the cases which preceded it and on which it was clearly based.

20.99 In *Jarvis* v *Swans Tours Ltd* (1973), damages for lost enjoyment were awarded in relation to a contract for a holiday. In that case:

> Mr Jarvis booked a winter sports holiday with Swan. The holiday was described as a 'house party'. The brochure referred to afternoon tea and cakes and a yodeller evening and stated that ski-packs would be available. For the first week there were 13 people there, but for the second week Mr Jarvis was the sole member of the 'house party'. The cakes for tea were merely crisps and dry nutcake. Full-sized skis were only available for two days. The yodeller evening turned out to consist of a local man coming to the hotel, in his work clothes, and quickly singing a few songs.

Mr Jarvis claimed damages for breach of contract, as the holiday was not as promised in the brochure. At first instance he was merely awarded £31.72 as the difference in value between what he contracted for and what he got. The Court of Appeal awarded £125. It considered that he should be compensated for his lost enjoyment.[37] Plainly, a holiday contract is a contract the

37 See also *Jackson* v *Horizon Holidays Ltd* (1975).

'very object' of which 'is to provide pleasure'. A further example of a contract to provide pleasure is to be found in the Scottish case of *Diesen* v *Samson* (1971), where a bride was awarded damages for the distress (the loss of enjoyment) caused when the photographer she had booked failed to turn up to take photographs of her wedding.

20.100 In *Heywood* v *Wellers* (1976), the purpose of the contract was to provide relief from anxiety. In that case:

> The claimant had employed solicitors to obtain an injunction to prevent a man from molesting her. The solicitors were negligent and he molested her further.

Damages for mental distress were awarded. The contract was not for a commercial purpose, but to provide relief from distress, just as in *Jarvis* v *Swans Tours Ltd* (1973) and *Diesen* v *Samson* (1971) the object of the contracts was to provide pleasure.

20.101 The cases above provide plain examples of the 'objects' exception as stated by Bingham LJ. The 'very object' of the contracts in those cases was to provide pleasure or relief from distress. They contrast with *Watts* v *Morrow* (1991) itself, where the survey contract was not regarded as one 'the very object of' which 'is to provide pleasure, relaxation, peace of mind, or freedom from molestation'. However, that must again be contrasted with the somewhat different survey contract in *Farley* v *Skinner* (2001), where the House of Lords expanded the exception to an extent, although distinguishing the case before them from the ordinary survey contract in *Watts* v *Morrow*.

20.102 *Farley* v *Skinner* (2001) was concerned with the survey of a house in connection with its purchase by a successful businessman, who was retiring and wished to buy a 'gracious country residence'. He had been concerned that the property in question might be seriously affected by aircraft noise and he specifically instructed the surveyor to address that issue. The surveyor reported it as 'unlikely' that the property would suffer greatly from such noise. He was negligent in doing so. The question was whether the purchaser could recover more than nominal damages for that breach of the surveyor's contract. (The purchase price paid by the purchaser was found to have reflected the impact of noise on the house's value.) The House of Lords took the view that the case fell within the exceptions to the general non-availability of damages for mental distress. In particular, they addressed the argument that the provision of pleasure, relaxation, or peace of mind was not 'the very object' of a contract to survey a house for potential purchase. The line taken by the majority was that the exception does not only extend to cases in which 'the very object' of the contract is an appropriate one, but also (Lord Steyn) where 'a major or important object' of the contract is an appropriate one (at 812), or where a specific and important term of the contract is directed to an appropriate object (Lords Clyde and Hutton).

20.103 The extension of the exception is significant, as *Farley* v *Skinner* itself illustrates. It was applied, and prevented the need for a difficult distinction to be made, in *Hamilton Jones* v

David Snape (2004).There what was in issue was a solicitor's negligence in failing to see that a father did not take his child out of the jurisdiction. Neuberger J made the point that the mother's primary concern in instructing the solicitors might have been the child's interests. But whether her own interests or those of the child were uppermost

> both the claimant and the defendants would have had in mind that a significant reason for the claimant instructing the defendants was with a view to ensuring, so far as possible, that the claimant retained custody of her children for her own pleasure and peace of mind. (at [61])

Damages for mental distress were awarded.

20.104 However, *Farley* v *Skinner* (2001) should be put in its broader context. The point was made earlier that, in *Watts* v *Morrow* (1991), Bingham LJ said that the law would be 'defective' if it did not provide damages for mental distress where the 'very object' of the contract was to provide 'pleasure, relaxation, peace of mind or freedom from distress'. In effect, that was taken a stage further in *Farley* v *Skinner*. It was recognized that some further availability of mental distress damages was necessary to avoid a distinction of 'form and not substance', that is, the 'objects' exception as stated by Bingham LJ would have allowed for recovery if a house purchaser made a separate contract with a surveyor to report on aircraft noise, but not if that was simply specifically made part of a contract to survey the property more generally (per Lord Steyn at 811). However, a still broader perspective needs to be applied.

20.105 The basic principle on which contract damages are awarded is to put an injured party in the position they would have been in had the contract been performed. There are those who see this purely in terms of the financial position which the injured party would have been in had the contract been performed. Such a narrow view seems unconvincing once the exceptions noted here are considered. So why are damages for lost consumer surplus, or for mental distress, regarded as something which should only be exceptionally available? Basic principle would argue for their general availability. This needs to be considered further, but first we should look at another line of cases.

Cost of cure or market value?

20.106 We must now consider a line of cases which began with the question of whether the claimant's loss should be quantified on the basis of the cost of 'curing' the defective performance, or the difference in the market value between what the claimant should have had and what he or she obtained. The problem arose in relation to situations where someone contracts for work to be done on their property which will not add to its value, but which will add to their enjoyment of their property. Such situations have raised difficulties in the calculation of damages where the builder does not carry out the work according to the contract terms. The defective performance makes no difference to the value of the property and the builder has contended that damages should merely be nominal, whereas the homeowner has argued that a substantial amount will need to be spent to cure the defect and that he or she should be awarded that 'cost of cure'. It seemed at one stage that the award of damages had to be based on one of these two sums, but, as we shall see, a reversion to basic principle has now shown that not to be the case.

20.107 The first case to consider is *Radford* v *De Froberville* [1977] 1 WLR 1262. In that case:

> C had sold part of his land to D, D contracting to build a wall to separate her land from C's remaining land. This she failed to do. The wall would not have added to the value of C's property. C claimed the cost of building the wall on his side of the boundary.

Oliver J did not confine C's recovery to nominal damages. He awarded C the 'cost of cure'. He said (at 1270):

> Pacta sunt servanda. If he contracts for the supply of that which he thinks serves his interests—be they commercial, aesthetic or merely eccentric—then if that which is contracted for is not supplied by the other contracting party I do not see why, in principle, he should not be compensated by being provided with the cost of supplying it through someone else in a different way, subject to the proviso of course, that he is seeking compensation for a genuine loss and not merely using a technical breach to secure an uncovenanted profit.

The vital issue in such a case would seem to be to establish what the injured party's 'genuine loss' is. That will depend upon what 'interest' of the injured party the relevant contractual requirement served. However, the convenience of the simple pecuniary measure of 'cost of cure' being available meant that the nature of that did not have to be openly faced up to.

20.108 The difficulty in this area is that the injured party has contracted for a purpose which is not reflected in an objective market value. The injured party has contracted for the 'consumer surplus' (i.e. 'the excess utility or subjective value' which would have been obtained from the contractual performance—D. Harris, A. Ogus, and J. Phillips, 'Contract Remedies and the Consumer Surplus' (1979) 95 LQR 581 at 582). If the difference which the contractual performance would have made to the objective value of the injured party's property is smaller than the 'consumer surplus', then the injured party will be undercompensated if the injured party's recovery is restricted to that objective value (often nothing). In other words, damages ignoring the 'consumer surplus' will not put the injured party in the position he or she would have been in had the contract been performed. It may then be appropriate for the injured party to recover the cost of cure, as occurred in *Radford* v *De Froberville* (1977). Certainly that will be the case if the 'consumer surplus' is equal to, or greater than, the cost of cure. In that situation, an injured party will be mitigating their loss by curing the defect. However, the point should be emphasized that if the 'consumer surplus' is less than the cost of cure, awarding the cost of cure overcompensates the injured party. In other words, where a 'consumer surplus' is involved, it is not always appropriate to calculate the damages simply on the basis of either the cost of cure or the difference in value. If neither such sum is to be used as the basis of calculation, it must be admitted that the identification of the correct sum to award cannot be very accurate, but it is the only way to comply with basic principle. The need to depart from the simple dichotomy of cost of cure, or difference in market value, was recognized in *Ruxley* v *Forsyth* (1995).

20.109 In *Ruxley Electronics and Construction Ltd* v *Forsyth* [1995] 3 All ER 268:

> C contracted with the defendant for the building of a swimming pool with a maximum depth of water of 7 ft 6 in. C made it clear that the depth was important to him as he wanted to be able to dive and he needed that depth to feel safe to do so. The defendants built a pool with a maximum depth of 6 ft 9 in, and it was only 6 ft deep at the relevant point for diving. There was evidence that, as constructed, the pool was, objectively, safe for diving and the difference in the depth made no difference to the value. In order for the pool to be made to comply with the contract depth, it would have been necessary to rip out what had been installed and put in a new, deeper pool, at a cost of about £21,000. At first instance C was awarded £2,500 general damages for loss of amenity and pleasure. The Court of Appeal (Dillon LJ dissenting) found that the appropriate measure was the cost of cure.

The Court of Appeal viewed the awarding of the cost of cure as the only means of placing C in the position he would have been in had the contract been performed—that is, in possession of a pool which he felt safe to dive into. Obviously, in awarding the cost of cure, the Court of Appeal in *Ruxley* was protecting a non-commercial interest of C, but it was doing so inappropriately according to the House of Lords, which concluded that it was not restricted to awarding either the cost of cure or the difference in value. The House of Lords restored the award made at first instance.

20.110 In *Ruxley*, the House of Lords reasserted the basic principle that contractual damages should put the injured party in the position he or she would have been in had the contract been performed. Obviously, the Court of Appeal had also attempted to comply with basic principle but Lord Lloyd pointed out the basic fallacy in their reasoning. He stated the basic principle for the award of contractual damages and said (at 282): 'This does not mean that in every case of breach of contract the [claimant] can obtain the monetary equivalent of specific performance.' In economic terms there is a substitute for the injured party's loss of the enjoyment of diving into a 7 ft 6 in swimming pool. The injured party might derive equal enjoyment from a holiday, costing far less than the cost of cure. The lost contractual 'end'—the lost pleasure—can be compensated in money terms without the need to furnish a sum which would provide it through the equivalent of the contractual 'means'. In other words, contrary to the view of the Court of Appeal, having decided that a nominal difference in value was not an appropriate award, there was an alternative to awarding the cost of cure: directly awarding a sum to deal with the loss suffered.

20.111 In *Radford* v *De Froberville* (1977) and *Ruxley Electronics and Construction Ltd* v *Forsyth* (1995), in deciding whether the cost of cure was an appropriate award, the courts referred to whether such an award was 'reasonable', and this has received some emphasis. However, the duty to mitigate means that the injured party will not recover for a loss which he or she could have avoided by behaving reasonably on breach. A lost 'consumer surplus' exceeding the cost of cure should be mitigated by behaving reasonably and 'curing' the defendant's performance, and it is appropriate for the injured party to recover the cost of cure in damages. Similarly, if the cost of cure exceeds the 'consumer surplus', it is in keeping with the duty to mitigate that the injured party should only recover the 'consumer surplus' and not the larger cost of cure. Although 'reasonableness' has been addressed more bluntly, in terms of proportionality,[38] it is contended that the references to reasonableness in *Radford* and *Ruxley* should be understood as reflections of the duty to mitigate.

20.112 In *Ruxley Electronics and Construction Ltd* v *Forsyth* [1995] 3 All ER 268, Lord Mustill said (at 277):

> The law must cater for those occasions where the value of the promise exceeds the financial enhancement of his position which full performance will secure. This excess, often referred to in literature as the consumer surplus . . . is usually incapable of precise valuation in terms of money, exactly because it represents a personal, subjective and non-monetary gain. Nevertheless, where it exists the law should recognise it.

If it does not recognize the consumer surplus, then the injured party may either be undercompensated or overcompensated.[39] In *Radford* v *De Froberville* [1977] 1 WLR 1262, Oliver J awarded the cost of cure to compensate for a non-financial loss. He refused to accept that the injured party had to be left with nominal damages because the building of the wall would not affect the value of the property. Under the circumstances he regarded nominal damages (at 1268) as 'a result so strange and so monstrously unjust that Mr Bumble's animadversion on the nature of law seems, by contrast, a restrained understatement'.

20.113 In that case injustice could be avoided because the consumer surplus could be appropriately compensated for by an award of the cost of cure. However, in *Ruxley* the court had to deal with a situation in which awarding the cost of cure would have overcompensated the injured party, and been unjust to the other party. It was necessary to recognize the possibility of directly compensating for a lost consumer surplus so that (per Lord Mustill at 278) '[t]here is no need to remedy the injustice of awarding too little by unjustly awarding far too much'. Even if it certainly cannot be said that all the statements in *Ruxley* are in accordance with that, it should be recognized that avoiding both forms of injustice requires damages to be generally available for a lost consumer surplus.

Basic principle

20.114 Fully complying with basic principle, and putting the injured party in the position they would have been in had the contract been performed, raises issues in relation to the limitations

38 *Birse Construction* v *Eastern Telegraph* (2004).

39 In fact this has perhaps been put even more broadly in terms of the need to recognize the injured party's 'performance interest' if an inappropriate level of compensation is to be avoided—*Panatown Ltd* v *Alfred McAlpine Construction Ltd* (2000) per Lord Goff and Lord Millett.

currently placed on the award of damages for mental distress, and fully recognizing the award of the consumer surplus.

20.115 Lord Scott's judgment in *Farley* can be seen as taking a significant step further towards the general availability of damages for mental distress than the rest of the court. He said (at [79]):

> The *Ruxley Electronics* case establishes, in my opinion, that if a party's contractual performance has failed to provide to the other contracting party something to which the other was, under the contract, entitled, and which, if provided would have been of value to that party, then, if there is no other way of compensating the injured party, the injured party should be compensated to the extent of that value.

This approach would allow all 'consumer surplus' losses to be recovered, that is, all cases where the contractual performance would have provided some 'excess utility' or 'subjective value'. In other words, damages for loss of enjoyment or relief from distress could be recovered in all cases where some element of the contract was to provide enjoyment, or relief from distress, whether that element was a 'major or important object' of the contract or a minor one. *Farley* and *Ruxley* may be seen to provide a pathway to that.

20.116 However, if the non-availability of damages for mental distress is seen as a matter of policy, it should be asked what that policy is and whether it provides a sufficient reason for not complying with basic principle. There has been no clear identification of what that policy is. However, in the Court of Appeal, in *Hayes* v *James & Charles Dodd* [1990] 2 All ER 815, Staughton LJ did say (at 823):

> Like the judge, I consider that the English courts should be wary of adopting what he called 'the United States practice of huge awards'. Damages awarded for negligence or want of skill, whether against professional men or anyone else, must provide fair compensation, but no more than that. And I would not view with enthusiasm the prospect that every shipowner in the Commercial Court, having successfully claimed for unpaid freight or demurrage, would be able to add a claim for mental distress suffered while he was waiting for his money.

There would seem to be two points here: first, a fear of 'huge awards' and secondly, concern about inappropriate awards of mental distress damages in commercial cases. These should be considered in turn.

20.117 In relation to a fear of US-style 'huge awards', the point can be made that if mental distress has been occasioned by a breach, then damages covering it would only amount to 'fair compensation' in the sense that the award would simply be complying with a basic principle and putting the injured party in the position that that party would have been in had the contract been performed. However, the assessment of the sum of money which should be awarded in relation to this type of damage does pose obvious difficulties, and that may well be the real concern here, but first the point can be made that it seems unlikely that the English courts would succumb to any temptation to make US-style 'huge awards'. In *Farley* v *Skinner* (2001), in extending the 'objects' exception somewhat, Lord Steyn noted that in the lower courts 'non-pecuniary damages are regularly awarded on the basis that the defendant's breach of contract deprived the [claimant] of the very object of the contract' and that 'The awards in such cases seem modest' (at 810). Secondly, in relation to any broader concern simply with the uncertainty of the quantification of an award for mental distress, in *Ruxley* v *Forsyth* Lord Mustill made the point that:[40]

> In several fields the judges are well accustomed to putting figures to intangibles, and I see no reason why the imprecision of the exercise should be a barrier, if that is what fairness demands.

20.118 The final point to consider here is Staughton LJ's concern about inappropriate awards in commercial cases. However, the point which should be made is that it is not the commercial area which should be determining the rules as to the availability of these damages. Commercial contracts are primarily concerned with profits, and contract damages generally cover such losses. Unlike consumer contracts involving an element of mental distress on breach, generally the rights and obligations under commercial contracts are not going effectively unenforced. However, although one can simply say that raising what happens in commercial contracts to block the general recovery of damages for mental distress is a misconceived focus, the point can also be made that it seems unlikely that such awards will be significant in the commercial context. Even without any additional restrictions on the availability of damages for mental distress, in the commercial context the rules about remoteness and mitigation would often provide significant barriers to recovery. It will, for example, be difficult to argue convincingly that having to derive the expected profit by finding a substitute contract in the market, thus mitigating the loss, and claiming any difference in the price has caused significant mental distress, when finding such contracts is what the claimant does on an everyday basis. Further, even if there was significant mental distress in such a case, it will nevertheless be difficult to argue that it was within the reasonable contemplation of the defendant and, if the approach to remoteness propagated by Lord Hoffmann in *The Achilleas* is applied, it would also be difficult to argue that the defendant could be regarded as having assumed responsibility in relation to the risk of mental distress losses. The duty to mitigate and the remoteness limitation must be kept in mind when concerns about mental distress damages in everyday commercial contracts are raised.

Summary

- Basic principle—putting the injured party in the position he or she would have been had the contract been performed.
- Usually awarded to cover the expectation loss, that is, what was expected to be derived from the contractual performance.

40 [1995] 3 All ER 268 at 278; N. Enonchong, 'Breach of Contract and Damages for Mental Distress' (1996) OJLS 617 at 629.

- May be awarded to cover the reliance loss—subject to the limit that the injured party will not recover for losses which would have been suffered had the contract been performed.
- There is limited scope for restitutionary recovery to allow recovery of all, or part, of D's profits from the breach.
- Losses will not be recovered which are too remote. The traditional remoteness rule encompasses types of losses which were within the reasonable contemplation of the parties as not unlikely to result from the breach. The *Achilleas* suggests a test of assumption of responsibility.
- The breach must have been a sufficient cause of the loss.
- The injured party is under a 'duty' to mitigate, that is, the injured party will not recover for a loss which he or she could have avoided by taking reasonable steps on the breach occurring.
- The injured party's damages may be reduced where he or she has been contributorily negligent and the breaching party's liability in contract is the same as it would have been under the tort of negligence independent of the existence of any contract.
- Under the traditional approach, penalty clauses are not enforceable whereas liquidated damages clauses, as a genuine pre-estimate of loss, are enforceable. Both state the sum to be paid on breach.
- However, the rules on penalties have been considerably relaxed with the landmark judgment in *Cavendish* and *ParkingEye* (2015).
- The extent of recovery of damages for mental distress, or the 'consumer surplus', is currently controversial.

Further reading

M. Bridge, 'Mitigation of Damages in Contract and the Meaning of Avoidable Loss' (1989) 105 LQR 398

B. Coote, 'Contract Damages, Ruxley and the Performance Interest' (1997) 56 CLJ 537

D. Friedmann, 'The Performance Interest in Contract Damages' (1995) 111 LQR 628

L. Fuller and W. Perdue, 'The Reliance Interest in Contract Damages' (1936) 46 Yale LJ 52

D. Harris, A. Ogus, and J. Phillips, 'Contract Remedies and the Consumer Surplus' (1979) 95 LQR 581

Lord Hoffmann, 'The *Achilleas*: Custom and Practice or Foreseeability?' (2010) 14(1) Edinburgh LR 47

A. Kramer, 'An Agreement-Centred Approach to Remoteness and Contract Damages' in N. Cohen and E. McKendrick (eds), *Comparative Remedies for Breach of Contract*, Hart Publishing, 2004, pp. 249–86

A. Kramer, 'Remoteness: New Problems with the Old Test' in R. Cunnington and D. Saidov, *Contract Damages: Domestic and International Perspectives*, Hart Publishing, 2008, pp. 277–304

A. Kramer, 'The New Test of Remoteness in Contract' (2009) 125 LQR 408

E. McKendrick, 'Breach of Contract and the Meaning of Loss' [1999] CLP 37

E. McKendrick and M. Graham, 'The Sky's the Limit: Contractual Damages for Non-Pecuniary Loss' [2002] LMCLQ 161

E. Peel, 'Remoteness Revisited' (2009) 125 LQR 6

A. Robertson, 'The Basis of the Remoteness Rule in Contract' (2008) 28 LS 172

A. Tettenborn, 'Hadley v Baxendale Foreseeability: A Principle beyond Its Sell By Date' (2007) 23 JCL 120

Chapter 21

Specific enforcement

Specific performance

21.1 An order for specific performance has the effect of ordering a contracting party to do what he or she has undertaken to do. However, an award of damages is the main remedy for breach of contract; it is available as of right, whereas there are restrictions on the availability of the equitable remedy of specific performance, and it is subject to the court's discretion. Sometimes, an injunction may, in effect, enforce performance of the contract; when it would have that effect, it is subject to the same limitations as specific performance.

Adequacy of damages[1]

21.2 Damages provide the primary remedy for breach of contract, and specific performance is not available where damages would provide an adequate remedy (*Harnett* v *Yielding* (1805) 2 Sch & Lef 549 at 553). The basis of the precedence is historical, in that the courts of equity would provide a remedy only where the remedy available at common law was inadequate. However, the question of adequacy of damages continues to be the first hurdle to be overcome by a claimant asking for specific performance.

21.3 The question of whether damages will be an adequate remedy for a breach of contract is often put in terms of whether the injured party would be able to purchase a substitute performance if given damages. A contract for the sale of shares which are freely available on the market will not usually be specifically enforced. The injured party can buy substitute shares (*Cud* v *Rutter* (1720)). But replacement shares will not always be available. Specific performance

1 See A. Burrows, *Remedies for Torts and Breach of Contract*, 3rd edn, Oxford University Press, 2004, ch. 20.

might be ordered where, for example, the contract relates to shares determining the controlling interest in a company (*Harvela Investments Ltd* v *Royal Trust Co. of Canada* (1985)). In contrast, the courts always seem to assume that any piece of land, no matter what it is wanted for, is unique, and damages will always be an inadequate remedy. This even applies where it is the seller, rather than the buyer, who is asking for specific performance.

21.4 Section 52 of the Sale of Goods Act 1979 provides that the courts have a discretion whether to award specific performance to a purchaser of specific or ascertained goods, but the courts still apply the common law test of adequacy to the question of whether to award specific performance under s 52.[2] In relation to a sale of goods contract, damages are nearly always considered to be adequate. A substitute is usually available, although occasionally the goods will be considered to be unique and damages inadequate.

21.5 'Unique' goods are usually thought of as being those with some artistic merit, such as the Chinese vases in *Falcke* v *Gray* (1859), where Kindersley V-C said:

> In the present case the contract is for the purchase of articles of unusual beauty, rarity and distinction, so that damages would not be an adequate compensation for non-performance.

The argument has occasionally been successful in relation to essentially commercial goods.

21.6 In *Société des Industries Metallurgiques SA* v *Bronx Engineering Co. Ltd* (1975) the goods were not considered to be unique and specific performance was not ordered.

> The buyer had ordered a machine from the seller. A dispute had occurred and the seller contended that he was entitled to treat the contract as ended. The buyer was trying to prevent the seller sending the machine abroad to another purchaser before the trial of the main action. The buyer could obtain a substitute machine, but only after 9–12 months' delay.

The court was immediately concerned with whether to award an interim injunction. It decided that an interim injunction would not be awarded if specific performance would not ultimately be available if the buyer was successful in the main action. On that basis, the court considered the adequacy test and concluded that damages were adequate because a substitute was available. The long delay before another machine could be obtained was not seen as preventing that conclusion. A similarly restrictive approach to the question of adequacy of damages was taken in *The Stena Nautica (No 2) (CN Marine Inc.* v *Stena Line A/B and Regie Voor Maritiem Transport)* [1982] 2 Lloyd's Rep 336. That case concerned the sale of a ship. In breach of contract, the seller was refusing to deliver the Stena Nautica to the buyer. In deciding that damages were adequate the court placed reliance upon the availability of a substitute ship, despite the fact that the substitute was 'substantially less convenient' for the buyer (at 342).

2 E.g., *Société des Industries Metallurgiques SA* v *Bronx Engineering Co Ltd* [1975] 1 Lloyd's Rep 465 at 469; *The Stena Nautica (No 2) (CN Marine Inc.* v *Stena Line A/B and Regie Voor Maritiem Transport)* (1982).

21.7 In contrast with *Bronx Engineering* (1975) and *Stena Nautica (No 2)* (1982) is the decision in *Behnke* v *Bede Shipping Co. Ltd* [1927] 1 KB 649. In that case, specific performance was ordered of a contract for the sale of a ship on the basis that the ship was:

> of peculiar and practically unique value to the [claimant]. She was a cheap vessel, being old, having been built in 1892, but her engines were practically new and such as to satisfy the German regulations, and hence the [claimant] could as a German shipowner, have her at once put on the German register. A very experienced ship valuer has said that he knew of one other comparable ship, but that could now have been sold. (Wright J at 661)

The claimant wanted a ship for immediate use and Wright J concluded that damages would not be an adequate remedy. Specific performance was ordered. On the basis of the 'uniqueness' of the goods involved, there seems to be little to distinguish the three cases. Perhaps the main point to make is simply that specific performance will rarely be awarded where the contract is one for the sale of goods.

21.8 In *Sky Petroleum Ltd* v *VIP Petroleum Ltd* [1974] 1 All ER 954 the question of substitute goods was considered in the context of the sale of commodities, which were usually readily available, but which events had rendered scarce. The *Sky* case concerned a contract for the supply of petrol under which the suppliers were refusing to continue to supply. An interlocutory injunction was ordered against the supplier after the court applied the adequacy test. The test was applied as the circumstances were such that an injunction would be equivalent to specific performance (at 956). Damages were found to be inadequate because the oil crisis at the time meant that the purchaser could not obtain supplies of petrol elsewhere and there was a serious danger that he would be forced out of business if the seller did not deliver (see also *Howard E Perry & Co. Ltd* v *British Railways Board* (1980)).

21.9 There is a further difficulty, in addition to that of the question of adequacy, where the contract is one for the sale of goods which are not specific or ascertained. As was indicated earlier, the Sale of Goods Act 1979, s 52 envisages specific performance being available where the contract is one for the sale of specific or ascertained goods. Basically, goods are specific if identified and agreed upon at the time the contract is made (s 61) and ascertained if they have been identified subsequent to the making of the contract, that is, goods are specific or ascertained if it is known exactly which goods are to be used to fulfil the contract. Where the contract is for the sale of a quantity of oil, or steel, or citrus pulp pellets, the goods may not be specific and may not have been ascertained by the time specific performance is requested. The question is whether specific performance is possible if the case does not fall within s 52—it has been indicated that it is not (*Re London Wine Co. (Shippers)* (1986)), but *Sky Petroleum Ltd* v *VIP Petroleum Ltd* [1974] 1 All ER 954 at 956 would argue to the contrary.

21.10 Focusing on the availability of a substitute emphasizes that the adequacy rule helps to prevent the remedy of specific performance from rendering the duty to mitigate largely meaningless. We saw earlier that an injured party will not recover, in damages, any sum which they would not have lost had they behaved reasonably when the breach occurred. If specific performance was readily available, this incentive for an injured party to take reasonable steps to limit their loss would be removed. Under the present, restricted approach to the availability of specific performance, if there is a substitute contract which a reasonable person would make—a substitute within the duty to mitigate—then damages will be adequate. Specific performance will not then be available and the duty to mitigate will not be circumvented (see G. Treitel, 'Specific Performance in the Sale of Goods' [1966] JBL 211).

21.11 The test of adequacy of damages is often translated into the question of whether a substitute can be acquired from another source, but that question is not always helpful. In *Beswick* v *Beswick* (1968) the problem was whether specific performance should be awarded because the privity rule would have produced an award of nominal damages. In that case:

> Peter Beswick was a coal merchant. He handed over his business to his nephew on the basis that the nephew would pay him £6 10s a week during his lifetime and £5 a week to his widow after his death.

The nephew ceased payment on the death of Peter Beswick. The question was whether any remedy was available to meet the nephew's breach of contract. The widow could not sue on the contract personally, as she was not a party to it. However, the widow was also the administratrix of Peter Beswick's estate and she could sue, in that capacity, for the estate. The problem with the estate suing was that the loss was not to the estate but to the third party, the widow, and the estate could only have recovered nominal damages. To meet that problem, and avoid the difficulty caused by the privity rule, the House of Lords ordered specific performance of the contract and the nephew had to perform. The fact that damages were nominal did not mean that they were an adequate remedy in the instant case. (A promise for the benefit of a third party to a contract may now be directly enforceable by the third party under the Contracts (Rights of Third Parties) Act 1999—see **Chapter 17**.)

21.12 The adequacy of damages limitation on specific performance has been examined in terms of economic efficiency (see A. Burrows, *Remedies for Torts and Breach of Contract*, 3rd edn, Oxford University Press, 2004). The non-availability of specific performance can be seen as economically efficient. It is part of the efficient breach theory (see para. **20.65**). It allows a breaching party merely to pay damages, where that is an adequate remedy for the other party, and keep the additional profit, the prospect of which led them to breach in the first place. The argument is that if specific performance was generally available a breaching party would not have been able to make that extra profit. They would have been inefficiently held to his contract. In answer to that it can be argued that the greater availability of specific performance would not lead to inefficient performance, but merely to a party wanting to breach having to pay a proportion of their extra profit to the other party as a way of negotiating their way out of the readily available specific performance. However, it is not easy to say where economic efficiency truly lies, because of the transaction costs. There are costs involved in a party wishing to breach having to negotiate their way out of the contract. There are also transaction costs involved in an award of damages, and it is not clear which are likely to be the greater. In other words, there is no obvious economic justification for the adequacy rule (Burrows, *Remedies for Torts and Breach of Contract*, 3rd edn at p. 475).[3]

Supervision

21.13 If the contract requires performance over a period of time, so that an order of specific performance would involve the court in constant supervision, then that has been seen as a reason why an order of specific performance should not be made. In *Ryan* v *Mutual Tontine Westminster Chambers Association* (1893):

> The lease of a flat obliged the landlord to provide a resident porter who would be 'constantly in attendance'. The landlord employed someone who was absent for several hours each day while he worked elsewhere as a cook.

The Court of Appeal refused specifically to enforce the landlord's obligation to have a porter 'constantly in attendance'. Such an order would have involved the court in constant supervision.

21.14 In *Co-operative Insurance Society Ltd* v *Argyll Stores (Holdings) Ltd* [1997] 3 All ER 297 the House of Lords reaffirmed that specific enforcement would not normally be granted where it would require persons to carry on a business, and considered and explained the question of 'constant supervision'. In *Co-operative Insurance* v *Argyll*:

> The claimants had leased the largest unit in a shopping centre to the defendants for 35 years for the purposes of operating a supermarket. There was a covenant that it be kept open during the usual hours of business. The supermarket became unprofitable for the defendants, and they shut it. The claimants were concerned that the closure would impact upon other trade in the shopping centre and sought specific enforcement. That was refused at first instance, granted on appeal, and then refused by the House of Lords.

Lord Hoffmann, with whom the other members of the court agreed, explained that specific enforcement would not normally be granted when it would require someone to carry on a business and would thus require 'constant supervision'. He pointed out that it could lead to the need for an indefinite number of rulings by the courts, and that was undesirable. He explained that the only means available to the court to enforce its rulings was the 'quasi-criminal procedure of

3 R. Posner, *Economic Analysis of Law*, 2nd edn, Aspen, pp. 88–93 and 95–7; H. Beale, *Remedies for Breach of Contract*, Sweet & Maxwell, 1980, pp. 13–14 and 142; C. Goetz and R. Scott, 'Liquidated Damages, Penalties and the Just Compensation Principle: Some Notes on an Enforcement Model and a Theory of Efficient Breach' (1977) 77 Col LR 554; I. R. Macneil, 'Efficient Breach of Contract: Circles in the Sky' (1982) 68 Va LR 947.

punishment for contempt of court' and that meant that the situation was unsuitable for specific enforcement. He said (at 302–3):

> The heavy-handed nature of the enforcement mechanism is a consideration which may go to the exercise of the court's discretion in other cases as well, but its use to compel the running of a business is perhaps the paradigm case of its disadvantages . . . The prospect of committal or even a fine, with the damage to commercial reputation which will be caused by a finding of contempt of court is likely to have two undesirable consequences. First, the defendant, who ex hypothesi did not think it was in his economic interest to run the business at all, now has to do so under a sword of Damocles . . . This is, as one might say, no way to run a business . . . Secondly, the seriousness of a finding of contempt for the defendant means that any application to enforce the order is likely to be a heavy and expensive piece of litigation. The possibility of repeated applications over time means that, in comparison with a once and for all inquiry as to damages, the enforcement of the remedy is likely to be expensive in terms of the costs to the parties and the resources of the judicial system.

In other words, it is inappropriate to use the threat of contempt proceedings to compel someone to run a business that they had decided should be discontinued—and the possibility that the 'constant supervision' might require repeated recourse to such proceedings also makes specific enforcement too costly, in terms of the resources of the parties and of the courts.

21.15 Lord Hoffmann also explained why specific enforcement in such cases as *Co-operative Insurance* v *Argyll* is usually refused, at a more general level. He pointed out that the likely result of ready availability of such an order would be that the parties would negotiate so that the claimant would eventually accept, instead of actually enforcing the obligations, a sum of money which would be far higher than if specific enforcement had not been available and which may be in excess of any loss caused by non-performance. Lord Hoffmann pointed out that 'the purpose of the law of contract is not to punish wrongdoing but to satisfy the expectations of the party entitled to performance'. He regarded as 'unjust' a 'remedy which enables [the claimant] to secure, in money terms, more than the performance due to him' (at 305).

21.16 However, Lord Hoffmann distinguished between contracts requiring someone to carry on an activity over a period of time and contracts for results. In the latter type, the same possibilities of repeated applications to the courts would not generally arise. The court could usually simply view the end result. This distinction was used to explain the fact that specific enforcement has been ordered in relation to building and repairing contracts (see, e.g., *Wolverhampton Corpn* v *Emmons* (1901); *Jeune* v *Queens Cross Properties Ltd* (1973)). The point can also be made that such contracts often specify the work to be done with precision. Another factor indicating that cases in which a defendant has contracted to carry on a particular activity will normally be unsuitable for specific performance is that of uncertainty. If specific enforcement is to be granted, it must be clear what the defendant must do to comply, and the obligations in such contracts are often not set out with that degree of certainty (*Co-operative Insurance Society Ltd* v *Argyll Stores (Holdings) Ltd* [1997] 3 All ER 297 at 303–4). Building contracts, on the other hand, are usually set out with the required degree of certainty. However, in *Rainbow Estates Ltd* v *Tokenhold Ltd* [1999] Ch 64, it was said (at 73) that 'the problems of defining the work and the need for supervision can be overcome by ensuring that there is sufficient definition of what has to be done in order to comply with the order of the court'.

Personal services

21.17 The general rule is that the court will not order specific performance of a contract requiring personal services, for example a contract of employment. If specific performance were readily available in relation to such a contract, it would place too great a restriction upon the freedom of the individual. In relation to an order of specific performance against an employee, the restriction upon making such an order is embodied in statute. Section 236 of the Trade Union and Labour Relations (Consolidation) Act 1992 states that no court shall compel any employee to do any work by ordering specific performance of, or granting an injunction in relation to, a contract of employment.

21.18 However, exceptional cases where it is appropriate to give specific enforcement against an employer have been identified. In *Hill* v *CA Parsons & Co. Ltd* (1972):

> Mr Hill was 63 and had worked for the defendant for 35 years. The defendant made a closed shop agreement with a union, DATA. Mr Hill refused to join DATA and, at the insistence of the union, the defendant purported to terminate his employment on one month's notice. Until the dispute, Mr Hill had every expectation of continuing in that employment until he retired. The relationship between employer and employee had not broken down. Union pressure was the only reason for the dismissal of Mr Hill.

The Court of Appeal (Stamp LJ dissenting) granted Mr Hill an interlocutory injunction in circumstances which made it equivalent to temporary specific performance. The court ordered the defendant to continue to employ Mr Hill for the proper period of notice which he should have been given (i.e. six months). This may seem to be a very short-term benefit, but Mr Hill was hoping to postpone the ending of his employment long enough for the Industrial Relations Act 1971 to come into force and provide him with protection against the closed shop agreement. Sachs LJ emphasized that the relationship between employer and employee had not broken down.

21.19 *Hill* v *CA Parsons & Co. Ltd* (1972) is regarded as an exceptional case (*Chappell* v *Times Newspapers Ltd* [1975] 1 WLR 482 at 501 and 503)—specific enforcement of a contract of employment will not normally occur. The lack of breakdown of the relationship of employer and employee in *Hill* was emphasized by Geoffrey Lane LJ in *Chappell* as the key factor in justifying the exception (at 506):

> Very rarely indeed will a court enforce . . . a contract for services. The reason is obvious: if one party has no faith in the honesty, integrity or the loyalty of the other, to force him to serve or to employ that other is a plain recipe for disaster.

21.20 Great importance was placed upon the continued trust and confidence between employer and employee in *Powell* v *Brent London Borough Council* (1988), where it was seen to require that the employer should view the employee not only as competent but also as able to work sufficiently well with fellow employees. In that case, the facts were as follows:

> Mrs Powell was employed by the authority as a Senior Benefits Officer. She applied for the post of Principal Benefits Officer. After the interviews she was informed that she had been appointed and she should take up the new post. However, after a query by another candidate, the authority decided that its selection procedure might have been in breach of its equal opportunity policy and informed Mrs Powell that it was going to re-advertise the post. The authority claimed that Mrs Powell had never been appointed to the post, and that she should return to her job as Senior Benefits Officer and re-apply for the post. She claimed that she had been appointed. When Mrs Powell commenced legal action, the authority gave an undertaking that it would treat her as a Principal Benefits Officer for a month. The pattern of events was then such that she had been working as a Principal Benefits Officer, without complaint from her superiors, for four months by the time the court came to consider the granting of an interlocutory injunction to order the authority to treat her as a Principal Benefits Officer and to restrain it from filling the post before the trial of the main action.

The Court of Appeal granted the interlocutory injunction because it thought that specific enforcement, by a full injunction, might be granted when the main action came to trial. The four-month period provided evidence that Mrs Powell could perform the duties of the Principal Benefits Officer and there was no evidence of a breakdown in her relationship with those with whom she would be working. The authority was ordered to continue employing her as a Principal Benefits Officer until the trial of the main action.

21.21 In *Robb* v *Hammersmith and Fulham London Borough Council* (1991) Morland J took the line that where the contract is to be kept alive in only a limited way, it does not matter whether confidence still exists between employer and employee. Under those circumstances, the enforcement envisaged would not produce a situation which required confidence to exist.

Mr Robb sought an injunction to restrain the council from giving effect to the purported dismissal until the proper disciplinary procedures had been carried out. He was willing to give undertakings that he would remain suspended on full pay. Morland J thought that to obtain an injunction, there was no need to show continued trust and confidence where all that was being asked for was the right to have disciplinary procedures properly carried through, without any actual work being done by the employee.

21.22 An inroad on the basic restriction on specific enforcement in this area is where an injunction is granted to enforce a negative term in a contract for personal services. However, it should be noted that such an injunction will not be granted where its effect would be to compel specific performance of a contract in relation to which specific performance, as such, is not regarded as appropriate. An injunction will not be granted where the negative term states that the employee is not to take up any other employment (*Whitwood Chemical Co.* v *Hardman* (1891)). Enforcement of such a negative term would, in effect, leave the employee with no option but to continue to perform the positive terms of the contract of employment. However, the courts have not always taken the same approach as to which negative terms can be enforced without, effectively, coercing the employee to keep his or her contract with a particular employer.

21.23 In *Lumley* v *Wagner* (1852), the facts were as follows:

> Mlle Wagner had contracted to sing at Mr Lumley's theatre, Her Majesty's Theatre, on two nights a week for three months. She had also contracted, negatively, that she would not sing elsewhere during that time without Mr Lumley's permission. Mlle Wagner was offered a better rate of pay by Mr Gye. She decided to break her contract with Mr Lumley and to contract with Mr Gye to sing at the Royal Italian Opera, Covent Garden.

The court granted an injunction to prevent Mlle Wagner from breaching the negative covenant not to sing elsewhere during the three-month period. Specific performance of the obligation to sing at Her Majesty's Theatre could not have been granted, but the injunction was not regarded as doing indirectly what could not be done directly. It did not matter that the injunction might persuade her to fulfil her contract with Mr Lumley.

21.24 The approach taken in *Lumley* v *Wagner* (1852) was followed in *Warner Bros Pictures Inc.* v *Nelson* [1937] 1 KB 209. In that case:

> Mrs Nelson, who was known professionally as Bette Davis, had contracted to render her services as an actress exclusively for Warner Bros for a number of years and, during that time, not to perform for anyone else. In breach of that contract she agreed to act for a third party.

Warner Bros could not obtain specific performance of the obligation to act for them or an injunction which would have the same effect. Branson J said (at 216):

> [T]rue to the principle that specific performance of a contract of personal service will never be ordered, [the court will not] grant an injunction in the case of such a contract to enforce negative covenants if the effect of so doing would be to drive the defendant either to starvation or to specific performance of the positive covenants.

However, in the instant case, an injunction was granted to prevent Bette Davis from acting for anyone else. That was not regarded as indirect specific performance. The court was not persuaded by the argument that she would be compelled to perform for Warner Bros because of the difference between what she was likely to earn acting in films and doing anything else. The court thought that, although the injunction might tempt her to perform the contract with Warner Bros, it was not equivalent to granting specific performance. She could earn a living without breaching the injunction. The case seems all the more extreme because of the time span involved. *Lumley* v *Wagner* concerned a covenant for three months, whereas the covenant in *Warner Bros* v *Nelson* related to a period of years.

21.25 A more realistic approach to the question of whether an injunction would amount to indirect specific performance was taken in *Page One Records Ltd* v *Britton* (1968). In that case:

> The Troggs, a pop group, had contracted to employ the claimant as their manager for five years. The Troggs covenanted not to employ anyone else as their manager for that period. The group broke that agreement by employing another manager.

The court refused to grant an injunction preventing the Troggs from employing anyone but the claimant as their manager. It was recognized that they could not function as a pop group without a manager and that any such negative injunction would effectively amount to specific enforcement of the contract of employment.

21.26 The decision in *Page One Records Ltd* v *Britton* clearly takes a more realistic line than the previous decisions on what will effectively amount to specific performance. The court did not take the view that the Troggs would not, effectively, have to continue to employ the claimant, because they could always have taken up some occupation other than that of pop group.

21.27 In *Warren* v *Mendy* [1989] 3 All ER 103 the Court of Appeal preferred the approach taken in *Page One Records Ltd* v *Britton* (1968) to that of *Warner Bros Pictures Inc.* v *Nelson* (1937), which was regarded as a very extreme case. In *Warren* v *Mendy*:

> The boxer Nigel Benn made a contract with Warren for Warren to act as his manager for three years. The contract contained a covenant that Benn would not enter into an agreement with anyone else to carry out the functions of a manager for that period. Within a few months of the agreement being signed, Benn claimed that he was not bound by it. He made an agreement with Mendy for Mendy, effectively, to act as his manager.

Warren sought an injunction to restrain Mendy (a) from inducing a breach, by Benn, of the contract with Warren and (b) from acting as Benn's manager. The Court of Appeal refused to grant the injunction. It took the line that the question to consider was, basically, the same as the one which it would have had to address had Warren chosen to try to enforce the negative covenant in the contract against Benn—that is, was the court being asked to make an order which would have the same effect as an order for specific performance, compelling Benn to perform his contract with Warren? The court thought that:

> Compulsion may be inferred where the injunction is sought not against the servant but against a third party, if either the third party is the only other master or if it is likely that the master will seek relief against anyone who attempts to replace him.

The judge at first instance had gained the impression that Warren would take action against anyone in Mendy's position. On that basis, the question of 'compulsion' had to be considered more generally, and in the same way as it would have been looked at had Warren taken action against Benn. The court looked at 'compulsion' in the context of a contract for personal services, 'inseparable from the exercise of some special skill or talent'. Nourse LJ, delivering the judgment of the court, said (at 114):

> Compulsion is a question to be decided on the facts of each case, with realistic regard for the probable reaction of an injunction on the psychological and material, and sometimes the physical, need of the servant to maintain the skill or talent. The longer the term for which an injunction is sought, the more readily will compulsion be inferred.

In other words, the court thought that the need to work to maintain a particular skill, or talent, might effectively compel an employee to perform a contract if he or she was prevented from exercising his talents otherwise. This is akin to the line taken in *Page One Records*. It is very different from the suggestion in *Warner Bros* v *Nelson* that Bette Davis would not be forced to act for Warner Bros because she could always take up some employment other than acting.[4] The reference to the length of time covered by an injunction should also be noted; it was indicated earlier that the time involved was one factor making *Warner Bros* an extreme case.

21.28 In *Warren* v *Mendy* (1989) the court made the point that it was considering a contract which related to the use of a particular skill or talent. If a particular skill or talent is involved, it may need to be exercised if it is not to decline or be lost and, even without that, there is every reason not to take the line that the employee should be required either to waste his or her skill or talent for a time or to perform the contract. The view has been taken that this should apply even where there is no question of the employee starving because the employer is willing to pay him or her to do nothing, provided that he or she does not work for anyone else for the contract period. It should apply whether the skills are those of the artist, sportsman, or chartered accountant:

> The employee has a concern to work and a concern to exercise his skills. That has been recognised in some circumstances concerned with artists and singers who depend on publicity, but it applies equally, I apprehend, to skilled workmen and even chartered accountants. (*Provident Financial Group plc and Whitegates Estate Agency* v *Hayward* [1989] 3 All ER 298 at 304 per Dillon LJ. See also restraint of trade.)

Discretion

21.29 Specific performance is an equitable remedy.[5] It cannot be asked for as of right. It is a discretionary remedy, but the discretion is not arbitrary or capricious. It is governed, as

4 *LauritzenCool AB* v *Lady Navigation Inc* (2005) is best explained on the basis of a limited personal element in the time charter contract, rather than as a reinforcement of the older approach.

5 See A. Burrows, *Remedies for Torts and Breach of Contract*, 3rd edn, Oxford University Press, 2004; D. Harris, D. Campbell, and R. Halson, *Remedies in Contract and Tort*, 2nd edn, Sweet & Maxwell, 2002, p. 178ff.

far as possible, by fixed rules and principles (*Lamare* v *Dixon* (1873) LR 6 HL 414 at 423). On that basis, factors affecting the court's decision can be identified. For example, the court will consider whether there has been a delay in asking for specific performance (*Milward* v *Earl of Thanet* (1801); *Lazard Bros & Co. Ltd* v *Fairfield Properties Co. (Mayfair) Ltd* (1977)). It will consider whether the person seeking specific performance is him or herself prepared to perform his or her side of the contract (*Chappell* v *Times Newspapers Ltd* (1975)). The court will weigh the difference between the benefit one party will gain from specific performance and the cost of performance to the other. If the cost is disproportionate to the benefit, that is a factor against the making of an order of specific performance (*Tito* v *Waddell (No 2)* [1977] Ch 106 at 326). Further consideration is given below to some of the factors identified as relevant to the exercise of the court's discretion. It should be noted that the parties cannot fetter the courts' discretion in their contract (*Quadrant Visual Communications Ltd* v *Hutchison Telephone (UK) Ltd* (1993), and for a more recent decision which comments upon the scope of the court's jurisdiction to grant specific performance see *Jones and another* v *Oven and another* (2017)).

Hardship

21.30 Someone against whom specific performance is being sought may argue that it should not be granted because it will cause them substantial hardship. In *Denne* v *Light* (1857) specific performance was refused of a contract for the sale of land. After making the contract the purchaser refused to continue with the purchase because he discovered that the land in question was 'landlocked' and the vendor refused to guarantee that he would have a right of way over any of the surrounding land.

21.31 Specific performance has been refused because of the substantial hardship which it would cause to the party refusing to perform, even, in exceptional circumstances, where that hardship arises from circumstances which occur after contracting. The hardship was sufficient to justify a refusal of specific performance in *Patel* v *Ali* [1984] 1 All ER 978. In that case:

> In July 1979 Mrs Ali contracted to sell her house to Mr Patel. At that time she had one child and was in good health. Mrs Ali spoke English very badly. Through neither party's fault, completion was initially delayed. By the time the court came to consider whether Mr Patel should be granted specific performance, Mrs Ali had two more children, and cancer had resulted in the amputation of her leg. She claimed that specific performance would cause her great hardship. She would have to move and her poor English, coupled with her disability, made her very reliant upon assistance from friends and relations who lived close by the home she had contracted to sell.

Goulding J exercised his discretion not to order specific performance. However, his refusal was subject to Mrs Ali paying a sum of money into court to ensure that Mr Patel would receive his damages, once they had been calculated. In deciding to exercise his discretion, and to refuse specific performance, Goulding J acknowledged (at 981) that:

> in the majority of cases the hardship which moves the court to refuse specific performance is either a hardship existing at the date of the contract or a hardship due in some way to the [claimant].

However, he was satisfied that the court's discretion was wide enough to refuse specific performance in other cases of hardship. In the particular case, although the hardship was not caused by Mr Patel, specific performance was refused because, in the circumstances, it would inflict a 'hardship amounting to injustice' to grant it. The delay was not due to the fault of either party and an order of specific performance would force Mrs Ali to move in circumstances very different from those which she contemplated when contracting.

Consideration

21.32 It is said that 'equity will not assist a volunteer' and specific performance will not be granted of a contract which is merely under seal and for which there is no consideration as such, or of a contract for which the consideration is purely nominal (*Jefferys* v *Jefferys* (1841)). It also seems that inadequacy of consideration may be relevant to the exercise of the court's discretion, particularly where it supports other factors indicating that specific performance should not be granted (*Falcke* v *Gray* (1859)).

The party claiming specific performance

21.33 Specific performance was refused in *Walters* v *Morgan* (1861) 3 De GF & J 718 because it was thought that the contract had been obtained by unfair means. The defendant bought land and was immediately hurried into granting the claimant a mining lease over the land, before he had time to discover its true value. By 'contrivance of the [claimant] the defendant was surprised and was induced to sign the agreement in ignorance of the value of the property' (at 723). In many cases irregularities in formation will now be covered by duress, undue influence, misrepresentation, or mistake.

21.34 In *Shell UK Ltd* v *Lostock Garage Ltd* (1977), Shell was refused specific enforcement of its contract with Lostock. Shell had acted unfairly in its performance of the contract and had inflicted hardship on Lostock. In that case:

> Shell had contracted to supply petrol to Lostock Garage on the basis that Lostock would not obtain petrol from any other supplier. The agreement could be terminated on 12 months' notice. During a petrol price war, Shell subsidised the other garages which it supplied in the same area as Lostock. Shell did not subsidize Lostock but charged them the full price. Without the subsidy Lostock could not sell petrol at a price which would not make a loss. Lostock told Shell that they would obtain petrol elsewhere. Lostock found a supplier from whom they could buy petrol at a price which would enable the company to make a profit.

Shell asked for an injunction to prevent Lostock from breaking their agreement not to buy petrol from any other supplier. Shell was effectively asking for specific performance of the tie agreement. On the basis of Shell's discriminatory treatment of Lostock, and the hardship it had caused Lostock, the Court of Appeal refused to grant the injunction.

21.35 In *Lamare* v *Dixon* (1873) a contract had been made for the lease of some cellars. Before the making of the contract, the owner promised that he would make them dry. The promise was not a term of the contract and it was not regarded as a misrepresentation (it related to the future). Nevertheless, the owner's failure to make the cellars dry led to a refusal of specific performance.

Mutuality

21.36 It has been thought that, in order for one party to obtain specific performance, the remedy must have been one which could have been available to the other party from the time when they contracted. On that basis, mutuality meant that if the obligation of one party, X, was such that it could not be specifically enforced, then X could not obtain specific performance. That was so even if the obligation of the other party was one which was otherwise appropriate for specific performance. At its most extreme, mutuality meant that specific performance was not available even when the party asking for specific performance had already performed. In that situation there would be no possibility of the other party performing, as ordered, and then finding him or herself able to ask only for damages in the face of a breach (E. Fry and G. Northcote, *Fry on Specific Performance*, 6th edn, Sweet & Maxwell, 1921). However, in *Price* v *Strange* [1977] 3 All ER 371, the Court of Appeal made it clear that mutuality is to be tested at the time when the court has to consider whether to grant specific performance. In addition, it seems that the question of mutuality is more appropriately regarded as a factor relevant to the exercise of the court's discretion rather than as a bar to specific performance. In *Price* v *Strange*, the facts were as follows:

> Mr Price was the tenant of a maisonette and Miss Strange was the lessor. Mr Price's lease came to an end and Miss Strange agreed to renew it if he carried out certain repairs to the building. He carried out some of the repairs but Miss Strange prevented him from completing them. Miss Strange refused to grant him the new lease. She completed the repairs herself.

Mr Price asked for specific performance of Miss Strange's promise to grant him a new lease. Miss Strange argued that he could not obtain that remedy as she could not have specifically enforced his obligation to repair, that is, that there was no mutuality. The Court of Appeal stated that the question of mutuality had to be considered when the action came to court. By that stage the repairs had been completed and Mr Price was willing to reimburse Miss Strange for the cost of the repairs. There was no question of Miss Strange being ordered to perform only to find that Mr Price was refusing to repair and could not be ordered to do so. However, Buckley LJ went further than simply considering the time at which the potential non-performance of the claimant's obligations should be assessed. He thought that where damages would provide an adequate remedy, if the claimant failed to perform, then that might satisfy mutuality. He said (at 392):

> [T]the court will not compel a defendant to perform his obligations specifically if it cannot at the same time ensure that any unperformed obligations of the [claimant] will be specifically performed, unless, perhaps, damages would be an adequate remedy for the defendant for any default on the [claimant's] part.

In the particular case, the potential sufficiency of a damages remedy to satisfy mutuality did not have to be considered. The repairs had already been carried out. However, the line taken by Buckley LJ seems appropriate. There should be no difficulty with the question of mutuality, and an order of specific performance against one party, if damages would provide an adequate remedy for that party. It also seems that mutuality should be regarded as a factor in the court's decision on the proper exercise of its discretion, rather than as a bar on specific performance. Goff LJ said (at 381): 'want of mutuality raises a question of the court's discretion to be exercised according to everything that has happened up to the decree.'

Injunctions

21.37 An injunction may be used to prevent a breach of a negative undertaking in a contract. As indicated earlier, where such enforcement would effectively compel performance of the positive contractual obligations, the question of granting the injunction will be considered in the same way as an order for specific performance. Where an injunction would not amount to effective specific performance but is purely negative, even in its effect, it is readily available and may even be the primary remedy (*Doherty* v *Allman* (1878) 3 App Cas 709 at 720; *Araci* v *Fallon* (2011)).

21.38 A mandatory injunction may be used to order the undoing of a breach which has already occurred. The granting of such an injunction will be subject to the 'balance of convenience' test, that is, the court will weigh the benefit to the injured party and the detriment to the other party from the order (*Sharp* v *Harrison* (1922)).

21.39 An injunction may provide the means of securing relief until the trial of the main action. An interlocutory injunction is basically granted in the light of the principles stated by the House of Lords in *American Cyanamid Co.* v *Ethicon Ltd* (1975).

Damages as an additional remedy

21.40 When the jurisdictions of the common law and equity were divided between different courts, damages could not be awarded by the Court of Chancery, the court to which a claimant would have to go to obtain an injunction or specific performance. Lord Cairns's Act (Chancery Amendment Act 1858) provided for the awarding of damages in addition to, or in substitution for, specific performance (Supreme Court Act 1981, s 50). However, as an injured party may now ask for both the common law remedy of damages and an injunction or specific performance in the same court, there is little need for the additional damages remedy.

Action for an agreed sum

21.41 A contract will often require one party to pay money as that party's performance. If one party has fulfilled all contractual requirements for the money to be due to him or her, then if the other party refuses to pay, he or she may be able to claim the sum due under the contract rather than damages. An action for the sum due under the contract is a form of specific enforcement of the contract but, as it involves only the payment of money, it is not hedged round with the same restrictions as an action for specific performance or an injunction. In addition, it is not subject to the uncertainty and restrictions of the rules on damages.

21.42 Where the contract has been terminated after the duty to pay has arisen, the action for the price may be maintained. The price cannot be claimed where termination has occurred before the duty to pay has arisen. Where the party to be paid has to decide whether to terminate in the light of the other party's wrongful refusal to perform, he or she will often have no effective choice. He or she will probably not be able to continue to perform without the co-operation of the other party. However, if he or she can continue to perform, so that the other party's duty to pay arises, he or she will then be able to claim the price rather than damages. That was what occurred in *White and Carter (Councils) Ltd* v *McGregor* [1962] AC 413 (see para. **18.40**). We have already noted how uncomfortably this case fits with the duty to mitigate, and the limitations on it.

Summary

- Traditionally specific performance is only available where damages do not provide an adequate remedy.
- Specific performance is a discretionary remedy taking account of, for example, hardship to the party in breach, behaviour of the party asking for specific performance, mutuality.
- Specific performance is not normally granted where it would involve the courts in constant supervision.
- It is not normally granted in relation to contracts involving personal services.

Further reading

A. Kronman, 'Specific Performance' (1978) 45 U Chicago LR 351
G. Schwartz, 'The Case for Specific Performance' (1979) 89 Yale LJ 271

Index